Red Socks

\+

Pink Knickers

By Karen Melissa Genge

THE THIRD TESTAMENT

Published by New Generation Publishing in 2018

Copyright © Karen Melissa Genge 2018

First Edition

The author asserts the moral right under the Copyright, Designs and Patents Act 1988 to be identified as the author of this work.

All Rights reserved. No part of this publication may be reproduced, stored in a retrieval system or transmitted, in any form or by any means without the prior consent of the author, nor be otherwise circulated in any form of binding or cover other than that which it is published and without a similar condition being imposed on the subsequent purchaser.

www.newgeneration-publishing.com

New Generation Publishing

FOREWORD

Here is my life explained through the parables and different gospels
That's how a Christian would read this.
A non-Christian would find the parables and certain gospel passages
explained through my story.
That was the premise on writing this book.

ACKNOWLEDGEMENTS

I thank my family for sticking by me through my illness and my husband Matthew. A special thanks go to St Paul and St Peter for giving me the gift of this book. I thank James for always being there for me doing this book as I prayed to him every day.

Chapter One

When you're born and you're being held in your mother's arms for the first time I believe that's when you first experience how powerful and pure and how unashamed God's love for you actually is, (through your mother's love)

SEEING GOD FOR THE FIRST TIME

The charts were playing David Essex's 'Hold Me Close' as number one on the hospital radio softly in the background as Mum held me in her arms. She was in a warm room by herself gently pressing me against her for food. It was near midnight on a Thursday. The birth had been easy and at 7lb and 11oz I became a healthy little eater straight away and as a Thursday child, according to the saying, I was going to have far to go. Mums long red hair brushed my face so she pushed it out the way. Looking very pink I'd hurt my mother initially before latching on real tight.

Dad had left not long after the actual birth to give Mum some sleep, but my mum, Avril, was completely in awe of the little bundle in her arms. The nurse came in to take me back to the hospital bed as Mum was left to drift into a very deep sleep.

Upon wakening to the clutter around her a breakfast tray had been brought in with toast that my mother barely ate. Apparently her parents were waiting to come in and see me to be introduced to Miss Karen Melissa Burr for the first time. I couldn't see much but blurred grey shapes against a very bright light and apparently was told "Now this is your grandparents come to see you and give you a cuddle." I felt the warmth of the strong arms lift me up and heard plenty of cooing and gentle chatting with Mum telling them my weight, Dad had called me Karen, they both came up with Melissa.

Mums parents moved around me and gently placed me in my mother's arms yet again. I'd been a hungry baby and apparently never cried when I'd come out of the womb.

It wasn't long till the lunch tray came in and my new grandparents left making their excuses. I'd had plenty of snuggles afterward and we both fell asleep together with mum's hair resting against my cheek.

Just two more days the nurses said at St Peters hospital in Shepton and Mum could go home.

Home was in Evercreech and as I got carried across the threshold in to the hallway I was being introduced to the place where I'd been about to live in. The passageway led out to the kitchen by which was the door to the dining room with a big dining table with two long blue benches either side which was where all my stuff got dumped in a big bag.

Mum pushed a stray hair behind her ear with one hand while I was cradled by the other arm and she placed me into a white Moses basket. Mother moved by the wells dresser in the dining room with china plates, just for show on, on the shelves. With me in her arms she moved the Moses basket out into the back yard that was basically a concreted area, with a bit of a garden that Dad tended to vegetables in. All around the yard had been a low wall and Mum placed me on a stand so that I was up off the floor and she picked off the runner beans for tea. Sat outside she cut them up to put in a saucepan. It was quite sunny and Fiona was perched on the bouncy chair. Fee, as they called her, had a sunny disposition and gorgeous blonde locks.

The bell on the front door rang loudly out to the back garden so Mum got up to answer it. It was my Nan Burr, my father's mother asking where the new little one was. Mum told her that I was out the back with Fee so Nan walked into the living room. The green sofa with a hole in the back was covered in a yellow crocheted blanket, the telly was in the corner by the front window, and there'd been a fireplace and a cupboard with a hi-fi on top with all the LPs and cassettes underneath.

Outside Nan held up a yellow cardigan saying that she'd knitted it just for me. It was a bit big as Nan placed it against me but Mum said "Never mind she'll grow in to it." And just as Nan spoke the doorbell went again and it was my other Nan at the door.

"Where's my new grandchild?" She'd asked and Mum took her through the hallway, then the kitchen and into the backyard. "Let's have a hold then." Nan had said and Mum scooped me up and placed me into her arms.

Fee was staring hard at Nan until she looked down at her and gave her a peck on the lips. "Nice to see you too my lovely." She'd said, and Granddad came into the garden after briefly talking to Dad who'd just got back from the shops.

Dad was classically handsome with dark hair, side burns, of medium build and in jeans and a t-shirt. Mum had been the type to wear jeans and comfy jumpers, was of medium build with ginger, straight hair.

Mum had been beginning to realise that she couldn't just get on with tea and left the beans with the knife to one side, suddenly realising that they were bound to get visitors.

Uncle Cyn came on his own next and said he'd just popped in for a quick look at the baby and said Aunty Caroline would come over another time wanting us to settle in first. Uncle Cyn had been a wartime baby and was much older than Mum and he had an incredible very distinctive laugh. he had to have a cuddle too and said "What a good baby." With a smile on his face. Aunty Nola looked over his shoulder having crept through the front door and said "She doesn't seem to mind being picked up by strangers does she?" Uncle Cyn just laughed again and pointed out that they weren't strangers. We were all family and then passed me to Aunty Nola, my mum's youngest sister. She had lovely, naturally curly auburn hair and was very beautiful. Cradled in her arms I'd been aware of a sweet scent that wafted over me and I inhaled the smell. She'd had a bag on her arms that knocked me slightly off balance which Mum relieved her of. "There's a few things in there that Graham and I thought you might need." She said. The bag was full of nappies, Johnsons Baby Oil, wet wipes and talcum powder. Mum had been grateful.

The garden got a bit crowded and Mum noticeably to the other adults was getting tired and drawn, so in turn, I got plenty of kisses, goodbyes, lovely to see you's and we'll come again's from everyone as they left one by one.

Mum soon picked up the greens again and finished chopping them up. I was put back in to my basket. The sun was high and mum, dad, Fee and I ended up eating outside on patio furniture.

A couple of months later I was big enough to be put in a highchair next to the dining room table for meal times and I'd developed a lovely little giggle whenever I got attention but was mainly quiet. Mum gave me some keys to play with and she'd noticed by now that my hands had to be kept busy as I'd had a tendency to pick up and play with anything I got given. Jangling the keys at least Mum knew I'd been happy. Fee kept giving me toys to play with too. Then the baby food came out. Fee had fish fingers, mash and peas while my parents had large bits of fish with their veg. Mum let her food go cold while feeding me while playing the aeroplane game and I got frustrated with the flying spoon and kicked and waved wanting to hold the spoon myself. I knocked the food flying and got in to a bit of a mess.

"Oh well," Mum had said "as Thursday's child we're going to have a long way to go with this one." Mum beamed at me as I started pulling off my socks to take them off. Fee had said, "Pooey, smelly feet." And held her nose up in the air.

After dinner I dozed off and so Mum took me upstairs to my room. Once there though I woke back up again and stayed moving round the bed a lot. Mum felt exhausted and put Fee down for a sleep too. I'd kept waking up at night quite a lot during the past month so Mum had the idea to try the radio on in my room. The dulcet tones of presenters and quiet music eventually lulled me to sleep. At last Mum had found a cure for all mine and hers restless sleeps and she had the best night sleep ever since I'd gotten home.

The next day, fully rested, I'd been put in the garden in the bouncy chair that was yellow and had black squares. Attached to it was a dangly thing with a character from the Muppets on, a mirror and something to squeeze on. I'd loved to kick it more than anything and Fee would squeeze it for me making my eyes light up in appreciation.

As a passive baby I didn't really make much noise though I'd come across as a contented little person always playing on my own with toys while

Fee needed constant attention. Mum noticed the air getting cooler and decided to get the pram out and take us girls for a walk. Tucking me into my new blue crocheted blanked and taking Fee by the hand she took us to the local park.

Fee got pushed on the swings while I sat in my buggy just taking it all in with a couple of toys on my bedding.

Dad had finished paternity leave by now and Mum had started me on the bottle. Outside in the families white Moses basket, Fee once used, Mum put the radio on and noticed that I dozed off quite nicely to the tunes playing. Mum smiled to herself as the housework was being completed with the help of Fee flicking the pink and yellow feather duster about.

At six months old, my Mum noticed me starting to crawl through the hallway, the kitchen, dining room and living room keen to explore. The stair gate was the only thing stopping me from going upstairs. All this crawling around made me not only hungry, but got Mum to put little jeans on me so as not to let my knees get hurt.

That meal time Mum tried me with a cut of carrot for the first time and I bit hard on it, as Mum had run her finger over my gums and had noticed two teeth before feeding me. It felt cold in my mouth and a crunching sound while eating was new to me and I banged the highchair with my hands. At the point I'd finished the carrot and wanted more of which Mum gave me along with breadsticks. That day I had my first solid poo which made Fee run into the other room as Mum changed me. She sang a nursery rhyme to me and tickled my tum to stop me wriggling about and I soon got clean.

Outside in the sunshine I bounced around in the bouncy chair while Fee was tickling my toes. Mum came out with breadsticks for both of us as she cooked tea. Mum poked her head out the back door from the kitchen and noticed Fee sticking a breadstick up her nose laughing at the same time. Unfortunately though she never got a laugh out of me.

Mum suddenly had a light bulb moment at me as Fee unstrapped me from the chair, then held my hands to stand me up and next thing I knew Mum brought out a push along black and white dog with orange wheels on. I was elated. This was to help me walk round the back yard.

Mum booked the church for my christening a few months back and decided, while we were outside, to dig out Fee's old christening gown. Mum guessed that it was about the right size for me now and decided to try it on me as everything was cooking. It was a beautiful fit just ready for the next day.

It was a cosy countryside church called St Peters' in Evercreech that day. The sun was shining, the birds were singing, the hyacinths were in full bloom. I'd been dressed in the same white long frilly gown my Dad had been in at his christening. Outside the whole family took turns to hold me for photographs and I'd been feeling cosy and well loved. Aunty Nola, my mother's sister, was there of whom had been asked to be my godmother and Nan Burr also. Uncle Cyn was my godfather.

Fee was running about trying to get everyone's attention while everyone in seventies fashion stood around for the camera in the grounds of St Peters.

Barney, my Uncle and auntie's dog had been there all excited by the foray. Other Uncle and aunts had been there, both sets of grandparents, cousins Scott and Lyn, even dad's best friend Mike Smith with his wife and Graham Burr.

God was shining on us that day and as I'd been carried down the aisle I never whimpered even when the vicar made the sign of the cross on my forehead. Everyone hummed and aahed and repeated, in a church full of witnesses, their vows to keep me in the faith and to protect me from harm.

I smiled through my eyes up at Mum cradling me with one arm while singing the hymns from the service sheet in the other hand while gently swaying me back and forth.

There'd been a real feeling of togetherness and warmth. This was my send off into the Christian faith. We all bustled up the aisle back outside into the glorious sunshine. A few more pictures were taken just before we all walked together back to my mother and father's home and we all went in through the back gate. Most of us stayed outside, mostly the men as the women took off foil, cling film and tea towels from the endless tray, plates and bowls. The men tucked in first, I'd had my bottle and Fee cooed over me glad that she was in the middle of all the attention with probably wishing she'd still had her christening whilst in the same dress.

Mum took me outside and passed me around until someone had put a blanket down for me to crawl in normal clothes. Happy and content I played with Fee who then took centre stage showing everyone how much she loved her little sister by passing me toys and helping me to stand up. Everyone oohed and aahed us, some of them were even laughing happily.

Scott and Lyn were just that little bit older than us so decided to stay on their seats and enjoyed the sandwiches, carrot sticks, and sausage rolls, etc. Scott was especially a healthy eater with an athletic build, glorious tan and blond hair. Lyn was the younger of the two also with blond hair.

I eyed up everyone looking with my smiling eyes to my coloured Uncle Cyn hoping for a cuddle. He caught my eye, lifted me up and swung me in the air laughing with me as I said Dad to him. He tried to coax Cyn out of me. I wriggled in his arms but his strong arms kept me safe.

The sun had been strong all day, the drinks got passed around a lot. Mum decided enough was enough as she saw me fall asleep so she picked me up and put me back in my cot.

The next day I was sat in the back of the car strapped in my Moses basket with Fiona. The sound of the engine hummed along lulling me fast asleep. Fee had been laid out on the seat willing herself to doze off as Mum gently spoke to her and sang a lullaby, Rock-a-bye-baby. Dad looked at her briefly and smiled secretly wishing she'd been a boy, but appreciating us three girls, Mum included. The car sped up along the main A-road from Yeovil on to the sea front at Weymouth. The sun was smiling on us that day and Dad pulled into a bay at the top of a place called Nothe Fort overlooking the harbour.

Out of the car I got placed into a pram. Fee got carried on dad's shoulders as we walked into the top end of the high street to take us down into the main town. Nearing the harbour we went along the bridge overlooking the boats bobbing up and down on the water. Mum pushed the pram over a grate which made a loud rumbling sound which woke me up. Looking about me all I saw was peoples' legs and small children holding their parents' hands and I spied the sea when passing the steps down to the harbour wall. I blinked at the strong sun through under the brim of my hat. Fee had been chatting happily to Mum and dad. Turning my head there was a road and an endless array of shop windows promoting lovely things. Mum pushed me in to a charity shop right next to the toys that Fee reached out to play with and got me to press the buttons that lit up and played beautiful songs. Kicking my feet out at the same time while laughing through my eyes, Fee laughed out loud and got me to giggle. "Da" I'd said and Fee told Mum as she got back from looking round the clothes. Other ladies in the shop turned and smiled indulgently at us. Fee was used to the attention and in her pretty dress said "Hello" of which they responded to by saying the same. Mum took one look at the toy we'd been playing with and took it from my hand to pay for it. Wandering over to the cash register with us Fee smiled and said "Thanks Mum."

We wandered round all the shops before going along the esplanade. There was a bit of a breeze and our parents took us down a ramp to the beach. Tired of pushing me around Mum let me down to walk along the beach with me falling on the soft sand every so often getting covered in the stuff. Dad brushed the sand off and put a high factor of 50 on.

In and out of the sea we went splashing around. Mum took turns with Dad to hold our hands swinging us up and down in the water and encouraging us to swim. It had been a glorious day. I'd started on solids and had finger food for lunch which Mum carefully broke up and got me to hold careful not to get me messy. Dad saw to Fee's food then she disappeared for a bit with my father to see a puppet show Mum had said. I had her full attention now and she gently kept talking to me telling me to say mum...I just giggled in her arms making funny noises and naturally coming out with the word "Da". Mum hugged me and showed me how to build a sandcastle with one of the buckets and spades they'd brought along.

Mum noticed my cheeks and my nose going red and slapped on some more sun screen just as Dad came back with Fee who had a lolly in her hand.

It was nearly half past four and I heard my parents saying they were going to pack up and get an early night. Mum said they'd cook tea when they got back and I was soon back in the car gently talking through my own little sounds to Fee speaking with me most of the way home.

The next day we were moving house from Evercreech to Shepton. On that day there was an air of excitement that I'd felt all around me.

> *Proverbs 14:13*
> *Laughter may hide sadness. When happiness is gone,*
> *sorrow is always there.*

There was a removal man talking to my parents in the kitchen. I'd been placed in a buggy. I'd been asking for food by saying "Da," and putting my finger in my mouth. I'd wanted to get out of the restraints to feel the floor under my feet desperate to want to walk not understanding why I couldn't. There was a tension in my legs making me kick out. No-one was paying any attention. Fiona had gone outside with Dad taking what she could lift to the van, like our toys. They were pleased with her for wanting to help. I was too young and not aware yet of exactly what was going on.

The move will give us a home of our own at last." They'd said.

Once pushed into the warmth of the sun outside I'd felt the heat warming up my veins. Squinting up to the sun I sat patiently watching, quietly observing the removal man with Dad lifting the furniture into the back of the van. The doors soon closed. I heard the engine roar off into the distance. I'd heard Mum tell me that she'd take me up the park to let the men move the big furniture in first. Mum sang to me all the way there trying to get me to sing, to make a noise, she was happy. Fiona helped Mum push the pram feeling pleased that she was helping. They walked by the pub on the corner. The green field caught my attention. I remembered the voices of happy children there from visiting these places before. The desire to run there coursed through me. I kicked hard on the pram and said, "Dad?" I saw muck look at me quickly, she looked grim and had stopped singing. I'd enjoyed her singing, why did she stop?

In the park Mum placed us both on the swings and pushed each of us in turn. A delicious thrill went up the back of my spine. Kicking my little legs, forming words in my little head, trying to say push harder. "Push." Came out of my mouth. Fiona giggled as she knew what I meant. Then Mum having heard pushed me just that little bit harder. I felt the rush of the wind on my face it felt deliciously cool. Mum slowed us down, there were other families turning up who wanted the swings. We stayed for another few minutes before Mum lifted us out of the swings and placed me in my pram then grabbed Fee's hand dragging us to the ice-ream van.

"Two mini-milks please." She'd said and handed over the change to the man in the van. I'd said, "Mini." And my little face lit up as I had grabbed the stick.

Mum took her time to push us back to the old house. When we stopped I can still see her pushing the strands of hair about her face around the back of her head.

Back in the yard she left us to play. I'd been pushing around doggy desperate to walk. Fiona sat on the dog pushing me on with her feet digging in to the ground. Mum came in to the back yard dragging boxes with her. Fee abandoned me to help Mum but she told her to just play with her little sister, me. Fiona did not obey and picked up a toy tired of our play. I turned to her and started walking my first few steps. Fee noticed and went to grab my hands to help while dropping her toy. Walking by a lot of boxes piled high after Fee had helped me through the house to the outside. Then the van turned up again. Mum helped them put the boxes inside as Fiona and I watched.

Mum then bundled us into the car to drive behind the van all the way to a place called Shepton Mallet.

"Over the hills and far away," Mum sang about a family of ducks as she was driving over the hills and round the bends. I felt the wind across my face coming from mum's side of the car, nice and gentle feeling tingly on my warm skin.

Pulling into the driveway I'd heard the door click. I didn't know what this was but instinctively knew that I was getting out of the car.

We got into the house and upstairs Fee and I had the biggest room that had jungle wallpaper. I loved the giraffes. They made me smile and then the next day a long drive was hard for me as a young baby down to the seaside. Fee would have been talking then as I was only saying mono-syllabic words with Dad being the most heard out of my mouth. Mum had given me a teething toy to pick up and grab and even a couple of bread sticks to keep me going while I'd wriggle my toes and sway slightly to the songs on the radio.

The woven rugs were put out on the beach with the blue and orange windbreak around us. Fee was happy with a spade and bucket. I'd been toddling around getting used to the feel of the sand beneath my feet. Constantly looking up to see my family happy and content. Feeling strong enough to walk further I found myself gently feeling the lapping of the water through my toes cooling my skin nicely.

Next thing I knew two strong arms were picking me up while Dad waded into the sea just a little bit further up to his waist. With his hand firmly placed under my belly the cold water was a shock to the skin and made me wriggle wildly. Dad gave a coaxing laugh and I could hear Mum and Fee joining in. Feeling swept away by the water slightly I firmly griped dad's fingers feeling a rhythm pulsating through me caused by my kicking that was calmly slowing down. Laughing up to my father's twinkling blue eyes I felt safe. He let go briefly and the water went into my mouth but Mum noticing my struggles came up from behind placing her hand under my belly as Dad had been distracted by Fee splashing him in the face. Mum then took my hands and glided me across the water walking backwards with me.

> *1 Timothy 2:15*
> *But a woman will be saved through having children,*
> *if she perseveres in faith and love and holiness with modesty.*

The tempo of my kicking had become nervous making my whole body shake this time. I struggled out of mum's grip as she was holding me and my arms flailed about.

Fee had been a more confident swimmer with her arm bands on following us moving about while Dad had swum off out to sea to get some exercise. With Dad out of the picture Mum swooped me up in to the air into her arms and she gently sang in my ear a lovely lullaby. Fee getting jealous started to sing louder a nursery rhyme Mum had been teaching her. With two different tunes surrounding my head Mum and Fee started laughing at me as I'd just tried to sing for the first time. They never told me what I'd done though and they just cooed and continued to laugh at me instead while coaxing out another tune. It was Humpty Dumpty and Mum tickled my tummy, suddenly feeling dry and warm my feet were desperate to feel the cool water running through my toes again so I wriggled hard. Mum lost her grip and fell backwards so fee quickly grabbed one arm too hard which hurt. At least she'd stopped me from drowning.

Dad had come back after hearing the commotion and started gently teaching me to swim again. As he moved away with me gliding through the water Mum decided to get the picnic out and asked Fee to help her. I just smiled up at Dad with my piercing blue eyes matching his smiling back to saying Dad again.

It was a long time till Dad and I got out of the water. Fee was back to using the bucket and spade. Her and Mum had made a lovely castle that I just happened to stumble into feeling suddenly tired on my little legs. Mum had said, "Never mind." And sat me on her knee for feeding. Fee had eaten and felt put out so Dad got out a little story book to read to us as she sat in his lap with a promise afterward we'd all make another castle.

There were few people on the beach that day; the odd couple holding hands, a stray dog wandering away from their owners and a couple of other little families with their children not quite old enough for school yet either.

The radio soothed us girls in to sleep in the car as Mum and Dad talked amongst themselves about what to do on our up and coming holiday with gran and gramps.

During September time we were having an Indian summer and with Dad desperate to teach us to swim before our holiday Mum and Dad pushed us in prams up the hill from us to the open air lido in Shepton Mallet.

There were two arm bands underneath the buggies plus swimsuits and towels underneath with a couple of nappies for me. In the ladies Mum put on my blue swimsuit and Fee's pink one. Then we waddled towards the baby pool. Dad had jumped in at the deep end nearest the changing rooms in the big pool intending to have a swim first. Ten laps later he joined us and I splashed him in the eye he just laughed and I just laughed back. Mum took her chance to swim in the big pool. With Fee and I walking through the water Dad began eyeing up the other females, especially ones in bikinis round the pool. Getting a bit bored he took us girls towards the shallow end of the large lido. Fee wouldn't get in and walked back to the baby pool by Dad started pulling me around in the water just like he'd done in the sea a month before while watching Fee. Mum had noticed her on her own and came back to join her. I was in my element I'd begun to really love playing in the water getting my dad's attention and because I'd smiled with my eyes, Dad's were always twinkling back at me.

Now Fee being there was beginning to notice how much attention I got from father by the only loved teaching me to swim. To him Fee was all grown up being able to swim with her arm bands and Mum was with her. So we took a long time each enjoying the moment.

Psalms 84: 11 – 12
The Lord is our protector and glorious King,
Blessing us with kindness and honour.
He does not refuse any good thing
To those who do what is right
Lord Almighty, how happy are
Those who trust in you!

Fee started to learn how to wrap Mum round her little finger and was soon asking for sweets. Mum told Dad would get them but we were playing happily so next thing I knew Dad was carrying me to the sweet shop and he got little ice lollies. Two milky cow ones for us and big chocolate lollies for them.

I began to get cold and Mum saw me shivering wandering round the side of the pool so she took me into the changing rooms to towel me down. Put a nappy on and into warm clothes. Fee took her time with her lolly glad to have dad's attention. They were happily talking when Mum and I came out.

It was then Fee's turn to get changed. When she'd finished and we were being happy being pushed back down Shaftgate Avenue to Coombe View.

On the next day we all got packing to go on our first ever holiday this year with Nan and gramps, Aunty Nola and Uncle Graham to a cabin at the end of Burnbeck Pier. The coastline road had been long and with the window slightly down I know I'd been sound asleep with the gentle overtones of a song in the background.

He'd have taken the scenic route my dad. During the journey with Fee I'd have sung some nursery rhymes with Mum and Dad first.

When the car was parked the bags were hoisted out and we looked in on Uncle Steve's t-shirt printing business to say hello. He knew we were coming and gave us girls, Fee and I, a present each. I had a blue teddy bear I called Bluey.

At the wooden cabin we checked out our beds. Fee and I had a blown up mattress upstairs on the balcony overlooking the downstairs living room where there was a sofa bed for Nan and Gramps to sleep on.

It turned out to be a wet and windy holiday. One night when I found it hard to sleep I wriggled around so much I fell off the balcony and onto grandad's big tummy down below. Everyone was shocked when they woke up and believed that I could have really hurt myself. The holiday itself became less memorable after that thunderstorm of a night of where the waves kept crashing onto the cabin. The whole highlight of the trip was me falling out of bed.

Arriving home from hour holiday Mum and Fee helped Dad unload the car and I, stretching my legs bounded upstairs. In front of me was a large bookcase with all sorts of classics on including a row of green hardback books along the bottom. The right was the bathroom all decked out in pinks and reds. I needed the toilet and climbed on the seat to do a wee, carefully holding on to the radiator to pull myself up. Ever independently minded and not asking for help I wiped my bottom and got off the seat and yanked hard on the flush but the paper floated on top. I wanted to wash my hands but couldn't reach the sink so ran the water in the bath to clean my hands under before drying them.

Fee came trudging upstairs and I asked her to help me with the flush. Fee was busy with clothes in her arms helping Mum by dumping it in the wash basket outside the toilet door.

Just happy to be home I walked by Mum and dad's bedroom door on the landing to get to mine and Fee's room and started digging out some toys. Wanting Fee to play but getting no response I started carefully putting Bluey on the bed with my dolly and gently talked to them. Fiona did eventually come in to see what I was doing.

"Finished unpacking?" I'd asked and Fee went to get her dolls out in response. She'd had an orange and white teddy bear from Uncle Steve and we put them together on the bed. Mum called upstairs to see if we wanted sandwiches. Fee yelled down a resounding "Yes" for both of us.

Two minutes later we were downstairs sitting at the table munching into hammy sandwiches with a bit of red sauce. It was to be my birthday that week and no-one asked what I wanted. Oblivious to what was coming I always focused on the now and wanted Bluey at the table so Mum let me run upstairs to get him as there had been a spare seat. Fee huffed she might have wanted a chair for her own dolly but as usual I got my own way first. Happily munching away Fee decided she couldn't eat it all but I was famished and Mum was pleased that I had a clear plate.

Dad took the crockery out to the kitchen to wash up and have a chat with mum. I toddled off looking for play things with Fee. I plunked the keys on the piano in the dining room it was always begging to be played.

Dad put on some music on the record player and I wiggled to the music happily playing with my toys. Mum called from the kitchen that she was going to join us.

Life had been a lot of fun back then and the week soon rolled into my birthday as because what it says in the bible;

> *James 5: 5*
> *Your life here one earth has been full of luxury*

On the door step was soon Uncle Graham, Aunty Nola, Aunty Caroline, Uncle Cyn a very young cousin Casey, Aunty Wendy with Scott and Lyn as well as my grandparents. Taking over the whole house I soon got presents off everyone. Tearing open the paper Mum had a rubbish bag handy and I had a hair set, a Sindy, colouring books, plain drawing paper with pencils and some clothes. Off of Nan Burr I had a Silver Jubilee colouring in book. Mum told me to say thanks and I hugged everyone in turn as they all sat round the living room with drinks in their hands. Music was on in the background as everyone chatted away.

I overheard Uncle Cyn ask Mum if she wanted a washing machine, not knowing what one was, I'd said what I'd heard Dad always saying. "Mum's the washing machine." Uncle Cyn laughed as Mum said she'd get one, one day when they had enough money and that she'd been struggling but managed to wash everything in the sink. It had been a dry day and she took her brother outside of where the washing was on the line. Other uncles and aunts followed and I struggled for company so went looking for Fee. She was talking animatedly with our cousins, Scott and Lyn, and was cooing over baby Casey in her crib. I looked at her wondering what they were talking about and ended going back to my toys in the living room where I'd left them and carried my drawing paper outside with everyone else.

Content with pencils and paper the family were tucking into party food. Mum asked me to help myself but I struggled to reach the table so Fee put some food on a plate for me. I got food all over my drawing and made a bit of a mess so soon gave up eating.

At this point everyone who'd turned up for me were cooing over Casey's crib outside so I happily kept on making pretty pictures.

It was long afterwards that everyone started to make excuses to leave and all said they'd had a happy time. I got brief kisses off everyone before they left. Tired and full I had a goodnight's sleep and in the morning Mum put up cereal for Fee and I. I liked snap, crackle and pop. Fee liked co-co-pops from the multi cereal packets.

At breakfast Mum told us that her and Dad had made a beautiful crocheted blanket together before they got married and she laid it out on the living room carpet with our tea-set to play with it. Fee went upstairs hunting for dollies and was ages so I placed the cups around the blanket on their yellow saucers, then the plates next to them and plastic cutlery in appropriate places. Fee and I stretched out this game all morning.

That afternoon Dad drove us girls over to Evercreech to see dad's parents. They greeted us at the door to their little bungalow and ushered us in through the hallway and out into the kitchen. Nan asked us if we all wanted drinks. Cola and lemonade were for us girls so we went for the coke. Mum and Dad had cups of teas.

I went out to the conservatory just off the kitchen to have my drink on the long blue bench like seats. I left my drink on the floor as I'd pulled over the bench for some paper to draw on. then juggled my work and drink to get down the steps into the garden but managed to trip over sending my glass smashing to the floor. Nan noticing through the kitchen door came to my aid saying "Woopsey-a-daisy. Not to worry Karen. We'll soon have this mess soon cleared up," and Fee was asked to get the dustpan and brush while I sat down outside on the ground outside with tears running down my face. Nan told me that she'd get another drink and she place it on the low wall outside. Getting a little table outside for me and a chair I soon perked up to do my drawing outside.

At this point Dad had come outside as Granddad asked him to see to the veggie patch and do some weeding.

Genesis 1:11
Then he commanded, "Let the earth produce all kinds of plants, and God was pleased with what he saw.

Dad took his shirt off to show off a tan to get it topped. Mum came out with a tray of everyone's drinks on and placed it on my table. I had to take my drawing to the wall to lean on.

Mum had been heavily pregnant at the time and looked awkward wherever she went to sit down. She was big at the front and I remember Nan saying to her it would be another girl. Nan knew this to be true as she spouted an old saying "Big at the front a girl, and big at the back a boy."

Mum had looked sad as her brother Uncle Steve's death shook her hard that year of 1977. So Nan and Granddad sat with her for a while. I kept my head down drawing a lovely picture I'd thought would cheer Mum up and make her smile. Fee was flitting in between Dad and the oldies. Mum said her head was spinning and kept saying "They're coming, they're coming." Nan gave her hand a hard squeeze and started counting trying to get Mum to regulate her breathing and kept her walking. Mum kept wincing, nearly doubling over, and holding her side.

Dad looked up from the gardening and asked if he should call an ambulance but Nan seemed fine and said give it twenty minutes and the feelings would pass. Upon hearing this I stopped staring and went back my drawing ever trusting that older people knew what they were talking about. Fee had been worried though and stayed with Mum afterward all afternoon.

Mum did ask Gran and Gramps if us girls could stay the night if the new born baby was about to come and Nan said that was fine. Mum had been worried about lack of toiletries for us but Nan said she'd get toothbrushes from the Spar shop. My mother looked relieved at this conversation and took my queue to show her my drawing of the family.

"That looks nice dear." Nan had said but I wanted to show Mum. "Lovely." She'd said. I'd been getting used to platitudes.

That night Fee and I shared a bed in Nan's spare room but we couldn't sleep as we talked about the new baby. Fee knew Dad wanted a boy but I told Fee about Nan's saying of how she knew it would be a girl. I did eventually get to sleep but Fiona kept nudging me awake, telling me off for snoring.

Later on that next day we heard from Mum. She'd been shopping round Bristol for some reason as the doctor had told her to keep being busy and walking about. The next phone call had been that Mum was in a Bristol hospital and had given birth to a healthy 7lb little girl of whom, apparently, had a fair set of lungs on her. We were told there'd been complications as the baby had come out with her foot facing the wrong way. Fee and I desperately wanted to see her. I also heard Nan asking on the phone what they'd named the baby. "The baby's name is Eve." I heard Nan parrot back and she soon came in the living room to tell us.

"We heard." Fee and I said together but Nan went on and explained that it would be another day before Mum was to be transferred to Shepton Mallet's hospital and into a proper maternity room all to herself.

Fee and I couldn't wait to see our new baby sister so as soon as Mum came to Shepton Dad took us round to see them. I was curious about her feet but my hand had been batted away from the blanket. Mum wanted to keep her warm. I'd heard the nurse recommend a specialist podiatrist in town to help with Eve's feet. I'd always been interested in adult conversations and liked the pink crocheted blanket that my new baby sister had been wrapped in.

Walking behind Dad going through the door I misjudged where I'd been walking and Dad take us all over home. Cooing over Eve in the car Mum turned round and smiled at us.

A couple of months later Eve had been settling in quite nicely. She cried a lot but Mum had been patient and kind with her, always fussing.

With Fee and Eve barely being a baby a few months on, sitting in the back of the car Dad said that the grandparents were following us to Sandy Bay out passed the Burback Pier near Weston for the day.

It was a lovely beach and the tide was nearly in. Mum changed me in to a blue and yellow dotted swimsuit on a white background. She dressed Fee in red and white. The place had been heaving with people and we just managed to get a spot bot far from the water's edge.

Gran and Gramps all tall and majestic looking as Gramps was in a brown suit and Gran in a long skirt and blouse turned up to sit next to us. Nan stripped down to a swimming costume and followed Fee and I down to the sea. Eve woke up and mum had to feed her to stop her crying. Evidently the noise on the beach awoke her. Gently placing Eve in Dad's arms all three of them walked down to the sea leaving gramps with all our belongings.

I laughed up to Eve in Mum's arms as her feet were dangled in the water and gave Eve a bit of a splash on her face. She started crying so Gran grabbed my hand to have a walk along the water's edge together at which point Mum took a photo. Nan had to crouch down to get in the picture.

Mum took Eve back to our stuff which left Dad swimming in the sea with Fee in her armbands. I needed mine really but didn't know how to ask. I then got promptly splashed in the face by older children swimming right by me. I liked the crowds but not others getting in my way. I tried to swim but flailed around miserably with a mini wave knocking me over. I'd managed to find my feet and stand up and noticed Nan had gotten my armbands. Wanting to shout 'yippee' my face lit up and Nan knew that I'd want to go out further in the water. With a guiding hand she pushed me through the crowds and I bobbed up and down ferociously kicking my little legs out behind me. My arms felt heavy as I didn't like the restrictions of armbands but at least they kept my head above water.

Coming back to shore I threw off my fluorescent arm coverings in favour of grabbing an ice lolly that Mum had in her hand for me. Luckily I didn't have far to walk to our beach mats that were made out of cane all woven together. Not liking the feel of it I sat on it any way at this point with everyone sitting down. Gran and Gramps were on the deck chairs. Dad sat on the sand and after eating Fee and I buried a leg each of his in the sand. Dad just laughed, Mum encouraged us to use the buckets and spades and I'd gone to Eve in her moses basket to talk to her and to try and get her to hold my spade. The oldie's looked and laughed but Mum thought that I was going to hit her so Dad was told to take it out of my hand. It had been a fun filled afternoon on the beach and we wer all soon drying off and putting on our clothes again. Mum declared fish 'n' chips for everyone and after bundling into the car we stopped off on Weston's sea front for chips in cones for Fee and I while everyone else had fish with theirs.

When finished Mum had to breastfeed Eve followed by her burping and a nappy change. Walking along the seafront on the promenade the sun looked a deep orange as it was setting over the sea. Full and happy we were soon on our way home after kissing Nan and Gramps goodbye as they were heading back to Evercreech.

Back in Shepton a lot of stuff had to come out of the car. Fee shoved a bucket and spade in my hand as Mum carried Eve and her and Dad shared the rest. "Ah well," Mum had said "Red at night Shepherds delight." She'd said.

It was Monday next day and I was pink all over. Fee had amazingly stayed white. Mum's freckles were more pronounced and Dad had gone off to work looking lovely and brown. Fee and I had woken up quite late that morning so Mum got us out some colouring in books for us after breakfast. I took my new Jubilee colouring in book into the living room and rested on the glass coffee table. Fee stayed at the dining table. It was a lovely easy going day.

By the end of the week jumping into the car Mum turned to Dad and said "Let's try somewhere different." Dad responded "Well we'll just see where the car ends up shall we." As he turned round and spoke to us girls. We all smiled it was like going on a mini adventure until the road seemed to get longer and longer on a wide A road. Fee moaned and Mum winked at Dad finally knowing where we were going as we'd passed the Weymouth thirteen miles to go sing. Mum turned to Fiona and told her to wind down the window as she was feeling sick telling her "Another twenty minutes love, just take some deep breaths of fresh air."

Fee had gone paler than her pale skin was possible but Dad could not pull over on such a busy road.

Once in Weymouth Mum took us to the local Spar shop to get my eldest sister some water. I'd asked for a drink too and got some lemonade. Then we sat on the wall by the harbour. Fee gradually got some colour back to her cheeks and we all made our way to the beach. I noticed the swing boats, trampolines and helter-skelter and asked to go on the boats. Dad said later after settling down on the beach and encouraged me by walking down to the sea to have a swim. Eve stayed with Mum. I found that I was getting better at swimming with armbands and that they were beginning to rub my skin. Dad told me to take them off. I did and spent a long time dancing through the waves. Fiona had joined in too and at five years old could swim unaided. I wanted to be just like her and jumped into a wave and feeling the waves on my forearms it was lovely to be free from restrictions. Dad told me to use my arms more and let me get on with it. We were in the shallowest part of the sea even though the water came up to my waist and I kept standing up every time I'd felt like I'd been sinking. Dad kept an eye, Fee was swimming nearby and Mum was encouraging Eve to walk on the beach by holding her hands. A lot of work still had to be done with her feet at the specialist chiropodist in Shepton but Mum was determined to get her walking the same way as other children.

Fed up with being in the sea and having had a nice picnic Dad took me over to the swing boats. He lifted me into one end while he jumped in the other side. My little face lit up as Dad strived to get us higher and higher. I loved it and yanked the rope harder and harder. I could have stayed on there all afternoon but we only had thirty minutes and were soon off again.

The afternoon flew by and we were soon walked across to a little stage in a red and white hut. It was three thirty and Punch and Judy made me wonder what all the other children were laughing at as the red cheeks, nose and cackling laugh gave me the creeps. It was to be my birthday the next day and I didn't really want this in my memory. I didn't cry but was haunted.

The next day I'd had a couple of friends over for my third birthday. A boy named Jonathon and his sister, Jennifer. I think they were both twins. My grandparents had turned up too and my Aunty Nola and Uncle Graham.

It had been a lovely sunny mid-October day and the presents seemed to have a theme of most things being knitted like a cardigan, a jumper, matching hat, scarf and gloves and a rubber ducky.

Us children played our first game of musical statues in the living room with Dad on the LP player making it stop every two minutes. I giggled a lot and so did my friends. We even had cake and lots of party food with multi-coloured party hats with poppers too that seemed to make a mess everywhere.

I was soon saying goodbye to my friends and had been busy making plans with them to see them again soon. Mum seemed pleased with this friendship and after everyone left she beamed at me and got me to open my mouth and close my eyes to get a surprise. It was a sweetie and I spent ages sucking on it before something came out of it to fizz on my tongue. Mum did the same to Fee and both us girls burst out laughing. I started to choke and needed some water. Dad handed me the glass and tipped it into my mouth slowly while moving me on to the sofa to sit down. This was when Dad gently rubbed my back till I'd felt better and could breathe easier.

"I think it's time we thought about bed." Dad said to me so us girls were soon in our nighties and cleaning our teeth.

Fee was only at school for another two months before the Christmas period. This time flew by as our days were filled with something to do every day. We even had a Christmas party at Fee's school before they broke up which gave us a chance to dress up into our prettiest dresses. I loved to dance and always felt sad to leave.

The beginning of that Christmas period was one of my earliest memories which was of me watching the Water Babies on TV for the first time. The boy's hairstyle was a bit like mine from the film only darker. I'd thought, back then, that he'd died and gone to heaven whilst singing 'High cockerlor-um' and finally felt pleased for him after being rescued by the girl from the big house of where he'd been a chimney sweep. I'd looked around me at the white dust sheets over the lounge furniture and can remember watching our chimney sweep putting the endless extensions on what looked like a big toilet brush and him making a mess that would make me cough. He cleaned up his dirt though before he left and Mum had to pick up the sheets behind him.

We woke up the next morning and when Mum opened the curtains everywhere was completely covered in snow. The house roofs were white with the sky the same colour we were itching to get out into the snow to play. Mum got our coats, scarfs and gloves to put on while listening to the radio to see if Fee's school was closed. It had been. Also they'd said that the pond up at the park was completely frozen over for the first time in so many years.

On the way there we kept stopping to collect up snowballs to throw to each other. I'd tried to stuff a ball in Fee's hood as one she threw to me sent icy cold water down my back. All across town I liked to leave deep footprints in the virginal snow and look back at the trail I'd left. Mum wanted to keep us going as Fee marched on.

We went through the big wrought iron gates to the park and were soon at the pond. Sure enough there were adults being foolhardy walking on the ponds ice. Mum knew I'd wanted to try it and so did Fee so she held our hands and told us not to do it, but we watched for ages.

Fee and I started to turn blue with the cold as we stayed there to see families with trays to sit on to slide down the incline over the other side of the pond. Mum eventually pulled us away saying that we were going back for some hot soup with rolls of which we did after just taking our time enjoying snow again all the way. The hot thick chicken and mushroom soup was delicious. I savoured every taste feeling the warmth spread through my tummy. I finished first as I couldn't breathe very well. Every mouth full was rushed so I could inhale and exhale through my mouth more easily. Fee told me to close my mouth while eating as Eve had her milk from Mum's breast.

Thoroughly warmed up I'd felt quite sleepy so Fee, Eve and I curled up in front of the telly watching Bagpuss, a pink cat, and Button Moon not really absorbing what was going on as I drifted off to sleep, so did Eve.

The curtains in the morning were opened to even deeper white snow. Mum decided we were to stay indoors. The crayons and pencils came out as I made my way downstairs in warm comfy clothes. Fee and I gotten the utensils out but Mum told us not yet as we were to have breakfast. I had jam on toast and tried to feed Eve. Mum laughed and held Eve against her for feeding telling me that she wasn't on solids yet. Dad couldn't go to work or drive the lorries that day so we played games or watched television. On the news it was white all over the country and Dad phoned his brother, Uncle Keith, to see how he was in Cumbria. I never got to find out but was always curious how everyone was. The cars had come to a standstill completely buried on the roads. The day went by slowly and Fee was getting bored. I enjoyed Mum's attention in the kitchen while she'd been getting lunch for all of us and I chatted away happily mainly to myself running up and down stairs with my dolly bringing down new clothes for her to wear. Nan Burr had knitted her a lovely blue and white patterned dress. It was a big baby and I loved to sit her in the living room and talk to her asking Mum in the kitchen if she could sit with us at the dining room table for lunch.

Mum unusually cooked for all of us as she normally cooked for us in the evenings but as we were all home she wanted her kitchen clean for the rest of the afternoon.

I wanted to talk but Dad flicked his newspaper at me when in the living room so I spoke with Fee instead chewing her ear off. I'd had a nursery rhyme going round in my head and would randomly start singing throughout the rest of the afternoon leading in to the evening. Snuggled up in front of the fire watching Dad poke it with a stick, occasionally picking up a coal that fell out, the fire guard had to keep being moved and I wanted to put a white fire stick on to keep the flames going but dared not ask.

The following day Mum had the radio on and schools were still shut for the foreseeable future. Propping my arms up on the window sill I itched to go outside but as me and my sisters were still relatively small Mum did not want to venture out fearing she'd lose us in the drifts.

The snow stayed deep for a few more days until we saw people coming out of their homes to shovel up the snow on their drive ways. I'd put up permanent residence looking out the front windows until one morning when Dad wanted to get outside for a walk with us all to relieve the boredom that had settled upon us like a cloud.

Chapter Two

Mum wanted to stay indoors with Eve though so Dad took Fee and I outside with him to find out what the fields and the roads looked like up behind the Horseshoe Inn. It was a long old walk and the hood on my thick coat kept flopping over my eyes. Fee and Dad had snowball fights but I hated the feel of wet snow in my coat every time a throw was on target. Gritting my teeth I tried to scoop up my own ball of snow and made it as big as possible, but it kept crushing down small as it kept melting in my glove covered hand.

Up the hill we trudged through sludge and I looked to the side of me to see the very high drifts as far up as the highest hedges. Dad took a photo so I went and jumped in the snow but it came up over my legs and the soft snow seeped in through my trouser legs. I was getting very wet. Next we walked near a barnyard and outside in a very large drift we saw the hood of a mini which Dad identified from the small square roof.

The air was very still and out from the sky it gently started to snow again. I stuck out my tongue to catch the flakes and loved the taste of it melting in my mouth.

Dad started to tell us to avoid the drifts as dog owners passed us and Dad was worried about us standing in shit. Because of the flurry coming down though he guessed it would come down harder so we went back down the hill towards the family home of Christopher Casenove.

My father picked up speed to get home as the snow was coming down harder. I had to rush to keep us and as my chest was soaking wet by now as well as my feet and back I struggled to breathe. My nose was running and Fee managed to stay up with Dad. At the bottom of Bowlish Hill Dad decided to walk up through the meadows to come out in to Hillmead of where we walked pass the pub and up on to the main road opposite the Wimpey Estate. I was beginning to sneeze and Dad finally turned round to look at me and looked concerned so he picked me up.

> 'Luke 13: 12-13
> *When Jesus saw her, he called out to her, "Woman you are free from your illness!" He placed his hands on her, and at once she straightened herself up and praised God.'*

All the way back through Shaftgate Ave to him I'd been carried while Fee's hand had been held. My father was anxious to get back.

Mum took one look at us girls coming through the front door and said she'd run a hot bath. All Dad wanted to do was have a hot drink.

Ten minutes later I started playing with the bubbles with Fee and I'd been put at the end with the taps. Banging in to them I had to learn early on about sense of space so they wouldn't hurt my back and I wouldn't get in Fee's way. Mum bought out the shampoo bottle that looked like a Russian doll that was called Matey and gently rubbed it in to our hair. A bit got in my eye and it stung so I rubbed it out making the stinging even worse so Mum took extra care with the jug of water to get it all out. I was always happy in a bath but soon had to get out as Dad was coming up for a shower. Mum afterwards put us in fresh clean clothes and served us up with a hot casserole. We all took our time and I really loved the doughboys.

Mum thought we'd had enough of being up afterwards so I wasn't long before I was put in to bed. My head barely hit the pillow before I was asleep.

The sun came out the next day and Fee had to go back to school down the hill to Bowlish. I always enjoyed walking down with her and Mum while Eve was in the pram. The pavements were still precariously icy and sludgy but we could still look out across the fields and through the woods down the steps to lots of thick white snow.

It was hard for Mum to push the buggy down the steps so Fee tried to help pick up the bottom. I just trudged on oblivious as no-one asked me to help. At the bottom Fee had been looking grumpy. I think she just didn't want to go back to school.

At home Mum fancied doing some baking so I helped her and kept wanting to feed Eve. The dough I noticed tasted nice. Mum, it felt, laughed at me, my parents did that a lot and back then it made me feel warm inside and well loved.

Like the snow my heart would melt easily.

About a week later the family went for a walk across the fields. Eve was in a pram but Fee and I had been walking with Mum and Dad. Under the pram was a blanket and a picnic. As we walked along Dad pointed out the buttercups. He picked one and held it under my chin and I was told that I liked butter. I just smiled up at Dad and watched him do the same with Fiona and Eve. I noticed a yellow glow under their chins created by the flower and was told that it was the glow that proved your love of butter.

Through the long grass we kept walking with green fields all around us. Mum and Dad occasionally stopped to look at cows in neighbouring fields. The hedges looked tall and I had to look up to see the top of trees trying to see the birds my parents would look at.

Ecclesiastes 1:8

Everything leads to weariness – a weariness too great for words. Our eyes can never see enough to be satisfied; our ears can never hear enough.

With the sun in my eyes I had to squint and I bumped in to a tree. Mum had said that I always bumped into things. My eyes I'd heard were going to have to be tested. Dad had picked up a massive leaf called a Doc leaf he said that it would take the sting out of nettles.

Across three fields the blanket was laid out for our picnic. Nice eggy sandwiches, Battenburg and crisps with orange juice went down nicely. I loved to wonder and eat instead of sitting still.

we sang nursery rhymes and I loved us all singing together before we finished our picnic and decided to walk further after being satiated.

Across Friars Oven we spotted things that Dad said looked like raisins but Mum decided to put us straight by saying there must be rabbits and lo and behold we saw one pop out from the trees. Mum started telling us stories about baby rabbits and their families. Mum was always telling us stories. Luckily, because it was a dry day we hadn't needed boots, but the bushes were tickling my legs as we couldn't avoid them walking back across one field to which we had to climb over a concrete style. the pram had to be lifted over it empty and Eve afterwards.

With the sun getting low in the sky and we passed the cows again there was one last field yet to cross before we walked down Bowlish Hill down to Bowlish Lane. The pram had to be carried up the steps leading to Shaftgate Avenue and was then pushed back home with Eve back in it.

It was a typical day the next day for Mum doing the daily chores, feeding Eve her bottle and cooking for the rest of us in the evening when she'd realised Fee was coughing funny. It didn't sound like a usual cough.

A few days later Eve and I had developed an unusual raspy cough too. By this time Fee had developed a hoarse voice and Mum decided to keep her off of school. We had all come down with something called croup. It took a long time for us to go through all the other symptoms such as difficulty breathing and inspiratory stridor (a snoring type noise when breathing in).

Mum was getting at the end of her tether after a month of this and it didn't seem to be getting any better as we'd also come down with a fever. Mum had tried the natural remedies like taking us out in to the cool air from time to time or keeping us in a steamy room caused by a hot bath she'd have been in to wash. Mum was so worried that she kept a constant vigil but it had been getting to her what with Dad being away every day in the lorry. Mum had also come that close to doing something silly as she got more and more depressed, but thankfully, at her lowest ebb the croup passed all at once. It was like, finally, God had listened to her prayers and life started to get back to normal.

A few weeks had passed when we were soon off camping by a cliff side and were in our eight berth orange tent with our Aunty and Uncle, Nola and Graham. The tents were side by side. The scenery was amazing looking over the cliff edge out to sea. It got windy from time to time on the cliff and we'd walk down to the beach of where I'd spend hours in the sea while my sisters would get fed up with swimming. Eve would watch the fishes and Fee liked Mum and Dad's attention and so would stay with them. They'd have the old fashioned windbreakers because Fiona was always cold. We all had orange lollies.

Up at the tent we had a little camp fire to cook our meals on and we'd all warm our hands round it. In the evenings the whole family would sit around either singing songs or nursery rhymes. Before us girls would go to sleep Mum would sing a lullaby or tell us stores of Naughty Art, of Mum's made up little Imp.

I remember one night when I stuck my head out the tent really late and watching Fee wandering around in her white nightie looking like a ghost. She was sleep walking and I thought nothing of it and went back to sleep.

It hadn't been a long holiday, only a week, and we were soon getting back to the comforts of being at home. Woke up one day to tea and biscuits Mum had left for us. I took a little bit of time dunking my biscuits in my drink but one bit got so soggy it fell into the cup. I'd had to fish it out with my fingers.

Eve and I had bathed together the night before and as per usual I'd sat in front of the taps which I didn't mind but it did prod my back. Eve would always get our first leaving me to swim in the bath anyway. There was nothing like soaking in warm bubbles. Mum called me a water baby.

Mum came up eventually to choose my clothes for me and she put me in to my favourite dungarees just right for playing in and to make cakes in.

Fee and Eve went outside to play in the sun as Mum and I got out the mixing bowl, the mechanical whisk, the eggs, sugar, flour and sieve. I loved to mix it all together and often got flour all over my nose and on my dungarees. Mum would talk me through the process and tell me to take out the cupcakes tray and the paper cups to go in them. The paper always stuck together for me and I was amazed at how many paper cups were in a packet. I got down the wooden spoon from the bowl and started spooning the mixture in to make the fairy cakes licking my fingers as I did it.

Mum called out the front door for Eve and Fee to come in and share licking the bowl out while I had the spoon. We went to the armchair to fight over the last of the cake mixture making a mess over the sofa. Next thing we knew Mum had placed paper and crayons on the table to distract us. I fell for the distraction every time as I left Fee and Eve for the bowl to go and colour in my jubilee colouring in book that my Gran had given to me.

The morning passed in a haze once we were all at the table trying our best with dot to dots, colouring in, and using the play dough on the silver tray.

For lunch there'd been sandwiches and crisps and us girls had to stay at the table.

We all rushed outside in the afternoon playing in the sunshine with Fee on her bike with stabilisers, me on my tricycle and Eve clambering on and off a push along cart. Mum took a photo of me on my tricycle with my red cheeks aglow in the sunshine.

The three of us were happy and Mum brought the chalks outside to scribble on the yard. Mum drew out the squares and the numbers for us to attempt hopscotch on.

Then much later Mum brought out orange juice for we were getting thirsty and I helped Eve drink from her cup.

Into early evening around five o'clock it was getting chilly so Fee and I were asked to bring in the chalks and the blanket in the backyard which was put there in case we needed a nap. None of us had succumbed.

Something yummy smelling was cooking on the hob and Dad came in the front door just in time for tea. Nice baked beans, sausages and potato waffles.

After that weekend I was due to start nursery and upon walking into nursery I looked all around me in a very long and narrow looking room. There were lots of high up windows running the length of both walls. On the walls was lots of pictures of flowers, paintings, drawings and one big picture of a park with a duck pond in it with lots of scarily large animals like squirrels, birds, and even a worm sticking its head out of the ground looking like it was winking.

Mum had dressed me in jeans and a t-shirt ready for messy activities. My friends Jonathan and his sister were starting with me. There was a large group of us and we were all told to sit on the floor in a circle and had to tell each other our names. I wasn't shy and said Karen as clearly as possible. Never one to absorb too many details all at once I couldn't recall any ones names, but did get stuck into singing The Grand Old Duke of York, This I could remember after singing and I was introduced to other nursery rhymes too like Humpty Dumpty, Jack and Jill, Incy Wincy Spider and many more.

Feeling dry, glasses of orange juice came round on a tray for us to help ourselves. Sitting cross legged and sipping gently, everyone chatting noisily just washed over me as the sun streamed through the windows. I'd only been there for the morning and we got the paints out after juice. Putting on a bright red pinny I had to talk to the next child to me to share the paints. Red, blue and green were the favourite colours for grass and people. I then painted a yellow sun taking great care over every detail. I was quite pleased with my long sticks of grass, oval bodies with round heads with stick thin arms and legs, both people had bright smiley faces and sticky up hair and that glorious sun embodied how I felt perfectly. The paintings then had an hour to dry.

It was then free play. There was a kitchenette to play with, a book corner and big climbing pads all brightly coloured. I loved the kitchenette with all sorts of plastic ingredients to mix up pans and bowls to make cakes and cook eggs and pretend cans of baked beans to shake over a saucepan. I was in my element using the stove, then the oven, and pretending to put on the fan. There had also been a little sink next to it to put all the utensils in afterward to pretend to wash up then put everything away. That last hour flew by with me in my own little world.

The lady in charge of the nursery had pegged our painting son a line in the corner of the room and told us that our pictures were dry to take home as parents started turning up to the doors. They were two big French doors at the front of the building and I hung back as all the other children raced around trying not to get caught to have to go home. I smiled at all the children playing their parents up and Mum was soon there waving at me to look at her. I ran in to her arms excitedly telling her about everything I'd done all the way home while singing The Grand Old Duke of York. I could tell Mum was pleased and Fee just seemed quietly happy to see me while Eve was in the pram.

All afternoon I wouldn't stop talking and Dad that evening, got a full rendition of what I'd done that day too. I didn't stop to ask what Fee or anyone else had been up to, though luckily when they got the chance to speak, Fee shared that she'd had a friend round and Dad mentioned he'd been up country in his lorry. Eve had been happy in her highchair.

I slept like a log that night as my mind buzzed with happy dreams. Up with the lark Mum got me ready for nursery again and that day the theme was about trains.

We'd sat round in a circle on the floor again, with us all being roughly the same age, and had singing time. I was really enjoying this time throwing myself into every nursery rhyme really loudly. To start off the theme of trains. We all had a group story before fruit about a train that had been struggling to get up a hill and could talk. At first his mantra was 'I think I can, I think I can,' as he struggled with his load up what I thought must have been a mountain. Then at half way up the nursery assistant started chatting more loudly, "I know I can, I know I can." Before reaching the summit of the railway line before letting out a loud "Choo-choo", as the train heaved itself over the brow and chugging happily along on level ground. I thought "Wow," and said this mantra over in my head as some of us sat in the book corner later on trying to stand on our heads as a group of us had a competition going of who could stand on their heads the longest.

Now I'd left a plasticine model of a train on a tray before playtime and I was hoping that I could show Mum, Fee and Eve my model when they were to come and get me. this was when I'd pushed my way to the front door first that morning before grabbing Mum's hand to bring her inside with Fee. I loved to show them around and feel proud of what I'd done going on about how I could stand on my head the longest. To prove the point when I got home I started to stand on my head on the sofa for long periods to the point of hurting myself. Dad soon came home and I had to show him what I'd learned at nursery that day too.

The next day was a Friday and the whole family went up the big park together. At the park the first thing us girls ran towards was the swings. there was only two so I went down the slide several times enjoying the fastness of sliding down it and in my head I went "Wee" whilst it felt like taking off like a bird.

I noticed Fee had gotten off the swing so I walked across to it and had a go. Swinging back and forth, higher and higher, for a long time and Eve and I didn't get off for ages. Then we got on the see-saw giggling as the two little girls we were. Dad kept pushing down Eve's side with Mum doing the same my side. Afterward Mum put a crocheted blanket on the grass and layed out a picnic consisting of yummy food and drink. We lounged around nibbling and drinking in the midday sun with us all enjoying our company. Dad bought along a football and after about an hour of lounging around I'd been the only one to get up with him. We stripped off our jumpers and turned them into goal posts. It was so nice to have his attention to myself. I ran at the ball to kick to him in the middle of the goal posts. The ball went wild and started rolling down the park towards the ducks. I found that I had to run for it and laughed trying to kick it back up the grass. First with my left foot then my right while looking up to Dad after every kick making sure it was going in his direction. Two more kicks later I notice Mum walking down the side path with Eve and Fee in tow after they'd finished on the swings. Eve wanted to join in with the football while Fee sat down on a bench with mother. Eve toddled around falling over the ball a couple of times. I laughed at her and Dad decided to help her out more. I felt pushed out of the game a little bit as it was me whom had to run all over the grass chasing the ball every time it went the wrong way. I started to get out of breath and walked to Mum on the park bench to grab a drink. We all watched Eve running around with Dad trying to play football and at two years old she looked really cute but soon got tired so Dad picked her up to put her in the pram to get pushed all the way home.

At home we slouched around together humming and aahing what to do so Mum got out some crayons with a happy smile on her face. I knew it was my birthday the next day and found life amazing.

At least we never drew up the wall and Mum loved us for it, because she said, "Well done. At least I don't have to clean the wall like I had to when you were two years old.

The next day I woke up happy it was my birthday. The whole family turned up and I remember Charlie and Casey sat on the sofa looking very close. They had nice clothes I knew Nan Sheila bought them for them. Fiona said something to me that made me realise for the first time that she was jealous of their nice clothes. I turned to my friends Jonathan and his sister to start playing games with my cousins.

Running around happily the day swam by. At the end of the party Mum introduced me to a golden Labrador. I shied away behind Fiona. It looked quiet and shy. Then Dad took him outside into the garden to run around, we all carried on talking together. Shy as I was Mum kept us on the floor and we danced to a happy tune playing musical bumps.

The friends had gone home but the family had stayed. I looked around me and saw Casey and Charlie sitting down first and I was out. I felt incensed as the birthday girl should have been helped to win.

Afterwards in the hallway I said goodbye to everyone. I got picked up by my Uncle Cyn who made me laugh. I can picture my blue eyes shining up at him as he'd tickled my feet and I loudly laughed again. He was the last one with Aunty Caroline and my cousins to leave.

Afterwards, I can see this as clear as day, in front of me the puppy barking at me while I stood in front of the garage. I cried so hard that I wet my pants. Mum came out and saw my tears and swore at the dog, patted its head then she turned round as the dog sloped off and she gave me a big hug. Mum soothed me by constantly talking and wiping my brow.

"That naughty dog." She'd said "I'll get rid of him for you." As she carried me inside.

Mum then started to look through the freezer and pulled out some ice lollies. "Here's one for you. It's to cheer you up."

I said, "Won't my sisters want one?"

Mum replied, "I've only got one left and it's just for you."

I smiled and started to cheer up. A little song went through my head that went "It's my party and I'll cry if I want to, cry if I want to, you would cry too if this happened to you. Do, do, do, do, do, do."

I went into the living room afterwards and got Mum to put on a song. I got carried away dancing, then put my arms out to spina round like the rotors on a helicopter. I spun around so fast for ages. I found myself wobbling about too much as I stopped and fell over on to the corner of the fireplace and hurt my head. It stung real bad and I cried again.

Mum came rushing in and gave me a hug and just held me for what seemed like ages. Then I felt physically sick and threw up all over her. My birthday had been ruined as my lollipop and party food went everywhere.

Mum decided to put a wet flannel on my forehead to bring out any bruising she said.

A couple of months later it was Christmas time and each Christmas we would put a pillow case at the bottom of our beds ready for Father Christmas to put our presents in. I hadn't twigged about Father Christmas not being real at this point and was always determined to stay awake at night to see him. I think we always used to put a carrot out for Rudolph, a mince pie and a drink of sherry out for Santa. I was awake at 4 o'clock this Christmas day in the morning and I found a drum amongst my presents. It was the type of drum that had red, blue and yellow xylophone keys on it. I started banging on it waking the whole house up, because in those days when everyone was up we couldn't go back to bed.

Going downstairs Mum asked us who had taken the chocolates out of the wrappers lft on the tree. Not one for blaming others all us girls stayed quiet. I saw the empty wrappers and instantly knew that it was Eve.

We always had traditional turkey for lunch and would go to Evercreech to see Nanny Burr and Gramps in the afternoon for more presents and games of cards in the dining room on a thick brown table cloth or we would take it in turns on Nan's wood and green pinball game. This would be when my Aunty Sue and Uncle Keith would visit from Cumbria, Broughton-in-Furness.

Aunty Sue was a school teacher who taught French and German and Uncle Keith was a chemist. They were super intelligent to me as they would speak in French amongst themselves and I learned the word 'oui' that meant 'yes'.

Happy in the company of my family it was soon time to go home.

On Boxing day morn we all got ready to go for a walk across the fields before getting back for lunch of which was bubble'n'squeak, a left-over of all the Christmas dinner.

In the afternoon we'd go to Gran and Grampy Erns to see them for their wedding anniversary in to Wells. There'd been lots of food layed out for us to tuck into. Uncle Cyn, my black Uncle, who was thin, wiry and very handsome, Aunty Caroline, who was brown haired and average build, and my cousins Casey and Charlie were there along with Aunty Sue, Uncle Roy, cousin Ashley, plus other extended family members. It was a warm cosy feeling I got from all the family around me.

Into the evening the adults started to have alcohol while us girls played charades with everyone sitting around in the living room and kitchen having a laugh. Even my cousins Scott and Lyn would join in. They were both older than me and had blonde hair and piercing blue eyes. I looked up to my family and loved them very much. The evening ended in a warm glow in my tummy and the next day that golden glow came up in the west on the next morn.

The cockerel crowed far too loudly and woke us with a start. The window had been ajar all night as the breeze caressed my warm fuzzy head.

As the months slipped in to March I remember being outside in the warm spring air all morning. Then in the afternoon in the back garden Mum bought out Fee and I some lollies. She pulled the wrappers off carefully and slowly and gently put them in to our hands. We grabbed them tight thirsty and hungry at the same time. I sucked on it, then licked it gently before shoving it in Eve's mouth. Mum turned to us and she winked, and gave a girlie little laugh. I laughed back feeling a nice tickle in my tummy as Eve swayed back and forth in the black and white bouncy chair.

My Aunty Nola of who was very beautiful with long and naturally curly auburn hair had just turned up with my Uncle Graham of whom was a handsome man, quite tall, with lovely bright orange hair and a moustache which tickled my nose when he'd kissed me an hour later just before they left.

Left out in the garden us girls started to dig the soil under the Beech tree and found some worms. I accidently cut one in half. They stayed still for a while before they both started wiggling again. Then Mum came out and noticed the mess I'd got in to with the mud. I scratched my nose and Mum laughed. My face was covered in it she said and laughed. She looked at the others and pointed out that we could all do with a bath. She told us to strip off as we came in and to go straight upstairs for a wash. Then we had fun in the bath.

During the summer we went to Butlin's on holiday at Minehead. I remember a hall full of ping pong ball games and pool tables. I used to love playing table tennis especially with Dad who was always dead keen on teaching us how to play properly and learn the rules, the more I learned about rules for things the more I thrived on wanting to be the best at playing. Fiona used to try and cheat but because her type of play was obvious it gave the rest of us a bit of a laugh.

There would be outside games too as a photo Mum had showed us playing team games outside with other children on this holiday. We all had these peaked sun visor croupier hats. Eve's was green and I assume mine was blue as it was always my favourite colour. I'm sure Fee's was yellow.

Near the end of the holiday Fiona got on stage with lots of other young girls to see who was the prettiest, I think, and Fiona with her blonde hair won hands down.

Just before we went home we took out the pedaloes. I usually pedaloed with Eve on the big lake. I used to love creating journeys on the water round and round trying to get as much mileage as possible before giving the pedaloes back.

It had been a lovely sunny holiday and great fun had been had before we all headed back towards Shepton.

The next day I'd played that morning running around with my best friend Eve. I'd felt a sensation between my legs, I'd actually enjoyed it.

We were playing on the front lawn racing about feeling alive and free.

Psalms 103:5
He fills my life with good things so that I stay young
And strong like an eagle.

Eve touched my arm gently and I felt it. I knew it was my turn to chase her. I'd smiled up to her twinkling eyes and the chase began again. Screaming and laughing we ran around time after time with my head in a whirl. I'd felt that sensation between my legs yet again. I actually enjoyed it. The game seemed endless as Fee came out to join in too all around the front lawn.

In the afternoon we went up to the park and Mum got approached by an older couple who seemed to know her and they took one look at Eve and I and asked if we were twins as we had the same red hair. Mum stayed for what seemed like ages with these kind strangers and I hung around to be introduced behind my Mum's legs.

All around us were stalls with endless bric-a-brac on. I even browsed through the puzzles, toys, books and a looking glass. I'd picked it up to look through it over my hand to make my fingers look big. Ever curious Fee and I walked to the big tent at the side of the park to look at the flowers and the produce proudly on display. One odouress posy of flowers made my nose twitch making me sneeze having set off my allergies. The tent seemed huge as the family stayed together wandering around. Not talking much to my sisters I stayed close as upon walking out the tent we headed for the ice-cream van by the swings. We queued for ice lollies. I'd had an orange Solero. My sisters went for Rocket lollies with hundreds and thousands on. While licking on them we moved on by the bouncy castle. I hadn't been that eager to get on as it was packed but Fee and Eve got money out of Mum for a bounce. I'd shied away from the amount of children on there.

Walking down the park the stalls seemed tempting with the big tombola in one tent. Mum got out money for us each to have a pound a go on a raffle. I'd needed a five or a zero to win an orange fruit shoot, Eve won some cards and Fee never won anything. We moved on to the moat to see the boats bobbing up and down on the water with little children using their wind-up toys. The birds were accepting crumbs from passers-by kind enough to throw them scraps from their bags.

All along the front of the pond were small tables outside the boot out cars with endless household objects on. I'd eyed up a pretty lamp Mum called a Tiffany lamp. I did not have the guts to ask for money to buy things.

Trailing behind the rest I walked up to the main arena to watch the girls dancing, then the gymnastics display with the blue mats in the middle for them to run along and cartwheel and back flips across. I'd felt a twitch of envy. The family had come to stand by me. The day slipped by effortlessly into the early evening.

Feeling happy the next day Eve, Fee and I went across the road to Patricia Oakley's house to play. Eve seemed to play effortlessly with these friends and went to sit on an armchair that I'd wanted to plonk down on. I felt jealous and hurt at being left out of their games and being pushed away from sitting down so I lunged at my sister with both hands. Gripping her throat in a pure rage of jealousy, time seemed to stand still as the heat surged through my arms in to my hands pressing harder into her neck. Upon looking up I saw the colour drain from her face. The anger and hurt I'd felt pulsated through my veins until my hands just fell away. Bursting into tears her face became a blur but I remember staring into her eyes until they registered the enormity of what I'd done.

I ran out to the kitchen to get some sandwiches and came back in again. Eve looked a bit lifeless and I realised that I wasn't going to that chair. The rest of the day went in a complete haze with no-one disciplining me.

Every year when we were young we'd enjoy Christmas parties at the Showerings headquarters at the top of Shepton, passed the traffic lights heading out on to the Bath road. Opposite would be the factory with the Babycham deer on top. In the hall on the left hand side was where we'd later have a disco. Where as to the right of the building was a reddey-brown carpeted area of where we would eat and then have games afterward like pin the tail on the donkey and play musical chairs of where the chairs would be substituted with pillows. Santa would come in after the games with presents and this was where I'd sat on Father Christmas' lap and had my photo taken for the local paper. My Mum kept the black and white picture.

We'd had a running buffet in the evening by the dance hall where I loved dancing as close to the flashing lights as possible while happily stomping around to 'Come On Eileen' by Dexey's Midnight Runners. We would all be tired but happy come the end of the evening.

The next day the sun was shining, the birds were singing and I laid in bed looking at the shadows on the curtains that our two beech trees at the top of the garden would create. I'd thought that I'd have liked a full day of fun and stayed in bed for a while with my arms behind my head. Mum came in with a tray of teas and biscuits on. I clambered down the ladder from the top bunk and got dunking with my custard creams. I sat there with my sister Eve of whom jumped up first and went to the toilet. We'd had baths the night before. I soon got dressed. I was only five years old and Eve and I went outside on the back lawn.

"Do you want to play ball games?" Asked Mum.

We'd said "Yes," full of happiness and joy. Me and Eve, 'cause Fee was at school, went to the garage and we found out a cricket bat, two squash rackets, two tennis rackets and a football. We hunted high and low for tennis balls and squash balls. Now we settled on tennis balls and used a toy sized net halfway down the lawn that we pushed the sides down into the earth. I gingerly threw the ball in to the air and aimed to hit it on the way back down to Eve. It went over the net and Eve connected with the ball before it hit the ground but it went in to the net. Mum said that it was fifteen points to me. I served again and again Eve hit it in to the net.

"Thirty points to me!" I exclaimed and Mum beamed. She had to help Eve so stood with and held her arm up. Eve was only two bless her and I began to get carried away.

My next ball went a bit wild as Mum created a nice run of hitting the balls and it went over the fence to Aunty Dot's.

"You'll have to go round there Karen." Said Mum.

"Ok Mum. I undid the latch on the side gate, went down the drive and across by the front door over the little fence and then I knocked on their door.

"Come on in." They said, "I actually saw the ball come flying over the fence." I walked through the house and got told, "It's by the back door."

"Thank you." I said as I picked it up. "I'll try not to do it again." And then threw it back over the fence. I was soon back home trying again. The game, with Mum's help got up to deuce and I hit the ball wrong way again and went in to Aunty Mary's the other side of the house.

We kept going and used up four balls in the tube. I went round Aunty Mary's and she told me off. "Stop hitting the balls over here they're in our vegetable patch. You're not getting them back."

"Sorry Aunty Mary." And she shut the door on me and back at home I called her a dragon over the fence out loud. I told Mum and Eve when I got back and that became her nickname.

The next day it was lovely and sunny again. It was an Indian summer as Mum would say and the air was crisp. Mum said "Let's all go to the fayre later."

"Yes please." Said all three of us and we played outside for a bit. I sat on the edge of the path and pretended I'd been in a bumper car and made loud brumming noises and the occasional honk, honk. I really was looking forward to going to the fayre.

"Just wait till your Dad gets back he's at your Nan's working on their vegetable patch. Then we'll have some lunch all five of us."

I got a bit grumpy thinking of the balls I never got back from Aunty Mary the dragon lady and when I finished my driving game I got Daddy's football knowing I'd get away with using it. Fee, Eve and I threw it to one another at first but Eve kept missing the ball. I'd ran around in a sweat. We then kicked it around by Fee who wasn't interested.

Dad soon came home and we all sat out in the glorious sunshine to have sandwiches, fruit, chocolate and a bag of crisps. We had our Robinsons squeezy boxed with it.

Afterwards we got to the car to go to the fayre for the first time.

At the fayre we wandered around for a little bit and the bumper cars caught my little yes. "Dad I've been practicing in the garden can we go on the bumper cars?"

"Sure K. B. Anyone else want to go?" But no-one else was interested. We soon got into a car and Dad took the wheel and floored it. Dad moaned about mystifying strategies the older children were using in their little cars as we got bumped a few times, but I just laughed and loved watching Dad get all uptight. The game was soon over and I jumped out and asked if Eve and I could go in the toy cars on a roundabout. Mum said "Fine." And got her money out. Fee just stood there and asked if she could go on a hoopla. She looked as white as a sheet.

Eve and I were soon on the roundabout. I pushed all the pretend knobs in my vehicle. They didn't do much except either light up or make a honk, honk noise. The ride was soon over and I wanted to go again.

"Let's look round the stalls for a while." Said Mum, "and look at what Fee won. It's a teddy bear."

I looked at a stall and asked, "Can we hook a duck? It's only a pound to go."

"Ok." And all three of us took a turn and I won some fruit juice. We stayed at the fayre all afternoon and Dad took me on the big Ferris wheel. It was really high and I loved to look at everyone down below us. I could see for miles and as we went round Eve and I with Dad waved at Fee and Mum. We all soon had toffee apples to go home with.

The following Friday us girls, Eve and I got out our little bikes from the garage and Mum said to me. "I'll push Eve along on the bike with the stabilisers." I had some too on a pink little bike but was left to peddle on my own. I smiled at Mum helping my sister out. We had a lovely little morning as we went up and down our hill and Mum took a photograph of Eve on her first proper bike looking cool and calm.

I on the other hand was getting hot and bothered cycling hard up the hill so I could just take my feet off the pedals at the top to fly down the hill. Then I kept doing that up and down the hill several times. I'd felt really happy and free with no-one telling me what to do.

I had a brilliant day playing on my bike with my sisters. In fact way into the afternoon we'd gotten most toys out of the garage like hula hoops. I liked to twizzle them round my waist. Then Mum called us in for tea to have potato waffles with peas and fish, our favourite. I sat there and ate it all up. I soon jumped up and helped Mum in the warm in the kitchen while Fee got sent outside to put the toys away. Then Dad soon came home and had fish 'n' chips put back for him. Then we settled down for the evening and put on the box. We soon went on to bed after a cheese and crackers supper.

On the Sunday the whole family went to church at St Peters and St Pauls. We got there in the car and settled in pews near the front of this massive church and sat down in total silence. the rest of the church soon filled up and I remember Mum in particular talking to friends she'd made in church and I felt really jealous. I didn't really know anyone to talk to so I said hello to Mummy's friend Pat. I looked around me and admired the pictures in the windows. I then craned my neck to look upwards to admire the ceiling. My love for traditional churches started here as everyone sang the first hymn. I didn't really know it as it was my first time in a service.

The vicar said afterwards for all small children to follow the lady at the side of the church for Sunday school. Fiona, Eve and I trotted along behind the lady to a place called Peter Street Rooms. We all sat down at desks and learned all about Adam and Eve and how they were made out of sand. I got the notion that my veins were made out from roots found in the sand. Then they taught us how Adam was tempted by Eve who was tempted by the snake to eat the apple from the tree of knowledge with the consequence of being banished from the Garden of Eden. We then coloured in a picture of a tree, a snake, undergrowth and a man and a woman with a massive leaf over their bodies.

Coming back from church we were all happy. Fee decided to try and balance me on her feet again on the living room carpet. Then Mum decided to start a wall chart in the kitchen. She'd found a massive giraffe chart from a comic Fiona had and stuck it on the wall in the kitchen by the door. Mum stood next to it first and put her hand on her head. Then without moving her hand she twisted round and found out that she was five foot and two inches.

"Who's up next?" She smiled at me.

"Me, Mum." I'd said. I'd turned five years old that day and Mum put my age by two foot two inches. Dad came in from work and picked me up.

"Where's my kiss?" and I kissed him, "Happy birthday." He said. I blushed and burst out into song singing, "Happy birthday to me, happy birthday to me." And I had a small chuckle to myself.

"Hold out your hand and close your eyes. Now open them."

"Thank you Dad." I beamed. It was a Sindy doll and I cuddled him.

"Now stick out your other hand." And he started tickling my palm singing "Round and round the garden like a teddy bear. One step, two steps tickly under there." And he tickled underneath my armpits. I let out squeals of laughter. Dad picked me up then and turned me upside down and the blood rushed to my head. I started kicking wildly begging to be let down.

"I'll let go in a minute." He turned me up the right way first before putting me down gently.

"Look at how much I've grown Dad. Stand there too." And he did. Dad was a little bit taller than Mum at five foot four and he put his name and age at thirty by his height.

"Where are my other beautiful girls?"

"Eve's in the living room." Mum said, "And now I've got to pick Fee up from school."

"I'll go with you Mum." I'd said.

"Oh I'm going to walk down."

"Not take the car?" Dad said, "I could go down Bowlish school if you want?"

"Actually I'm swamped here." So he picked up his car keys and said to me, "Do you want a ride out?"

"Yes," I'd said and Dad let out a whistle. Then I tried.

"Blow through your teeth." He said and I let out a harsh trill. Mum laughed. "You'll have to practice that one K B."

"I will." And I remember trying to whistle the Whistle While You Work song from Snow White. To me it sounded really good.

As soon as we got back from school Fee decided to balance me on her feet and I let go of her hands to pretend to fly. It was my birthday and I was getting a lot of attention. Mum gave me the family card with Dad's, Fee's, hers and Eve's name on. I thought it was sweet that Eve had scrawled her name herself.

For my birthday my whole family turned up to celebrate with me. My cousins and my sisters would play musical chairs by using pillows on the floor. When Mum was ready she put on the music and we danced round and round the pillows. Then Charlie got out and Mum put a cushion back on the sofa and started the music again. Wiggling around the cushions the music soon stopped again. It was a mini pips LP and I started to sing with it. I soon sat down as the music stopped. Fee and Eve sat on the same cushion and Eve was told to get off and she got in to a strop saying that she sat down first and sat on the sofa aggrieved. Casey, I and Fee were left and we just walked around with the music putting our hands on each cushion.

"No cheating," said Mum and she drew out the music. Casey got out next. Then Fee and I literally butted heads and she started crying as I won the game. Mum decided that one game was enough before my party tea.

I can always remember eating jelly and ice cream too with lovely soft eggy with cress sandwiches. Everyone sang happy birthday when the cake came in. I blew the candles wishing the day would never end. It soon did though and I was happy.

The next day Mum said that we were going to a carnival concert matinee down at Wells Little Theatre. It was Aladdin and amazingly listening to the songs and getting caught up by the songs the afternoon flew by.

After the concert Morris the compere came on the stage in front of the big green stage curtain and asked for a willing child. Eve got pushed forward by Mum and she got up on the stage to sit on a stool. Then Morris started singing to he and she burst out crying.

It didn't take us long to get back home for Mum to comfort her.

A week later on a Saturday it was Shepton's bonfire night and Dad taught us how to keep our hands warm by cupping them together, blowing warm air on to them and rubbing them together. We also had sparklers after we went on a caterpillar ride. The caterpillar was a child's version of a roller coaster that had a snake like canvas come up over you while on the ride. It was lovely and warm that night watching a huge bonfire and fireworks after the carnival queen and princess paraded first.

It was a typical day at home. We awoke early for school and after tea and biscuits I got ready for Sunday school all excited about what I was going to learn about the Christmas story. At Peter Street Rooms there were several of us with our versions of Mary and Joseph's trek across the desert. A picture to colour in, of a few town houses and a man and a woman on a donkey. We were learning about the service to be held in the evening done by candle light.

At the evening service I loved the atmosphere with my family all around me and the glow of the candles. I loved to sing the carols in my loudest voice.

I cuddled up in my sheet, continental quilt and blanket when I got home in the evening happy and contented. In the morning I found myself tangled up with all my bed clothes on the floor of the bedroom as I'd had yet another dream of falling through a kaleidoscope of colours just before waking up from being on the top bunk.

Tina Brine came round that day and was playing in the mud with the rest of us and her and Fiona came indoors with their faces covered in mud. Mum had to laugh when she was asked why did she let us get so messy. She'd said it was their first face masks and that they were happy.

Mum had been bringing up tea and biscuits one morning and I actually been awake before she came upstairs. Now going purely by instinct I thought it would be funny to climb on the windowsill behind the curtains to wait for Mum. My legs were hurting as I'd crouched down on the ledge and I was at least small enough to not make the curtains bulge out. Eve was asleep and I waited patiently to hear the door being opened. As soon as I heard it creak I leapt out from my hiding place in front of Mum of whom's face went white as she dropped the tray of biscuits and tea all over the floor. I didn't stay to help pick it all up as I'd scared myself at this point as having not expected such an extreme reaction. I desperately needed the toilet. Eve had woken up wondering what the commotion was about and even Fee came in to the room offering to help mop up. Mum sent her downstairs for a tea towel. What amazed me was that I hadn't even been told off but got promptly left to finish getting myself up.

Downstairs I got my own drink then went back up to bed having avoided everyone else as Mum was getting Fee ready for school. Eve and I were left to lay in bed wondering what the day would bring. I even felt happy as the sun was creeping through the curtains. There was no anger or recriminations later on either as Mum must have been prepared to forget the whole incident and I went on and enjoyed my morning at playschool.

I went to bed that night and had my first nightmare. Running around Shepton we were all playing tag. Adults and children alike were involved. Every time someone got tagged they got turned in to a big grizzly bear. That was the scariest part and I was frightened of bears chasing me desperate to tag me so that they could turn back into being themselves. Someone did tag me and I felt myself growl really deeply with my brown hairy arms outstretched desperate to tag another person to be myself again.

Now in the morning Mum had found that I'd wet the bed so decided to put the plastic covering back on the mattress.

Outside in the back garden later in the freezing cold I'd wrapped up warm in my big thick coat. I had a watering can that I'd filled up from the kitchen several times to water the bottom of a tree trunk. I kept pouring the water over a dead branch trying to bring it back to life and I enjoyed watching the trunk getting darker under the old H2O. Eve came out to see what I was doing so engrossed was I in my task I never saw her creep up behind me with another retainer filled with water to do the same thing.

Having been out in the cold Mum had a hot stew in the oven for lunch. Fee was at school, Dad at work, so it was just us three girls.

Thoroughly warmed up from the food we stayed indoors and played games. I plunk-plunked on the piano and asked if I could have lessons. Mum knew of a Mrs Bosley in Wells, she'd been getting to know through my Nan, her mother, of whom had had lessons with her years before. This had been the first time I'd asked my Mum for anything.

Dad came home past five o'clock from being on the road all day. Us girls had had our hot food but there was plenty over for Dad and he put on some music on the LP player to drown out the howling wind from outside. It made a lovely cosy atmosphere.

That night in bed wriggling around getting comfy on my plastic covered mattress I put my arms behind my head and stared at the shapes on the curtains. The trees in the back garden were making creepy shadows while moving through the strong wind. There were red flowers on the walls in the room and as my eyes were adjusting to the light, while being given the creeps by the wind howling outside, I noticed a tiger face on the curtains. Staring at this shape hard my body began to relax until all I could see were a pair of eyes staring back at me. My subconscious had found a way of making me less scared as I drifted off to sleep.

Chapter Three

Nan She's house at 2 Woodview was always full of clutter and I loved it with all the old drinks bar in the corner with drinks packed in behind it. The big old fashioned alcohol posters in frames on the wall. On another wall was a glass cabinet with lots of ornaments in. Family portraits ordained the walls too. There was a beautiful photo of Aunty Nola with a halo of brunette curls framing her face. A picture of Mum looking as though she was still at school above a dark wood cabinet stuffed with glasses. There was a photo of Uncle Steve looking tanned and shirtless in the sunshine somewhere. Along the wall opposite was a mosaic of mirrors and underneath were shelves of brass ornaments that us girls were sometimes asked to polish with Brasso and a cloth. My cousins were there too with their eighties style big hair and smart clothes. I'd always felt at home in my Nan's and there was a lovely smell of one of Grandad's stews on the cooker with chopped up large chunks of carrots, swede and potatoes and lovely doughboys in a lovely type of gravy. some of us tucked in to it sat round the table and the others sat in the living room with bowls in their laps. Uncle Cyn laughed distinctly in his own unique way at some adult jokes with Mum, Dad, his wife Caroline and Gran and Gramps.

Nan got out some alcohol for the adults but Uncle Cyn always declined. Nan and Mum hit into the wine and the men cans of beer.

Then they'd sit around playing cards, mostly three card brag for small change. We'd all been there for Gramps birthday while all us girls sat around the telly with Aunty Sue, Aunty Nola and Aunty Caroline and particularly Nan and Mum sat around watching the telly. Gran had on Rainbow and I always found the character Zippy laughing in a way that reminded me of Grampy Ern.

They all soon came into the living room and someone turned off the lights for a rousing tune of happy birthday. I'd been licking my lips as I always did for a bit of chocolate cake.

Putting down my etch-a-sketch that I'd wiped clean we all stuck in to the cake.

The next day I awoke to tea and biscuits in bed with my two sisters. Fee came in with us. Mum told us to get some clothes on as we were all off to church. The service was to be about the evening Christ's body had been taken from the cross to his family's tomb.

In church we all sang the first hymn together then Reverend Woolmer told us children to go off to Sunday school. I took my service sheet with me.

We did some colouring in and the project was put on to teach us some hymns. This morning we learned the words to the hymn The Lord of the

Dance. I loved singing but the words were a bit sad even though the music was upbeat.

It was soon time for us to re-join the church service and we slotted back into the pews with Mum and Dad as the congregation stood up for one final hymn. Singing as loud as I could we all sang the Lord of the Dance together. Dad leaned over to give me a protective hug. I looked down at my service sheet when eventually closed and saw the picture on the front. This was when I saw that black cross of where the sun usually set in the west with a golden sky that made an arch in the background of the old style service sheets. It had been of the first Ascension Day when Christ had died at the age of 33 everybody knew that back then. This was the morning I'd started thinking of Anno Domini as being after Christ's death. Just to help me start remembering those two little words. I learned the letters B.C. that day for the first time that mean Before Christ's conceivement.

Hand in hand, walking by West Shepton the next day the whole family headed for the park. Eve was still in the pram as I helped push with Fee holding Dad's hands. There'd been a football in the bottom of the buggy so that when we'd had enough of the swings at the top of the park we'd have a kick about on the open grass. Mum and Dad would use their coats to create two goal posts and I really enjoyed kicking the ball to Dad the goalie. All along each side of the park were footpaths going down to the pond and we walked down them after a heated run around playing football. In amongst the flowers and the bushes I spied a red squirrel darting about and with the birds in the surrounding trees that we walked through we came to a halt. Mum fished out the bread from the bags and gave us girls each a chunk, for some reason, as the birds came out from the trees and the ducks ventured out from the little island in the middle of the pond, most of them gravitated towards Eve. We would enjoy feeding them and laugh at Eve chasing the birds and ducks around and we nicknamed her the Queen of the Ducks.

The family ended up sitting on the benches round the pond to share a picnic before more running around over by the steam and the aviary with brightly coloured birds in before making our way home.

There were no belts on the back seat of cars when my sisters and I were really young and I always had to sit in the middle always straining to see through the front window to a) see where we were going and b) to try and listen to Mum and Dad to be able to talk to them that following weekend. Eve had led out asleep and Fee would happily stare out the window while maintaining conversation with Mum and Dad easily. I was the one desperate for their attention.

We seemed to be driving a long way until the car got parked by two large lakes by one of which there was an ice cream van. I'd been happy with everyone's company but Eve was crying at being jolted awake and Fee wanted something to eat, so we all had lollies this seemed to keep my sisters both quiet. I'd have loved to have known what the different birds and ducks were but every time I went to ask Eve or Fee needed my parents' attention, so I just remained quiet enjoying the scenery.

This was Chew Valley Lake and lots of other families were there wandering around and taking a look. It had been an afternoon and I'd have wanted a walk but Mum hadn't bought the buggy for Eve.

The next day we got in to the car and headed for Evercreech through Fosse Lane, Prestleigh and then by the Bath and West we soon turned in to the little village. Now through the winding lane we came upon a clutter of houses and went by huge factory gates. Then we cruised in to a cul-de-sac of where there was Nan and Gramps bungalow at number eight.

We got out the car and Dad told us "When I was learning to drive at fifteen I sneakily took your Gramps car out and crashed it across the lawn." I looked at the front garden and I imagined Grandad's brown and white car trashed on the front lawn and laughed a bit with embarrassment as Dad was meant to be a class A driver. Shit hot.

In my grandparents I took off my shoes in the hallway and dug my toes in the carpet thoroughly loving the feel of it. We stayed for a while chatting happily and having drinks in the kitchen before Fee started asking to go out to the park. Mum looked at our bored faces and took pity on us.

At Evercreech park pass the pub I'd enjoyed playing on the climbing bars and pulling myself across on a ladder, I'd had a lot of strength in my arms.

I stayed in the park with my sisters while Mum and Dad went to the pub to bring out drinks. Us girls had coke while Dad had a lager and Mum had a shandy. It was a warm day and the drinks felt lovely and cool down on our throats. We had a wonderful afternoon and I felt tired from all that playing.

On a warm spring day Dad was ushering my sisters and I upstairs to go to the toilet before putting our shoes on downstairs. Upon putting on our coats Dad was shoving us out the door. The plan being for us to get out the house that Saturday, to go somewhere different for the day. Mum took the longest to get out the door as she'd been making up a big hamper for us to eat.

Once in the car I'd paid no attention to where we were going as I'd hummed to myself the songs on the radio feeling a little bit jealous, as Fee knew all the words to the hit record on the radio. Dad was talking to Mum the whole trip and I'd overheard bits of conversation knowing we were going somewhere near Frome on the Longleat Estate called Shearwater.

Happy and content with playing I Spy in the car with my sisters, Fiona and I trying to get our parents involved. Dad soon pulled up by a large lake under some trees.

Looking out over the water while alighting from the car the scenery was stunning as all around the lake, as far as we could see, was endless trees to go exploring through.

I was always at the back while we were walking just enjoying myself by Dad kept telling me to keep up. I loved to see the flowers all around me like the endless bluebells, occasional buttercups and primroses. Every time I had to run to catch up my breathing would become tight and I'd miss looking up to see how tall all the deciduous trees were. In and out of the trees to walk by the water I noticed Dad finding some smooth stones to create ripples across the lake so I'd tried to do the same. Fiona got a few more ripples than me after all my attempts I'd gotten as far as two.

Dad smiled at us as Mum and him pressed on through the trees to find a suitable clearing for the picnic rug. I'd had my head down learning where to put my feet as I dodged brambles, twigs and the roots of the trees poking their heads out through the grass.

We stopped at a large clearing right by the lake and the sun was high signalling noon time. A little disinterested in the food I picked up some paper Mum bought and started playing noughts and crosses with myself. I was very good at winning. Noticing everyone was talking and Mum had been cuddling into Dad getting ready to lounge out, my need to explore took over. I slipped away feeling excited at being able to wander round on my own pace following my feet. I remember seeing a lone looking duck with a longish neck and what looked like wings on his head. I didn't know what type of duck it was but it looked kind of regal and looked right at me.

The lake was intermittently in view so that I knew that all I had to do was turn around at any time and find my way back easily about an hour later. Mum and Dad were calling me and my heart was racing thinking I'd get told off but my parents had packed up the rug and picnic things to come find me. They weren't cross but Dad put his arm around me protectively saying not to run off like that and touching my nose. It felt tickly and I rubbed it.

The whole family reached a point where we couldn't walk on any further so we all turned round making the day twice as long and this time we all walked slowly to keep together. Mum was looking bogged down with the picnic hamper and blanket so Dad took his turn to carry it all on the way back to the car.

Once in the vehicle I soon fell asleep in the middle of the back seat of where I'd always sat as my sisters preferred to sit by the windows.

It was quite cold by the time we got back and out the car again. Mum told us we were going to have stew for tea and to tidy ourselves up and wash our hands before settling indoors for the evening.

In the morning I'd put on the TV and switched on an American film there was an oversized American laughing at a young lady. I said to myself why as I'd never understood the joke and thought why were they together. All this I said out loud.

There was another scene of where people were standing around laughing. I understood the joke but didn't find it funny. I analysed out loud why was that so funny? I never understood the plot and kept saying why all the way through it. It really annoyed my parents and they told me to shut up which made me feel awful I'd only been enjoying the film.

After the film in the morning we had lunch and cleared things away. It was coming up to two thirty and we all jumped into the car to watch my Dad's football team play at Wookey.

Once there we stood around together and watched Dad proudly talk to his team before they started.

The whistle blew and we stood by the paper mills team goal. This was my Dad's team. The ball got passed back through the opposing team as they tried to push forward at the same time. Now inside the box next to us my heart was in my mouth as a player kicked the ball on target pass the defender towards the goalkeeper. Luckily he caught it and the Paper Mills supporters all clapped and cheered.

Now a defender caught hold of the ball and ran with it all down the pitch and scored for my Dad's team. It was a little crowd that went wild.

Matthew 5:12
Be happy and glad, for a great reward is kept for you in heaven.

Dad shouted praise to the team of a "Well done lads." The goalkeeper picked up the ball from the net and kicked it halfway down the field.

One to nil held to half time and the teams were soon trudging back to the changing rooms for half time.

The family had chocolates and a drink at half time. The game soon started again and the teams swapped sides on the pitch. I strained to see the ball down the other end which was where most of the action was until one player broke free and dribbled the ball all the way down the pitch. The shot on goal was way off target leaving everyone on our side clapping at the attempt. The other goalkeeper took the ball and kicked nearly in goal the other end. It was an amazing kick. There was a scuffle over the ball and the referee blew his whistle. The player was offside as there was no-one between the ball being kicked to the next player.

There was some swearing from the other crowd but I knew the referee had done nothing wrong.

All the second half the other team pushed forward more putting us on tender hooks but towards the end, in the dying minutes, one of ours broke free again to score a second goal. The crowd went wild and Dad seemed really happy.

After being in the clubhouse we walked around the grounds and on an incline Dad and I spotted some rabbits. Dad pointed out the pink eyes on one of them and said what they had was myxomatosis. I agreed with my Dad when he said they should be put down.

Back at home I saw a big bag of washing in the kitchen and Mum put it in the machine moaning about having to do the whole football kit.

Now in the morning us children went to Sunday School and we learnt a new song with the chorus of 'From the old I travel to the new, keep me travelling along with you.' We read the words of the projection screen and we did some biblical picture colouring in. Before we knew it us girls were back in church in time to be able to go up to the front, during communion, for a blessing. It was my first time as the vicar put his hand on my head.

It hadn't been long until the last hymn and it was the new song we'd learnt that morning. I went out of church on a cloud. We had a brilliant day.

The next day Mum got up early to take Fee over to her friend Claire's house because she was about to walk with her into school at Bowlish. On the way back I remembered seeing Mum's knitting lying about the house which was a lemon coloured cardigan and I'd asked her who she was knitting for. She'd said my cousin Charlie, a nickname for Charlotte. Because I'd expressed an interest in her knitting Mum offered to teach me how to knit when we got home.

Mum would get up at 5 o'clock with Dad every morning and would stay up to do the house work before us children would wake up. This was done so that she could spend all our waking hours with us.

At home Mum had some spare orange wool and while Eve had been set up with toys on the living room floor in front of us, she carefully showed me, by holding my hands whilst grasping the needles, to wrap the wool round both needles and to tie a knot. By keeping my hands tightly grasped on both needles Mum's hands guided me to wrap wool around the right hand needle then to pull the thread through the hole attached to both needles. Mum kept doing this with me until we had ten stitches cast on. Then she showed me how to push the knitting utensil into each stitch to make our first line by carefully guiding my hands to do it and together we created my first ever square.

Psalms 37:4
Seek your happiness in the Lord,
And he will give you your heart's desire.

Chuffed I gave Mum a kiss on the cheek and said, "Thank you Mum." She then diverted her attention to sitting on the floor with Eve while I carried on knitting to turn my square into an oblong. Getting carried away I dropped a couple of stitches so Mum sat with me guiding my hands again to put them on to the needle again. I quite enjoyed this and went to knit a scarf for my dolly which took all morning. In the end though Mum had to show me how to cast off. The article soon became part of my big dolls outfit and got into playing with Eve on the floor as she'd had all the dolls out including the two black dolls we had. There were three Sindy dolls, and three big babies too that we dressed and undressed while sitting them around the tea set and Eve played hostess.

Lunch had been a snack as we'd filled the whole morning.

Mum got some wooden puzzles out afterward and Eve was playing with one that had a blue bunny rabbit, a yellow duck, a frog and a goldfish on. I'd been putting together a twelve piece puzzle together with a rabbit with clothes on standing on its hind legs with a round lolly in its hands. The time flew by that day and we were soon down the hill to pick up Fee from school.

After taking off Fee's school uniform she got changed and got ready to go outside for a walk with our mother into town. We passed the Anglo Trading Estate and walked into the sweet shop on the former. Picking up the sweet jars one by one we made our selections and put them into our white paper bags. I'd grabbed an egg sweet and felt my teeth sink into it, it tasted nice. Walking on by the police station we crossed to the co-op, Mum told us that she wanted food for a picnic for tomorrow as we were told we'd spend all day across the fields in a village. Mum picked up the multi-bags of crisps, box drinks, chocolates, apples, bread, cheese and a Spanish onion. After, wandering round the aisles and us eyeing up the sweets we wafted out the main doors down towards the library.

Fee and I chose our favourite books. I chose Five go to Kerrin Island, Fiona chose an American book. Mum wanted us to have something to read across the fields at a place called East Cranmore.

At home Mum did the sandwiches. I saw her glance at her watch. I'd heard her mumble it had been ten o'clock. She said out loud, "It's getting late love." Then Dad came downstairs. I saw him fresh from the shower. I noticed that he cheekily picked up a bit of cheese and pop it in to his mouth. He helped her wrap up the sandwiches. I'd stood back realising a moment of intimacy between them. I'd come out wanting to help. They put it all in a rucksack. I followed them blindly out the door while looking at my feet with my sisters trailing behind. A thrill of excitement went through my spine making me look up to get in the car. We were off in my mind for another adventure. I saw those green fields Mum described exactly how I'd envisioned them as we pulled up down the lane to get out at East Cranmore. I heard them talk asking each other about where to go for the trains but opted for the open fields.

They placed the picnic blanket on the grass and I'd watched them place the bag of food by it as my sisters and I ran off to play in the long grass. I felt free as we chased one another playing tag. It felt like the moment could last forever. Thoroughly invigorated I put my arms out twirling round and round making me dizzy loving the feeling. Eve had noticed me and told me to come and eat. I hadn't realised they started the sandwiches and went to sit down with them.

In the grass it felt like we were shrouded in a moment unforgettable as my family laughed and joked together liking the sound of our own voices. The day floated by in to early evening. Dad looked at his watch reminding Mum of having to go on somewhere. Mum brushed her hair back off her face, looked at us and Fee, Eve and I went to help pack up but I'd never got there fast enough to pitch in. All I remember was picking up a stray empty bag of crisps and stuffing it in to my pocket.

Dad said, "We can't stay out all night. I promised luv to get up early to go to church in the morning remember?"

The next day Dad drove us across town and parked in the big car park on the Bath road going out of town. The air was brisk as he grabbed mine and Fee's hands while Mum took out the pram for Eve. We got on the pavement and walked through a little alley way to come out in to the bottom of the high street. Looking up I saw a bridge coming over head and forward I spied the entrance to the church. The bells were ringing, they got me excited and I beamed up at Dad still holding my hand. We found a long pew near the front of the church and Mum and Dad hugged one another. Mum was happy she got Dad to come with us.

The family soon stood up for a rousing first hymn, St Peter and St Pauls were massive and I enjoyed hearing my own voice resonate inside my own head. My favourite part of any service. Not staying for communion my sisters and I got shepherded out the side door to go down a cobbled alley way towards Peter Street rooms. Fee had the responsibility of holding our hands while the other children and we were soon in the hall.

Plonking ourselves down on chairs there was a print out of the basic story of David and Goliath, the giant, I was intrigued about how a tiny sling and a stone could be a weapon. We even got to colour in a picture of them together. Pleased with the work we were allowed to keep my sisters and I were soon shepherded back up the path for the end of the church service and one last hymn for me to sing loudly to. Sunday School had been brilliant that morning.

Back at home I started popping the buds on the fuchsia bush at the bottom of the drive, something Fee had gotten me in to. We stayed outside Fee and I until lunch was on the table and the whole family sat round the big table together. Happily eating I let everyone talk around me and soon gobbled all my food down.

In the evening Dad would love playing with us girls like with snakes and ladders and then when the telly was on Dad liked to play, 'Row, row your boat', on his knees then he would flip us over backwards so that we were upside down in turn which would make us giggled and make our heads briefly hurt. After a lot of attention from Dad, Mum would love to tuck us all in bed with an adventurous story that she'd love to make up. It was about this little Imp called Naughty Art of whom would wake up in the mornings thinking of naughty things to do that day like using a sling shot to attack cows. At the end of the story the cows decided to get their own back by chasing Arthur out of the fields. Sitting on the fence gasping for breath the little Imp, as big as Mum's finger, promised not to hurt the cows ever again and he went to bed realising that he shouldn't have done what he did with a heavy heart.

Fully rested and stretching, then rubbing my eyes to get the sleepy dust out I'd missed Fee going to school so I went over to find Eve of whom was already downstairs with Mum. Fishing out my silver jubilee colouring book Nan had given me I sat at the dining room table with pencils waiting patiently for breakfast. My favourite Weetabix came out with plenty of milk and sugar on and I'd watched Eve playing on the floor in the living room.

It looked warm and sunny outside but I stayed contentedly indoors with my colouring in book inwardly laughing at Eve playing with her toys with Mum helping her.

The Duckson and Pinkerton upright piano was begging to be played by the table so I decided to have a bash long enough for Mum to get the message to take us out. Mum always took a long time deciding what to do with us as she liked to plan a few hours of fun for us at a time. Having let my frustration of momentary boredom out on the keys I was soon on the floor playing with Eve.

I enjoyed alphabet spaghetti for lunch with mash potato and a Cornish pasty. I'd asked Mum where Dad had gone in the lorry and Mum's answer was always "Up country somewhere." That day we'd been round Wickham Way with Uncle Roy and Aunty Sue playing in the back garden of where they had their three year old tortoise. I found it hard to spot him at first being so small and looked up into their trees and saw a big bird feeder with little golden, yellow and blue birds attacking it. Always fascinated by the things around me I'd forgotten who we'd come to see, and just then Mum called me to come in for a drink and a biscuit in their little kitchen. They offered us sandwiches but I'd only taken one not really that interested in food but politely said thank you. Letting the adults' talk I went back outside.

The evening sun was getting low and Sue and Roy came out to give us a kiss to say goodbye and told us to come round any time. "It was a pleasure seeing you." They'd said.

Next day was the beginning of a holiday a we jumped in to our yellow Datsun. Dad chucked the luggage into the boot. The car sped off down the road. The luggage soon got slung in the accommodation and we walked to the nearest beach. Stopping at the pier Mum got out her purse to pay a gentleman for us to get on a ride. I'd sat on a red and black dotted lady bug waving my hand in the air while trying to turn the wheel. The merry go round went round and round while my Babycham bag flew off my arm. Getting off my ride we walked up the pier. In my hand I dangled my bag loosely and I remember at having dropped the comb and I'd heard the money, the silver coins, drop on the pier. The tide was coming in and it fell in the water. I got scared that I was going to fall through the slats on the pier.

Another day while we'd been on the beach all day Dad had carved out cars in the sand for Eve and I. They looked brilliant and I soon got sat in mine happily to pretend that I was driving. Next thing I knew something was being put down my back. It had been Eve with a red and white polka dot bikini on. A shudder went down my spine and I heard Dad laugh and he called out "All right winky." Mum laughed. It had been a crab that went down my back. I didn't like it but I just carried on going in and out the sea and at one point Eve and I buried Dad's legs in the sand as he didn't seem to mind at this point. Then Mum appeared with ice lollies.

We loved our lollies, we all had rocket lollies by licking the hundreds and thousands first then biting the brown bit in the middle with the white bit round the outside. I crunched feeling the ice cold sensation down my throat to taste the raspberry underneath. I'd been in my blue and white polka dot swimsuit.

A whole day passed lovely as I'd felt the sun drawing the heat out through my face. I can see my Dad touching my nose and I can see the blue twinkle in his eyes. I smiled back.

At home Eve recounted the moment she put the crab down my back trying to wind me up. Mum heard and called her evil Eve. I was shocked so it soon shut me up so that Mum wouldn't call here that again.

The next day we went shopping and while we were out we stopped at a newsagents. At the shop us girls looked round at the stickers and found some transfers. I'd eyed up the cherubs, hearts and flowers tattoos. I liked the look of them and picked them up. Eve and Fee did the same. We stayed there and looked at the cards and I had a laugh to myself over the funny cards.

Now coming out of the shop we went up to Haskins to have another look around. Mum wanted some new bedroom furniture she said. I quite liked looking round the furniture. In the sofa section I admired all the settees in the large room and had to try several out. I mooned over the extra comfortable ones that were brown or beige. They were my favourite colour. Then we went upstairs and looked at the beds. They all looked very welcoming and comforting. I lazed out on a couple until Mum told us to get off because you weren't meant to lie on them.

Now in Haskins there were a lot of furniture that I used to dream about having in my own home one day. I loved the lamps and light shades too and enjoyed the pretty patterns and the different colours of light. We went down a corridor full of cupboards and hats and scarf stands and with mirrors on the wall.

Then at the end of the corridor there was a till that mother ordered a bed from. I got bored and started to dance around. Mum told me to find a toilet so I went off on my own to find one. I'd noticed toilets back down the corridor so I retraced my steps to find them. By the time I came back everyone was waiting outside wanting to go in the supermarket that was situated next door. We went round and Fee pushed the trolley around the shop floor as Mum filled her up. At the till there were chocolates and we all threw one in for ourselves. Mum gave a pretend shocked look and laughed, "Alright. Only one then." She said.

At home we went through the bags and I grabbed my transfers as Fiona helped Mum put everything away.

Mum said to us with our transfers "Let me help you." And she put water on our hands with a flannel over the top of our transfers on the back of our hands. Then I had a flower and a heart on my arm. I showed them off all day.

Then the next day on the green that day there was a brass band playing in the bandstand. The tuba pelted out louder than the other instruments calling me to dance with a wonderful beat. I tapped my foot and twirled like a ballerina. My sisters were running around driving my parent's nuts. Fiona would have most of the attention. I can see her out the corner of my eye talking away to our parents. The heat from the sun made me feel all aglow and my cheeks were burning. The band struck up another tune. Eve looked at me all cheekily holding out her hands and I'd grab them swinging round and round. Feeling dizzy we fell to the floor laughing. Having had enough we ran through the grass to the gate racing each other towards the swings. Two children were already on them so we jumped on the see-saw, with Eve's wicked grin looking at me. Pushing up and down the playground toy squeaked noisily. Fiona stood and watched with Mum and Dad with the strains of the music in the background. In the background there were lots of children running around. I could see a boy pulling a girl's hair, she cried.

As we got off the see-saw we clambered all over the climbing frame going every two minutes down the slide. Getting in the way of the other children we decided to climb back down the sides of the frames and play tag around the grass. Fee joined in and we all ran around together. I imagined the other children around us joining in and smiled at everyone.

That day had been an adventure and we all went home happy.

The next day I came to school in my uniform a bit late and queued up outside for our form rooms. I stood behind a girl with short blonde hair and blue eyes of whom I got talking to. Her name was Lynda.

Starting the day in a play room with toys and what the teacher called ephemera, and utensils. I found myself talking to a boy called Trevor. He was playing in the Wendy house by the wall with me pretending to be doctors and nurses. I got a bandage and put it round his head. Then took a dolly to do the same with while beaming up at him and saying, "I helped your baby." He beamed back at me then took the baby to doctor him back to health.

We'd made the best of the day out of it and at break time I noticed all the children had paired up. I went to pair up with Lynda for activities in the playground and said. "Why are you playing with me?" and she said, "Because I like you."

Starting the end of the day there was a bell for everyone to come inside to make us all get together for one last activities afternoon. I went to the toy kitchen pretending to make a meal throwing in a plastic egg, tomato, bacon, beans and toast cooking it in the saucepan. The room was full of noise and there was a plane that flew across the air that somebody had made. That day was brilliant.

In the classroom the next morning I paid attention and listened to the teacher and played with toys all strewn about the room as she'd said, "Just enjoy the morning and get the toys out." So we did. I found a baby and a bottle and pretended to give her milk by sticking it in the little hole in her mouth. Then I found some clothes and put it on her plastic little body. A little jumper and a skirt with knitted knickers attached to the skirt. Then I held her hand. The bottle dropped to the floor as I pretended to go for a walk with her. The other children were running around knocking things over, all was in chaos so I found a quiet corner, picked up a comb and did my dolly's hair. Then holding her hands I twirled her around pretending to help her fly.

Juice came on trays and we sat down politely and sipped. I felt like Mum crossing my legs feeling cheeky and happy. I turned to Lynda and said "Will you play with me and dollies?" She said, "Yes." So we walked back to the children's corner and just sat down for the rest of the morning with their dressing up clothes. Then we flew around the room bumping in to things and children. We made so much noise it was funny. The bell rang and I grabbed my coat to go outside with my lunch box to walk over to the canteen. Sitting together with friends I was happy. Towards the end of eating, myself, a boy named Thomas, and my friend Sidwell decided we stayed behind after lunch. We became the last ones in there. In our coats alone Thomas dropped his pants and he said, "Have you got one?" So I dropped my knickers to have a look and we giggled. We pulled up our clothes quickly. Sidwell just stared. I knew what boys had down there after that and with Thomas in a green weatherproof coat and orange felt lining and orange fur around his hood. Then I felt a bit creeped out. the canteen ladies were in the kitchen then dropped something and made us jump so we went outside.

Plenty of children filled the yard and I ran around finding my friend Lynda. She was with Georgette playing skipping so I asked to join in. They had a handle each so that I could jump rope. Faster they turned the skipping rope and it whipped the back of my feet a couple of times. They soon got fed up so we swapped and took one end to let Georgette have a turn. Then it was Lynda's turn and we played till the bell rang.

In the classroom I found myself gravitating towards the kitchenette set and then met Trevor and said, "Hello. Play with me." He said "No." And ran off round the room with the other boys with guns. The babies caught my attention again and I pretended to heat the bottle on the little cooker in a pan. I timed it for five minutes with a little egg timer and turned a knob that went 'click, click, click,' over and over again till it went 'ping'.

The bell rang again and we all trooped outside with our stuff ready to go home. Mum picked Fee and I up and took us home with Eve, by walking back up the hill toward Shaftgate Ave and Coombe View.

Feeling full of beans I ran upstairs when I got home and decided to sit on my bottom at the top of the stairs to bump one by one down them.

"Bumpety, bump." I went in my head down the stairs. It was funny. "Don't play on the stairs." Mum said, but that spurred me on to do it again. Three more times and my bottom began to get a little bit sore. Mum came out to the hallway and dragged us to go outdoors to play in the sunshine of where we just ran around shouting playing tag. All three of us had some fun building up a sweat getting up an appetite while Mum sorted through the kitchen cupboards as I heard her slam a drawer. Dancing around the lawn I wiggled my hips with a tune in my head. I spotted a tennis ball and played catch with myself by pounding the ball against the side of the garage wall but then I stupidly threw the ball too high and it disappeared on the roof.

Mum called us in for some drinks as she could sense that cordials were necessary to keep us going. Fee, Eve and I sat down on the path or on the edge to catch our breaths.

"What do you want for tea?" As I sipped I dreamt of baked beans, an egg, and potato waffles and sausages. Eve trumpeted baked beans with Fee and Mum laughed and said, "It's coming up."

Half an hour alter we were sat at the table eating exactly what I'd dreamt of and I predicted the food coming right. Mum asked us if we wanted to go to the fayre tomorrow. I beamed and inwardly thought great.

The next day it was a Saturday and we all got up at the break of dawn. I grabbed a 'Read it Yourself' book and read Billy Goats Gruff and then William Tell about a man who shot an apple off someone's head. I felt cosy and warm sat on the sofa as the TV played in the background.

I got up and looked for my Sindy doll and found her a Wonder Woman's knitted outfit so I ran round the room pretending that she was flying. Mum was adamant that we all needed something cooked inside of us before going out that afternoon to the fayre. We were all looking forward to it.

Sat around the table we discussed what we'd like to see and in my mind's eye I wanted to see the animals like the elephants. We were eating a lovely hot stew with big chunks of bread and I put on big dollops of butter feeling very hungry. I said out loud, "I'd love to see the elephant." Everyone laughed and said, "We're going to the fayre not the circus." And I grinned feeling like a twit but pleased we shared a joke.

Helping Mum wash up afterwards made us all feel really close as a family. We were soon putting on our trainers and coats to walk all across town together as one big happy family.

Going through West Shepton, toward the Cenotaph, by the Ridgeway Estate and to the fields the fayre was there. My little face lit up as soon as we got to the field gate as I saw a food bar to the right and to the left there was a round stall under a red and white canvas with toys attached to the poles around it and inside was a large paddling pool with yellow ducks on. Some were turned over and you could see the purple numbers on their bottoms. We had to wait for them to be pulled back over for a go. I looked at Mum who looked at Dad and he said, "She's only had a go on one stall. It's only fifty pence," so he dug into his pockets after rubbing his hands together to warm up and I could see him shivering with the cold. I felt lovely and warm in my bomber jacket and I copied Dad by rubbing my hands together excitedly. I grabbed a pole with a hook on the end and three chances to hook the hoops on the ducks noses. I picked one up first time and the owner of the game looked at the number underneath and matched it to a bag full of a couple of fish in water. I didn't bother having the other two goes so Eve had the next one and Fee had the last go. Then we walked by the arcade of where the older children were hanging out and Dad spotted the bumper cars opposite. Dad and I jumped in one and Fee and Eve jumped into another. Giving the money to the bloke who told us to use the pedals Dad put his foot down cruising through other bumper cars all trying to miss each other but wanting to secretly go bump. Dad bumped in to my sisters' a couple of times and I turned to Mum smiling at us with the pram and the goodies we'd won. We were on the bumper cars for twenty minutes and when we went round and round avoiding the cars bumping into each other I beamed up to Dad again as he brilliantly mastered driving around lovely and fast until we finished. When we got out I looked at Fee and she looked as sick as a dog. She declared, "I do not like fairground rides." And promptly threw up.

We walked on round in the grass of where some bits were slightly muddy and dried grass was scattered in some places to soak up the wet ground. I could hear feet jumping off metal stands so I looked up and there was a mini rollercoaster. I grinned and said, "Can I have a go on that one please?" Dad looked at Mum who looked at Fee and Eve and they shook their heads. Fee still looked pale but I soon jumped on the steps up to a car. Dad followed and we pulled the bar up at the side before the tout took our money. Feeling a frisson of excitement up my spine the ride moved slowly at first and Dad put his arm around me but I shook him off feeling uncomfortable. The loud music pounded inside my head and a voice over the tannoy said, "Scream if you want to go faster." So I screamed and the ride jolted forward faster. So caught up in the moment I had another frisson as the ride jolted again to go even faster. Round and round three times till it began to slow down and then it slowed to a halt and we got off. I was laughing and shaking at the same time when we got off and Dad's suggestion was we got some food. We went by huge barrel filled with water and apples and I questioned what you had to do with it. I'd read the sign 'Apple Dunking' as Mum explained that you stick your face over it, pull back your hair and grab an apple with your teeth. Mum and Dad had a go and ate their apples while we had toffee apples with hundreds and thousands all over them.

We all wandered round the fairground one last time soaking up the atmosphere. Swaying to the songs playing loudly on each ride my cheeks felt rosy and pink. Then we walked all across town to get home again feeling warm inside and happy with my rosy cheeks.

That night I felt euphoric as I cupped my hands round a mug of Horlicks with a red beamer of a nose as we all warmed up together. Sipping the hot drink slowly everyone was talking happily saying what a lovely time we had and Fee declared that she was never going on a ride again.

Mum offered up cheese and biscuits so we sat around at the table eating different cheeses from a wooden board and pickled onions with crackers and having to put on butter ourselves. Feeling full up Mum told us to get ready for bed.

In the morning I was cold inside. I'd picked up my Sindy doll and played with her boobies. My nail grazed her but I preferred to use my thumb and forefinger on that sensation between my thighs. That old familiar sensation made me rub my legs together and so fast I grabbed for a pillow and got on top pulling the middle of it like riding a horse. I'd pulled it through my vagina getting familiarised with that particular area. I'd be writhing around on the bed for ages I'd make a 'Pa' sound with mouth. Then I'd sink into the pillow and fall asleep.

One Saturday morning Eve and I gotten up early in our nighties. We'd been huddled up together in the bottom bunk scared of the storm the night before but had awoken the next day back in our own beds.

Eve had had our story book in her hands, as she'd read the line, "It's easy as falling of a log!" Just like Penfold who was a mole with glasses on would hear from Danger Mouse, D.M. I would jump off the top bunk at the same time. This was when Barren Greenback was pursuing him he had been that great big frog his arch nemesis. I'd then seen in my mind's eye the back of Danger Mouse and remembered what he looked like with his big ears, slim body and the red D. M. on the front of his yellow shirt.

As I'd land with a thud on the floor Mum came in wondering what all the noise was about. I'd woken up everybody in the house all moaning at me intermittently throughout the day.

The television set had been put on early that day and downstairs I remember Ant and Dec being on SM:TV Live. This always made me smile.

That Saturday afternoon we all went out to enjoy the sunshine doing our usual walk across the fields before coming back home for tea, the usual spaghetti hoops and waffles and an egg were placed on the table that day by Mum.

It was on the following Sunday that I'd woken to a flapping noise and a loud bang against the bedroom window. It scared me half to death. I grabbed my hair and started chewing feeling my nervous. It tasted salty then I got out of bed. Went to the bathroom and had a shower to get nice and clean. I put on a nice little dress for once that was checked with the colours of red and black. Feeling posh for once I floated downstairs to meet with my posh upper middle class, very conservative family. I went to church with a very freckly impertinent stuck up nose. I had tiny dimples in my oval face pronouncing themselves as I smiled up at my Dad. My hair was half way down my back and golden by then which swayed proudly as I walked to the car. The whole family as we went to church and there we prayed together. Listened to the vicar and the sermon was about idiots on Pentecost who stupidly thought everyone would understand them when they didn't. It was written that some people thought they'd been on the wine again. We floated out of church just satirically having a laugh wondering what the hell speaking in tongues was supposed to have been about. I got nervous again as I'd cried during the sermon and chewed my hair again.

It was the last day of school and we all had the chance to make decorations. We had a brilliant time cutting up orange, pink and yellow paper into strips and hooked them round each other to make a chain to hang up on the ceiling at home or on the tree. I was pleased. Then I got the scissors and snipped away at drawings on gold paper of stars of all shapes and sizes of which one cut out I used a hole-punch on. Through the holes we put ribbon and piled our Christmas decorations up before we made cards for family. I chose blue card for all four family members. White cotton wool and green cotton. I had felt pens for the res and on each card I placed white paper with everybody's names on in red writing. The first picture I put together was on my eldest sister Fiona's card. I had white clouds, green strands of grass made with the cotton and I drew a red sleigh on white paper with brown sacks and a Santa on, of which I cut out and put on the card. It looked brilliant to me. On Eve's I made a snow field with a snow covered house on and for Mum I made a cotton wool big snowman. For Dad's I tried a nativity scene I copied from a book and took one of the gold stars I made that didn't have a hole in and put it over the top.

This took most of the day up and I was very pleased with myself. When I was going home with everything in my bag I'd been happy swinging my bag under my arm. I was holding court with my sisters all the way home loving the sound of my own voice. I couldn't shut up about how brilliant Christmas was going to be.

At home Mum had put up the tree and the other decorations but the tree looked a little bit bare. I beamed and told Mum I had some decorations for the tree. So did Eve from home and Fee from the first year of St Pauls, so Mum had loads of home-made decorations.

We watched Mum stand on the sofa and chairs putting up our home-made chains. She laughed because apparently the schools and Eve's from home had had the same idea. The dining room and the living room ceilings were soon decked with chains as well as shiny paraphernalia. Then my stars, Eve's stars and Fiona's went on the tree. We all laughed and said, "Fancy that we've all had the same idea."

Dad came home in the evening and after tea we heard Christmas music outside while we were watching the telly. It sounded in the distance and we all pricked up our ears as the music got louder until bright lights shone through the room. Me and my sisters jumped up with excitement and asked about going outside to see what the commotion was about. Mum twitched the curtains, smiled and said, "Santa's come early. Do you wanna go out and see him?"

We all said yes and rushed for the door. "Put your shoes on." Mum yelled but Dad said "It's alright I've got to pick them up to get on the cart anyway."

"No." Mum said. "They'll hurt their feet." We were a bit confused as Mum started going through the shoe cupboard and Dad said, "Well hurry up then." Dad picked me up as the tension between Mum and Dad heightened and he carried me to the float as the engine started but we got there on time. I felt heated from the glow of the lights and embarrassed as Dad pushed my little bottom to help me clamber on the sleigh. I felt sheepish as Santa spoke to me and said. "What's your name?"

"Karen." I'd said.

"What would you like for Christmas?"

I replied embarrassingly. "A toy would be nice." And I was desperate to get off his knee as he handed me a bag of sweets. I looked up and my sisters had wandered outside looking cosy and warm ready to do the same thing. Then we all went back inside and I was elated.

Chronicles 12:40
All this was an expression of the joy that was felt throughout the whole country.

I'd seen Father Christmas and heard the music for ages as he seemed to stay on our estate all night and I went to bed happy.

Dad asked me if I wanted to go round Aunt Sis's next morning and he told me that she was Grandad's sister. It wasn't far he'd said as her house was just up the road pass the swimming pool. It was a nice sunny day as we turned into Cornwall Road. I'd felt a bit nervous as we approached No. 6 on the corner and swung open the gate to pass by an overgrown lawn that had definitely seen better days. Dad rang the doorbell and a frumpy older woman with long brown hair opened the door. The hallway was filled with clutter and as we entered the living room the dust filtered through the air and the particles showed in the rays of sunshine coming in through the windows. Everywhere was cluttered, there'd been a stack of newspapers by the sofa with a great big magnifying glass on top. Dad and I managed to find some place to sit while Aunt Sis just sat in her armchair.

After offering a drink and then plonking herself down. I sipped at my orange juice while Dad had a tea. I stared at her face while she talked and noticed a mole on the side of her face with a hair sticking out of it. I'd got side tracked by a noise behind me and turned to see a large white cockatiel. A horrible smell emanated from it and noticed droppings all over the bottom of the cage. I'd always been polite with 'p's and q's' but barely spoke. The bird was speaking more than me which left me animated.

I turned my head and got back into hearing the conversation and heard Aunt Sis talk about her bunions while showing them to us and how she'd wished that she'd always worn the right sized shoes. I just stared and wished the floor would open up. Dad saw my face, stretched and put his cup down squashed into the side of the newspapers. He rubbed his hands together and stood up saying that we'd better get back for tea. I left most of my drink with a bug in it and awoke from a daze of looking into the rising dust in a yellow ray of sunshine. I smoothed down my trousers and said goodbye to my great aunt.

I'd had a long day what with school and everything and was soon tucking into a hearty well-cooked tea. It wasn't that much longer until I got dressed into my favourite blue nightie ready for bed. My sisters did the same and in bed I snuggled up with Bluey my teddy bear to listen to one of Mum's stories about a naughty Imp called Naughty Art. Every time I yelled out, "Naughty Art the Farty Art." When his name first got mentioned it made Eve laugh. My sleeps were beginning to get more dreamless.

The next morning I began with rubbing my eyes a lot as the tears were streaming from them. I hadn't had a bad dream and sniffing Mum called upstairs with a cup of tea rousing us up for an early morning walk. There was no church this Sunday.

The air was crisp and cool against the back drop of rolling hills of a myriad of green coloured hedges, trees and grass. It was nearing the end of spring so the lovely flowers were still abloom. There were primroses, daisies and dandelions and each one Mum told us to pull up were amidst the dewed morning grass. My nose was streaming as I picked one up and I sneezed but Mum wanted a few to take home for the garden. My parents had said the pollen was high, even Dad had bought a handkerchief and let me use his. As my eyes wept I couldn't stop rubbing them to see making them more and more sore and itchy. In the end it became a vicious cycle so Dad took my hand and told me not to rub my eyes so much but I couldn't help it and started to wheeze. I'd gotten a rub on the back from Dad and told Mum to turn around and go home, but Fee and Eve were busy helping pick the flowers so we had to lead the way and turn back.

The rest of the family soon caught us up in the bottom field before the hill down to Bowlish Lane.

Mum wasn't cooking that day as we were all going out for lunch down the Horseshoe. In the pub we were told to sit still but I needed the toilet. Us girls had cola while our parents had shandys' with a lovely cooked roast dinner served promptly for our growling tummies. The beef was delicious and got cut up for Eve as she had only been four. I raced to finish just so that I could relax and breath properly afterwards. Dad wasn't paying for puddings he'd said as Mum had made an apple pie waiting for us at home.

Next morning we'd have started off the day in class while all the races were being set up outside. I remember an obstacle race including cones and hoopla's. I'd taken part in an egg and spoon race and a sack race.

The skipping competition would have been the last order of the day as we went straight in to collecting awards. We even had three podiums of where a girl called Georgette came first and I came second standing proudly on my box. The best end to a good day. That was how it should have been but Mum spoilt it. When the skipping competition had been in progress, in the school yard, I sat down from skipping thinking I'd won as I couldn't see anyone else skipping, but behind me Georgette was still jumping rope. Nobody told me even though Mum had been watching. What irritated me more than anything was Mum afterward going on and on about how someone should have said something about that girl behind me, but Mum herself could have told me. I'd been proud of myself for getting on podium two too. This was the first time Mum had ever upset me. I went home afterward happy that I had at least something to show for my day.

The next day at lunch time I'd sat by the cold concrete wall on the bench. I went to a quiet place inside and drooped my head and I saw sand all around my mind. I felt a hand on me. I sensed it was Sidwell but I shrugged her off unable to explain how I felt about my Mum.

Chapter Four

The next day was a fun day as I got to dress up as a bumble bee all day and Dad dressed up as Buzby from the BT adverts. I remember Dad winning a knobbly knees contest and I was strangely proud of him. The fete was held in the school yard with lots of tables with bric-a-brac on and a raffle, and a barrel with shavings in with lots of presents. It had been a lovely sunny day but as the afternoon wore on the school yard stone wall produced a shadow across us which caused a chill. We all did a parade in our costumes to the tune of 'Come Follow the Band' to top the day nicely.

Then the next day Mum dropped us girls off at Nan Burrs for them to take us off for the day. Bundling us in to the car Granddad took the wheel and he drove us to where they called Lyme Regis.

Carving up the countryside and gliding through the main A37 road us girls happily chattered away. I'd been happiest just feeling a part of everything so when I ran out of something to say I sat back content to let everyone talk around me. Nan passed around a bag of mints and we were soon on the coastal road heading towards a place called Lyme Regis.

Now there was a small town we had to go through with poky little roads carrying an awful lot of traffic. Gramps parked at the bottom of the hill near to a shingled beach. When getting out of the car Nan took us round a few shops and I noticed coloured sand in one of them for the first time in a clear plastic container. I loved picking things off the shelves and looking at the different fossils trying to imagine what sea creatures they had been. Completely enthralled Eve was getting tired so our Grandparents decided it was time to hit the beach so Nan bough us a couple of buckets and spades.

On the beach Fee and Eve nabbed the buckets so I had been left to bury my legs in the sand and then spent ages digging a deep hole to Australia while getting in and out the sea. Nan came in with us girls a couple of times and then Fee started to get hungry. We'd had a lolly while being on the beach but it was getting on for two o'clock so we walked off the beach to go to the chip shop that was well known for having pictures of famous people on the walls. I stared at the black and white photos thinking that one of them looked like Rock Hudson from an old fashioned film I'd watched called 'That Darn Cat' with Doris Day.

I'd been getting in to thinking that people we bumped into from time to time looked like famous faces.

The fish 'n' chips were lovely but a bone got stuck in my throat and I started choking. I heard someone yell to get me a drink. My eyes started watering and I felt my face go hot as I struggled to breath. Grandad put a drink to my lips and encouraged me to hold it. This was the first time I'd choked on a bone and I had to sit down. My sisters fussed round me while we all sat on the wall and the panicky feeling left me as I threw up starting to put me off eating fish. But I was hungry and tried again. Fee told me to pick through the bones but where the last one felt as though it had scratched I couldn't finish the meal. Then Gramps decided we needed to stretch our legs. We started to walk round the harbour.

Under the warmth of the strong afternoon sun I felt tired. It was three thirty and Nan told us to turn back half way along the harbour wall to go to the car.

I still felt as though my throat hurt as Fee and Eve grumpily had enough anyway. I let them moan for a bit to Nan and Gramps feeling sorry for myself not letting anyone else know as I missed the beach.

The next day we all had breakfast early and headed off for church. There'd been a rousing chorus of Morning Has Broken before my sisters and I were shuffled off my Mum into St Peter Street rooms for Sunday school. We were introduced to a story about a man called Job. At first the tale was told to us as we'd all sat at the tables and I started to see out my mind's eye a great big whale like that in Pinocchio swallowing the man whole into his tummy then being spat back out onto the sand of where he then strolled purposefully, thoroughly afraid of what God would do to him next, into the town of where he managed to turn everyone from the evil ways back to worshipping God.

The story came with photocopies for each of us as an illustration for us all to colour in. My whale was navy blue and I drew water coming out of his air hole. The mouth was wide open with Job flying in the air towards what I coloured in as a very bright yellowy beach. The man was quite small and I praised myself for staying inside the lines very well as no-one told me well done. I did it myself. I put my name and date on and proudly took it to Mum while Fee and Eve were already there. I'd always taken the longest to colour in oblivious to anyone else as I always concentrated very hard on my work.

It was soon time to go back in to church for the last hymn and I remember singing loudly about the purple headed mountain. Mum and Fee shot me a look but I just carried on until it was time to go back for a nice roast dinner.

In school the next day I'd been engrossed in learning about frogs and toads, mushrooms and poisonous fungi, completely fascinated and pleased to be learning about something totally new. When I handed my work in the teacher looked pleasingly at it and gave me a good mark.

After lunch it was P.E. and we were practising country dancing out on one of the school fields in the sunshine. Dosy-dohing I kept looking at my feet to judge my steps and I thoroughly loved the exercise and being whizzed around when linking arms with the other children. We all had to line up in pairs and create bridges with our hands in the air for us to dance under and go to the back of the line. We were rehearsing for our school summer fete.

After quarter passed three on our way home Mum asked us if we wanted to go up the park. I'd been dead keen but was told to wait till Dad got home and until after tea.

We had waffles with a fried egg and baked beans for tea and as promised we all traipsed up the park with a football. Instead of going on the swings Dad pulled off his jumper and Mum took off hers to make goal posts. Then me, Fee and Eve took it in turns to tackle one another on goal before aiming the ball at Dad. I'd been determined to get the ball pass Dad and was upset Dad caught it. I kept wanting to go again and kept getting frustrated with Dad wanting to tackle us girls and because Dad was so good showing off in front of us eventually just passing the ball between his feet and kneeing it up in the air several times. I watched in wonderment wishing I could do the same. Fee and Eve had left for the swings with Mum but I stayed and actually scored a goal wishing we all kept playing together.

I soon caught everyone up on the swings but had to wait my turn. I was starting to hate waiting for things.

Getting out of bed early, after being called, us girls were dead excited to be going away on holiday for a week. Dad had told us we were staying in a caravan and I was keen to shower and dress before running downstairs and wanting to get in the car straight away. Mum and Dad were all smiles as they piled up the car for everything to take away with us. Fee looked a bit glum lugging stuff out the door blissfully unaware that I was not helping too as no-one had asked me to.

In the car, without a grumble from me, I'd had to sit in the middle of the back seat yet again. I'd have rather sat by the window but Eve and Fee claimed travel sickness if they couldn't sit by the window themselves. Fee and Eve always seemed to get what they asked for but I didn't want to cause a fuss. Always happy Dad pointed out the different places we passed going by all the rolling green fields, but I couldn't see the area stuck in the middle as Dad said we were heading towards Yeovil to Mum. Not really knowing the direction we were going in Dad had gone into Honiton on the A30 and headed towards the A376 to the coast then before the signs for Exmouth headed towards Budleigh Salterton and on to Ladram Bay Holiday Park.

I was just finally pleased to jump out the car by our caravan. We were finally here and my immediate thought was to do some exploring. Not really paying a thought to help unloading the car and with no-one telling me to do so I'd wanted everyone to hurry up to find some fun. Why couldn't my parents ask me to help out like they did my sisters? I'd have been more than happy to do the unloading to feel more a part of the family. I thought it was me who had to take the lead in all the fun.

Dad promised we'd explore where the beach was after some food and all of us eventually tucked into our picnic of sandwiches, crisps, chocolates, and juice. Mum asked Dad if we could find a shop to stock up for more food, then the whole family started walking through he caravans down a lane passed a shop, Mum said we could stop in on the way back yup and not long after the road widened down to a very pebbled beach. All the pebbles looked orange and the cliffs nearby looked like they were made of clay. Dad said we'd probably drive off site some days to explore the rest of the villages nearby. We'd tried a day on the beach the day after getting there but after sitting on the pebbles we all noticed ourselves getting covered in red dust. Eve and I used our lilos out on the water. Mum had had a blanket on the red shingles that turned the blanket a funny colour. We never went on the beach again after that and toured round Dawlish, Dawlish Warren, and Torquay instead. Happy to just be all together we'd had a lovely holiday.

In the morning the next day the sun was shining, the birds were singing, there was a skippity skip beat in my heart. I ran downstairs after showering and dressing to find loads of things to do. I found out some knitting and decided to knit some dolly clothes. I loved the yellow and white, orange and white, blue and white dresses my Nan Burr had knitted for our babies and I wanted to knit a dress as good as those for my Sindy. I got pink wool and size nine needles. Casted on twenty five stitches and knitted twenty rows before casting off every other stitch to create the waist and knitted five rows for the waist band. I then created enough stitches in between the other ones to make thirty stitches. I then knitted fifteen rows before I decreased the stitches at the sides to create the arm holes. Then I created a turtle neck at the top and then did exactly the same again to sew together to make a completed dress. This took three hours to perfect. It was a lovely sleeveless dress I then put on my naked dolly and was well impressed with myself.

Mum brought out lunch consisting of yummy sandwiches with cut carrots and celery with salt that I put on the side of my plate.

Now afterward Mum gave out some comics to us three and Fee spotted a colouring in competition. We all went upstairs after lunch.

I lay on my bed with my headphones gently humming away and pretending to be a conductress with an orchestra as my favourite Famous Five tape began with a very famous Beethoven piece of music. It was very atmospheric to begin a mystery.

Afterward Fee called me to her room and she showed me a beautiful zoo picture she'd coloured in all by herself. I'd said, "It looks great."

Then she asked, "Can you fill in your name and age please to help me win this?"

Ever considerate I obliged.

The next day it was sunny and we all played outside and I'd come across some French tapes Dad was learning the language for in case he ever went there on a holiday. I put it on my personal stereo and wondered around outside learning the very basics loving the sound of my own voice, I said "Bonjour mes amis." With a laugh and "Bon nuit." Finding out how to say good morning my friend and good night. I finished the day on a natural high after tittering about all day.

A week later I was heaving up sick and not feeling very well when Mum shouted up the stairs. "Fee there's a large delivery for you. Can you come downstairs and open it please?"

I heard Fee run down the stairs and she brought back up a massive pound puppy even though the form had been filled out with my details. I felt really hurt that Fee claimed the prize as hers but she explained to me that it was her colouring in skills that won it.

Now in the morning the next day I'd been round Lynda's early as her parents were taking us in the car to a place called Cranmore. There was a great big picture of an old fashioned steam train above their fire place and had never twigged that they were train spotters. They'd slung a picnic hamper in the boot of the car and headed out of Shepton towards Frome.

At East Cranmore they'd pulled in at the train station and everyone jumped out then we all made our way to an embankment looking over the railway line. To our left was a bridge with a brick wall either side and we just sat there in the sunshine watching the trains go by. It was very peaceful apart from the choo-chooing down below and more families turned up through the morning to do the same as us.

We'd had a tasty picnic, some nice sandwiches and tit bits with the family favouring savoury foods. Then afterwards we walked on the bridge looking down on a locomotive coming through. We all cheered when the horn blew and steam came billowing out from the little chimney encompassing all in its path.

The day was so lovely with the sun smiling on us. Lynda had a happy family and I got on well with them.

It was a heady summer and everyone was going off places enjoying the sunshine and Mum and Dad headed towards Wells, then Wookey and out towards Weston-Super-Mare. We'd had our swimming suites and towels slung in the boot of the car and met my Aunty and Uncle and Gran and Gramps at the Tropiquaria. We were there to have some family fun.

On the sea front we had to queue to get in and we could hear the noise coming from the swimming pool inside of children running around and playing in the water with their parents. I could feel the excitement running through me as we stepped in to a world of pools and water slides. We were all soon in the pool splashing around and having some fun with barely any room to actually swim. Mum had taken the camera to shoot what was one of the best times of our childhood. It was an open air pool and really hot so we relished walking around in the shade or jumping into cool down, or going down the slides to hit the cool water at the bottom. We were there for the best part of the day and we all had ice creams when we were dried and back in our clothes taking a stroll along the beach watching the sun slowly disappearing over the horizon. Happy and satiated we made our way home.

The next day we drove through the sand dunes at Brean Down with the gulls shrieking overhead we pulled up on the beach. In the back of the car we had a barbecue that we set up in front of a high dune. Dad started the fire and got it going before the football team started to show up ready for training. Dad got them warming up running up and down a really high sand hill and I went wandering off bored to tears. There was a certain sense of freedom to spending time on my own alone with my thoughts letting then just blow through my mind. I disturbed a man peeing, at least I think that was what he was doing, as he turned round and flashed me while in his light blue trousers. I got freaked out and hurried back to Mum and Dad.

The barbecue was in full swing with no-one running anymore but were eating the sausages and burgers. At least I got back in time for lunch. I tried to tell Mum about the flasher but she acted as though I hadn't spoken. I got that a lot when I was small. The football team soon got back to their training and we stayed on the beach all day. I felt inclined to stay with the group after the mornings going on.

On the way back to the car while walking along the pavement Eve pointed out she could see someone's bum. We all looked at two butt cheeks through holes cut into the back of a man's pair of black trousers.

It had been a strange day and in the morning school began at quarter to nine. We all lined up in the yard behind each other and the girls either side tried to talk to me or so I thought so I went to join in their conversations and they gave me an 'I'm not talking to you' stare. I turned round to face going into class and looked around me for Lynda and she gave me an encouraging smile. I said. "Morning." And shut up ready to start the day as a good girl of whom would be quiet in class.

Once sat at my desk the work seemed easy soaking up every bit of information like a sponge.

At the end of the school day I went home with Mum and sisters and I asked for a cuddle. I just hated cuddles that lasted too long as I didn't like Mum's heavy hot breathing on me it made me feel uncomfortable.

Back at home I just wanted to sit quiet on my own wanting a chat with Fee. I asked her for a rubber from her collection to get her talking and I got yanked off the sofa by me feet and tickled. Every inch of my body came alive to my sister's touch and I writhed around on the floor caught up in every single moment of a different mainly over my belly and under my arm pits tickle. With one hand she tickled a foot at the same time which seemed to go on forever and thought she was never going to stop and started wheezing terrified of not being able to breathe. I'd started off laughing but couldn't take that harsh tickling any longer. I nearly passed out until she just stopped. I'd had a really bad asthma attack.

By the Paper Mill out at Wookey was a lush green field with a football pitch on and I remember the club house was long and had a skittle alley. Dad was the manager of the team back then and had a friend who had a mop of black hair, a moustache and beard who asked if I'd enter a design-a-football-kit competition. This had been while the whole family had just watched a game and were sitting in the club house while us girls had crisps each and a coke. We all felt very at home with Dad's friends and I started planning the colour of the kit straight away. I chose the colour dark purple. I'd felt very excited that I'd been asked and spent time that afternoon with a pack of pens and some spare paper.

On the walls of the clubhouse were old team photos and in the middle of the skittle alley on the far wall had been placed a big picture of the team's logo. This I copied having a real eye for colour and placed it on my purple and black striped shirt in the top right hand corner. After carefully spending an hour doing the shorts, boots, socks and the player too I'd signed my name, age and telephone number with address on the back. Dad gave me a pat on the back and told me it looked good then he handed it to his friend. I smiled up at him with my eyes smiling.

Eve and Fee had gone outside to play by running around on the grass. We were all happy Dad's team had won. I could hear Mum grumbling when picking up the dirty kit to take home.

Glancing at my school books on the Monday I concentrated on what I was writing excited about learning English. We were learning about adverbs and nouns. My answers had been spot on.

When I'd gotten home that afternoon Mum was proud of my achievements as she flicked through my little blue English book and seen how many red and gold stars I'd had. Pleased as punch I watched the telly with my sisters getting into my favourite cartoons. Exhausted that evening I still found it hard to get to sleep and started to lie facing the room with my hands firmly between my knees to keep myself still knowing I'd get nightmares by now if I faced the wall.

By the end of the week, of which flew by, it was soon time for us all to go back to football at the Paper Mill. As soon as I'd seen Dad's friend he told me that my football kit design was being used for the next season.

On the Monday I sat on the sofa and imagined how God used his influence on the world. I thought about it and it came to me in an inspirational thought that God was actually a couple, a man and wife. The men took the credit for everything back then. All the apostles were men who had wives, so I deduced that God took credit for everything while his wife used all her love to encircle the earth in her warm embrace. That was in the morning as I waited to get in the car and then went to school and met Lynda Ball at the gate. The yard was heaving with children. At the sound of the bell we all lined up ready to go in our classrooms. Lynda and I were in Mrs

Chivers class on time ready for lessons. We'd been having reading time and I'd had out my Read it Yourself book and it was all about the story of the Ugly Duckling. The poor duck was deemed ugly by her own family and swam away to live with a duck family then was shunned by them as he wasn't really a duck. The poor thing ended up on their own and a year later they turned into a beautiful swan. I liked the happy ending to that story and then the bell rang to signal morning play out in the playground. Lynda and I would play together for some of the time but she kept talking to the other children of which I didn't like so went off by myself wandering round the play yard watching everyone play happily. I was pleased to see and hear happy children.

The next lesson was basic math and we learned our twelve times table of which I'd been practicing at home in my head. I could quite easily get up to 12 x 12 equalling a hundred and forty four which was as far we were expected to get. I liked maths and should have been teacher's pet and couldn't understand why other children gave time to talk with the teachers and never had a conversation with them myself. Not that it bothered me that much as I always by then just focused on how good I'd been at learning things.

Afternoon bell came and we all ate in the canteen together. I was usually the last one in there watching the canteen ladies put the hexagon tables and chairs away. Not worrying where Lynda was or anyone else for that matter I strolled round outside looking through holes in the wall obsessed with pulling out weeds or pulling off moss while thinking about putting it all together to create a carpet while at home. Feeling full from my sandwiches, crisps, chocolate and fruit I stretched, and yawned feeling satisfied with myself before bracing myself for afternoon classes.

It was soon home time and I wanted to show Mum what I'd learned. Coming out of the classroom I had spotted Eve's red hair running towards Mum so I'd followed them to the yellow Datsun by the pavement outside. Mum said she'd been coming back later for a parents teachers association meeting so I was dead keen at home to talk about the book I'd read. Mum smiled and sang the song about the ugly duckling and I sang along with her while Eve learnt this song too. Fee already knew it and I was dead happy we all sounded really good together.

Mum put tea on the table then went to the PTA meeting when Dad came home on his own.

Springing out of bed I found my clothes and put them on. Mum called for us girls to go downstairs and have breakfast as we were going off in the car. The birds were singing. The sun was shining and I had a song in my heart and in my head I was singing that popular song. It was from a musical and it went, 'Oh What a Beautiful Morning, who what a beautiful day. I've got a wonderful feeling everything's going my way.' I danced to the car with a skippity beat tapping my toes wholeheartedly. Getting on everybody's nerves and not caring.

The car sped down the road and over the hills by endless green fields and high hedges. Coming into the car park there were loads of spaces and dad chose the space nearest the entrance.

With the National Trust pass we all trooped in together by the golden leaves and the large pink chrysanthemums, at Beaud Gardens, on the bushes. I darted in and out between the bushes telling stories to myself of how I could have spoken up for myself in the last conversation I'd had with my parents. My sisters would talk animatedly with Mum. Then I would catch up with them from time to time wheezing and dying to talk to them about fir cones and animals I'd found.

There came a clearing for a nice place to sit and put down the picnic blanket. We all sat down and Dad put his arm around me to make me feel protected and I smiled up at him with our blue eyes twinkling together. He teased gently and touched my impertinent nose and I inwardly giggled but my sister Fee turned to look at us sharply.

Mum took out some paper and pens and put squares of dots on them. We took turns to join up these dots to make our own squares to put our initials in. I nibbled at my food from time to time and felt a bit itchy over my face it felt like there was spots on my nose, chin, cheeks and forehead and I kept on wanting to pick several spots on my back. My Mother told me not to wander off again as she thought out loud that I'd picked up a rash from a bush or a flower or something.

Dad put his arm around me for a while as we walked through an arboretum of trees and he tried to point out the different birds and animals, but Mum tried all the time to get us to look for red and grey squirrels. I always had to squint my eyes to see them though. I'd been told I was short sighted.

Through the woods I imagined finding a squirrel and walked off again following my feet through the trees careful not to trip over any roots and to avoid any brambles. Lost in my own little world we soon got home.

That evening I watched old newsreels on the telly of two girls playing in their garden based on an old story of true life.

They'd had an old fashioned camera and while they were running around the bottom end of their garden they got pleasantly surprised when they saw two fairies flying around and took photos of them. They showed the picture on the telly of what they took and the bush in black came out and you could make out the shapes of the leaves and the fairies were white and very clear with wings on their backs hovering over a bird bath. I really believed that they were telling the truth. I liked that story.

All that day the next day I kept scratching while trying to distract myself by watching the telly. I watched my favourite cartoons like the Get Along

Gang with animals like Portia the sheep dressed in human clothes along with the other animal characters. There was a moose called Moose who wore a blue jumper with a M on and I used to find this cartoon cute. I'd holed myself up in front of the telly watching my other favourite cartoons like Duck Tales with Scrooge Mcduck and his three annoying nephews with their annoying voices that I used to find cute. Scrooge had a cave filled with gold and jewels that in the opening credits he used to swim in with his nephews.

I loved the Chippendales about twin beavers and the gummi bears. I loved singing "Da, da, da, Chippendale rescue rangers, cha, cha, cha, Chippendale rescue rangers," over and over again loving the song at the beginning of the cartoon not realising it was annoying. Why? 'Cause I was a happy child.

While I'd been dosed up on my medicines because I'd had chicken pox I gave into scratching a main spot on my forehead that eventually I'd scratched off that day.

The afternoon was full of homework that I had to catch up on but each time I went to write my English essay my itches were beginning to get the better of me and I couldn't sit still for long and concentrate as my mind kept going blurry. Then my eyes would blur over. I tried to do knitting at mother's request to keep my mind and hands busy as by this point I felt that I could knit simple things with my eyes closed.

The afternoons were very long as I got more on edge and uptight. For the past three days I'd had my sisters stay away from me. I'd had colouring books of where I would go over and over again everything with the colours red, green, blue and yellow pencils from tiny little packets that came with large felt lined pictures. My mind was always full of things to do and Mum one afternoon gave me the paddling pool outside to play with as Mum knew that the cold water would soothe my itching up my arms, over my belly and my face. My sisters joined in and we had some fun.

I tried a few hours on the piano and urged my fingers on to play faster and faster scales to take the urge away to itch.

The weekend came and Mum ran out of soothing cream she'd kept putting on me but noticed that the pox was clearing up. By the Sunday after eating my first hearty roast dinner for a week. I was feeling much better.

It had been Dad's idea to go for a walk out in the sunshine for a few hours for all of us to get some fresh air on our skins. The whole family walked towards the steps down into Coombe Lane and at the bottom we went by the Horseshoe Inn. Part way up the hill I looked to the right and saw a big house Dad steered us round to the left. We went by some lovely cottages and on the right hand side was a long high wall with trellises and trees hanging down over it. There was a blue door with a piece of wood on of which was carved a sign that Dad claimed he'd made at school for the Casenove family that lived there. Christopher, he'd said, was a child of whom Gran used to babysit there years ago. Apparently he was a famous actor I'd seen on the telly.

I looked up the winding hill and towards loads of hedges and beyond gates as we passed to lots of lush green fields. The hill grew steeper and I found it harder to breath so I went slower lagging behind everyone, but Dad always frog marched everywhere making me run to keep up. He would turn to me to say, "Keep up Karen." And rub his hands together.

Further on up the road on the left hand side we encountered a huge yard outside of a barn by a large farmhouse. We could smell a strong odour of poo so knew that cows were in the barn. I spied some through the slats in the barn sides and through the door. Some mooed gently and jostled about they were all black and white. So we'd stopped and looked climbing on their metal gates swinging on them.

Walking on Dad got talking to Mum of whom I could tell was trying to hang back with me as my sisters stayed up the front with Dad.

The road was long and arduous just for me as everyone led the way then it veered round to the right, but in the middle of the road was where you could tell the cows had crossed the road that morning.

For another mile the lane seemed longer and longer. We stopped regularly to look over several fences and gates to gaze out over endless sky and the fields with the houses in Shepton in our vision. Dad would point out whereabouts our house was, the Anglo Trading Estate was and where you could see the large Clarks factory building was.

A crow had been perched on a hedge right next to me and I asked, "Is that a blackbird or a raven Dad, or is it a crow?" Dad being the smart Alek said it was a crow and I smiled cheekily at him glad I'd gotten his attention again. I'd constantly sought my Dad's eye.

The road started to slope downwards. It felt better to walk that way and it wasn't so painful on my legs anymore and felt jubilant when Dad pointed out we were on our way home. Down the hill I looked at Mum and started to run a little bit keen to get back before it started to get a bit darker.

The evening came and back at home quite late we had cheese and crackers with onions for supper. Mum and Dad put the telly on softly and told us girls to go to bed. We raced upstairs to brush our teeth and put our nighties on. I soon cuddled up in my sheet, duvet and blanket to drift off in to a dreamless sleep.

That morning I had a good night's rest. I felt well again and Mum told me that I had to go to school. I felt elated about going to see my friends.

Nehemia 8:10
"Today is holy to our Lord, so don't be sad. The joy that the Lord gives you will make you strong."

At school in the playground I met up with a friend called Sidwell of whom was blonde and in pigtails with blue eyes and there was a girl called Georgette who spoke to me and said, "Good morning." So I was polite back and said the same to her. I still looked out for Lynda of whom was my best friend. I had to ask her if she'd had chicken pox too and we got to talking in line for the first class of the day. Everyone at school, even though they didn't say it, were glad to have me back as the teacher said it at the beginning of the day.

The morning was taken up doing an English class and Mrs Chivers a tall slim, dark haired lady with spectacles on used to emulate me every time I stuck my hand up to spout letter by letter she'd copied on the board as a new big word the class learned through me.

Straight after this lesson we went outside to go to a dinner lady who had a tray of sweets and drinks for us to buy and I didn't both to buy as Lynda queued up. I eyed her up and down glad she was my best friend and felt full with pride.

The following lesson was an art lesson of when I'd used up a lot of different coloured paints to cover a great picture on the floor with everyone else. Then looked up after trying really hard with the paintbrush to see smiling eyes at me and I wondered why? Turned out I'd had splodges of paint all over my face when I put my hand up to go to the bathroom. I'd noticed in the mirror and secretly smiled to myself as I used a wet paper towel to wipe it off.

Lunchtime came and went as Lynda and I asked for skipping ropes to play with and we roped Georgette into holding one end of the rope while Sidwell held the other wooden handle. The red and white rope was then turned for Lynda and I to jump over in turn. The two other girls got faster and faster. I knew they wanted our turn to end quicker as they pounded the school yard harder and harder with it whipping under my feet. I then caved with my feet hurting from all the jumping. I'd wanted to sit down and have a drink after the tuck had gone back in. I knew that I should have taken the rope for the other girls. I'd held it for one minute before getting faster and faster doing the same for them, Georgette and Sidwell.

The afternoon lesson after the bell had been a mathematical lesson concentrating on basic times tables of up to six by six. We'd had dominoes to demonstrate this as we all had a pack each to place each number by number in turn to copy in our text books ready for the teacher to go through each multiplication sum on the board for us to say out loud how the sum was thought out. This took us up to the last bell.

Out in the yard full of yelling and screaming children I waited for my Mum who always picked up me and my little sister Eve first then we went all across town together to pick up Fiona from St Pauls School.

Back at home Fee taught me how to play with our hands "Up above." She said of where she put her palm up to get hit then, "On the side." She'd said and turned her hand to get hit again. Then quickly said, "Down below," while moving her hands quickly then said, "You're too slow." As her hand went ultra-quickly down by her side and she laughed. I did the same to her. Then Eve joined in our little game.

It was June 21st 1982 the next day and I'd heard there was a big street party laid on down the road that Mum wanted to take us to in the morning. At the bottom of the road the atmosphere was thriving with loads of happy families with stalls outside their houses with either food on or with things to do on. Someone had got an old gramophone the party music was blaring on. I looked up in wonderment looking at endless union Jack banners tied to the lamp posts and I noticed table cloths were either, blue, red or white. On poles were pictures of Charles and Diana the prince and princess of Wales. The place was buzzing with happy children either, dancing, running around or playing together nicely as I noticed the adults standing around drinking and chatting nicely.

Mum pulled us away by about 2 o'clock saying thank you to our neighbours who'd said we were welcome to come back later round their houses to play.

At home we put on the television for us to see what the fuss was about and there was Diana and Charles outside a hospital with their first born son in their arms. All I can remember was that they'd said their son was called William. Princess Diana was in a blue dress with a white collar and her husband was in a boring grey suit. The flashes of cameras were going off all around them. The whole family sat transfixed.

On that day Mum gave us a mug each with Princess Diana and Prince Charles and mine was blue. The other sisters had each a different colour.

After the news they'd put on a documentary about both of them during their single years. One half was of how Charles had been a cad having been seen out with a string of beautiful women on his arm. There were also a couple of scenes of when he first courted Camilla Parker Bowles. The other half of the documentary was about Di with pictures of her brother, mother and father as a young family and how she'd been a lady.

A week later the journey was a rough one across the waters to Eire. Everyone was sick on the boat except me. I remember going up on deck with Dad to watch the waves crash over the boat while looking up to the dark sky that seemed to have no moon. Then I remembered that it was the middle of the day. A perfume spillage at the end of our row of seats was what made Dad heave. Luckily, by the time we got to our holiday cottage at the top of a cliff face overlooking a long stretch of beach out to the peninsula we were all feeling fine. One of the first things we did when we got there was to turn on the television and Mrs Mangle and Jane were in a scene on Neighbours that I had seen before. Apparently Irish TV seemed behind us. The living room and kitchen was decked out in pine furniture and we soon allocated bedrooms at the back of the cottage. One of the first things we did was explore the cliffs behind and we went over a stile to follow the cliff face a little way. We were all in our bomber jackets to keep out of the icy wind.

The next day we explored the beach and up in the sand dunes, because we were situated right by the Atlantic, the sea was too rough and too dangerous for us to get in and have a swim. I lost my red sandals up in the dunes.

In the evening, after tea, back at where we were staying we found a local pub that looked over the sea and we sat in the window seats. Dad gave me some of his Guinness to try and I remember saying it tasted of tin. The locals at the inn seemed friendly.

The next day we went for a long walk exploring the roads round where we stayed and a stray dog started to follow us. We called the dog Timmy because of the Famous Five I loved reading so much. He followed us for miles. He'd even stayed with us as we found a wooden picnic table to stop and have lunch with woods around begging to be explored. Timmy enjoyed our food as much as we did. When we got up to move on Mum, Dad, Fee, Eve and I passed a row of lovely cottages terraced together with box lawns and lovely flowers out front. This was where Timmy got left as we assumed the second cottage was his home.

The next morning we heard a lot of noise coming from outside on the front lawn. We opened the curtains and there was a flock of sheep standing outside the front window. We were going off into the capital today and even though us girls started off in matching short jump suits all pink, purple and white the day started to descent into bad weather. We had to get changed.

There were lots of shops in the city that we trailed round and a horse and carriage ride caught out attention. Up in the carriage we rode round the more scenic areas of Dublin, even down through a very pretty tree lined road when the heavens opened. The guide was very broad accented and I never understood a word he said as we sat without a hood over the carriage and got thoroughly soaked.

As we trudged back through the streets we heard, 'There Must Be An Angel' by the Eurythmics blaring out from one of the shops next to the cinema. We looked at the films playing and decided on seeing the Never Ending Story to escape the bad weather. The boy in the film I could identify with as I was a bit of a dreamer too and I felt really sorry for him as he jumped into a dumpster to avoid the bullies. The large talking ferret didn't do much for me but it was a nice story. We went back to the cottage afterward tired and ready for bed.

The rest of the days passed in a blur before we headed for home on the boat on a calmer Irish sea.

Back at 10 Coombe View, Shepton Mallet, we all settled back down in to ordinary life that was a bit boring at times. Now on the next day the weather turned out nice so me and my sisters went outside into the back yard of where we stayed. I loved outside. On the grass I went to the left with my arms outstretched and let my hair fall over my face. I thought I was going to bump my head but my hands hit the floor first. I then elevated my legs sideways over my stupid little head. Then I decided to do the same over and over again each time trying to extend my legs further and further outwards to create an upside down 'V' shape.

Mum came out mid-morning with Coca-Cola for us to drink and Eve spied a funny looking stick that had blown off one of our beech trees while we had been away. She showed it to Mum who told us, what I thought was a little porky pie, that this special kind of stick could help us find water.

I finished my drink and wanted to find that special kind of stick for myself that I realised was a V-shape. I fell for the game of holding out the pointed bit to the ground pretending, after a while of walking around, to make the stick quiver to point out where the water under the ground would be.

We got trowels out and I started to dig underneath of where I'd pretended the water had been. I picked up flower pots dotted around and filled them up with earth. The morning soon flew by. Then Mum came out again with soft door stop sandwiches and coats but we decided to go in to the warm.

The next day was a cold afternoon and Eve and I were bored indoors so we decided to go outside and get our cricket bat and some tennis balls. Eve threw the first six balls as I went to bat in the yard and as it was French cricket we had no stumps so I ran back and forth to the back wall of the house to the bottom of the garden. it was an easy enough game and Eve and I took several turns by which time we were sufficiently warmed up and were full of beans so one of us went to the garage beyond the gate to get a couple of skipping ropes. We'd gotten Mum outside by this point, and her and Eve held the rope for me to jump over. I wasn't very good at skipping this way though and soon had a rope by myself skipping far more easily on my own. I'd usually try and do one hundred jumps while Eve skipped more slowly. I wanted to be like Dad skipping for England to keep fit. As we got more and more heated Mum brought us out some squash each and as we sat down at the edge of the path through the middle of the garden the cold air started seeping through our bones. It was time to go in. We managed a game of Buckaroo of where you'd laden up a donkey to the point of it kicking out to make you the loser before having tea. We loved to have baked beans on waffles and my face was all aglow from being outside and my freckles were more prominent.

The next day armed with our sticker albums Mum and Dad put us girls into the car to head for the beach. We were off down the coast heading for

Cornwall and the first place we got to was somewhere Dad called Constantine Bay.

It was a lovely sandy beach of where I'd thrown off my shoes to dig my toes in the sand. I went to run into the water but Dad said the red flag was up so took all of our hands and the whole family walked out to the rocks. Not liking the feel of the rocks under my sandalless feet I dared myself to come closer to the pools of where Dad was pointing. He told us that there was a crab in the water. I stared fascinated and noticed the feet of a young boy in trainers walk up to us to see what we were looking at. He'd been on his own and said, "Hello." I promptly looked up and said "Hello." Back noticing a mole on the side of his face.

Having stood there too long I turned around and noticed Mum, Dad, Fee and Eve had moved on to a bigger rock pool so I left the boy to it to go after them. "Nice to meet you." I'd said and ran off towards them. it was a bit windy so I tugged on my coat to do it up. Wishing I'd kept my sandals on I started to wheeze while everyone was talking around me. They were looking at tiny fishes and I went to ask what kind of fish they were but no-one could answer me. Eve slipped a bit on the rocks that were all black. Mum grabbed her hand to keep her upright. The wind was getting cold.

Dad wanted us to move on over the rock pools to look for more crustaceans. I could hear the waves beginning to crash on the beach so I'd turned to look and missed watching the sea come in fast towards us through the rocks. The water had been a shock coming up around my feet especially as it was nice and cool. In came tiny little fish flailing about. I never looked up much and danced around in the water singing a current hit single. Fee joined in with me singing. A part of me suddenly realised that I didn't know where my shoes went and noticed that Mum had them in her hands. I was beginning to get bored as other families walked around us.

Dad told us to head back towards the beach. Eve began to cry as she began to get colder. Fee wanted a lolly but Mum explained that we were nowhere near any shops. We all seemed to be cut off from civilisation as the beach came into view as the family were the only people there. I'd wanted to sit down and dig a hole in the sand and let the feel of it round my toes dry my feet. Wishing I'd brought trainers and some socks. Sniffing I wiped my nose on my sleeve.

Mum suggested we went back to the car and have our picnic in it, and it became a long trek back to the vehicle. Mum watched me rub my nose with my sleeve again and said she had a tissue from which appeared from up her sleeve. "Here have this." Dad said to blow hard which I did making my head hurt. Then Mum gave me my sandals so I'd put them on.

After nibbling on some sandwiches and mini cheddars I'd had enough. Dad told us to strap up as we were driving along the coast. Next stop had been a sleepy little village and Fee, Eve and I got ice creams. I'd had an orange Solero with plenty of ice cream in the middle. Eve had a Fab lolly and Fee had a Feast. Wandering in and out the souvenir shops everyone kept moving on too fast for me as all I'd wanted to do was read the funny postcards while inwardly chuckling to myself. Following my feet I bumped into the family standing around outside one shop just eating lollies and chatting, not knowing what they were talking about I felt left out. "You caught us up then," Dad said rubbing his hands together and giving me a smile.

Taking our time walking back happy I'd felt the day had been a pleasant one always content spending time with the family. I wished my sisters would give me a window seat in the car but they were always afraid of getting car sick. That's why I never really got to see any scenery out the window and never really learned the routes to anywhere. Dad would always be our tour guide telling us about the monuments, towns and villages we passed through and Mum would try and get some singing going of which I loved.

Out of the window Mum spotted a little church and asked Dad if we could stop and have a look around. Fee needed the toilet so Dad found an available space in a car park of where there were latrines and we all got out. Mum advised us all to go to the loo as it was going to be a long way back and before we knew it we were wandering around some beautiful thatched cottages until we got to the church. Once inside I'd wandered round the side of the pews taking everything in. Dad pointed to the ceiling so I craned my neck and saw some beautiful carvings above us. The picture of Jesus was in the stain glass window at the front of the pontiff of which I stared at. I wandered over to the lectern and saw an open book of war heroes. It was a beautiful book with gold leaf edgings and with big fancy letters at the top of each page. I looked across to Mum and she was writing in a book. Moving through the pews to get to her I grabbed on to them and swung my feet to walk quickly to see what she was doing. She said that she was signing the visitors' book and inclined the pen towards me asking if I wanted to write something so I grabbed the pen and complimented my surroundings. My eyes looked towards lots of pamphlets and notices. I walked over and picked some up intending to have a read later at which point I looked around and realised everyone must have gone outside. They were wandering around the headstones reading each one so I'd done the same thinking I'd recognise a name wondering if that was what they were looking for but no names were familiar to me.

Dad ushered us back to the car saying that he wanted to drive on back home. We still had a long journey ahead of us.

Back on the A30 we came across a McDonalds and Mum made the decision for us to stop there for tea. Pulling into the parking lot we jumped out the vehicle with our tummies growling. I wanted a pink milkshake. At the restaurant my sisters ordered banana milkshake and a chocolate one with

Big Mac meal deals. Dad found seats for us all by the window and we all tucked in hungrily.

Afterwards I found myself yawning in the car and dozing off to the humming of the engine and the lull of a ballad on the radio.

At home I asked Mum where my sticker album was. She'd brought it in and I sat reading the Great Mouse Detective story that had been a film I'd seen at the cinema and I took it to bed with me later on.

The next morning came round quickly and tip toeing downstairs early I'd heard Dad scraping at something over the sink. He was cleaning our Clarks shoes that had been left by the back door the night before. I smelled a strong smell of seaweed.

In the kitchen with him I just stood and watched taking it all in. Now the sink was on the left hand side near the back door and he put each pair of shoes outside to dry in the sunshine. It was a beautiful day and we were off to school that day. I'd been getting excited about going on a trip. When I heard we were only going to Streets Clarks factory I thought great a day away from boredom of home.

Now when we got there we parked up by a low ceiling long dark brown building situated by some houses. I thought that I'd meet Granddad Burr. The teacher got out first and waited for us all to get out.

Once in the building we looked round the patent room, and round the shoes made stacked in boxes. We also encountered sewing machinery that they used to put together the shoes. I met Granddad and he said, "Hello." I beamed at him and said "Hello Gramps," back.

After the brief tour we went back to the foreman's office of where a man offered to let our feet be measured one by one. I got into a queue of five as the others were told to either go to the toilet before we went home and some went with another teacher to the nearest shop for snacks. We all took it in turns to do all three. We were curious.

> *Ecclesiates 1:8*
> *Everything leads to weariness – a weariness too great for words. Our eyes can never see enough to be satisfied, our ears can never hear enough.*

I got curious about Gramps work and asked him. Then I bought a little fudge chocolate bar before being the last one to go to the toilet. The class was told to congregate in the car park afterward.

When it looked like we were all outside the head teacher took a roll call to make sure we were all there. Then she said, "There will be a Mr Clark coming to school in September and I am very pleased at the turn out for this trip as I know you've taken time out from your summer holidays this year so thank you."

We jumped back on the coach and headed for Bowlish of where our parents came and picked us all up. Mum was first in line at the gate when we got back. I'd been pleased to see her on her own, Mum said my sisters had been waiting for me as they had been playing Buck-a-roo and all our other games that day for something to do. They wanted an extra player that was all as it was getting boring.

I soon got into the swing of snakes and ladders and I had to be a blue counter. Eve was yellow and Fee was red. We chased each other round the board and I got caught in the middle of my sisters getting more and more competitive with one another.

It wasn't long before it was teatime and not long till I flopped exhausted into bed.

Chapter Five

It was a Saturday morning the birds were singing, the sun was shining and everyone was awake early. Mum came in early with our cups of tea and said to us to dress quickly as we were going off for the day. Yawning I stretched and wriggled my toes, then stretched again finding it had to wake up. An adventure was to be had and we all got dressed after showering very quickly.

I was the first to the door. Fee was helping with the hamper and Eve was in the kitchen with them. Dad had been in the hallway calling for everyone to hurry up. He rubbed his hands together and winked at me saying at least I was ready. The three of them came wearily to the door one by one as they had all been moaning. Dad was pleased with me though and didn't really care about everyone's moans and groans.

Eve and Fee wanted to sit by the window, I'd have liked to have done that but wanted everyone to be happy so I gladly sat in the middle. Dad drove and told us we were going to Heaven's Gate. Moving forward in my seat to look out the front window I wanted to talk to Mum and Dad, but the radio was on. Fee started singing so I sang too. We were a happy little family.

The car pulled into a gravelled car park and we all jumped out. Mum, Fee and Eve shared carrying the picnic, blanket and pencils and paper as they walked along the path through a lush green field with tall trees either side giving me a glimpse of where I could explore. Dad knew what I was thinking and told me the roads through the trees went by the lions and tigers enclosures intending to scare me to not go exploring but I did think that that could have been a cheap way to get into Longleat.

The birds were singing and Dad stopped once in a while to point to animals to show us but I needed extra encouragement to be able to see things. Dad would tell me to just follow his finger. I could see for miles across lush green fields and as we came upon the precipice we all looked down to see Longleat House and to the right of a long river just in front and lots of cars lined up by it. I could see people on deck chairs and soaked up the sight right before me. Gulping in large bits of air to get my breath back I turned around and saw the picnic blanket spread out before me with food laid out. Mum passed out the mini cheddars of which I accepted and took my time nibbling I silence as everyone talked around me making me feel content.

Fee took out the pens and paper of which I'd used to doodle on. I loved to draw basic shapes like stars, squares, triangles and circles that I would always colour in the same colour of blue then I would put borders around them and end up colouring those in too. Mum and Dad were talking. The midday sun was high in the sky making us feel hot.

Desperate to explore on my own I remembered Dad's words about the lions and tigers wondering where they were and laid back to put my arms under my head to drift off to sleep. Dad woke me up to tell me he needed to put suntan lotion on my arms and legs. The cream felt lovely and cool on my skin as Dad gently rubbed it in. I noticed Mum putting sun cream on Eve's face gently stroking her freckled nose. Dad didn't do my whole face and just put it on my nose as it would go red easily and flake off.

I needed a wee after waking up so Mum went to give me some tissue but didn't have any so Dad told me to use a leaf. Crouching behind a tree

I'd grabbed several doc leaves and was soon back with everyone else. There was talk about what was on at the cinema so Dad looked through the local for five o'clock screenings and they found the new Star Wars movie was playing at the Regal in Wells.

"The Return Of The Jedi is on." Dad had said, "Who here likes Star Wars?" We all said yes, anything to stay out and enjoy ourselves.

Keen to get going I jumped up and did a cartwheel and tried a backflip while everyone helped to pack everything up to go to the cinema.

Mum asked Dad about tea and Dad thought a take-away would be a nice treat. it was agreed. Fish 'n' chips.

Getting back into the car I'd have loved to sit by the window but didn't say anything as Fee and Eve would have been sick if they couldn't sit where they wanted. Making the best of sitting in the middle of everyone I started singing but Dad put on the radio and Eve and Fee fell asleep. I sat back a bit miffed. Mum and Dad started talking so I just relaxed, felt the movement of the car but couldn't sleep and then felt uncomfortable. I moved around and woke up Fiona as she was the light sleeper. She groaned to Mum so Mum turned to talk with me and I thought we could have a natter but she told me to try to sleep before getting back into Wells.

The Regal was huge and we all traipsed upstairs to the balcony seats. I loved the opening orchestral music and read the words floating through the heavens about a galaxy far, far away. The plot was a bit complicated but it was a classic tale of good against evil and I kept second guessing what was going to happen in Han Solos, Lukes and Leah's relationship.

Surprised that Hans got to marry the princess and was even more surprised that Darth Vader was actually Luke and Leah's dad. I really enjoyed the film.

I had a good sleep that night and in the morning found myself in a heap amidst my blankets on the floor yet again. Downstairs Mum asked me if I wanted cereal but I fancied jam on toast.

That afternoon after lunch Mum took us up to the big park. Once there Eve and Fee met up with their friends and Lynda Ball was there so we went straight to the great big heavy wooden roundabout. All us children were jumping on and off so I decided to push everyone round as fast as my little legs would carry me. Some children screamed with joy and laughter which spurred me on then I jumped on as it was turning and grabbed the handles to lean backwards. Eve wanted to get off and put her foot behind her on the ground to start to slow us down but let out a piercing scream of pain as he foot twisted under the roundabout rim. All the parents rushed over to take us off and Mum decided to bundle us into the car to go to the local hospital out by Waterloo school.

In the corridor for ages Eve had been put into a cast. I'd been in a daze and Fee was asking our little sister if she was alright. I saw the cast as something Eve could show off to her mates at school.

The next day she was hobbling around on crutches and had everyone running around after her. I'd felt put out at the attention but smiled at her, wanting her to talk to me and play like we usually did. Her friends came round though and had signed her cast.

Everything stayed normal for me though and found myself turning to read my Enid Blyton books more as I craved adventure. Timmy, Anne and George had been left to pack a picnic which always included ginger beer before they went off with their friends to Smugglers Cove. Imagining myself with them I could see myself hiding in the shadows waiting for the bad guys to turn up. The eldest boy had told his parents where the Famous Five were going and after hours of waiting the gang were surprised that after the smugglers came the adults had come down looking for us bringing the police to nab the vicious thugs. I finished reading the book in under two hours missing going out into the garden with my sisters as I noticed Fee was putting out knives and forks for tea. Eve's friends had gone home.

The next day my sisters and I had been playing outside the front of the house all day with the hula hoops, jump ropes, pogo sticks, etc. and late in the afternoon I got my bike out wanting to stretch my legs. Up and down the hill I went outside the house and along Wickham Way, up through the lane passed Jo Trimm's house, the road behind ours and along Shaftgate Ave several times before I dared myself to do something wonderful. At about the sixth time at the top of Coombe View I went to stand on my seat and I lifted my hands off my handle bars and stretched them out to balance myself before I flew down the road. It was like a walking on water moment. At the bottom I'd been amazed I hadn't fallen off as I made a grab for the handle bars and plonked by bottom back on the seat. I felt elated. My Mother's walking on water moment had been when she told me that she had walked two steps on thin air. Her feet hadn't touched the ground. In bed that night I could feel myself floating in my dream high above the town. I'd felt intensely alive like I was flying and for the first time ever I never fell out of bed the next day.

It was a Sunday morning and Mum rounded us all up for church. The vicar John Woolmer took the service as half way through my sisters and I headed off for St Peter Street rooms out the side of the church.

I can't remember who led Sunday School but I do remember learning my favourite hymn for the first time as we'd learned hymns at Sunday School. We'd been looking at the words on a projector and as soon as the words Colours of Day came up I was singing as loudly as possible, with a rousing chorus of:

> "So light up the fire and let the flame burn,
> Open the door let Jesus return,
> Take seeds of His Spirit
> Let the fruit grow
> Tell the people of Jesus
> Let His love show."

The words rang so powerful and true with a strong tune to back them that I was always going to remember this one.

Back in the church to join my parents we all sang the last hymn together before returning home to a lovely roast dinner.

At the morning prayers in assembly the next day I put my hands together and said the Lord's Prayer under my breath deep down needing a new friend. Kim was finding other children to talk to she didn't seem to need me anymore. I felt that she was slipping away.

Moving out of the hall with everyone else I bustled about going to my lessons.

In the afternoon at lunch break I'd had sandwiches, crisps, and biscuits. I'd sat on my own not really bothered about anyone else. I'd been happy and went to my classroom to put my bags away on my peg. I went to the toilet and heard the noises of the children playing happily outside and got drawn to them. Floating downstairs to the play yard I began pacing across the basketball court marking out where my living room was in the centre lines. In between the lines near the canteen I'd imagined my kitchen down the other end of the court was the dining room I imagined walking in to with a meal in my hands. Someone caught my attention it was a boy I remember vividly, a young handsome lad with jet black hair. Handsome features, he was white in a white shirt and black trousers. I stared not recognising him. I turned my head and looked back quick he wasn't there. Floating around pretending to sit on my sofa munching my crisps happily, talking to myself inside my head. The presence of that boy stayed with me all through my day. He was there in my heart for the rest of the day with me in all my lessons.

On the way home in the car I mentally hugged myself.

In the morning I floated into school and up the stairs two at a time. At the top I went into my first lesson and I smiled when I saw my teacher with his guitar knowing we'd have a bloody good singing lesson. It was to be about war songs that morning.

The first song was called the Siegfried Line which went:
"I'm gonna hang out the washing
On the Siegfried Line
Have you any dirty washing
Mother dear
I'm gonna hang out the washing
On the Siegfried Line…"

I loved the tune I had it in my head all day. Come the end of that day I finished all my work and was happy with myself.

At home I discovered some money down the back of the sofa. I went upstairs and put it in my piggy bank. It was a nice evening kicking back on the sofa watching the TV and next day was a Saturday and I woke up to more TV. I loved it.

Mum tried to drag me outside in the sunshine tempting me with scones to eat with jam and double whipped cream and a cup of tea. My sisters were already out there. It was such a nice lazy day and I picked my belly button fluff out.

> *2 Thessalonians 3: 6-7*
> *Our brothers and sisters, we command you in the name of your Lord Jesus Christ to leap away from all believers who are living a lazy life and who do not follow the instructions that we gave them. You yourselves know very well that you should do just what we did. We were not lazy when we were with you.*

That evening Mum wanted us in our smart garments laid out for us the night before. It was Remembrance Sunday, the birds were singing and the sun was shining, streaming through the curtains bathing us girls in a warm ethereal glow. All dressed up in our brownies outfits that were cute little dresses. We got told to wait by the front door but I never listened as we all took turns to fly down the stairs one by one and I'd taken too much time over my hair putting it into a ponytail.

Four minutes later we were in the automobile cruising down the road to the Catholic Church across town that was at the top of the big park. Jumping out of the vehicle Fee, Eve and I approached our friends in our separate little groups and we took our flags for each group leader. My leader's flag I looked up to with the Sprite logo on.

The ladies that ran the guides had a massive navy blue girl guides flag to walk in front of us as we all approached the church to troop down the aisle together.

The older children led the way and we all sang a marching hymn. As the service progressed we all got to sing some war songs in my section at the front of the church as we stood up in turn to sing the songs we all learned each. The voices rang out very loudly encouraging me to sing even louder to hear my own voice. My mother and father were in the congregation somewhere and I could feel the pride emanating around the sides of the church from all the adults put together.

The next section called the Elves got up and sang leading from the front with a wonderful song that went, "You are my sunshine, my only sunshine, you make me happy when skies are grey…" It was my favourite war song and with the last section leading they trumpeted the White Cliffs of Dover which sounded wonderful.

From the front row all the Scout leaders with their groups led the way out up through the aisle with all the masters from the other Baden Powell groups started from a million years before.

At school one morning I walked through the main doors of the old nunnery and to the right I noticed everyone already in lesson. They were waiting patiently for me to turn up. On the floor next to them were tambourines, triangles, drums and recorders. One was just waiting for me. I picked it up not knowing about the hole at the back and it sounded funny. I looked round the room and the teacher actually told us to put our thumbs over the holes at the back of the recorder. After going round us each to teach us our parts of the tune I got taught Three Blind Mice. I loved the sound it made as my fingers danced over the notes. Getting carried away I didn't notice some of the other loud noises of the children banging away. Totally oblivious I kept playing and playing till I'd perfected that lovely trilling noise and ended up taking the recorder back home with me.

Riding in the car over Prestleigh Hill down passed the Bath and West Showground then turning left through a winding road with high hedges either side we approached some houses. Turning right passed M. Purses, the pharmacy, we then made a left in to Nan and Gramps cul-de-sac and Dad parked the car. Dad looked towards the bungalow and their brown roofed and white car. It wasn't there. My parents made up their minds then and there to walk us girls over to the park. On the way there Mum pointed out the village hall on the left hand side of the road, the newsagents on the right hand side. Then we went passed the pub on the corner of where the park came into view, the heavy wooden see-saw was in the middle of the view and back near the wall was some swings.

Eve, Fee and I ran into the park. me and Eve made a beeline for the see-saw. Eve looked at the see-saw and was unsure of how to climb on as she looked at the end of it higher than her in the air. Not thinking about Eve I jumped on the end near to the floor patiently waiting for my sister to get on. Now Fee was being pushed by Mum on the swings chatting away happily with her while Dad broke away to lift my little sister Eve on to the see-saw. As she was put on Dad moved to the middle and started pushing us up and down and as we got used to the motion my little legs began to push hard on the encounter with the ground. Dad moved away and left us to it. I got carried away and started jumping up and down on my seat banging the wood against the floor at which I got fed up and jumped off leaving Eve to crash to the floor. Why did I do that really? As next I heard Eve burst into tears as the see-saw had come down hard on her ankle. Everyone came running to her aid. I stood there transfixed knowing we wouldn't have fun on the see-saw again. No-one even looked at me as they fussed around Eve and Dad let her lean on him back to the car. I remember Mum saying they'd have to get her to a hospital she said the nearest one was in Shepton. I felt tearful at having hurt Eve and needed comforting myself and felt left out. Feeling brave I choked on my tears, I felt my chin tilt obstinately in to the air and felt a bit bereft from the group. No-one was talking to me or even looking in my direction. I'd wanted someone to comfort me, to say it was just an accident and to reassure me that Eve would be fine.

Dad put his foot down coming out of Evercreech determined to get to the hospital quickly. Through Prestleigh into the top of Pilton turning right into the top of Shepton and through the winding lanes down a hill under the bridge then left by Nan's old house into the Old Wells road then turning right down to St Peter's hospital.

We were in the hospital for what felt like hours. Eve had been crying the entire time. Fiona sat with her on one side holding her hand with Mum on the other side gently rubbing Eve's back saying soothing words. I felt totally ignored. Dad had gone off to get teas. On the way back a man in a white coat came over to Mum and said they'd had to put a cast on her ankle that covered her foot. Then they all walked away together leaving me on my own wandering the corridors looking for them.

Lost in my own little world I followed my feet with my head down feeling dejected for ages until I quite naturally came across Dad, Mum, Fee and Eve in a room where my sister, I could see, had a cast on. Looking around until someone caught my eye I walked over to them determined not to show my tears and be strong for my little sister.

They told me Eve would be off school for a while and I can just hear Dad say I'd have to look out for her when she did get back to school.

While Eve was at home Mum fussed over her trying to create fun for both of us and I remember quite vividly Mum dragging out our continental quilts to go over the garden path out back spread over the lawns. Then she clothes-pegged her crocheted blanket over the line and got some old red bricks from the back of the garage to anchor the blanket out on each corner to make a make-shift tent.

Eve hobbled in first and I thought of asking her if I could draw pictures on her cast. Eve looked pensive as if she was thinking about it. Mum had bought out crayons and paper out next to us of where I got my idea from. I'd been overheard as I'd asked and Mum said, "No you can't." There'd been a line I crossed by asking and I felt down in the dumps again feeling sorry for myself as I felt bad over Eve's ankle.

Mum brought out lots of toys for us to play with in the tent and we chatted happily together and Eve cheered me up. She was my best friend really and I ended up wanting a lot more of a friendship than I got.

Mum left the tent out afterward overnight as it stayed dry and then in the morning it was a nice dry sunny May day. Then Mum came into our room to give us a cup of tea and biscuits and stayed for a chat. She wanted to know what was going on in our ordinary lives. I didn't have much to say so I told her I loved her and that I felt too much pushed out with the attention Eve got and that I felt truly sorry for her bad ankle and cried expecting a warm cuddle which Mum gave me. "Eve will be alright." She wiped away my tears and then suggested we all three went up to the park for the morning.

Eve couldn't walk very far though 'cause of her ankle. That's what I thought as I looked at her and Mum interrupted that thought with, "Let's go up in the car shall we?"

Eve and I grinned at her and then she told me to help her put the tent away. We went outside and I helped her fold up the crocheted blanket and the duvet and was told to put the bricks up behind the coal bunker.

When that was one all three of us were soon in the car heading for the big park. Mum said over her shoulder to Eve, "You must take it easy today." And Eve wickedly said. "Yes Mum."

I knew what she was thinking though and as we walked through the park there was a lot of other children there. We had a blanket between us and instead sat out on the grass. There were lots of daisies around us and Mum said, "Let's make some daisy chains until the swings are free."

I started picking them up one by one and made holes in the bottom of the stems to link them together. Eve did a longer chain than me and Mum helped her make a tiara with them and put them around her head. We all smiled but I looked down and mine broke in my hand. "I'll help you." Mum said and I ended up with a bracelet of flowers.

We never got to the swing set that day but it was lovely just lazing around in the sunshine and on the way home I was blowing dandelions trying to tell myself the time.

During brownies that evening while sat around in a circle in the hall we were all told that a camping trip was coming up and they wanted to teach us some songs. The Owls told all of us to be proud of who we were and where we came from of which was the first song they taught. It had been a song that all brownies would use on camp to announce ourselves it went:

"Everywhere we go, people always ask us, who we are, where we come from and we tell them…" and then everyone yelled, "We're from Shepton. Lovely, lovely Shepton!" And there was another one about never getting to heaven on a four poster bed. There were angels and little red devils in this song of which I loved to sing. We had also been playing games that evening. I particularly remember winning on tee Ludo game.

Everyone was excited about going to camp and letters were given out to give our parents explaining what was needed to take with us. I'd briefly snatched a look at the bit of paper but knew that Mum would sort it all out. I had absolute trust in both my parents to always be there for me no matter what.

In school the next day I'd been a little swot, completely engrossed in my books and learning till after school.

Next Sunday morning while in Sunday School we sat round praying on the floor. Then the project was put on and we saw a new hymn to learn. All singing loudly together I had to sing louder than the rest to be able to hear my own voice. Getting up afterward we all had orange juice while milling around a table by the front door of where the adults got their hot drinks. I danced back to a seat and sat down by a table happy to be part of the group as everyone else took to seats. bits of paper were handed out with a small island on and with a man on it. The teacher told a little story about the story of a man stranded on an island who prayed to God to be saved. Then a plane turned up but the man said he was waiting for God to save him so the plane flew away. Then a ship turned up after lengthy prayers and again the man turned the help away saying that he was waiting for God again. The same happened with a balloonist but the balloonist turned around and said to the man, "But it sounds like your God sent me to save you." So the man gripped on and was saved.

We all turned to our bits of paper and I started colouring in the golden sand before giving the man some blue trousers and a green top. In the background was the boat and the ship to colour in of which I drew and the hot air balloonist hovering overhead. Finishing up we all trotted back to the church. It had been a lovely day all in all.

The following Saturday getting up with a spring in our steps Mum wanted the family to go out across the fields before coming back for lunch. With the sun coming up over the house we put on our summer dresses and sandals. Outside on the drive way while waiting for the others I did a handstand up against the wall and scraped my leg. Everyone came out by that point and not one to make a fuss I rubbed my leg to follow the family up the hill to Shaftgate Avenue. There was a path to some steps that seemed very high up but we all made our way down quite fast to Bowlish Lane. At the bottom of the road there was another little lane going up through some woods behind Bowlish school. Undaunted by the pebbles I imagined all of us as the Famous five and hit the fields up ahead. The little lane seemed endless while I was wheezing a bit at the back. The morning dew dripping from the brambles on the bushes and making my feet wet from the occasional bits of grass protruding out along the path was playing up my hay fever. Dad told me once that I'd grow out of having asthma as he had.

Eventually coming out into the first field I gave a loud sneeze prompting someone to say, "Bless you." I looked to the right where Dad was pointing at the other fields across the road into Croscombe and saw the cows grazing happily, glad they weren't in our field.

Dad picked up a blade of grass placing it between his thumbs and blowing in to it making a funny squeaking noise making us girls laugh. Eve was the first to pick up a blade of grass to do it herself while Dad was showing Fee how to make the noise. I tried on my own as Mum stepped in to help Eve. Fee made the first squeak, I gave up and Mum was struggling to help Eve. With the grass making our feet wet with late morning dew Dad blamed the grass being too moist as we walked into the next field. Up by the hedges were yellow flowers Mum said were primroses and buttercups. Mum and Dad picked a buttercup each and held them under our chins saying we liked butter. I didn't understand till Dad pointed out the golden glow the flower made under Eve's chin. It was obvious to me the flower would give that glow under anyone's chin though but I smiled at what they were doing.

Stinging nettles caught my ankle but I ignored the pain anxious to catch up with the others as we made our way through three more fields. Then Dad pointed to what he called raisins in the fourth field. He made us stop in our tracks and pointed to a hedge down a slope to our right. I squinted and saw a white bobbly tail disappear into the foliage.

"Ah," I thought, "Rabbit droppings."

There was also cow pats we had to dodge and thistles that kept scratching our feet. Dad was on a frogmarch at this point with my sisters following his path to dodge the sharp thistles. I just ambled behind anyway suddenly becoming aware of a really strong awful smell.

Fee spoke up first, "Ooh, where's that strong pooey smell coming from Dad"

"Oh. That's the sewage farm over the road." That prompted questions from me about a sewage farm and he told me that that was where all the poos and wee went from people's houses. At least I'd stopped sneezing and desperately trying to catch my breath at this point as we'd all stood still.

We were all glad when we turned to go back the way we came. Behind the hedges in the second from previous field I noticed a railway sign and thought that looked odd. At least through this field there'd been cows behind the border of raspberry hedges that we kept picking the fruit from and eating.

The midday sun had gotten hotter and at this point the grass had dried out but that pooey smell seemed to be following us.

Back in the first field and looking at the greenery all around us Mum had picked some primroses she said that she was going to put in the front garden at home. The longest part of the walk was the passage way back down the hill to Bowlish Lane again.

We were all getting hungry and we soon got home for tea. I started looking forward to goin off to brownie camp the next day.

In the bus toward Cheddar I'd been singing happily with my friends with us all excited over our first brownie camp. The bus pulled up by a wall near a gate. Mum jumped out to pull this gate open for us to drive through up a wide path to a field enclosed by some tall trees.

Us girls jumped out in our jeans and jumpers ready for activities to help put up the tents. I remember watching the others assemble tent poles jumbled all up over the floor not really knowing how to help. I'd been in a happy daze and the leaders having taken charge didn't notice me holding a pole in my hands awaiting instructions. Hands were everywhere searching through the poles and assembling them together. Someone had taken the pole out of my hand to slot in to place so I just stood and watched. Our tent was soon up and so were the others.

The next task was to explore the woods together for twigs and I remember Tawny Owl saying you could rub two sticks together to make a fire. I'd rubbed two together in my hand but just accomplished rubbing the bark off.

Us girls had found lots of twigs, branches and sticks to build a fire with when we got back. For tea we sat around our little camp fire keeping warm while the meat was being cooked on gas fires. We had to go to Mum's tent to collect the baps and finger rolls one by one as the food was ready. The smell of onions were enticing as I'd asked for a hot dog and picked up the ketchup bottle. Ambling around the campsite there were several tents in our enclosure and hundreds of brownies. I'd been one of the last ones to eat and noticed other girls in light yellow t-shirts and brown shorts of which I hadn't yet unpacked for that day. Yawning to myself I took a strong gulp of fresh air swallowing some of the smoke from the fire with my slightly charred food. Then I heard someone yelling for us all to assemble back at camp together. Which I turned round and followed the noise to where everyone else was.

The greeting songs were to be sung that we'd learned the week before. This was wonderful all of us feeling a part of the group. There were other songs too and afterward we were to wash ourselves in wash basins to clean our teeth and get into nighties.

I'd been sharing a tent with Becky but as other girls came in to talk with us I snuggled down in to my sleeping bag to get warm feeling tired but happy and drifted into a deep sleep.

Some girls coming into the tent the next morning woke me up and so I dressed quickly into my shorts and t-shirt just like the other girls. Wriggling my toes into my socks scrunched into my trainers I was soon ready to walk around the place.

The air was brisk, the sun was waking up and everyone had been going for breakfast. I strolled over half asleep to muesli, Frosties and snap, crackle and pop. Frosties were my favourite and I'd placed a lot in my bowl with milk. Becky didn't like milk with hers which was Weetabix. Sitting down outside the guide leaders' tent my friend and I ate together with both of us chatting happily. Thinking Becky was bored of our conversation I put the crockery back for washing off where there was a group of us. I remember Becky coming over to tell me something but I just thought that she'd been talking to the other girls. Feeling ignored and excited all at once I decided to follow my feet and explore the woods. Not one to look over my shoulder I took off all by myself and explored right to the perimeters occasionally coming to either a wire fence or a brick wall. I'd done a lot of walking. My tummy started grumbling and so made my way back following the noise of the camp.

There was a lot of hustling and bustling when I'd got back with everyone sorting our lunch rifling through boxes of packed sandwiches, crisps and fruit all in and out of the tent.

That afternoon I remember faffing around with ropes to tie a certain type of knot called a slip knot. Quick at picking things up I wandered over to my friends keen to join in with them and help out. No-one noticed me though so I kept asking for their attention by thinking that they'd at least talk to me. Now it took them a while to achieve their knots and we were all to go off and play games together afterwards through the woods. We even played hide 'n' seek through the trees and I got caught far too easily.

Back at camp I remember a heap of new potatoes someone was peeling to get ready for tea and I saw a big silver canister that was bubbling over nicely a I'd been warned not to touch. A nice big casserole was being made for all of us and I stood there with a bowl first in line. Then the others came and joined me creating a queue. The casserole was delicious after being served up. Sometime later it never occurred to me to offer to help out with the spuds before. All tucking in we were happy.

Becky and I were chatting away happily but she kept stopping to talk with the other girls of which I hated. That evening girls were coming and going in our tent and I found myself hitting the pillow and falling into a sound sleep.

Everyone was always awake before me as their chatting would rouse me. Looking at the ground I'd wander round the site not noticing anyone else as they were all talking around me. I tried to butt in and would laugh happily not caring about the adults working to put the tents down.

It had been a warm weekend and the objective of the weekend had been to gain more badges that my mother would sew on my sleeve later when we got them. It was also an exercise in building relationships, and raise confidence in team work to help us to gain skills in real life.

Tired and happy on the bus back we were all singing songs and I remember joining in with a rousing chorus of getting into heaven with angels on a bed post.

Back home I looked forward to the next day as I was going off in Dad's lorry.

Dad and I cycled into work with me sitting on the cross bar, across the main road in Shepton, down to Hillmead, under the bridge, by the doctors and across the road pass the King's Head, which we called the Dusthole. Along this lane towards the end was the lorry depot. Dad had to go look for his large vehicle and found a cabin for us to jump into. Then he drove round the yard looking for his trailer already full of Babycham crates and lots of other drinks besides.

Terry Wogan got tuned into and his soft dulcet tones would send me off to sleep on Dad's bunk of where we'd sleep later on that night, because Dad and I would get started in the dark early hours of the morning. The daft little girl that I was, missed the rolling countryside pass us by until we hit the M5 of where my eyes finally opened. The tunes on the radio had changed. Dad had tuned into a different station with lots of upbeat modern music on. As Dad sped pass many other vehicles on the motorway I'd got excited and would egg Dad on to fly down the middle lane.

Matthew 5:8
Happy are the pure in heart;
They will see God!

Exiting for the M6 the hedges were high but we were even higher as I could look down over the next motorway we were heading for. Learning the words to the songs on the radio was easy so Dad and I didn't talk much but Dad knew that I was happy. At the speed Dad was going the lorry was soon changing on to the next motorway the M55. I'd started jigging around to the local sounds of the area as we'd tuned into another station again. Dad and I would guess the artistes. We even played eye spy as the road behind us fell into the distance.

The first stop in Blackpool was at a supermarket and Dad skilfully manoeuvred the lorry in backwards to the yard. He told me to stay in the cabin with the stereo on. 'Money For Nothing' came on and I sang away listening for the forklift truck taking the pallets off and Dad closing the side of the lorry. He came back to the cabin with paperwork in his hands to fill out before telling me to 'stay there' while he went to the office.

We were soon on the road again with the seafront panning out in front of us. It was a gloriously sunny day and I had to squint into the sun to see out front. I'd missed what my Dad, Mike, had been saying but he sounded excited as the lorry screamed to a halt in a lorry park. The tachograph for the day had to be filled in before we both alighted and headed off to get some lunch. Our tummies were growling. The food we had was basic, beans, toast, bacon, egg and sausages. Then Dad suddenly realising I hadn't heard him before began to tell me that he'd always wanted to go up Blackpool Tower. He asked me if I was up to it with a knowing twinkle in his eyes that knew I'd say yes.

It was the most amazing experience ever and we climbed the last few stairs at the top. It had been so cold and windy I had to catch my breath and hold on to the scaffolding behind me as Dad was trying to point out the different places he recognised along the skyline. I inched forward a bit to show I was listening but my head began to swim at which point Dad turned and saw my pale face. It was time to go back down.

The rest of the evening went by as both of us took in a bit of sightseeing round town, but the trip up the tower was always going to be the highlight of the trip.

The toilets where we cleaned our teeth and had a bit of a wash before clambering into the cabin head-to-toe to fall asleep.

As per usual I awoke with Dad already driving on the M5 heading back into Bristol. By the afternoon we were listening to Steve Wright and Dad would take the piss out of their sad stories.

We stopped off a Sal's greasy spoon for sausage sandwiches for lunch before heading back to Shepton to see Mum and my sisters to tell them all about our little adventure.

The following morning turning into Nan's driveway into Evercreech Dad told us of the time when he'd driven across the front lawn when learning to drive. I laughed. jumping out we went into the two bedroomed bungalow all saying hello and being ushered into the flue flecked kitchen for drinks. I had a Coca-Cola and Fee started asking for her presents. We were then ushered into the living room and it was always cards first. Fee had some stamps from Uncle Keith and Aunty Sue in her card and some money from Uncle Cyn's card. My card was next. I made mine but everyone else's were expensively bought. I hadn't bothered with a present but was excited for Fee as she tore into all the wrapping paper leaving a mess on the floor so Nan got a black bag. Grandad had a bag of mints he started to dish out so I sat on his lap while the adults disappeared back into the kitchen.

I happily stayed in Grandad's lap listening to his war stories of being in the navy on the great big ship. I pictured in my mind's eye the massive tin can warships with the military guns on, and on the mantelpiece was a picture of Gramps with his navy uniform on giving me a hazy picture of military life as Granddad talked. I ended up dozing off as we were all called out to a birthday tea and it wasn't long till the birthday cake came out. Dad told Fee to make a wish before we all burst into song back in the living room. I hoped Fee's wish would come true as we all happily tucked into the soft sponge and the creamy icing.

The sun had been shining that day and before it went down the family went outside for drinks before the last rays of light went down.

The next day I'd been excited getting out of bed as my class were due to go on a school trip to somewhere called Slimbridge and I had to be at St Pauls for seven thirty. Assuming that was where we were going I was surprised to be turning up at the leisure centre, but Mum explained that had been the plan all along.

I stared out the window at the dull grey sky and recognised the Bath road still excited to be going somewhere instead of being at school. I'd sat with another girl and we got chatting. Someone got up to push their lunch box back into the overhanging compartments.

We sped up along the motorway and the teachers were talking about the weather hoping the rain would hold off. I'd sat by the aisle on the left hand side and looked briefly through the front window and saw the sign to Dursley of where we exited the motorway.

After another half an hour we were clambering off the coach in cold weather with the sky very grey. The class wandered up to a pond to look at the wildlife and while standing on the gravel the heavens opened. Apparently we'd been booked in to see a film about the area and so were ushered into the centre out of the rain.

Sat in the front row of the auditorium the news reel started to tell us about the founder of Slimbridge was Sir Peter Scott in 1946, and how the place is situated around a part of the Gloucester and Sharpness canal. Its 2,480 acre estate owned by the Ernest cook Trust and looks after many migrating birds such as various gees and American widgeon with the emerald coloured heads with white looking tiaras. We saw reels of numerous birds making the reserve their home such as swans, pochard, coot, and tufted duck amongst many others. The video went on about how they were all cared for and looked after.

I had to blink to adjust to the light once outside and another coach load of children were lined up waiting to come in. We all sat or stood around with our lunches taking our time. I'd had cheese sandwiches, crisps, an apple, chocolate (Mr Penguins), and a little box drink Mum had put together for me. Afterward I went to find a bin and wandered around the nearby ponds for a bit to look for the wildlife but was soon called back to go to the coach. Clambering into a seat I'd been tired and nodded off a couple of times on the way back leaning my head against the window particularly when we were on the M4.

Getting off at the leisure centre we walked back along Charlton road to the school for our mums to pick us up ready for the end of the day bell.

That evening Eve and I had turned up to brownies as usual in our smartly pressed brown dresses with our recently sewn on badges on our sleeves. Mum, brown Owl, took the session and had invited a man to talk to us with an unusual pet. Now we'd been having beetle drives and bug projects recently of where we'd gone outside in the local countryside tracking down and logging all the different bugs we could find. Thankfully this session was in the warm back at St Peter Street rooms.

The man that came in had a big tank and we all crowded round to take a look at a massive and very hairy red and black spider. We were told it was a tarantula and if we were very brave it would be placed on the back of our hands for a couple of minutes. I'd felt brave and pushed myself to the front and stuck out my hand. This massive spider felt tickly on my hand and the man explained that they were poisonous spiders but I wasn't in the least put off.

It wasn't long before we were singing in a circle and collecting our coats to go home.

Then the next day I got up for school, washed and dressed and headed out to the car with my sisters. it was a warm summers day I'd been thinking ahead to seeing Paul Allen and my friend Lynda. At the school yard I'd been a bit apprehensive about my first lesson boring maths but as I sat down to actually learn I'd actually got excited as I flew through my sums feeling pleased with myself. With a golden warm glow about me I drew my friend Lynda to me in the school yard to play tag during 1st break round the grounds. We ran around the copse of trees at the top of the school field tiring ourselves out. Then we played pat-a-cake, pat-a-cake, baker's man with our hands before hearing the bell. I told her excitedly about my piano grade I'd been about to take that was my first exam but she didn't listen and went in at the front to lead us indoors.

In the afternoon I rushed through English soaking up the ABCs on the big chalkboard and stood up at the front of the class and we came up one by one to write down the next letter making a line underneath. It was a big room and I'd been squinting to see and at my turn I wrote the letter W in the clearest letters. My teacher was pleased a I'd looked at them and saw a warm smile which I responded with a twinkle in my eye too.

I sat down on my seat waiting for the next person to get up. No-one got up as the teacher had ran out of pupils so I'd volunteered for all of X, Y and Z.

"Teacher's pet." I'd heard someone say. I ignored that comment and mentally hugged myself. The teacher was pleased with me.

Floating around peacefully for the rest of the day with other children pushing and shoving while I'd glided peacefully into the canteen for the table. I got my lunch box out and sat with Trevor and Sarah. Lynda came sauntering over with her tray and sat next to me. I'd eyed her cooked meal, sausage, chips, and peas and felt enticed with the smell. Mum never gave us money for a cooked lunch, prepared to do it herself later on that night.

Talking about our lessons I secretly wanted what Lynda had on her plate. Eating with a great group of people I'd slipped into my own little world just feeling cosy letting them speak. I desperately wanted to tell them about my piano exam that afternoon in Wells.

Late afternoon lessons were actually taken outside of where they let us play with chalks on the school yard marking out a hop, skip and jump game while others got the chance to skip. I'd joined in with a big jump rope held at two ends with others for me to jump through. They were getting faster and faster and as I stepped to get out of the rope it hit my ankle making it sting. Hobbling over to a bench I sat down to sit the rest of the lesson out.

It was nearly the end of the day as we all came back in and were all told to get our jumpers, cardigans and bags to take home. Mum picked me up but not my sisters who had to go home with friends as she took me into Wells for my piano exam.

Apprehensive at first, seeing that I was going into an imposing large white building I'd spied a lovely grand piano of which I'd never played on before.

The room had a thick dark carpet but the walls were white. There were pictures on the wall that looked imposing and I tentatively ran my fingers over the keys. The adjudicator Ronald got me to run through all my scales out at first. Feeling nervous at first my fingers seemed to have a life of their own and took over. My sight reading I'd been told was very good and my listening ear to decide which key he'd been playing was very good and I got it right first time.

After spending what seemed a long time that day Mum finally took me home.

A holiday was coming up the next day and coming out of Shepton towards the A37 and Yeovil the car sped along with the windows down, the sun blaring and the radio on, us girls were getting excited singing to our favourite songs. Queen's 'I want to break Free' was playing loudly.

Nehemiah 8:10
The joy that the Lord gives you will make you strong.

The sign to Weymouth passed us by as we turned into the A road towards Bournemouth then Poole where the caravan park called Rockley Sands was. 'Karma Chameleon' was playing in the background.

When we were there it had its own private beach not far from our static caravan and the sites entertainment. Our days were filled with trips to the beach although one day Dad decided to take us in the car to explore a picturesque village of where us girls posed for a photograph with our sunglasses on and arms and legs akimbo, looking daft.

Fee had been up most mornings with Dad doing a mile run round the camping site and to the beach. The onside radio station would blare out, 'Come on down to Rockley Sands', that me, Fee and Eve would parrot all holiday.

I'd had a go on the go-karts zooming round and round the tyres not hitting them once. Eve would go on the go-karts too.

Life seemed always exciting back then and fresh and new. I lived for the day and it was with a heavy heart and plenty of sun-kissed skin with which we all returned home with the memory of the seaside dipped behind us.

In the morning I woke up to the lovely sounds of birds singing, whistling and chirping. It would have been nice if I knew the birds that matched the separate calls. I layed there enjoying the noise and the shadows the beech trees at the bottom of the garden on the curtains created in the wind. It was lovely. The simple things always made me happy all the things that were free.

I went to school feeling full of life and happy skippity skipping when I got out the car down the hill from the school gates. I walked by the railings and fleetingly thought they looked like prison bars. Why? Because I'd have loved to enjoyed the sunshine all day.

In a good mood no-one annoyed me for once and I kept my head down in the classroom, inwardly grinning to myself imagining the stars and ticks I'd be getting from the effort I'd put into my writing all day.

By the end of the afternoon lunch break I sat by the window in the next lesson and the sun streamed across my face. I had to squint to see properly and had to focus really hard on my geography lesson. It was about waterfalls and I learned about Victoria Falls, Angel Falls, and Niagara Falls straddling Canada and America. I imagined the water cascading over rocks and by trees poking out the side of the rocks with the water falling into big rivers. I got a lovely feeling of something washing over me as I wrote and my head got stuck in the moment.

In my mind's eye I wanted to write a story about it and of how I swam in a pool at the bottom of one I visualised very strongly. No-one ever knew what I was thinking as I worked very hard and diligently with the task of finding the 'falls' in our books and writing about them. I gave good descriptions as pictures were given out to colour in to stick in our books with our descriptions.

I'd developed eye strain and wished I hadn't sat by the window in the strong sun light. My old friend Lynda sat two rows over and had a couple of key rings on her desk along with a sharpener, rubber, ruler and other things. It looked a mess. I kept my desk clear and thought about my collection of key rings back home.

At home that afternoon I went straight for what was my sisters Showerings bag I'd nicked and dived in to look at my key ring collection and though of Lynda. It was her birthday soon and we'd fallen out of friendship so I thought of one last titch attempt to win her back. I took the bag down her house to give them away. Her mum answered the door and Vicky was there. I knew I lost her but she took the gift anyway. I stood there like a limpet watching them play and just decided to go home early. No-one stopped me.

Mum asked me why I came away early and I shrugged my shoulders finally accepting the friendship was over and it was all because I'd either cut her hair or got set up by Lynda to steal Vicky's gloves of whom had a policeman as an uncle who had come round the house to scare me into giving them back.

Later on Fee asked me why did I give all my keys away to ape-face-Ball and for the first time it was said. I slapped her down and admitted we weren't friends any more.

I'd been dropped off at school early next day with my sister Fiona and we walked up to our classrooms for the start of the day.

The morning was a busy one with a lot of work getting down and in one lesson we were asked about what we'd dreamt recently. Brian was asked about what he'd dreamed recently. He'd said that he had a dream about a train in his bedroom rushing past the foot of his bed. I'd wanted the teacher to ask me about my most recent dream as I'd dreamt about chasing a boy called Rocky along a country road with high hedges either side. On approaching a triangular shaped grassy verge at the end of the road Rocky vanished and I flew over it all to see where he went but I couldn't find him. Landing on my two feet walking back along the route I'd just walked, behind the hedge were some swings and all of a sudden the scenery around me changed to that of a courtroom I was all alone in before I had awakened. I was bummed that I'd never gotten the chance to recount that dream and headed off home that afternoon a little dejected. Though what we had for tea soon cheered me up.

At piano lessons I met a girl called Alice Berkley of whom I was supposed to do duets with and we first went to Cluttons to where she lived so that I could practice duets with her. We found a row of red bricked houses we were looking at them from the back gardens. One had a red see-saw at the back and a swing with a broken down gate from the pavement. We walked down the path, Mum and I, calling out to Mrs Berkley and she told us to come in. I felt Mum's nose go in the air as we found Alice's Mum sitting on the carpet with a long skirt on but with her legs opened wide. You couldn't see anything because of the long skirt but I soon scarpered to the piano with Alice to practice. Alice had long brown hair and dressed like her mother. I'd been playing the beat and the trill of Alice's notes I thought sounded fantastic. We played for a whole hour all over the keys before Mum had had enough to drive us back to Shepton.

Chapter Six

On the following day for May Day celebrations my sisters and I were up at Collett Park. I remember being in my country dancing outfit that made me look like an old scullery maid with my pinafore and cloth hat. We danced round the Maypole weaving in and out of each other through long ribbons.

Afterwards we went round the endless stalls and played the tombola, did a raffle, watched gymnastics and jumping dogs. I watched Morris dancing for the first time and after a while the music started to grate. We queued up for ice-creams and had a laugh at the brilliant paintings on the other children's faces and wanted one ourselves. Mum willingly paid for tigers and butterfly pictures. Thoroughly happy us girls trudged across town back to our abode.

In the morning on the Monday we went into town to go round the library to get some books. I browsed round them all taking my time looking for an easy read. Eve went straight for the box shaped book stalls with the hard-backed easy to read books in. Fee disappeared to the teenage section of where I'd found her and thumbed through all the books till I'd settled on American Valley High books. I took home a couple of them remembering how the librarian looked all grumpy, while putting her fingers to her lips and telling us to be quiet.

Starting to read one as I walked I'd lagged behind the rest absorbing the American lingo enjoying every word. Mum announced that she was cooking us all lunch and would do us all waffles.

In the morning I got up for school and enjoyed doing my writing in English class. It was about a funny subject to me encompassing all that life entails. It was a ditty that went:

Sugar and spice and all that's nice, is what little girls are mode of, and something about snails and puppy dog tails are what little boys are made of. It made me smile. I wrote it decadently down the middle of the page and drew lovely pictures around it of candy, snails and a dog with a little boy and a little girl skipping. I coloured it in and made it look really nice. I broke a pen in my hand from squeezing it too hard and it cracked. I'd been concentrating too hard.

Next lesson was a bit more enthralling as they pushed all the chairs and tables to the side of the room and the teacher got us all to sit on the floor in a circle. Then musical instruments got passed around for us to learn a couple of songs. They were good fun and at the end of the day my grandparents came round to visit. In the dining room we all sat around the table chatting and Nan started spouting with Mum what they thought us girls would grow up to be. I heard them say that I was brainy enough to be a teacher or librarian one day. I scowled at them as I couldn't think of anything worse to do. Most other children, especially boys were horrible and the librarians, who always insisted on us being quiet, always seemed dull and boring especially on TV as uptight squeaky people.

Now the next day Mum dressed me in a purple denim dress with a white polo neck top on underneath with white ankle socks and black and shiny sensible shoes ready for school photos that day.

First class of the day us children were told that throughout the day we'd be called for photos and so to come straight out of class.

Now first class was lovely. I got to learn about star constellations. We heard about the bear and the saucepan that hung above Shepton and I was enthralled. We had to write about it and I found it very interesting as I dreamed about outer space.

The second lesson had me in stitches as we worked out how and what things lived around the school grounds and I spotted a helicopter plant off a tree. Then someone called out my name. I had to go for my photo to be taken. I sat in a classroom decked out like a studio of where there was a blue background of where I had a lovely photo. It was taken on a polaroid camera and I had the picture there and then. It cost seven quid for one big photo and two little ones to keep safely to take home. One would be for Mum and the other two for the Nans'. I saw them that afternoon and had a wonderful time with them and the evening was lovely and I went to bed happy.

In the morning Mum bought in tea and biscuits. I hungrily attacked four custard creams and drank my drink hot. I got into the shower automatically drying myself and walked into my bedroom of where Eve had gotten dressed. Mum had my clothes pressed and hung up for me. I put them on still keen to go into school. Face the day and enjoy learning.

My English book was bulging with red and mainly gold stars as I opened it to write down home work after the lesson. In maths my subtracting was getting harder but I easily took it all in enjoying all of it.

The afternoon was swimming in the school's private pool. I jumped in and swam from side to side and really enjoyed myself.

From the corner of the room there was the teacher calling out my name begging me to stop swimming as I'd not heard him to the last minute. I'd been called to swim up and down the length of the pool for my certificate. My grade two. They asked me to swim on my back for two lengths. It was lovely floating on my back looking up to the ceiling kicking my feet out and flailing my arms about a bit. Getting near to the end of the pool I put my arm back behind me anticipating the wall. Doggie paddle was the hardest flapping my arms about very close to my chest. Breast stroke was the easiest but I had to keep dipping my face in and out the water to learn to breath properly and I kept on getting the chlorine water in my mouth. I was told that we were doing very well and were introduced to a new way of swimming called the crawl and the breathing exercises were even harder.

We got out in the warm pool area that felt as hot as a conservatory on a hot day as the pool was covered in the same as a conservatory trapping the heat. Drying by the side of the pool we stripped off and got changed.

One lesson later and we were on our way home. Eve and I got home and got changed into our jeans and comfy jumpers to walk up the fields together with Mum and Fee. Down the steps, and up Bowlish Lane there was a large grass verge with a couple of conker trees Mum said were full of conkers ready to pick. We looked on the grass between the leaves first. Mum told us to pick up the green, hard, spiky balls. I'd been curious enough to stamp on one to see what was in it. The green shell broke very easily to reveal a lovely nut. This made me find loads of other green cases under all the leaves.

Then we took them home to play conkers together in the living room and put them on strings to dangle and hit each other till they broke.

We did this till tea time of when we had potato waffles, baked beans, and sausages all together. The family stayed up till about ten o'clock. Then Mum gave us supper of bread, crackers and cheese before we went to bed.

It was a typical September morn with the sun bursting through the curtains waking us all up early. Being a Saturday my parents took one look at the weather and decided we'd all go off for the day to a safari park just under an hour's drive from home to Longleat.

Jumping in the car. Picnic in back. Dad drove the yellow Datsun along the Frome road out of town with us all chatting away happily. The radio was on with us girls singing our hearts out. I'd loved trips out together as a family and when we drove through the gates with large trees either side Dad paid at the hut for us all to enter Longleat House's ground. The trees dropped behind us to reveal stunning scenery and we took the car to the river parking in a line with the other vehicles. The backdrop was the large house and I wandered if we'd bump into Lord Bath of whom lived there.

The first port of call was the land train that we all clambered into choo-chooing passed all the animals in their enclosures like the lions, and the tigers and we all craned our necks to look up into the trees to spot monkeys and looked out over the sprawling grounds to try and spot the giraffes in the distance.

Pulling into the station there was a large maze nearby that we paid to get lost in and can only assume the whole family found their way out of. There was an ice-cream stall close by and I loved the orange Solero lollies with the ice-cream in the middle but Mum and Dad had said to wait till later.

Us girls played in the castle climbing all over it before Dad called Fee, Eve and I to go back to the car for our picnic lunch. We all took our time going to the car getting slightly tired and hungry. It was lovely sitting on the red checked picnic blanket together tucking into sandwiches, cake and crisps with our boxed drinks. I'd been tempted to paddle in the river as it was hot but no-one else wanted to so I never bothered.

Afterwards we made our way towards the house's gardens that we looked round very decoratively bedecked with many flowers and shrubs and there was even a mini maze you could easily find your way around.

Dad asked us if we wanted to see the Doctor Who exhibition and the 'yes' was unanimous. Outside it just looked like the size of a big blue telephone box but inside was a bit of a museum with a massive, original Dalek in, that was a massive robot. The consoles and all the other exhibits made you feel that you were actually in Doctor Who's Tardis. I'd felt creped out by the Daleks that randomly said they would exterminate and it wasn't long before Mum, Dad, Fee, Eve and I came back out again.

Fee wanted to see the doll's house exhibit with Mum but the rest of us weren't interested as we lazily ambled about in the sunshine. It wasn't until about four o'clock that I'd finally got the lolly I'd asked for. Feeling slightly sore from the sun the whole family made their way back to the car and we were on the road again by five o'clock all feeling happy and tired.

At the time of being in the Brownies there was a movie star called Anthony Andrews and us girls were told that we were to stay where he was filming in a hall somewhere. When we got there us Brownies in our uniforms walked by many trailers of where the actors and production team lived and worked. I even caught the inside of one of them. Mum had talked to the producer and he'd told her that the Brownies could have a walk-on part in the film of us just crossing the road.

All us girls were excited and that evening our sleeping bags had been layed out around the sides of the hall and I got talking to a girl named Kerry from Holcombe of whom had lovely long brunette hair. She taught me how to write a fancy 'K' for my signature and one afternoon we pretend to get married and I had to be the man. Kerry put a white pillowcase on her head as a veil as we pretended to say our vows. Sometime afterward, that day, I walked by a room with the door open and a pile of money was on the middle of a table. I gasped and ran to tell Mum. She told me that was how everyone in the film got paid.

Outside we all dressed as pirates and we clambered all over a bit of an adventure park with rope ladders in the trees. On this holiday when we got filmed walking across a zebra crossing I'd heard Eve had run into the side of a park bench and had to have an ambulance to put stitches into her bottom lip.

The next day it was my Sprite's group that had to cook breakfast. We did bacon, eggs, baked beans, toast and I think that I had just done the washing up.

That day we were soon on the bus singing that 'we'd never get to heaven on a bed post' and 'who we are and where we came from' making the journey home a happy one.

Next day I turned on the telly to watch War Games about a boy who hacked into military computers to download games at first but got embroiled in their reality with real warships, real submarines, tanks and rockers and had to convince the inventor of one of their own machines that what he'd started wasn't real. Then ended the very real prospect of World War Three with a simple game of tic-tac-toe. I wanted to be that smart as Matthew Broderick's character and enjoyed the thrill of the film.

That evening the family enjoyed a meal together round the table engaging in conversation but I sat and just enjoyed my family's happy chatter as I struggled to eat stuffing my face. I couldn't breathe as my nose was blocked and Dad told me not to open my mouth while eating.

At school while in my classroom upstairs I'd been working happily away before looking up and dreaming out the window when a sharp voice made me turn my head. It was a boy called Rocky and they called me gormless. I knew the intent was nasty and was really hurt by it. I sunk my head back into my books and shrugged my shoulders to carry on while my eyes watered up feeling stung.

It had been an Indian summer and while we were back at school we were all dead keen to get outside in the sunshine. Lunch time was hectic as everyone wanted to get outside on the grassy playground to play and instead of playing with friends I went for a wander round the huge grounds. At the top of the field was a copse of trees of where I'd noticed conkers on the ground and I started picking through them for the best ones. I'd put them in my skirt pockets. Still wandering round the grounds I went behind where the school's pool was and had a look through the window. I could feel the heat from the pool radiating through the glass and could smell the strong chlorine. By the time I'd finished walking the perimeter of the field the bell went to go back to class.

Mum picked Fee and I up at the gates and I showed my sister my conkers, she said she knew where more conkers could be found. Mum, upon hearing our conversation took the car to the top of Bowlish Lane and we all walked up the grassy hill to look for more conkers and we had to look for extra for Eve to play with.

Back at home I used a knitting needle to pierce holes in my conkers and my blue wool I'd used to thread through the conkers to tie the end into several knots so as not to pull the wool through. Mum went to get a cork screw for Eve to poke into her conkers and Fee tried to pierce hers with scissors. A couple of mine split so I gave up with my needles. mum finished them with the corkscrew and more wool. Then we ended up with five each to play a game of conkers.

Eve and I went first to swing them at each other. They missed so we tried again. Then the conkers collided but nothing happened to them. I tried to swing mine harder the third time and totally missed hers and hit her nose. I laughed nervously. Then I held mine still for her to hit my conkers.

"Hurry up you two. I want it to be my go." Fee said.

Eve took one wild swing at mine and chipped the corner and we told her she won that game. it was Fee's turn then with the winner and theirs just flew at one another and parts of Eve's flew across the room. Fee won that one and took me on. The score was one, one. Then I managed to destroy one of Fee's. It became a one all draw. Four of our conkers later the score became 1, 2, 3. One to me. two to Fee and three to Eve.

We had a lovely evening watching the TV and having dinner that was nice and hot. Stew with dumplings and apple pie with custard. We all went to bed early. Then in the morning my parents washed first then I was in the shower next. Fiona came across the landing. I can see her going to the toilet, while I could see Eve waiting. I could sense it in the air an internal battle was going on with sisters for the bathroom. I went downstairs out of the way for my breakfast. Sat at the table waiting for everyone to come downstairs I looked forward to my Weetabix. Mum came from the kitchen to ask me to get what I wanted so I'd got down the box from the cupboard. Put on three Weetabix with sugar and a little bit of full fat milk that I knew had been left on the doorstop that day. Tucking in my sisters soon joined me and ate their own food. I'd eaten mine down really fast and soon got down from the table.

The TV was on in the background showing channel four breakfast news, so I went to watch it. Sat on the sofa I was transfixed by the presenters, with my hands on my knees. My sisters joined me and lounged out. Starting the day happily this feeling I had inside of me was bliss.

I got up and walked into the hallway to get on my school shoes and to pick up my bag from upstairs. All excited about my birthday the next day I felt elevated looking forward to what was to come. In school at my desk all thoughts were pushed into the background as I got stuck into my work.

The teacher, I felt, looked at me which made me vaguely aware of them. I looked around the classroom and the atmosphere felt so alive. Everyone had been working with their heads down too so I got back on with my books. The sun streamed through the window on us giving a wonderful golden glow throughout the whole room. Suddenly there was a noise as another teacher came into the room. I could hear them talking saying my name. My ears pricked up and then my hair rose on my neck stood up. They were talking on and on about what I thought was the standards of the school, secretly smiling to myself.

Next to me was Kim busily doing her writing while I did mine. Her head had been bowed low. The bell then rang for a break so I went to the lady's room across the orange carpeted corridor. Then went outside for five minutes for fresh air.

That afternoon I stood at the start of a storm brewing over the heavens at the end of the playground. I took control of the situation as I was always in control of storms. The thunder rolled overhead and everyone was forced to go inside the hall. The rolling reminded me of a game of marbles. In my mind's eye I could see me getting out by Babycham bag later to get my marbles out.

Back in the classroom my chair squeaked as I sat down. It sounded really loud. Then I sat down and started writing a story about myself of some of the daydreams I used to have. The pen flew across the paper. Half an hour later I had several pages worth of a really nice story.

Next lesson started very sweetly with a nice little old lady teacher who talked in dulcet tones about the future. Painting a lovely picture of a pink orange sky with utopia in the background. It was to be the front page of a folder. There was a list of topics to cover about worldwide peace. On the list was geography, politics, history, economics, and governments. I had to choose two topics. I chose history and geography. The first page I headed History and wrote about my favourite peaceful year in the whole wide world 1886. The armies of the world had defected from their governments. It was in a huge history of the world book and a separate encyclopaedia. Putting the article together I had to work out where, when, and how throughout the year everyone downed arms.

After the lesson it was the end of the day and the storm was still raging making me think of my marbles.

Then at home I got out my blue Babycham bag and tipped my marbles all over the floor. Eve did the same in the living room. We sat in front of the radiator and with our separate piles of marbles. Then we flicked one each towards the middle of the room trying to hit one another's, and we missed. Eve went next and flicked her marble to where the others were hoping to hit one. She never. I rolled one towards it and actually hit it. Then I could claim it as my own. We did this five times and I won six marbles back. Then Eve and I crouched forward further across the carpet to chase the balls around the room. We pushed the marbles along harder and harder with bigger ones claiming them one by one by themselves. Racking them up into bigger piles on the other side of the room. I noticed my pile was smaller than my sister's so I'd urged her to play again, using the bigger balls first, some chipped as we played making a clicking noise. Urging each other on she got more and more excited about winning. I didn't care, it was such fun being caught up totally in the moment. Over and over again with my hair flopping in my eyes so I kept having to push it out the way. Eve gave up first but I kept on going. Then tidied up, counting out the same amount for each bag. One was brown the other was blue with a Babycham deer on the front. I sensed somebody coming through the door.

I'd remembered bringing watercress in a white little pot from school that day and putting it in the living room window to be in the sunlight with Eve's pot.

The person behind me made me turn around to see Mum of whom said that my sisters were to go to Wells so we jumped into the car. Driving along the way there we were all happy going to see Aunty Nola and Uncle Graham first. We ended going up St Thomas Street towards the Bath Road. Turning into the left lane into the housing estate and the second house we parked by. Walking u her driveway, Barney, the dog. came out to meet us wagging his tail. His nose always looked happy and wet with his eyes shining. I patted him on the head then tickled him by the ears. He led my family out into the garden down some steps onto the lawn shrouded by trees and bushes. I picked up a stick and dangled it in front of his eyes for a bit, teasing him before I threw it across the grass and then went into the house through the patio doors. Once in the living room I flopped down on the sofa and spied Aunty Nola using a knitting machine in the corner of the room opposite the telly. She got chatting to me about her knitting business so she said, "This is my first jumper that's nearly finished," so the demonstration began with her pushing the stitches into stitches to completion. It was a lovely light purple colour, and I sat for ages talking to her for a while till my Uncle came into the room to join the discussion.

The older members had cups of hot drinks in their hands while us girls had a cold drink each.

That evening we went passed the Cathedral, round the moat and watched the ducks with their families playing happily on the water chasing each other around. Stopping every two minutes to look across the fields. Eve then pointed to a flasher by one of the benches. I didn't want to look, so we walked straight by them. We got in the car by Tor Woods to head off home for the evening.

The next day I came flying down the stairs grabbing my things for school, some things were going to go my way that day. I just felt it. In school I sat next to a boy called Wayne. I didn't even like him very much but I had nowhere else to sit. I'd been about three rows from the front. I'd been squinting at the board writing everything down wanting to know everything which was what drove me. Wayne disgustingly kept shaking dandruff out of his hair all over the table.

In the middle of the day I went to lunch and sat on a bleacher in the school with a friend Kim. She sat there the whole time ignoring me talking to the other girls. I felt jealous but rose above it enjoying the rest of lunch. I went outside the main doors and lazed out on the steps and went asleep with my head on my lunch box. I'd got woken up by my legs being grabbed by a

Damian and someone else. I felt a presence behind my head and my arms were raised. They'd said they were giving me the bumps and carried me out into the yard. They threw me up into the air and dropped me. The back of my head hit the floor first. I winced and held the pain with my hand and took off across the grass up to the park to sit on a swing. I was angry.

> *Job 40:11*
> *Pour out your anger and humble them.*

I just wished I was back at home, I really should have shamed those boys.

Finally feeling as though my mind had cleared I made my way back to school.

I turned up to the classroom where Mr Lock looked up and said, "Welcome back to the classroom Karen." He didn't ask me where I went and I slotted back into the lesson.

By the end of the day it was time for my birthday party and we gave my friend Kim and Paula a lift back to mine. I'd never told anyone about my accident. I'd found a way to cope with the bad things in life to just rise above it.

We had some music playing in the background, and it was loud not letting us speak. The adults had complete control over us as we played musical statues. I danced really hard wiggling my hips. I got my hands on my hips letting myself go even shaking my hair around. Losing myself completely in the moment. The music stopped. I stood still. I eyed up the others around me. Eve twitched. I tried hard to stay still expecting my little sister to go out but Paula did. I hadn't noticed her. The music pulsated through my veins making me pound the floor hard with my feet. I banged too hard feeling a shooting pain going through my foot and then my leg. My head span as the music stopped and I swayed expecting to get out. My vision had blurred and Eve went out. The music started again. There was only three of us left. Boogying hard the tune changed. I expected to stop too soon but kept on going. The tempo increased. I span around with my arms out not realising I'd hit my big sister on the arm. The music stopped. I fell over and got out. Fee and Kim were left each one, I could tell, were slowing up. Dad jumped in and told them to move apart and move more. The music went on and on. Dad pushed them to dance harder. Kim actually shook her head and toppled one way as the music stopped. Fiona had won. My parents gave out sweets.

We played the game two more times and I never won as I wriggled around too much. Then we played musical bumps. I wished they'd just let me win. It was my birthday. It wasn't till all of us sat down to play pass the parcel that they made the music stop for every child to get a chance to win. I won first for a little toy. It was all wrapped in newspaper and wrapping paper. We had several games. I never won again, but was pleased that everyone was happy. I revelled in the pleasure but when we split to lounge around with drinks everyone was talking but I stayed silent loving the atmosphere.

All of us were absolutely exhausted. I could feel the heat in the air and the smell of sweaty feet. Someone went, "Pooey." It was Fee holding her nose. I looked up to her as her little nose went creased. The food was on the table. I went and joined my friends to sit down with them completely lost in their company as they all chatted together. I had nothing to talk about. Picking up one sandwich I shoved it into my greedy little face but I got all the left overs as I'd waited too long for my turn with food.

Next thing I knew the lights got turned off. Mum came into the room with a chocolate cake that I knew instinctively had ten candles on. All of us burst into a resounding song of "Happy birthday to you, happy birthday to you, happy birthday dear Karen, happy birthday to you." Mum placed the cake in front of me and my Dad told me to make a wish. I blew the candles out quickly not really thinking about a wish. The lights went up and it was nearly time for everyone to go home. Kim placed her present on the table with a card. I went to open it and it was a little present that I liked. My card was soon whipped out of my hand to be put on the side. One card came from Paul with a bigger parcel. I beamed with happiness enjoying the attention as they all placed their cards and gifts to me one by one. I felt jealousy emanating from sister Fiona so she claimed the attention by talking to everyone. I was left to tidy my parcels up but I gave all the paper on the floor to my parents to put in a bin bag and gradually the room thinned out as they all went home.

Then in the morning I went to school euphoric and I played the fool all day long happily doing lots of work loving the feel of the ephemera. Flicking through loads of text books in every lesson.

On the way home I looked forward to going into the living room to relax. I went to sit on the sofa with my homework and wrote my spellings down in my book before Mum was ready with our tea. We had baked beans on potato waffles with sausages for tea as we all sat up to the table together after Dad had come back from his travels in the lorry. He'd just gotten a new one that day and it was parked outside for Mum to take a photograph of him with it. Then he had to take it back to the yard. When he got back he helped Mum to tuck us into bed and we were allowed our headphones and audio cassette tapes to help us get to sleep.

The next morning there was a really nice sunrise streaming through the curtains. Jumping out of bed I soon went to the bathroom to get ready for the day. Shrugging my clothes on I shivered slightly in the cold bedroom as it was chilly. Eve sat on the edge of her bed while I'd been dressing and rubbed her eyes saying she'd get in the shower next. Fee jumped in quickly after and then that day at school, first lesson, I was inwardly mortified remembering that I'd had a wet dream of a boy at school named Darren I really liked.

We had current newspapers to look at for the lesson and had to cut out pictures of the Royal family. They'd been snapped out and about for a fashion article. I inwardly loved girlie fashion of skirts, blouses and dresses but rarely got to put them on.

> Job 10:12
> You have given me life and constant love.

On cutting the pictures out all we had to do was a collage of favourite clothes. Then I had to write under each picture why I liked the colours, the shape and what I thought the material was. I loved the idea of the feel of satin, silks, sued and leather.

Next lesson was easier again as all I had to do was tell a story from a Jackanory programme of where the orators own spin of Cinderella was of a social climbing gold digger. I knew that was all she really wanted at ten years and that the dwarves were emotionally stunted put together within the Cinder's story was funny.

After lunch I took gymnastics and we all went into the main hall. Blue mats were put out everywhere all over the floor. In my blue, black and pink striped little leotard we had to do stretches up and down and to the side stretching everything akimbo all the time for twenty minutes. I knew I was shit hot at cartwheels and especially back flips to prove my contortionist self. I did these twice from one corner of the mats to the other corner. We all lined up and done these in turn.

I had a great day and I remember that by the evening that day my asthma had gotten really bad. I couldn't breathe, my eyes were streaming from really bad hay fever and I was throwing up everywhere. Mum was panicking with me in the little box room. She'd called the doctor at first but when he came and saw me an ambulance showed up. The first thing they did was give me an oxygen mask as I was laid down. Then I heard the sirens whirring and my heart beat sped up feeling the excitement of being rushed to hospital in the middle of the night. I didn't know which one I was going to but when I woke up in the morning Eve was in a bed opposite. Apparently Eve had felt upset by me being there, taking the attention away from her having her adenoids out. I heard that a friend called Rebecca of hers was going to stop by.

I only stayed in hospital for a couple of days and I was soon home again looking forward to a Halloween party that Saturday.

In the evening I dressed in a black mask with pointy ears, black bodice with a tail on the back and with black tights, so I was a cat. Eve dressed in a black leotard with a bats hat on and some wings. Fiona had put on a black bin bag with a witches hat and hair round the brim on. Mum had the costume of a zombie bride all dressed in white with blood make-up all over it.

Dad was already there having watched the football match at the club house that day. He was in a torn tuxedo and we all danced the night away hand-in-hand swinging around.

The next day Dad had seen an advertisement in the local paper looking for athletes or aspiring athletes to run in the Shepton Mallet Fun Run. It was decided that Dad, Fee and I were going to take part. The race started outside Whitstone school and we all geared up in one big group to get ready to run. The intention had been there to run all the way round but as the race progressed and Dad shot out in front with the adults and Fee disappeared out of view with Tracy I ended up walking round the lanes with the ambulance. There had been another woman with me to whom I got chatting. We were swapping life stories and aimlessly following the back roads around the outskirts of Shepton only knowing which way to go because of the route the ambulance was taking. I learnt that the other lady and I had asthma in common and as we ran back to the school over an hour later I was at least pleased I'd completed the course as my family were there to greet us clapping happily. It turned out that they had been waiting a long time for me as Dad got back in twenty minutes and Fee in half an hour. We were the only ones at the end of the Fun Run still there, though with a happy sense of accomplishment we all went home.

That evening went by quickly as we all took turns to shower, change and have a spot of tea. Mum and Dad talked over us about the following day. Mum was saying that our uniforms were going to be ready for the next day as I listened the realisation hit me there was a momentous occasion the next day.

In the morning it was a Sunday and us girls, after showering, dressed ourselves quickly for church then headed out the door. There was a chill in the air and I felt so alive.

In the church there was a hymn I got in the moment singing loudly as possible getting trilling. I stood next to Mum with Fee on one side and Eve next to Dad the other side of Mum taking up half of one of the front pews. It was in a place though of where I could not see around the pillars to watch the vicar giving the sermon. Feeling frustrated I'd fidgeted in my seat getting an annoyed look from Mum in return. Fiona looked around at me too. With an impertinent nose I though sod it and launched proudly into another hymn. Right at the end of the service my parents milled about getting drinks for all of us by the side door of the church.

Somewhere deep inside my world emanated out a very bright yellowing glowing light all around me.

Nehemiah 8:10
Today is Holy to our Lord, so don't be sad.
The joy that the Lord gives you will make you strong.

Standing outside in the dim November haze we all headed towards the big car park through the bottom of town to reach the automobile to take us home.

That had been an amazing weekend and in the morning we were told that it was the week before Remembrance Sunday. In first class the teacher got out his guitar and got us to repeat back to him three little wartime songs.

'We're going to hang out the washing on the Siegfried line'. Of which the whole class parroted back. Then he sand 'Is there any dirty washing mother dear?' I inwardly snorted and stuck my nose into the air while sat right in the middle of the rows of children on the floor. The first line got repeated again for us to mimic before leading into 'cause the Siegfried Line's still here'. Over and over again all the words resounded round inside my head before we learned 'Whether the weather maybe wet or fine we'll just muddle on without a care', at which point my voice got even louder blending in with what I thought was the teacher's loud boom of a voice before singing the last bars of which I'd dropped my loudness down to suit the rest of the school children.

Another song, 'You Are My Sunshine' was learned that way too of which really made my morning at school that day.

I'd felt like winding others up that afternoon at lunch and tried hanging around Kim for all of it, getting caught up in groups of children in the school yard. Instead of having the chance to wind anyone else up though because I thought I'd be alone with my best friend to do it, I'd found them winding me up. I wanted to laugh ferociously with them but instead had found myself justifying my every word with my voice getting louder and squeakier around me. I started to hate my loud very squeaky voice as it grated around my brain. Everyone, it felt, as the moment stretched out around me seemed to hurt me deep inside. That moment I knew what it was like to be laughed at by everyone.

A pain seared through my side that felt alien to me and I started to see Kim through a different light. She then looked right at me but didn't return my smile so I felt perplexed so frowned. The tables were about to turn in our relationship.

After lunch in the classroom all my emotions that had catapulted outside came together to propel me to try even harder with my work. A golden glow was all around the classroom right up till the end of the working day.

At home my piano resounded gladly to my touch the keys perfectly to the tunes I played. Happy the music was coming together as I tapped the notes along. For hours my fingers ran over the piano blurring the lines between songs and scales of which sounded euphoric to my ears. I eventually turned round to a lovely smell of food to see tea on the table. I'd felt the tug of my tummy growling away to receive the food. It wasn't till after eating, when we were all slumped in front of the telly that a film called 'Big' came on for the first time. I loved the scene where Tom Hanks woke up one morning in a man's body after the scene at the Zog machine at the fair had given me the creeps and wondered if I could do that. My bestest moment of the whole film had been when the main character and his boss danced on the large keyboard in the middle of his shop. That song resounded round in my head for a few days in which time I'd found myself finding the notes on the piano to fit the tune. Every note matched the music in my head perfectly. I knew I'd drive everyone nuts just playing it over and over again so placed the song in between the tunes I had to play for my next concert, exam pieces and scales.

That night feeling euphoric Mum bundled everyone into the car as it was Dad's turn to drive to go to a carnival. Down the hill from home into Wells we parked by what Dad said was the park and the recreational field. It was heaving with people round town and it had been dark. All around us were bright lights coming from food vans, the odd shop front window and the odd people with funny wiggly lit up fluorescent wands. There'd been a man with lots of helium balloons in his hand. I inwardly giggled picturing him flying off with them into the heavens. I'd heard my sister Eve asking for one of them. Mum said, "No, I'm sorry they're five pounds each. That means they'll be fifteen pounds for all three of you."

I felt and hard the sulks so dropped my head. I'd inwardly heard myself saying, "Where are we going?" Then Mum and Dad propelled us through the edge of town of where I'd constantly look up and around me at all the sights and sounds. The atmosphere was electric and we walked under some trees that felt slightly eerie causing dark shades even though bright lights seemed to be everywhere. Round a bend and through some traffic lights as we walked in the road we came to a big pub in front of us.

The next thing we knew we were all being traipsed upstairs to go to what was called Annabel's flat that I knew was above an Argentinian Falklands War shop. We all sat round in the barest looking of living rooms in chairs or a sofa and had drinks each and every one chatted animatedly, happy just to be there. Caught up in the moment a loud boom of a noise rebounded off the walls and a golden glow came through the window creating round and laser shape white lights around the room. I jumped up first to look through the window and was enthralled by the magic of all the shapes, colours, lights, dancers, the wonderful costumes and imagined in my mind's eye being one of the girls in the white leotards with feathers on their bottoms and heads. My little face was animated. I noticed my sisters were either side of me getting a look.

I asked later for a burger and us girls together insisted on cheese burgers. The other two wanted chips, I didn't really want chips, so Dad offered to get food on the street corner right by the pub, The Mermaid. We were still gazing out the window for a while at the moving parts and inwardly I'd been dancing along to the music singing along with one of the songs inside my head. A loud noise distracted me later on and Mum stood at the door with burger and chips in her hand. I wiped my nose on my sleeve as I'd sensed the heat from the food causing my nose to block up. I'd been so hungry and munched gingerly away happily watching the end of the parade. The music was so loud resounding round inside my brain putting me in a daze loving the moments they all passed me by. It didn't even occur to me that everyone else had been outside for most of the night.

Then it dawned on me that the show might be over as there was a huge quiet interlude in between carts so I went downstairs to find a toilet. Outside I saw Dad first rubbing his hands together in the cold night air. I could see the frosty smoke come from his hands while doing this and the same white smoke came from his lips. I stayed there with the rest of the family with Dad's arm around my waist as I looked up to him inwardly smiling not aware of those in the crowd wanting to push past. Safely in his arms I started juggling around to more music I could hear coming so caught up in my surroundings. I bloody loved carnival this lead into a really good mood for the rest of the weekend.

That morning after, at school, I found myself working even more ferociously putting pen to paper starting with English, starting to see so easily the words I needed to write in my mind's eye. Having pure faith in my abilities I'd managed to complete the set tasks and homework set during the lesson by the end of the English lesson.

Next came history we were learning about a war called the Battle of Hastings, they said was set in 1066. The books had lots of pictures on the pages. One picture in particular was of a wagon with hay on of where a man in navy blue uniform leaned on the cart with his back to me. There was smoke on the horizon and through this I could see the picture of the canon. There was nothing to write we just had to read and memorise the words for an essay to do at home alter. I grabbed my books and all my utensils that were neatly arranged on my desk and ran outside without my bag after putting it on my peg.

Somewhere outside there was my friends. I never looked for them as I wandered round happily noticing out of the corner of my eye the same brunette of whom I knew to be Emma but wanted my best made Kim. For the first time I actually acknowledged that she wasn't there when I needed her.

That afternoon through geography learning about how the earth's core looked like while looking at very basic charts, I realised, myself, that the core was still perfect in that it resembled the sun in every way.

Last lesson was maths of which I enjoyed. I looked at each sum methodically and made sure I saw the numbers in my mind's eye and saw each answer correctly each time. The answers got more and more instinctive.

At home later Fee sat next to me on the sofa and got my attention for once leading me into a conversation about a card game called strip poker. I turned to her with a blank look on my face. Then she described where she and another girl used to go to with the boys near a stairway in the changing rooms during lunch break that day. I pictured, out of the corner of my eye, that room looking through the hallway first of the old nunnery building and honing on that scene in my head. Fee told me *that* she'd gotten as far into the card game that she had taken her top off.

It was a chilly November morning and I'd been chatting away happily to Rebecca not really concerned if she was enjoying my company at all. We were with a gang of other girls all in our brownie uniforms and I'd been proudly showing off my new badges, sewn on by Mum, for being creative.

Matthew 6:2
They do it so that people will praise them. I assure you.
They have already been paid in full.

Standing by the cenotaph, at the top of town, we were getting ready to march down town to the church for Remembrance Sunday. All happily chatting away standing near our proud parents we called to attention. Then the Last Post was played and the wreaths were placed at the bottom of the cenotaph. Looking around me I saw the scouts all smartly dressed and the girls and boys brigades as we all headed off down the hill by the shops. Martin's newsagents on one side then Daniella's pastry shop on the next, over the crossroads and down to the market place.

The vicar took control as we all gathered round after finishing singing 'Onwards Christian Soldiers'. Prayers were said and then after the sermon about how the brave soldiers had fought, specifically, in both world wars although other battles were remembered in our prayers. The Lord's Prayer was said and John Woolmer led us passed the Amulet and the public toilets round to the church for anyone wanting communion. There was the last hymn and everyone stayed afterward for teas, coffees, orange juice and biscuits. I was still chattering away to anyone who'd listen oblivious to how I'd actually sounded as everyone politely seemed to nod and agree with me in all the right places.

I'd enjoyed the songs as I loved to hear my own voice resonating round the church. No-one told me I might be too loud. It was obvious to everyone that I'd been really happy.

Sat in the classroom the next morning I found myself mentally checking the time watching the round clock upon the wall. The teacher was rabbiting on about a new book we had to read literally about bunnies, a fox and other animals who tried to catch the moon in a pond. It wasn't even funny to me as the rest of the class giggled because I knew the whole scenario was ridiculous so humphed to myself. We were having a story reading morning and I'd had nothing else to do but listen of which made my eyes stray yet again to the clock. It was quarter to ten and my fingers were itching to do something so I found myself picking up my pencil and tapping it lightly on the table. My body quivered in anticipation of getting up to go out and play. I kept looking round to the door as everyone listened to Beatrix Potter books too. This was boring but I did manage to still hear the instructions of us having to write about each story and what we thought of them and compare their difference of which I found myself mentally preparing in my head. My note book filled itself with ideas as we were eventually being told to leave for break time. I stayed in the classroom though to work through my notes and write my essay.

After the mornings work I headed outside to play on my own running around playing tag with other girls and then someone found a ball to play piggy-in-the-middle with and I ended up in the middle most of the time and found myself hating this game, so I waited for the girls to get bored with me. Clouds rolled overhead and the sky got quickly dark. I found myself in the bottom left hand corner of the play yard and I heard my Mum say my name of which echoed in my head. She wasn't there though and it sounded like Mum had been calling me through, what could only be described as a coma like state in my brain. This chilled me to the bone before I became the last child outside to go into class.

That afternoon we learned about Valentine's Day and my head was in the clouds hearing of Saint Valentine. Till the end of the day we were happily using glue sticks, coloured card, different coloured paper, glitter, felt pens and paint. I'd used white card and cut out a large red heart from the coloured paper to glue on the front. I then outlined the word happy along the top of the front page. Under the heart I'd outlined Valentine's Day. In between the outlines I pasted on glue very cleverly then sprinkled gold glitter over each letter carefully till it made two lines of gold. I patiently waited for five to ten minutes before picking my card up and shaking the excess off over the bin the corner of the room. I'd been pleased at how glowingly the letters were perfectly accentuated. I decided to copy a little cherub blowing a trumpet from a book I'd seen one in, once in my mind's eye and was quite pleased with it as the picture fitted inside the card quite large to put writing inside the cherub's robes. With a red pen I wrote happy valentine's day again and wrote it to Mum and Dad writing lots of love from Karen at the bottom.

When I came home from school that day I switched on the TV with school books all over the floor to watch my favourite cartoons like Duck Tales, the Get Along Gang and the presenter Philip Schofield with Ed the Duck. Then would watch John Craven on Blue Peter.

At church the next Sunday I'd been listening intently to the sermon and something about what Revd. John Woolmer said made me cry. Afterward I couldn't remember what the service had been about even if anyone had asked. I'd always anticipated questions that were never put to me and would imagine conversations in my head. This would make me feel quite lonely really in a house with two adults and two sisters always doing their own things.

At home I grabbed my dolls and did their hair raking the comb through over and over again making ends come out. Focusing on myself I never noticed if anyone needed my company. No-one asked for it as Mum was cooking in the kitchen. Dad was out the back cleaning our shoes and my sisters were off playing together. I touched my Sindy doll's boobies enjoying the sensation going through my thighs. Why wasn't anyone paying attention to me?

Mum interrupted my thoughts just then and called us all to the table to sit up for lunch. It smelled delicious as our usual Sunday roast came out. I'd had my usual chicken leg with me and Eve would eat what was left over.

We all ate heartily and afterward Mum asked us girls to help with the drying up. Fee dried two things, made her excuses and went to the toilet. Eve didn't dry much more before she'd made an excuse to leave which left Mum and I finishing up the dishes. Mum offered us rocket lollies with hundreds and thousands on as treats for helping with the washing up.

Dad had the newspaper looking though it on the sofa for things to get out to do. Mum came in and sat down with him saying we'd eaten early enough for us all to go on a drive somewhere. She suggested going to see the white snowdrops out at Pylle. Dad agreed. He groaned that he'd just cleaned all our shoes so Mum suggested that we all take our wellies to walk through the fields.

Slamming the door shut as I got into the car I got told off by Dad saying I'd break the hinges. Fee opened the door again to sit next to me. Eve had gone over Helen's her friend's house for the afternoon.

I was quite pleased to be sat by the window for once and turned the handle to wind the window down as it was becoming a hot day. No-one seemed to mind.

Going through town I'd spotted very few people about. Shepton always seemed dead. On the top road along Fosse Lane it looked like we were heading for Evercreech until Dad turned off in another direction looking like we were going in one big circle around Shepton mallet. then he turned left before the road into the top of Pilton at which point I gave up figuring where we were going.

We were soon driving through some winding lanes, Mum said to find the snowdrops. Out the window I poked my arm out to try and catch the berries on the bushes as Dad drove slowly round a bend just before he pulled over to let someone pass. Mum spotted a pull-in just up the road for us to park, so Dad slowed down even more as I managed to grab at a twig and yanked it off.

Dad told me off after alighting from the car because, he'd said, other drivers would have gotten confused through seeing my arm waving about. We all went to the boot of the vehicle to get our wellies out and swap our footwear ready for the fields. There'd been a gate next to where we parked with a sloping path into some woods the other side. Walking along my parents pointed to the flowers and Mum set a competition for the first one to spot a squirrel. I told Mum that I'd seen a red squirrel at Collett Park once but Mum walked on in front with Dad and I lagged more and more behind squinting as I went to see what everyone was looking at. The snowdrops were in abundance and more seemed to be on the left hand side of the path.

Nearing the bottom of the path there was a stream. Dad told us that the flowers we'd been looking at grew more by water and on through the undergrowth we went to coming to a field. Looking out over there'd been lots more of exploring to do, but Mum said, "Two more fields then we'll turn back."

My feet hit some icy mud and I felt the cracking of the ice underfoot. I liked the sound and started jumping on more dry ice to crack. I really enjoyed this little exercise but I could hear everyone moaning about me to keep up.

It hadn't been overly cold and at least the weather was dry. We still had to be in thick coats because as it was February time it had still technically been winter.

Getting bored with making crunching noises and staring at my footprints as I walked Dad halted so we all stood still. Dad beckoned us over to look up a tree to see where a chopping sound was coming from. Squinting up into the green foliage of the tree the noise got louder and sharper. Mum told us it was a woodpecker. I couldn't see it but could definitely hear the bird. Thinking of Woody Woodpecker off the telly I'd been baffled that a red and blue tall bird wasn't up the tree. I didn't see what I expected to see and gave up looking after ten minutes saying, "Yeah I saw it." When really I'd never. Then we continued walking over the first field into the second one but when we got there the grass seemed taller than me and my sister. Dad looked for some sort of path to walk along but then Fee started talking about poisonous adders being in the grass that she'd learned about at school. This made me curious to see one, Fiona got scared and Mum looked worried sot the trek across the field did not happen as the whole family turned round to make their way back.

No-one was in a rush to get to the car and thankfully they were all walking with me so I started chatting to Fee. I tried to tell her what I learned at school about birds and she did seem interested. Inclining her head every now and again in acknowledgement of everything I was saying not really being able to get a word in edgeways.

Mum heard me jabbering and I heard her giggle. Thinking she was laughing at me I stopped talking. The scents of the white flowers reached my nose and I just focused on getting back to the car. The cold was getting on my chest making me wheeze a little bit. Dad put his arm around me to push me on.

Back in the car we all piled in for the journey home.

Chapter Seven

After school I'd changed into my usual jeans and jumper and told Mum I was going out on my bicycle. Cycling down our hill to Wickham Way aiming for Linda's cul-de-sac part of the road I turned right up the path through the metal bars onto another cul-de-sac of where Jo lived in the corner. Dumping my bike on the drive way before knocking on the door. Jo answered and was pleased to see me. Saying hello to her Mum, and with us both asking for juice we headed upstairs to make a tent. I can't really remember the layout of her room but we'd put up a white sheet over our heads with the ends probably tied onto the posts round the edges of her bed and tucked into drawers on the other side. Jo and I decided to try a séance by holding our hands together, closing our eyes and asking if anyone was out there. Giggling nervously we asked that if anyone was out there could they knock on the door three times. We'd forgotten about our drinks and tried to blank everything out while concentrating hard. Next thing we knew there were three sharp knocks on the bedroom door. Jo and I screamed as a pleasant face appeared from behind the door with our orange juices on a tray. It had just been Jo's mum.

We went downstairs for sandwiches afterward as I'd stayed on for tea before I'd said my goodbyes.

The next day we woke early as Mum dragged us out of bed tempting us with tea and biscuits. Everything had already been packed all we had to do was get ready. Throwing on my trousers and jumper already picked out for me we all ran down to the car pointing in the direction of Great Ostry road.

We were going to Brighton and I fell asleep as we headed towards the A361 and then onto the Causeway on the A27. With the radio on low Dad was driving passed the M3/London/Southampton/Winchester/Portsmouth junction to merge on the M27 and then back on the A27 through Devil's Dyke Road. I woke up with the sea in sight having missed Dad's tour through the countryside and saw the imposing Grand Hotel that was to be a Butlin's Holiday resort. As per usual I watched everyone put their stuff away and felt the need to explore.

Over the following days we explored the sea front but the sea was too rough for us to go in so we were content to use the indoor pool. On one occasion in the swimming pool I recognised a famous face. Dad asked me if I saw something missing on his face. Nothing was obvious to me but Dad pointed out the celebrity had no eyebrows. I was reminded of his name. Duncan Goodhew. I'm sure my parents said hello but I wasn't bothered trying to be cool. Dad went on and got a certificate for competing in a fun run.

I remember playing golf outside in the rain, just a small putting range and I can recall taking a turn when I swung the golf club back hard to take a swing and hitting Fiona in the face. I missed the ball as Fee screamed as blood flowed from her nose. I had broken it and felt so bad everyone could see how sorry I was and so I wasn't reprimanded. A trip to the hospital meant Fee was bandaged up for the rest of the holiday. Silence from her and no-one actually dealing with me spoke volumes. I was actually allowed to enjoy the rest of the holiday but this had started the ball rolling to me feeling alienated from my family.

One afternoon after school I actually got keen to jump in the shower and wash as I'd never done it after gym class that day with all the other girls, 'cause I'd actually felt embarrassment that day and didn't want to.

After washing I heard Mum had been calling me to hurry up and get in the car to go see Granddad for his birthday. I soon dress in jeans, t-shirt and a jumper. I wished that I had lots of soft and flirty dresses but Mum always brought me all practical clothes. I always wanted a word with her about it but never got round to it. When had the chance it was never in the back of my mind as the moments came when there were higher agendas.

Down the road I started to panic I had no card or present. I looked at Eve and Fee. There were no obvious signs they had anything either. Mum read my mind and said, "Don't worry I've written a family card from all of us."

A tangible thought went through my head that a key ring I'd bought from before could be a present as Granddad liked whistling just like me. The reason I thought the latter was because the key ring I'd had was all the rage. You whistled, it bleeped and helped you find your keys. I'd made it as part of my key ring collection I'd been proud of, before I'd given my collection away to Lynda years ago as I'd never wanted them at the time of not needing her friendship after she dumped on me with Vicky.

I came out of my reverie from staring out the front window. I wished that I wasn't always in the middle of the back seats but never had the guts to say anything as my sisters always claimed they got car sickness.

Luckily the journey didn't last long and we were soon at Tor View number two knocking at Gran's door. Gran always answered with a big smile and a hug came from Gramps and we all said happy birthday one by one.

In the kitchen we all sat down and I always sat on the leaf patterned bench, inwardly praying no-one spoke to me a I didn't know what to say but really wanted some attention for some emulations that never came.

Aunty Nola, Uncle Graham, the dog Barney, Scott and Linda were there. It was a nice house full but I could feel pushed out but included in a shared family warmth.

Later on there was a chocolate cake with a few candles on for gramps to blow out and afterward I decided not to give him my key ring 'cause I'd spied his keys in the living room with a whistling key ring on it. Mum parroted my earlier thoughts by saying, "It's the eighties Dad they're all the rage at the moment," as she gave him that particular key ring herself that day. I didn't mind it, it just made me inwardly laugh as I shared a private joke with myself.

The evening wore on and the sky outside got dark early as the telly went on to keep me amused. The company had got boring as everyone hit into alcohol and the whirring conversations round my head seemed to be endless. I didn't know how, when or where I could join in and got fed up. All I looked forward to was when they'd cut the cake so I could have a piece.

Tired at nine o'clock as I'd been watching the clock I heard Dad mention it was school tomorrow and the family was going to have to move on.

We all soon left and that night after having so much excitement at the party I fell asleep as soon as my head hit the pillow.

Going to school next morning I'd been humming a tune all the way there but thinking ahead to the door in front of me. I knew that I'd be watching the programme I was thinking about when I got home that day.

Slinging my bag on the floor next to my chair I got my first work book out for the lesson. Mr Rossington wanted to talk first about what we were to write for English. Highlighting where the reference books were that he wanted us to read by pointing to them in the room and going on about the school's library our topic was to choose a foreign country and write about it. I had in my mind to write an essay on America the place where all my favourite movies were filmed. Wishing I could talk about my favourite films I knew that some research was in order. I'd come across one book, a travel book to sunny California that I'd actually found at home that afternoon after school. Mum had got some travel brochures and to me the hotels, swimming pools, and local attractions were enough to talk about and I hit into my writing in front of the TV on the floor.

My favourite cartoon called Ulysses came on and I ended up singing along to the theme tune whilst flicking through the holiday brochure. I thought of where to start on the assignment and decided to lead in talking about the buildings and surrounding areas in Florida. Some hotels they said were not far from Orlando's Walt Disney's studio. I was going to make my assignment about the glamour of Hollywood. In a daydream I did a lot of writing while the programme changed to Grange Hill. I looked forward to seeing Tucker and the scrapes him and his friends got into.

An hour later fed up with writing I sat on the sofa and picked up some knitting determined to knit some trousers for my Sindy doll. She was going to look glamorous.

Dad poked his head round the glass doors and asked for his hug as he'd just got in from work. He put his arm round Mum asking her to wait serving up our tea until after he'd had a shower. Dad winked at me and said that we'd have an arm wrestle later. my little face lit up. Down from the shower my father did not forget his promise and we sued the arm of the sofa to lean on. I flexed my muscles rather proud of them and really grabbed Dad's hand hard. We were tussling for a full ten minutes before Dad's arm pushed mine over. I'd really thought I'd been in with a chance of winning. Mum beamed in at us saying that tea was on the table. I'd had fish fingers, peas and waffles with my sisters while Dad had mash, and a big piece of cod. He always had more than the rest of us, but Mum would say that he was the man of the house.

Mum wanted us girls to help in the kitchen. Fee did her usual disappearing act, Eve dried up a couple of things and I was always left to finish up. I'd told Mum about my day as she'd always asked while with her before stopping off to find an array of dollies that I would line up on the sofa to pretend they were watching TV with me. My big baby had an arm out of its socket and I tried to put it back in without much success. Comparing the arms to that of my Sindy dolls I noticed that their arms were held together with elastic bands and spent a long time pulling legs and arms out of their sockets on the dollies to see how they were put together. it never solved my problem with the big baby though as it seemed all you had to do was push it back into the shoulder. I'd been well impressed and fussed over their clothes next. After that I'd found a little comb for fussing over their hair.

Letting out a yawn and stretching my arms out Mum got the message to take us up to bed. We had to clean our teeth first after we'd put on our nighties. I was in my favourite blue one and with Bluey in my hand I turned in for the night. At least I'd learned by now which way to face to avoid getting nightmares.

In the morning, after tea and biscuits, I struggled to get out of bed, stretching and yawning as I went. Rubbing my eyes I heard Mum shouting up the stairs to hurry up and got in the shower. I did as I was told and the shock of the water cascading around me woke me up.

My clothes were neatly pressed ready in the wardrobe to put on. I reached for my shirt, jumper then underwear and skirt. Then put on my long white socks ready to go downstairs for breakfast. I'd had Weetabix with milk and plenty of sugar on top. My sisters were nearly out the door so I had to rush to put my coat and shoes on.

At school my day was full of learning new things of which I'd absolutely loved soaking up everything like a sponge.

Psalms 37:4
Seek your happiness in the Lord, and He will give
you your heart's desire.

In country dancing I pushed myself forward to get up first for the dancing and prancing around under the arches of hands and Dosy-dohing. I thoroughly enjoyed my whole day.
With my head buzzing at home I carried that joy until Dad got home of whom I completely idolised.

> *Exodus 23:13*
> *"Listen to everything that I, the Lord, have said to you.*
> *Do not pray to other Gods; do not even mention their names.*

Sat with him on the he asked me if I could rub my tummy and pat my head at the same time. I giggled as I'd tried. Dad explained that it meant you had good co-ordination skills. We kept the bonding moment going for a while and Eve and Fee joined in.

I'd followed Fee up to her room afterward and she put on a tape which we tried to sing to. After the tape played we both burst into a rendition of 'I know him so well'. Fiona was Elaine Paige and I was the other one. We just loved to sing.

I'd watched Fee's golden hair shining under the rays of the sun coming through her window. I really envied her beautiful blonde hair.

Mum called us down to dinner and the smell of the food was delicious. For afters Mum done our favourite apple crumble with custard and she asked who'd wanted the skin. I'd said "Me," Fee didn't like it but Eve said "Me too," so Mum divided up the skin for both of us and heated it all up. We all tucked into dinner really quickly. I burnt my mouth. The food went down and Dad told me off for chamming telling me to eat with my mouth closed. Mum stuck up for me though by saying that I only did it because I couldn't breathe through my nose.

That night Eve and I had a really nice talk about school, friends and our family. I used to feel really close to Eve and we talked and talked till we naturally just exhausted ourselves and fell into deep sleeps.

Opening my eyes slowly I felt a lot of sticky goo that had glued my eyes together. I'd rubbed at it to get it off and it looked yellow. Mum came in with the tray commenting on me rubbing the sleepy dust out of my eyes. I'd heard Eve say, "Ow." I hung my head over the top bunk to ask if she was alright and I saw her rub her head. Eve had sat up too quickly. Mum encouraged me to get out of bed and have my tea and biscuits on the floor that morning. Tucking into bourbon I wished that Mum had put the custard creams into the tin. Eve asked if there was any custard creams and Mum went downstairs to have a look. Coming back in quick time she emptied a packet in the tin and luckily my tea was still hot for a dunk but being too keen the biscuit crumbled into the mug. It looked disgusting in the cup and didn't bother finishing it so I aimed straight into the shower while no-one was in the bathroom.

At school we got out our maths books. the sums were getting repetitive in our lessons, it was always the times table these days and I already felt confident enough to do all my tables up to 12 x 12 makes 144 as I'd kept singing that song on the Hans Christian Anderson film. I'd always pushed myself to do all my times table to fit in with the tune of inch worm. I felt really clever.

Back at home later after doing more homework in front of the telly I sat on the sofa and started messing about by going cross-eyed and looking at my nose. When Fee came into the room I asked if she could do it too. We giggled as we both noticed how funny our eyes looked and got Eve to do the same.

It was Eve's birthday part that afternoon and she told us that Mum said she was getting a surprise. One by one her friends turned up, mainly Kelly and Helen with a couple of others for a birthday tea of which they had outside in the garden. Mum put the stereo on in the kitchen for after food and we had games outside, mainly musical statues. Mum told us not to do musical bumps out on the concrete as we'd hurt ourselves. We didn't mind, we just enjoyed ourselves anyway. Eve had been made to wait for presents and we soon found out why as Dad came through the back gate from work with a hutch under his arms. he placed it on the step for us all to have a look at and inside there was a grey looking rabbit. This kept us enthralled for a while and Dad asked what Eve wanted to name it. She said Thumper after the rabbit in Bambi.

Aunty Nola and Uncle Graham had been at the party and I really liked their present for Eve which had been a big blue bean bag that was outside with Eve lolling about on. Dad had wanted to disappear upstairs for a shower asking Mum if she'd saved the cake yet. With my ears pricked up I'd started to get excited and began to look forward to a piece of cake. There'd been a bit of a breeze as Mum eventually bought the birthday cake out to a rousing chorus of 'happy birthday'. the wind blew the candles out. Mum asked me to go into the kitchen to bring the big box of matches outside. They'd been left on the sideboard and I passed them out to Mum as she'd tried to light the candles again. Dad cupped his hand round each one as Mum lit them and she told Eve to hurry up and blow them out. Dad rubbed his hands together and blew on them to keep warm and told Eve to make a wish. Aunty Nola had positioned herself to take a photo and shouted to say cheese to Mum and Dad who grinned from ear to ear as Eve blew the candles out.

Everyone stayed for about another half an hour before their parents started showing up two by two and they all said goodbye and thank you for the party.

It was soon Collet Park's fun day and the Mendip Hospital Carnival Club were running a stall. They were hosting a spinning Jenny with bottles of wine as prizes. Chris was in charge for most of the day which left me able to go round all the stalls. I didn't have much money but spent the od twenty pence on tombola's and raffles that were placed all round the main arena in the middle of the park. I went and helped with the rest of the family win a tug of war contest and I remember being right at the back and slipping up on my bottom in the mud and ended up not helping much.

I stopped to watch the gymnastic display and the dancing and started to get bored. Having one last trawl round the stalls for a bargain. I went back to our stall to have a go on the spinning Jenny, a great big brightly coloured round wooden board, of where wine was among the best prizes. I won a bottle of wine and unscrewed it there and then. Feeling cool I'd hit into it getting more drunk out in the sun by the minute. Feeling like something was drawing me to the Salvation Army tent I'd found myself signing up. I started to sing my favourite hymns feeling happy; 'Colours of Day, 'Morning has Broken' and 'Amazing Grace'. I'd even gotten Keith, Sue's husband, of whom were both thin with brunette hair and pleasing faces, singing my favourite hymns along with me. I'd been in the grip of the Holy Spirit. This near enough ended the day for me on a high note out in the sunshine. Mum had noticed the state I'd gotten in and insisted I had something to eat so she gave me some money that I got a cheeseburger and chips with. The sun was making my head pound and it was beginning to get late. We were one of the last ones packing up our stall. I told Mum that I'd wanted to stay for the dance in the evening feeling buoyant. Mum was unimpressed and we never went back up the park once we got home.

Next day, at home, in the middle of the day I went up to Nan's in my head and wanted to be alone, all by myself, I thought that I should have been an only child. I'd been sat on the sofa dreaming of having my own personal space but never got it. Now Fiona had been keeping on at Mum for a lift. Eve went out with her friends, the fights were endless and all I craved was some peace. Through the post came a clunk. I ran to the door and ripped open a brown envelope with cardboard in it. Inside was mine and my sister Fiona's cycling proficiency certificates we'd been training for, for three weeks at the top of our hill that was arranged through school. I'd been proud of our accomplishments.

Later on that day I had a go on Eve's orange space hopper in the back garden but could not balance on it at all.

Next day putting on my usual jeans, t-shirt and jumper I'd jumped out of bed as soon as Mum woke me up with tea and biscuits. I raced downstairs for some toast for breakfast. Dad was taking me on an overnight trip in the lorry to a place called Margate.

Slinging on my coat, to wrap up warm, Dad and I got on his bike with me on the cross-bar. In the dark with only the street lamps and passing cars for light we headed into Hillmead and under the bridge towards the yard.

Dad soon found his lorry, then I clambered up into the passenger seat dead excited while slinging my overnight stuff on the bed behind. I'd asked Dad if we were going on the motorway and my father said yes the M3 and the M25.

I still didn't last long in the passenger seat before I'd curled up on the bed to sleep to some lazy tunes on the radio and Terry Wogan's voice with the loud engine grating underneath.

I awoke after being on the A303 and Dad was overtaking lots of cars in the middle lane. The M3 seemed really busy and Dad and I got chatting about what was on the radio. I'd been told what monuments we'd pass but quickly forgot. It was exciting being up high in the lorry and being able to look over hedges and walls to the green fields and beyond.

On the M25 the channel changed on the radio automatically and I asked Dad if I could put his Dire Straits tape on. The answer was always yes and I sat there playing air guitar singing loudly. On the A2 Dad said we were almost there. Beach in view we had a few more roads to go before the loading bay was insight at the supermarket.

Dad took a long time, while I sat in the lorry, unloading the lorry then pulling the side of the lorry across. Jumping back into the driver's seat I'd been told that the last of the load was booked in for the next day at another supermarket.

We found somewhere to eat, a nice greasy spoon, for a fry up and then Dad took me shopping. There were nice shops and I brought a t-shirt then we'd noticed Sleeping Beauty was on at the cinema. Dad paid for us to see it. This had been the first time I'd seen a film and I remember the three fairies flying around.

When we'd come out of the cinema it was dark and ornate lights were dangling on a wire by the sea along the promenade. Dad showed me a train on a bridge reaching out across the water. I can't remember where it exactly went.

Back at the lorry park we freshened up and went to bed. Dad soon unloaded the rest of the crates the next day and were at home again in time for tea.

In the morning it was dark when I woke up. I'd heard the ticking time bomb of a clock in my parents' room. It was eerie and their alarm went off. Dad came out of the room and fannied about in the bathroom. Then he went downstairs to clutter about in the kitchen. I went down the stairs rubbing my eyes and yawning to see him off to work. he was surprised but happy. Then as he went outside the door while kissing Mum he told me to go back to bed as it was only half past five. Then I trudged back upstairs and couldn't sleep so picked up some knitting by the side of the bed. I was knitting a long scarf. After an hour I dozed off and woke quite late to Mum coming in with a cup of tea and biscuits. I'd noticed my knitting was on the floor and smiled at Mum. She sat on Eve's bed with me and her cup of tea and she got to talking about when herself, Aunty Nola, and her brothers were younger. It was about their holidays to Bowleaze near Weymouth and how Uncle Steve and Uncle Cyn were in a band. Apparently Uncle Cyn played the guitar. Then she told me how her, and Aunty Nola liked to go out dance and sing outside the restaurant there. They'd gotten jump change for entertaining the public and they really enjoyed themselves.

Later on for lunch we had a nice cooked meal and afterwards rhubarb crumble that I had to say I did not like. I wished Mum would pay attention to me about that.

Showerings garden party, the next day, was at Kilver Court in Shepton, in the sprawling grounds out back with all the azaleas and blooms and blossoms showing wonderful colours. There were white gazebos and tents, with rock pools here and there with the viaduct in the background. In the tents I wandered around accustomed to being on my own picking up the little wine testers and cider tasters. I poked my head out of one tent wondering where my family was. I figured they were with everyone else who'd gravitated towards the press taking photographs of a white tiger from Bristol Zoo.

When I'd caught up with Mum and Dad they were sitting around on fancy white chairs, and I remember giggling and lolling about on my heavy wrought iron white chair, No-one seemed to notice or even care that I had gotten drunk. By this time no-one seemed to know how to talk to me any way as I was always in a little world of my own but at least I was enjoying myself and feeling carefree on a gloriously sunny day.

Next day Mum and Dad went on holiday with their friends Mandy and Graham to Tenerife and left us three girls at Nan and Gramps in Evercreech. Turning in to the cul-de-sac I got excited as this was a new adventure for us to spend a week away from our parents. Eve and I had the main bedroom and Fee had the side room. We were told that we'd go off for days to the beach like Lyme Regis, it had a lovely little beach, a small harbour, and a fish 'n' chip shop we'd always go in with famous visitors' faces on the wall. That night Nan offered us Ovaltine before bedtime.

Nan had a lovely big garden and I remember this year they had a blue tulip imported from Amsterdam. They had hula-hoops and various other toys and a tea set to play with. Some days we would walk around to the park stopping off for a drink at the corner shop on the way. on the last day I remember knocking over a plant pot in the living room window spilling compost all over the carpet. Nan was furious and her coldness, as she turned her back, spoke volumes as she went for the dustpan and brush.

I was glad to be going home and was overjoyed when Mum and Dad came to pick us up. They stayed for a cup of tea and a chat before driving us home.

When we got back my grade 3 certificate had come through the post and I'd passed with a distinction. My piano playing must have been brilliant.

Up at big school called Whitstone it had been a typical day at school with double maths in the morning and with me struggling to make sense of algebra. I mean, I'd been alright with a maths problem with one letter in it but two letters made me go quiet as the teacher wanted us to call out the answers before going through the thought process involved in order to get to the answer.

English was always easiest and I'd always felt like I coasted along nicely in lessons. Dad had always said you had to put your head down and just get on with school.

After lunch, was CDT, which meant craft, design and technology. We always had to stand up in class to high desks. As we were settling down to get out our books Rosie came in with a twig in her hand and I jokingly called her Twiggy, but bright spark Nicky upset me when he told the class that Twiggy was a white woman who was a model. I bawled my eyes out afterward because Nicky had twisted my words to make me sound racist and it had been an innocent comment. The teacher called my Mum out and she complained to my form tutor Nick and as far as I knew Nicky got reprimanded.

I had been so upset when I came home that I drifted off to Dad's Van Morrisons album, particularly the 'Have I Told You Lately' song. I felt so at peace in my dream that I know I was seeing the world through what we perceive as God's eyes watching us all through the clouds. I started praying hard after this to always be able to see the world through God's eyes.

I couldn't look at Nicky or my form teacher when he told me that he'd dealt with it the next day. I was well embarrassed about Mum's involvement and resolve not to tell her of anyone hurting me after that. I had to stand on my own two feet.

In the morning I was late for school again. Running up the corridors living in my head as usual I was actually walking to my first lesson having missed registration. I dumped my bag on the table as French was about to start and the teacher looked sharply at me. I'd sat down on a chair in the middle row by the wall and had to squint at the board 'cause in French they used pink chalk, and sometimes green in small writing that I struggled to read. I wanted the writing to be very clear in white really.

After the lesson I walked down the corridor to English language. Mr Jeremiah was lecturing us on a certain book about Charles Dickens of who he was, and what he was about. We made a list of his books like Scrooge and the Tale of Two Cities. There was about twenty books in the series. We had to choose a book from the list, read it and write about what Charles had been thinking when he wrote it.

Break time came. I never bought anything but I hung around outside with a girl named Rheann of whom I made a friend with, just talking and needing each other's attention. We walked about together for fifteen minutes.

Next lesson I went to a drama class but the teacher wasn't there and all the boys started to jump on one another and it was the one they always picked on, on the bottom. They made me blush. As a Damion joined in he looked at me embarrassed with a cheeky grin. The teacher walked in and one by one they got off each other. They sat down and said "Hello Mr Casey," in a unified voice. We started the lesson in silence while the teacher passed around a script to read. I got a name Terry to read the line from and there were enough characters for everyone to play. We sat in a circle and spoke in turn of the script. I got to speak on three separate occasions as Terry. Now I put my all into my words and spoke very passionately like I was talking to young children. We were supposed to take the script home to learn the directions as well as the lines.

Come the afternoon there was a certain smell emanating round the classroom. One boy I assumed had farted and all the other boys laughed. He looked squarish faced, with dark twinkly eyes, sunken cheeks, with curly hair and laughed himself inanely. His name was Rocky.

After school Mum gave me a card for a new baby, one of her friends just had, her name was Louise. Her parents were friends with Mum and Dad. Their middle daughter Helen was still friends with Eve and Claire the eldest was still best friends with Fee. It was a lovely pink card of a girl baby with blonde hair toddling about with the words engraved in gold were 'Congratulations It's a Girl!' It had been really cute, Mum had signed it from the whole family. I had to walk down the steps and up Beach Avenue towards the house at the top of another hill. I knocked on the door and the mum Jan opened it and said, "Oh. Hello Karen what are you doing here?"

I said, "Hello. Can I come in?"

It was a warm welcome. The walls were cosied coloured and there was a crib in the living room. I looked in and cooed and thought what a cute baby. With the card in my hand Jan had said "Would you like a drink?"

I said, "Yes please. I'd like an orange juice." I couldn't take my eyes, totally mesmerised, off of the baby.

There'd been a fireplace behind radiating heat. A creamed coloured sofa, a warm rug on the floor and presents been opened on that rug looking like an organised mess. When Jan came in Phil, her husband, followed her in and said "Hello." To which I responded similarly and then exchanged the tumbler for the card while still staring at Louise. They said, "Thank you Karen."

Jan stood there opening the pink envelope and beamed. Then moved towards the fireplace and put it on the shelf above it with lots of other cards. I looked at Jan and said, "Can I look through the cards?" As I'd made my way towards them to open each one in turn. The sisters had given their own card, which were sweet. I'd seen two sets of grandparents' cards and from aunties, uncles, godparents, and several friends. There were two sets of cards exactly the same.

"Sit down Karen." Jan said, "Stay a while," so I said, "For half an hour then as I have to get home for tea," and I blushed in the warm room not used to making excuses for myself. I sipped my juice slowly and asked, "When is the christening?"

They replied, "Oh. In about two years' time. We're not focusing on that at the moment." Then Helen came downstairs straight into the living room and said, "Hello Karen. How's Eve?"

"She's find thank you." I replied still blushing from the attention and from the warmth of the room. Sipping slowly, sinking into the sofa I was getting fuzzy headed and really cosy.

Phil looked at his watch and said. "Hadn't you better get going Karen your tea will get cold?"

I hadn't realised till I'd gotten home I'd been out for over an hour.

The next day I awoke in a temper. I'd had a nightmare of not being in school on time and of wandering in and out classrooms not knowing where my class was meant to be, and the reoccurring part was going up and down the communal stairs. I came downstairs with a sore head expecting cards as it was my twelfth birthday. I came across my sisters who only said, "Morning Karen," sarcastically. I then realised from the clock that it was nearly mid-day.

I wandered round the house all day wanting someone to say happy birthday to me but they never did. Mum and Dad were quiet all day with me and I was beginning to feel really ignored. It was my twelfth birthday for goodness sake and when it came to six o'clock Dad snapped at me and said "Go put something nice on Karen."

I found a nice dress and flirty sandals as outside it had been lovely weather all day as since September it was a lovely Indian summer. Grumpily walking downstairs I'd felt that I'd been the only one to make an effort to dress up and felt out of place and like I was the only good girl. Dad looked at me and said, "Put a cardigan on Karen," So I ran back upstairs feeling told off and found a lovely lemony coloured cardigan. He yelled upstairs to my sisters.

"Come on. Get ready. We want to go out."

At least I hadn't been the last one to get changed as I always felt like the good girl who did things the moment she was asked. I overheard Eve moaning downstairs. "Can we give them to her yet?" I started to twig and got curious as to where we were going.

In the car we sped across town. Then towards Frome and wondered where we were actually going. For one, with my curiosity piqued, I looked out the front window with everyone strangely quiet as my sisters were usually moaning.

> *Ecclesiastics 1:8*
> *Everything leads to weariness – a weariness too great for words.*
> *Our eyes can never see enough to be satisfied; our ears can never hear enough.*

I turned to the left and saw Eve's face strangely pale, "Can we stop Dad please? I need to get out," so Dad found a side road at which Eve jumped out like a trapped tiger and promptly threw up in a hedge. She held her stomach, doubled over and had to inhale and exhale really deeply. I was getting impatient. Then Dad went over to her and held her and said audibly. "Come on get in. Not much further to go," and I heard Mum say, "I hope she can eat something in a minute."

I realised we were going out for a meal. Eve got into the car and Dad turned the wheel to do a U-turn in the road to drive by a little village park and by the entrance to a school. Then we drove by some fields till we hit some more buildings until we stopped at a big pub that I knew was called Pacher's Pocket. Parked by loads of other cars I got worried until I heard Mum inside at the bar say, "Where's the Burr table please?" We were shown to a large table to hold twelve seats around and I saw the rest of the extended family sat there.

"Happy birthday Karen!" They all shouted in unison and I glowed before sitting down in the middle of everyone round the table. Everyone had a menu each and the waiter came round ten minutes later for us to order.

I said that, "I'd like some spaghetti Bolognese please,"£ then was asked what I'd like to drink and replied, "A Coca Cola as well please."

Fee, with eyes bigger than her belly, went for an adult's portion of half a chicken meal. Eve had beef and so did my parents. The extended family with Uncle Cyn, Aunty Caroline, Casey, Charlie, and both my grandparents order next and we sat and chatted. Then one by one they gave me cards and presents. I had to open them straight away although Dad told me to do it later. I remember having two cards from uncles, one that wasn't there, and one gave me a fiver in his card. My other one up in the Lake District given to me by Dad had a five pounds Boots voucher in. Everyone else gave me their cards and presents and then the waiter took it all away to put on a spare table next to us. I loved my record from one of my sisters that had the song 'First Time, First Love' by Robyn Beck on it. I was getting more elated and my grumpy mood was slowly going away. Somebody had put a huge helium birthday balloon by the table. By then all the food came out and we all tucked in eating and joking and laughing, even though I stayed quiet all through the meal. Half an hour later Eve and Fee were struggling. Dad looked over, I'd finished, and moaned at my sisters. Even Mum joined in and they said together. "Can you please just eat the meat for once you two? You know that the meats the most expensive part of the meal."

Eve finished. Fee moaned and groaned and in the end gave up. The family laughed as Mum said, "You've got eyes bigger than your belly again."

All patting our full stomachs the room suddenly went quiet. I became expectant as the mood changed around the table. The same waiter came back in with a big cake and everyone started singing happy birthday to you, and I felt a nice warm glow inside as the cake was put in front of me. Mum grinned with me and said, "Make a wish Karen." and I did want this feeling to last forever. We all tucked into a bit of cake for pudding and I had the biggest slice for a change. Thoroughly filled up and happy Dad ordered some hot drinks for the adults and they all had coffees with mint chocolates each. Us girls had cola each with ice, and it went very slowly down my throat tickling my insides with lovely refreshing ice taking away the burning sensation down my throat from all the chocolate I ate.

Uncle Cyn started laughing the loudest and we all turned to listen to him and Dad sharing a joke. It went over my head but I smiled at them both anyway.

Then Dad said, "Let's give a toast to Karen," even though I'd already started my drink.

"To Karen on her birthday," they all said in unison.

We all finished our drinks and happily fell out the front door joyfully laughing. I went quiet as I just enjoyed the merriment all around me.

Jumping in the car, after giving everyone hugs and kisses, we headed off home.

In the morning at school I remember feeling elated. I glided up the stairs taking two at a time, after being dropped off, to the form room for registration. Mrs Newman was her usual detached self from a daft boy who put his hand up and loudly shouted, "I'm not here!" And everyone burst into giggles and I groaned inwardly. It was an old joke.

Gliding to the next lesson across the other side of the corridor. We had, I noticed as I sat down a stand-in teacher from religious education who looked as rough as sandpaper called Mrs Robinson who had dyed blonde hair, but you could see her black roots. With my head down working hard on an adventure story. I wrote about a hot and randy couple in the jungle together finding a ram shackled building to sleep in. As they walked there they got into amazing adventures and there were locals who came after them. While they were walking together he gave her a hug with a pat on the bottom. Now this whole story was loosely based on a film called Jewel of the Nile with Michael Douglas and I adopted Dad's behaviour towards my Mum with the pat on the bum scene.

While everyone was working hard I heard a boy named Aaron being singled out for being gobby and he said "Fuck off," which wound up Mrs Robinson to the point of coming over to him. When she got to the table she yanked his ear that went bright red and said, "Now I'm taking you to the headmaster." I knew in my mind's eye that he was being dragged by the ear all the way downstairs.

I put my head back down to concentrate on my writing and I finished the whole story covering several pages before everyone else finished. because I'd looked round and some of the class were still working looking a bit sheepish and scared of the teacher. I leaned on my arms covering the book with my hands so as not to reveal to my teacher that I was doodling and the bell soon went for break time.

At the end of the day I went home with Mum in the car. At home I threw my front on the floor in front of the telly and watched it while doing my homework.

After de-mentally trying to get through as many maths book as I could. I got up afterward and spent a good two hours practicing on the piano.

When Dad came home that evening he sat with me on the sofa and had a bit of reminiscing with me. The stories just spilled out from the days of his youth while at the same school as me.

Apparently he'd been in what was a house group. One of four and they all had to win points for their houses. He told me of how they all looked after one another on the school field at lunch times. The older ones would organise rounders with the younger children while Dad and his friends would go and play football together with younger lads.

"One," he'd said, "I wagged school all day with my best friend, Mike Smith, to go off with him in his lorry. The next day after this I got told off and was offered a whip."

I looked at him horrified. Then he said with a glint in his eye "I got to choose a thin one or a thick one so I chose the thin one." He told me why, "Because the thin one only stung for a while and left a sore mark of which I ran to the cold tap outside the school and ran it over the sore bit to take the sting out with friends showing off my war wound as a badge of defiance."

I had an artificial laugh but with a twinkle in my eye not fully understanding his attitude but knew it was all a game to him. Trying to see the boy in him had been easy, it was the defiant side of me.

Next day I fought off extreme tiredness by stretching a lot and yarning a lot as Mum cried out to get out of bed.

"Your teas are on the floor," she said about half an hour before I actually got up. I picked up my tea and spat it out as it was cold. I had a biscuit out the tin and dunked it in my drink, it just crumbled and I didn't want it anymore. The drink and biscuit looked disgusting.

Washed, dressed and ready for downstairs in my uniform with ankle socks on I had my breakfast and sloped out the door stretching again and yawning. Mum got us to school just in time that morning and my first lesson was drama. In the lesson I got out my little book with my script in it and rad through Terry's lines again. I'd been early. The boys came in laughing about children in long white socks and found them hilarious. I was glad I had my ankle socks on and felt cool. The lesson started and we had to create a courtroom with the table and chairs. The jury was in a line of chairs down one side of the room. The Barrister had a desk and two desks in front were for the defence and the prosecutor with their clients. There was a chair to the right of the Barristers desk. As the courtroom drama was in process there was a camera that the teacher used to film us. We had a bright white light in our faces as we were videoed.

When it came to the jury scene that I was in the light behind the camera shone in my face brightly and I froze. then all I could remember to say was exactly what the person next to me had said. My right lines had completely gone out of my head so I just reiterated the previous comments blinking madly. The three other jury members tuck to their scripts and the blush I had for feeling an idiot soon went away.

> *Proverbs 12:15*
> *Stupid people always think they are right.*
> *Wise people listen to advice.*

There had been a hung jury so we had to do it all over again and the script had to be re-read because of my stupid reaction. The rest of the lesson we re-hashed the story. The beginning tied me up in knots as I knew we were gonna have to start again with the scenario announcement of the murder. We started with the witnesses. Then the Lawyers tied them up in knots. The one playing the Barrister got carried away with the hammer banging for order every two minutes and I got tied up in the stomach worried about my speech again. I'd been asked if I wanted any water. I said "Yes." My next line was when the jury went out of the room for deliberation to decide the court case. When we came back in they went through the jury one by one for the reasons of their answers and that camera was right in my face again with the light glaring at me and I was told just to say, "Yes," instead of the whole line that I forgot.

By the time of the end of the week it was Friday the thirteenth and Halloween month. Everyone at school kept on in the classroom to stay safe if we went trick or treating. The boys kept trying to scare us girls by getting in our faces about it being Friday the 13th but I didn't care 'cause as far as I was concerned I'd been born on the thirteenth and felt that it was a lucky number for me.

Come the Friday I rushed through my English language class by writing a stupid little story about two little boys from school who hated one another. They had endless scraps in the play yard over me and I didn't want the attention drawn to me. I hated the way the girls envied me as they were either the most bright intelligent little shit who was gorgeous or the most self-important little twat who thought every girl should have been after him. It was only seven pages long about a boy named James and Stuart. Two random names I picked right out of my head. After the fight when James won I walked off with him across the school yard to try and talk some sense into him about not getting into any more fights because I hated them. While all the girls swarmed over Stuart to help him out.

"I hate violence." I'd hung around him all afternoon but by the end he was having me in stitched telling me to grow up and that boys fight sometimes. Then he gingerly put his around me. It felt nice and tingly.

The bell went and I stopped dreaming. Pleased with my story I floated into the next lesson after lunch into a whole afternoon of craft, design and technology. I sat at my desk and my eyes glazed over at the blackboard. Twenty minutes later I woke up from my reverie and we were told to draw a diagram of how to make a wooden dog with a block of wood, a chisel and sandpaper and a little hammer. My diagram was overly simple so as the teacher pointed out while looking over my shoulder.

The school day ended without a catastrophe as I knew it would, because I always felt blessed on the thirteenth of each month. I walked home with my friend I'd made called Rheann.

At home I got changed into a big long skirt that made me feel beautiful that was beige and frilly with a white tight shirt that I tied up around the waist to look like a cowgirl shirt that shows your belly button.

While I sat in the living room Mum pulled out Haribo spooky sweets that were shaped like spiders, webs, rotten eggs, witches, cauldrons and pumpkins for us to dip into as she told us to encircle her on the floor. She said not to take too many as they were for later. Then Mum burst into a rendition of a story about a lady called Nancy Camel. Apparently she'd lived in the woods after being pushed out of her community. Then by gossip she was classed as a witch and she lived a very lonely life and children and adults were too scared to go by where she'd lived. This story gave me the creeps as Mum said she'd lived in local woods down by the steps. Being Halloween Mum enjoyed the scared look on our faces.

That evening Mum made us all hotdogs and put on creepy music in the background like War of the Worlds borrowed from our neighbours. Then the Thriller album. Fee decided we were to play a game called Murder in the Dark. We put names into a hat and pulled out one for the murderer. Then pulled out another for the detective and then one for the victim. Mother turned the light off then Eve the detective went outside the room. The murderer, who knew who they were, pushed the victim to the floor and we all screamed. Eve had to question us about the immediate situation until finding out the murderer amongst us.

Then we played the game again and I was the detective. The screams came and I had to ask who was the murderer?

I asked "Where were you?" To Dad, "When it happened."

He said, "By the window," he smiled and I thought he was lying.

To Fiona I asked, "Where were you when it happened?" She went quiet and said, "Well I sat on the sofa."

I knew that was obvious so I asked her straight out. "Was it you?" I looked at Dad who was still smiling and I asked "It was you wasn't it?" And they said, "It wasn't us." I went to the kitchen to find Eve and asked her "Did you do it?" And realised she'd gone to find food. I got confused over Mum's suspicious death and gave up questioning. I was pretty sure that it was Dad and said "It's you isn't it?" Again and felt fed up.

We went to play again and I turned all the lights off. Just as I did it there was a loud ring on the doorbell just as somebody screamed. Mum quickly turned the lights on and I followed her to the door after she told me to get the tub of Haribos. There were two little witches at the door who looked horrified they'd obviously seen the place go dark and heard us all scream.

Mum and I said, "Trick or treat?"

They said, "Treat please," so we delved into the pot and dropped a spider into each of their buckets. I sat down on the stairs with the sweets and waited for the doorbell to ring again in the dark and the coats hung up on the wall were giving me the creeps while Mum put the music back on and an evil voice was cackling at the end of the Thriller song. The bell rang out again and I jumped out of my skin.

Deuteronomy 1:17
Do not be afraid of anyone, for the decisions
you make come from God.

A ghost and a Gremlin stood at the door they both said "Trick or treat?" in unison and I said "Trick please." They told me a limerick and I gave them a handful of treats anyway. Mum came out and said, "You don't have to wait in the hallway in the dark Karen. You can come in the living room," so I did. Then she moaned "And not too many sweets at a time or we'll be passed out money next."

I sat on the sofa with my family and inwardly wished the creepy songs would turn off. Over the course of the evening endless streams of children turned up at the door literally begging for treats and Mum and us girls took it in turns giving out the sweets until it was getting really late so Mum told us to go to bed.

Two weeks later it was carnival time in Shepton and the school was buzzing as it was also mufty day. I'd gone in my jeans, t-shirt and a warm jumper. I had a pound in my pocket to give to the teacher for being able to wear my normal clothes, for a charity.

I went to my lesson about paper folding and we had a book of diagrams given to us to make things. There was a stack of paper on the desk and a stack of tracing paper next to it. We had a stand-in teacher for the morning she'd said as the others were either ill or training in another part of the school.

I found a nice complicated diagram to follow to make snowdrop hangings for a Christmas tree. I had to fold the bit of paper several times and copy an eighth of a picture that was really pretty. Then I had to cut round the picture and cut out the various holes that were different shapes. I undid the fold and had a sixteen pointed snow star. I punctured a hole in the top of the paper and strung some string through it which I was pleased with. I then did it again a couple more times.

Going back to the teacher's desk I picked up a handful of paper and sat down on my seat intending to be clever and do three at once but I encountered a bit of a disaster as I ended up shredding half the paper.

At lunch I ate with my mates that I'd been getting to know. There was Rebecca with her bright ginger hair, I felt envious of. Then there was Barbara who was fat, and had long brown hair and Emma who was quite tall, solid and dependable. Then there was Rheann. I got out my lunch box with my sandwiches, crisps, chocolate, fruit and drink.

We all sat around a blue hexagon table. Us girls chatted about the school and our lessons. Becky said she was struggling in class and Barbara and Emma said the same. They weren't in the same class as me as they were in the remedial set. I sat there quietly and let them talk.

Chapter Eight

In the afternoon I went to history class in the middle building down the corridor. I sat at a table at the back of the room by the door with Rheann and there was a boy who introduced himself as Simon. he was my build with a round face, dimples, freckles and with tight curly blonde hair. He wore spectacles and seemed quite bright. The three of us sat with our heads in our hands and I started writing on a bit of paper backwards for the first time and tried my name. It came out neraK in mirror writing. Rheann looked over my shoulder and pushed it to Simon to have a look. He cheekily laughed in his eyes, and asked what I'd written, it said 'hi my name is Karen'. Looking impressed he tried the same. He put hello in a ridiculous way so I got the paper and put it down in mirror writing properly. He didn't get it at first and tried again and put my name is Simon. He nearly got it so I had to help him. Mr Rees stopped talking and looked over at us and Simon was told to take the paper to him. He looked baffled and Rheann piped up and told him he'd need a mirror to read it. He scratched his ginger beard and said, "Don't do this again," But all three of us inwardly smirked. I stared at him and thought that Mr Rees looked like Henry the eighth. The lesson was boring but I managed to get a little bit of work done.

Come the end of the school day the sky had come with grey clouds in the air and I walked home with Rheann through the big park, towards West Shepton and on by the swimming pool towards home.

Sat on the sofa when I got home I felt nice and warm slumped out dreaming of being in America and living in the suburbs somewhere walking down the avenue with adults and children on roller boots and skateboards. My house had a porch with a big swing on the front. I'd been stuck in a movie I'd watched recently called 'The Goonies' about young children looking for treasure.

Dad came in after work and sat with me. Then talked me out of my reverie by talking about his childhood days and of when he got his first job of when he used to have a bicycle with a basket on the front with bread rolls, tin loafs, French sticks, and baps in. Dad said he would deliver the bread to his neighbours and the roads in his area for the local bakery. He told me that he just walked in and got the job on the spot just by asking. Dad also told me he'd had a job chopping off chicken heads and turkey heads for Christmas. He even described how the turkeys would run around the yard with no heads on and I could just see it out of the former of my eye.

Another day came and went to school. It was a Friday and I was looking forward to a charity event taking place on TV that night called Children in Need. The whole family sat and watched it and we enjoyed one daft stunt of bungee jumping for money. The celebrity was an idiot as they took off and they had to start again as he wasn't harness on right. This scenario raised hundreds of pounds. Then Roy Castle did a tap dance on a special floor that counted all his taps to break a world record. I sat watching completely enthralled captivated by the numbers. They went up by thousands and the money went up by millions.

There was a scene of hundreds of people behind a presenter in Blackpool urging a head shave of a beautiful long glamourous haired girl. Her eyes twinkled as she had the shave on live telly and raised twelve hundred pound and the crowd cheered. It was amazing. Mum pledged a five pounds a pound for all of us on the phone.

Come two o'clock in the morning the next day the programme had raised thirteen million pound. We finally went to bed feeling elated.

In the morning there was no Fee or Mum about and Dad, when I saw him, said they'd gone to Birmingham NEC to watch T'Pau.

Eve said, "Don't you pay any attention to what's ever going on around here?"

I instantly felt jealous and asked "Who have they gone to see?"

Dad said, "Carol Decker of T'Pau."

I couldn't believe it Mum had never taken me to a pop concert. I hated her for it.

Ecclesiastes 4:4
But it is useless. It is like chasing the wind.

I loved my sister but never myself enough to lie to myself for a while that she actually deserved it. Dad said later that Fiona had won the tickets.

I found myself that day reading a good book all about adventures by Enid Blyton. The book had an ephemera torch, pick axe, lunch box, compass, plus other things to use in a made up action adventure story that I could create myself. The stores ran from one different stage to another through different pages like it said, as I'd completed a task, to go to page 56 to carry on the adventure.

It was a Wednesday at school and I'd been told to wear my own clothes. I put on jeans, a shirt and a cardigan as I'd been told that it was a mufty day. I had to bring a pound to war my own clothes.

I liked shoes and I put on my Clarks shoes that were black and sensible. In the classroom that morning I got asked what I'd be doing in five years' time. I planned in my head an office job of where I got to do a lot of paperwork because I loved paperwork. I told the teacher and I had to write an essay about how my life would be. This was in English.

Then in maths I used my textbook and loved trying to get to the end of the book as quickly as I could and the teacher loved me but I just didn't realise as I always kept my head down and got on with things. At eh end of the day I was happy.

The next morning Fee came into my room and she lay on the bed with me to have a chat. I'd gotten undressed and was about to have a shower but stretched out on the bed. Chatting away Fiona absentmindedly ran her finger nails over my nipple which went hard and left me breathless. It had been one of those things and was never spoken about. I soon got in the shower and Fee had to wait for her turn.

Feeling cold coming out I shivered and dried as quick as I could. Putting on something warm and cosy my first thought was to go downstairs and put on for the Christmas films.

It was a cold morning outside as I could see out the front window so I curled up on the sofa in the warm. The telly flickered on at the touch of a button. The introduction song came on for Mary Poppins and my twelve year old self's eyes lit up as I knew I was about to be transported back in time to my much younger self. I loved the bright colours, the stereotypical costumes of a bankers upright upper middle class clothes. The words to the songs hit right on the button and got you swept along to every scene. Every now and again I felt looks from my sisters as I felt myself singing along. I was right in the moment when Mary Poppins and the children jumped into a chalked drawing and could still fully believe in the power of imagination years on from when I first watched the film. I glorified in singing the word Supercalifragilious to expealidocious very loudly. In my teens I felt that I should have been cooler, but in the safety of my own home I could get swept up in each moment to moment. Come Feed the Birds still had that magic twinge on my heart which gave a very bittersweet moment.

The end soon came when Mary took off into the wind on her umbrella and I felt elevated myself pretending in my mind that I could try that sometime with an umbrella in bad weather.

Mum soon called me out of my reverie for some sandwiches on the table and she said there were still pressies to be wrapped for Christmas. I shrank at the idea realising I had no presents for anyone so thought I could get out of wrapping. My sisters soon got stuck in with their presents for their friends and close relatives. Their banter was annoying me as I got stuck into another film on the telly called 'The Little Mermaid'. Following Ariel's adventures were more enthralling to me than heaps of paper to wrap resents with. I thought I'd averted doing something I never felt inclined to do. It came to the scene of where she sang to the prince on the shore and he fell in love with her voice. That voice haunted me throughout the film as she'd traded that voice with Ursula, a witch, for legs. I always loved the ending but was still caught up with that initial tear at the heart moment when she finally, out of desperation, got her voice back and the singing in my heart felt like it could last forever.

That same day we were told to dress up to go to church for a candlelight service. I couldn't really tear myself away from the telly as another film was half way through about a stray dog looking for owners after owners for affection. Too caught up in the telly I told Mum absentmindedly I wasn't getting changed as I was fine as I was.

Mum said, "Could you at least see to your face and comb your hair." I ran my fingers through my hair several times to get the knots out and went to the hallway to look in the mirror at my face. There was nothing wrong. Then Mum came at me with a warm flannel saying, "Let me sort your face out. There's black on your nose."

I squinted into the mirror, "No there's not Mum," and ended up biting into my flannel. I went "Ugh." I felt mortified and blushed. Dad came by with my gleaming black shoes. "I've cleaned them and polished them. Put them on please," He'd said.

Feeling like a princess, fussed over, I glided out the door being the last to get to the car. It annoyed me that Eve was waiting for me to get in as I hated sitting in the middle every time. Why didn't I say something? Because I didn't want to cause any arguments.

The church wasn't far to go and we soon pulled in the large car park at the bottom of town. We got out. I slammed a door and felt singled out yet again as dad told me not to bang the door so hard. Why couldn't my family just have a normal conversation with me instead of always giving orders. It really got on my nerves.

I gingerly held Mum's hand and we walked through the alleyway into the bottom of town. We crossed behind the library towards the front of St Peter and St Pauls imposing doors to allow us into the large church. The family entered by the left hand side door and picked up paraphernalia to help us learn the service and the carols. Another man held out a box with wax candles in cardboard to us to take to our seats.

The service covered the nativity of Jesus and we had to crane our necks as children re-enacted out the biblical story all over the aisles. With Mary and Joseph coming from the back of the church. The Wise Men came from the side aisle then we sand 'We Three Kings of Orient Are'. I loved singing and the sound of my own voice. We had sat by the right hand side door and after the song we sat down. I put my candle on the shelf behind the pew in front of where Eve's lovely hair hung down over. I was concentrating hard, with my eyes closed, on the Lord's Prayer and I heard Mum say, "What's that burning?"

I looked up and saw Eve's hair alight. She turned round angrily as I'd burned the back of her head. I didn't know where to look. I wanted the ground to swallow me up as everyone in the side pews turned to stare at us. I got told to blow my candle out and luckily there was only one more carol to sing before I hung my head to follow everyone back out of the church. No-one told me off as the stares did the trick.

Back at home Mum put on some stew for tea and everyone laughed at Eve. I didn't want to know and was soon back in the living room on the sofa watching the telly.

The next morning I sauntered downstairs after throwing some clothes on hoping to watch more Christmas TV and turned on vintage Wurzel Gummidge with Aunt Sally always wanting cram teas and a slice of cake. At some point the scarecrow gave me the hee-be gebees which meant scared me half to death as he unscrewed his head which looked so real. It tore at me inside and I had to keep on watching till he put his head back on. Now how Aunt Sally never fainted was beyond me.

I looked outside to the winter sun and saw my sisters out there with friends that came round but saw none of my friends. Without the encouragement of my friends they have never visited me. I had a small tear in my eye as I turned back towards the telly but felt in a strop so I sauntered outside anyway. I picked up some rope from the open garage to skip with hoping someone would notice me, but as I walked to the front of the house to be with my sisters everyone had disappeared and the front door was locked. I found myself picking up hula hoops, a pogo-stick and more jump ropes. I dumped them in the middle of the garage. I went to go inside but Dad came out and said, "Don't dump your toys there Karen as I need to put the car away later."

Feeling frustrated yet again that I couldn't get any company I sloped back into the living room of where Mum told me off for missing lunch. Apparently when I'd gone outside everyone had sandwiches and mine were left just for me. I asked Mum where everyone had gone she said, "Oh. They've gone to each other's houses."

I can't even remember who my friends were meant to be and fleetingly I wondered what Rheann, Becky, Emma and Barbara were up to. I knew where Rheann and Barbara lived.

Mum said, "Why don't you go round your friends' houses?"

So I took off down the steps towards Barbara's house. It was the only time I ever went round hers and the front door was wide open. I expected her house to be a tip as she was never a trend setter and always on the outskirts of normality, reminding me of a gypsy, to the rest of the world. The house was dark. It never occurred to me to call out if anyone was there. The place seemed empty. I want back through their hallway and out the front again and got putt off ever coming back as no-one was there. I went back up the steps towards home and watched cartoons on the telly instead like my favourite Ulysses, She-ra and He-man all set in a futuristic world. The fantasy world I seemed more at home with than reality that I was alone and into the evening when my sisters came home.

I got up from a cooked meal on the table early to watch more of the telly and found myself watching Dr Who of whom had a Tardis and scary robots saying they would exterminate me. I found myself hiding behind a pillow as the family watched this together. I felt a nice glow of having those I really loved around me.

This was Christmas Eve and we all had to go to bed early.

On Christmas day up with the lark, we were all excited and grabbed our pillowcases at the bottom of the bed stuffed with presents. I got the usual mixed box of chocolates and loads of other presents that were a bit boring really.

Later on after I'd fallen back to sleep. I got out of bed after hearing voices underneath my room. I sneaked downstairs rubbing sleepy dust out of my eyes. The family were having breakfast and were dressed. I was told to go back upstairs in my blue nightie to wash and dress. My usual orders were my only conversations so I did as I was told. The shower woke me up and I yawned making me choke on the water, so I coughed and soon got out. It was nearly lunch time and my stomach lurched ready for a huge turkey roast blow out of which we thoroughly enjoyed.

After helping washing up we all got our shoes on to get in the car to go to Nan burrs for the afternoon.

When we were there Uncle Keith, Aunty Sue and little Katy had stayed the night at Nan's. In the living room they sat around talking in French. With my limited knowledge I tried to join in and impress. Fee looked pissed off and then my Aunt and Uncle tried to get Katy, my cousin, to speak in German. I was well impressed realising the atmosphere had changed a little bit as I'd felt enlightened with new knowledge, as I loved learning other languages.

It was soon teatime and afterwards we all tried playing cards and as per usual Dad was winning everything. I loved competing and enjoyed the whole evening before my family made their final excuses and left.

On Boxing Day we would all go round Uncle Cyn's for a party. Today had been Gran and Gramps anniversary. At these parties would be Aunty Caroline, Charlie, Casey my cousins, Uncle Roy, Aunty Sue, my sisters and I with Mum and Dad and Gran's other relatives. Most of them would sit round the living room talking and enjoying the party food.

Grandad owned a karaoke machine that was kept out in the yellow walled back room. he loved to get it out at these parties and Mum would ask him to sing old carnival songs, particularly the old duck song. I loved to sing along to the Four and Twenty Virgin's song and the Down in the Valley song with Gramps. We would laugh together while singing and I would itch to take the mike off Granddad and hog it myself like Granddad would always do. I felt ignored as everyone was talking and I had nothing to talk about, it was boring.

As the evening drew on I got tired of listening to everyone else and wanted to go home. I'd eaten too much and felt bloated.

We woke up on the third of January on a brilliantly sunny day. The air outside was cold and crisp making our room feel cold as Mum had left the small window open all night. I'd yanked open the curtains to shut it and soon got washed and dressed.

Someone was crying in the kitchen I'd heard as I'd walked down the stairs. It sounded like Eve and I saw Hammy in her hands. She held him up to me and I saw blood coming out from his behind. Now Hammy was a hamster and my first thought that he was a girl and they'd got the sex wrong. Then I remembered Dad having done the test before so I knew it was a boy.

I heard Mum say to Eve, "We'll have to take him to the vets."

"Mum I'm scared why would he bleed out the back passage?"

I just stood there and watched as Mum pushed by me to get on the blower. I crouched down with Eve wanting to give her a cuddle but I held back waiting and listening for Mum on the phone. She soon came back in and said, "It'll be ok, we've got an appointment in twenty minutes so we'll go out the door now. Karen will you get your shoes on you're coming with us."

I thought "What about Fee." She wasn't there and so us three trooped out the door to the car. All across town by the school we went to the vets just before the lights along Charlton Road.

I remember sitting in the car. I had no interest in going inside.

The car was parked by the side of the road and Mum and Eve were ages, when they came back Eve was in floods of tears.

Mum said, "We just had a little burial ceremony for Hammy, so be quiet Karen."

I sank back in my seat not knowing what to say anyway as eve in floods of tears just sat there with her shoulders hunched over. We were both strapped in so I stared out the window thinking that my sister just needed to cry things out as Mum steered the car back home.

After we got back I decided to slope off to the local park by the swimming pool. It gave me a chance to maintain my own perspective on life that everybody and living creatures had to die sometimes. I never voiced this opinion to anyone as I was well aware I sounded cold. Even to my own ears but that had been my cold hard clarity. I pushed myself to get a lovely thrill running through my body as I went higher and higher on the swings. Even twirling the chains round as tight as a bow string gave me a thrill as I just let go to spin round ultra-fast back the other way.

After finishing in the park I got back on my bike and rode around the whole of the estate going by the familiar houses. I inhaled the air with an impertinent nose and pushed the bike into third gear pedalling harder before coming back down Coombe View hill of where I flew passed the house going down to Linda's road. There was a garage open that showed a very old but up together black classic car. I put my foot on the floor and stayed there watching a man tinker underneath it. The shine on it gleamed in the afternoon sun. I was well impressed. Now I'd been told to come back in time for tea and my estimations of time were pretty good. I'd had nothing but a t-shirt on with nothing covering my arms and as it got cooler I could feel a tingling while sun got dimmer in the sky. I smelled cooking come from a house so went through a passageway of where Jo lived and went halfway round the circle again back to home for tea. I wasn't that bothered about food but knew I had to be home.

At the drive way I had a favourite hymn reverberating round my head called 'Colours of Day'. The words floated inside my brain with me inwardly just knowing 'Colours of Day', dawn into the mind, the sun has come up, the evening's behind and I whistled simultaneously with the words. I felt happy and light hearted as I approached the dinner table of where Eve, Fee, Mum and Dad sat.

"You're here in time then," Dad said, and I looked up at him with my eyes shining. Not aware anymore that anything sad had just happened. Mum noticed my hair flopping in my eyes and recommended a haircut. I said, "Sure."

After being back at school for a while the weeks soon slipped into the next month when it was Fee's birthday.

At school one morning I remember a fight breaking out during the lunch break about a watch between Rheann, my best friend, and an idiot called Richard. He accused her of stealing it. The argument took place by the side of the canteen on a pathway next to the netball courts. It was me who'd spotted a teacher called Mr Beasley watching the incident while in his usual tracksuit bottoms. He'd shouted after Richard but the bell went for after lunch and as Rheann was the closest he told her to explain what was going on to the head teacher Mr Schofield. I went to the head with her and sat outside waiting. When she came out she looked vaguely petulant. I mean I would never had used that word before to describe her personality as he was normally cock sure and arrogant. This made her look vulnerable to me as tears sprang to her eyes. I remembered that evil Richard asking the teacher for him to help him get his watch back, but I knew my friend wouldn't steal. She wasn't the type and had been there to defend her but was never asked if I knew anything or what I'd witnessed. I walked on late to my next lesson after Rheann thanked me for being there and she walked in the opposite direction.

It was French. I sat down by the wall and overheard everything said perfectly but my eyes glazed over as I stared at the picture caption sheet. It looked like, in every picture, someone was asking for something as they pointed to bread I put Je voudrais du pain s'il vous plait. Then they pointed to what I thought was a bottle of wine so I put Je voudrais du vin si'il vois plait. The milk and other necessities like cheese and peas. I chose the easiest way to write this only changing one word each time as it became Je voudrais du petit pois s'il vous plait.

French was too easy and in my head I parroted to myself all the lines in my sexiest French accent.

It was soon home time as it was Fee's birthday. We all sat in front of the telly in the living room waiting for guests to turn up. They were Katherine, Claire and Helen for Eve for her birthday tea. For ages beforehand we all sat around decadently talking because to me we all should have talked about what was going on out in the real world like poverty homelessness, wars, and diseases. I wanted a debate about what had been on the news lately but all I'd heard was what who had been where and when with her other friends she knew at school and felt totally lost with their gossip going on and on all around me. Eve knew where to chip in and seemed to know the children they were gossiping about as the conversation progressed onto which girls were going out with which boyfriend. I inwardly yawned genuinely not knowing what they were going on about. At least they were happy.

Tea came and went with pretentious little fondants, sandwiches, dips with carrots and celery, bowls of crisps and a trifle. Afterwards Mum turned out the lights and she carried a big sponge cake in with fourteen candles on. Then we burst into spontaneous song and I yelled to Fee to make a wish. Then she blew her candles out with a poof of an exhalation of air.

After the decadent little tea party we sat around with hot beverages. I had Coca-Cola with lots of ice, I'd helped Mum make the day before in an ice tray. I was pleased with myself that I had helped but still couldn't join in with the conversations about what I thought were completely inane subjects like how the girls got rid of zits. I never had any trouble. Then they started on about cream over their faces and cucumbers over their eyes.

Fee and Katherine the hypochondriac of whom had a cast on that day on her leg tried the cream and cucumber thing after her other friends went on first. I remember Mum taking a photograph of them laid out on the sofa together. I'd gotten into the armchair feeling pushed out so I'd put the telly on.

Come eight o'clock everyone finally went home and us girls got to stay up late on a school night and I remember watching Nightmare on Elm Street. It gave us the creeps. Now all night long I'd heard Fee shout out at every noise she heard all night long. Every time I woke up intermittently to another moan or scream from Fee being scared of slight noises and creeks all up the stairs.

In the morning, downstairs, I remember Fee put on her shoes and sat on the sofa with Mum and I overheard Mum saying something comforting to her, so I poked my head around the door. I saw Mum tuck strays of hair behind Fee's ears saying, "Why become scared of ghosts Fee. It's real people you should be scare of. She burst into tears and they cuddled. Just watch out for strangers Fee," she said and I remember thinking that I couldn't have put that better myself. I wished I'd gotten in with those words as my mind went blank to any more consolable words.

I put my shoes on in the hallway getting ready for going out the door for school. That day I had a chemistry lesson and we used blue and green chemicals that we dripped one by one into a tube on a piece of gauze over a Bunsen burner blazing a strong flame. I remember a bang noise as the chemicals mixed together in the heat. I didn't know what they were called but the answers were in the instructions on the board of which afterwards I assumed we just had to copy down. I made my work look aesthetically pleasing with a bright colourful graph of how different elements mixed together culminated into different coloured clouds of mist and different smells.

Then in history with Mr Rees we did a pop quiz of dates to see if we remembered dates that wars and battles took place in. I never spoke up as the one I really knew came and went as Simon knew that 1066 was the Battle of Hastings. Battle of the Somme came up and the War of the Roses. I got stuck on the latter struggling to remember the date as the lesson flew by. I never realised I had to write several passages from my history book down too as I found myself writing a note passed round from Rheann to Simon in mirror writing. I*t said please help I want to get out of here. I could tell by their smiles they wanted it to.

After school that day at four o'clock I got to Mrs Bosley's my piano teacher's house in Wells. As I walked in clutching my music bag there was a familiar smell of cooked cabbages. I took it to mean that they were doing some sort of a casserole for later. At the stool there had been another girl with long brunette coloured hair and a pleasing countenance with a long pleated skirt and nice blouse on. She turned to me as Mrs Bosley introduced us, "Afternoon Karen," she said, "This is Louise, Louise this is Karen. You will be duetting for the next music festival at Longwell Green at Weston."

We were to have three months to practice and straight away Louise and I hit it off. As usual I sat on the left hand side to keep the beat as this was my stronger side of playing any music. The hour soon flew by as Mrs Bosley kept pushing us to attempt the whole tune so that by the time we left the song resounded round our heads so that Louise and I knew perfectly well practicing what it should sound like.

Our parents soon got us and they stayed for introductions and a bit of a chat. Mr Bosley came out and said "Hello," and I remember his bald head, beauty spots on his face and wonky teeth.

Then on Saturday morning I sat in front of live TV with Ant, Dec and Cat Deeley being prats on SM:TV live. I sat on the sofa inwardly laughing and secretly fancied Declan with a gorgeous twinkle in his eye. While sat in front of the television I day dreamed of being on an old Carry On movie set of where there was an old dusty road with a desert either side and an old ram shackled wooden house was there on the right hand side. I got the impression it was the Carry On Cowboy set as to the left I walked into an editing suite or a music studio. There was a huge console with lots of buttons and lights blinking on it with audio visuals written and cut ins, cut aways, and megahertz and all the other stuff written under the control switches. I knew from then onwards that I didn't want to be alone in the world as I knew it was an old abandoned movie set with nobody else there. I'd felt abandoned, bereft from everyone. I got the impression that the movie industry was a lonely place to be.

> *Lamentations 3:28*
> *When we suffer, we should sit alone*
> *in silent practice.*

That day the loneliness stayed with me as I went to the park up the road on my own to spend a few good hours on the swings and trying to swing high enough to see over the wall of the open air swimming pool. I'd dare myself to get so high as the top bar on the swings without losing control.

Into Sunday after coming home from church with Mum and Nan the day was panning out to be an open road full of possibilities for my future.

Then on the next morning I set off for school with a spring in my set while jumping into the car. Mum yawned, let off the brake as we rolled to life down the driveway with the engine struggling to kick in. It was a cold February morning and Mum had asked me to put the window down to clear it of a thin frost. I did it with a crackling noise and was afraid I was cracking the window. Mum had on the wipers to the bottom of the driveway until the windscreen cleared. I watched her look out the left window into the side mirrors of which I used to gaze at myself in all the way to school as I looked out the window myself. All the way there I'd been looking forward to lessons and seeing my mates.

At the little car park we always pulled in at the top of a long slope I got out and practically ran into school feeling shivery once out of the car into the frosty air. I could see the air freeze as I exhaled. I did Dad's trick and deliberately blew as much hot air from my mouth into my hands and rubbed them together. My rucksack with my books in was always slung over my back. It was black with red stripes and was always proud of the good condition I kept it in.

> *Proverbs 18:11*
> *Rich people, however, imagine that their wealth protects*
> *Them like high, strong walls around a city.*

I always felt my main folders edges though through my clothes that my timetable was in along with spare lined paper and extra work I did. I made registration on time and had been glad to get the rucksack off my shoulders. My left shoulder blade twitched and sent a shiver down my spine. I rubbed the back of my neck flexing my muscles in my arms as I did so not paying the teacher or anyone else any attention. I was the only Karen in the class and was used to giving an automatic response, "Yes," to my name. I heard Damion quip, "That's my name don't wear it out."

I never looked round but I felt the amusement in the atmosphere too geared up for the coming lessons. I even found myself for once flicking open my black folder to make sure, from my timetable, where and what my first lesson was. It was geography. We all stayed with our form teacher Mr Badman for our first lesson. It was about all the European countries in the world and all I had to do was not get drawn into saying one of them that got put on the board as everyone else got drawn into competing with one another to say them out loud. I just wrote diligently all the names in my text book as they got called out.

Well that lesson seemed confusing. Was I supposed to learn the country names in Europe or was it just something else designed to prove I was doing work in the classroom? I learned nothing. I remembered the usual names England, Eire, Northern Ireland, Scotland, France and the Nederland's etc., but I already knew them. I felt that the teacher was just filling in an hours lesson was something they just made up to do on the spot. Was this teacher deranged or something 'cause I swear he knew I twigged that he hadn't prepared by winking at me? I'd eyed him up and down at the time and he looked like a big huggy bear. Had he been thin his looks would have encompassed classically handsome with black hair, nice height, and yeah what could have been tight buttocks had he not let himself go.

I sashayed down the communal stairs to the next lesson halfway down into the door on the right into the rusty coloured carpeted room. The drama room.

The teacher Mr Casey came in and said, "Margaret Thatcher," really loudly, "What does that name mean to you?" Without waiting for a response knowing it was a rhetorical question he launched into emulating spiel about the last Prime Minister of the country England. Was she the best woman ever for the job?

I realised that I needed my orange drama text book and wrote down furiously all the good points of having a female Prime Minister.

"Why are you writing?" The voice said sharply, "Just look at me and think. I am telling you your next assignment."

My head snapped up to look at him and in embarrassment realised that Mr Casey had made everyone look at me.

"Our assignment is to write a script emulating the greatest Prime Minister of the country to encapsulate the epitome of all countries leaders."

We had to write this down I was sure of it for a heading. Then we had to re-arrange the chairs to act out his little script to show us exactly how to set our word for word to write an excellent adaptation.

At the end of the lesson I was sure how to do the homework set to make up a play all on my own.

Four lessons later Mum took me shopping after school into Wells to where I knew I was finally going to get to feel like a grown up. She took me into a big clothes store and asked the lady to measure me for my first ever bra. The lady put the measuring tape around under the boobs as she told me to put my arms up. I'd been told I was 36cms round and then she looked at my boobs and measured round the nipples over my t-shirt and told me I was an A cup size. I got a white training bra and felt all grown up while Mum encouraged me to get two of them to start me off. Then she hurried me up as we had to get going to Louise's house in Croscombe. It was the girl I'd met at my last piano lesson.

I walked up to her bungalow that looked quite posh on an incline. There was a nice, well kept, sloping garden with neatly placed colourful flowers dotted around the borders and over rocks to hang down all in different shades of red, orange, yellow and violets, encapsulating a beautiful riot of colours with a well-kept mown lawn in the middle. The bungalow was attractive from the outside of where the walls looked freshly white painted and I poked my head through the window before pushing the doorbell. Clutching my music in my arms I stilled my nervous bossom that I could feel my heart race erratically behind.

I got led into her living room, the décor was soft cream colours and at the end wall was a big keyboard on a stand. The first words that sprang to mind was what a heathen. I preferred my proper upright fifty-two white keyed Zender piano. It was snobbish to feel this way I know and I'd had to get over myself. I said hello to her and her mother and father. I followed their outstretched arm pointing out the keyboard to slowly move my immobilised self towards a seat in front of the keys. I found myself blush at them because I couldn't help but look down my nose at this situation.

Louise's father offered us a drink and we both said yes to orange cordial. It was placed on the coffee table behind us. I went to put up my music and shook out the tension in my neck that had built up briefly. I had to get over myself and I'd, out loud, started to tap my foot and count in my head to start playing in time with her. My hands were steady ploughing through the beat pulsating through my body. In tune with her playing and noticing her notes at the same time. I realised when she tripped over keys and missed out beats with her next notes.

At the end I said, "Let's start again." We played the tune more slowly so that the top tune she was playing could fit in perfectly with my bass beat. Five times we kept going over it till we were both satisfied we matched each other to make the sound right. We both looked at each other and knew it was time for a drink. I sank into her nice soft sofa and decadently with my left hand sipped my drink as I was very aware of the expensive furniture and didn't want to spill anything.

We chatted about the up and coming festival and decided we'd pick her up along the way and take her. Mum sounded pleased with our practice as she'd sat there the entire time working out what was going to happen in a couple of months' time.

We were soon saying our goodbyes and thank you's arranging when Louise would come to our house to practice and I pretentiously thought on a real piano.

On the way home I looked forward to seeing everyone and Mum went straight to the kitchen to make our tea. I sat in the living room with everyone with their heads in the TV for once begging for silence around them so that they could listen to it. My head was buzzing though as I'd actually wanted a conversation for once about heathens with keyboards instead of having proper pianos.

The oven smells wafted into the living room and feeling deflated realising no-one would match my point of view. I got up and realised my favourite Fray Bentos steak and kidney pie was part of our tea. I tucked in, cheered up and didn't pursue the conversations I wanted to have.

In the morning I went to school and had an idiosyncrasy that drove me mad because my Mum had told me to do one thing and my sisters were telling me to do something else. I had my own ideas of how to be. I didn't want to keep my long hair but everyone's opinions were clashing with mine.

In first class I spoke in an American accent with a wry smile to Rheann. She laughed and led me to a derangement that showed me that I loved her as the biggest matriarch in school. The derangement was lying. I didn't like lying but knew where she was coming from.

Sat next to a boy I got slightly embarrassed as the lady talked about body functions. I thought too hard and a little squeak came out my bottom. Now feeling slightly mortified I blushed and the boy sat next to me moved away slightly. I felt hurt at the movement feeling rejected. The whole lesson went over my head as I wallowed in feeling rejected.

Psalms 31:12
I am like something thrown away.

Later on that day I had a light bulb moment and helped a girl in class next to me in understanding some big words. I actually felt pleased I helped her as she parroted back the sentences she put the words in and could see the pride of her work in her face.

After school I walked home with Fee for once as I spotted her at the front gates on her own. We walked partially in silence and partially talking. On the way we walked over to the fields down the bottom of the steps and up Bowlish Hill.

It was such a lovely day and we lazed out in a field that sloped down to the road by a river. Chatting away we decided to while the time away counting cars. I'd said I'll take the blue ones and she'd said I'll take the red ones. Annoyingly mainly white cars and vans flew down the road into Croscombe. I got to count to about fifteen and Fiona counted twenty in between giggling as she tried to engage me in a gossip that I didn't understand. My gut reaction to gossip every time was that I didn't like it.

Ten more cars each later I sensed Fee was getting bored with the game but I could have quite happily played it forever totally caught up in the happiness of the moment. I lounged out on my back and put my arms behind my head and stung my elbow on a stinging nettle. I didn't care I felt really happy. At forty eight vehicles and Fee had reached fifty she was itching to go home. A little bit annoyed. I stretched and got up to follow her all the way home.

At home when we got there the first person we noticed was Eve and Fee went off to talk with her. I felt a little bit envious but relieved that the gossiping Fee would rather talk to Eve. Those two I felt always shared secrets making me feel left out but strangely off the hook so that I could concentrate on the telly and homework. Home and Away came on and then I got called for tea up to the table. Dad sat at the head of the table. Mum sat at the other end. Fee and Eve sat on one side and me on the other in front of the wall. The food was delicious and I ate all of it. I smiled up at my father and he winked at me. Then I softened. My sisters noticed and kept talking about their day and gossiped about their friends. I used to shy away from gossip just not getting it. How they found so much to say about other people I just don't know. I'd thought it was boring.

I finished eating first and slipped off my seat to switch the telly on and Dad told me to switch over for the news. I sat on the sofa with my head in my hands concentrating on why there was so much evil in the world. There'd been another death of a young lady who'd been night clubbing a few months before and they'd found her body dumped somewhere.

Dad interrupted my maudlin thoughts and asked me did I know the answer to a cryptic clue in a crossword from the newspaper. I smiled up at him again knowing he was distracting me from the harshness of the news report.

I said, "Look Dad can I do your Puzzler?" not really knowing the answer to his cryptic question.

His eyes smiled at me as he'd rolled up his Puzzler and tapped me on the head with it.

I said, "Thanks Dad," and went looking for some colouring pencils in the welsh dresser in the dining room. I sat back down with the rest of the family and found a colours-by-numbers picture that I knew was easy. I was there for an hour colouring in diligently all the colours in the rainbow, a nice scene of sky, balloons, two trees, a rainbow and a clown in a field. Now 1 represented blue, 2 represented orange, 3 yellow, 4 red and 5 green. I took liberty and used different shades of green to do the foliage to add depth to the picture.

To make myself intellectual I did a skeleton puzzle. I worked out where to put several black squares into the grid asymmetrically as much as I could to match the question numbers and started to answer the question. In another hour I completed the puzzle feeling smarter than the average bear as I had Yogi Bear in the back of my mind and I laughed. It was a Friday and Dad told us that a friend had been away for the week in the land of Down Under and he'd brought back Dad as a present a didgeridoo. A musical instrument that was a long wooden cylindrical object that people blow into.

He showed it to me that evening while we were all still glued to the television and he pointed out that it was all in the tongue action. I tried it and my lips went fuzzy as I blew too hard on it. I laughed and blushed briefly from the power needed in the puffing. Dad passed it to Eve and the first time she blew into it, it made a loud boom noise and I got jealous wanting to do the same.

Proverbs 14:30
Peace of mind makes the body healthy,
But jealousy is like a cancer.

Eve sat there for a while and made lots of noises with it. I was itching to have another go. I'd blown into it twice whereas Eve was getting carried away with it and used the didgeridoo several times.

My sisters took themselves up to bed early and I seized my chance by taking the didgeridoo back from the corner of the living room where the stereo was and tried again. My lips kept going fuzzy as I kept blowing too hard and getting red in the face all over again. I got all jealous again and wouldn't give it up till I got a noise from it. I blew lightly tapping my foot at the same time imagining a beat to intro into it and I shocked myself by producing a little loud boom from it. I was that deranged to do it. I realised the time and took myself up to bed and slipped into my cute little blue nightie. The girliest item I had to wear.

The weekend started the next morning and I jumped out of bed to get into the shower. I went downstairs in my clothes for breakfast. It was toast and jam which tasted delicious with a cup of tea. I sidled down from the chair to turn on the television to watch my favourite presenters on live TV. I loved Saturday viewing and was happy slouched on the sofa.

Back at school on the Monday I started humming a hymn in class stuck in my head from Sunday, my favourite one Colours of Day annoying everybody but wasn't aware of it. Church had been so full of life that day before with everyone emulating Christ and god all morning with prayers and other adulations.

Now this was a nice physical education lesson of where we're country dancing round the main hall doing the dosey-dough. I thoroughly enjoyed the exercise with the boys dancing around. Holding their hands and mooning over them, particularly Aaron of whom I enjoyed watching his hips wiggle. Feeling free, dancing around, the lesson was soon over.

At the end of the school day Rheann and I went round her house for the first time. We went into the kitchen for a drink and they had all the mod cons. Her mum reached for two glasses from the dishwasher and asked us what we wanted. I asked for orange juice. I looked around me and propped myself up on the side and liked the warm colours in the room admiring the cleanliness of the cupboards and sides. I took a sip of my drink and Rheann said, "Let's go upstairs for a chat."

We walked by the dining room on the way into the hallway and I couldn't resist a peek into the dining room. They had long heavy dark brown curtains hanging down over what I assumed were French doors behind a music stand with a double bass propped up next to it of which was behind the table and chairs.

Rheann said to me, "That's my mother's. She is learning the instrument."

I felt impressed and followed my new friend upstairs by a few pictures on the wall as I looked around me I felt a warm family spirit in the home. In her room we sat on her bed. I surveyed the place which had pink walls and lots of personal things lying about. Now my friend was keen to talk about her family. "I've got two brothers Evan and Glyn," and I asked, "Which is which?"

She replied, "Well Evan is the blonde curly haired one of whom is the middle child and there's Glyn who's got jet black hair who is the youngest."

I propped my head on my hands lazing on the bed getting comfy and let her go on. "Then there's Meesha and Moneesha my cousins," she said. I thought of mine Casey, Charlie, Katy, Lyn and Scott but let her speak. It didn't feel like we were there long before I decided to leave and walk down the road to the bottom of Bowlish Hill to walk up the lane to the steps leading home. I floated all the way back feeling cool, calm and collected to tea on the table just as I got in. I felt famished and ate it all up very quickly before settling down for the evening.

The next day at school I found myself glazing over my books first lesson with my mind elsewhere really and strained to concentrate. The work seemed pretty straight forward but because it was easy I was able to push what I had to do to the back of my mind thinking I'd do it later. My mind wandered again as the bell went. I slung on my coat and pushed my hands into my pockets thinking of the next lesson.

Chemistry was not my strongest point and couldn't focus properly in the lesson. I was getting a headache but enjoyed just setting up an experiment on my desk that included the usual Bunsen burner. The ephemera had pictures of the utensils involved and instructions of what to do. The room was cold and I felt like my headache was beginning to go as I put in the minimum of effort on my experiment. It seemed easy and I filled in the results in the most simplest way possible.

Dragging my ass over to the next lesson over the other side of the school I was looking forward to lunch as my stomach was growling. The next class was maths. I enjoyed maths and really put all my effort into it. We were being introduced to trigonometry. I sort of understood and got out my green pencil case. I had a protractor, a ruler and a calculator ready for the lesson. What we were learning was a bit confusing but I never dared ask what to do. I liked to figure things out by myself.

At lunch time I met up with Rheann and we ate together in the canteen before deciding to go outside the school grounds. We went outside the side doors from the canteen to walk round by the tennis courts and the sandpit to find the stile at the back of the school.

We were soon in the bottom of town walking round the shops. Rheann and I lost track of time a bit and decided to walk back to school through the grounds again. The school field was deathly quiet and there was no-one about. My next lesson was in the science building and I walked fast to the room of where I'd been due to take my craft, design, and technology lesson. I got the look of death from my male teacher as I turned up halfway through the lesson but got largely ignored. There was writing on the blackboard that I wrote down as quickly as possible while everyone else seemed to be making something and I started carving an otter out of wood before the end of the lesson that I stuck on to a smooth stick that went into a stand. I sanded it all down as best I could and varnished it. This had been a double lesson and was pleased that I caught up by the end of it. I was gasping for a drink and didn't speak to anyone as the boys discussed the lesson with the teacher. I'd always been impressed with those who could talk to teachers as I couldn't.

There were two more lessons before the end of the day and at home I remember having a conversation with Mum about my day. I can recall mother saying to me that there's more than one way to skin a cat. I think she was proud of the way I'd caught up in my CDT lesson that day. I liked her praise as it came very rarely about school work to my face.

Needing a release of some emotions I began to practice the piano. I loved the feeling of my fingers running fast over the keys. I did my scales first and went through all of them over and over again. I had such a rush of emotions that drove me to play three songs I was learning. One was a classic tune, a French one I think, and the others just sounded beautiful to my ears. I raced over the keys too fast really as I gained more and more confidence in my playing.

That afternoon, afterwards, I heard Mum and Dad discussing taking down the glass doors in between the dining room and the living room and was worried I wouldn't get any more privacy on the piano. I never voiced my fears though.

Chapter Nine

That evening I picked up a good book I'd been reading by Alexander Dumar. D'Artagnan defeated an army and got to be one of the Three Musketeers' with Porthos, Athos and Aramis. I loved the book as the backdrop of France really came to life through the power of the brilliant words. In the background while I was reading the telly was on and I laughed as a cartoon ironically was on about a dog called Dogtanian. It was a cute take on the story of The Three Musketeers'.

That night as I crawled into bed I slept soundly and awoke very full of myself feeling a strong life force coursing through me.

Psalms 37:4
Seek your happiness in the Lord,
And he will give you your heart's desire.

I felt so alive as Mum dropped me off at school. I loved the lesson of French that day as we did orations and I loved my sexy voice. Ooh la la I thought as I skipped to my second lesson of biology in the science block. We were talking about the biological make up of frogs and I thought to myself I hope we don't have to dissect them. One class made even put her hand up and asked that very question and the whole class squirmed out loud with a loud groan. "Ooh," we all said and the teacher replied, "We don't do that anymore."

All the groans put me off wanting to know anything about the rest of it and ended up completely forgetting the work.

I was soon on the way to a morning's break for tuck that I didn't want but it was a chance to get fresh air and I loved standing around outside in the cool air, while everyone else got some food.

I talked to Becky and she told me about a boy she fancied called Gary. I smiled wondering how they would get together and saw it in my mind's eye that they'd make a lovely couple. Now Barbara and Emma were nearby and looked jealous of our talking. I liked the jealousy vibe and kept talking to Rebecca till the end of the break. I then walked into the maths block to go and sit down for a lesson that I actually liked and understood. Numbers were my friends as they never changed. You could rely on them. I waded through the lesson a bit though getting slightly stuck on trigonometry again. I'd wished I'd asked about it but just never had the nerve but diligently, bit by bit, made my way through the book. Halfway through the lesson the teacher called me to the front to mark my work she said that she hadn't marked it for ages. I had to stand there as she ticked more than crossed out what I'd done so I became pleased with what I'd done and stopped worrying so much.

> *Deuteronomy 30:11*
> *"The command that I'm giving you today is not*
> *Too difficult or beyond your reach."*

Then I sat down feeling strangely elated that what I was doing was nearly actually right.

The next lesson was history and I had fun reading about a large National Trust house and the lineage and owners of it.

Come the end of the day I walked home with my friends and at home Eve was there first and I heard about a doctor's appointment she'd had the day before about a knee problem. I knew this problem had been going on for a while but for some reason the doctors couldn't get to the bottom of it.

In the living room while we all sat down Eve was in the armchair facing the front window and her knee was bare so I placed my hand on her knee and it tingled then went really hot. I warmed up Eve's knee by it and I really believed that I could heal her. My hand stayed there for a long time radiating the whole area with heat and her knee went pink. I'd said a little prayer in my head for Jesus to help me heal her until the area went cold and I moved my hand away.

Eve said, "That felt nice. I can't feel any pain anymore." I smiled and thought it was freaky but I'd cured her. I just knew it and felt happy for the rest of the day.

The evening soon went by and the next day I awoke to the loud chirping of the birds outside. It took me a while to realise that it was a weekend. I'd had a bit of a nightmare that I was struggling through an air vent that I'd felt trapped in crawling around, I think it had something to do with a move I'd watched called Die Hard not so long ago on the telly.

That morning I found a book in my sister, Fiona's room, called Hollywood Wives by Jackie Collins. Now within the first few pages a girl was touching herself washing in a shack. I felt turned on and thought this was going to be a good book. I settled into it on the sofa not aware of what anyone else was doing and read half of the book and learned a lot about relationships in Hollywood. Come mid-morning though I'd had enough and found a game to play with my sisters of whom wanted to play Ludo. It was fun with the different coloured counters. I wanted to be blue the other colours were red, yellow and green. Fee was red and Eve was yellow. The game went on for a long time as the dice were giving low scores. It was fun though until lunch as we had to keep going until Eve won. I won twice. Fee three times and I never really worried about winning anyway. Eve was happy winning twice in the end as Mum made us a hot meal. We were all famished enticed by the nice smells.

It was all soon gobbled up and we needed a bit of bread and butter each to go with it, and also glasses of lemonade of which we liked.

It wasn't a lot but it was Eve's birthday celebrations that afternoon and her friends turned up at about three o'clock of whom were Kelly, Helen and a few others. It was her tenth birthday. We had a lot of pop and little sandwiches with tit bits covered up on the table ready for five o'clock Mum said.

We played a game of musical bumps. Fee didn't want to bother but there was six of us to play. Mum started the music. We started to dance and wiggled around with our arms in the air and our feet barely moving already wanting to collapse on our bottoms. Mum pressed stop and we fell on the floor. I fell backwards and hurt my back and soon shot upright. Then I was out as I was the last one to sit down, but was thankfully to be relegated to the soft sofa watching everybody else. The friends were openly daring each other to move more by holding each other's hands to do twirls, but mid one Mum turned the music off again and Eve and Kelly fell on top of each other laughing after twirling. Mum said they were both out. Helena and the other two were still in looking as though they were smiling in their eyes. I knew they all thought they were going to win but the other two got out two stops later. Helen won and got a bag of jelly babies before they played again twice. I knew Mum fixed it so that the birthday girl won one game.

Then Eve started to demand another game called pass the parcel. They all sat round on the floor in a circle and even fourteen year old Fiona wanted to join in this time. Mum put on a record of a pop song and pulled the arm across to start it. Then a package got passed around the group of seven with every now and again just dropping it into each other's laps. They laughed each time as they didn't want to give the parcel away to each other but Mum stopped the music at me. I tore open the paper and found more paper underneath. It was quite a large package and I tried to guess what was underneath. It felt squidgy and I imagined more sweets. I soon got told to pass it round the group again as the music had got restarted. It was fun as some pushed the parcel around quickly to get it back to them before the music stopped again at Fiona who carefully unwrapped the next layer. There was nothing there. Five more stops later it landed on Kelly B and she unwrapped the last layer to find a bag of boiled sweets.

Afterwards we sat around giving Eve her presents and she beamed up at us as she opened them to find a big eagle kite from Mum and Dad that they put away in the welsh dresser saying we'd use it during the summer months. She also got I Could Be So Lucky by Kylie Minogue on record and the first Live Aid record to help feed the world they'd said on the telly. She got other nice presents and we were soon having the tasty food up at the table.

Everyone laughed and joked. We were all soon singing happy birthday to Eve as Mum bought out a lovely sponge cake that I drooled all over.

I said out loud, "Make a wish."

Eve then went pink in the cheeks as she blew her candles out. I secretly wanted to know her wish as I prayed for it to come true.

The evening ended wonderfully as her friends went on home and it was soon Sunday morning with us getting all up for church. In our warm clothes we were soon sat on the cold pews listening to the sermon that was all about love as I listened to a part of James gospel and I smiled really believing I understood. Then afterwards we all stayed for coffees and cups of tea while Mum and Dad stayed and chatted to their friends. Pat and her husband of whom I thought looked and sounded like nice people. I knew they ran the local jewellers in town. I willed them all on to get out of church and we were soon home looking forward to a roast dinner. It was delicious that nice roast beef, carrots, swede, Brussel sprouts and roast potatoes. I looked forward to going outside in the sunshine to play. I soon came in again bored and sat down at the piano instead to go over and over again my favourite pieces for a concert coming up. I sat there for a couple of hours loving the sound of the keys always enthralled by the wonderful music I could eek out by my fingers.

I heard Eve asked when was tea?

Mum moaned, "Didn't you have enough at lunch?"

Fee chipped in, "Couldn't you make us some sandwiches?"

She said, "Fine. I've got some beef left over. Sit to the table the three of you." but I kept playing on the keys on my piano.

Fee said, "Can't you stop that Karen?" I tried to ignore her. Then Mum piped up, "Two more minutes Karen and you must sit down at the table."

I heard a groan from my sisters but I didn't care I loved the sound I made. Mum then came in balancing three plates in her hand and moaned at Eve, "Get your books off the table then Eve."

I was reminded of the book I started to read and thought I'd pick it up again after tea. The beef and mustard sandwiches were delicious and afterwards we finished off Eve's birthday cake. I licked my fingers and my lips as they got sticky from the soft icing.

Mum looked at me and said, "Wash your hands please. All of you. Before you touch anything."

We all went to the kitchen and used the Fairy to wash our hands. My sisters offered to wash up but soon disappeared and I was left to help to do all of it with Mum while Dad was outside cleaning the car she said and we had a bit of a chat. The sun streamed through the window shrouding us into a perfect moment in time.

School next day was lovely. Everyone seemed happy and I bumped into a girl called Nicki on my lunch break who said, "Hello."

I said, "Hello." Too and looked right through her as I wondered where my friends were for lunch so I had to seek them out.

The end of the school day came and Mum decided to take us to Nanny. She's in Wells.

My sisters said to Mum, "Happy anniversary." I joined in realising it was March eighteenth. I mentally did the maths and realised it was their fifteenth anniversary. Then blushed a bit mortified as I hadn't got them anything.

At Nan's family were there to make a fuss over Mum and Dad. They had a chocolate cake, my favourite part of the afternoon. Now my cousins were there and my uncle and aunts all chatting happily away as I tucked into the cake. I took it into the living room with Casey, Charlie, Fee, Eve and Lyn and Scott. I turned the telly on and let everyone speak around me about life and love. I wondered what they all had to talk so much about. I caught parts of the conversations and couldn't make head or tail of why they repeated themselves.

2 Samuel 22:29
You, Lord are my light; you dispel my darkness.

It wasn't like the clear conversations that were obvious on the telly that always seemed to have more of a purpose. They all rambled on as I got into Neighbours and followed the lives of those on Ramsay Street. Scott and Charlene were walking down the aisle together and I had a little tear in my eye. The music was very touching as they played flashbacks of the best parts of their relationship. I didn't want to miss this. The brandy snaps, that were delicious, got handed around.

Everyone came into the living room afterwards to watch the news and I got a nice arm and cosy feeling with my family all around me. I got asked if I wanted a drink. I said, "Yes please," and had a cordial. I gulped it down greedily as if I'd been dying of thirst. Dad stood up, and jangled his keys in his pocket and said, "We'd better go home." and so with a groan we all got up for our coats and trudged out the door down the passageway to the road. The car wasn't that far away. Just round the corner in front of the pub and we were soon on our way home.

That evening the family watched Surprise, Surprise with Cilla Black, Bob Carolgees and Spit the dog. Fee, Eve and I loved to sing the song how Cilla sang it with her Liverpudlian accent. The words were 'Surprise, Surprise. The unexpected hits you between the eyes'. We always laughed mimicking her.

I finished Hollywood Wives that evening and was shocked when the main character set a boat alight. I wanted a nice story to read afterward.

A week later we went back up to Nan's again just to see her and have a bit of tea. Now Aunty Nola was there with her dog Kipper and I nearly tripped over him as he ran at me licking my hand. I touched his nose and Mum told me that a wet nose was the sign of a happy dog. He yapped. We laughed and I held his paw to shake it like I always did saying, "How do you do?" and grinned to myself giving him a little treat that was a bone to chew. I looked at Aunty Nola and she was happy with me. Looking more beautiful than ever I talked to her happily asking her how she'd been. She told me what she'd been up to and I asked her about Uncle Graham. Apparently he was at work.

There was a lovely smell coming from the cooker. It was a huge pot of stew that we went on to have some of with the lovely doughboys in that Granddad had made. It was delicious with chunks of carrot in and swede, and other vegetables with nice chunks of potatoes in with a nice stewing mix. Mum stood with Nan in the kitchen afterward to help wash up with Aunty Nola helping to. Us girls sat in the kitchen having been told to wait for pudding.

> *Amos 8:11*
> *People will be hungry, but not for bread; they will be thirsty*
> *But not for water.*

Nan's signature for sticky toffee pudding was coming to be put in the microwave with nice hot custard. my mouth was watering as I couldn't wait. Then listened for the ping of the microwave knowing that it was coming. Hot and steaming on the table I mashed it up to let the steam come out before tucking into it. It was sickenly sweet and very delicious. Afterwards we all said, "Thank you," my Nan and Gramps seemed pleased with us.

Now I'd bought a new book along about a Mrs Pepperpot a spin off from Mary Poppins. It was in a green hard back edition of one of the books from a series. I sat in the living room zoning out to everything else completely absorbed in a fantasy world.

The next day in the morning I had to put my bathing suit and towel in a bag for a swimming lesson that afternoon. The sun had a habit of making me leap out of bed and having put all my books in my rucksack too I was soon out the door for school. Still managing to get in late for registration. I could put up with anything. I was happy. Nothing could get me down.

In Home Economics, Mrs Feebrey, was having us sew all lesson which was time consuming enough and couldn't wait for swimming. Wandering around to the English building for French I'd started to learn the male and female words for objects. We couldn't say anything out loud but I'd have loved to practice my French accent. Katherine was sat in front of me as I'd overheard her gossiping. It was always about the other girls. I wasn't interested, although, if I had been a gossip she'd have been the best person to gossip with.

About half an hour after eating lunch my stomach was growling again because I hadn't eaten much but was just as well as we were being frogmarched across town to the public swimming pool. I could always get changed quickly and we were all soon lined up along the deep end ready to take it in turns to dive under the water for a black breeze block. Easy, peasey, but the water in the outdoor pool was freezing especially in the most shaded spot in the pool. We all had two turns at diving under the water and it was a pain in the ass waiting for turns. Freezing cold and still hungry when I got out I raced into the cubicle to change and to get an ice-cream at the little shop before traipsing all across town to get back to school which was a pain as I lived only down the road from the lido.

During the summer of this year my family and I went to Doone Valley to ride horses. I remember the horses coming out of the paddock through the big gate and us trotting up a hill through a lot of trees to the open fields of bracken. There we were allowed to gallop. I was surprised at how fast my horse ran leaving Eve at the back. Next thing I knew there was a scream and I turned round to see Eve flat on her backside in the gorse having fallen off her horse. I couldn't stop myself from smiling. As we trotted back towards the stables through the trees my horse stopped suddenly to eat a patch of grass and I started sliding down his neck and had trouble pulling his neck up. The guide had to do it for me. Trotting down through all of the fir trees we ended up back at the stables and the guide came to give me their hand to help me down then they helped Eve and the others alight.

Mum and Dad had been for an hours walk while we'd been riding and they met us at the gate in front of the stables yard.

I felt invigorated from being on the horse but Eve was just glad we'd got back. The trainer told my parents what had happened. My horse had been named Silver and we were allowed to feed our horses as a thank you. I got given an apple to give to my horse and gave them a pat on the nose and I'd said, "Thank you," to my horse anyway.

We then all went for a walk together and found a small little church tucked away into a hillside. Mum loved taking us around churches and she'd told us the story of Lorna Doone and of how her shot gun wedding was supposed to have taken place where we were. I visualised a woman in a tight white lacey dress stretching at the seams over a baby bump and someone actually standing over her with a shot gun. I stifled a giggle.

Coming out of the church we began to walk back to the car of which we carved up the countryside in to get back home. Dad loved to take us the scenic route.

The next day I got up early and was the first one in the shower singing away happily a Madonna song called Holiday. Now while I'd euphorically danced around all morning getting ready for school. I pissed everyone else off when getting into the car by banging the door shut too hard. Mum told me off.

At school there were two lessons about a classic book by dickens called Great Expectations and all I got from reading it out, as there was no teacher, was there'd been an old woman sitting in a grand dining room wearing a wedding dress with cobwebs everywhere. The rest of the book never made sense. I'd propped myself on my arms yawning trying not to go to sleep. Apparently the teacher had been ill as the deputy head told us what to do.

Later at lunch time I'd sat by the window with the sun streaming across my face. I sat with another group of girls for once of whom didn't seem to mind me sitting with them. One girl was a lovely blonde called Shelley who always spoke to me with her fit friend Vicky. I talked to them briefly and they were both kind to me and made me feel popular as I ate my sandwiches with a little bit of turkey, lettuce, cucumber, and a bit of salt sprinkled over the top. I munched away at my salt 'n' vinegar crisps. Passing them around Vicky and Shelley took a crisp each and said, "Thank you," they made me feel happy and warm inside. I then nibbled on my choccy bar that was a Marathon and my favourite. For a drink I had a Coca-Cola bottle that made my lips feel fuzzy trying to drink out of that little hole at the top. I wanted to ask the dinner ladies really if I could have had a glass. After the meal the other two said, "See you around," and they sauntered off together looking happy. Then I spotted Rheann outside and went to talk to her and spoke about my other friends Becky, Barbara and Emma.

Now a Sarah walked by looking pretty with lovely dark curly hair and said, "Hello." Then Rheann and I had a chat with her. She was scrawny looking but nice. Then an Emma Race joined her friend Sarah. They got chatting and they walked away leaving me with Rheann and we went up the field together having a laugh and a joke.

On the field we sat on the grass. I kept looking towards the sand pit as there was a gang of girls throwing someone up and down counting up to fifteen. Then they dropped her in the sand. I thought that was cruel.

Now in the next class after lunch I found myself doodling on my hands a phone number that Rheann gave me for her house. I remember it very well 4549, with the area code at the front. Then I concentrated hard on my lessons for the afternoon praying inside to just wanting to get home.

In the afternoon the following day word had gotten around school that Richard's watch had still not been found. Rheann and I were walking towards the crowd of children on the play yard by the tennis courts. A teacher came towards her from the science block pass the front of the courts and they yelled and signalled across to Rheann to go to the headmasters again. He even pointed to his watch I figured she was lip reading back, "Why?" I'd had my face to the crowd and one girl was shouting obscenities in my face saying in between intelligible words saying it was about time my best friend towed the line and stopped getting away with so much. I slapped her down by shouting, "I am English you know and not deaf stop being horrible about my best friend!" And she backed off. I had rolled up my sleeves before hand to just face the cow out.

I went down the corridor afterwards towards the head's office intending to wait with her and she was there pacing the floor completely on edge. It wasn't long after I'd showed my face that she went in to see Mr Schofield so I sat outside on a chair waiting for yer yet again for the same issue. It seemed to take ages and I'd been expecting shouting from behind the door but it was eerily quiet. I flicked through a magazine waving about my face like a fan.

I ended up missing out on lunch that day after a non-contrite Rheann came towards me. I believe she was off the hook.

In social education that afternoon we went through safe sexual practices and STIs. They brought along different samples of varying condoms and a diaphragm. They explained that STI stood for Sexually Transmitted Infections. This was the days when AIDS were all over the media and the teacher got complete attention. The protection got passed around and the embarrassed laughs and crude comments came from the boys. Up on the board was two diagrams, one of being an inside picture of the vagina as they demonstrated how and where the diaphragm was. The teacher made the mistake of passing around a life sized dick to practice putting condoms as some of the boys started to blow into them trill they were huge making jokes that their dicks were bigger than that. Much hilarity followed from that but not me. The girls were pissed off. I could sense the attitude, so the life sized penis got put away before all the samples were ruined. I still ended the lesson confused as to how a diaphragm was mean to be used.

I met up with Rheann by the school gates with Becky, Emma, and Barbara to walk home together. Emma left us to go through the park and all across town Becky and Rheann did most of the gossiping. I just chipped in where necessary. When we'd gotten as far as West Shepton, Barbara disappeared down Bowlish Lane as we went up the hill onto the new estate towards Rheann's house.

Outside her home Rheann's mother greeted us and Becky explained to Mrs Griffiths about what happened at school and I'd overheard Rheann's mum say that obviously Becky was the better friend. I felt hurt and left my friends to it to turn round and go back home crying.

Psalms 31:9
My eyes are tired from so much crying;
I am completely worn out.

In the morning I went to school laughing my head off inside with a skippity skip. Very few things made me laugh but the Big Breakfast on Channel 4 that morning made me laugh and I pictured in my mind's eye the egg in the cup on the blue and white checked table cloth. I recalled Denise Van Outen's last joke with Chis Evans. It was hilarious and I'd have loved to have phoned them up that morning to play their games.

In school I sat like a good girl in history class daydreaming of working in the telly while Mr Rees handed out work books with all the Tudors in. It was for our next assignment. I looked at one man in a picture looking dark, dangerous and horny with his whiter ruffles around his neck on his shirt. I felt a nice sensation between my legs.

After the lesson I floated off airily to cookery class and I found Miss Jackson there first setting out pots and pans on the desk. She told me that there were assignment sheets for us to come up with our a la carte menus. I'd forgotten my ingredients and I soon remembered I was going to make a casserole. I was gonna cheat with for pudding to just be put into a microwave.

"I've forgotten my ingredients Miss."

"You'll have to sit this one out then Karen and write a new menu during the lesson instead."

I sat there bored the whole lesson just dreaming up mainly sweet puddings. I put down for starters soup of the days, prawn cocktail, pate on toast, and garlic mushrooms. For main meals I put a salad, a roast, and a vegetarian pie. For puddings I put down apple crumble, hot chocolate fudge cake with ice-cream, and a cheesecake. The whole task was too easy and I saw Miss Jackson's all-knowing look that told me, "I knew you'd do this."

It was soon lunch time and not long before I was back in class doing maths. The teacher always let us get on with things and I put my head down working ferociously through my maths number to number in each book.

Next lesson was stupid as I plonked myself down in the science block. I'd dropped my bag and all my stuff went all over the floor. I felt like an idiot but Nicky came by and helped pick up my books. I really liked him. I considered him a friend and if he'd asked me out I'd have said yes, instead I said "Thank you," and asked him how his day was.

"It's fine thanks." He was the most popular boy in school as he was handsome and a very nice person who had time for everyone.

I sat down at the desk at the front of the room and glazed at the board. My eyes went funny and my contacts dried out so one fell out and I had to rush to the toilet. I put my hand up and the teacher let me leave. In the toilet I took out my other lense and washed them in solution and let them stand in their pots for ten minutes. I didn't care about chemistry anyway but was soon back in class with them in my eyes.

After school Mum took me shopping in town and we went in New Look as Mum said that I needed a new jumper. We looked through endless rails. Some were nice but too fluffy and I knew they'd go up my nose and make me sneeze. Mum got fed up with me being choosy and told me to grow up. She got my back up and I never answered her. She suggested we go to Yeovil. I said "Yes please," thinking we'd trail the shops. Mum saw my expression, "No we're not trailing the shops. We're just looking for a new school jumper and a shirt. You're looking scruffy lately. Your school kit needs updating."

"I need my hair cut first remember," Mum looked at her watch and said "We'd better go see Ashley at GJs in the middle of town." Ashley was my cousin third removed as he was my Nan's brother's third eldest.

Mum took us girls to Asda shopping down at Yeovil to find our school clothes and once there I fell in love with a turtle neck jumper that was navy with a lovely design on. I knew it was going to be my favourite.

I felt fantastic with my new haircut as Ashley had cut it before swishing about half way down my back.

At the start of the new term day there'd been a lot of fuss about a boy band having been in town as part of touring the country during the summer holidays. I hadn't read any papers with it in but picked up the gossip from overheard snippets of conversation. Some girls thought they were hot. I'd never heard of them being a mainstream band. Apparently they'd been a big group from the seventies that, my parents had never mentioned before.

The teacher was late to take the register that morning and the boys were pissing about sticking their hands up and saying, "I'm not here," or "I'm here," before their names were called. I just smiled vacantly loving the atmosphere.

I drifted absentmindedly from one lesson to the next that day not taking in the new timetable we'd had to stick in our black binders that morning. I'd felt a bit lost going towards first lesson following the wrong groups of kids losing my fellow classmates so I poked my head round each door in turn as I walked about. I was lucky. The first door I looked through the window of my friends were in so I just walked to the nearest available chair and sat down. My eyes started to glaze at the pink chalk all over the blackboard and from the back of the room I couldn't see what they were writing about. Teachers rarely ever used other coloured chalks besides white. I had to go to the board after lesson to start taking down the notes and became late for my next class.

The communal stairway was taunting me. Up or down so I looked at my new timetable and thought French right or was it drama? I hadn't had time to fill in the blanks that morning so went to the door to the left and everyone was already in there. Luckily the teacher hadn't appeared yet, but when Mr Casey appeared full of books he actually apologised for being late and dumped his load on the first table he came to, expecting us to pick up a book each. They were orange booklets with very basic storylines in for a couple of drama exercises. The exercises had poses in for us to enact and stay still in the moment of say a charade of a court case. This took an hour to complete as he went round three groups of us studying the differences in our interpretations of the same story. We were told to write about why we interpreted the scenes we posed for homework.

At lunch Rheann and I went for a walk round the perimeter of the grounds to look for a way out, but it wasn't until we were back by the tennis courts we spotted a stile leading down into a housing area. Rheann stood by a low hanging wall by the edge of the grass, so I took the opportunity to tackle her about the missing watch as she had one on her writs I'd never noticed before. My friend just stood there and took it. All my shit. She just shook the watch in front of me as if to say what but at least my anger came and went just like that. Then we decided to sneak off the grounds to go for a walk.

Less than an hour later Rheann and I turned up to registration in our own classes just on time for the bell. Starting the afternoon all wheezy with my nose running from being out in the cold my afternoon lesson came and went in the blink of an eye.

The last lesson of the day was a bit dull as the teacher monotonously droned on and on about the same thing as the week before as no-one had got the homework right. The lights in the room flickered as we heard a thunderstorm rage overhead. Some of us were looking out the window as dark clouds rumbled overhead. I'd been glad Rheann and I made the most of the good weather at lunch time. I could only dream of what the day would be like at the end of the week for my thirteenth birthday and was looking forward to it.

That next morning starting the day full of anticipation for what was to come I noticed the sun was streaming through the curtains smiling down on us. Throwing on my school uniform that was neatly pressed I was actually on time that morning for form room and the boys were good for once. After registration I wafted around the room flashing my legs in front of everyone. I felt cool.

Five minutes into the next lesson I studied hard and didn't notice any distractions going on around me. With my head down and focusing hard I tried to keep my hand writing as neat as possible writing a whole essay about a book we'd been reading of the future. I stretched out my lovely legs feeling the warmth seeping through my loins. Enjoying every sensation. I put my left leg across the other leg and sat up straight thinking I'd been going asleep. I blinked a couple of times and played with my eyelashes to get the sleepy dust out while yawning like made amazed I'd made it in to the lesson while half asleep. Over my shoulder I saw the teacher approach me as I'd gone to doodle on the book so I shaded my hand. My hair fell over my face and the teacher went the left side of me so I flicked the text book open again so that she could pull the work towards her and have a brief look. The teacher gave a toothy smile so my eyes twinkled back.

She said, "Good work. Lovely and neat." and walked off to the next unsuspecting victim. Pleased I'd finished the essay by the end of the lesson. I'd flicked back and forth through endless books to do the report for the next subject that morning.

Come break time I went out to enjoy the sunshine. Rheann and I went to queue for the tuck shop but the line was too long. Then we wandered around the school rounds while talking about gossip then the bell rang.

Starting mid-morning group discussions in class I found myself just letting the others speak animated around me in a circle. I could understand what they said perfectly but had no inclination to offer any opinion of my own as none sprang to mind. One thing went round and round in my head but everyone was sharing different variations of my thoughts anyway. While listening I got out my note book to write down actual opposing views to keep my analysis very clear offering my opinion as they talked in my note book ready to write up on A4 later. Yawning and stretching as I put my pen and paper away everyone shot me a look which I ignored.

My hair being half way down my back that day with the sides pulled back I felt very beautiful but was realising fast that no boys ever wanted to ask me out so I resolved to myself to dress more sexy. It was a subconscious decision that day to wear tighter clothes to emphasis my pert shape.

At dinner break Rheann disappeared as I'd got talking to Lisa, Rachel and others by the tennis courts. I told them that it was my thirteenth birthday the next day so next thing I knew seven of them were grabbing my legs and arms flicking me up into the air. They'd said that they were giving me the bumps. While moving towards the sandpit I started to wriggle about kicking wildly and throwing my whole body about convulsively until I'd managed to connect my foot hard with someone's stomach and they let my feet go. One foot went on the edge of the sand before they dropped me over it. I wobbled a bit and became free and ran off glad I hadn't been completely covered in sand. I'd picked up my school bag where I'd dropped it by the playing courts and headed towards the canteen of where I ended up sitting down round the big octagon shaped blue table with Rheann.

After that lunch time in class I'd felt really smug knowing I'd gotten away from those nasty children outside. Starting the farts was a young lad who looked Mediterranean and scrawny. He was a new boy desperate to fit in trying to cause a giggle which never came and I felt his embarrassment.

Flicking my hair over my head I just turned over another page of my curricularised texts in front of me desperate to know what some big words meant. Keeping my head down I'd heard my father's voice echoing inside my brain for me to just do exactly that. I kept out the way just picturing Dad having just had a thin cane at school then going to the outside tap to keep the sting away. Day dreaming while scribbling away desperate to make sense of what I was writing. My eyes glazed over for a second and water streamed from them making them sting. My head started to pound concentrating too hard by the end of that lesson. I was wishing I'd put my hand up about the two words I didn't understand.

Walking home later I still had that same pounding headache. My nose and eyes were streaming. I'd ascertained the pollen must have been high that day and tried refraining from wiping my nose in my sleeve.

At home I asked Mum for a handkerchief and Mum came to me saying, "Here have one of your Dad's." I took it gratefully giving my nose a big blow. I went cross-eyed for a second and noticed my nose was bright red. Fee popped her head round the door offering a pamper session upstairs she wanted to show me.

In her room Fee got me to kneel on the floor as she carefully brushed my hair talking about giving me a French plait. Fiona had a firm but tender approach with her hands as she deftly but surely started to make knot after knot using lots of strands all down the back of my head. This took about half an hour before she grabbed a hair band from her nightstand to wrap my strand of hair up.

"There," she said, "I hope that makes you feel better," and I looked through a desk mirror while Fiona had a hand held one to the side of my head to show me what a French braid looked like. I really liked it and told her, "Thanks Fee," as some colour came back in my cheeks from the warm room. It looked really good and resolved myself then and there to attempt this plait in my hair again sometime. I then turned to her knowing that my eldest sister was expecting me to attempt something with her hair. Fiona sat in front of me in the same way but as her locks were very fine I'd tried unsuccessfully to knot them together in the same way. I eventually dug my nails into her had making her flinch so I dropped my hands admitting that I couldn't do anything with it.

Mum called from downstairs for tea and said that bangers, mash and peas were on the table. I raced down feeling hungry soon sitting erect at the dining room table as Mum milled around putting everything out.

> *Isaiah 55:2*
> *Listen to me and do what I say, and you*
> *will enjoy the best food of all.*

It was manna from heaven for my cold which resulted in me using my hankie a lot and Dod told me off for sneezing over my food.

"I can't help it." I squeaked out with my voice sounding annoying to my own ears all of which made me sneeze more so Mum got up to make me a glass of water as it was soon placed by my plate. I sipped slowly letting the steam off the food waft up my nostrils as I ate noisily not too aware that I'd been chamming away. The food tasted delicious and warmed up my belly. A nice hot crumble with custard came afterwards and I didn't have the guts to ask for more skin as Mum had always split it up equally.

Getting up from the table afterwards the others offered to dry up but as usual I ended up doing it all with Mum. Mum then asked me if I had some piano playing to get on with so I sat back in the dining room on the piano stool for a long session of scales.

Now that weekend I'd heard a new song on the radio by Madonna called La Isla Bonita and I found myself tinkling on the right notes with my right hand creating the tune. I did this over and over again with it sounding amazing of which I'd really liked and did it so many times with all the words to the song going through my head so I sang them out loud. This was done a few times before I heard a shut up from Mum of whom went on to say, "Please play something else your sisters are getting annoyed."

The faith in my heart of always being able to play was so strong I sat there till bedtime trying the first bars of a song over and over again of a song called The Gavotte until I could push myself to finishing the whole tune.

That night I had a dreamless sleep for once then the next day as I awoke I'd actually heard a cockerel crowing. I stretched out and one hand hit the head board and it hurt.

Mum came in the room with what I assumed was our usual tea and biscuits, but as I'd jumped down of the top bunk I spied pink and yellow fairy cakes with our drinks. Mum smiled as Fee came in and then Eve and Mum burst into a rendition of 'Happy birthday to you, happy birthday to you, happy birthday dear Karen, happy birthday to you'.

They were all soon pressing cards into my hands urging me to open their ones first. My face glowed as I tore them open and beamed at the lovely words and looked into their eyes one by one to say thank you to each of them. Mum promptly said I'd have to wait till the afternoon after school to get my presents.

It was a rush to get into the bathroom after that with Fee and Eve squabbling for time in there together. I just waited for my chance. Today was my birthday and I was feeling glad.

The school never acknowledged my birthday but my friends in turn that day, Becky, Emma, Barbara, Rheann, Caroline, Hayley and Rosie, Lisa and Rachel all gave me a card each when they saw me whether in the classroom or outside during break times. I'd asked them all to come to my party after school but I knew deep down that Wanstrow and the surrounding villages of where most of them came from were too far away for them to come from.

My school day swam by and I remember walking back to mine with my main friends Becky and Rheann in tow. Barbara and Emma said that they'd catch up with me later after going home first to get changed. When I got back with my two friends I ran upstairs to quickly get changed into black leggings and a tight shirt. I quickly brushed my hair out to return downstairs. Mum yelled out she had a surprise for me later. I just assumed that Mum was on about my present.

I had to go outside when downstairs and in the garage all the tools had been covered up and Dad had positioned a shiny disco ball into the main light. A big car torch was on full beam at the side of the room and a cassette playing out the hits of the day from a Now tape. My friends followed me outside. I tried boogying to a couple of tunes to get the party started but no-one was interested in dancing so we went indoors.

The table had been covered in food so we all sat down and tucked in with everyone a bit quiet. It was nice as I'd remembered everyone's presents having been placed in bags by the sofa ready for later. The food was delicious as I fingered it all not quite knowing what to have next. Mum soon turned all the lights out and I noticed a chocolate continental cake with candles on as everyone burst into a rendition of happy birthday.

Half an hour alter while sat in the living room everyone passed me their presents and I'd been enthralled at the seemingly endless gifts even though I'd twigged most of them came from Mum and Dad. Drinks were passed round and then I thought that if I got up and headed into the garage that everyone would follow me. Fee followed me and we had a boogie to a couple of songs but no-one else came out. Perhaps it was because it was cold in the garage? I'd felt cold and a bit despondent no-one else came out so went back inside. My friends were still chatting with drinks in their hands and it was cosy inside until about eight o'clock until everyone had to leave. They said their goodbyes and I thanked them all in turn for coming.

Then I remembered I'd had a Tiffany record from someone so I put it on the turntable on Mum and Dad's hi-fi for a dance. I'd gotten up my family for a dance to that one and was happy. Mum said to put on a party album after and to turn the sound down as the table had been cleared and Dad got out the Scrabble board. Everyone paired up except me as I'd been the little English genius in the family and I started with the worst letters possible. An 'X' and 'Y'. It took me ages to get the letters out. Dad had an Oxford dictionary close to hand for all of us, but I couldn't be bothered to use it. Dad always took his time on his turn with Eve and Fee with Mum whom had the giggles as they placed the letters for something rude. I seized my chance with the Y to turn that word into something else and got stuck with two more letters. Dad looked over his glasses to study the letters left in front of him and had to turn to the dictionary we were all waiting for him to make his move. Each letter was meticulously placed around the board creating a new ending to one word and creating a whole new word when he declared he was out. Mum and Fee looked baffled and couldn't go and I realised that

I'd been stuck with a couple of consonants that I couldn't use. We counted them up and I lost. It had been a brilliant birthday anyway and I basked in the glow of the warmth of my family.

In the evening the next day we watched a movie at the cinema into Wells at The Regal. We had seats upstairs and we sat in the front row so that I could lean on the wall at the bottom to look at the screen underneath. It was an action thriller with a James Bond in. I got geared up for lots of thrills and spills with loads of gadgets and hot 'n' horny women of whom I adulated and loved. I looked at the film in a daze and there was a chase in a speed boat and the camera zoomed in on a woman spy who looked just like me having lots of fun. I loved her clothes she looked glamourous and at the end of the film I had to stay for the music.

In the morning there was a disaster on the news. There was a terrorist attack that killed a baby up in London in a café and I watched it on Channel Four news on The Big Breakfast. I was getting ready for school and I had a memory block about a piece of work to hand in at school. Through my head I found a dilemma I was going to have to make it up for my assignment for English. My book was a classic that I missed while being ill and I panicked.

In school that day I felt out of place in the lesson and zoned out to what we had to do next. I saw everyone hand in their work a bit baffled.

In a girls toilet I found a used condom in a sink and threw it in the bin. Afterward I'd heard a rumour during lunch that the boys had been found messing about in the girls' toilets. Outside there was a wet patch by the canteen and I figured out they'd been filling condoms with water and had been throwing them about like they were balloons.

After lunch a boy named Rocky challenged me to a contest during a lesson as to whom would complete their word search first. This was in a social education lesson situated in the science block. I found my words methodically from the top, from left to right, eyeing up each individual letter and every letter around them. I found two words this way that were down the list in alphabetical order. The letter 'C' came next for chemistry words. I looked across at Rocky and he laughed at me so I glazed and tried to find words without being too methodical expecting them to leap out at me. Some did and I looked up at Rocky and his friends were laughing I was determined to win this contest. I drew out the lines down the words in order getting faster and faster and I surprised myself when I finished as I shouted out that I'd done it. I could see Rocky was still writing and was jubilant that I won.

This was the last lesson of the day, and at home I couldn't stop smiling and was surprised that no-one asked me what I was grinning about.

Now after having getting a buzz out of doing that word search I found one of Dad's monthly Puzzlers and flicked through to each word search pushing myself to do them really quickly before I could settle down. The first one I did methodically but instead of ringing the letters of which took time I just put a line through each of them. I'd convinced myself it shaved off half the time and noticed it was a puzzle I could send off through the post. The left over letters though had to be put together left to right to create a saying that was: 'Nothing easy is worth doing if it's worth doing well'. I filled in the form and cut it out. Finding an envelope I went through Mum's purse but couldn't find a stamp. Then Mum made me jump as I put it back.

> *Psalms 51:3*
> *I recognise my faults;*
> *I am always conscious of my sins.*

"Mum, do you have any stamps?" I asked and she replied, "Look in the Welsh Dresser I think there are some in my black purse."

I found it straight away and said, "Thanks Mum."

"What are you sending through the post anyway?"

"A competition in Dad's Puzzler." Dad walked in at that point and quipped. "Make sure you win it," and he grinned at me. I did two more word searches and did a bit of homework in front of the TV and I had a relaxed evening.

In the morning I got up very early with Dad and we had breakfast together. Dad soon took my bowl away to wash up. I grabbed my shoes and coat then put them on as Dad sat on the stairs tying up his laces. He went to the coat hooks by the door too and grabbed his denim jacket. He told me to wait there while he got his bicycle from the garage. It was a large dark green bike with a cross bar in the middle that I sat on and rode with him side saddle. I gripped onto the handle bars as hard as possible and down the drive way the bike wobbled a little. I felt a little bit scared but Dad just encouraged me to hold on tighter. All across the estate, then down into the road of Great Ostry through Hillmead and under the bridge we soon turned up at the Showerings lorry yard. Dad said, once he'd chained up his bike, "I need to find my lorry and we need to wait for it to be loaded up this morning."

I grinned up at him and we soon found his cab and he said, "Get up on in and wait for me." So I clambered up on in and Dad put on the radio for Terry Wogan to keep me company.

In the cabin shrouded by darkness with just the console lights on I yawned and loved the soft dulcet tones of the Irish Terry. Then I got lulled into sleep and when I woke up the engine was very noisy and the radio was louder playing a modern contemporary tune. I bopped along to the song and grinned across at Dad and mentally became a conductor tapping out the beat shaking my little head with my hair swishing around in my little pony tail. I was in jeans and t-shirt with a jumper on and I felt really hot so I took my little jumper off. I couldn't stop mentally grinning inside my head.

Cruising along the A303 Dad said we were going to London to two supermarkets to offload our load. I started to look out the window more and Dad turned down the sound of the stereo. I didn't realise he was trying to encourage a conversation as I naturally zoned everything else out and took in as much scenery a I could enthralled by the long open road. I always felt a thrill when overtaking other vehicles. I still bopped up and down in my seat to the tunes over the stereo.

Dad smiled over to me and started to tell me of the landmarks we were passing so I strained to see out the window at them loving every minute of being with my Dad. I'd told him that I was getting a bit peckish and he said, "We'll be pulling over soon at the nearest greasy spoon café."

A hundred yards down the road we pulled into a car park and used a coach parking space. Dad pulled on the brakes and they made a huge whooshing noise. I sighed with my tummy grumbling and I envisaged a lovely sausage sarnie with plenty of brown sauce. We were soon hitting into our food and Dad had a bacon butty of where he flirted with the waitress like he always did with a twinkle in his eye.

I said to Dad, "What time are we getting into London?"

He said, "About twelve o'clock." Then he replied, "If you want to go to the toilet go now."

I said, "Why do you wanna go?" He grinned and said, "Yes. I'll meet you outside back at the lorry."

It became a bit of a race in my mind and soon got back before my Dad ready to pull myself up the steps and back into the cabin. While I was standing there I looked around and something caught my eye on the grassy incline. It was a squirrel and it made me smile. I stood there transfixed as Charlie the squirrel, as Dad called him, then broke into a nut and it seemed like a moment hung in time as I saw him nibble. I turned to Dad and shared a little smile. Then we got into the cab. He turned the engine on. It roared and then the radio came back on and we cruised into the motorway and I looked out over the hedges and the fields.

Job 25:2
God is powerful; all must
Stand in awe of him; he keeps his
Heavenly kingdom in peace.

It was enthralling as I rolled down the window a little gulping hard in the thin air. I loved breathing the fresh air deeply and got annoyed at the new presenter on prattling away on Radio One.

Dad piped up saying, "Sometimes the radio picks up new stations as we get nearer to new places."

As we neared London we got caught in loads of traffic and strained to see what the hold-up was. The lorry had stopped and after a while Dad began tapping the steering wheel with his finger I liked to notice these little things about Dad. Then he whipped out a choccy bar for himself and me. He got my favourite Marathon chocolate. I nibbled slowly and I could tell Dad was trying not to get so uptight. He went to pick up his tachograph to study it at the wheel. I wasn't sure what the wiggles were all about but I knew it was to do with how much time we had.

The queue began to move slowly then he put his paperwork back and started to indicate. Then said, "We'll go another way. We're booked in for one o'clock and I don't wanna be late."

I said, "Ok Dad."

We ended up taking a much better scenic route anyway and Dad started to point our famous landmarks round that part of London.

I remember going by Trafalgar Square and pulling up by some park surrounded by black wrought iron gates and Dad then struggled to find the right way to the supermarket. I can't even recall seeing one in sight, but we soon pulled up. He jumped out and I looked out the window to see him pulling back the sides of the trailer. I'd seen the Babycham picture crumple up as the curtains drew back then the forklift came out and took four large drink filled crates. I watched enthralled. Dad came back to the cab, opened the door and grabbed a bundle of ephemera that he said he was just taking to the office to get all the items ticked off and to do what, I assumed, to grab an invoice.

He'd turned on the radio for company and half an hour alter he caught me singing as he came back. "We're going to lunch. Then we're going to drop the trailer off before we're going to go back."

We soon found a side street of where we both jumped out after parking and then walked to a supermarket. Dad soon found the fridge aisle to grab some sarnies each and a packet of crisps. Then we sat outside on a park bench. The weather was lovely and we watched the world and his wife go by. I nibbled politely and I asked what the trees were in the park. I knew they were beech trees but I just wanted to start a conversation.

"Oh." He said, "They're just the same as the ones we have in our back garden."

Then I asked something else pretending I'd seen something. "What's that moving over there?" Dad looked round and pointed to something at the top of a tree and said, "Do you know what bird there is up there?"

I didn't answer straight away as I strained to see and saw more birds land round the bottom of the tree.

"They're ravens," Dad said, "That you get around the palace."

I said, "Can we go there today?"

Dad said, "No, we haven't got time." Then I remembered the trailer had to be dropped off.

I asked, "What time do you think we'll get home?"

"I promised your Mum we'd be back by five o'clock." I smiled and Dad said, "Take the rubbish and put it in the bin over there."

I obeyed and we were soon back in the cab. It had been hard for Dad to manoeuvre round central London and took all his concentration until we headed out to one of a run-down borough's just out of town. We were there quite a long time as Dad and another man had to undo the crowbar holding the trailer.

Dad came back to the cab and heaved a sigh of relief, "That feels lighter," he said, "We'll soon be back home."

As the ignition flared up, the engine roared and we were soon back on the motorway. Then we were soon back at the Showerings yard and I jumped up on the cross bar of the bike. With the wind in my hair it was relief. I'd enjoyed the day with my Dad and Mum was soon pleased to see us and so were my sisters.

I kicked off my shoes under the stairs and hung up my coat hungry as my nose lifted into the air following a lovely cooking smell.

"That smells like a casserole." I thought and Mum broke into my thoughts.

"Wash your hands," she said and the whole family were all soon sat round the table for dinner.

Chapter Ten

The next day I was back at school and I'd been in a social education class. The whole class were given children dummies and they said that we're going to learn basic first aid. The teacher asked us what we knew CPR stood for and the whole class looked blank so she put it on the board and went on to tell us about the kiss of life and chest compressions. After being told and the words went onto the blackboard, she did a demonstration. Then we all had to copy. I pinched the nose of my child, tilted their head back and blew into the mouth. Then pumped the chest five times and did it all again until the green light came on. That'd meant that I had saved a child's life.

When the dummies got wiped cleaned they took them back. Then we were given bandages and learned how to do a sling by folding it in the middle from corner to corner and tying it round the neck with the arm poking through it. I'd quite liked this lesson and it was soon over. Before I knew it I walked over to my art lesson that was upstairs in the maths building. I did a brilliant drawing that I went on and painted from the back to the front layer by layer till the end of the lesson.

Then mid-morning there were snacks to be brought by the canteen but I never bothered. I wasn't hungry and got put off by the queues.

After break I mentally skipped to Mrs Freebey's home economics lesson to do stitching and we started a picture for Christmas. I'd decided to do a snow scene against the back drop of a night sky with a snowman. I started it from the top and worked my way down the weave diligently bit by bit. It was a nice peaceful lesson and there was something quite therapeutic about sewing that I really enjoyed. I yawned at the end of the lesson feeling pleased with myself.

After lunch I had a double English lesson and learned all about Samuel Peeps and his diary. Then around the same time there was the plague caused by brown rats that burned up in the Great Fire of London. It had been a lot to read and we had to do an assignment on what we had just read answering questions written on the pages of the history book. It took me all lesson to read back through everything to try and remember it all. By the end of the day I'd felt I'd done enough.

In the morning I found my shoes at the last minute after foraging thoroughly through the shoe cupboard before putting them on really quickly. I half ran into school that morning as Mum had a really bad fever because of the flu.

I pushed myself really hard to run across town kicking up leaves as I went really enjoying the crunching noises I made running through them. I even stuffed a few in my pocket for leaf rubbings to do in art class that day.

After the register was taken and I had been the last called out as I'd rushed into the class out of breath I went on over to my art class. The assignment was to cover the weather and out of my pocket I pulled out five completely different leaves. At first I copied the shapes and coloured them in to match each leaf colour that was five different shades. Then on tracing paper I copied the shapes gain and then put the tracing paper over a decent piece of ephemera to copy it out again for comparisons with my free hand drawings and coloured them in again. then with a thin bit of paper and crayons I did some rubbings of which were crap, as I made holes in the paper so I had to do it several times. I wrote on each bit of ephemera what I'd done and put my name and the date on each one to hand in to my teacher.

Break time came and went really quickly and it was soon an intellectually challenging lesson. The questions came thick and fast in a history lesson for a pop quiz to see if we could remember dates for famous people of when they lived and created what they were famous for. Like 1066 was the Battle of Hastings in my mind I got right but couldn't get in there quick with. In 1666 I knew the plague and the fire of London was and I put my hand up and actually got that one right out loud. It was an intellectually tiring lesson of which I let out a loud yawn at the end of the lesson.

Feeling thoroughly challenged for one I was famished and went to lunch with my friends Rheann, Becky, Emma and Barbara and really enjoyed my sandwiches, crisps, fruit, chocolate and box drinks.

At home that afternoon I picked up Dad's Puzzler and learnt to do a skeleton crossword. Now I had to do the black squares in an asymmetrical way and fill in the numbers in the right order. Then answered the questions that didn't give the game away of how many letters you needed that I actually finished for one in front of the telly. My favourite news article came on Blue Peter with John Craven of whom reminded me of my father. It was only a five minute news segment and I liked the music that led into the items of news. It kept me in touch of what was going on in the world.

Then I looked at the Puzzler book again and did my favourite backwards crossword of where I had a grid of letters and I had to find the answers to cryptic clues laid out asymmetrically in the grid. I blacked out the unused letters and put the numbers in at the beginning of each word to create a completed crossword. I did this while watching Mrs Mangle's scenes with plain Jane and Henry on neighbours. Then it was Home and Away when Mum told me to turn off the telly for tea and I jumped up quickly, and did an about turn into the dining room. I then sat down and wondered what we were eating. It was a funny green and pasta looking mess. Mum had said it was broccoli pie. It looked disgusting so I then started to pick at it making lots of funny faces. I struggled with it for half an hour before I finally gave up as it had gone cold and that was my excuse for leaving it.

In the morning, the next day, I found a spider in the bath and I felt a little queasy as it was huge. I called out to Fiona and she came into look to see what I was on about.

"It's only a spider."

"Touch it then and throw it out." I'd said, but she wouldn't as it scuttled down the plug hole. I then got the guts to get in the shower. I lathered myself all over then let the heated water run all over my body really fast, twirling around and letting wash all over my hair as well to get the shampoo out. I stung my eyes and let the water run over my face for ages to take the sting out. It finally worked and I got out. Towelling slowly after putting a turban on my head I walked back into my bedroom of where I put my white slightly see through shirt over my new white bra on. Then I put my navy knee length skirt on and put on my little white ankle socks. I felt my legs, they felt nice and smooth. I put my hair up into a ponytail and I'd left a lump on the top of my head of hair that never seemed to go flat.

I then ran downstairs and felt flushed cheeks as I'd grabbed my shiny black Clarks shoes. I'd soon done the straps up and beamed feeling pretty. I loved how I looked. Then I closed my eyes and did a little girl's squeaky fart as I moved towards the door feeling mortified.

Psalms 39:8
Save me from all my sins,
And don't let fools laugh at me.

I heard Eve and Fee's laughter as they pushed pass me to get to the door. Jumping in the car I had to get in the middle seat of which I hated. I really wished I'd said something as Mum put her foot down to go up the hill. Then out of the Wimpey Estate by the Anglo Trading Estate, then across the crossroads through the middle of town and the other side of the lights we went by the road that led down to the prison. Around a big bend we then came to the entrance of the school and pulled up by the middle building of where me and Fee jumped out after we'd stopped off at St Pauls with Eve first.

I trotted over to my registration class and learned that I'd nearly got in first for once. The teacher looked very tired that day and a bit grumpy and he went through all of our names hurriedly. We then went down to assembly in the big hall and sat four rows back. I turned my head around and we all looked like a sea of navy blue uniforms looking very tidy. I felt proud to be there.

2 Samuel 22:28
You save those who are humble,
But you humble those who are proud.

That day I'd had a lovely few lessons of teachers being nice to me. In English I got an essay back with a 75% pass mark on that I'd felt really pleased with, with also a grade B on.

Then in physics I got a ten out of ten mark on my last assignment back to put in my book. At break time I found a friend in Rheann who said she'd had straight A's that morning and the teachers were nice to me all day saying my work was very good and that I'd put in a lot of effort.

That afternoon after school Mum sat with me on the sofa and told me straight out that she could have made it into the England's Olympic squad on the trampolines. For years she was the best at back flips and forward roly polys in the air. Just before she got selected for the England squad they were told to get brand new leotards and Nan said they couldn't afford it, so Mum missed out.

Mum then got up to peel the potatoes for tea and we had mash, peas, carrots and Brains faggots for a delicious meal. I actually said, "This is a wonderfully tasty meal Mum. Can we have ice-cream tonight please?" Mum beamed at me for being nice about the food for once. Then I got up and offered to do the washing up. Mum said thanks and scraped all the plates for me before stacking them up with me by the side of the sink.

Then I went to the sofa for the evening and sank in between my bedclothes happy for the night.

The next day my showering was really quick and I jumped out feeling a bit wobbly on my feet and I realised that my tummy needed feeding.

Now in the bathroom window was my saline solution that my contacts had been in overnight and I'd easily put them in with my just freshly cleaned finger. Then downstairs I'd gotten out a bowl from underneath the sink and then reached up into the cabinet overhead for a bowl of fruit 'n' fibre, and reached into the fridge for some milk. I put it all together for a lovely breakfast and took my time nibbling away like a little bunny rabbit.

Now, when at school, I got there last in the registration class but the teacher looked down her nose at me and I laughed as their spectacles slipped down onto the edge of their nose. She looked a wise owl. Then I glazed over and turned to sit down. My teacher called my name out. "Karen. You're here aren't you?"

I bit my lip, blushed, and said, "Yes," before having to get straight back up to follow everyone down to assembly. The head teacher lead prayers that day and we were all soon grumbling. Picking up our books, cramming ourselves in down the corridors to go to our first lesson.

My mind was on overload with lots on it just waiting to burst out and encourage me to talk to people. I burped loudly, put my head down, and avoided the other children's eyes.

In the first lesson I'd felt really opinionated in the French lesson and wanted to tell the teacher I already knew it all and wanted to scream with frustration going over the same stuff we did before. I wanted to learn something new.

Ecclesiastes 4:6
Perhaps so, but it is better to have only a little,
With peace of mind, than to be busy all the
Time with both hands, trying to catch the wind.

The next lesson was a copycat lesson because I'd felt like I'd done all that before too. It was like a de-ja-vu day as we had to parrot word for word old newspaper articles in a geography lesson covering world catastrophes like famous earthquakes that happened in San Francisco, along the fault line. We learned all about the Richter scale and the one we'd had to study about had been the highest on the scale since records began. I'd really enjoyed that lesson. It had been a real eye opener learning about the rest of the world for once.

After break I headed for the science block to my biology lesson and we got handed out work sheets about the internal workings of a sheep. Now there was a diagram recently put on the wall indicating where the lambs liver was, the heart, the kidney and the bowel along with everything else. I was surprised at a picture of a sheep's skull but we had to study it and memorise where everything went. My stomach heaved just looking at it as it had the eyeball still in it. I put my hand up and asked if I could rush to the toilet. The teacher said yes as she looked at my pale face and I only just made it to be sick down the toilet. I'd realised that I couldn't stomach looking at a dead animals eyes. I swilled my mouth out afterward with loads of water.

Back at the classroom I wasn't there for that much longer before we broke up for the next class. I walked slowly over to the middle block downstairs towards the end of the corridor for my history lesson and Mr Rees wasn't one of those who liked the sound of his own voice so he told us to get on with it. I took out my text book and was on the chapter about Mary Queen of Scots and how she was the sister of Elizabeth the first. I got very interested in their early life together before they grew up and apart. Then how she became the Queen of Scotland. I had to write my own version of that information and I formed a story in my mind that really wasn't what I had to do. I pushed a mirror writing letter to Rheann and Simon to ask them did they want to meet after school and Simon said that e couldn't as relatives were coming over. Rheann looked lost in thought and didn't answer me.

In the next lesson I had to get upstairs to geography with Mr Heaphy of whom was determined to teach us about the geographical lines all across a map of the Middle East and showed us on a large map the other countries the equator went right through. I had to draw the map myself and use a graph over it to show that I understood about geographical lines.

My tummy was grumbling as I reached for my bag after that long lesson that seemed to go on forever and I satiated my desire for food very quickly giving me a little bit of heart burn. I'd been the last one in the canteen just before going into afternoon registration of where the teachers had to prove the children were still there before they faded away from heart attacks from any child possibly missing.

The afternoon shot by in a bit of a blur. I remember distinctly the words in the French lesson that I though was ménage-a-trois and I blushed then looked at the actual word that said menagerie. I had a blood good laugh under my breath as I then thought I saw a sentence that sounded like the words in a song I knew called Jo La Taxi that was sung by a sexy French songstress. I laughed again and went to the next lesson a little bit confused.

Isaiah 19:14
The Lord has made them give confusing advice.

I was very glad it had been the last lesson of the day coming up and it was craft, design and technology. We learned all about the wires and buttons on a board that went into a computer which was something my Mum knew lots about as she put something similar together at the EMI factory in Wookey once, so she told me.

After school I played Sonic the Hedgehog round Darren's at his home in his bedroom who was a cousin of whom was about six years old. He showed me a rose afterward that he was going to give his first girlfriend that evening on the first date that Aunty Sue had encouraged. I thought he was being really sweet. I went home as he went to his date and at home Fee demanded tea and said she was starving. Mum didn't like the word and reminded us there were starving children in Africa to encourage her to eat.

In the morning I went to school and flopped down in my first lesson that was physical education. Now in the hall after putting on my flirty little skirt and white top we sat on the benches and watched the teacher Mr Beasley put out hoops and cones for us to do an assault course with some balls. Then we all got off the benches and sat down in four rows in front of the gymnastic materials to start the assault course. I took my turn last to jump through the hoops, to run round cones bouncing a ball, to do twice and on the way back we had to put the balls where we picked them up and jump back through the hoops to sit down at the back again. We were the first team to finish as we sat there good as gold. The teacher said, "Well done," and we were happy.

After the showers I got dressed and went to Mrs Robinson's class to de RE which stood for religious education. We had to get out our dark green text books and look through our information manual. We had to read all about Buddhism of where there once was someone called Buddha who had been a fat little man I never really cared about. Apparently the faith is about recycling humans into animals. There had also been a picture of an army of Buddhists parading about in orange robes in the middle of a high street somewhere in the Middle East.

It came break time and the lesson after had been a social education one. We learnt how to keep a diary detailing every aspect of our lives and to analyse thoughts and feelings to help turn us into responsible adults.

Next came an essay to write in an English class about aliens from outer space as we watched a newsreel about something called Roswell. Apparently it had been a disaster in America of where extra-terrestrials crashed down to earth. I think it had been when Buzz Aldrin and Neil Armstrong went into outer space, or perhaps it happened after the first man landed on the moon. I got so bored I started giggling to myself. Nobody heard as I just floated in my mind till I got out of the lesson.

By the time I got to Mr Greenway's lesson in the afternoon I was getting fed up. Rheann had sat on one side of the classroom and I just picked up my ruler and deliberately zoned out thinking it would be funny to flick something across the room. The trouble was I'd been focusing so hard on zoning out to act cool I mentally found myself in a dark tunnel. Then I pushed my mind back to reality and let in the light from the classroom again. I noticed that the rubber afterward had gone across the room after I flicked it with the ruler. It was a shame I came back to earth as I'd wanted to zone out till the end of the lesson. No-one seemed to notice my state of mind for the last five minutes. Reality had been getting so boring.

In the last lesson of the day I sat next to a boy I did not like and put my head down to study hard till the end of the day.

After school it was bliss as I put on some nice leggings and a flirty little top.

During assembly one morning I remember doubling over in pain with really bad PMT. I was getting fed up feeling like this every month. At the end of the school day I'd still been hurting really bad. I told Mum thinking I'd get sympathy and advice on how to deal with it. Mum, however, was unsympathetic and told me to get over it. Well she didn't actually believe me and I was still in a lot of pain. I told my sister Fiona while crying on her shoulder that Mum didn't care and Fee suggested Feminax pills she was taking for the exact same thing. They came in a pink packet. I took one of Fees and they worked straight away. At least Fee cared but I never found these packets in the shops.

Next day I wandered into home economics class and sat down at my counter. Miss Jackson asked us to get our ingredients out and I went blank. I'd forgotten to prepare for this class. Luckily there were ingredients at school for me to use. I had to think fast about what to do with them and wrote down my own made up recipe to make a ginger cake. I guessed the cooking time to be about 30 to 40 minutes. I actually did a good job mixing the ingredients together to make a nice consistency. In to the oven they went and I set the dial to 200 degrees. Twenty minutes later everyone could smell burning and me and the girl next to me saw smoke coming from our oven. The other girl screamed "My cakes!" We pulled both our cakes out of our oven and they were all burned. it was near the end of the lesson and Miss Jackson came over to serve up detention for me. I had to stay behind during lunch to tidy up the kitchen utensils cupboard and what I heard was to take everything out, wash it up, and put it away more tidily. Half way through washing up the teacher came in to see how I had been getting on and was surprised at seeing me still there. She explained that I should have just tidied the cupboard and sent me to lunch. I left feeling as though I'd just pissed her off and had my lunch quickly before the bell went for afternoon class.

Next day the whole family set off really early in the morning up the A303 towards London. Lots of things were on my Dad's agenda for us to go see. Madame Tussauds, being one of them. When we got there I remember seeing the red tour bus going round and thought excitedly about us going on one, unfortunately we never. The part of the day that was the coolest had been when we went underground to see a part of old Victorian London. It was mainly dark with oil lamps everywhere.

There was a mannequin of an old fashioned dressed policeman that helped to create the whole ambience of the place. It was weird going out of there back into the daylight of modern London, but I really felt like we'd gone back in time.

Next place was Madame Tussauds and all I can remember seeing was Michael Jackson's and Barbara Cartland's dummies.

It was a lovely day out though and I can remember walking past a monument called a needle by the River Thames. Along that stretch you could see through iron wrought railings in front of the National History museum I had gone round the year before with school. We even seen the Queen's jewels and went over London Bridge.

It was sad to have left London behind.

There were two of us who got to do work experience at my cousins Ashley's hairdressers. I was quite excited by then thought of washing people's hair and perhaps cutting some hair too. The first day was pretty uneventful. There were a handful of clients and I got to sweep up hair off the floor. I'd also got told to sort out all the hair grips, curlers, hair clips, and little combs, etcetera while the hairdressers got to do the exciting bit of cutting the tendrils on some women. At least I got to work alongside them creating their magic. It was a light and airy hairdressers, with big windows and no need for electric lights to be on. Everything was done in natural light.

I went up town to Daniella's for lunch and said hello to Nan Burr working there. A pasty and a drink were all I needed before walking back to GJs hoping at least to get to wash someone's hair.

The girl from school who'd been working alongside me had been having a better experience of the hairdressers than me. At the back of the main mirrored floor were the wash basins running along the middle. There were three in all.

The second day in she got to wash a customer's hair whereas al I had to do was stand and watch. My fingers were itching to do something and I ran them through my own hair getting agitated. One hairdresser saw this agitation and told me that they'd like to say thank you for the effort I'd been putting into tidying up by giving me a perm. I leapt at the chance as I'd have loved my hair all curly. As it was the end of the day the offer of a restyle was to take place the next day.

Being at home I watched my usual Neighbours before having tea placed on the table by Mum. A lovely beef stew. The aroma was deliciously enticing as I hungrily attacked the food. I should have complained about the lack of doing anything worthwhile at the hairdressers but instead told everyone about my up and coming brand new hairstyle. My contact lenses had already unleashed a confident new me and complaints were never my style anyway. A small part of me still wanted to at least be able to wash someone's hair if not do some cutting. Mum told me of when cousin Ashley used to work in GHs and we laughed together.

The next day during lunch break I went into Boots to do some shopping for Dad's 39th birthday and Mum had told me to get his favourite aftershave Old Spice. Down at Martins, the newsagents, I got a card and some crisps to eat walking back up the high street to Co-op to get some sandwiches.

At the salon it took all afternoon for curlers to be pasted into my hair and to be sat under a massive heater hat but the end result was worth it. I loved my big hair. It came just in time for the end of year school dance, everyone was looking forward to.

On the Friday I felt like a new woman in my jeans and tight top turning up for the last time to help with brushing the floors and tidying up. I'd pretty much should have learned at least all the tools a hairdresser uses but hadn't been paying that much attention. It was all to do with hair right?

In the evening I put on clean jeans and a t-shirt to meet with Rheann at school. She looked her usual self and we went for a drink by the drinks stand in the canteen. At the top of the stairs we manoeuvred ourselves round the biggest crowd we'd ever seen at a school dance. I finished my drink first and pushed myself to the front of the crowd dancing around and clapping the band not worrying where Rheann went.

Later on in the evening I went looking for her as the crowds thinned out wandering why she'd disappeared on me and found her coming in from the school entrance. I didn't ask her where she'd been. We got chatting and waited like good girls for our lift home with my Dad.

In the morning Dad and I walked around town together. I can see Dad with a newspaper rolled up in his arms in the glorious sunshine while walking up through town. I asked Dad why didn't he wear sandals and he told me in no uncertain terms, "Not those Jesus Creepers," in his tight clipped tone.

I spent that day in his company while reading the paper helping him with his crossword while sitting outside with the whole family in that glorious sunshine the following day too.

Next day I'd gotten up way too early with a very empty stomach that was growling at me so I tiptoed downstairs in my nightie and grabbed some bread from the tin to put in the toaster. I stood there for what seemed ages and put on the kettle. I took down four cups for the family and Mum came padding into the kitchen after having cleaned the living room. It was the first time I realised how early she got up in the mornings.

"I do this every day," she said, "I get up with your Dad at half past four. Do his lunch box and clean downstairs before I get you all cups of teas to get you up for school."

I blushed embarrassed, "I didn't realise Mum. I always thought you went back to bed afterwards."

"Maybe on the weekends," she said, "When your Dad's home. Although I still can't resist the routine of a cup of tea and biscuits in the morning for all of you. I like to get you up so you can get on with your day."

"Well I've put the kettle on Mum." I said.

"Let me take over I like doing it."

My toast popped out and Mum went to the fridge for me to get some Flora, that my Dad liked. I grabbed a knife from the drawer.

"Do you want jam, or marmalade Karen?" I thought that Mum should know by now I didn't like marmalade so I really emphasised my words when I spoke to her.

"Uh. I do not like marmalade Mum."

"Strawberry or raspberry?"

I said, "No thanks Mum," and had put the margarine on by then. "I'll have it plain." I took the plate back upstairs with Mum following me with the tea tray. When in my room I sat on the floor and had a conversation with Mum and Eve as I nibbled on my toast and as I sipped my cup of tea.

"Right. Who's going to get in the shower first?" Mum asked. We just smiled and were soon in school.

That morning in class we were in the middle of a biology lesson all sat around talking when Nicky looked at me with a little twinkle in his eye and he started singing, "You got that sweet little mystery," and my eyes glazed over and thought that was sweet. He turned away then and carried on talking with his mates. I put my head down and carried on with my work. Today I had an affirmation moment of a boy actually liking me for me. I had always felt beautiful and put on a pedestal of where boys never knew how to speak to me properly.

By the end of the day I'd managed to finish two maths books, read the rest of Great Expectations and learnt yet again how to do trigonometry, but it still went in one ear and out the other.

My art lesson went slowly as I took my time over a large picture of my face that I'd coloured in perfectly as part of a self-portrait session.

I happily walked home and found myself dreaming of being an actress.

In the morning it was sunny but quite cold, a real chill in the air ran through the family. Nanny Burr sat with Eve and I while Mum, Dad and Fee went to Aunty Nola's funeral. I wanted to say goodbye at her funeral really and walked up to the local park whistling my favourite hymn Colours of Day all the way up there.

On the swing swaying back and forth pushing my legs out to go higher and higher, laughing at the delicious thrill going through my whole body, while arching backwards and feeling the shudder of the cold hard chains going through my fingers, as I felt lonely.

> *Job 19; 13-14*
> *God has made my own family forsake me;*
> *I am a stranger to those who know me;*
> *My relatives and friends are gone.*

I stayed for over an hour that afternoon. The sun was shining with the cold seeping out through my bones and my bare legs were going pink and my bare arms felt lovely and tingly. I needed to think.

A few hours later Eve ran to Mum for comfort, Fee looked like she had shed a lot of tears and so did Mum. I'd felt so liberated I never even noticed.

That same sun got even hotter the next day when we all undressed and got ready for school. I'd put on my school skirt, shirt, and smart school shoes and headed out the door with Mum driving to Whitstone.

We all got on the bus and I remember sitting next to my friend Paula. All the way down I'd sat mostly in contemplative silence. I was by the window with my head on my hands wishing I'd said goodbye to my Aunty Nola. Paula finally broke through my silence by sharing a sandwich with me. She'd tried to share a little secret but I'd blanked her out.

The coach purred nicely down the hill by all the shops to an archway at the bottom on the left hand side. Gingerly the coach manoeuvred itself onto the small concrete area right by the sea. to the left was a high concrete step for us all to alight off the coach. We were at Lyme Regis.

Feeling the breeze from the sea on my skin and round my neck as my hair was in a ponytail. I'd felt aloof, cool, calm, collected and warmed through by the mid-day sun. Everyone was around me grouping together in their little cliques. Paula approached me for us to walk around town together and I tried to keep up with the rest of the group. Words failing me I wandered round the fossil shops of where one caught my eye, it looked a like a snails shell with the lines looking like bars.

After going up the hill we turned around to where the shingle part of the beach was and we wandered to the harbour wall to sit down and have our picnic lunches together.

On the beach we walked all together. I'd actually felt bereft from the group starting to lag behind feeling the glorious sand between my toes.

We didn't stay long and soon made our way back to the coach to head off home.

Fiona set me up with a boy from her year called Richard and on that same day we had our first date. It was a sunny day as Richard and I went for a walk round Shepton. Up Bowlish Hill Richard started making jokes and I wet myself laughing. I mean here was this big guy with golly-wog hair desperate to be really good company and he was. I quite liked this Richard.

Next day at school I'd forgotten my gym kit again and had to wear a tatty second hand gym skirt and an old white airtex top. Everyone in class were climbing up the ropes on the climbing frames. I attempted the rope climb and deliberately took my time over it, but I got a leg burn. Gym class was not my favourite lesson. In the communal showers afterwards I raced to get out back to my bench where my clothes were hanging up, no-one would ever talk to me in the changing rooms. I'd been looking forward to maths class, the last lesson of the day. The teachers didn't care about me much so if I kept out of trouble till the end of the day I'd be fine.

I was to meet up with Richard later at his house down Bowlish Lane where he lived with his mother. It was a nice area down in like a ravine with sloping gardens and a wooded area by some steps that I walked down after school to go see him. His house was one of a terraced red brick houses and when I first went in Fee was there with another Richard too but they soon left us in a nice warm and cosy living room together. Cuddled up on the sofa we watched a bit of TV. I tried to initiate sex by climbing on his big tummy but he just lay there so I soon climbed off again. It was starting to get late and I was getting hungry so I left Richard in front of the telly a I left and made my way back up the steps along Shaftgate Ave to Coombe view and then home.

In class the next day my English teacher was getting us to read Animal Farm and I had to read a paragraph to the whole class. I loved reading out loud even though it was a bit embarrassing. I'd stared hard at the words before it was someone else's turn. The rest of the day passed in a bit of a blur and I raced home on my own. Tomorrow was Friday and Richard and I had arranged to go across the fields after school. I couldn't wait. Rheann had been avoiding me during lunch that day and I could never work out why she'd occasionally do that to me. I'd witnessed Linda, my old best friend with her gang of mates together at lunch and I'd eaten on my own.

Friday came and my date went with me through the meadows, over the hill, and towards the old railway tunnel. It was such a gloriously sunny day with a hint of frost in the air. We'd never kissed before so I was pleasantly surprised when Richard moved in for one and he'd tried to invade my mouth with his tongue. I reciprocated but he bit me and the moment was spoiled so I realised this relationship was over. I'd told him that in the worst way possible when walking up his road by shouting he was a bad kisser and that I really fancied Damion. I didn't really pay that much attention to him slumping his shoulders dejectedly as he went one way and I went the other.

I'd got into school just on the bell and ran upstairs to my form room to hear my name called by Mr Badman. Ferreting through my bag I checked for all my books ready for the day. Double English was first and I had anxieties about finding the right classroom as we were having our lesson in a different room again.

> *Psalms 116:3*
> *I was filled with fear and anxiety.*

I thought it might have been downstairs at the end of the corridor. Luckily it was the right room as I found a seat. Lessons were either interesting or boring and this morning my interest was piqued by not the teacher or the lesson but the gossip going round the classroom. Today was the day when some of the class were chatting about a trip to Berkley Castle the next day. I loved going on trips away from school and I could see Rheann and myself going off on our own round town.

I worked hard at concentrating on the lesson but I was starting to get a headache. We had a break afterward for those who wanted to get some tuck but I wasn't interested and prayed to be able to just get through the day. Two more lessons were coming up, maths and home economics. Algebra seemed easy and so did cooking, maybe I could just float through the lessons but I still couldn't shake my headache and come lunch time I finally started to feel better after something to eat.

In the afternoon it was P.E. and biology. Mr Beasley was always pushing us to try harder in gym and I felt refreshed from the exercise. Biology came and at least I felt ignored enough by the teacher to just be able to keep my head down and wait for the end of the day bell. Minimum effort necessary as I just wasn't that interested in the internal workings of the body. Home work was set, but I never bothered with biology.

In front of the telly at home my French home work was due in the next two days so I'd thought I'd better do it copying the text in French I felt reasonably pleased with that at least I'd tried. yet again Mum wasn't impressed with my books all over the floor and asked me to tidy up for tea.

I went to the piano to practice 'Fur Elise' for my next competition and at least, finally, I was doing something I really wanted to do for the first time that day. On the piano again after bangers, mash and a crumble with warm custard, I practiced my chords and scales with my fingers racing over the keys. Mrs Bosley had told me I had the tendency to let my fingers race but the best bits were what gave me a real buzz.

Dad came home and Mum told me to stop playing for a bit of peace and we all snuggled in for the evening to watch the telly.

The following day Fiona got up early to go to France and she'd gone before I awoke for school. I was jealous of her visualising her getting on a boat, having croissants for breakfast in her hotel room and her making friends when coming in from school that day.

Our evening meal consisted of us four, me, Eve, Mum and Dad sitting round the dining room table talking about Fiona, Mum talked about giving us croissants for breakfast the next day seeing as I shared my earlier visualisation.

As we were eating that hot food we heard a familiar trill of the ice-cream van from down the road. Mum had asked if we wanted ice-creams for pudding. Us girls said, "Yes please!" as our little faces lit up. I licked my lips in anticipation and wolfed down the rest of my meal. Mum sent Dad to get some money for our highballs. In my mind's eye I could see Dad at the ice-cream van so I turned to watch him out the window in a queue with other parents.

I'd sat in front of the telly with the news on watching about the Argentinian war. My mind absorbing the footage of the heartache while knitting. I'd gotten from the corner of the room down in the cabinet with the small lips. I was trying to knit a blanket making segments I could estimate as big as long as my bed.

Dad had come in the side door of the living room and made me turn my head to the left. I grabbed for the ice-cream offered and sat back on the sofa. The delicious taste slithering down the back of my throat until the chewing gum in the bottom that I used to love to champ and make bubbles with. Absentmindedly I placed my hand on my tummy and felt the fluff in my button hole. I looked down to flick it out.

Watching the news again there was an actor who felt the need to lie to the cameras on him facing a court case. I saw right through him and thought basically he was a bare faced liar. Which made me think that acting was a form of lying as you pretend to be someone you're not which could spill over into everyday life making me think about something going on at home. My nerves were so tight while chamming at home.

That next morning Mum kept her promise and gave us croissants in the morning with butter, a knife and some jam. I picked at the bread not liking the taste very much not really wanting any food. It was too dry and got up from the table to watch Saturday morning telly. I was the only one who watched it as Mum cleared everything away.

Sabrina the teenage witch came on and I loved the immaculate clothes, make-up, and the imaginative storylines. I'd lost myself completely in the plot.

By lunch time I'd had enough of the TV. Eve had gone out. I sat at the piano running my fingers over all the scales looking at my music for my next competition for the Kingswood Festival at Bristol. Pounding the keys, looking at the cadences and matching them with each note it felt good to make a sound so wonderful to my ears. It was a classical piece I'd been getting used to hearing, before I knew it that weekend flew by while Fee was away.

On the Monday morning back at school I lived in each moment trying to soak up the new things we were learning finding some things repetitive.

In the afternoon H.E. lessons I didn't have to think and felt soothed by sewing a bookmark together using orange wool first then blue wool to make a pattern. By the end of the day I walked home to the top of my road with Rheann who left me to go down the steps to her house. I walked home completely relaxed and calm with the world.

Going through the front door Mum said "Welcome home love," and grinned when she saw me. I relaxed all evening till the next day of when I had to go back to school.

During lessons I learned that Thor was the God of war and that they were the God Thursday was named after of whom was Roman. I also found out new names for the different bones in biology. One name made me inwardly laugh as they said it was the real name for the funny bone in the arm. I'd also found a little bit about the Muslim religion and saw how beautiful the insides of Mosques are and also how beautifully the women were dressed in traditional clothes.

In history we read about Queen Victoria and Prince Albert which made me laugh when I overheard some boys talking about prince Alberts.

In the afternoon an age old argument broke out between Mum and Fee I'd heard over and over again about clothes and Fee needing a lift somewhere. It was bubbling up in my chest with my mind's eye focusing on a white and blue dot out of the corner of my left peripheral and all I could think of was saying, "It doesn't have to be this way." I'd felt very clear minded and heard myself saying those words very distinctly of which made Mum turn and say, "Stay out of this Karen." Fee then got hysterical getting

Mum's attention back to her and I saw Mum giving her a short sharp slap round the face saying that would stun her back to earth. Then she turned to me ferociously but instead of listening to what I had to say, which was what I'd been expecting, she shoved me hard through the living room door and into the hallway and I felt my head slam into the sharp edge of the under the stairs door frame. Tears rolled silently down my cheeks. I felt angry.

> *Job 40:11*
> *Lord, I know you will never stop being merciful to me.*
> *Your love and loyalty will always keep me safe.*

Mum never even said sorry to me afterwards as she'd turned back to Fee finally getting a sensible discussion out of Fee and my sister, I heard, said, "Sorry," to Mum. Not wanting any solace after hearing these words I just stood up with a short sharp pain tearing through my head proudly sticking my chin up in the air realising that was all Mum had really wanted from Fee, not a solution from me.

My mind felt clearer after that and I began to realise that no-one needed my help. I'd only been quoting a line from an American movie that I'd watched years ago. That epiphany came and went just like that.

I found myself alone up at the park kicking out wildly going as high as I could loving the feel of the adrenaline rush. It felt like a long time before going home pushing the need to belong as an equal in my family with an opinion someone would actually listen to.

At home I grabbed yellow and blue wool to make squares side by side together on one needle to speed up the process of making my blanket without having to sew up lots of individual squares afterwards in front of the telly.

That next day in the afternoon Fee and I walked round to a bungalow on the Ridgeway Estate with Jason, his girlfriend Jenny and a couple of more friends. I cosied up to Jason on his sofa to watch a film called In the Name of the Rose. At the raunchy part I felt my thigh tingle by his legs getting me all turned on. We finished the film then went into the back garden of where there was a barbecue in front of a fir tree. We all had hot dogs and afterward, as they thought the fire was dying out, someone threw what they thought was a used aerosol can on the fire which made a large flame and caught the tree alight. We were scared and had to get damp tea towels but the fir tree lit up like a big bonfire so we ran in and out with buckets of water. The whole thing sizzled and the whole yard became a pool of water. At least we save ourselves from a total catastrophe.

We soon went home Fee and I to a warm bed that night.

The next morning I woke with a start as I'd heard a loud cockerel crowing somewhere. I looked out the window at a golden glow in the sky to look for the cockerel it sounded so close all along the skyline on tops of houses. I propped my arms up on the windowsill just gazing at the glorious sun knowing I had no school that morning and I could take my time to get up.

I eventually moved to get in the shower and stayed there for ages. It felt nice and tingly over my taught muscles making me feel more alert.

The phone rang downstairs as I was drying and Mum shouted up to me to answer the phone as it was my best friend Rheann. I ran down totally elated in my dressing gown.

"Morning Rheann. How are you?" I'd said patting my face with the towel.

"I'm doing alright thanks. How would you like to come round for lunch with my family?"

"I'd love that. What time do you want me round?"

"Well I've just got up," she said, "Make it in two hours' time."

"I'll see you at eleven then." I replied.

After dressing I went downstairs to the living room and found my knitting. I whacked on children's television and did pink and blue squares for an hour and a half. I then went into the hallway and got out my trainers. After slipping them on I put on a little summer jacket to keep my shoulders safe from the sun. It took me twenty minutes to fly down the steps and up Beech Avenue to get to Misburg Close.

At Rheann's I pressed the doorbell and her mother answered.

"Hello Karen. Come on in. She's in the living room."

I walked through the hallway and met with Rheann on the sofa. I sat with her and asked, "What are we having for lunch?"

"Ratatouille and apple crumble with cream."

"Are you vegetarians?" I asked and she said. "No. We're having steaks with it."

We talked for a while as I took in everything in the room. It was quite big with a large cabinet running along the back wall and had another corner cabinet to the left with the TV on. I found myself going through the bottom drawer of the large cabinet noticing hundreds of cd's of classical music, one being of Madame Butterfly.

Lunch was soon called and we sat out in the dining room. I met her bothers at the table. One had a mass of blonde curls on his head of whom was thin and wiry. That was Evan and the youngest brother was Glyn who had black hair, was short and had been really cute. A girl at school called Lisa said she'd fancied him once. The food was lovely and I complimented the mother.

After the food we sipped cordials and had a chat together. her brothers' seemed really sweet.

At least I'd finished my food that afternoon having talked to everyone. Then we went up to her room and Rheann got out a pack of playing cards. She asked me what games I played.

I said, "I know rummy, three card brag and pontoon."

"We'll play pontoon," she said. Rheann dealt two cards each and I had to get as close to twenty one as possible. I got dealt a three and a five so said, "Twist," that meant I got given another card. I got a ten of hearts and stuck at eighteen. Then Rheann stuck at the two cards she had.

"You lay first," she said and I felt pleased with my hand, but Rheann had nineteen so she won that game.

Five games later we'd had enough and went out for a walk to walk off our food. All around the estate and back again. Rheann talked about boys and I told her I liked a boy named Damion. Then she shared with me that she liked someone called Simon of whom had dark brown hair and was of medium build and I knew his parents were pillars of society as they went to church most Sundays. I soon went home after that.

Chapter Eleven

The next day was a Saturday. I awoke with a spring in my step as I knew I'd been invited to a barbecue that day. I went downstairs and switched on a programme called Going Live with Philip Schofield. I laughed at watching it liking the presenter as he was very good looking.

I got a bowl of cereal with a cup of tea to go in the living room with, but Mum spotted me and coughed, "Excuse me but up at the table p-lease, and don't forget to dress up smart today Karen as you've got a barbecue to go to this weekend."

I said, "Fine. I'll put on a dress Mum."

"Which one? As I can iron it for you."

I gobbled up breakfast quick and dived in my wardrobe quickly. I went through everything to find a nice warm flirty blue and white dress that was fully lined. It didn't look creased so I slipped it straight over my head feeling beautiful.

It had soon slipped into the afternoon and I'd been sitting at the piano when Mum told me to put my shoes on.

"Come on Karen. We're off to the vicarage."

"Ok Mum." I'd said and soon put on my sandals. How long is it going to be Mum?"

She said, "Oh about three hours."

I beamed and we got into the car. All across town I felt happy always liking the thought of a party.

Now the barbecue was in Reverend Woolmer's garden and it had been filled with French exchange students. I noticed a boy on his own and thought he looked bored. Feeling confident I said to him questioningly, "S'ennui?" and he said "Oui." Not knowing what to say next after hitting the nail n the head he looked at me questioningly.

The Monday started out lovely and sunny as Mum drove her and I out to Mrs Poling's school. My sisters had other plans for the day. One had gone off with Dad in the lorry while the other one was with Gran and Gramps for the day.

In our summer clothes we waited outside Mrs Poling's grand home and Mum told me about the ghost her employer had seen once at her house that had turned her hair white.

Surrounded by a handful of children we got on a bus. Mum told me to sit with the two children I was to look after for the day. Sitting there day dreaming I never paid that much attention to what my two children looked like. I just assumed they'd follow the pack.

In the zoo it was my first time there and the place seemed huge. It was soon lunch time and everyone sat out on the grass to have a picnic. Mum and Mrs Poling decided to do a head count and my two were missing. I was told to go find them so I naturally wandered over to where I'd last been with them and with Mum following she found them first at the butterfly enclosure.

My instinct had been correct. It wasn't long before we were heading under the Severn Bridge in the way back home. Mum hadn't been in the least bit cross with me at all or if she had nothing was said, so I stuck my nose up and stared back out the window again.

When I was about twelve, Dad used the word kids to describe something we were all going through and that was when I took umbrage of the word kids and said that I wasn't a young goat. This was when I started to hate generalisations or generalistic comments therefore lumping my feelings in with everyone else's. I didn't bother asking what Dad had been talking about. I'd been insulted.

Job 20:3
What you have said is an insult.

We vegged out in front of the telly that evening and I remember watching Benny Hill of where he'd ate a goldfish alive straight from a bowl. It made me feel sick. He'd done a striptease of where he'd peeled his skin off of which really disturbed me.

Galatians 5:12
I wish that the people who are upsetting you would
Go all the way; let them go on and castrate themselves.

Then there was a girl with a knitted skirt on and a loose strand got caught in a door and the whole skirt unravelled, which turned me on.

That Saturday my family and I went round the agricultural show of the Bath and West showground. Not taking much notice of the stalls and anything going on around me not least of all the discussions the family were having I soaked up the atmosphere and headed for the rides by the main arena. Dad let me go on the Mexican Hat which was like a big cage ride while everyone else lazed out on the grass with ice-creams watching the horses in the main arena.

I was soon a bit wobbly as I'd made my way back towards them and was content to just sip a cold drink to calm down.

It was lovely and warm, Eve and Fee were getting grumpy and bored so it wasn't long before my parents had had enough but I could've stayed there all day.

It was on the news when we got back about Martin Scorsese's film The Last Temptation of Christ and in my youthful idyllic mind I couldn't understand what the fuss was all about. Why couldn't our future King have a Queen, a family, and a normal happy home. He above all others deserved to find happiness surely? I thought this as I took my time over combing the tail on my little pony over and over again while the news broadcasted the outcry over the film.

In the morning we'd packed up our big five berth family tent and headed for Swanage. It was a long drive and we ended up getting in a huge queue of traffic for the boat to take us to Bournemouth. Whilst in the queue we waited for so, so long that we actually found the time to get out of the car and walk to the nearest garage for drinks, crisps and chocolate and back again. We had our magazines in the car but were getting bored reading them.

When we drove onto the boat our car was one of the first ones to get on for that trip so we parked right at the back to be one of the first ones to get off. I remember, once we were there walking through some gardens of where there was a lovely string of lights running alongside the path. Going towards the beach we headed for a big enough space on the sand for all of us.

In the evening we went to the cinema with really posh comfy seats. We sat near the back and instead of taking my contact lenses out as I should've done after ten hours of wearing them I left them in. I had taken no glasses on this holiday. This was one of the first screenings of Batman with Jack Nicholson. I always liked the scene of where he'd asked Kim Basinger's character if she'd ever danced with the devil in the pale moonlight. I liked the fear it created.

Psalms 3:6
I am not afraid of the thousands of enemies
Who surround me on every side.

We walked back through the gardens with the twinkly lights on afterwards heading towards the beach. As we approached the sand it turned out to be the first time I'd seen a nude man's body that wasn't my Dad's. I can picture in my mind's eye the white back and bum. He must have been about to do a skinny dip.

We all got back safely to our tent after this and that was when, whilst having a bit of supper, that Dad scared Eve through smiling at us through the window trying to sound like the Joker. Because Eve screamed she set me off.

The holiday seemed uneventful after that before we headed home.

It was Nan's birthday when we got back and in Evercreech when we saw her I remember seeing old photos and I thought Granddad looked so handsome in his old naval uniform while in his twenties.

The party went really well and everyone exchanged presents and cards except me, 'cause I just thought what was the point? Everyone else has got one and zoned out just enjoying the family atmosphere. The drinks came round then we went to the kitchen for food. It was a lovely evening.

The following day Mum took me to a piano lesson into Wells. I thought we were going to Mrs Bosley's as I sank back into the passenger seat. It was a lovely sunny day as the golden glow of the morning sun glinted off the windows on the houses around us. Turning by the garage to the right off Bath road and I wondered where we were going. Mum talked animatedly about Jane my piano teacher's daughter. I then twigged that the bungalow, that we turned up at, was our final destination.

Going to the front door Mum drove off. I actually felt a bit apprehensive and rang the bell. A tall lady came to the door with long blonde curly hair with a cigarette in her mouth. She told em to come on through while she went to the back of her home to put out food for her cat. I slumped on the stool and put my bag on the floor. I then take out a piece called Fur Elise, put it on the stand, and waited for Jane to come back.

As she sat down she decided to play the whole piece through for me and I got dead excited listening to the different cadences in the tune.

> *Proverbs 14: 14*
> *Good people will be rewarded for their deeds.*

Itching to play myself Jane took me through the first stage of the piece bar by bar. It was quite repetitive until I got taught a lovely fast bit that I found my fingers just danced over as it was a bit like a long scale. The whole hour was spent learning that whole song bit by bit which I really loved the sound of. Towards the end though I'd had to go through some new scales by which point the doorbell rang. Jane stubbed out her cigarette in the ash tray on top of the piano and left to open the door to let her next pupil in. I was surprised expecting it to be Mum. Jane asked me did I mind waiting by sitting on an armchair and letting her get on with this man who'd come in. I'd felt like I'd had no choice. He had to go through his scales first not playing them half as fast as I could but Jane explained he'd only just started learning. I felt awkward until the bell finally rang again of which made me jump as it was sharp and shrill. Mum came wandering in. I looked up and she apologised to Jane for being late. She wanted to talk to her so Jane ushered her into the hallway for a chat. I blushed at the man still struggling on the piano till I realised I'd better stand up and sidle outside. Mum was giving her money for the lesson and saying thank you for waiting. I clasped my music to me then followed my mother out. My Mother said we'd get a drink at home as I'd said that I was gasping.

The sun was still shining all the way back and I shut my eyes feeling my face warm up through the windows. I nearly fell asleep.

At home Dad came in from being out in his lorry and I remember him talking about a cousin called Carolle of his and that they'd asked us to come round and visit. This visit was apparently set up by Nan Burr as Dad said he'd promised his mum he'd go see his cousin and her children ages ago. This trip was to be in Yeovil.

The next day was a Saturday and Mum spent ages on getting us ready in matching dresses that were multi-coloured patterned on a mainly blue background. We'd all washed our hair the night before and our locks were shining either bright red or a lovely golden blonde colour.

While at Carolle's we all had a drink each and headed into the backyard for a photo. The sun was still gloriously yellow from the day before and it wasn't long until we had to go home but her daughters seemed pleasant enough. Even though I hadn't spoken with them.

We took off from there and headed towards Weymouth out of Yeovil. Tearing up the miles I looked out the front window to see the hills rolling by. Dad promised us a trip to somewhere a little bit different.

Passing through the sea front in Weymouth the roads were surprisingly clear and I rolled down the window to breathe in the sea air. The music on the radio was blaring a tune but Eve and Fee weren't listening while they were talking to Mum and Dad. Wondering where we were going I took no notice of the conversation going on around me. Realising we were going out of the town we went over a bridge of where I'd looked out over an estuary and I spotted some birds as I squinted into the sun. Dad told me to sit back in my seat so I slumped down with an oomph. Looking out the side window over Fiona's shoulder I could see some dark rocks of where waves were crashing into and Dad pulled up by them first.

Getting out of the car Dad warned us not to get too close to the geyser. I didn't know what he was on about and edged forward over the rocks. We stood still for a while waiting for something to happen with another family there looking through a large hole until someone yelled to stand back. Suddenly a lot of water shot up into the air after waves had come crashing up the sides of where we were standing. I looked down at my feet and they were soaking wet. Dad told us to look up again as more water came shooting up through the hole. I heard another father shout. "That's a geyser kids."

We stood there for quite some time watching the display unsure of whether I really liked getting wet feet or not. Fiona was transfixed with her nose in the air while Eve was getting a cuddle from our Mum. I looked to Dad and he came over to put his arm around me. We stood there for what seemed an age before Dad steered us back towards the car. My feet were sopping wet and I had to take my socks and black shoes off. I felt miserable at first until Dad explained that we were off to look round a lighthouse into

Portland Bill. I perked up but refused to put my socks back on as we got out of the car again.

Walking past some houses we saw a lighthouse and Dad led us up a spiral staircase inside. Looking up at it made my head spin as we walked round and round in a circle to the top. We were made to look up at the big light shining out through a massive porthole. The man who owned the place guided us away from his living quarters, but I peeked through one of his doors anyway forever curious looking at arched shape furniture. A perfect shape for a round house and this stopped me from feeling giddy as we wandered round the spiral staircase downwards.

Outside I breathed a sigh of relief and took a gulp of fresh air. I'd developed a sniffle what with my wet black shoes on. The family led the way back to the car and I slumped into the middle seat wishing I could sit by the window, but never dared asked if I could knowing my sisters said they suffered with car sickness.

Dad drove us into the town more and came across a pub of where we alighted. Mum told us we were stopping for a meal. Through the doors Dad made his way to the bar and told us girls to look at the specials board. I fancied sausages, mash and peas. I didn't notice what my sisters ordered as I'd asked for a Coca-Cola. Sat down at the table we all tucked in. I fell silent and enjoyed the warmth of the room warming my feet up. My shoes were starting to get dry. Each mouthful of food tasted delicious and I shovelled it in. No-one noticed my chamming for once as my nose started to run. Mum offered me a hanky to blow on and I sneezed really hard making everyone look. We were asked afterward if we wanted pudding and all us girls asked for a banana split.

Ten minutes later large glass pudding bowls came out with bananas cut in half with masses of ice-cream in the middle with chocolate sauce all over the top with some strawberry sauce too. I let it all slip nicely down my throat. Finally full we all finished our drinks before getting up from the table. Dad went to the bar to pay for everything then we all waved goodbye as we went outside. It was getting dark as we all got aboard our car and Dad drove us out of Portland the way we came. I looked out towards the sea where the rocks had been where we'd stood a couple of hours before. The rocks looked dark and foreboding which gave me the chills as the waves crashed upon them.

The drive hummed along all the way home as I felt myself dropping off while leaning on my sister Eve in the back. By the time we got back Mum had to rouse all of us before we got out the car. She offered to make us all hot drinks that we said yes to. A nice Ovaltine sorted us all before putting on nighties to head up to bed. We did our teeth and soon jumped under the covers and my mind went back to the creepy rocks.

In the morning Mum and Dad drove us into Wells to see our grandparents but we parked up by the Cathedral Green finding nowhere else to put the car. Fee and I walked side by side into town as we were sent on an errand while the others went passed the Fountain Inn to Nan's.

This was when Fee trusted me with a really big secret that she'd had a pregnancy scare after being with her boyfriend Nick on the sofa one day. I promised that I wouldn't tell anyone and it was the first time anyone had ever trusted me with a secret. It made me feel special as we walked by the Wells Cathedral in the sunshine together.

I woke up early the next day and clung to my bed willing myself to go back to sleep but I could already hear Mum coming up the stairs with the tea cups clanking. I managed to roll over and have a snooze anyway finally waking up to lukewarm tea and bourbon biscuits. They weren't my favourite but I dunked them into my tea anyway and drained the cup. I stretched and yawned and heard Mum banging on the ceiling under me yelling to me to shower and get dressed. I washed quickly in the sink and chucked my school clothes on. Dragging the comb through my hair I used a hairband to put it up into a pony tail. Mum yelled again that they were going. I grabbed my school bag. Fee had already left for school as she walked in with her friends.

Mum and I turned up, in the car, to the top car park and just as I got out I heard the bell. I raced down the hill on my own to the languages block to my registration class and got there just in time to hear my name called out. There were instructions in a letter given out to take home at the end of the day about when all our homework was due in. I then raced down the stairs to my English lesson. We had in a relief teacher as our usual teacher was off sick and someone had put a whoopee cushion on her chair. She saw it and ended up in tears for the rest of the lesson. No-one had any sympathy and I got bored as I got on with my work.

It was double maths after lunch when Rheann and I'd have hung out together up in the field. I enjoyed maths as it was simple enough, but I just couldn't seem to catch up with anyone else so I was determined to get through one whole maths book when I got home from school that day. I was jealous of Fiona in the top maths group in her year. I wanted to be that good at maths too.

> *Proverbs 14:30*
> *Peace of mind makes the body healthy,*
> *But jealousy is like a cancer.*

I lay on the floor, once at home, in front of the TV watching Ulysses, I loved singing to the theme tune of. I'd had my maths book in front of the telly working really hard to get through it probably not even actually reading the sums properly as it was algebra. But I did my best. I'd also had a sheet from

French that day to work through and was learning what to say in a patisserie. I loved French and liked to use my French accent out on my sisters. I got jealous of fee though who did better at French than me and was allowed to study German.

At quarter past five I'd put my homework away to watch Neighbours. Mum then called us for tea and I helped to wash up afterwards. Fee had crept off to the toilet and didn't come back.

The next day I got up early. Mum brought us in tea and biscuits. She left them on the floor and I licked my lips ready for the custard creams. I'd dunked one into my tea for too long and it dissolved into the hot wet liquid. I saw the bits floating on the top and didn't want it. I'd tried to fish it out with my fingers but couldn't pick it up so I just left it to go cold. I jumped into the shower to get washed and dressed. I put on a skirt and shirt to look smart for the day ahead. I was going to play in a piano competition and was totally looking forward to it. I grabbed my music after putting my shoes on. Mum was at the door ready and I jumped through it onto the path kicking up the gravel.

In the car Mum turned the ignition and pointed the car in the direction of the beach. Mum churned up the countryside and I just daydreamed out the window gazing into the sunshine. Mum turned the car into a lane, a place I didn't recognise, but knew that we were going to the Longwell Green Eisteddfod near Weston.

Going through the gates into the car park there was a low ceilinged building. I met with Darren in the lobby and the rest of the musicians. Jane's daughter, Emily, and her partner were looking smug with her long blonde curly hair and that perfect look golden girls have. The partner was older and they were told in front of us they were bound to win as they'd passed higher grades than us.

In the auditorium Darren and I got up first and sat down on the stools side by side. I started to play the beat before Darren started pounding the tune out louder than me. The tune resounded out loudly over the whole room, each bar got louder and faster till I felt like that the beat was thumping through my very soul. I was so happy that I didn't even look at my partner being completely in tandem with him. I was pounding the floor with my foot in complete synchronisation with my fingers. The tempo slowed slightly and Darren turned the page without missing a beat. The tune got faster, we got so lost in the moment. His foot blended the notes together in a louder way by pedalling a foot pedal to the floor. It made a crescendo before coming back to a softer sound that I found myself swaying to. The beat changed slightly and Darren's fingers changed tempo to meet mine. It sounded fantastic to my ears. Darren turned the page so quickly all I had to do was look at the music while my fingers had a life of their own coming back to the original temp. The build-up was coming to a massive crescendo and I could feel the tension coursing right the way through me. Pounding the last chords together one by one we eased into a lovely blend of a bittersweet ending as though we were actually signalling the arrival of a beautiful queen. Everybody clapped.

Two more couples got up to play simple little tunes that tinkled together perfectly. There was clapping every time. Then Emily got up with her partner. They sat down gracefully together with their noses stuck up in the air. Her long blond locks caught my attention and the tune they played everyone knew. It was by Beethoven, a tune very popular on the telly. In the way it was played the tune lazily danced around and the audience were quiet, completely silent, expecting a long complicated composition just like the other songs. The adjudicator stood up. It looked like he was going to applaud them but he moved towards them to make the two of them start again, or so I thought but the music kept on playing very sweetly resounding round the echoey hall. People clapped.

There was one more duet with two boys who played their own way. Then laughed all the way through the song and enjoyed a long hard complicated tune that twirled and danced louder and louder then faster and faster till the tempo changed. The tune got sweeter. They were completely in tandem. I got caught up in their magic. It was a brand new song to me.

At the end of the competition the adjudicator read out the results. He praised all of us. The first couple got a good result. The second couple got third prize. It was just a certificate. They read our names and there was a pause of anticipation before he told us we'd won and that there was a trophy to keep for a year.

The two boys went on and got second prize and Darren and I got surprisingly first prize. We were elated.

The next day the sun beamed through the living room window round at Nan Sheila's, and you could see the wall down the alleyway just outside. The net curtains were tinged slightly yellow and all around me there was dust over everything. I snuggled up on Gran's brown sofa to watch Home and Away on the big television by the window. My sisters and I used to watch together at home but some gossip that the adults were on about always seemed more interesting to them these days. Mum, Dad, Gran and Gramps never worried if I should be privy to anything they were on about even if I became the topic of conversation. I overheard Nan say, "She'd come out if she was interested."

"Who was she?" I'd asked myself, "The cat's mother?" and felt insulted watching Danny Minogue's character get all stroppy about something.

Job 20: 2-3
Now I'm impatient to answer. What you have said
Is an insult, but I know how to reply to you.

The characters' lives on the telly always seemed more interesting to me anyway.

Mum called out to me. We were all about to leave, we'd been there all afternoon. Us girls were still in our school uniforms which was unusual for us and besides Mum had to get back to cook us tea.

The next day we set off for East Grinstead in 'Betsy Ann the third' heading towards Frome. Dad loved to take the scenic route wherever we went. As the car glided through the country-side we passed by a lot of green fields, Dad called them a plain, next thing we knew there was a great big circle of rocks nearby. This was the first time I'd seen Stonehenge.

Jeremiah 33:3
"Call to me, and I will answer you; I will tell you wonderful
And marvellous things that you know nothing about."

Dad told me about the ghost town opposite of where the army practiced. I felt intrigued. Further down the road this trip that was starting to seem endless until we started to pass more landmarks and Dad would point them out to me trying to engage me in conversation to make the journey less long. On the way we passed Guildford which seemed alive with planes flying overhead. We ended up going through Redhill town on the A25 which led to the hospital at East Grinstead.

At the hospital it was a bugger to park and the place seemed huge as we wondered round looking for the Peanut Ward. We eventually found it opposite the ward with old people in. This was to be my home for the next three weeks.

As I settled in there was a girl called Fiona Foster in the next bed on one side of me and a girl called Sarah Burr on the other side while opposite there was a boy called Alexander. His dad caused quite a stir complaining as they were with Bupa they should have had a private room. I liked the look of Alexander as he reminded me of the girl in the move Santa Clause but figured I wasn't allowed to talk to him. I think he'd have made a good subject for a story as I had an English text book given to me to keep me occupied.

I did get chatting to the two girls either side of me and would play with Sarah in the toy room. She was there because of a mole on her face that had grown so large it covered her whole cheek and was getting it removed. I told her that I was there to get my cornea replaced as my contacts had scratched my left eye causing korneacosis while I'd been on holiday to Swanage. I also told her that Mum had fainted when she was told I had a hundred stitches in my eye after the op.

I learned they had to drill a hole in the back of my eye as I'd contracted glaucoma during the operation.

When Mum turned up to see me she'd stay a couple of nights at a time and we would love to pull the television into my cubicle to watch films. I remember watching a Herbie film, but the one film that really stood out was Popeye with Robin Williams and Shelley Long. My Mum and I loved singing to the song, "And he's large." We would giggle at it.

One time when Mum came to visit she'd brought some alcohol from Dad's lorry with her to give to the older people across the hall. Mum went looking for Nigel Havers during one visit as apparently there was filming there.

The rest of my time was pretty uneventful but I did leave with Sarah and Fiona's addresses. I had asked Fiona if she was related to the actress Jodie Foster. She said no but we all did go on and be pen pals.

In the morning, back at school, I had a really good lesson of art and another one of music. In the classroom we learned about African instruments and we'd even had some in the class that got used in a traditional song that we were all enthralled by.

Then on the lunch break I went up the Youth Centre. As you'd first enter, there were padded bench chairs either side of tables and as you walked through them there was a confectionary counter to your left. At the far end of the room there'd been a comfy sofa facing a telly on the corner wall. This was in the same room the pool table was hogged by the boys. There'd also been an entrance to the squash courts of Shepton mallet Leisure Centre and toilets down the right hand side.

I'd sat down that day opposite Leigh on the computer game table to wait for him to finish. He was too good at Pacman though and I didn't get to play. Afterwards he irritated me by suing the table to doodle on scraps of bits of paper.

> Proverbs 10:26
> Never get a lazy person to do something for you;
> He will be as irritating as vinegar on your teeth
> Or smoke in your eyes.

He did these wonderfully complex mazes and I tried to draw them too on my bits of paper but mine were not so intricately drawn and ended up with lots of dead ends. My favourite doodles were usually hearts, flowers, and eyes.

Now after school that day I watched Grange Hill and I wanted to hear what a teacher in the programme had to say about doodles as she tried to set up an extra-curricular activity in studying them and what they meant, but the students never turned up. I'd have liked to have known what my drawings said about me. That bugged me.

The next day I got to school and I got to a drama class and acted the part of a Shakespearian character from Romeo and Juliet. I had a few lines in a passage with Mercutio and felt romantic as it had been a fight scene. I imagined two boys fighting over me and one of them was in the classroom a I dreamed away and blushed in front of him.

That afternoon I'd been up to the playing fields with Rheann and we passed by Caroline, Rosie and Hayley.

Caroline said, "I really admire your spirit as you're in and out of hospital a lot with your eyes."

I said, "Thank you," but I felt slightly bugged by that.

Friday came quickly and I lugged my heavy rucksack with all my folders and books into school. It occurred to me that a boy who wanted to help me could actually have offered to carry my bags for me. Wandering down the corridor to the classroom for roll call. The teacher called our names out and I slumped over the table letting out a large yawn while leaning on my bag. Dreaming of the boys in school knowing none of them really noticed I needed a bloody good friend. I let a tear trickle down my face. Names were called and I laughed when the same lad from before had put his hand up and said that he wasn't there. Always making the class giggle.

Slinging my heavy bag over my shoulders realising it was easier to carry it with both my arms in the arm holds. I marched about to my first lesson. Head held high I noticed Simon slip into a room downstairs and wandered in after him praying it was the right lesson. Never really checking my timetable. I sat right at the front of the class determined to see the blackboard that morning.

Mr Jeremiah always enthralled me reminding me of a comedian off the telly. I leaned back into my seat and sat up straight for once instead of slouching determined to take the lesson all in. My hair felt lovely and long that morning as I felt it glamorously swaying down my back. It had felt like all eyes had been on me that day and I couldn't stop grinning. It had still felt like, by the afternoon, someone, anyone, a good looking lad could offer to carry my bags in a mature way just like in the American movies I'd watched recently. I think it had been in My Girl.

Feeling beautiful in gym class of where the benches were and all the girls got together to put their bags on the hooks above hour heads. I actually had my own PE kit for once. Mum had given me a nice clean navy short skirt, kind a looking like a ra-ra to show off my lovely legs, my best feature. I also loved to put on my white airtex polo shirt. Feeling more beautiful than the rest and slightly envied we all made our way into the main hall. We had to set the chairs up in a big circle in the middle of the room leaving one spare free for musical chairs. The teacher had a large brown stereo that they put on the stage and they pressed play.

Never one to get all hot 'n' sweaty running around I just floated letting my hair float around like a halo. I stayed for about two rounds and I found myself battling for one seat and fell on to the lap of Aaron who actually seemed to blush and like it. I got up thinking this lesson was boring and sat on a chair in front of the big windows leaning into the curtains. I slouched trying to do my model pose of where you let your hips lead. The sun shone through the window and I noticed my hair looked golden as I sat there twirling my locks in my fingers.

Rushing back up to the showers I flashed my sexy legs to the boys knowing they were all staring. Stripping off back at my bags I grabbed my white towel and headed for the communal showers. I stood under the water that had initially made my whole body tingle from the freezing cold shock of it and let it warm me up. Standing there lathering myself up and pushing my face under the cascading water gasping for breath. My hands were all over my body getting myself nice and soapy. I eventually had to make my way through the steam seeing glimpses of the other girls' bare bodies. Feeling pink from the warmth I stepped back into the changing room of where the cold air hit me. I dried myself off really quickly trembling with the cold remembering Aaron's blush. It felt wonderful stepping back into my navy blue long skirt emphasising my little hips. I put on my white shirt leaving a provocative gap at the top. I felt really alive, glad to be able to go on home.

Running down the stairs I made my way across to the little car park to head off across town.

At home I'd had to wait for my sisters so I got into my skin tight jeans and a skimpy t-shirt. I looked down myself and admired my body in the mirror.

> *Proverbs 21:24*
> *Show me a conceited person and I will show you someone*
> *Who is arrogant, proud and inconsiderate.*

Mum called up the stairs to tell us we were off into Wells to see my Nan and Gramps.

We all clambered into the car. I'd have loved to have sat by the window but my sisters always got their own way. I just stared into the sunshine beaming in through the front window. Dad put the radio on and I sang inside my head humming and singing intermittently to where I could have butted in out loud.

Pulling up by Tor Woods we all got out the car and walked down the hill. I'd put my hair up in a ponytail letting it caress the back of my neck. Swishing it about, keeping cool.

On the way Mum asked me that if Gran gave me the money could I go get some fish 'n' chips. In their house that was the first thing Nan did. I can picture her get her small purse out digging deep into all her coins to pull out some notes. I felt pleased to be able to go and get them. Down the passage way trying to dodge the cracks in the floor I was soon inside the chip shop. The waiting area was quite large and as I ordered I could see the kitchen in the back where everyone was busy. I stood around for a long time reading the flyers on the wall. Mentally drumming my fingers on the counter. The food soon came out. Hugging it all to my breast to keep me warm I inhaled the smell and breathed deeply.

We all sat together in the living room tucking into our food. The sun streamed through the window trapping us in a moment unforgettable as we silently ate.

We all had a lovely meal together and the family stayed all evening just chatting. I enjoyed all the smiles and the talking patiently waiting to be spoken to. Never had I felt so warmed up from such nice food.

The evening ended implicitly as we all wandered up back up the road to the car. Slamming the door shut Dad went on and drove us home.

At home we went for a walk round the block before deciding that it was getting late. I took myself off to bed after having a bit of bread and cheese. In my nightie I snuggled up in my warm bed dreaming of the nice day I'd had.

In the morning I stretched out lazily in my bed and yawned slumbriously putting my hand to my mouth. I wandered downstairs for a drink. Opening the fridge I fished out some milk, poured it in to a glass, and gulped it down.

Everyone followed me downstairs all washed and dressed. I shivered from the cold, stood there in my nightie, and decided to get washed and dressed myself. I slung on my red dress. Sat down and picked up some knitting always trying to make squares.

Dreaming of being outside I just sat there with everyone milling about doing their own things. My Mum came to me with a drink, a nice cold orange juice, asking me if I was going to the carnival meeting with her that evening. I gave her my secretive smile and said yes. Getting up from the armchair I gave myself a mental hug.

The day was my own. Lunch was soon at the table. It was a lovely roast dinner. The pudding was a nice apple crumble and I got the skin from the hot custard.

We all soon got up from the table together and Dad sat down with the newspaper in the armchair. I picked up my knitting and it wasn't long before Mum was telling me that it was time to go out.

We were at the carnival meeting at The Crown at Pilton and I remember sitting upstairs in the big room that was normally a skittle alley. Feeling bored with the adults conversation going on and on around me and they were on about having a casino night up at the pub. It was going to take a lot to organise and Mum said she had sun visors at home for the croupiers to wear.

It had been a nice meeting and ended amicably.

In the morning in the corridor outside the history classroom I witnessed Lisa being chatted up by Damion. She looked flattered but she slapped him down. I felt jealous and pleased she didn't want him. I ventured into my lesson with a smirk on my face and I sat down with Rheann and Simon of whom had golden curls, a cheeky face, some freckles and was of medium build. We sat around smiling at each other as Mr Rees took the lesson. He reminded me of a king with his big build, ginger hair, with a moustache and beard. He was trying to get a discussion going and as always I held back not knowing when to butt in with my thoughts enjoying the foreplay. I wrote a note to Rheann in mirror writing to say look how clever I am and she wrote back I can do that too. Simon was watching and I could tell he wanted in what we were doing as he grabbed our note. He looked bemused to start off with and attempted the backwards writing himself. He was brainy, but scratched his head and put down the first thing that came into his mind about how intelligent he was too. It was a kind of flirting with him and sneaky with Rheann and we kept it going all lesson.

At lunch afterward Rheann and I sat on the grass and we had our food outside. We discussed very little just relaxing in the sunshine with the all-weather pitch in the background and hardly anyone else on the grass. I looked across to the bike shed and spied some bikes wondering where most of the school had gone for lunch.

Back in the classroom I'd felt happy and content just letting the afternoon lessons wash over me.

At home my homework came first in front of the telly sprawled out all over the carpet. I stuck to simple answers just to get my homework done and soon picked up my green and blue squares to knit with. Self-involved as always enjoying my own company the needles with my fingers soon created four squares and I pushed myself t do some more. There had been no-one around as far as I could tell. No-one sought my company. The hours flew by and tea appeared as if from nowhere on the table. Dad had come home. We all sat together mostly in silence with Mum and Dad sharing some of their news at interjections into the silence.

Sat in the living room we turned on Children In Need. The opening credits gave the line-up for the evenings viewing but I was looking forward to watching the amount raised on the screen go up and up. They started with the band playing their charitable song. I picked up the song very quickly and hummed and sang along to it. My face aglow I watched the presenters happily telling the viewers where the money would go and they said all up and down the countryside. It gave me a buzz and then a heart rendering story came on about a boy in a wheelchair needing friends and an active life. They said that a children's centre needed the money to expand to encompass more special children like this boy. In the building they showed those with Down syndrome and various degrees of disabilities. My heart went out to them. I loved the bits where they filmed all over the country with the crowds cheering on the amounts being raised. I remember in Scotland a man having a sponsored shave there and then on the stage. They lathered up his face with shaving foam and cut to the main audience back in London. The crowds were cheering a celebrity come to endorse and promote the charity. My mind was wondering if they secretly donated a lot of their wealth.

I wanted to stay up all night and watch excited about how much they would raise. Mum made a five pound pledge, a pound from each of us over the phone and later on made us crackers and cheese for supper.

It wasn't until about 2am in the morning when the programme finished that we all went to bed.

That Saturday there was a game of football on the telly on BBC1. It was a match with Eve's favourite team Liverpool. We'd sat and watched the whole game cheering inwardly with Mum cuddled up with Dad. Mum talked all the way through and Dad with the patience of a saint tried to explain the rules. Mum just got swept up in her own emotions sounding forced irritating me as the rest of us stayed silent. It was like she was deliberately putting it on to impress Dad.

The end of the game came and Liverpool won. That evening we went to bed quite late and my mind was buzzing and I felt euphoric that Ipswich Town and Wimbledon won their games as I liked their blue football kit. It was my favourite colour.

In bed that evening I found it very hard to sleep. I'd lain awake for most of the night as my sister Eve recounted the whole football commentary of the match we'd watched in her sleep. All the while I smiled secretly to myself.

In the morning I woke up to feel fully awake and alert for the whole day. Mum wanted us to get ready for church and we got into the car that shot across town to pull up in the large car park at the bottom of town. We soon got into some pews and were attentive. I got into the first hymn that I sang really loudly and enjoyed myself. Then there was a gospel reading from *Peter 1:24-25*

> *As the scripture says:*
> *"All human beings are like grass*
> *And all their glory is like wild flowers,*
> *The grass withers, and the flowers fall,*

But the word of the Lord remains forever."

I had a really good sing that morning and the sermon was really long. It had the synopsis of everyone having a beautiful soul inside them like the bud of a flower waiting to open up to God and grow. At the end of the service I had a wonderful day having a roast dinner for lunch and then going for a walk with the family.

In the evening I went to The Crown at Pilton with Mum for a carnival meeting and she did the work of a secretary. That night I slept peacefully.

On the Monday my sisters were packaged off to school and I stayed behind in my jeans and t-shirt waiting to go to hospital. It was the first day for my stitches to be removed from my eye. I'd been looking forward to it. Yawning and stretching I put my hand over my mouth. The cold air outside woke me up as it hit my face. I put my hands in my pockets ready to go on a nice long journey with Mum and Dad. I saw it as an adventure. Slamming the door shut Dad had a go at me saying I'd break the hinges. I silently seethed that I didn't have the strength to break a bloody door and sat passively in the car waiting for the engine to roar.

Not speaking to them I sank into the side seat with my head against the window silently humming to myself with a song on the radio. I went to click my fingers but didn't make much of a noise, so I kept trying. Queen came on the radio singing "We'll keep on trying to walk that fine line," and I sang my heart out with no sisters looking at me to slap me down. It was a long journey and I, like my Dad, enjoyed the freedom of the road. I looked out the window and Dad told me about the army ghost town story again. I strained my eyes to look into the distance looking for beige empty buildings and I could feel the echoes of the guns. It made me feel empty inside. The moment was implicit. The sky looked so blue and I was at peace with the world. Mum and Dad were quiet.

It took us a long time to get there and the hospital looked quiet. The halls were echoey as we headed for the Peanut ward. The lady at the desk said there were no beds available. We'd come all that way for nothing. I went into the children's' play room as I was told to and played with the toys reminiscing about when Sarah and I played there together. I'd been there for a while sat on a push along toy before Dad poked his head round the door. I was told to go and sit on a spare bed to hang around for a while but the operation couldn't be fitted in that day. They'd made a mistake and was told to go home by Dad who'd said, "Sorry luv, we have to go home," with his hands in his pockets looking contrite.

The sky outside was getting dark there was a storm raging overhead, I hadn't eaten for twenty four house in anticipation of having the hundred stitches taken out of my eye. The storm raged overhead as we got stuck in traffic. The whole sky turned black, it was like demons swirling overhead against a red sky. I fell asleep till we got home. I felt weak as I went upstairs to bed.

Now first thing in the morning the telephone rang and I leapt out of bed to run downstairs and answer it. Picking the phone up I blanked out. I could hear the phone banging against the radiator. As I came round I was flat on the floor. Dad poked his head out of the kitchen door looking scared. He told me that he'd get me some dried toast. I was too weak to get up so Dad had to force feed me gently until I had the strength to do it myself out in the hallway. Dad got me a drink of fizzy water then I went back to bed after saying thanks. I hadn't eaten for twenty four hours.

A few weeks later in the early morning as Fee and Eve got ready for school. I dressed in jeans and a jumper to go to hospital with Mum and Dad again. Today was the day I'd been going to have my stitches out and I felt happy. Pulling my hair into a ponytail I traipsed off behind them jumping in the car. They sped off. Dad was in full control. The car ate up the countryside. We flew passed Stonehenge. The fields were gloriously filled with rape and lush green foliage. I really enjoyed the scenery.

Pulling up to the massive old fashioned stone building of the hospital in East Grinstead we swept up the gravel to park.

Walking through the wide entrance doors we looked for the Peanut ward and I got shown my bed. The nurse came to speak with us to tell me what time the operation was. My eye was throbbing with the excitement of finally getting my hundred stitches out.

In the operating theatre they put a needle into the back of my left hand and I counted backwards from ten not getting to one. Next thing I knew my eye had been propped open and saw them take the strands of each stitch out. The bright lights were making me want to close my eyes to blot it all out.

I came round a few hours later and my eye sight was the best it had ever been. My mind felt so clear. The first thing they did was come to me with a drink and sandwiches. Mum and Dad were allowed back into the room to see me. They had been full of smiles telling me that they were proud of me. Mum brushed my hair back from my face and I responded with a bright smile of my own looking into their bright blue eyes. The colour matched the sky outside and Dad rattled his keys in his pocket. He told Mum that we'd stop off at McDonalds on the way back home for tea. I pulled out my shoes and my clothes to get dressed and took my time putting it all on. I'd felt elated thinking I was finally free of all hospitals.

Dad said, "We'd better go," while looking at his watch. Finally pulling on my shoes I jumped off the bed.

Following them back through the hospital we made our way to the car. I slammed the door feeling triumphant and Dad gave me an irritated look and said, "Don't slam the door."

All three of us were soon carving up the countryside heading for a McDonalds. I'd asked for a cheese burger and chips and ate hungrily. Mum and Dad had Big Macs.

Back in the car Dad put the radio n not inciting any discussions. I lazily propped my head up with my hands leaning on the door and stared out the window. The whole world seemed to float by encouraged by the sound of the engine I drifted back off to sleep with the sounds of the songs drifting through my subconscious. Mum and Dad talked quietly until some familiar landscape came into view at the top of Shepton.

I wasn't really aware of this at the time but Mum and Dad liked to encourage our competitive streak. I just enjoyed doing things with the family and being active. There was a phase we went through playing some sport on some weekends called squash. We'd all take it in turns to partner up. I remember one time in particular when I was the one watching Mum with Fee and Eve with Dad on the opposing courts from the bridge running through the middle. I would see them pound a little green ball against a wall back and forth to each other, not really understanding the rules. All I knew was that if you didn't get to the ball in time the other person scored a point. When it was my turn I would struggle to run round the court chasing the ball as my wheezing would play up but it was fun. I had no regular inhaler back then and felt fit enough to join in.

Chapter Twelve

First lesson on the Monday was physical education and I had to borrow an old gym kit. The little skirt was a royal blue colour. I loved the way it floated round the top of my thighs showing off my best feature my legs. Putting on the airtex top that was light blue it was creased. I didn't even care then made my way downstairs, after looking down over the balcony watching the teachers setting up in the gymnasium. At the bottom of the stairs I was the last one in the room. The blue mats had been put out over the floor. I did a cartwheel showing off my knickers I didn't even care. It was gymnastics. We took turns to do cartwheels and back flips from corner to corner of the mats. Mine weren't even that brilliant but I tried. Hot and sweaty after my time I cooled off by sitting on the bench just watching. I was living in the moment watching the fit boy enjoying their physiques and their rippling muscles.

Feeling cold after cooling down the lesson was over and we all got changed and went to lunch.

I dallied in the school hall and went to the gymnasium equipment, the weights. I sat on the bench and put on 20 kilos and lifted them in the air feeling so strong. I witnessed my muscles flex and admired them.

That afternoon we had a history lesson and learned about Florence Nightingale and how she trained to be a nurse and did her share of all the cleaning. She was famous for it and they called her the lady of the lamp.

It was coming up to Christmas and the whole family got together for the 25th. We really enjoyed ourselves.

Then on Boxing Day the family got together at my aunty and uncles to celebrate Nan and Gramps wedding anniversary. I'd wanted to buy a card myself but realised Mother and Father bought a family card. We all sat around in the living room and I spied a drum kit at the side of the room. It looked tempting but I sat and watched everyone stuff themselves. Everyone talked together animatedly but I had nothing to say. The others wanted nothing more than to talk. I'd have some music to dance to for a proper party. It was boring for me. I went over to the drum kit and picked up the drum sticks. I'd started to tap the left drum then the cymbal while tapping my feet I made a wonderful beat. Casey and Charlie got me off the drums saying it was too loud.

I went out into the hallway and found the karaoke machine that Granddad had gotten on first. He was singing the old fashioned love songs animatedly. Looking pink in the cheeks from booze. The evening went on and on until the early part of the morning. Uncle Cyn started to see us out of the door chatting animatedly and made us all laugh.

In the morning I put on the TV and during January, Christmas break from school, I watched Sleeping Beauty, of which I wanted to tape and keep. I remember vividly the prince slaying the dragon whilst over what looked an erupting volcano. I'd seen that bit while up at the table in the dining room. I'd been doing homework at the table and wanted to keep that film to play back later. We were playing Christmas games like snap with the cards. I was looking forward, not, to going back to school and when at school a week later I got talking to a younger lad at school in a year below me. He looked cute with his sandy coloured hair and handsome face so I asked him out.

He said, "Sure. We'll walk home after school together."

"That would be nice."

It had been a lunch break and I was looking forward to the date with Jason. I thought we could walk through the meadows together holding hands. I thought about this during French and we were learning the words to objects around the home. One word made me laugh it was couche as I'd heard somewhere the words Voulez-vous couche avec moi c'est soir? And I believed it was something to do with sex but learned the word le couche as being the shower.

After school I walked with Jason all across town and we chatted nicely even walking down the hill towards the meadows, but from there we parted. Jason walked on home by himself and I turned and walked onto the Wimpey Estate to Coombe View.

A year later in the morning during Christmas week the family went to Uncle Cyn's for a Boxing Day party. The whole family was there talking, eating, drinking and I felt like I was being ignored as nobody spoke to me.

> *Ecclesiastes 2: 1-3*
> *I decided to enjoy myself and find out what happiness is.*
> *But I found that this is useless, too. I discovered that laughter*
> *Is foolish, that pleasure does you no good.*
> *Driven on by my desire for wisdom, I decided to cheer myself up*
> *With wine and have a good time.*

So I hit into the wine. I needed clarification that they actually wanted me there. I sat in the living room all night drinking away watching the TV trying to listen into other people's conversation wanting to put my point of view across.

Now come the end of the evening Casey and Charlie's mouse had gotten loose and we all panicked. Everyone had to stop what they were doing and find it. It wasn't even their mouse it had been the schools, they gave it to my cousins as a pet project. The cage had been in the corner of the room adroitly behind the sofa. I'd been the one putting her hands down on the floor ready to catch it if they shot out of the sofa. I braced myself like a goalkeeper with their hands almost touching the ground. Then I saw him creeping out from under the fireplace. It freaked me out as I thought the fire would have burnt the poor thing.

"Don't worry cuz, the heating's not on."

"Phew. Oh look there he is again," and it flew out of the windowsill as it jumped from the armchair to there.

A lot of us gave up an hour later while I was still down on all fours at the side of the sofa I soon got fed up and Charlie found the mouse under the table the cage was on. She picked the mouse up. That was the highlight of that Boxing Day.

That Saturday we all wanted to go our separate ways. Fee had been asking and asking Mum for a lift and for money to go shopping with her friends. Eve had already gone out. I'd been upstairs at first sorting out my Sindy doll house cutting out a nice lot of squares from old pieces of carpet laying them out on the bottom of the drawer under my bed. The voices got louder coming up through the floor. I had watched so many American movies by now to know how I'd go downstairs and instinctively use my sweet little calm voice to make Fee and Mum stop shouting. I'd hated the shouting so much by now that I went to walk through the living room and saw a ferocious face on my sister angrily snapping at Mum.

"Mum will you please just give me a little bit of money and a lift into town with my friends!"

I interjected and said, "Mum, it doesn't have to be this way, it doesn't have to be this way."

Mum threw a ferocious look my way and said, "Butt out of it. This doesn't concern you," and she shoved me hard against the shoe cupboard door frame. I sunk to the floor instinctively touching that sharp sting on the back of my head. My eyes blurred over for a second and I mentally shook it off in time to see my mother slap her round her left cheek. I sensed that same sting in her. Her face went white with shock. Mum used a softer voice this time and asked "Why?"

Fiona gave a sensible answer in a cold clear voice. The answer Mum wanted and I knew they never needed my help at all.

Fee went out the door any way coldly and calmly probably to walk to her friends down town having reached a compromise with Mum over money. The war was over and Mum stormed off in a rage. I just picked myself up Mum never even turned round to see me as I blinked back tears.

Job 11:16
Then all your troubles will fade from your memory.

I stuck my jaw up in the air feeling resolute enough to want to just go up the park by the swimming pool.

No-one came looking for me and afterward no-one asked if I was all right or what I'd been going to say. Coming off the swing had been a real buzz for me after going higher and higher in the air matching the height of the top bar flying through the air with that same old frisson of excitement running through me. Feeling alive in my mind I'd ended up thinking that no family was at home when I got back. So I let myself back in through the garden and sat down on the concrete path at the edge of the garden oblivious really if anyone was at home.

Waking up next morning I could still feel that sharp pain a little bit at the back of my head I'd pushed my head into the pillow real hard all night to get rid of my pain. There was no cup of tea and biscuits for anyone that morning and my mind started emanating an aura around my head that looked crystal clear.

Sat on the sofa later wishing I'd been at church I'd never felt so alone.

Job 19:13
God has made my family forsake me;
I am a stranger to those who know me.

I'd felt a cold cut through my heart and I saw a white light feeling like a knife shoot into my side.

Then and there a part of me felt something was missing but the light grew and in my head I thought that there must have been a twin sister in my mother's womb that had died. I was going to put myself first.

In the hallway at the cafeteria I'd found Rheann on the pay phone she was talking to her mother and on the top of the phone there was a packet of Maltesers. I cheekily put my hand inside the wrapper and popped a sweet into my mouth, but before I put it in she bit my hand and was shocked for a moment.

The end of the day came and I decided to find a friend to walk home with, Rheann got a very determined stance about her marching us all the way back to her mother's house. We went up to her bedroom and had a nice discussion about boys and life. I went downstairs for a drink.

I found myself walking home on my own afterward in the sunshine. Flashing my lovely legs and at home Mum greeted me. We sat down together and talked about our faith. I'd always felt a real spiritual connection with her.

My mind felt clear about Jesus's ministry and the parable about the sower. My mind was made up that I'd found a friend who's head was in the brambles as Mum told me we were two mixed up individuals. But I wasn't.

That evening I went up to my room to watch the TV and stayed there till bedtime.

That morning at school the form teacher was asking for little actors and actresses to try out for our year's school play. They said that they needed a pianist and I thought great that could be me. I never actually put myself forward though that day and went about my lessons as normal. I'd had PE class of where we went outside to play netball while the boys played football.

The next few lessons were mathematics, English and physics.

After that school that day by the car park on the top road I'd actually had a conversation with a boy named Dan, of whom was a bit robust, but had dark hair and a pleasant face. I thought I could have had a potential boyfriend in him as he was good looking and I'd liked his attention.

When I got out of school I walked home with Rheann all across town until we got to Beech Avenue. We walked to the little shop and got some drinks and sweets before going to Simon who'd come from welsh Wales. We went to his house and banged him up. He was in. he came to the door and invited us in for a drink. We all had juice. We stayed for a while for a little chat. Simon had gorgeous blonde curly locks and a tiny birthmark on his face. He was about my size, average. It wasn't long before we made our way home after saying goodbye.

I had a lovely evening at home and next day when I got into school a little bit late and I'd missed assembly in school. I had to get my folder out to see what first lesson was. It was music and I had to make my way to the back of the school hall and I managed to catch up with the queue going into class. We all sat down and I automatically eyed up the piano with the lid up begging to be played. I had the chance to get up and sing and Rocky said he liked my voice of which I'd always remember. I learnt nothing that lesson only that Rocky liked me. Then afterwards I had a PE lesson of where we did country dancing in the main hall. We doesy-doed all round the floor and had to swap partners and when I got to Aaron he enjoyed hugging me. That's what he said and I liked being flattered.

After morning break I had a French lesson and I sat behind Katherine and before the teacher came in she was being a bit of a bitch gossiping about naughtiness that I'd supposedly done.

> *Leviticus 19:17-18*
> *"Do not bear a grudge against anyone, but settle your differences with her, so that you will not commit a sin because of him. Do not take revenge on anyone or continue to hate her, but love your neighbour as you love yourself. I am the Lord."*

Now I sat there, in revenge, yanking her lovely long curly hair out of her head. I yanked harder and harder with my left hand while I still wrote my work down with my right hand.

When home the family watched a film together called Three Men and a Little Lady. No-one believed me when I said that it was the character Jack who was the vicar impostor. While I was watching it Dad gave me a bit of paper and a pen to take dictation of a football match he wanted in the local paper. I sat there and wrote it out very neatly about Wells the team he was a manager of.

The next day Miss Davies in maths class singled me out to talk to me in the middle of a lesson. I giggled nervously at being spoken to in front of the whole class and she thought I was laughing at her and so got told to stand outside the classroom till the end of the lesson. She put in my yearly report that there are times when her attitude is wrong and her work suffers. I thought that was totally unfair as she had never spoken two words to me before that incident.

It was after this lesson a fight broke out at the bottom of the stairs between Aaron and Elvis over a girl named Jasmine. I was scared as they blocked the bottom of the stairs. I hurried to get passed while shaking like a leaf.

I got up the next day and felt pleased to be going to school. I enjoyed my lessons in the morning and sat with Becky, Barbara and Emma and Rheann for lunch.

After lunch I had maths and sat next to Damion, the boy I'd fancied and spent the entire lesson staring at his long strong artistic fingers. I still managed to finish my maths book.

In the next lesson it was Physics. I thoroughly enjoyed it, for the lesson I had to draw a graph and answer questions from a text book. I laughed to myself doing the whole assignment in mirror writing and it looked very clearly written. I handed to the teacher as soon as I'd finished and soon got the assignment back. Mr Greenway had put on there krow doog and 10 out of 10 in mirror writing too and I felt really proud of my work. I also learned about a split atom and that split down enough there was nothing holding everything up so I ascertained that was where God was.

At home later I did a last minute go through of my tunes for my exams for fifth grade. I enjoyed them and was soon in Wells on the grand piano. I thought that I did very well and was pleased with myself. I'd thought I'd get a merit.

A few days later I got a letter through the post, it was my certificate. I'd got a pass grade and knew I was going to have to give up lessons for exams at school were about to take priority.

The next day Lisa, the object of my girl crush, had asked me if I'd liked knitting as she was knitting scarecrows. Upon saying yes she gave me the pattern for the scarecrows hat that Lisa had told me was to be in green.

I soon got stuck into knitting a hat. As it had been easy to make. I was soon hitting into my second hat too. My knitted blanket and dolls clothes were soon taking a back seat.

In the morning, while packing my school bag, two hats were ready to give to Lisa and I'd started another one to also take with me to school.

It had been a lovely sunny day to end off the school week and it was soon the afternoon and Physical Education. We were all outside. The teacher had announced it was to be rounders and I'd actually brought my own PE kit for once and was surprised as I'd gotten picked for captain. Beaming proudly I'd chosen the best boys for my team like Rocky and Gavin and he'd told me that he was into masochism. Blushing madly I got ready to bat and was soon out. Lisa had got out before me and had been sitting underneath the large tree at the bottom of the school field happily knitting. My bag had been slung under that tree so I took my knitting out and Lisa and I sat there quietly watching our team win. I'd felt really happy and at peace that afternoon.

In the evening I got near the end of my latest book by James Herbert.

The next day I found myself in history again writing in mirror writing just to impress my mates, Rheann and Simon.

By the afternoon I kept going through the alphabet backwords from z to a as I walked through the canteen to go outside.

Rheann said, "What are you on about?"

"The alphabet backwards," and I laughed. I thought of EastEnders and srednetsae and laughed again. I was trying to think of the way to say things backwards.

It was chilly next day when Dad and I set out for the lorry. With our bags packed for an overnight trip to Cumbria to see my Aunty and Uncle, Dad and I got in the cabin. As the engine roared and Terry Wogan's lovely voice wafted into the air I soon fell asleep.

I awoke on the motorway and clambered down onto the passenger seat from the bed. Dad couldn't speak as he'd been concentrating on the road so I looked around and got excited by the height of being able to look for miles and the speed of the vehicle overtaking cars and other lorries. The music on the radio had me humming along and I stretched out happy and relaxed.

The sun was getting higher as we pulled into a service station for an early lunch. I always had a sausage sarnie and Dad had a bacon butty. After drinks, the toilet, and being able to stretch our legs Dad said there was another three hour drive to the Lake District.

On the way there though there'd been hold ups and Dad had a phone call to pick up Uncle Keith from work.

Around five thirty I remember driving towards an ethereal golden glow over a small expanse of water with green hills either side and there was a small white building that was the pharmaceuticals where Uncle Keith worked.

Once Uncle Keith was in the cabin I had to clamber back on the bed and I listened in on the two brothers chatting about where to go to get to Uncle Keith's home.

We went through a very idyllic looking village and I remember a tall house that looked like the colour of sand with a gravel drive way. Dad pulled the lorry in from the road.

Aunty Sue said the housekeeper had gone home so put on a prepared spaghetti bolognaise into their microwave for us to eat. We all watched a bit of telly before making my excuses to go to bed, and I remember looking down over the balcony over the living room watching the adults in front of the telly before sloping off in my jammies to sleep.

I think they had a relative visiting the next day and have a brief recollection of looking round their decadently landscaped garden out the back before Dad and I left to drive all the way home.

In the morning it was a Friday the 13th and I got up out of bed happy. I went to stand in front of the big mirror to get dressed and I suddenly had to lean on it to put my socks on as I wobbled. Next thing I knew I'd pushed the glass on the floor smashing everywhere. I got scared as I knew that a mirror smashing meant seven years bad luck. Being a Friday then thirteenth I had been in a good mood thinking that all thirteenths were lucky days for me as I was born on the thirteenth.

I got up the big pieces of glass then Mum came in and said, "What's that noise?" Then told me off for picking up the pieces saying she'd do it with a dust pan and brush.

I got on with going into school and had a weird feeling about the next seven years. I started with a music lesson and we were learning about music out in Rio and their big carnival. I looked at the pictures of the big wonderful costumes all very brightly coloured and very beautiful.

In RE I rocked on a chair tapping my pen on my book. Looking at the Jewish religion and their Bar Mitzvah of when they have a coming of age ceremony for twelve year old boys. I also learned that Bar Mitzvah for thirteen year old girls of whom had come of age. Traditionally, my book said, the father of the Bar Mitzvah gives thanks to God that he is no longer punished for the child's sin {in Genesis Rabba, Toldot 23:11} a different kind of Bible.

After break I went to History and we got some books each to read about Cleopatra and Antony of whom were lovers. They both died for each other after being the two most powerful couple in Egypt. They died not long after the battle with the Romans.

Next, after the bell, was Physics, that was downstairs over at the science block. In the lesson we learned about the power of gravity and Sir Isaac Newton's law about it. I thought the mirror that morning had a certain gravitational pull on it and glazed. I heard that it was based on Coulomb's

Law and that it had something to do with inverse square laws. I looked at my bit of paper with the diagram on and I had to fill in the gaps Mr Greenway said. I'd been getting quite good at algebra but spent the whole hour trying to work it out.

The next two lessons were a double class of mathematics. I sat by the window and worked my cotton socks off ploughing my way through two more books.

On the way home I was on my own as everyone had gone early. It was a sunny day. Now at home I threw my books on the living room floor and lay on the floor to do my Physics home work. I tried really hard to get the mathematics of Newton's Law of gravity. It gave me a headache. I did a bit of history, my maths and RE homework before spending a good two hours on the piano.

When Mum, Dad, Fee, Eve and I and Gran and Gramps went on holiday to C'an Picaforte together we stayed in a hotel on the sea front. We were all soon spending days on the beach and us girls all had lilos. Eve and I spent all afternoon on our lilos one day just leisurely drifting out to the small red and white lighthouse about a mile out to sea. I was a bit scared of seeing what was under us so far out and on top of lots of rocks and green seaweed with possible sea creatures swimming around. Eve and I dared ourselves to sit on the concrete step but I was scared of leaving my lilo and losing it out to see. We soon came back into shore again but Mum looked worried as we had been out to see so long.

One afternoon after having spent most of the day on the beach we took a family bicycle that sat five of us with a canvas shade on the top around some of the coastline roads. I remember stopping at another beach and grabbing a coke with lots of ice in even though wee weren't supposed to drink the local water the ice soon melted.

That evening Gramps was conned into eating squid because my parents told him it was pork, he hit into most of it until they finally confessed as to what he was actually eating and he didn't want it after that.

In the mornings there wasn't much of a selection just mostly cold meats, salad and cheeses.

At night Fiona and Eve would hook up with some lads and attend the evening discos in the hotel. One lad was German of whom I remember sat at a table talking to him while Eve got drinks and I remember her being off with me not getting my own drinks.

Towards the end of the holiday we all became ill and thought it had been the local water being ice in all our drinks.

There was an underground nightclub not far from our hotel a bit old school with fancy dancer that we'd said we'd go to see but never got round to it.

Not long after we'd gone back home there was a news report that our hotel had shut down due to food poisoning. Apparently it had been in the cold meats.

Back at school in the morning I went to Physics and there was a young stand in teacher. His name was Matthew and looked a bit green behind the ears and very young. Lisa told me that she fancied him as I walked by her and we ended up having a little chat before the lesson started. I laughed inwardly thinking of a private little six joke with myself as I pictured them together. Then I walked off to my table to enjoy sitting by myself as I'd chosen Physics to take the exam of later on because we'd all chosen our favourite subjects to do for the rest of school.

I'd chosen Physics, History, French and Music but English, and Maths had to be studied till I finished school. I loved those subjects but the Biology teacher put me off that subject and so did the Chemistry teacher. When I saw Mr Casey he was a bit mystified as to why I never took Drama he said I was very good at it but everyone told me to take Music as I played the piano.

Now in the next lesson I had physical education and we were all outside to learn the long jump and the high jump for our own mini-Olympics. I had a go at the long jump and leapt into the air to land a metre away, for me the teacher said that was really good. Next I queued up to do the high jump with the pole vaults. I grabbed hold of the stick and amazed myself at ow high I jumped over the pole vault it was set at four metres high. I had a lot of fun and enjoyed stretching myself physically.

Then we had a mini-break to get some confectionary but I never had any, so my best mate Rheann and I went for a chat just walking around the grounds for half an hour before going our own sweet ways to our next lessons. I went to music as she went to drama. At music I went to the far side of the school. There were lots of windows for me to stare out as th lesson was boring we were learning something about sitars and other weird instruments that I'd never heard of.

That afternoon I went to my usual music lesson with Mrs Bosley's and she presented me with a violin. She asked me, "Would you like to know how to play a violin?"

"Yes. What violin?"

"Don't worry," she said, "I've got one here. You should try a second instrument."

I said, "Ok," and picked up the instrument and used the bow. I started writhing it across the strings and it sounded like a cat being strangled. In other words it sounded bloody awful. I endured the noise to be taught some of the notes but each time the noise it made went straight through me and made me wince each time.

I had to put my teacher straight, "I cannot endure this sound trying to learn this instrument. I've inwardly winced at each try on it."

"That's ok. You clearly won't develop a love for it. I thought you'd just enjoy a second instrument."

That Saturday Mum took us girls to see Nan and Gramps in Cheddar at Nan's souvenir shop, this was situated in the only shopping centre at the bottom of the Gorge. Three shops up from Nan's was an amusement arcade of where I liked to go and play space invaders for about an hour at a time.

At the amusement arcade there was a penny making machine which reminded me of the Zog making wishes come true machine from Tom Hanks film 'Big' and out of its mouth and underneath was a white card with a prediction on. It gave me the creeps. I really enjoyed visiting Nan's shop as she would occasionally let me serve on the till. When I would go up the Gorge I loved the ice-creams opposite the pound shop overlooking the river usually just before Mum would take us home.

At home I went and played chopsticks Aunty Nola had taught me and picked up by ear the song on the piano in the film 'Big'. I'd felt proud of myself and imagined being right in the moment of when I'd seen that scene of when Tom Hanks' character was dancing on the keyboard.

Next morning we saw my cousin Katy turn up, with my Uncle and Aunt, Keith and Sue. They stayed for a little while but asked if Katy could stay with us for the day while they went to a place called Bath. I'd heard Mum say that was fine.

Fee, Eve, Mum, Dad and I from under the stairs found six tennis rackets and a tube of little yellow balls to take over to the council owned tennis courts by the Shepton Mallet football field. Then we all walked over town to these courts and there were two free. Mum, Eve and Fiona took up one court playing two against one with a ball while me, Dad and Katy used the other court.

Dad served the ball first expecting us girls to run around after it. I did all the hard work running around while little Katy stood there bemused striking out sometimes. She looked so cute with her golden hair, blue eyes in all innocence tried to keep up. Dad played unfairly a bit though as he took competing against us very seriously and we could barely keep up. I loved tennis and soon built up a sweat as the sun rose higher in the sky.

We played all morning and I learned more rules like playing an ace serve that was basically a ball hit straight down the middle of the court with no-one able to resound the ball back. Dad's competitiveness was irritating I just liked the exercise. Katy and I just enjoyed playing the game.

There was constant shouting on the court by us as Mum and Fee kept declaring the balls were out and John McEnroe's voice kept resounding round my head from off TV saying, "The ball was out man." I laughed to myself saying this line in my head in an American accent. I didn't realise

I'd said that our loud and Fee, Eve and Mum just laughed at me and I blushed but I loved hearing their laughter.

I gave up after a while as I started wheezing from laughing and running around so much. Dad wanted us to stay on right up until a late lunch to help get our appetites up he'd said. I took a tennis ball and started pounding it against a wall that had a white outline of a football net, on it, very hard. This took a lot of my frustrations of losing against my Dad anyway.

At home afterwards we all regressed with Dad back to when he was a little boy at school. He was telling us about his brother Uncle Keith and of how he used to recall whole programmes while sat in front of the telly while doing his homework. I felt not pride about his brother coming from Dad but a feeling that he'd had a real chip on his shoulder. That Uncle Keith had been the one who'd followed his dreams and gotten everything that he wanted. It was a nice getting to know you session with who Dad actually was.

In the evening my Uncle and Aunt came back. They spouted a bit of French between one another of which Fee would say later on that it pissed her off. I enjoyed their talk though trying to pick up new French words as I went along.

One afternoon I remember having asked Mrs Bosley if I could learn the guitar. Mum took me straight up the Bath Road out of Wells to her house. She dropped me off and I walked up the steps feeling wheezy with my books clasped against my chest and my new guitar with me. My heart beat racing finally I was going to learn something that was going to be easier than the piano. I'd loved the sound of a guitar especially on the LPs Mum and Dad used to play at home in the evenings. The sound of a wooden Spanish guitar was my favourite. Harold greeted me at the door way to lead me through their pokey hallway then to the left was the music room. All the books were a bit of a clutter but there was a large place round the piano. I sat on the stall facing Miriam and she handed me the guitar I'd bought from having had my birthday.

The feel of the strings were harsh against my soft fingers but she gave me a guitar book and taught me the notes going through the scales bit by bit. By the end of the lesson I'd been taught one little tune that went like: da, da,da…, da da…, da da da da. Happy with my accomplishments and pleased at the way Mrs Bosley taught with plenty of pictures. I'd always remember her telling me that she used to teach my Nan, Sheila, the piano in her house too.

Mum soon came to pick me up at the door and neve ever not come in to chat with my Nan's old friend. We'd sit there for a while as I'd itch to leave and go home. Feeling frustrated listening to a conversation I'd felt not included in and remained tense.

Job 6:11
What strength have I got to keep on living?

Mum never noticed as Harold went to open the front door and it frustratingly took us ages to get outside.

Running down the steps first without a care in the world I hadn't noticed Mum pick up my guitar and music. My teacher was a lovely old lady as I slipped into the passenger seat just waiting for Mum. I'd slammed the door hoping Mum would get the message. Then ten minutes later we were finally on the way home.

At home I'd wanted to play for my sisters and I still had time to do homework and practice the piano too before settling in my room to watch my little black and white telly.

I loved to watch Drop the Dead Donkey with Stephen Tomkinson in that I'd fancied to bits. I'll always remember that episode of where he'd bungee jumped with a girlfriend he was having sex with while dangling in the air.

The following day excitement was brewing as I was looking forward to going back to school and did some gruelling last minute homework. I liked to speak French while getting on with it front of the telly. I'd also hit into an English essay as that was based on one of my favourite books by Shakespeare. Writing effortlessly I didn't put much thought into my work and was ready to go back to school. Always being a last minute worker.

Blowing off steam in the back garden I did endless hand stands and back flips, of where I'd arched over backwards on all fours pushing my legs up into a handstand and over again.

Mum called us all for tea, she'd even called Mrs Blackers looking for Eve. I noticed as I'd crept in being the first for the dinner table always wanting to be the good child. Mum then came in telling us girls Eve wouldn't be home as she was staying with her friend Kelly for tea with Helen too.

Never one to complain about food I ate hungrily eating everything on my plate. Fee on the other hand asked for too much and couldn't finish her meal. Mum always maintained that we couldn't get pudding unless we ate everything and so my sister had to eat it all up. Mum took our plates to the kitchen and all she asked for was for us to dry up. Fee had done a few things then made her excuses by going to the toilet. I'd stayed and finished it all up by myself. Mum was pleased with me and told me that Dad, when he got back, would want to watch the snooker. I turned it on anyway getting out my knitting needles to do some yellow squares for my blanket. I'd smiled up at dad when he got in and our eyes twinkled at each other before he turned the channel to BBC2 for world class darts. The close ups got me excited, sat next to Dad, watching them get their 180 scores of the voice of which I loved and I'd shout with them, "One hundred and eighty!" Dad and I laughed together.

At eight pm we had to dress up but I stayed in my jeans to go off to Showerings Social Club. It was summer skittles and Mum and Dad played in a mixed couple's team. I loved to stand there watching the balls thunder down the alley, but it was too loud for me with the clapping and the cheers. Dad tried to wind me up which was easy for him as I found my voice got ultra-sonic and hated him for it.

Turning my back Eve and I went into the bar and I picked up the shove half penny game with all the chalk on it. Eve and I were so close we'd marked up each other's scores, with the loud cheers coming from the alley. We then noticed the skittles board. It had been on a green table and you had to swing a ball to hit down as many pins as possible.

We always had Coca-Cola and a packet of crisps while going back into the alley winding up being ignored as we watched our parents happily winning their game.

They joined us after that and took us straight home.

It was Sunday the next day and Mum never insisted we wore our best clothes to church. Mum and I opened the kitchen cupboards that morning with Fee to take harvest goodies to church. I'd taken a nice long shower and slung on my shirt, jeans and shoes passing everyone in the hallway watching them load up the car with one box of fresh vegetables and another box of flour, cans, and cake making things. I was always happy.

At the church the display of harvest food was amazing. The whole front of the church by the black piano was covered in fresh vegetables, and fruit in wrapped boxes turned on their sides and bags of cans laid out looking like a feast.

The first hymn was 'We plough the seeds and scatter the good food on the land, but it is fed and watered by God's almighty hand'. I sang loud and proud joyously with a packed church.

My mind was buzzing after all the singing with 'Morning has Broken' and my favourite one 'Colours of Day'.

This feeling lasted all week and on the following Saturday us girls were told that we were going to see the cast of Carla Lane's Bread act on the stage at Bournemouth. I'll always remember Joey, the blonde one, the fat one and the red haired woman and their mother. They were just exactly as they were on the telly.

Mum, Fee, Dad, Eve and I had balcony seats right by the stage looking down on them in the best seats in the house. They really made me laugh by the simplicity of their storylines. The flaming haired woman was always teetering around in her high heels reminding me of Aunty Nola. That evening flew by and on that Wednesday we were all back at school.

Sat in French I wished I'd studied harder as Fee was taking German that year.

> *Ecclesiastes 4:4*
> *I have also learnt why people work so hard to succeed:*
> *It is because they envy their neighbours.*

Jealous I'd struggled to keep up in class and I remembered Fee teaching me Ines, vines, dry, 1, 2, 3 while at home during that summer. Also knowing Auf Wiedeshen as farewell from the TV programme I'd watched all summer too. My mate Rheann had gotten to study German that year too. I'd started to get a bit of a complex.

That afternoon when back at home I'd sat on the sofa with a puzzler on my knees and pictured myself, as clear as day, sitting right on the edge of a new world bathed in a cool blue light emanating out over the planet. I'd felt on my own.

Through Mum being a Youth Worker she was asked by some record breakers to help organise the local youth to hold hands with as many adults as possible from in and around Evercreech to create the longest human chain in the world. We mad it on the evening news and I recognised myself with my blue bomber jacket on. It was a quick segment too so I was really lucky I got on TV.

Now at the beach one day I came across a sweet looking dog and a little old man who was very talkative. I wanted to tell him to not have his dog on the beach because it made me hurl at the thought of poo and wee on the sand and in the dunes. In my mind I'd said, "You realise lots of children on the beach and catch diseases from the excrement your dog leaves behind," but something stopped me from saying that to him. He was a sweet little man but I was angry with him.

> *Genesis 27:44*
> *And stay with him for a while, until your*
> *brother's anger cools down.*

I had been there with my parents and my siblings, Fee and Eve. We had a lovely time on the beach.

Then in the car coming home from Weymouth my eyes were playing up. I felt sick, the lights round my eyes were a blurry white as the sun had burned them. It was my glaucoma playing up. I couldn't even see. Mum took my hand and led me indoors and I had to wait for my eyes to get better and for the sickness to go away.

I'd always felt like one of the cool girls at school and had been attracted to Damion for a long time. Finally I thought he'd noticed me when at school one day he actually asked me out. It never occurred to me that he wasn't serious or that he was actually seeing someone else at the time. This was my chance. After school I waited ages for him to show up. I'd even traipsed up and down the road outside the house in case he couldn't find us. It occurred to me when I came back in for tea and it had become really dark that perhaps I'd got it wrong. I was used to feeling wronged and misunderstood at this point anyway.

It had been November time and I'd been in the hospital that evening from five o'clock onwards with my carnival club stripping off all together getting changed to get on the cart. I was a Chinese lady. With Mum getting changed not paying attention to anyone else putting on my black wig on last. Then we had to have our make-up put on one by one sitting at the make-up table with my Nan putting eye shadow on.

On the cart I stood at the back of the float by then Chinese take away and I remember fixating on a man's tight little ass called Jon. I fancied him from that moment on all the way round the Bridgewater circuit till we got off at the end of the route not recollecting anything else afterward.

Two days later at school I had double English that was really hard to follow as we had to wade our way through old essays to red to help us with our up and coming mock exams. They were supposed to give us ideas but me, feeling cocky, glazed over it knowing I'd do well with the subject anyway and it didn't cover the subject we had to cover for our assignments.

I'd played a mind game with myself pre-empting what was to come in my head leaving the chance to daydream through my lesson. I really wanted to get on with ding some actual work.

At the end of the day I'd had a conversation with my sister Fee about going on a blind date with a boy she knew called Neil who apparently went to college with her and he studied accountancy. Fee told me that he was really handsome looking.

We'd gone to Nan's that afternoon and I dressed up in tight jeans and my favourite turtle neck cable knitted jumper. Feeling beautiful I got into the car with my parents and we picked up Neil on the way there. Sat next to him I felt a very strong sexual tension and at the carnival I remember hanging back with him while the others walked in front and for some reason I talked pure gobbled gook. I had a real complex about him that made me feel stupid. He walked on ahead. I realised that evening that I'd embarrassed him and put him off me when I'd got home.

It was late when we got back and Neil got dropped off on the way. I was soon in bed.

In art the next day I came into class and saw a girl with lots of paperwork with girl models that she'd drawn on and they looked really professional. The dresses they'd drawn next to them I was really jealous of, they looked like she could create new designs for clothes for a living. While looking at them I got confused over what I could do that would be remotely as good for my own assignment to count towards my mock exams. I sat down worried as I hadn't even made a start on an idea so I got a really big A1 sized bit of paper, got out some paints to try and be like a famous scenery painter. I sketched out a scene of trees and bushes and a skyline with a faint line through the middle of the paper so that each tree became a thin outline from the back ones to the front. Through the middle of the picture starting from the skyline I drew two wiggly lines getting wider and wider to look like a river. I drew a bridge over the river then started painting. I painted across the sky first to the line with thin light blue paint and waited for it to dry. Then I dabbed white paint on with cotton wool for clouds.

After drying out I got out two shades of green and with an orange and black I mixed the colours together in a palette of six different retainers to make different shades of green, orange and brown to do the leaves n the trees first and with a very delicate brush did as many individual leaves as possible trying to give depth and a nice arboretum of colours from the front of the picture to the back. I painted the bridge and washed out the palette's colours while the paint dried at the end of the lesson.

There were two lessons next then after lunch there was English and I fired up the teacher with a nervous girly giggle as she got me to stand up and read out a passage from a book we were reading different sections from. It was a bit embarassing but as I got into it I loved the sound of my own voice as I focussed less on the uptight teacher and more on my words, then I sat down quite pleased with myself.

Then it was history and Mr Reese gave us certain passages to read about Samuel Pepe's and Rheann, Simon and I got through the words really quickly and wrote notes to ourselves in mirror writing which caused a giggle inside our heads as we pushed the paper to and fro from each other. Simon was always a bit baffled by mine and Rheann's writing and I knew he got more and more determined each lesson to copy our style of writing. Mr Rees caught us out and poor Simon had the letter so he had to hand it to him. The teacher looked a bit baffled and Simon blurted that he'd have to have a mirror to read it. So why did I start this? It was to keep ourselves deliberately misunderstood to save ourselves from embarrassment. As he sat there confused the bell went and I found myself exhaling glad we got out of being told off. The teacher didn't even bother to reprimand us.

At home that afternoon I just relaxed with maths books all over the floor in front of the telly of where I lay down on my stomach and spent a good couple of hours watching Grange Hill, Blue Peter, the Australian soaps and the news trying to chase every maths question desperately wanting to get into the top group of maths like my sister Fiona was in. At this point she'd been moaning she couldn't keep up or manage with the work and was almost considering going back down into the second group I was in. I envied her and tried so hard with maths to be as good as her. I did some French it was too bloody easy and I loved spouting the words out loud as I spoke in my sexiest accent. I could muster loving the sound of my own voice, but started to miss the point of female and male spellings as I'd just copied them into the boxes under the pictures. We had to do this to match the scenes.

I'd finished as much a I was gonna do and got up for a late tea as Dad had only just got home and had come in to hug us and say, "I'm back. What's for tea? Wait for me to have a shower."

The next day I'd sat in my nightie watching the telly in my bedroom. The presenters were hilarious and I couldn't lay down comfortable. I'd sat up against propped up pillows at first but started squinting at the goggle box but after a while I was itching to get up really but couldn't tear myself away from what had been going on with Sabrina the Teenage Witch. I turned around and led upside down on the bed propping up my head with my hands. After a while I got pins and needles. Then I heard a yell.

"Karen. Are you getting up today?" And I felt at fifteen I had all the time in the world to do absolutely anything I wanted. As far as I was concerned the whole world was my oyster and one day I'd live it the Melissa Hart way who was the girl who played the teenage witch. I'd been obsessed with living in America of where all the girls wore these gorgeous shift dresses while in pumps of white daps in this country.

I eventually got my ass out of bed and noticed a lot of sun outside so I found out one of my shift dresses to wear that was red. I then went to the shower to wash body and hair. I'd ended up feeling more beautiful than anyone in the world when in my dress and decided to go for a walk round town by myself.

Now I'd gotten as far as the sweet shop on the corner and remembered a discussion with my Mum about dressing up too much like a woman as she saw me put on a bit of lippy that morning too. I'd just wanted to look like Sabrina off the telly. Mum had pointed out not to rely on my beautiful looks with my long golden hair brushed out like a hundred times and I loved my kinked fringe that fell to the left shielding my left eye.

Now somewhere at the top of the Bath road out of Shepton opposite the big car park at the bottom of town I ran into two good looking young lads. One with blonde hair and one with dark hair. I laughed and giggled feeling lovely and in control of the situation. This three way conversation made me feel intelligent for once as my conversations with my family never let me feel that way.

At the shops when I eventually got to town I headed towards the cheap jacks shop and decided to start looking for Christmas cards basically believing in myself. The cards were nice enough but they had to be cheap. I spent the whole day out and about round town. I'd even visited the video shop called Becks and went through every video in the rental shop with no intention of buying one.

I got fed up with the shops and walked out of Shepton towards the viaduct towards Bath and went into the local graveyard to have a look for anything with Burr on it or any other family name.

> *Ecclesiastes 1:8*
> *Our eyes can never see enough to be satisfied,*
> *our ears can never hear enough.*

I wandered around for about an hour before jumping over the wall into the neighbouring fields called the meadows and walked down to the main path running along the bottom of the next two fields and came out at the bottom of the hill that I had to go up again on the pavement back to the entrance to the Wimpey Estate of where I'd lived. I then turned into the bottom of Shaftgate Avenue. I got chatting to the same boys again and they said, "Hello again. Where did you get to?"

Appearing casual I'd said, "Oh around town and through the fields." I liked these lads and asked if they were brothers. They said no and went into the opposite direction as I headed for the top of my road.

I noticed on the front lawn Eve had friends around as there were bikes about that I'd never seen before and I knew that Kelly and Helen were there. When going indoors I said, "Hello," to both of them but I don't think they heard, but I always liked my sisters friends. After going indoors I overheard Kelly telling everyone that her mother came originally from Liverpool and was somewhere down the line related to the famous Paul McCartney from the sixties band The Beatles. I loved that bit of information and was desperate to know the how, but the phone rang. It had been a telephone call to tell Kelly to go back home. I heard Helen say that she had to go back home too.

Later on that evening while watching the news I got into the political debates thinking that I was intelligent enough to understand what was going on. Afterwards there was a documentary about Florence Nightingale. I assumed it was going to be all about her but apparently another nurse in the Caribbean existed at the same time of whom was black and worked with the full force of the Holy Spirit.

The next morning I felt happy to go to school and I had gym class straight away. I'd actually packed my gym kit for once; my ra-ra little skirt and white t-shirt with trainers in my rucksack. When in the changing room getting changed I stuck to my corner of the changing room trying to just focus on myself and no-one else. The changing room, I could see, was embarrassing for some girls but not me. I took my time and was the last one to go downstairs hoping to just be able to sit on a bench out the way as I'd heard them upstairs bouncing balls around. I was dreading the class thinking they were playing basketball. I'd gotten downstairs without being spotted and sat on the bench. Thankfully the teams had been chosen so I thought, "Oh well. I'll just sit this one out." The lady teacher never noticed me anyway so I always did what I wanted to do in her class.

The next lesson was in the science building doing Physics and I ended up copying the answers down from the text books. I'd thought I was brilliant answering the questions right the teacher was throwing at us.

> *2 Samuel 22:28*
> *You save those who are humble,*
> *But you humble those who are proud.*

By the middle of the lesson he said to open our books to page thirty two and I had been going through the answers at the back of the book for page thirty two and onwards. I realised that I was rubbish at cheating. I screwed my work into a ball then realised I'd gotten the answers for the second part of the lesson. I got bored and realised that if I copied the questions from the book I had the answers ready to put down when finishing the work at home later, but realising that I'd need the answers to what Mr Greenway had put on the board. I wasn't in synchronisation with anybody that lesson.

After break I went to music class and we learnt about Tchaikovsky and Beethoven. I knew beforehand that Beethoven was German and that the most popular song he ever wrote was Fur Elise. I put my hand up in class and proudly boasted, in my head, that I could play Fur Elise off by heart. I never got the teacher's attention though. Everyone I saw, as I looked around, were looking at me. I blushed and put my arm down again. I promised myself I'd show up with my Queen of Sheba music to impress the class with.

Lunch time came and I sat on the grass with Rheann. There was Caroline, Rosie and Hayley there too but I never paid them that much attention as they chatted happily away amongst themselves. I actually liked Caroline's clique but could never think of anything to talk to them about.

In afternoon class I had maths of where I plonked myself down by the window. The sun was streaming in and I actually had my back to the teacher of which I loved as she never, thankfully, paid me much attention. I flipped through the pages as fast as I could write all the answers down and surprisingly got through a book and a half in an hours lesson. I always knew how to push myself in maths class. As usual no-one spoke to me and I headed off downstairs just after two o'clock for the last lesson of the day over in the English block for a literature lesson and we learned a bit about who George Orwell was.

Chapter Thirteen

The next day we watched an autobiography on the TV on a cassette player at school. I propped my head on my arms as the room descended into darkness to take the glare off the telly. I stared at the black and white picture taking in as much information as I could in my memory. There was no way I'd been capable of writing anything in the semi-dark. Right. As well as not being able to see much with my failing eye sight stuck at the back of the room I mentally took notes. The film was long and a soon as it was over the blinds went back up and the lights came on again and every child sighed with relief. I also heard several yawns along with mine afterwards. I loved my English but new information given to me without the aid of pen and paper to hand to write information down with made me want to wake up more than anything and take large gulps of air as Mum came to the school that day in the car to take me home.

   I had a lazy late afternoon just sorting out my physics homework making it look like I'd been listening in class and tried to do the honourable thing with the latter answers by changing them a little bit.

   It was six o'clock when we had tea and I threw some jeans on with what I thought was a classy red top for the school disco. Dad was popping Rheann and I in the car to after she arrived at my house.

   We had a lovely dance that evening to modern early nineties music and I never left the dance floor all night not even when the lights went up and I felt like the best dancer in the world.

> *Luke 12:19*
> *Take life easy, eat, drink, and enjoy yourself!*

Which I did with my eyes closed.

   I went up the park the next afternoon to have a go on the swings. I did that a lot and on this particular occasion Damion, the boy I liked. turned up with a friend to kick a ball around. I watched them put their jumpers down for posts, and I really enjoyed watching them. They called me over to talk with them as they were playing so I walked over to a copse of trees to stay out the way of the ball and I distinctly remember Damion asking me who I fancied. I got all embarrassed and stayed quiet and I think they got really bored with me after that and carried on with their game. Trouble was the ball ended up flying at my head and hurting me. I ran off in tears with a bruised ego and a painful head. My Dad saw me when I got back and asked me who made me cry. I told him and because Dad knew his Dad Skip. he went up to his house to talk with him. Dad found out that it had been the other boy with the fatal kick and Damion said sorry for what happened.

The next day first lesson was music and I had gone to the trouble of finding out my Queen of Sheba sheet music. I had every intention of playing it in class so I sat down at the piano with it and started to play the bottom half. I went all the way through the song. It sounded brilliant to my ears and wanted to do it again. I thought that I was impressing my class and the teacher.

"That's very nice Karen," the teacher said, "But I want to get on with the lesson."

I felt a bit embarrassed and grabbed the music to put in my bag embarrassingly.

"Look it's obvious you can play the piano and you're really good but I need to get on with the lesson." Which they did as while I'd been playing they'd gotten a lot of musical instruments out.

Now just before lunch I had a physics class and breezed by Mr Greenway who said good morning. I said, "Good morning," back.

"It's nice to see you well," he said. "Now class open your text books. We're learning about black holes in the universe."

I gulped was this going to turn out to be one very long algebraic mathematical sum to explain it. I got simple algebra wrong enough times as it was and sat in class feeling a bit confused all through the lesson.

2 Samuel 22:29
You, Lord, are my light;
You dispel my darkness.
You give me strength.

I went straight to lunch afterward with my lunch box. I had sandwiches, crisps, a chocolate Penguin, an apple and a box of orange juice drink. It was very nice.

That afternoon I did physical education and I soon put on my flirty little skirt and white t-shirt to go downstairs to the gymnasium. Everyone was in lines so that we could play a little tournament of basketball. I thought great I really don't want to play this and just stood around all lesson just letting the ball drop when it came to me till everyone got the point not to throw it at me. I predicted this and it happened.

Now at the end of the day I went home happy determined in my mind to really push through my maths books when I got home. At home I went to fling my books on the floor in front of the telly but Mum jumped in. "Can you please not do that and get changed first please?"

"Ok Mum, but I gotta do homework. It's late again."

"I don't know why you leave it all to the last minute."

I wheezed, "I can't keep up with it all Mum so I just let some drop until I know I've got to do it 'cause sometimes I forget that's all."

"I need you on the table not all over the floor."

When I sat at the table though with no distractions after about half an hour I began to get a headache. I gave up completely trying to do the work thirty minutes into my headache and I knew that I could've done more in front of the telly. I then put everything away in my holdall and cosied up n the sofa to watch my programmes.

Tucker was having a bit of fun that day in the classroom and his sense of humour reminded me of my Dad on Grange Hill. As I sat there Mum sat down with me and started to tell me stories of her and her sister Aunty Nola. Now carnival for the year was over and Mum decided to recall an old memory of just after Shepton Mallet carnival once of where Aunty Nola looked down at the road and found a twenty pound note once. Mum was always jealous of Aunty Nola about this as she'd had wide expressive eyes that looked like they could take in everything. I loved talking about the past with Mum and we had a long chat.

The following morning I had English literature lesson about Charles Dickens, A Tale of Two Cities. I loved these types of lessons as all I had to do was read a passage out loud which talked about love. I had the boys staring at me and so embarrassingly at first started to orate. Then as I got in to it I rather enjoyed talking out loud. I'd seated myself and just listened to the other children reading paragraphs out loud.

Next lesson was history and in Mr Rees' class we had a lot to learn about Queen Elizabeth the first of whom was so-called the virgin Queen. I loved the way she'd been portrayed as a self-righteous woman. Perfect to me to be running the churches and unifying them to create the Church of England. This was done through her influential friends and colleagues of whom worked in the churches and parliament.

In the afternoon I went to music and we learned all about music from Pakistan and of how snake charmers got their snakes to dance and a bit about their culture of music. In a picture we had to find as many instruments as possible. I found a sitar, a banjo, and basically all variations of guitars and a harpist. Apparently there had been fifteen different instruments to find from a list we were given so as to learn what this eclectic array of instruments looked like. I had a lovely day that day.

On the Wednesday morning it was a languages day and I got my usual lift into school from Mum. Running down the hill I'd been late for assembly and I raced along the corridor up to the main hall of where I sneaked down to sit behind everyone. The Lord's Prayer was being said then Mr E Schofield started off giving school notices before we all headed off towards our own lessons for the day.

English was first and we had to draft a poem and I wrote one about The Daytime which went like: the sun is warm and lovely, the children come out to play.

After English I sat in the middle seats of French and strained to see the blackboard copying down as much as I could learning about French cheese, French wine, and their bread. Du borsin, du vin, du panne and asking for them in French by learning Je voudrais… and s'll vous plait. I imagined actually being in France and practicing the words in my sexy accent so stayed quiet. Katherine was being a pain by gossiping in front of me when all I'd wanted to do was learn.

By the afternoon classes I'd developed a cold in the nose and couldn't stop sniffing. Rubbing my nose in my sleeve I started to drift in my mind during afternoon classes and after the first afternoon lesson I'd developed a cough. Longing for some warmth and comfort I slung my rucksack over my shoulder to walk down the stairs to the science block to Mr Greenways lesson for Physics. I sat at the front on a stall at the front of class and learned all about the mathematics to describe the law of gravity. I struggled to understand as I wrote it all down but couldn't form an intelligent enough question in my mind that would help them to help me make sense of the algebra. I'd sat next to Rheann who seemed to know what she was doing and admired her understanding.

Back at home after school I snuggled up on the sofa to watch the TV and Fee came in with a friend. I'd felt lovely and warmed through not thinking about my cold then Anna sat down next to me. She looked a bit boyish with her short red hair. I tried to talk with her but she seemed transfixed. I'd asked her about her family and if the programme the A-Team we were watching was her fave TV programme.

Fee had been up to the table doing homework and looked up at the juncture and explained that Anna had never had a television at home. It was about nine o'clock before she left.

After school the next day Rheann and I walked all the way down passed the meadows after popping in the pub on the way through Hillmead. Feeling like queen bees we ended up sticking our thumbs up to the traffic together and instead of standing there Rheann wanted to walk on. I wanted to stay by the bus stop but didn't stop to have a go at my friend so I followed her. We walked a long way it seemed by the high wall, Bowlish school of where I'd stopped to look in at the grounds of almost hearing the happy voices of years ago when I played there.

Nearly up by the 30 mph sign some woman pulled over to pick us up. Rheann breathed a sigh of relief. I was just excited to go to the pub with her. I'd felt like a grown up.

At The Mermaid into Wells, Rheann set up the pool table and showed me how to do it. The music Rheann put on was by Queen. I'd been determined to win a game pushing the balls really hard around the table going for the obvious holes. Rheann seemed to keep winning, but as my turn came again I had a fluke shot of where the ball at the top end of the table bounced back into the right hand corner by me. I was happy that I could do the same sort of shots Rheann could easily get away with and won one game.

Several games later we had to go home so we walked across to the bus station to make our way back. Rheann was the biggest matriarch in school and I was proud to be her friend being all grown up and going to pubs with her and drinking Woodpecker cider.

At the bottom of Bowlish Lane we stepped off the bus and went our separate ways. I'd only had two drinks. I could handle anything. Mum and Dad never asked where I went so I never told them. My life was my own. I seemed untouchable.

My sisters were sat down ready for tea when I got in so I sat with them. I still couldn't believe no-one could tell I'd been drinking and tucked into my steak pie with peas and mash potato. Thoroughly warmed through that feeling stayed with me and made me want my bed. Pulling my blanket I was knitting round my knees I hit into knitting my pink and blue squares. Trying to knit more quickly by the minute I soon remembered I had a piano competition coming up and sidled over to the stool.

The glass doors had been taken down. It was sunny outside and bathed in a warm glow my playing soothed the soul. First through my sight reading, my endless scales, trying out new octaves for harder scales. Then I hit into my tunes for my grade 5 piano pieces getting more and more ferociously faster on the keys. Thoroughly pushing through my inner emotions I'd felt that delicious warm yellow glow around my fingers.

In bed that night I'd had a deep sleep and awoke with a start in the middle of the night with a strong presence of Queen Elizabeth the first on the back of my bedroom door. She was dressed in her coronation outfit and gave me a freaked out moment. That vision stayed there for a long time until I went back to sleep.

After school the following day I'd been day dreaming about my dream home.

> *Numbers 12:6*
> *And the Lord said, "Now hear what I have to say!*
> *When there are prophets among you, I reveal myself to them*
> *In visions and speak to them in dreams.*

It was to be a great big country house. I grabbed some plain paper while sat on the sofa, a ruler, and a pencil first. Leaning on my work books I set out to draw a basic outline of a big house with really thick lines to emphasise the main outside walls. Inside the walls I made ne whole side of the downstairs into a drawing room of where I drew the shape of the top of a grand piano near bay windows. This was where my little breakfast table and chairs would go. I'd visualised a lot of books on big cases up the walls and a fireplace. I drew a hallway and basic stairs. There was a kitchen, a large living room and dining room. I took another bit of paper and drew an upstairs with a ballroom in it and lots of bedrooms.

The next day at school I was looking forward to going to the school disco that night.

I learnt about babies and how they were conceived. Boys took the piss and the girls sat there mortified just wishing the lesson would end.

The end of the school day came excruciatingly about a hundred years later.

The next school day began with a bright smile on my face. Vacantly I walked into the English block for our names to be called out. Some clever dick put his hand up and said "I'm not here." Everyone laughed except me thinking that he was a twit. My name got called and I inwardly blushed, so I tuck my hand up. The boys watched me so I turned back to my books checking where first lesson was going to be in my folder. I wished that I'd stayed at home. It was going to be Eve's birthday that day and all I could think of was the up and coming birthday party. Sticking my nose in the air I walked around all day believing the boys were in love with me wishing I wasn't put on a pedestal and wanted to be seen as sexy like the other girls who could get boyfriends.

I floated around outside during gym class noticing one boy, Damion, ogling my legs and felt as completely detached from the world as I was going to get. Totally happy.

Back at home Eve's friends turned up. Kelly, Helen with other friends I didn't know including a boy named James who looked sweet but sat with me. I recall that he was one of the only boys there who didn't want to join in with the fun and stayed on the sofa out of the way.

Looking at the fun they were having I imagined a better American style birthday party for myself with booze involved.

I'd been visiting my grandparents on one particular occasion and as Nan Sheila came to the door she tripped over the dog, Kipper, a Doberman cross with what we never knew. As she fell she twisted her wrist.

We all sat downstairs together for a while and my cousin Scott was there too. I had to go to the toilet upstairs with the toilet overlooking Woodview's Lane. Kipper followed me into the toilet and I shouted at him to leave but he came at me with his tongue hanging out.

Leviticus 18:23
No man or woman is to have sexual relations with
An animal; that perversion makes you ritually unclean.

What could I have done to get rid of him though. I'd been in the middle of peeing! He'd come up to me and licked my bits out. I pushed him away and out of the door.

Feeling disgusted I went back downstairs and felt really awkward round him licking his bits. I still had to stay until my Mum decided on going home after convincing nan to go to the doctors about her wrist and taking her there first. They were gone along time as I stayed with my cousin Scott.

It was Saturday next day and with the car gliding through the Mary Bignall Rand memorial gate Dad manoeuvred the vehicle into a parking spot close to the football pitch. The family, minus fee, were going to watch Dad's team play.

Eve was keen to ogle a player called Archie, her favourite of Dad's players. I fancied the one who always had a flash car. In front of the stand the manager's boxes were where Dad always stood to egg his team on while standing with Geoff. I liked standing near the edge of the pitch normally but Mum and Eve wanted to sit down.

Mum was getting embarrassing as she kept shouting to the ref, apparently you had to be paranoid the referee was against our side in order to enjoy the game.

> *Hebrews 10:32*
> *Remember how it was with you in the past. In those days*
> *After God's light had shone on you, you suffered many things,*
> *Yet you weren't defeated by the struggle.*

Lance, one of ours, got tackled to the floor in our box so we had a penalty. The small crowd encircling the pitch went quiet as my favourite player took the penalty. I held my breath in that moment as the ball caught his foot an excited thrill shot up my spine as the ball shot through the air just under the top bar. We all spontaneously stood up and clapped. That was the highlight of the first half and I always wished there were more goals to watch in football.

Looking towards the trees on my left then backwards towards the expanse of field behind the pitch up to the club house I watched the teams go back into the changing rooms. We had just enough time to go to the wooden shack by the bleachers to get a hot drink and a Kit Kat. Mum offered to get it for us four, including Dad, but I followed her up the steps intending to help her carry everything. I always liked to have a wander for fifteen minutes before the game started again and watched the tennis players at the far end of the leisure area.

My cup of tea was lovely and sweet as I'd liked two sugars while dunking my chocolate in to it. The football teams soon came back out of the side of the clubhouse making a racket on the concrete with their boots before making their way back on the grass.

I stood on the opposite side of the pitch next to my Dad who rubbed his hands together, sniffed and winked at me saying, "Come to stand with your old Dad?"

I acquiesced with one of my shy smiles.

Job 29:10
Even the most important men kept silent.

My favourite player caught my attention as he'd got the ball at the halfway line and was running towards the penalty box. I held my breath as his left foot connected hard with the ball sending it careering through the air. The goalie had come out of between the goalposts and the ball was heading towards the top right hand corner. Before I knew it our Wells fans were standing and clapping and I was proud of my Dad's team as they went further ahead with a 2-0. Now because nearly everyone was near the opposing goal two of the other team's players went running for the ball after the goalie kicked the ball all across the football field. The moment was a bit of a blur as the opposing team caught the football fast and lobbed it right into the bottom left hand corner of our goal. Within the space of two minutes two goals had been scored.

The rest of the game became hard work for us to stay in front but every pass seemed to go our way until the final whistle. I looked to Dad who'd run on the pitch to congratulate his players and I rejoined Mum and Eve going towards the clubhouse for fizzy drinks and a packet of crisps. The air was chilly for five o'clock and inside we found some comfy seats. A game was on the telly but us girls weren't interested as we waited for Dad up at the bar talking amongst the players for the next two hours.

We'd had a bit of bread and cheese by the time we got home as Mum didn't want to cook and we went to sleep happy.

One afternoon on a hot sunny day the whole family was in the car going to Weymouth. As we hit the seafront Bryan Adams 'Everything I do I do it for you' came on the radio. I asked Dad to turn the radio up as this had been my favourite song and had been number one for several weeks. As I sung into the wind while sticking my head out of the window I had never felt closer to God. All the words in the chorus seemed to encompass exactly how God loves us as the 'walk the wire' bit described exactly the path to heaven and I'd die for you bit reminded me of the crucifixion. The title described exactly how powerful God's love for us actually is.

I had an utopic dream that evening of very bright balloons and rainbows all over brightly coloured green rolling hills.

I remember, the next day, starting the day all happy and calm really. One of my Enid Blyton books had been in my lap for most of the morning while I'd quietly read enjoying all the adventures George, Timothy the dog and the others got into. Outside I could hear a gentle thudding at first against the back wall which got louder and louder. It had been Eve with a tennis ball and racket slowly getting on my nerves. I kept trying to read but the ball became relentless so I jumped and ran into the kitchen and told Eve calmly to stop. She just kept playing with that damn ball at which point I wished I'd been an only child.

1 Corinthians 13: 1-2
I may be able to speak the language of human beings
And even of angels, but if I have no love, my speech is no more than a
noisy gong or a clanging bell. I may have the gift of inspired preaching;
I may have all knowledge, and understand all secrets; I may have all
the faith needed to move mountains – but if I have no love, I am nothing.

I so desperately wanted to finish my book in peace so I called out louder to get her to stop. My nerves were so on edge when she came in saying that she only wanted to play so I jumped on her back and held Eve to the floor. She struggled so hard to get back up but I held her there shouting out, "Why do you always press my buttons? Why can't you just stop when I want you to stop?"

Her breathing became laboured and her body stilled just as Mum came in and said that she'd better phone an ambulance. I was shaking with indignation expecting her to say Evil Eve had wound me up again but they just left and Fee stuck her two oars in saying that Eve was going to be put on a life support machine. I didn't care the little cow had wound me up and I had asked nicely twice for her to stop.

Mum and Eve had gone all evening and all I could think of was at least I'd finally gotten some peace and quiet to finish my book.

My sisters had been whining enough about the time I spent on the piano and I'd had to cut back, I could have taken my anger out on the keys to have annoyed her in return. But I never thought of that and my music had always been the one thing in my life that all my frustrations could be poured into to make brilliant music.

Now in the morning I awoke to get ready for church I'd had a lovely morning feeling close to God singing the lovely hymns. I turned to Mum and she gave me an annoyed look. Floating home on a cloud, clicking my heels together we were all settled for a meal around two o'clock. It was a lovely roast dinner. We all sat round the table having to sit in silence but Fiona kept butting while my parents were talking. When we sat on the sofa with the telly on I'd picked up the newspaper and opened to a page with something called a Sudoku. It said underneath to complete the puzzle in under five minutes. Without putting too much thought into it I went instinctively to the right numbers the first few times then started to think more clearly about where the numbers should go. I went about it more methodically in my mind starting with in the individual boxes first then along the lines down, then across until I completed it. It had been a nine by nine Sudoku puzzle. then I noticed that I could join Mensa. The form was underneath. I filled it all in with my name Karen Mellissa Burr and 10 Coombe View, Shepton Mallet, Somerset. I then cut it out, found an envelope, wore the address on it, and found a stamp in a drawer in the Welsh Dresser in Mum's purse ready to send it on my way home from school the next day.

Did stewarding with Mum the next day for our carnival club, the Mendip Hospital at Pilton Pop Festival. We stayed in a small tent and came back to it one night with it stinking of smoke. We guessed someone had come in to get high. Behind our tent was the wigwams where we saw men wandering around naked at night round a fire.

Our job was to guard a field of tents of where it transpired that the first knifing of a tent had taken place and something was subsequently stolen.

I sat with Neil in the circus field while I had my skimpy little pink shorts on. Afterwards I went in the circus tent and saw the end of the show.

Mum and I were kept awake each night by a lot of drums being bashed and a dragon with its music and lights going.

One night I went to see Shakespeare's Sister on the Pyramid Stage and I pushed my way to the front of the stage. Two tall older lads in the carnival club walked with me to see the Shamen afterwards and I experienced crowd surfing for the first time and so was glad that I wasn't at the front in the thicket of things.

On the Sunday morning I remember being with Aunty Caroline in front of the Pyramid stage watching Van Morrison live for the first time and he played all his greatest hits in the glorious sunshine. That was the best weekend ever.

It had been a lovely sunny day as Mum and I made our way to Glastonbury. On the way there we were singing Cliff Richard songs like Living Doll mainly while in the car. We were really looking forward to seeing Cliff Richard at the Abbey. We parked at the Abbey car park and went through the entrance to the lush green grounds. It wasn't obvious where we were going at first but as we walked by the beautiful ruins of where the monks used to live Mum and I came across a massive marque of where we found uncomfortable chairs to sit on. Cliff sat on a stage with audio equipment round him and to start he sang three or four of his famous songs like 'Devil Woman, 'Living Doll' and 'Summer Holiday'. We'd thoroughly enjoyed the singing and afterward he'd been interviewed and I remember him talking about one of his passions that was tennis. It came out that he thought our tennis players came from a highly elitist group of where really the game should be open to anyone. That made him a really decent sounding guy. He'd also talked of his Christian faith and I assumed the audience, that created a packed-out tent, were of Christian faith also. I had a highly memorable day.

Next day after school I can see as plain as day, the Mall in London and thought that I'd embrace in an instant being Queen of England. I could envision myself opening the door of Buckingham Palace to the homeless, let them in and look after them. They'd looked so closed off in that palace encased in a bubble so cold. I'd had my homework in my lap suspended in space and time.

Fiona came into the room telling me tea was ready so I closed my book and went to the table.

I had first met Martin at a carnival dance at Paulton Rovers social club. I had worn my favourite velvety green dress with tights on that night and my favourite kitten-heeled black shoes.

We had done a parade in our carnival costumes early in the evening and I'd ended up dancing with him for most of the night. He'd told me that he was the lead guitarist and singer in his own band. My best friend Rheann hooked up with a lad called Geoff that night too.

The day after I met Martin, Rheann and I were walking round a place called Hillmead when we came across a phone box. A black cat crossed my path and I felt that it was a good time to give Martin a call. He answered straight away and we arranged a date.

For our first date he'd turned up at Mum's in a white Skoda and we went to Weston stopping off at a cider farm along the way for him to get a litre of cider. In Weston I couldn't keep up with his long strides as I followed him to the guitar shop. It was hardly a mutually agreeable date, or he just couldn't really be bothered to impress me with any great plans for the day! He had told me during this date that he'd spoken to a street cleaner once and had given himself a mental pat on the back for it. I thought this was wrong as I've always just spoken to anyone who'd speak to me regardless of who or what they represent. his attitude felt wrong as it reminded me of a passage in the Bible of where you're not meant to give self-praise.

Samuel 1:2-3
Stop you loud boastings
Silence your proud words
For the Lord is a God who knows
And he judges all that people do.

The next date had been an evening out at a dance in a club somewhere and Martin bought me a Bacardi and coke. I didn't like the Bacardi once I'd tried a bit so I left it. My favourite drink was Woodpecker cider at the time and it didn't even occur to me to tell him that and he'd never even bothered to ask what my favourite drink had been.

We'd gone for a few meals together on dates at Downside Inn, the dust hole, and the Bird in Hand pub/restaurant where we had taken Rheann with us once. That had been a mistake as Martin ended up talking to her for most of the evening while I cosied up to the fire in the corner of the room. The dust hole was a pub at the end of a road where Martin's friend lived of whom we visited once. It had a great big satellite dish outside. It was nice to get to know his friend. I'd been picking up some good polite habits like saying excuse me at the dinner table for nose blowing, sneezing and needing the toilet and turning my head away from the food to blow my nose.

The one time we went back to his house together of where he lived with his mother, we tried cosying up to watch a film called Witness. I still remember the white thick rug on the floor of the living room imagining where we would end up making love. Martin and I soon ended up in his blue walled bedroom though. I'd felt cold and like my mind wasn't quite there as I looked down at myself and was mesmerised by the way my skin leapt to his touch.

The whole episode had never felt right though and I was left feeling bereft as though I'd gone through something clinical. Our bodies just never connected and it should have been my first time.

Martin had shown me his collection of guitars saying he'd 'accumulated' them along the way when I'd first arrived at his house on the particular date. Was he really only trying to impress me with one fancy word? How insulting! He also told me his Mum thought me rude whenever I called as I wouldn't tell her my name.

When I first went on a jamming session with him at a pub called The Star I'd first met Mandy, Bernie and their two little children. It was a good jamming session, they'd said. I did feel a bit jealous of Mandy though like there had been a relationship between her and Martin once. Martin had watched me get all misty-eyed the whole time he'd been singing 'Summer of 69' a Brian Adams hit. I was going to be haunted by this song for years after we split up. I did remember parking with him outside 10 Coombe View once and the kissing would steam up the windows and we would easily rock the white Skoda my eldest sister Fee used to take the piss out of.

Martin had once said that he preferred a lot of sixties music to that of most modern music. That was all he said but Fee took the piss out of that too.

In the morning I woke up and found myself looking forward to school. Full of the joys of winter. I leapt out of bed, shivered, jumped in the shower and screamed at the cold water before it started warming up. The needles of the water pounded on the skin and I felt tensions ease away in my neck. I realised that I must have lay funny that night. Half an hour later I'd walked through all the steam I created in the bathroom drawing a heart on the mirror with my finger and sighing as I walked out. Shimmying into my skirt and white blouse I felt all tingly remembering Martin's kisses the night before. I'd ended up focusing on studies eventually half way through my first lesson of English of where I felt very switched on for once really focusing and noticing everyone around me for once. Nikki was in the same room and she noticed me. I looked at her in the face and smiled. I realised that I'd been looking people in the eye more that morning. I knew the book The Taming of the Shrew synopsis already because of the class discussions and felt no inclination to decipher everyone of Shakespeare's words. They were a bit weird.

Now in maths that afternoon I found that I'd done the sums in two whole books in one double lesson. I always felt pleased with what I did in maths.

That day I'd been looking forward to seeing my new boyfriend Martin. I always did fantasise about him coming to my school to pick me up so that I could show off my boyfriend who had his own car and could drive.

I remember sitting next to him at the dining room table in my home while we carefully and meticulously put a poster together for my Mum's 40th birthday. That was the first time I'd seen the boy in him. I had started seeing what our children would look like as we talked and he'd told me of the time when he had done some brilliant art work at school and someone had trashed it. He'd subsequently had to start all over again. I was taking art at school and was thoroughly enjoying it. Anyway we put his beautiful poster up and we jumped out at Mum singing, "Surprise! Happy birthday!" Mum put her hands over her face and blushed profusely.

Martin had brought his guitar along that night and I remember sitting on the floor at his feet while he played and sang. This was my boyfriend. I'd felt so proud.

> *Psalms 10:2*
> *The wicked are proud and persecute the poor ...*

Had these lines in the Bible started going through my head?

> *Psalms 10:3-7*
> *The wicked are proud of their evil desires;*
> *The greedy curse and reject the Lord*
> *The wicked do not care about the Lord*

In their pride they think that God doesn't matter.
The wicked succeed in everything
They cannot understand God's Judgements;
They sneer at their enemies.
They say to themselves, "I will never fail;
I will never be in trouble."
Their speech is filled with lies...

I had gotten drunk that evening and felt confident enough to impress him with my piano playing. I'd played Fur Elise and he'd sound impressed that I could play so well while drunk. Martin had taken me upstairs as Nelson, one of Mum's friends, took over on the piano. We'd tried playing chess together and Martin said my game play was a bit unorthodox but that was because I'd wanted to kiss him and never stop. He ended up not staying late that night. Was I pushing him away somehow?

While we'd been together Rheann and I started to write a story about us. In this story I'd become a famous novelist whereas Martin became a famous musician who had the looks of a male model and largely resembled my Uncle. We lived in Hollywood together in a wonderfully spacious condo and I saw us going on and having twin raven haired girls. I never saw marriage in our future, as I was obsessed at the time, when I was still very young, with the idea of having a great career. I never told him this. In this story Rheann married a rancher called Simon and lived in a great big house with sprawling grounds. Rheann would come to our condo to visit us from time to time to be our cleaner and Rheann never even batted an eyelid about being portrayed like this. I'd also wrote about being a bitch of a director making Rheann rehearse with a Richard in the story though he was her ex and had abused her.

The first time I went to a proper gig Martin had told me not to come. I'd chosen to ignore that advice to my peril. I had sat next to a young boy who was to impress me with his magic tricks. I reached for a bottle of whisky right next to me. It was Teachers. I drank three quarters of it and promptly threw up everywhere. I had danced for a bit and remembered going up to the stage to twang the guitar Martin was playing, then going down the steps and blacking out. The next thing I remembered was that I'd tried to drag myself up on my feet in the ladies but couldn't. I'd crawled to the door to give it a hard yank out of Mandy's hands. I could hear her saying, "God she's strong."

Proverbs 23:29-35
Show me someone who drinks too much,
Who has to try out some new drink,
And I will show you someone miserable...,

Had I been getting miserable with Martin?

The next morning Martin rang me to gloat over a possible hangover but I had felt fine. I had just come down the stairs from out of the shower with a turban on my head. He had first informed me about how he, unsuccessfully, tried to carry me across the lawn that night as I'd kept on falling down. He'd then dumped me by saying, "It was a little bit me and a little bit you," and I coldly asked "Wasn't that a song?" and promptly hung up.

Reversing backwards a little bit I do remember kissing him out in the hallway at Mum's once. It had been the same night we'd been kissing on the sofa all evening too. He had pulled apart from me when I was still in a daze and told that my eyes were shining. I'd said his were shining too. When I recalled this episode later on in life I realised that what I'd actually seen in his eyes that night was the moon and the stars and the words to that Abba song had gone through my head. 'The game is on again…' just that one line. Why that line of the song?

Not long after we'd split up I went to Martin in the middle of the night with hardly any clothes on my back and no shoes on my feet. A disabled man had offered me a lift that night and had asked me where I'd lived. I lied and said Whitchurch. My pride had vanished. I had just wanted to go to him, make love with him and have him tell me everything was going to be alright, and we'd get back together. But as soon as I got there and he saw what state I was in he put me in his car and drove me straight home!

For a while I kept playing the tune of 'Love Song' from my seventies book on the piano as well as my old favourite Fur Elise.

I'd found one of Mum's Bibles and started reading from wherever I'd opened it up. the first thing I read was about a camel going through the eye of a needle an analogy given for wealthy people. I'd been dreaming of being a famous writer and thought of it being a way of getting into heaven. It became my new challenge.

Picking up my Mills and Boon book a few days later I knew that to have my dream relationship with a man I would turn myself into a strong, successful, independent woman.

Then turning to the Bible one evening I started reading Revelations for the first time. It had been the part about John's vision of the Holy City and thought I'd make it in my lifetime ambition to help all those outside the City. I had wanted to share this with Mum as I'd wanted to share my thoughts with her but never got the chance. I remember just sitting there just lost in thought wondering if I'd ever have someone to share these things.

The next day at school there'd been a fight with three boys and I remembered in the end I noticed how boys were around me. They were idiots, so I knew they fancied me really because they couldn't stop fighting each other around me. I grew frightened of them. I hated feeling this way and wondered why there wasn't anger management classes at school. I could just visualise boys being told to just aim their punches to hit a wall.

In a lesson that day I learned about politics because it was the day the Berlin Wall got knocked down to create an united Germany. We learned also about the word Fuhrer which meant father. To my mind I heard the word fatherland as it was used to describe their Prime Minister. I also learned that Hitler and his wife committed suicide at the end of the World War Two. Lord knows where they were buried and to be honest I didn't really care. This was an English language lesson.

Next was a maths lesson and I sat there during the lesson just staring into outer space while working away as my mind was in a whole other place like at a beach somewhere.

After school Mum and I went to Wells to go to a piano lesson. I clutched my bag full of music to take to Jane's at her little bungalow. I rang the doorbell and as the door opened the cat shot our and Jane said, "Hello. Do come on in Karen. Do you want to start with your new piece of music for your competition?"

I said, "Yes," and nearly choked on the cigarette smoke hanging in the air as she puffed away in front of me.

"Do sit down and open it up," and she sat there tapping her cigarette into the ashtray. It was a filthy habit to me and wished she wouldn't do it. I fully concentrated on my song. Then she said, after the first page, "Let's start again shall we and just go over and over again each bar," so I did as I was told and she started writing numbers down over the notes as I'd gotten into bad habits with her Mum of not using fingering properly. She took over in the end to show me where each finger should have been placed and I envied her long fingers being able to stretch a whole octave to play the chords. Then I tried the piece of music again and this time she didn't stop me from going on with the next page of music of which Jane didn't interfere with. She just put where the thumb should have gone as number one on every line. I wanted to race through some scales but every time I raced through one she told me to slow down and start to do scales using three octaves as I was learning to do my grade five.

In the morning the next day Rheann had her mother write a note to the local council saying she was kicking her out of the family home. On the back of this letter Rheann was able to get a flat at a place called Grace Harris House, a charity set up to house homeless teenagers situated at the bottom of town just across the bridge opposite York House. they had strict rules about guests staying over but I still smuggled in clothes and a sleeping bag in a bin bag to disguise it as rubbish in case I was asked. One night when I stayed over we had another visitor called James who showed up with weed. I took one puff of a joint and it did nothing for me. I did go on and hug my knees up against a wall and held my hands together over my heart and pressed hard to make myself pass out. Why? I'd heard that the girls in PE lessons were doing this at school. It was strange because as I'd passed out I found myself back in my old bedroom at home on the red mottled carpet. I really believed I was there before I came round again and found James gone and an awful smell, of which I shall always associate with weed, was hanging heavily in the air. I had hurt myself pounding on my chest. I wished I hadn't done it. I'd stayed all night and then went home in the morning.

I'd had fun in school, especially as the weather was lovely so that I could either stare out the window all day or go outside in break times to enjoy the weather.

Back at home I went out again to Rheann's with a sleeping bag a I didn't want to go home. At the flat we'd played a lot of cards which was a game called shit head. Rheann dealt first three cards turned down then another three turned up on top. Then another three to hold in our hands. She taught me to start with the lowest red card. We had to use each card placed in the middle to usurp the previous card. On one particular occasion that's all we did and nine times out of ten Rheann would always win but because I won occasionally it was enough to keep me interested in playing. We stopped briefly for Rheann to make us beans on toast.

Then we went down the road to the pub of where I'd let Rheann order our alcoholic drinks. Why? Because I looked too young and there was no guilt there letting her take control. It felt like we'd be friends forever.

At home Mum had to go out for the evening and I put on some lipstick hoping to go out with her. Why? I must have been deranged. I should have asked as I'd shared Mum's Lipsil that we'd used to seal on the lipstick.

I ended up mooching round the house with my sisters doing absolutely nothing. The odd bit of homework, playing the piano and watching telly.

The next day at school it was nice outside so we played a game called lacrosse with the little red poles with nets on. I thought that they looked like butterfly catching nets as we ran around the courts. I never caught anything in my net.

After school that day I remember watching Home and Away where there was a girl with blonde hair called Carly who had two suitors. One was in the army who was shit hot and he lost the fight and it was then she knew who she truly loved as she rushed over to the army man to look after him and balled her eyes out. As Fiona sat and watched with me she asked, "Wouldn't you want two men fighting over you?" I immediately said no as I thought they were immature to get into fights.

The next day I'd heard that Fiona and Eve had been nightclubbing with Casey and Charlie at Busbees. I'd been jealous as I was never asked and would never have gotten in any way. I knew that because my sisters looked like real women with big hips and big bobs of whom always looked older than me. I was also told by Fiona that all the Wells Blue School children stood on one side of the dance floor while Fee and Eve's lot from Whitstone stood on the other side of the room all night because of rivalries. In my head though I knew that Fee and Eve from Whitstone still would have talked to Casey and Charlie from Wells Blue School anyway so I never bothered to ask about their evening.

Next day was a little bird course day at school and afterwards at home looked forward to tea.

After dinner at home I went round Rheann's for the evening. When I got there Becky was with her boyfriend Richard. Prior to this Richard had been seeing Rheann but I always thought of him as Becky's boyfriend really. We were all sitting around chatting with the atmosphere tense when I got up to go to the bathroom and Richard followed me in. He went to kiss me with a high octane of tension running between us which made me bolt for the door. I was embarrassed as I ran out of the bedsit heading towards the video shop with Richard in hot pursuit chasing me through the town and down the steps into Hillmead. I felt scared.

>   *Job 3:2-3*
>   *O God, put a curse on the day I was born;*
>   *Put a curse on the night when I was conceived!*

I started to pray out loud as I came out n the top road opposite the Wimpey Estate of where I saw two men and my chance to shout for help. When I turned round my pursuer had gone and my heart beat returned to normal as I walked back home.

My day at school next day should have been a study day for our up and coming exams, so I went to lessons as per usual but some of the other children were not there probably studying at home instead.

The first lesson I got out every maths back. I'd had two and asked the teacher for one more and pushed myself to do all of the three books determined to be like Fee better if not as good as her. At first the questions seemed easy. My mind was clear as I used my protractor to work out angles and different ratios for triangular shapes which was all the first trigonometry book was about. It had been a little bird course before I'd tried maths questions with the letters a and b in them. It was a bit confusing. The teacher was there working away and I wished that I'd had the guts to ask her about it. The next book was the same but harder. I flipped through the pages for something easier and gave up to study in the French with someone. I ended up doing three test sheets in my head and to write down what the spellings were. I knew an oration test was coming up and got frustrated. The end of that day came and in the evening I went to Pilton Youth Club with my Mum where she worked. It was situated at the bottom of a hill amongst the houses near the church down in the Working Men's Club basement.

In the youth club we sat around chatting but I don't remember saying a blasted word just using the pool table with someone and having a chat with Mum every chance I got. I enjoyed feeling a part of a gang.

In the morning back at school in my flirty knee length skirt and tight white shirt I floated into the first lesson feeling all eyes on me from the boys that I thought fancied me. I sat down cool as a cucumber and kept myself to myself. My golden long hair gave me a beautiful feeling with my fringe seductively flopping over my eyes. I was happy as I took on the job of being a cool girl. The other children got on with their own studies that the teacher left us to get on with. The teachers were quiet with us all day leaving us in peace and quiet for once.

On the lunch break Rheann needed to make a phone call by the main doors. The conversation was so long lunchtime ended quickly. I can't even remember eating.

Back in class sitting near the back I always wished I'd sat closer to the board as I had trouble seeing Mrs Newman's writing on the board to have to copy down on how to compartmentalise our study regime for English. It looked really good but I knew I wouldn't stick to it. I copied it any way thinking at least I'd done something in my lesson to help towards my GCSEs.

After school at Rheann's flat I'd taken my C + G savings box from home thinking I'd take it up town with my friend to put it into my savings but Rheann got to it first. I'd sat bemused, oddly unattached, as she attacked it over and over again to take out my pound coins. I don't know why I hadn't stopped her but she just took the money away from me. I just stupidly let her have seeing a she was that desperate for it.

Psalms 69:5
You know how foolish I have been.

It was Friday the next day and in the afternoon after lunch I'd looked forward to maths and sitting next to Damion so that I could stare at his long, strong, artistic looking fingers. When I got there though it transpired he wasn't in school that day. We were being set our coursework to count towards 40% of our GCSEs. I decided on looking into how many square boxes would make up differing sizes of cubes which was coursework I'd really enjoyed doing. I carried on doing this course work at home but loving it enjoying understanding for once what I was doing and could control where my conclusions were going as to how to find out the one sum that would explain how to find out how many boxes were in boxes. I started with four cubes then 27 boxes and worked progressively through sixteen by sixteen by sixteen and never got confused once as the sum was always width, by depth by length. I did lovely drawings of which was my favourite part in doing the course work.

Going around Rheann's flat again that evening I started to feel like my best friend was a real diamond in the rough as the attack on my saving box kept going around and around in my head. I'd only stayed for about two hours mainly playing a game of cards that always seemed to go on forever.

By about five thirty pm I was home back at Mum's for tea. it was paella nicely cooked peppers with carrots, peas, spaghetti and fish. Later on the whole family settled down to watch a film called No Way out with a hot 'n' horny Kevin Costner. I remember the plot line of where he'd shagged his boss's wife and had to head her murder enquiry. The whole film hinged on a photo coming up on his computer that would have put him away. He had to find the real killer. I was the only one to get the plot line and I found myself explaining to my mother how the plot line worked. I'd felt cosy and warm sat in the armchair for once feeling like I was actually owning the room with my family giving the explanation. Fee came back afterward with her new boyfriend called Steve of whom I met for the first time in the hallway as he'd kissed her goodbye.

It was a Saturday and the family went to Evercreech to see Nan and Gramps. They were pleased to see us, the feeling of which was reciprocated. Granddad gave us our usual mint humbugs as we sat around the living room with the TV on.

Fee turned up in the afternoon after being out all morning with her boyfriend Steve. Nan being her usual self when she met him for the first time said, "Hello John, how are you?"

Fee told me that when she sat down that Nan had wound him up, especially having chestnut coloured hair and was tall, and quite handsome. I knew that he fancied himself.

Chapter Fourteen

I remember staying in a tent in Wells once for a summer Christian festival called Spirit of Youth. I'd gone there to stay with a church youth group from Shepton Mallet. It wasn't about worship it was all about church youth groups from all over the country getting together to have a good time.

There had been one day when some of us were canoeing round the Bishop's Palace moat. Rachel from my group was having a go but she'd rolled around and fell out into the water. I'd been afraid that if I'd done it my glasses would have fallen off and got lost in the water. The weekend was filled with activities. I don't remember any prayers being said or hymns being sung but I can recall there being a treasure hunt round the Bishop's Palace grounds that I'd enjoyed being part of.

One evening there'd been a Christian band playing in the barn next to Wells Park and I really got down and boogied feeling totally at ease in my surroundings with like-minded teenagers.

I never made a single friend that week but that hadn't bothered me in the slightest as I'd thoroughly enjoyed myself and coming away with a Spirit of Youth 92 t-shirt at the end was a definite highlight.

The following week my church youth group all jumped into a bus outside Peter Street rooms all happy and looking forward to a nice night out at Club X. Our youth leaders Rebecca and her fiancé sat up front to drive us all the way out to Bath. We parked at the bottom of town on the first floor of the multi-storey car park and all walked together to a big church.

Once outside there were many other youths all milling about mainly lining u to get some cordials. The church was illuminated with disco lights and the Christian band launched into some thumping tunes. Never one to miss an opportunity to dance I just joined the crowd at the back of the church and got stuck in jigging about.

Romans 16:5
Greetings also to the church that meets in their house.

I can't remember talking to anyone but I do recall having a very good night. Eventually I got to have a drink but we were all soon on the bus again going home.

With Shepton's youth group one evening our leader Nick drove us all to Bath. Darren, James, Mel and the rest were sat in the back of the bus happily talking but mainly I'd looked out the window.

The youth group soon got parked up at bath's multi-storey car park and we all jumped out to go to Pizza Hut at the bottom of town. The lads had beers or lagers. I had a Woodpecker cider with my pizza and I'd tucked into my pepperoni one. It was nice to just be part of a group and I enjoyed hearing their chatter. Relaxing with my drink the rest of them were gearing up to go to Quasar. I'd felt a bit of, do-I-have-to, but began mentally committing myself to getting into the swing of things. I knew what we'd be doing and compared it to paintballing of which I was glad we weren't doing as I'd heard Steve, Fee's boyfriend, had gotten hurt from the paint.

Inside the Quasar building it was all dark and all I could see was laser lights everywhere. I'd fired aimlessly and learned to hide. There'd been a lot of skulking about but no matter where I'd been walking there were lots of shouting and gunfire. I soon got shot as the red spot on my belt soon lit up. I'd felt a bit bored playing this game but at least could say I'd done it, and was happy as we all clambered back in the bus to head for home. Nick dropped us off back at our houses one by one.

I got up the next day full of the joys of experiencing the sunshine streaming through the window. The sun was warming the whole earth. I'd flown high in the sky the night before up above where the clouds should have been into the clear blue horizon. I'd felt so alive so free. It was Friday the thirteenth. I smiled feeling blessed.

Rheann called for me in a car with a new boyfriend. She got out the car looking all thin and gaunt but happy. I walked to the vehicle and got in. He put some saxophone music on. It sounded so sexy. Relaxing into the back seat we drove into Wells. We parked by Rheann's flat above The Mermaid. All three of us walked round to another pub. Philip told us that he was in a tournament that evening, a pool tournament.

We spent the day in and out of the shops. Philip disappeared for a few hours. Rheann came across a girl with short curly blonde hair. She abandoned me to go talk with her she didn't even introduce us. I felt abandoned as Rheann disappeared with her for a bit. I went and wandered around for a while. Then ended up at her flat just waiting. Both of them soon showed up then we walked round to the pub. He played pool and won each round hands down. We were all enthralled clapping each time.

After he won he gave me a chance to play him. I'd been sat in the window watching all night and tried after he split the balls up. I never potted anything and as Philip took over he was the cool, calm professional potting each ball in turn until he cleared the whole table. I'd thought I'd got my chance when his seventh ball went down to clear my own. I didn't realise the winner got to completely finish the game. Now this game was filled with lots of youths, part of a pool club.

I'd started college and that morning in typing class we all sat at our desks at the QWERTY typewriters. I placed my fingers over the middle keys and were taught to go to the 'n' with our forefingers. Having a transcript to type up we all pounded our keys really hard to type fast. Being a pianist I thought that I'd been doing really well.

I was doing a secretarial course and afterwards we went to learn T-line short hand and then in the afternoon I went to my leisure and tourism classes and there was a tanned athletic girl with tight brown curly hair who smoked and told us in class that she wanted to work as an air hostess.

I saw her again later on that day in her clique of friends lazily smoking. I'd sat on the grass waiting for the bus on my own enjoying the sunshine. I was keen to get home and found myself just enjoying the weather the next day.

On the Sunday that weekend I met up with my church youth group at St Peter Street rooms. Iain had his guitar and we practiced in the hall first before going up the little lane to the church to take the service.

Standing around on the stage there was someone playing the grand piano. We did a little skit preaching the good news from the Bible. I got up and said out loud something from James ministry that was all about with God and Jesus. My voice sounded good to my own ears and I wanted to stand there forever enjoying the moment.

The church was packed and everyone was enthralled.

A week later on a Saturday there was a beep outside. I chucked my shoes on and rain outside. It was Rheann and her boyfriend. A tape he had on was really loud and we shot off down the road. I heard him talking, with a gravelled voice about going over to Street to a garage to get his car sorted out. I saw his bare arms flex with a tattoo on the shoulder as he turned the wheel on the roads. There was a song on the tape called Baker Street and I loved the loud bloody saxophone making my heart race. I felt so alive with the car racing. Rheann's boyfriend seemed intense and cool.

There were five hours to kill before they left together for their flat and we didn't even care where the time went.

That Monday in the college library it felt good to be working with rows of endless books on a week's work experience. My first task had been assigned to put sleeves on, of which I threw myself into and noticed dog-eared books that needed sleeving.

My next task was in the office doing some photocopying to replace old newspaper clips for the micro-fiche drawer. The local papers pages could be found there and I got praised for my work.

Psalms 57:7
I have complete confidence, O God;
I will sing and praise you.

The next day I was tidying the books and started to get bored remembering the hive of activity from the day before.

I had a brilliant week and enjoyed myself.

It was the last day at college the following Friday before we broke up for Christmas and I got into college on the bus just outside the doctors in Shepton Mallet with a student pass. Then when I was there I walked into my first class of where it was QWERTY typewriting and I sat stretching my fingers and yawning. I felt like I was flying across the keys with my finger working in perfect synchronisation. I lasted out the class and went to another building during lunch time and saw the lid up on a piano and popped in, 'cause I couldn't resist and played 'The Wind of Change', a huge pop song over and over again. While I was playing I thought sod it I don't want to do this course anymore and walked outside to the front of the building of where I bumped into my best friend Rheann. She showed up looking pissed of.

"Let's just do a bunk and not come back yeah?" I'd said, so we went for a long walk out to the Butleigh Road by a long line of trees that got my imagination going of why a whole line of trees would look the same placed the same width apart all the way what I thought was an old Roman Road. Then across the fields there was what looked like an old Roman entrance way to what could have been a building behind as it was made of two colosseums. I imagined the road I was on having old chariots being trotted along on it as the trees looked like, on both side of the road, as having been deliberately put there years ago t signal the entrance way to an old Roman town.

I was with Rheann a day later with Philip and we went to Glastonbury for what I thought would be a look around. He drove fast of which I really liked. Once in Glastonbury we started to look round the shops and went down Benedict Street. I saw a great big church and wandered around looking for the entrance.

"I'm not going there," Philip said, "I'm going to the Twilight Zone."

"What to another planet?" I'd said.

"No." Rheann and Philip said in unison. They laughed at me.

"I'm getting a tattoo." Philip said. "On my shoulder. Do you want to come in and watch? I know you're not old enough for one but they might just let you watch," so I went in with them and watched unattachedly as I saw, what basically sounded like a drill, a big needle going into his shoulder. I'd heard him ask for a British bulldog picture and I stood there mesmerised and I'd seen him flinch a couple of times whilst trying to appear hard to us two girls. They were doing a good job actually until they put on the yellow which made him bleed. The blood oozed down his arm making the picture look messy they didn't even offer him a tissue to dab it with or a plaster. They just ploughed on drilling his arm. I looked up after they'd finished and

Rheann had fucked off. She was outside having a fag waiting for when we came out.

We walked up to the local pub and had a drink in the Billy. I had my usual Woodpecker that Philip bought for me and Rheann had a lager while he had a shandy. We had a nice evening.

Then the next day I was looking forward to my old school's Christmas concert. In the morning I turned on the telly and got up Big Breakfast on Channel Four and watched the idiots presenting like Denise Van Outen and thought I could do that and got carried away with answering questions for their silly quiz of where buckets of water were involved. I had fun watching the television for most of the day trying to follow a murder mystery with Angela Lansbury in Murder She Wrote and got completely tangled up in the plot line. I got the answer of whom murdered whom quicker than she did. Then I watched Dick Van Dyke lead another murder mystery. I had a spot of lunch and flicked back on BBC1s news to catch up with the rest of the world. There was an earthquake reported in San Francisco and wondered why people would live so close to where they knew was a fault line. It was the biggest earthquake ever recorded in the last fifty years and dominated the news.

Afterwards I decided to get all maudlin on the old Joanna. I played a love song and 'Didn't they have a lovely time at Bangor?' And other seventies music along with 'Mandy' and 'Snowbird' and 'I'm Not in Love'. I played for a couple of hours not worried in the slightest of what my sisters were up to or my parents for that matter.

In the evening after tea when everyone regrouped Mum asked me if I wanted to go to a Christmas concert.

I'd said, "I'd love to," and I rushed upstairs to change my top to get ready.

"Ready yet Kar?"

"No Father."

"Just your Mother's going I'm not."

I soon dragged on a red top over my jeans to look classy but kept on my trainers and put on a comfortable cardigan.

Mum and I with Fee and Eve got in the car and headed for my old school Whitstone. We parked by the entrance and walked in a little bit late so we didn't have to queue and went straight into sit down just in time. We came with Gran and Grampy Burr in tow and still got good seats facing the band. They played all night wonderfully the songs of the sixties and forties they were a swingers band.

At the interlude we all traipsed upstairs to get a little bit of wine and a mince pie each. I didn't have to wait too long. I timed it right. The crumbs went everywhere. I did not care as it crumbled in my silver foil cup.

Sat back down it was the forties music of where they played big band songs that would have been sung by Buddy Holly or Dame Vera Lynn. It was a really good evening full of a wonderful atmosphere.

Next day was boring and I'd gotten up late and wafted around all day until Dad decided we were going out for tea for a Christmas treat. It was a good idea.

"Now dress up warm." He'd said, "'cause we're going for a long walk first around the lanes near Pilton. Mum'll bring the car laters. I'm keeping you out while she cleans the house."

Along the lanes that Dad frogmarched us through. We saw a lot of wildlife and I asked my Father what each flower was called and he said. "There are usually cowslips here Karen and during certain times of the year you see bluebells and foxgloves."

"Thanks Dad." I'd said as I stared at a field full of cows, then sheep, then pigs and we ended up in Pilton walking towards a pub restaurant called Crossways. Mum was there waiting at the bar and we all went to a table thoroughly hungry. I could smell the chicken on other people's plates. It smelt delicious and I saw someone from school who looked as tall as a tree called Robin who looked handsomer than ever all in black coming from the toilets ready to come over to take our orders.

I said, "Hi. I would like a roast chicken please and an orange and lemonade."

We stayed for the rest of the evening and had a lovely meal. It was fan-dabby-dosey.

The next day I had a bee in my bonnet about something. I'd felt really angry after feeling really left out of things at home and hearing other people's discussions in the family of where I'd constantly hear that my sisters were tired of hearing Mum wanting to protect me. This gave me inspiration for a poem entitled Knowledge. It went:

    Leaks like toothpaste
    Heard not known,
    Catch a taste,
    Seeds are sewn.
    Live your life
    With hearts on fire to
    Hurt stupidity
    Leave it burning
    For eternity
    Keep yourself
    Secret
    Higher in intelligence
    Wiser than others

> Leak it out
> Heard not known Source?
> Knowledge.

I'd found a segment in the paper asking for poems to put a book together called A Passage Through Time so I sent Knowledge through the post.

A few days later I had a letter from the publishers asking for personal details and £70 to see my name in print in the finished book.

After ditching college just before Christmas Mum and Dad pushed me to get a job. In fact Mum had asked the owner of a card shop that was about to open in Wells to take me on. they seemed happy to have an apprentice.

The owner got me to do a lot of cleaning and the wage was poor. The only time I'd served at the counter with my boss showing me what to do we'd had a robbery. A man in army fatigues had come in asking to buy a pencil. A he passed over the pencil for us to swipe we opened the till to get change. The next thing we knew the man had hopped over the counter, had his hand in the till, and made off with a lot of cash. As he ran by the shop window he looked back at me. His face haunted me. This incident really shook me up so much so that I didn't feel like working there anymore. My boss had told me to get a cup of tea. I'd felt like having something stronger while she talked to the police. I had felt like she didn't care about my feelings. After having had my tea I found myself back in the shop just staring out the front window imagining myself as Margaret Thatcher running the country.

I told my Mum about the theft that very evening and all she said to me, with no sympathy in her voice, which shocked me, was that I should have been glad the owner had been with me at the time or I could have been accused of stealing. Like Mum thought I could have been a thief. This upset me more than the robbery.

> *Psalms 69:20*
> *Insults have broken my heart, and I am in despair.*
> *I had hoped for sympathy, but there was none;*
> *For comfort, but I found none.*

I did get on the bus to go back to work the next day though. This was a Friday and I found myself, once I'd gotten into Wells, jumping on the bus to Bristol instead. I'd thought of getting my hair cut whilst wondering round Bristol but I ended up watching a move called Toys. My moral guidance.

Afterwards I used my old student pass from college to get on the National Express up to Scotland. On the coach I got talking to a builder on his way to Newcastle to do a job and as we were talking he ran his hand up my thigh. It tingled. Next thing I knew he was pushing my head down on him like it was a perfectly natural thing to do and all I can remember was that there was a wart on it. After this he brought me an Irn Bru and a sandwich. At this point though, as far as I was concerned, I had run away from home and was never coming back. A plan was beginning to form in my mind to go round a high rise flat, to burst into tears the minute someone opened their door and claim that I couldn't find my friend Margaret's home and would I be able to stay the night? It was the first thing I was going to do when I got there.

After having stopped at a petrol station and the builder got off. I curled up on a seat opposite to go to sleep and woke up the next day to glorious sunshine in Glasgow's major bus station. My first port of call was a high rise flat of where I went up a couple of floors in a lift and banged on the first door I came to, I was yellow. They had led me into their apartment and squeezing passed a bike in their hallway they asked me if I was alright but all I ended up asking for was a drink, as the tears didn't come, and I got some cold water. Words managed to fail me at this point all though I did manage to ask if a Margaret lived in the building.

Nehemiah 6:8
I sent a reply to him: "Nothing of what you are saying is true. You have made it all up yourself."

They said no, it came like a cold dose of salts over my mind as I soon made my excuses and left. That plan did not go well.

I did all sorts that day after that. I had taken seventy five pounds out of the C+G the day before and headed off down a very wide high street. I went in MacDonald's of where I got a scratch card and won myself a free meal. I did have to get verbally aggressive with the lady on the till over this as I wanted it to pay for the meal I was just going upstairs to eat and really I shouldn't have used the token till the next day. I got really in her face and told her to prove it that I hadn't got the scratch card the day before. She easily backed down.

At a shopping precinct I went ice-skating of where the ice boots must have been the wrong size for my feet because they ended up hurting. There was a university too that was situated at the top of this beautiful park, with lovely flowers, park benches and pretty bushes and I really appreciated it as I took a leisurely stroll around while watching the joggers, the dog walkers and the couples.

I went back to the shopping precinct afterwards by which the ice rink was and I came across a man that was obviously drunk sitting on a bench. He gave me money to get him an alcoholic drink. I tried to do what I thought the right thing was by going to the local supermarket for him but they refused to sell me alcohol as I didn't look old enough, so I spent the money on a sandwich and a drink for myself thinking that I'd probably not come across the man again anyway as I took off in another direction to a nearby wharf. Staring out to sea I could hear the strains of bag pipes sounding lovely across the water from where what looked like was a castle. It was probably the military tattoo as I had my tea. Feeling calmer and so much more at peace I made my way back to the National Express bus station to head back home on another overnight ride.

Penniless I returned back to the fold to be greeted by a police officer asking me where I had been and how I was feeling. My response was that I'd been feeling self-absorbed.

No-one else bothered speaking to me as Mum said that everyone didn't know what to say but at least I got a little bit of emotion from Fee who said they were all angry at me.

I managed eventually to get a job in a supermarket called Somerfield. While walking through the double doors of the local supermarket on my first evening at work there I tripped over. I momentarily stood completely still swaying a little to get my bearings.

Psalms 107:27
They stumbled and staggered like drunken men –
All their skill was useless.

Listening to the tills bleep on the left hand side of me. Plenty of people were milling about. I'd felt slightly stunned and a bit nervous. Imagining butterflies in my stomach I put my hand there to steady myself while looking down at my tummy. Where was I meant to go?

Pushing myself forward I'd looked round for an office door wanting to see a familiar face and a man with hair flopping over his left eye came towards me. He introduced himself a my line manager to be and asked, "You're Karen aren't you?" and I said, "Yes." He walked me to the health and beauty aisle saying that was where I was expected to work and he told me that if I finished early to go help someone else out.

I noticed only one cage full of aerosols, beauty products, combs, etc. and though I could finish all this very quickly and easily. I'd been assigned a protractible flip knife that was yellow and black. Gliding the knife easily through each product they were all soon placed neatly on the shelves and it occurred to me to face up the products as I recollected what I'd been told to do. Proud of finishing early I wandered over to the crisp aisle to help out and instinctively went to where the warehouse had been shown to me to grab two big Monster Munch boxes of crisps and threw them on the floor in front of their shelves. The person who should have been there was nowhere around and it didn't even occur to me that they'd finished their cage early too to go off and help someone else and I felt a great deal of satisfaction from clearing stock out of the warehouse.

Thoroughly exhausted from the evening I went looking for someone to tell me to go home and my line manager came into view with a puzzled look on his face. He asked me to help someone else who'd got stuck n candy. Side by side we worked together not having time to chat. I wished, as we worked, for a conversation but focused purely on helping them out.

The evening flew by and I was soon back home having a good night's sleep.

In the morning I had to go up town to get some money out for a trip called a Christian festival. It was going to cost me twenty quid and Iain, my youth leader, who'd set himself up to run the trip wanted the money at our next church youth group meeting.

As soon as I turned up that evening, before I went in, I stopped Iain to give him my twenty quid. I gave it to him just outside of St Peter Street rooms in front of a girl named Sarah. I did want to be friends with her but she insulted me by saying, "Is that money clean?" and I just ignored her and said to Iain in my defence, "I just got out this money today from my C+G account." I felt misunderstood.

> *Psalms 109:20*
> *Lord, punish my enemies that way, those who say*
> *Such evil things against me!*

Looking back I remember turning to see Sarah a little bit confused and saw her pinched face. She actually looked like she was jealous and I didn't even want to know why. I knew my cousin Scott had been inside and thought Sarah was the type to listen to gossip rather than wanting to get to know me.

In that confirmation class we talked of nothing else than going to the Christian festival. Our trip.

A few days later we hopped on the bus outside of where we usually met for our meetings and we took off for a field in the middle of nowhere.

When we got to where we were going it was literally a huge field with marquees in and other students were there putting up tents. We found our spot and started to erect our tents. The gang took a while and I was getting confused with matching a 'C' with a 'C' and a 'D' with a 'D', sounded easy to me but they were making mountains out of mole hills. I just stood there and watched having a private laugh with myself.

Half an hour later with a fully erected tent the group started lunch and we all ate baked beans on toast together over an open fire. I was wearing jeans and a t-shirt feeling cold. Iain saw me shivering and nipped back to his tent to get a nice big baggy blue jumper for me to keep warm. I felt grateful and a snotty nose but thought, "I love you Iain," as I'd said, "Thank you," to him.

After lunch we were told to have a wander round and enjoy what was going on in the marquees. I wandered over to the far side of the field of where I saw loads of people going to sit down, so I joined them.

When the man came into talk he looked full of happiness and told us a joke about the Pharisees and the Sadducees, but the joke was that the Sadducees were 'sad you see' in order to get us to remember them.

The man talked animatedly for ages and got all of our attention brilliantly and ascertained that Mary and Joseph were around thirteen or fourteen years of age when they got married and had Jesus. From what he had said about biblical times and from people had investigated of back then. He made perfect sense and I really enjoyed myself learning about these things.

That evening after we'd regrouped to have tea we all went together to an evening service of where we all sang together brand new songs I'd never heard of before all emulating God and Jesus that was amazing.

Two days late I went home feeling a little bit sad that my holiday was over. I wanted to tell everyone all about it but I just felt flat.

I'd taken home with me, it transpired, Iain's jumper and his little wooden cross that I deliberately took from him. I'd fancied the pants off Iain and that evening I felt very warm and comforted in bed. In the morning I saw a big indent in the bed behind where I'd been sleeping and it felt as though Iain had been spooning me all night.

The next day it had been an evening service when I got confirmed. Me and a few others had stood in front of the church to make our vows to God. The church was packed as we all took turns to speak. I felt very calm and at peace.

> *Ecclesiastes 10:4*
> *Serious wrongs may be pardoned if you keep calm.*

During the service I'd sat back down for the hymns and became perplexed as we never said the Lord's Prayer.

Sat in the middle pews with my family beaming proudly, Mum especially, I enjoyed the rest of the service. Singing loudly and enjoying the sound of my own voice I remembered the film about Tina Turner and how she'd been the loudest singer in church when a child. I'd have liked to have been discovered for my powerful voice too.

In church after the service I approached John Woolmer, the vicar, and asked why they didn't say the Lord's Prayer. He'd said they didn't have time in the service for it and that was usually another favourite part of the service. I'd taken the time to learn the Lord's Prayer off by heart over the years through coming to church too.

In Peter Street rooms those having taken confirmation and their families turned up for some food and to meet the Bishop of Bath and Wells. The man praised us and gave out a handful of red bibles to each of us.

Through my Mum I managed to get a babysitting job with a lovely little family that consisted of a single mum with three small children, Oliver, Nick and Georgina.

I walked all across town to this job in Waterloo Road in my little pink shorts. I got wolf-whistled at by some builders. I was all about feeling cool and sexy then.

At first the job seemed easy as all the children wanted to do was watch the television. I was surprised when Nick looked up and asked me about sex. He was only about ten years old. I told him that fucking was like scratching an itch. They all wanted to go outside once their programme finished so I took them across to the grounds of the old hospital. Feeling like a cool babysitter I wanted them to watch me doing cartwheels, handstands and a back flip. We stayed outside for a while but the sun started going down and they were getting hungry.

Nick had a friend with him and I let them get their own tea. I wasn't bothered about food. Nick's friend didn't stay long and I soon got them all upstairs for bed with a promise of a film in their Mum's bedroom. They all got on the bed as they stuck on a Walt Disney movie. I tried to impress them again with another back flip. No-one paid me any attention and I made my back twinge. They were all very good for me really as I eventually got them all into their own beds. Georgia needed a story to get to sleep and they were all still awake when their Mum came home even though they were all tucked up in bed. Their Mum thanked me with fifteen pounds and the gentleman with her ran me home. I was never asked to babysit again as originally this was Eve's job anyway and I don't think they'd been too impressed with me.

It was going to be my first Spring Harvest festival so I and the rest of the Shepton Mallet's church youth group all set off on the coach for Butlin's, Minehead. As soon as we got there we found our chalets and I was bummed when I'd realised we had to make our own meals. Someone had bought pizzas but they had sweetcorn on them. I had to force the food down out of politeness and the need to eat. Our accommodation had been very basic with one small bed, a sofa bed and someone had to sleep on the floor in a sleeping bag. I'd had the bed.

That afternoon we all wandered round Butlin's together and I remember Louise and I coming across a ranchers bar, then upon coming outside we wandered round the other side of the building. There was a small rollercoaster so I got on and went round on it twice. Poor Louise just stood and watched.

The first Beethoven film was on in the cinema opposite. It was a good laugh seeing a giant St Bernard causing mayhem especially in one scene when he totally wrecked a garden party.

Afterwards we all met up again for some tea back at the chalet I managed to get out of organising food as a lot of sandwiches had been brought with us. It was tuna, sweetcorn and mayonnaise. Again I was not impressed but beggars could not be choosers. We went out again afterwards to look round the grounds and found a massive lake with deep undergrowth around the sides and I heard the choo-chooing of an old fashioned train's horn coming from behind the trees.

The sun began to get low leaving a bronzed glow in the sky and on the water. Louise had stayed with me but the others had gone. Turned out, when we'd got back to our rooms, that the others had gone along the seafront to watch the sun go down over the sea. It was getting time for bed so I changed under my covers into my nightie, then jumped out to do my ablutions, then came back and was soon asleep. The others had stayed awake talking.

The next day we all split up to find some seminars to go to and I'd headed off to where the majority of the other youth groups were going into a dark and a bit dingy large building. We all sat round discussing how we'd all like to help out in the world and came up with lots of ideas. I stayed quiet not quite knowing what to say and the man taking the group noticed this and asked me straight out about what was important to me. I'd said everything was important, diseases, famines, wars, etc. and I honestly couldn't choose one thing I could put my mind to help out with. The man thought long and hard about my answer and said that simply I was right all of it was important.

We were there all week and I did get down on the seafront with everyone else that evening as Rebecca and her partner shouted us for fish 'n' chips.

On the third day some stayed for seminars while the others went into town of which I did and got myself a milkshake outside a little café on my own. It was bliss in the sunshine with an ice cold, milky, ice-creamed strawberry flavoured drink slipping coolly down my parched throat quenching my thirst. I then wandered round to the gardens and caught up with Sarah from our group. I just latched onto her and followed her back to the Spring Harvest for an evening's worship in a big tent. I learned some new funky hymns that evening, one in particular was 'I'd like to see the kingdom of God in my generation. I'd like to see the kingdom of God while I am alive. I want to give my life for something that'll last forever. Oh I delight to do your will…' That was my favourite hymn of the holiday.

The next day I found myself at one point in another popular seminar and it was about going to poor countries to help during the famines. We all said that we'd like to do that and we had to write down the steps we'd take to do exactly that and point to the wall saying that we'd jump in feet first and just go. The lady taking this said that was the wrong answer as you'd have to take the time to study all about the culture you'd like to help first and get you're immunisations pointing out that most of us would have found ourselves ill or in prison without getting the most basic of information first. I was impressed but still none the wiser about what I'd do with my life.

Back at home afterwards Uncle Graham came to visit Mum to talk about his job as a mechanic was what I'd overheard. I'd sat in front of the television with a book in my hand. All I ever really wanted was read and dream about being a writer someday.

I got off from the sofa to go see Uncle Graham and he was just making his excuses to leave.

"Sorry I didn't speak to you Kar. But I'll see you again. Right. I'm off."

I went to give him a kiss and giggled when his moustache tickled my lips.

"We might be in Wells later," my Mum said to her brother-in-law while seeing him to the door.

"We going shopping Mum?"

"Yeah why not?" as she said while turning to look at me.

"Yippee," I'd said in my heart. A chance to get outside the house.

When in Wells Mum took me round the clothes shops and I had a good look through everything in each clothes shop of where I bought one item.

Then we walked into a shop called MacKay's and I had a really good look round there. On the way out a funny little noise went off as I passed by the alarms. I looked down at my bag and noticed a purse hanging off my bag.

Titus 1: 9-10
They must not answer them back or steal from them.

There was still a tag on it. Not wanting to draw attention to myself I went back into the shop and put it back on the shelf. Now I'd been there ultimately for a job interview in my Evie navy blue skirt and jacket that I loved to wear. It was just perfect colour co-ordination for my interview with my local conservative party. I walked up the steps to a building of flats near the Regal of where they were based full of nerves. I opened the door and it was a big office with propaganda all around me. I got up more nerve to push myself forward to someone on a desk.

"Excuse me. I've come for an interview. My name is Karen Burr." They held out their hand for a shake and I took it.

"My name is Richard Wilson. Nice to meet you." The interview got off to a flying start and I went back outside with a skip in my step. Two days later I got a letter turning me down. I didn't mind. I knew I'd get something. Then with Mother waiting outside we took off for home.

The next day I went round to Rheann's in the afternoon she had moved to Wells to live with her boyfriend Philip who had the same surname as her. We were happy for a bit drinking alcohol and I thought we were having a laugh until Rheann turned nasty and I realised I'd been having a dig at her boyfriend so she turfed me out of her flat in the middle of the night. I then found myself walking along the middle of the roads to go home. When I got there I used my keys to get in and sneak up to bed.

In the morning I woke up with a headache and took a paracetamol. My pounding headache was soon fine. It's an idiosyncrasy I thought as Philip just wanted time alone with his girlfriend last night. Rheann had wanted her friend there, me, and I've always thought Rheann was a laugh and brilliant company. She made me feel cool and I had a brilliant adventure last night walking home.

I leapt out of bed wanting to find my magazine before I got into the shower to read about looking after your hair. It said that you must not put a hair dryer any closer to your head than eight inches away. I washed my hair quickly and got out of the shower to touch myself all over with the towel. I put on the hairdryer and dried my body with it as well as my hair and got off on it. As soon as my hair was dried I put on my clothes and danced around in front of the mirror with my comb singing loudly.

Now I went downstairs and switched on the TV and watched Big Breakfast on Channel 4 with Denise Van Outen or Chris Evans and I watched TV for the rest of the day. I loved Jessica Fletcher in Murder She Wrote. I loved following a good murder mystery.

Ecclesiastes 7:25
But I devoted myself to knowledge and study;
I was determined to find wisdom and the answers to my questions,
And to learn how wicked and foolish stupidity is.

Then Dick Van Dyke's murder mystery would come on afterwards and I knew it was his son working with him but I had no-one to tell. Nobody cared.

The next day Mum and Dad decided to take the family to Weston Super Mare and on the scenic route we drove through Westbury-Sub-Mendip and the car broke down. It coughed. It spluttered and would not move. Dad got out of the car and asked to borrow the phone at somebody's house.

Next thing I knew Granddad came out in his little jeep to pick us girls up and told my parents we could sleep with them for the night. Mum and Dad had to stay with the car until the pickup truck came to take them home to put the car in the garage to get it fixed.

At Nan's we couldn't settle for the night and I felt well looked after and in the morning my parents came and got us home.

It was a Sunday and Mum and I went to St Peters and St Pauls church for a nice service. We enjoyed the singing and I loved the hymns a I knew all of them and could really belt out a tune. It got to the sermon and there was some jokes that the congregation sniggered at. They laughed out loud to others it seemed fun for me. I bloody loved church and Mum and I stayed for coffee afterwards and I let Mum get the drinks. We sat down and Mrs Penn came over to talk with Mum and noticed her cheek. "It's gone all puffy," she said to Mum and a spider came crawling out of her mouth and plopped into her cup. It must have been poisonous.

"Don't worry Karen, but it must have been that spider in my mouth. Don't forget it's your Dad's birthday tomorrow."

"Oh I won't," she had bought me out of my reverie. We went on and had an idyllic day with a roast that afternoon and cosy time with the family.

The next day, on the Monday, we got all excited in the morning as it was Dad's birthday and we all left for Nan Sheila's to go see them for Dad's sake and I think me Nan had forgotten his present as she gave him a Mr Potato Head with hair that grew out of it.

> *Ecclesiastes 7:6*
> *When a fool laughs, it is like thorns crackling in a fire.*
> *It doesn't mean a thing.*

Back at home us girls took the piss and laughed at him. "What the hell was your Gran thinking? It's a child's present," Mum said. We had such a good laugh that day it would be emblazoned on my mind forever.

The next day it was a hot summer's day and the family piled into the car for a trip to the beach in Weymouth. When there at Nothe Fort we got out. Had a stroll around town and down to the harbour to have a wander up to Radipole the nearest nature reserve. Then we went on the beach and lounged out with ice-creams each, before we went home.

Then it was Thursday and I had an appointment with the Inland Revenue offices in Wells. I turned up all smart and took a while finding the offices that were by Somerfield. I went up the stairs and found the door and knocked on it.

"Come in," they said and I did. The gentleman looked kind and I sorted out with him why I'd needed job seekers allowance and got it set up. I only went that day because Mum had kept on to get some money coming in. She reasoned it out with me and said, "Claim our taxes back. Me and your father have paid into the system long enough. It's about time we got some money back.

I'd said to her when I got home. "It'll be about seventy five pound a week."

"I'll take twenty a week," she said, "For housekeeping because that's what Fiona has to pay."

The next Friday I walked into town to get some shopping and I was in jeans and a tight lime green shirt to emphasise my figure. On the way back I stood by where Lyndy's chippy used to be and Micky walked by and started chatting to me. I always felt flattered when he talked to me.

"How are you doing?" He said.

"Fine thank you," and I blushed. I really liked him he had been popular in school. I turned away saying, "Well it's nice talking to you," and I walked over to home down Cornwall Road passed the park and into Coombe View.

Fee had decided to go to Paris for the weekend with Nan Burr. I'd felt jealous that Nan was taking Fee with her but when they got back Nan was bruised all over her nose and on her eyes. Apparently she had fallen down some steps while looking up to the Eiffel tower. Poor Nan looked awful. Until then though they'd had a lovely time but they never got up the tower.

A few days later I went to Bridgewater with my youth group on a bus and on the way there we stopped off at a youth centre by the road. I hung around the pool table watching others play and I'd hoped to have a game too but I never so just had a chat. Then the group went outside and played basketball in the courtyard. I stood and watched, then the ball bounded in my direction so I picked it up and aimed straight for the basket and the ball slam dunked. I was pleased with myself and continued watching quite happily with my arms across my chest in the sunshine. I'd proved my point that I could play and let them get on with it.

On the Sunday Nan and Grampy Ern, came round Mum's to go to the Mid Somerset Show and I went in their jeep and Mum drove my sisters up to the Ridgeway Estate. It was free to get in and we started to head for the main arena so that gramps could sit down on a chair and watch all the horses on display. The rest of us walked round the stalls and I had a go at picking a playing card to win a cuddly toy but the card didn't match the ones on the stand. We got some cheese burgers of which were extortionately priced at four pound fifty. The sun was shining and I had a t-shirt on with an open shirt over the top with shorts on and trainers. I felt like an American because I was dressed how I saw them dress in the movie. On the way out after seeing the dressage with Granddad Ern, my Mum's Dad, we looked round the classic cars and we felt happy having gone round it all and seen the animals too.

Mum and Dad had been looking into buying a bigger property because they couldn't get the extension built over the garage that they'd applied for 'cause Eve was fed up of having to walk through my bedroom to get to hers. So one day the family all went to a big house on the estate opposite the school we'd been to.

Dad said though, "Don't get your hopes up we're just having a look."

Deuteronomy 13: 1-2
"Prophets or interpreters of dreams may promise a miracle
Or a wonder, in order to lead you into worship and serve gods
That you have not worshipped before."

It was a big house, very spacious and my parents wanted us to see out the window across to the park and moony-eye over an indoor swimming pool they had. I felt the dreamer side of me coming out and felt inspired by the place to want to live in a place like that one day.

That very same day we went to Gran and Gramps and I let them talk and talk about the past and the family. Uncle Cyn came in to sit down for a cup of tea so he put the kettle on and I said, "Tea please," and sat with Mum and Dad. They talked about the house they saw and the Grandparents were enthralled. Then they started again talking about carnival and the good old days. They told me stories I'd never heard before and had a laugh. Then Grampy said to me about a female relative of whom lived in America and was a famous country and western singer. He said to me, "Would you like to hear her?"

Nan cut in, "Oh not now. they don't want to hear that," and they had a bit of a barny over it and I would have liked to have heard it and know her name to look her up. Gramps never told me.

That evening Mum and I and the rest of us stayed in Wells. We parked by the park in the centre of town and went to a barn dance of where we had to wear our wellies. It was a really good evening. We dosey-doed, and did a skit. We kicked out heels up and had a really good laugh making shapes all over the floor.

I woke up one morning feeling bored.

Ecclesiastes 2:1
I decided to enjoy myself and find out what happiness is.

Mum and Dad had gone to work and Eve was out. I was in dire need of something to do. It had been on a whim that I went through my sisters' money box and my parents Showerings bottle to make change for the bus. I walked all across town intending to go somewhere, anywhere just to get out. I jumped on the first bus that was heading to Wells. Whilst traipsing around the shops it was decided I'd only really needed some more wool for my squares. The wool shop was just up a little side street. I'd bought some blue wool.

My expedition to Wells didn't last long and was soon home again with no-one even aware that I'd gone out. With no lunch in my belly and determined to knit squares I set myself up in front of the telly willing the time on till Mum would cook tea.

My Dad was a lorry driver for BOC Interbrand and had an office to report to on the bottom floor of the massive BOC Interbrand building at the top of Shepton in Fosse Lane. I was out of work at the time so Dad asked around for me and managed to get me into the offices on the first floor to take over a 16yr old girls job who was on leave to take her GCSEs.

The work was easy writing out and typing out figures from sales and quantities of goods from the warehouse. I enjoyed going to work every day to a nice cheerful office. I was always good at picking up on atmospheres and one old gentleman in the office had to take on every job going and soon realised that most of the office workers feared for their jobs. The girl's Mum of whose job I'd taken over asked me to her office one day and it was just down some stairs at the bottom end of our floor and I just happened to pass a door where the bosses were having a meeting. I overheard they'd made a three million pound profit and I soon relayed this information back to the office. I thought it was good news to cheer everyone up with.

I soon left this job upon the other Karen's return after having had a decent wage for once and being able to adopt a child through World Vision, which was something I had to give up when I didn't have a wage anymore. This was when I got desperate enough to have to sign onto an agency.

Chapter Fifteen

I wrote a letter to the local press to get work experience and when I went to work on the paper they let me sort out their filing and working on the looking back article. I was lucky that week that after going through a lot of old articles I found a write up of when a prince attended Millfield School for the twenty five years ago section.

There was a nice lady called Emma who gave me a pack about journalism courses which I thanked her profusely for fully intending to take some training.

I did go down to the cutting and pasting room of where the printed articles were placed on a board to manually create the page layouts. All in all I had a very productive and an eye opening week. I really enjoyed myself.

I'd applied for Youth Training up at Bath and only got in because of our Bath and Avon postcode. I went to an office I'd found the address for in the paper to be interviewed then went straight there on the bus. I thought I'd have to have been sixteen, straight from school, but apparently my postcode swung it in my favour at eighteen.

Next I had to work out transportation and that was easy as there'd been a Bath bus every day from the Cenotaph.

I'd finally got my chance to train as a journalist on computers. It was exciting sitting on the bus that first morning and was a bit concerned about getting to Bath on time. The bus went into the bottom end of the city under the viaducts and into the station. Next I had to find Charlotte Street which was all the way up town. I noticed a Big Issue seller for the first time by the Disney shop and stopped to buy one that was a pound fifty pence as I'd thought of the poor homeless people they were helping to get back into work.

In the Queen Anne House where my Youth Training was to take place I had to go to the basement to a huge office area with load of computers on desks. There was a grey carpet and a huge photocopying machine against the back wall. I sat down next to a lad who looked handsome with ash blonde coloured hair. The teacher started by handing out worksheets and got us to announce ourselves as we received the work.

I had a great day finding my way around Word, Excel and spreadsheets. That day had been exciting and I carried that feeling into work at Somerfield's that evening.

The next day I got youth training again and loved walking by the shops. Through a park to Charlotte Street by a car park.

When indoors I sat down it was a bit cold and was glad I had a jumper on. At the same computer as the one I'd sat on yesterday I slipped into completing the day before's task. Then we were shown how to do another programme that took up the rest of the day. I got a great deal of satisfaction from this.

Psalms 103:5
He fills my life with good things, so that I stay young
And strong like an eagle.

What with work in Somerfield in the evenings too, the week soon flew by until the following Monday of when I was still enjoying brand new things on the computer. By the time I got on the bus it was running late to get me into Somerfield on time for work. As I walked into Somerfield late, my line manager saw me coming through the double doors. I walked towards him and panicked. Upon turning round he yelled, "I'll fire you if you walk out the door." But I just said to myself, "But I quit!" In my head and walked all the way home smirking to myself feeling that I'd found something better up at Bath. I was getting paid around £50 at youth training every week anyway.

My Granddad Burr, around this time, was on death's door with lung cancer in Shepton Mallet hospital. He wasn't long there before he died. I had dressed in an aquamarine skirt and matching jacket. The day went without a hitch. The whole family turned up for the funeral as we entered the church to sit near the front after walking behind the coffin. It was a warm day outside. The usual hymns were sung and Dad did a lovely eulogy before we all ventured out into the sunshine to follow the funeral car through the town and out to the graveyard at the meadows. At the bottom of where all the graves were Granddad's body was laid to rest. I remember Eve bursting into tears and needing to be consoled. I recall a bit of a chill running through me as I stood a bit bereft from the others. With the vicar's sermon finally over I held on to Eve as we walked back up the hill towards the cars and we headed back to Mum's for the wake.

There was a certain comfort drawn from the family members that showed up and we all drew from that as we all milled about chatting to one another. I particularly remember a handful of us talking in the living room and as I stood by the living room door with Mum and Dad for a photo. I memorised Uncle Mike standing in front of the radiator with the sun out the window outlining his shape with his arm up and a drink in his hand radiating his warm boom of a laugh that was distinctly his own. I didn't know at the time it was to be the last time I saw him alive.

That evening Mum told me that she thought I was the strong one about everything but I wanted to show her that I cared so I made myself cry just to portray that.

Timothy 1:2

May God the Father and Christ Jesus our Lord
Give you grace, mercy and peace.

Sometime later Eve had been in Germany for a week on a youth exchange trip through school. We were told that she'd stayed in a lovely big house overlooking the Hamburg football stadium. Dad was pleased but Eve wasn't interested in football. The girl Eve stayed with was called Corinna.

When she came to stay with us I found myself in her company more than what Eve was as this strong confident lovely tanned young girl loved to play the piano. Corinna taught me a German tune that was strongly evocative, and her grasp of the English language was very good.

While she was with us we all went to Weymouth for the day. I remember Mum parking at Nothe Fort and us playing tag on the rocks overlooking the naval marina. Corinna was like a mountain goat jumping from rock to rock and I was not that confident doing the same so I eventually gave up. We went on the beach taking ice-creams we'd had from the Nothe Fort little café with us, but apart from that it didn't feel like Corinna had been in our company long before she had to go back to Germany.

I sat in my bed one morning and I visualised the world and saw how the world perceived the Christian faith from a dream I'd had that night. I'd been in a church and I'd been rattling bars making it look like a prison. The sky was red, the church was white but it changed into red. My hair was wild with rage.

I'd been wandering round inside it with carpets on the floor looking at my feet wondering what I was doing there.

It had felt like the world had taken faith and had made it angry.

That day I'd found an advertisement in the paper needing people to sew pudding bags. The unit to where they were, was at the Anglo Trading Estate. I went there and picked up a hundred bags to start me off with plenty of string. They explained to me that Xmas puddings for all the stores, including M&S would be put in them.

I would sit there for hours threading the bags I got 2 pence each for. When I got more confident with them I would get up to twenty pounds worth of bags at a time. Eventually Mum was helping me with them. This job did not last long as it was money for old rope.

Mum called up to me one afternoon saying she'd been on the blower to a Carolle arranging for me to go night clubbing with her daughter. A taxi was due to pick me up at 8 o'clock. I'd said fine but wasn't really that interested in a forced friendship with anyone. The thought of dancing the night away stopped me from rebelling against this one.

Come the evening I'd dressed up in a nice clubbing outfit and with some make-up on. The taxi was on time and had to drive into Street first to pick up Carolle's daughter Mel.

In the back of the cab and Mel in the front we barely spoke two words on the way to Oscars. I was looking forward for a drink when we got there I'd headed for the bar. Mel had vanished. I sat on two stools as I'd outstretched my legs across another one as I gently sipped my Malibu and lemonade. The song Two Can Play that game came on so with the drink abandoned I hit the dance floor and stayed there all night not worrying about Mel at all. Well, she'd abandoned me so why give her a second thought?

Standing by the entrance to the club watching first light breaking through the clouds I wondered where the taxi had gotten to. I stepped backwards to look up through the trees and some warm big strong arms wrapped themselves around me. I leaned in and he whispered in my ear asking if I'd like to come back with him in his car. I'd said, "Yes." This guy felt hot and he explained to me that he was being escorted from the premises by two bouncers. Unperturbed we were soon in the back of his cab and I'd had nowhere to sit but on his lap. I got the full story of why the bouncers were there as Reg said he'd gotten into a fight after his friend kept winding up the other guy all night. I replied that really his friend was the instigator of the whole fight. I noticed a smile tug at the corner of the bouncers lips and snuggled in for a snog.

Reg's home was a bungalow and we headed straight for the bedroom. The heat surrounding us was intense as I'd got on top with no worries even though it was my first time. I looked down at his maleness after that first time and he was hung like a horse. I suddenly got worried it was too big and decided to try and sit on it with my back turned to him. I complained he was too big for that as he pulled me back into bed to snuggle into him for a nice long sleep.

In the morning his body was still wrapped round mine and his body still felt really hot so I slipped out of bed totally naked to find the bathroom. In the hallway I noticed the telly on in the living room playing Match of the Day. I heard Reg call that it was just his Dad and did I want to use the phone to get a lift home. I dialled Mum's number and she wasn't pleased as I explained where I was to get home. Mum grumbled she had Nan Burr with her but said she'd find me in Cole ford.

Still naked I was bursting for the toilet so I took my time getting ready and I left not really knowing what this Reg actually looked like. I knew he was tall and what his tackle looked like but that was it.

Mum and Nan sat in silence a they took me back home. I felt fucking embarrassed with my Nan in the car.

It was soon the next weekend and I'd gotten a cab from Mum's intending to meet Mel at her house in Street. I went into Carolle's to see where I was meant to sleep that night. Mel then jumped into the cab with me to go across town to Maxine's. Inside the club Mel did her usual trick of disappearing on me.

A man offered to get me a drink so I accepted a cider and black and as I was at the bar another bloke asked me to dance. Someone on my wave length. Abandoning my drink we danced to New York, New York, on the balcony. Kicking my legs out in my sexy little black dress and black kitten heeled shoes I soon found myself back near the bar drowning in this man's kisses and it felt like we'd been kissing all night. My whole body felt lovely and warm.

At the entrance to the club, while getting my coat, my mysterious kisser stood at the till with a pen and paper. He asked me for my name and number. I looked at his cheek it was clean shaven and very attractive, and he gave me his name Matthew and his phone number. Matthew offered to wait for a taxi with me to take me home but after ten minutes I spied Mel with some guys walking away from the nightclub. I thanked Matt for waiting and took off after Mel towards The Wessex Hotel.

In the hotel bar I got chatting to three Americans and a Christopher Jones did most of the talking and introduced his friends from West Virginia, and Texas. He'd said that he was from Virginia.

It was last orders so Chris ordered up ten beers all along the bar and I enjoyed talking to him. I appeared worried at one point and Chris asked me if I was worried about my friend. I'd said yes and he informed me that she'd gone upstairs with one of his colleagues.

Chris told me all about his family's home, their ranch, his sister, and the fact he went to a Presbyterian church. He told me all about his job in radar. I should have asked if he was scared of being out on enemy lines, but it never occurred to me. Religion, politics and war was our main topics of conversation.

About two hours later we went up to his room. I got in one bed and it looked like he was getting into the next bed. I went to huddle up underneath the covers but that was when Chris started kissing me. Bless him he'd been awake most of the night trying to pleasure me, but he kept going flat at the crucial moments.

Ten hours later he told me to get a lubricant. I asked if he had KY Jelly, he just laughed and got a shower gel from the bathroom to lubricate me and this time he felt triumphant as he'd found some release.

I remember him turning on the telly at this point and it was the end credits of EastEnders omnibus. Then Cliff Richard's Summer Holiday came on. I enjoyed this film as I ate sandwiches that came to the room. In my mind's eye as I sat in the window sill afterward I could see myself going back to Virginia with him and settling down there, but he was busy proving to me his name by saying it was written in his clothes and boots. Why bother?

I called the number I found on that bit of paper from the night before and got a man called Tom, but I wanted to speak with Matt. Apparently I'd just gotten his brother and Matt was soon on the phone arranging a date. Chris told me I could use the hotel phone to call a cab and it never even occurred to me to worry where Mel went as I'd just assumed she'd eventually gone home.

A few days later Matt came round my house and we were at my parents' house kissing on the sofa and because Matt's dimples got more pronounced when he puckered up for a kiss he reminded me of a fish pout. I therefore started nick naming him Captain Codfish, not one to give up on our light petting though I soon got the Matt back who would snog me for a long, long time when he first met me. This was warm and familiar making heat in my belly and it would spread throughout my whole body. We tried to have sex on this date upstairs in my sister Fee's old room, but my fuzzy bits got too hot and expectations got too high on both sides so I ended up in a cold shower afterwards just to cool down.

I woke up feeling satisfied and happy one morning in Matt's bed and I overheard Matt on the phone talking loudly and I heard the word Arsenal. My ears pricked up and realised as Matt was talking he'd been on about getting tickets for Arsenal v Leeds United.

It was my birthday in a few weeks' time and I felt gleeful inside. I could tell that Highbury was in my future up in London and I couldn't wait to have a giggle with him when he got upstairs.

As soon as the phone had been put down I just got dressed and headed downstairs with my face beaming like a little balloon. Happy I laughed with Matt as I told him what I knew.

> *Psalms 2:4*
> *From His throne in heaven the Lord laughs.*

So I grilled him for a little bit before realising that it was true knowing I'd got him to spill all the beans about my upcoming treat and beamed up at him even more. Laughing in his face. I'd asked him when and it was for that Saturday. I felt even more elated. I realised that Matt was a man I really needed in my life so I prayed to God for him to be the one and that I didn't want Martin anymore.

We went in the kitchen together for some toast that Matt's mum had put on for us and we sat down to put our own butter and jams on.

I had to go to college that day so I had to walk down to the library for the Bridgwater bus. In Bridgwater, in the hut we were given video cameras to do some filing within the local supermarket. I stood in the produce aisle by the front door feeling a bit like a twit with the video camera and tripod in my hand.

> *Psalms 39:8*
> *Save me from all my sins,*

And don't let fools laugh at me.

An older lady on the media course walked straight by me to the side of an aisle and I assumed she wanted me to follow her. She pointed to the floor on a mat and said to place it there. All I had to do was stand behind it and watch the reactions and interviews she conducted on unsuspecting customers. I soon came to realise this was a census assignment on favourite products people would buy in the supermarkets. My hob was easy as I zoomed in and out and panned around for background shots as well.

We went back to the editing suite to put it all in a sane way so that the worst interviews got edited out.

The end of the day came and I was looking forward to my day out on the weekend.

That Saturday morning we got up early to get on the National Express and it was exciting. We'd made a picnic to take with us that day as Matt had told me it was bloody expensive at Highbury.

As we turned up in London I was surprised at the amount of side streets through a housing estate we had to get through to get to the football stadium. Pulling up at the grounds we were forty five minutes early so we wandered round the souvenir shop and looked through everything taking our time and balking at the prices. Matt and I then walked out in the grounds to see how huge the stadium was and soaked up the surroundings. We then jumped in our seats facing a big TV screen in the top left hand corner. matt got hungry so we took our rolls out. After we'd finished eating all the players came out. They looked pretty fit and I basically followed my favourite play Ian Wright the entire game in admiration.

> *1 Thessalonians 5:13*
> *Treat them with the greatest respect and love*
> *Because of the work they do. Be at peace among yourselves.*

We clapped and cheered till the end of the game when Arsenal beat Leeds 3-0.

The coach trip didn't feel like it took us very long to get home and we were very tired as we went upstairs to my boyfriend's bedroom.

The very next day we got up late and went downstairs to a nice aroma of a cooked breakfast. It was too cold to undress in the bathroom as I went for a pee and decided against having a shower. I went back upstairs to put on my clothes that were nice and warm. I'd done this quickly as I soon had food on the table as I said, "Thank you for this," and tucked in hungrily not even thinking about what else I could talk about wondering why there was never any questions about me coming from Matt's parents. I shrugged their non-curiosity off asking Matt what he wanted to do later. We bandied a few ideas about Matt settled on going to see my grandparents in Cheddar. It seemed like a good idea at the time.

For a whole day we took my Gran's dog Kipper for a walk round the Gorge. Up by the caves, by the cliffs of where we saw rock climbers. Then back down the Gorge again then up round the back of Jacob's Ladder. We were tired when we got back to my Nan's souvenir shop. I offered to do the till for a bit as Nan and Gramps wanted to stretch their legs. I loved being on the till and they soon came back so we talked to the couple running the ice-cream stand and they told us about their famous daughter who played international golf Matt and I had really never heard of her.

In the week I bought a collection of cd's for Matt's twenty second birthday. I knew that he liked a song called 'Sit down' by James so I'd bought all their albums.

That weekend on the nineteenth I gave Matt a lovely card with his present in the afternoon. His mum told us not to go too far that day as she wanted to cook a meal for all of us in the evening for his birthday.

We went off in the car to my Mum's and pulled in off the road to go in and see her. There were plenty of hugs and pleased to see you's. Then we chatted for ages and caught up with the gossip about what my cousins and Grandparents, as well as my sisters, had got up to.

Mum then gave Matt a stack of cards. One was from her and Dad with a big parcel. It was a nice grey coat. From my sisters he got a couple of fishing vouchers and there were cards from the Grandparents.

We all hugged then said goodbye taking another half hour to get out the door. I couldn't get over the differences between mine and his family as Matt always opened up more with my family than his own.

We soon went back to a meal up at his Mum and Dad's in the evening. It was a lovely chicken roast dinner and Tom gave out the drinks after we brought back Scholoer from the supermarket. We all sat round the table. I was quiet and so we were limiting the conversations to polite niceties, like pass the sauce please and the stuffing and they always did amazing onion gravy that I thought I'd really like but ended up not being able to but I never said anything.

We just recounted the day at Highbury and talked about the weather and everything we did that day. I offered to wash up after birthday cake and birthday singing, but Bob and Sue told us not to bother and let them do it. It had been a nice evening.

On the Tuesday I went to my youth club meeting with the local youth that I'd gone to school with. Wendy, the leader, had an agenda that evening and she waited for us to be sat around on the comfy chairs before launching into the most important issue at the moment in the media about youngsters turning to drugs. She gave us scenarios of what happens to them and how to say no if we were asked.

She'd said, "Would you like to take part in educating your peers in the knowledge of taking drugs?" We looked at her blankly and she told us of how they were looking to youth clubs because they thought peer led education would be better than getting adults to lead safety discussions. She passed round some leaflets for use to learn more about drugs and then she asked us about what we though class A drugs were and we said the obvious, crack, cocaine, and heroine. Barbiturates were class B with the likes of marijuana being class C and we were surprised at caffeine and tobacco being on the list. It got us intrigued though so we said we'd get involved.

A week later we met again and called ourselves a Peer Led Drugs Education Team and we went to another youth club and joined in with a debate over marijuana. One lad stood up and told us the heart rendering story of how his friend started out only taking weed but ended up on harsher illegal substances that went on and killed him. He got everyone standing on his side of the room. Then I spoke saying that marijuana should actually be legalised and made as an over the counter prescription drug as a lot of older people crippled with rheumatism and arthritis deserved to be prescribed with the aid of week to help them alleviate their pains. One by one some of the others were swayed to stand on my side of the room. The whole debate was about the law on these drugs that evening.

In the morning I decided to call Matt to come and get me as I had nothing on that day. He came to get me to take us up to his Mum's. We went over Gran's first as they only lived next door. Feeling hot and randy in the kitchen, even though Gran and Gramps were in the living room, I had a wicked glint in my eye as I came down on him. He just sank into it and let me take over. The olds called to us and as I swallowed Matt soon made himself look presentable before we went into the living room. We had big cheesey grins on our faces as we talked with them. I wondered if they knew but Gran and Grampy Genge gave nothing away.

We'd talked to them for a while then Matt spotted his Mum in the garden and went out to talk to her while I sat in the quiet with Gran and Gramps. My mind was a blank so I went next door and found a cd of mine upstairs I'd left behind and decided to play it on Tom's TV player. It was Celine Dion and the music was all about love. One song came on that was really trendy called 'Treat Her Like a Lady or you'd make a good girl go crazy' and I sang it really loudly. Tom came upstairs and looked surprised. He said that he didn't normally like the high Celine singing but was pleasantly surprised by the modern beat of the song I was listening to and the singing wasn't high pitched screaming, so we laughed together and I asked him about Walls ice-cream sign he had in his bedroom that you normally see outside of shops. He told me that he'd stolen it while once drunk and I recoiled a bit thinking he's a thief.

Deuteronomy 1:16
Judge every dispute fairly

The next morning was a Sunday after I'd stayed the night again and we were up in time to hear Sue ask, "If you want to go to church with us you can this morning."
We'd said "Yes," to Matt's mother.

In church I remember hearing a song for the first time called 'Come and Join the Celebrations. It's a very special day'. Apparently it was Matthew favourite song and he sang it wonderfully. This was my first Methodist service and as we went up for bread and wine I noticed it was just black currant juice that I'd thought was different. it was soon the end of the service and we all went round the hall at the back of the church and I met Matt's family's friends while I'd had a cup of tea with them.

Afterwards we went up to Matt's parents for lunch. It was roast pork and his Mum did honey glazed vegetables which were burnt and I didn't like them but didn't have the guts to tell her so I just left them on the plate. We had chocolate torte for pudding.

That evening Matt and I went to the Railway Inn out across the moors at Meare and we ordered orange juice with lemonade. We sat down in the corner ready for a carnival meeting with Phantoms and Carly, her sister and cousin came in next. Carly bothered me. She was very beautiful and kept imagining Matt with her as he spoke to them. Carly was all in black and wearing black trousers. The meeting started and as carnival was approaching we discussed venues for changing in. Now one of them was the Full Moon at Wells for their carnival. It had been a productive meeting.

A week later turning up at the youth centre in my jeans, jumper and sensible black shoes. I met with the rest of my group to get in the bus to go to the countryside.

Once in the sleepy little village the bus parked up at a car park to let us get out for a wander round town. Looking through some windows I chose a souvenir shop to look round. Peering closely at some wooden garden signs that made me smile like: 'Friends and family allowed but don't slam the gate on the way out'. I looked at the key rings that had personal messages for best friends, mums, dads, and nephews, etc. I loved looking at souvenirs and was in the shop for a while.

Wandering along the road outside afterward I made my way to an old wooden gazebo at the top of the little high street and caught up with the rest of the gang who made their way back to the bus.

With the weather gloriously sunny the bus pulled in at a hotel of where we alighted to go see our rooms. I was to share with James of whom grabbed the bottom bunk bed. I got out some money a I'd noticed a red phone box outside and went out to call Matt saying I missed him and that we were going out again to a pub. It had been a bonding weekend.

When I got back from my weekend away I decided to take a tape called Space Cowboy by Jamiroquai up to Matt's for the day and decided to stay the night at his house. I was always staying up there lately and Matt told me that day. "You only want to be here to get away from your Mum."

I refused to admit it but life was boring at home and the occasional work from an agency. I put on the music in the bedroom and started to seduce Matt feeling sexy. We made love to the music on his bed. Then we went downstairs to sit on the sofa and got chatting. Being completely open with me Matt opened up about ex's and said he'd had a couple. One of them was called Andrea of whom, he'd said, owned her own flower shop in Yeovil. He told me that he used to go see her on the bus and how it was hard for him to go see her. I didn't want to hear about ex's but I knew he would have had some and actually got curious about how she looked so he told me, "Big and black hair, and frumpy."

We ended up cuddling on the sofa then he had to take me home. I'd been staying up his too many times his parents inferred.

In the car I put on the radio and sang along to my favourite songs all the way along the roads by the houses on his estate down to the bottom of town of where I put on the indicator for him. Across the roundabout towards Glastonbury and then by where he worked at Safeway's to go up Fishers Hill and on the top road towards Shepton.

At Shepton he dropped me off as it started snowing heavily and at home it was already knee deep. I got into bed that night happy but in the morning you knew that the buses weren't running from turning on Good Morning FM and they gave the train reports and I knew my tutor needed the train to get into work but it was cancelled. I spent the day indoors mainly watching the telly while dreaming of a better future full of money making in the movies. I phoned Matt that day and he said that he wouldn't visit me while it had been snowing heavily.

A week later the snow had vanished and it was carnival time. Getting in the van at Shepton to take my carnival club Phantoms to Bridgewater we all started chatting nicely together and having a laugh and a bit of a sing song. I tried to get an old carnival song going my Granddad taught me about four and twenty virgins but they didn't sing along but I sang anyway about them going to Inverness. We got to Bridgewater and parked up by the Bunch of Grapes and jumped out the van to go get changed for the carnival float. I dressed as a princess that was sat at the back of the cart next to a knight, a king and a queen and another princess. I had to keep still all night as it was a tableau. I remember my hair itching the side of my face and my nose kept twitching in the night air but I had perfect control as I fought it for two whole hours along the carnival route round Bridgewater town. On the cart was two horses with knights of the realm on. There was a tent that was red and white striped on a green back drop of fake grass being the battle ground. At the front of the cart was a canon and there were rifles in army men's arms.

After we got the chance to move again and get off the cart we walked all the way back to the Bunch of Grapes to get changed. I felt sniffly, my carnival cold was starting and I got ribbed by Chris calling me Rudolph because of my red nose.

When we all got changed we got undressed together and I could feel the men looking at me so I took my time letting them look at the goods. I felt sexy and alive with Matthew next to me getting changed too.

We got on to the coach and headed towards a pub called the Knowle Inn part way home to stop for a drink. The club got out and headed for the bar and sat in one corner of the room chatting for ages having a laugh. Some of us jokingly sat on each other's laps and pretended that certain things were happening down below and we laughed encouraging saying that they were happy to see each other. There were drinking songs too as I'd hit into the Malibu and lemonade all night and Matt hit into the lager. Gone 2am we were still in the bar the staff had gone home and the manager to bed so we were left to help ourselves till 5am in the morning. We just had to leave the money on the bar before leaving. It was a great lock-in that night before we all drunkenly piled into the bus to take us all home.

Twelve o'clock the next day Matt and I crawled out of bed together and Matt growled under his breath and held his head. We went downstairs to smells of lunch at his Mum's house. It was another roast. I was famished while Matt looked ill.

"Mum," he'd said, "Do you mind if I can't eat all this today?"

Her face looked a bit upset. "Can't you try and eat some of this?"

"Mum's worked really hard on this meal." Tom his brother chipped in. I could see Matt's chest heaving though as he sat down. He ran off and was sick down the toilet. Matt was ill for most of the day.

I stayed that evening and we cuddled up early on the sofa spooning in front of a movie which was called Disclosure. Tome and his parents had gone out. It had Demi Moore and Michael Douglas in it and she was his boss while his character was married. Then the controversial big scene came on in his office of where Demi's character wore a low cut top and Michael's character had a glass of wine with her. She was very aggressively flirting and you could see him getting uncomfortably hot. You could tell he didn't like the situation but was turned on anyway. At first chance she whipped down his trousers, got on her knees and blew him off. Matt and I could feel the heat on the sofa together getting hot 'n' horny together. Then we got a shock as Matt's Granddad's face appeared at the window as if from nowhere. I embarrassingly shifted position and sat up and so did Matt. He never bothered to come in as we both blushed Gramps must have seen the scene on the telly. We had a lovely sleep that night together and Matt had to run downstairs in the middle of the night throwing up again.

In the morning I got out of bed early and let Matt sleep and got in the shower to wash and shave. I was cold in their bathroom and soon got dried and dressed into the clothes I'd brought down with me. I had toast for breakfast and did it myself that morning using the grill and strawberry jam on butter. In the living room was Tom playing a street fighter game on the TV and he asked me if I wanted to play. "Have the other console if you want Karen," so I took him on knowing I couldn't always win knowing this was a real challenge and I'll always remember Tom telling me that he knew I'd dump Matt soon thinking I was some sort of user. I took umbrage. That wasn't me and I resolved myself to sticking around and proving that wasn't me.

Leading into the next day on the Wednesday Matt and I walked round Shepton Mallet up to the carts. On the way there it was snowing lightly and by the time we got by the Ridgeway Estate it was snowing quite heavily. There was a Santa cart at the start on a chimney roof and a circus cart with a ring master and a large elephant in the middle. As we went passed the first few carts the snow looked like a wedding veil about my eyes making me go misty eyed about getting married to Matt.

That afternoon, my free day off college I had a job with my agency working in an office at Shepton for a firm called Frampton's. In the office all I had to do was tear off stickers and put ten at a time into envelopes. The other staff were pleasant enough as I sat there diligently working through a whole box of stickers never questioning what it was all for.

In the evening I got on the cart with the others and I stayed still brilliantly all night.

That evening on the Thursday we had Midsomer Norton carnival to go to and we all piled into the bus over at the bus stop. All the way there the road was clear and we sang some of the hit singles to myself silently on the bus. At the town we all jumped off the bus and soon got changed. Then we all got onto the cart. I'd sat down behind Carly who'd stood up. We started off down the road and a few people were watching. The few that did watch were throwing things at us mainly coins and I just sat there and watched Carly getting hit. Half way around we stopped for a full ten minutes and an ambulance crew turned up to try and move Carly who'd gone completely stiff in the cold night air. I just sat there mystified at the fact they had to physically move her as she couldn't do it herself.

> Psalms 69:20
> I had hoped for sympathy, but there was none,

They were there for ages with blankets, and hot drinks for her to warm up. Ten minutes later we moved on without her back to getting changed.

In the morning I looked forward to carnival but after freezing my butt off in the cold air all week I had a really bad cold and sniffed, blew my nose, wheezed and coughed all bloody day and decided not to go to carnival that night.

Instead I got on a Badgerline bus after the club would have left from up Mum's and watched the carnival into Wells that night down Union Street. The carts were amazing. Matt didn't know I was there and I coughed and sneezed all night. Even when they passed by I noticed Matt had gone to sleep in the trenches on the cart so he never saw me. But I had to go to the Full Moon pub afterward to catch up with the club to go home back to Street with Matthew he didn't know I'd be staying the night.

In the following week I was soon back to college and we had to do some promotional work for our own made up products. I chose a drink called melonade with freshly squeezed melon juice with carbonated water. I hand drew some really good promotional pictures with a melon shaped moon. Underneath it simply said melonade. It was a brand new product I thought. I came up with a whole folder full of work.

In the afternoon, next day, I hopped on the bus glad to be able to go out of the house to see my lover Matthew. It had been lovely weather so we strolled arm in arm round the back of his mother's house along the lane. We stopped to go over a fence into an inclining field of which Matt and I walked towards the far corner. Matt, at the top, by the next gate told me that his mother called it the kissing gate, so we stopped, had a snog and walked behind the trees of where you could see the top road. Along this route I remember seeing a tethered horse by the car park for the Street Youth Hostel. The path took us to a bench on the crossroads at the brow of the hill and had a good snog fest. One car beeped at us while they hung out the windows and shouted. I felt embarrassed but high as a kite.

We were happy with our arms about each other all the way back to the house.

> *John 13:35*
> *If you have love for one another, then everyone will know you're my disciples.*

I never stayed much longer as I'd needed to go shopping for cards and presents for Christmas.

Round town I had in the back of my mind when Fiona once pointed out that I was always a skinflint growing up and that I'd horded my savings not really buying presents for anyone. I felt caught in a should-have – to-do trap. Deep inside I knew I'd feel happier if family were elated at what I was to buy. Fee had hit a chord so I went round the expensive shops in Clarks Village down Farm Road on the right hand side. I got videos and clothes mainly, and some nice expensive looking cards anticipating what was to come over the Christmas period. What with Dad's love of Roy Chubby Brown and Eve's collection of Walt Disney films. that's what I got them.

> Psalms 45:12
> Rich people will try to win your favour

A few days later it was Christmas Eve and I had to work in the kitchen for Brottens' Lodge. That Matt and I agreed was in the middle of nowhere. When my lover got me there he told me that he'd have to drop me off quickly to zip home to have a poo.

The same happened the next day when Matt dropped me off to help out for Christmas lunches that were to feed a gang of policemen. The waitress came in and out of the restaurant to me in the kitchen where I dropped one earthen ware pot and broke it. I soon brushed it up and the lovely blonde waitress, whatever her name was, said to me "You'll make it to being a waitress one day."

I gave her my biggest sap down, my not too impressed face and she soon wiggled her embarrassed as back into the restaurant.

> 1Samuel 10:27
> "How can this fellow do us any good."

I was feeling pissed off helping out with lunches on Christmas Day and secretly prayed for Matt to come on and get me to take me home back to Mum's house.

When we got there all the family had, had a Christmas turkey lunch. Mum had kept some back for me. I felt left out in the cold eating on my own while everyone had gone in the living room to let me eat. I'd finished quickly to join the rest for presents to be given out and Dad played Santa with everyone's presents that had been placed under the Christmas tree in the corner of the room. Our little faces lit up like little balloons at the presents and Dad and Eve seemed especially happy with their video tapes.

As the evening drew on the men went and played three card brag in the kitchen. Mum was seeing to supper. The Nan's and my siblings were left in the living room with me and I zoned out on to watch the TV. An ad came on for the next film so I went to ask Mum. "Can we watch Drop Dead Fred film please?" Right while I was sitting next to Nan. I asked two more times and was vaguely aware at that point that no-one wanted me to be there.

> Acts 28:27

> *Because this peoples' minds are dull, and they have*
> *Stopped up their ears and closed their eyes.*

It wasn't until later that Fee said to me, "Don't you realise that this is the first Christmas without Granddad. You really upset Nan earlier."

I went on and blotted everyone out as they left me to watch the last of the film. Fee had been the last one to be in the living room with me. I hadn't been aware of the date and Nan Burr so called silently sat weeping beside me. I didn't notice.

The next day it was Boxing Day and Mum, Nan Sheila and I went to Tramways together which was a social club. Cheap drinks, a telly by the bar and a room full of tables and chair that we sat down on by the window. We had come to watch horse races to place bets on. Grandad had been a bouncer on the door when Nan had smuggled a bottle of wine in her handbag. Though I'd asked mum for pink Babycham a lovely fizzy alcoholic drink. I'd felt like that I'd looked down my nose a bit.

> *Matthew 5:6*
> *Happy are those whose greatest desire is to do*
> *What God requires.*

Mum and Nan made use of her wine and we had a laugh placing bets on the races on the TV. Now Mum put on her hurt face that I giggled at when she ended up not winning anything. I didn't care if I'd won or not of which I never, but Nan after being clever with the drink won something on a 3 – 1 bet.

> *Proverbs 16:33*
> *People cast lots to learn God's will,*
> *Nut God himself determines the answer.*

I'd have tried to work out what she'd won at a two way bet. Betting systems all ways made me feel thick.

The three of us went to see Granddad one by one to talk with him over the course of the evening before we all left for home.

In the middle of January there came the usual Paulton Rovers Social Club do of where Matt and I went with the Phantoms Carnival Club. I'd thrown on the nearest dress to wear that evening which was a grey stripy slinky number that had been knitted. The club got there on a mini-bus and I wondered if Martin was going to be there.

When first there we headed for the bar and I distinctly remember hitting into the lemonade flavoured hooches. We were soon on the dance floor making shapes and Carly, the blonde bombshell, spoke to me and called me Olive. I asked her why. She'd said that I'd looked like the woman on the old TV show 'On the Buses'. I felt insulted and immediately recoiled back into feeling aware of how good I'd actually felt when I'd first put my dress on that evening.

It wasn't much longer until we had to get on the bus. I had a full bottle of Hooch in my hand as we boarded and sat with Matt at the back of the bus. He called me darling for the first time and I felt that it was too early in the relationship for him to call me that so I tipped the drink all over his head and made everyone look at us. I laughed and fell asleep a soon as my head hit the pillow back at Matt's that night.

The next day we went shopping together and looked in jewellers' shops and my eye kept straying to the bright twinklers. In the precinct next to Tesco's I found a nice emerald in clusters of tiny diamonds ring. It was only a hundred and fifty pounds. I'd always thought I'd have had a blue sapphire but I fell in love with the emerald.

On the same Friday evening Matt and I attended my first games evening with his Mum and Dad in the hall out the back of the Methodist Church. We'd been to Tesco's first to buy some Pringles to go towards our fair share of bringing food for our tea. There were tables of four dotted around with different games on like Connect Four, Battleships, and that one of where you've got to guess the right person. As I floated to each game I introduced myself to new friends of my in-laws friends, like Maureen and John, Mr and Mrs Petts, Viv Squires, etc. Happily chatting away I just got immersed in the whole evening winning some games and then stopping to eat. Matt and I moved together for food and sat deliberately side by side feeling elated. It was midnight before we got home.

Sunday afternoon after lunch Matt took me back to Mum's.

The next few days were a bit of a blur but I soon remembered going back to Bridgewater College and being back in the editing suite to use for another filming project we did that day. The sun gleamed through the port-a-cabin window as I enjoyed s putting finished touches to my work. I went tap, tap, tap along the knobs, buttons and the twirly things and the up and down things for the audio descriptions. That day at college went too quickly and I was soon back home with Mother getting ready that night to go to skittles.

In the car Mum said we'd have to pick up Nan Sheila along the way. Up at Seeley Crescent Mum pulled up by her driveway. I had to get out to go and fetch her. Bring her up the hill safely and into the car.

At the bar at The Britannia pub Mum got the drinks. Nan had lemon and lime. I had a Bacardi Breezer while Mum got an orange juice. It was a good night. We sat down like good girls and Mum seemed to ignore me all night. I never did quite work out how to talk to anyone else. I could say hello but that was how far it went. It, in my mind, felt as though I could carry the whole team to victory with impossible spares all night.

> *Job 20:8*
> *they will vanish like a dream, like a vision at night,*
> *And never be seen again.*

I don't know why I thought I could do it but at the time felt very strong willed and very capable. We won that evening and Mum and I were soon dropping off Nan again before heading off for home.

A couple of days later it was a Friday again when I eventually got back to Matthews. He told me when he saw me that his Mum believed me to be at their house too often. Luckily that afternoon we had the place to ourselves so I went to his brother Tom's room to play street fighter on his telly. Matt came into the room after seeing his Mum and I'd slumped forward nearly on my hands and knees getting carried away with the game and Matt got on the floor with me. Next thing I knew I had a wonderful kinky frisson come over me as Matt tit wanked and gave me a pearl necklace. I made a big exhaling bossom heaving noise. Matt soon disappeared downstairs and so did I.

Sue came home with Bob about 5pm and they found us outside in the large back garden eating the raspberries while putting some of them in pots. My future mother-in-law came up to us and asked me to stay for tea. I loved her cooking and looked forward to it but got surprised as she came outside with sandwiches with ham, cheese and tomato in. She beamed at us and asked if we wanted to come to a cards night round the back of the Methodist Church in the hall again.

I said, "I'll look forward to meeting your friends again."

At the church five tables were in the middle of the room placed together in one big square. There were enough chairs for us all to sit on. Then we got dealt thirteen cards each and had to make hands of runs in one colour, like one, two, three or hands of three or four of the same numbers. The jokers got used for the games too and could be placed in any hand. I didn't shout loud enough for each card you could barter for in the middle of the table. The same friends from the week before shared their own little laughs with all of us and I knew what the shared jokes were and joined in until the night ended at one o'clock in the morning. I wondered that night why these Christians, to me, were gambling. Sue told me that, that attitude in the Methodist Church in Street ended years ago.

Getting into bed that evening I struggled to sleep in the camp bed in Tom's room and I wriggled around hitting the metal on the bed. It hurt. I got out to cuddle into Matt next door but never got there as Matt must have heard me get up and he came into see me. He got into bed with me on the horrible camp bed and we writhed together getting hot 'n' horny and then we woke Tom up which prompted him to say, "Whatever you're up to could you please do it in your own room," and we both did just that. Then writhing around in Matt's bed together I had to get on top to screw him all night long, but we did it once and fell asleep.

In the morning I had to go home and get some clean clothes with Matthew driving me there. He went into town to buy a few things while I got my stuff remembering that he told me to get a nice dress for the evening.

In the early evening Matt shooed all his family with me next door to his Nan's and began cooking. he came over and said, "Teas on the table," and I went back next door and there was steak and chips on the table. It was very nice. Before we sat down to eat Matt got down on one knee and was shaking like mad with both of his hands elevating towards me with something in them and he said, "Will you marry me?"

I said, "Yes," and flung my arms around his neck totally happy.

> *Deuteronomy 20:7*
> *'Is there anyone here who is engaged to be married?*
> *If so, he is to go home.*

Then we sat down to eat. It was delicious, then we had hot chocolate fudge cake. We went next door to show the ring off and I put my jacket on. We were to go clubbing at the local night club. Both of us had a brilliant time and I ended up staying the night.

The next day Matt and I bummed around and Matt's Gramps with Nan offered to take me home to Shepton. I got out the car first to check if anyone was there and Mum came out to talk to Nan and Gramps. Gramps said, "They make a lovely couple don't they?"

Mum said, "Yeah."

"It's brilliant they just got engaged." Gramps said. I could've shot him. Mum laughed. Gran said "You've put your foot in it again Eric."

"Why what have I done this time?"

"Well let Karen and Matt tell them themselves."

They all had a big laugh but I felt they'd stolen our thunder.

"Come on in," Mum said.

"Oh we can't stay," said Gramps, "We're only dropping Karen off," and I went indoors.

"Let's have a look at the ring then," Mum said inside and I showed her my little emerald and diamond. I spent a happy day in the afternoon showing off my ring to my sisters.

Chapter Sixteen

After Matt had very romantically proposed we'd wanted to go away to celebrate. We didn't have much money and I remember discussing going to Butlin's, Minehead for a few days while in Matt's Mum and Dad's kitchen with them listening.

Next thing I knew a few days later Matt told me that he had a holiday booked to go away with his friends for two weeks. This caused many a row and one in particular of where I'd thrown the engagement ring in a bin at the Unity Club and gave him a slap round the face.

Proverbs 22:24
The second saying
Don't make friends with people who have hot, violent tempers.
You might learn their habits and not be able to change.

Matt promised me the next day that we would go away on our own somewhere when he got back from his lads holiday and we talked about going to Gran Canaria for a week together. I went back to the Unity Club after our heart to heart to go through the bin for my ring and as luck would have it the girl behind the bar had saved it for me.

During the course of the arguments though I'd asked Matt where he'd gotten the money for the Ibiza holiday from. He said his parents. I felt so worthless in my in-laws to be eye's. I felt self-righteously angry in my quest to make them pay. I felt like a snake that day I'd crept in the house when everyone was up in the garden and I stole all their change lying around the house. All one hundred and thirty pounds worth which was to pay for our holiday to Gran Canaria. I wanted them to pay for us.

Proverbs 18:1
People who do not get along with others are interested
Only in themselves.

I had a trip coming up with Russians on a youth exchange and the next day we turned into a field in the middle of nowhere where we all set up our tents. I was in one with a couple of girls, the boys were in another one and the Russians in theirs.

First day there we all went go-karting in another field of where tyres outlined a very basic course with more in the middle. It had been in a secluded spot amongst a lot of trees and bushes.

One was allowed at a time and I loved the buzz of putting my foot down whirring round the course but went too fast and ended up laughing as I'd bounced off the tyres in the middle.

> *Nehemiah 8:10*
> *"The joy that the Lord gives you will make you strong."*

Determined to get as much out of the exercise as possible before the next person had a go I kept my foot to the floor. But they all soon called me back as someone came to say one round left after I'd crashed of which I obeyed.

That evening we were all around a campfire cooking marshmallow and a tall chap with ash blonde hair was playing guitar and singing.

We were all in warm clothes and as we settled into our tents I'd heard that some of our lot had gone in with the Russians.

James being the ladies' man cracked on to Marsha's blonde haired friend. Nick was getting friendly with Marsha and I'd been getting bored so I sloped back off to my tent.

In the morning I'd heard that James had, had sex that night. I wasn't that interested but glad I'd heard the gossip. It was cold where we were and I could feel the damp through my clothes. the youth leader soon took us all home.

The next evening when I went into my cleaning over at Clarks, Georgina wanted a private word which made me feel nervous and I wondered what I'd done wrong. She got me to sit down at her desk and was asked if I wanted extra work on the weekends. my little eyes lit up with greed thinking we needed the money.

> *1 Samuel 8:3*
> *They were only interested in making money.*

I said yes and skipped, not literally, out of the office to the canteen to do the wooden floor first. I started singing to myself while mopping as no-one else was around to hear me and I got louder and louder loving the sound of my own voice.

> *Proverbs 14:14*
> *Good people will be rewarded for their deeds.*

I did this every day during work.

That weekend I started my work in the ladies at the far end of Clarks Village just down from Marks and Spencer's. I cleaned the toilets, wiped the walls and the doors, washed the sinks out, and changed the paper and soap dispensers, then mopped the floors.

I then went to the other toilets with a man with a cart and did the same again in the ladies behind Monsoons by the children's' fort. Afterwards I went across the road by where Kwiksave used to be and did the same again. I was tired but invigorated ready for a shower when I got home and changed then needed mental stimulation so I picked up my TV guide and did all the puzzles then I did a long and complicated backwards crossword and skeleton crossword in front of the TV.

I picked up some yellow wool that reminded me of custard or a banana and started cable knitting a jumper for Matt. The next day I was going to Russia.

On the plane over to Russia I sat with Darren, James and Nick the youth leader by the middle aisle. I took a photo out through the side window and caught the amazing view and the wing.

After landing we headed for the train station. There were bunk beds and we sat up and talked. I got up and walked about a couple of times.

At the station I was tired but elated at the capital city and the first place we stopped we saw Stalin and concierges dressed in national costumes posing for the cameras. Heading for Red Square we stopped off at Stalin's grave, of which I took a photograph.

I then proceeded to Marsha's to where I was supposed to stay. All her friends came round for tea. They were all teachers and I took a photo.

Ecclesiastes 7:10
Never ask, "Oh why were things so much better in the old days?" It's not an intelligent question.

Next day we went to their youth club to say prayers, sing and take part in dancing with dancers in national costumes of which was a hoot. I really enjoyed myself. That day we walked round Kirov town and went on a tram in the middle of a very wide road and saw a famous statue.

The next day the boys played football in the glorious sunshine while us girls stood and watched and afterwards we went back to one of the boys houses. We started to watch a video about the football match and by the end it was just James and I sat on the bed. Then he took his top off so I wickedly exposed my breasts and went to tit wank so he'd strip off completely and he became erect and completely naked. I took the clothes with me to the kitchen to drink Slabatskoy vodka. I got pissed and laughed my fucking head off telling everyone in the room that I made James strip off and he was there waiting for me with a hard on and I laughed my brains out. Getting really, really pissed.

The next day we went on a bus towards a huge forest then stopped at a huge youth hostel and we were introduced to communal beds just like at a boarding school with girls separate from the boys.

I remember going to a rock face to do climbing but I couldn't get any farther then up two stones. I was crap at it so I came down. I watched the others go up and turned my head and saw someone on a horse. That's all I remember as I took a photo.

The next day we went on a trip to some brown shacks where they sold cigarettes and I had fifty rubles to spend. I watched the others buy some and had to go to the toilet. The only toilet I could find was in a wooden shack and it was disgusting with dirt, leaves, a bad smell in a small hole in a wooden slat and I had to use tissue in my pocket to wipe my ass. It was disgusting.

I got on a bus and went to a nice toilet where there was a lady who looked very prim and proper sat on a chair by a table with flowers on. There were coins on a plate which I ignored to go to the toilet and it was a nice and clean hole in the floor. On the way out I gave her a tip and liked the smell from the flowers.

Later on that day we got back on the train and Nick was bragging about Marsha and about how he was going to get married to her one day and we all went home.

At home I got ready in my dark green Jaeger woollen skirt and my favourite red jumper. I felt really sexy and cool all dressed up ready for my first day at college. I trotted in, in my knee high boots and found the first room a week after the course had started and everyone was sat in pairs so I sat on my own. I noticed a brunette who was good looking and had make-up on and they were talking about our first assignment which was to be about first impressions. the girl I had been looking at was called Louise.

At first I wrote about her and said she looked beautiful with cruel bitchy looking lips but then explained that once I got to know her Louise was lovely and took me for a coffee at a café and did brilliant work with her in Street high street. When it was on the wall Louise had a go at me on the stairs and I grumpily said, "You've just proved my point," and just cut myself off from that burgeoning friendship and didn't care. I didn't have a conscience.

That evening Matt and I went round Mother's as Mum and I had pre-arranged to go to belly dancing lessons. We stayed for an early tea and talked around the dining room table for a bit until Matt wanted to leave while it was still light he hated driving in the dark. I stayed on though to stay the night and Mum got into the attic and got down some belly dancing outfits. She could only find one soft floaty pink and yellow, with gold dangly bits outfit. The head piece had lots of gold dangly bits over the forehead. There was a belt with gold sequins all over with see through material over the belly to show off a belly button. mum wanted to take the outfit to the lesson with her which she did.

The lesson was at Croscombe's pub in a skittle alley and we learned to wobble our bellies, swaying back and forth. I had flashbacks to days of when I took ballet lessons when they told us to do double pliat with our feet.

I went round to Matt's on the bus the following night and found him upstairs with a really bad fever. His Mum told me to take up some food for us and his pills. Which I did. We had some quiet time before Matt pulled me into bed and on top of him I felt his fever and writhed around hot 'n' horny feeling a different kind of fever myself. My loins were insatiably hot and I loved him all over five whole times throughout the night.

> *Jeremiah 2:24*
> *When she is on heat, who can control her?*

Fully satiated in the morning Matt and I got up feeling a lot better and mother-in-law cooked us a nice hot breakfast, so we sat down with Sue and Bob. They talked about going off for the afternoon to Westbay along the Dorset coastline as it was getting later on the morning.

We set off at twelve o'clock with matt and I in the back seat of the car to cruise along the A roads into Westbay in less than an hour and a half. The car then pulled up in a little car park by a tiny railway station. Getting out in the bracing wind we had a wander in and out of the shops. Then round the harbour just taking our time and walked back round the shops to the beach to sit down for a bit. We decided, after an early tea with fish 'n' chips, for one last walk around. That was when Matt and I spotted a fair over a bridge in a field and I asked him to go on the waltzers with me. He hesitated at first but his Dad egged him to go on so we jumped into a big round seat with a metal bar around us to secure us into our seats. It was amazing swirling around and around on a rotating floor. I loved every minute of it until we got off. As we alighted I felt sick as a dog and Matt and I found ourselves throwing up over the bridge into the wind. We decided then and there not to go on any more rides. Matt's Dad saw us and told me that he shouldn't have done it at all as Matt was the type of guy that once bitten he was twice shy. I accepted that but felt sad that I never had anyone to go on rides with after that.

Going home on the bus that night fee had been at Mum's and left a book behind that night. She asked me if I wanted to read a book entitled Pandora's Box and I said, "Yes why not?" Fee pointed out that it was about female sexuality and I got curious.

> *Ecclesiastes 1:8*
> *Our eyes can never see enough to be satisfied;*
> *Our ears can never hear enough.*

On the sofa I started reading it. Page after page the book got sexier and sexier. The first scene I still remember was about the woman looking into a tall mirror and fantasising about two men feeling her up from the front and behind describing every sensation pounding through her body.

I stayed up Mum's that night as I was going to skittles with the Rascals for the first night for a few years. I'd had to bring a raffle prize so I brought a shower gel with me hoping to win it back. At the pub I pulled up a chair by Tricia, Mandy, Mum and Nan and had a pint of orange juice and lemonade. I brought Mum a pint too. Talking about the songs on the radio Mum got up to play and she hit a seven. Mandy was next and hit an eight, Tricia hit a six. Then it was my turn and I hit another six hoping no-one would hit any worse. No-one got below a five all night and we won.

In the morning I had to walk down to the coach stop by the doctors to get to college. My first lesson was a legal class and the teacher put two headings on the white board. Plagiarism down one side and slander at the top of the other side. We were asked to call out words to describe what the legal terms meant. I put my hands up for plagiarism and asked if it was to do with copywriting and he said yes and wrote it down. Someone said slander was to do with lying which was written down. Another person came up with it's a term for an illegality, which was put down under both names. We ended up with two long lists we had to copy and write an essay about basing the topic on articles or essay writing. The choice was ours for homework.

I went from one building to a cabin at the back of the college to retake maths GCSE. I even used the same books I used at school, but they pushed me to cove as many aspects of maths as they could in the lesson so that I wasn't flailing about at home afterwards trying to make sense of it all like I'd done at school.

In the afternoon we watched a film and had to stay detached to analyse what I thought was to be every scene and how they shot the movie. This is how I wrote describing every storyboarded scene and special effects and edits as best I could during the film just scrutinising through simple lots of highlights.

By the end of the week I'd done a lot of work for college and managed to keep up with all of my work as well as maintaining a healthy attitude towards my life as I looked forward to going over Matthews for the night. As I got there Bob and Sue decided to ask me out to cards night while Matt went to male dominated skittles. I hadn't realised that it was his skittles night and was told to go to Tesco's with Sue to buy some food to add to others' food for tea. I was told to buy some Pringles salt 'n' vinegar as that would do. It was a cards night and we played a game I'd never played before called Chinese Rummy of where we needed thirteen cards each and we had to make runs or three or four of a kind to get our cards out. I had to get used to asking for cards I wanted in the middle of the table before anyone else did. It was a fast and ferocious game making everybody shout out loud or all at once, but it was the closest person to whose go it was to get the cards.

> *Matthew 5:8*
> *Happy are the pure in heart; they will see God!*

We played till one in the morning and nibbled at the food half way through.

I slept on the camp bed on the floor of Matt's room but always found my way into his bed at night to warm up and shield my eyes behind his back to blot out the light coming through his skylight.

In the morning, at first light, we got up and Matt fannied about in his Mum's garage as I dressed and was having toast and he kept making a ruckus outside by the back door.

After breakfast I had to find out what he was doing and saw a black Shakespeare fishing box with two nets and two fishing poles. I was intrigued and asked Matt where we were going. He'd said that Walton or Somerton Viaduct fisheries were an option. Out of helpfulness I picked up the fishing poles and a net to take to the car. Matt grabbed the long net and box then told me to get into the vehicle first to put a rod under the seat belt to prop the end up on the front console. The boot slammed down and Matt slipped into the seat. This was exciting as it was my first time going fishing.

At the Viaduct he sat on the box and showed me how to put a line, hooks, eights, and a float on through the hoops on the rod. I got it perfect first time after copying him.

After a few hours my arm and shoulder got stiff as I'd stared at the float for ages catching a little tiddler that I was pleased with. Then I relaxed more into the midday sun. The afternoon flew by and I didn't realised that I had so much patience. It had been pure bliss.

> *Ecclesiastes 2:1*
> *I decided to enjoy myself and find out what happiness is.*

I stayed that evening for tea and didn't want to go home so I stayed another night.

The next afternoon Bob and Sue threw a party and had a barbecue with a few family and friends around. I loved the friendly atmosphere and the whole afternoon was relaxing and perfect. I'd felt like I'd found a boy next door partner in Matt and loved the closeness of his family and friends.

Into the evening everyone laughed, talked and stayed while I'd got introduced to a Gwenda and Geoff partners of whom were a tall athletic looking brunette, and a tall balding red head of a man of who looked very fit. Then Brian, who was a big man, Sally his wife, brunette and buxom with their children Leanne and Verity of whom stood around sucking her thumb. She looked big enough to be an eighteen year old which looked weird but I asked her age and she was fourteen. Tom, Matt's brother, who was slim, was there and his Uncle Mike, who was small build, and Aunty Chris a nice big happy blonde woman with their sons Mark and Christopher of whom were big people.

At the end of a glorious Indian summer's day we all parted company happily and I still crawled into bed with Matt until the morning.

By the Wednesday I deserved a break from college work and decided to take a long walk from Strode. Through the town I walked out to West End and then into Walton the next village. By then my feet began to hurt and I felt thirsty so I headed for the village shop and got a pint of milk and sat down outside the church which was a fatal mistake. I downed the drink in one and when I stood up my foot was throbbing. I phoned Mum but she wasn't home so I left a message to say I'd be late home from a red phone box. I walked on along the pavement out by the Pike and Musket. Then on by a really fast road by some woods where there was no pavement but was enjoying this endless walk. I came to a junction on the left hand side and came across a pub that luckily was open and I asked to come in to use their phone as my feet were killing me. I phoned Matthew for a lift home. Luckily, by this time, he'd finished work. he took me back to his. I packed my stuff and he drove me back to Shepton.

In college the next day I took my photos of the Russians coming and staying in England with me to do a display on a different culture of people. It took me all morning to put together a big poster on black background paper. Then I had to caption what I did underneath. One photo I was particularly proud of was me in a red go-kart round a field and in the end I told the story of the week they stayed.

By the end of the day I'd worked really hard and had a decent night's sleep as Matt and I talked all night long and I was telling him about all my dirty little secrets like he was a confessional.

The next day it was a Friday and college was as interesting as ever as we explored the world of storyboarding in one lesson. I had to make up a story and draw each scene in a box. then put the dialogue underneath.

In another lesson I sat and played with my pen tapping it ferociously while I analysed an old script to a film to death completely soaking up stage directions, how a scene was wrote, how pauses in speech were written between the orations. It had been a thick script to read through but I soaked up every detail enthralled at how much paperwork was involved in the making of a programme.

It all seemed to be filled with paperwork until we did some acting for a studio project of where I had to be a presenter interviewing someone. I had a big boom over me for sound to speak into and I'd had fun pretending to be someone.

> *Proverbs 21:29*
> *The wicked have to pretend a best they can.*

Matt picked me up from college and took me up to his Mum's for dinner. Afterwards Matt stood in the kitchen and really opened up to his mother about what went on at work that day. He was telling her about the gossip he'd heard and they were talking of their neighbours and what they were getting up to. I tried to chip in, to ask about these people but felt left out of the discussion.

> *Psalms 31:12*
> *Everyone has forgotten me, as though I were dead.*

Getting fed up with Matt not telling me about the people he knew and never gossiping with me I decided to go next door intending to sit with his Nan for a lovely cosy chat.

Next door was lovely and warm. They never had the heating on at his mother's. I settled into the sofa opposite Nan and Granddad listening to their stories of Gran being the matriarch of the family always telling us of how bit the garden was and how much of it Granddad owned. It was eight acres. It was divided up once between Gramps and his brother Alan of whom had been a policeman. There had been a family argument over the premise and Gramps' brother never spoke to him again but it had been brought by Eric and Evelyn, Matthew's grandparents. The place had nothing to do with his brother.

Matt came over and sat with me for a cuddle and I just let them all talk together. Granddad tied to get me to eat liquorice and I said no thank you as the conversation just went another way. The conversation switch made me feel confused and made an awful silence so I cuddled into Matt.

> *Psalms 82:5*
> *How ignorant you are! How stupid!*

They gossiped about their neighbours and how rich they were and I felt a part of the family feeling as though I was getting to know everyone. Realisation dawned though that these people liked to pretend to have money in order to have decent friends. Kicking back with a cup of tea sipping slowly I just enjoyed the rest of the evening.

The weekend started with Mum and I cleaning the house from top to bottom. I did the downstairs toilet. Hoovered the living room and dusted before Mum made us a light lunch to sit in front of the telly to watch a film together. It was about American schmaltz of where a young lad grew up in the city from starting out as an orphan living on the streets to standing up for his rights. It was a film about how a famous political activist had started out. This lad made loads of friends and talked to politicians bugging them and as he grew older after being taken off the streets and been put into an orphanage. A family adopted him in another country completely famine and he learnt another language. Not forgetting how he started he went on and changed the world starting the first homeless shelter. The sad thing was the adopted family died in a war and he ended up living on his own.

Sunday came and Mum and I went to church with my Nanny Burr and very few people talked to us but I sang out loud and proud thinking I sounded like a proper nightingale in the middle of quite a large bunch of parishioners.

1 Samuel 2:1
"The Lord has filled my heart with joy;
How happy I am because of what he has done!"

Pushing my voice louder so that I could hear myself listen to my sexy warble.

Then we all took turns to go to the front of the church for communal wine and I felt cold as I followed Mum. The bread tasted different this morning as it felt like manna from heaven in my tummy. There was one last song before we all filed out from church into the cold air.

A nice hot meal was waiting at home as Dad got back from a Sunday morning's kick about at the top of Collet Park. I'd asked him if he won. Dad said he'd scored a hat trick and secretly smiled at me winking. I asked him again and he just said, "Yes." I loved my Dad.

The afternoon went by lovely as Matt came out and took me out on a left, right drive out in the car. We ended up going left, right, left, right round the roads all afternoon and by the time we got back we were smiling glad we weren't feeling a bit lost anymore. Matt looked at the dials and said we'd driven seventy mile. I went to bed happy that night and in the morning raced to the bottom of the road to get on the college bus. When it pulled up in Street I looked forward to camera class as I'd had rolls of pictures to do up. In that class we were introduced to a dark room for the first time and I saw pictures hung up in a room with a red ethereal glow in. My eyes took a while to adjust to the light. There were paper trays. I think three all together with different chemicals in and we dipped the photographic picture in and out to get up lovely black and white pictures. I hung them up on a line afterwards with pegs.

In the morning Matt and I went down to Yeovil early to the football stadium to queue up for tickets for the afternoon's game. Then we got in the car and drove round town to the Pickety Witch for lunch. I wore my black leggings and white shirt feeling hot 'n' horny. As we walked from the car Matt produced a possessive arm around my waist. It produced a delicious thrill up my back. In the pub I'd had my usual mushrooms and garlic for starters, gammon and chips, and then hot chocolate fudge cake with ice-cream all as a birthday treat before going back to the stadium.

> *Genesis 9:3*
> *I give them all to you for food.*

Going to the stands he protectively put his arm around my waist again of which I loved to sit down. The score ended up 3-2 to Yeovil and we yelled and cheered with the majority of the crowd.

When we got back to mother's everyone was waiting to give me presents and cards too and Matt brought me a lovely pink mottled woolly coat that I absolutely loved the feel of.

The next day Matt took a long time to show up and as I loved my new pink coat I wore it down the bottom of the hill looking for him. Then the red estate Vauxhall I'd called the Yak because of the licence plate whizzed by me. I felt hurt whilst being in my new snuggly pink coat as Matthew didn't even recognise me and stop to pick me up. I had to go back up Mum's to call him and his mother said sorry he was on his way.

Two hours later he showed up and we went out for the day. To Street and on towards Langport way, to some field for us to have a nice long walk in. I wanted to have sex in the fields. Back then Matt and I used to lie out together and make love in the grass together. It was just for a quick fondle and for some lovely long kisses. Twice he came before we lazed out and slept. It had been a lovely day out.

That Thursday after college I was all dressed up in my favourite green skirt, red jumper and knee high boots and I walked up to Middlebrooks to see Matt to have tea with my future in-laws. Afterwards we all walked down to the Methodist Church to wait with a gang of people to wait for a coach. I stood there talking to Bob and Sue's friends saying, "Hello. How are you? My name is Karen." To those I knew I'd asked if they were all right before asking them about their lives.

On the coach we were still talking about Phantom of the Opera as it was what we were all going to see.

At the theatre we went in through the side entrance as Mrs Parsons, Sally, walked through on crutches for us to sit together. Famous songs were sung about a man in a black tuxedo and a black and red cape of whom haunted a theatre. I remember them using the real chandelier in the theatre as a prop when the Phantom flew on obvious ropes round the ceiling and made us all jump. The heroine sounded as good as Sarah Brightman and was brilliant.

Matt's Gran and Gramps drove us to the airport, next day, at Bristol and hung around waiting to see us leave. We had to check in and go through customs and as Matt went through the metal detector something set it off so he had to stand there and empty his pockets. It had been a belt that had set it off but Matt was put through the embarrassment of having to pull out a packet of condom from his back pocket.

> Psalms 3:9
> And don't let fools laugh at me.

We both laughed and I'd set off the metal detector too and got my nail scissors confiscated.

At our hotel called Babalu we had gone self-catering and we'd had a nice kitchen which led out to a balcony right next to the pool. I had a song stuck in my head for most of the holiday which was The Fugees version of Killing Me Softly that I'd sang up and down the cold concreted passageway between rooms.

Our hotel had been situated half way up a hill and you could look right over the coat line and Puerto Rico and in the evenings, after lounging around on the beach going in and out of the sea, we'd go round the town's nightlife.

One day we went on a jeep safari touring the island of where we threw water balloons at each other and sand, "Ola, ola coca cola a-reeb-a, a-reeb-a," and what sounded like, "Underlay, underlay," with a Scottish couple we'd got on real well with. We'd seen the Four Tops that evening and they were brilliant we knew every song.

We really enjoyed our first holiday together and was soon flying back home to Bristol airport.

That Saturday I had been invited over by my mother-in-law to be, to go off Christmas shopping with her to Burnham. I got over there on the first bus to see Sue and she greeted me by the back door.

"Ready then." Sue said.

"Ready when you are." I'd said and smiled at her. I went to get in the back seat and she said, "In the front Karen."

I got the feeling she didn't want the position of chauffeur and wanted a chat. I couldn't think of anything to talk about so stayed silent so we had the radio on in the background.

Trailing about the shops, especially the gift shops, I kept looking for Christmas presents and ended up in Bastins afterwards for cards, wrapping paper, gift tags and plenty of Sellotape.

The morning flew by and before mid-day we went for tea and cake before we ended back up walking along the sea front as the pair of us headed for the car at the apex car park.

It was another hour till Matt was expected home and Sue asked if I wanted to wait for lunch till Matt got home.

I'd said, "Yes."

As soon as he got back from work we sat down together for sandwiches with nice thick bread.

Matt and I hung around the garden all afternoon lazing out in the grass underneath the cherry plum tree of where we loved to snuggle up and make love together out of prying eyes.

That evening Matt and I went to The Bear Inn for a drink with his mates. I got a bit puddled, so did Matt and I started flirting with Matthew's male friends of whom I'd grown rather fond of. Then I grabbed a packet of cigarettes on the bar. I'd been gasping for a fag and took a long drag after asking Jon for a light and puffed in his face. I got a shock and Baggy told me Matt was planning a September wedding for us. I felt anger emanating from Matt behind me of whom had a go at him. The cat was out of the bag and Matt and I promptly went home.

I floated into church in the morning for a preliminary nativity serve that involved all the young children on stage. I thought they were cute all dressed up as angels, sheep, and the nuclear family unit including God. The story was so cute with the little ones being kings, wise men, and shepherds.

The Genge's and I then progressed to the church hall to see the children running around still in their little outfits while the rest of us sat down for hot drinks and I had a cordial. They'd sat with their friends I'd never met before and so got introduced. I loved the sense of community spirit amongst this family unit and friends.

My life with mother when I got home was beginning to feel more and more boring and I began to compare my family to theirs. I realised that my Mum and Dad weren't involved so much in the community as much with such close friends so I had it in my mind that my family and Matt's should have gotten closer. To do more things together so I started whinging to Matt about getting family projects on the go to get both families together.

The next day I walked down to the doctors on the corner to get on a work's bus during Christmas break from college to go out to Ditcheats cheese factory out in the sticks.

When I got there I had to put a blue coat on and what looked like a shower cap but was made out of blue soft elastic. I'd clocked in then went down to the factory floor. They told me to stand at the front of the production line to keep lifting great big blocks of chees on to push onto the conveyor belt to go through the slicer to make small chunks of cheese. Then someone half way down the line had to check the wrappers. At the end of the line were two packers. One to box the cheese up the other to put the boxes stacked correctly on the pallets. I had to do this same job that whole week while nibbling at bits of crumbling cheese off the softer block. I was looking forward to the week the factory was closed between Christmas Day and the New Year.

On Christmas Day the whole family woke up late and went downstairs to have breakfast together before getting washed and dressed. We finally got all together in the living room to watch Christmas television together and I remember watching The Water Babies and Bed Knobs and Broomsticks. This I did while everyone drifted out into the kitchen until I got called to sit up for Christmas lunch. It was nice having all of us sat round the table. We laughed at the cracker jokes, put on the crepe paper crowns, and claimed our toys from the crackers. Mine was a spinning top.

Halfway through the meal Dad blew off and blamed it on the sprouts. I just stuck my nose in the air laughing with my eyes.

> *Ecclesiastes 2:2*
> *I discovered that laugher is foolish.*

Dad smiled at all of us. Then for pudding we had a proper brandy covered Christmas pud with cream. I was always glad it wasn't a traditional style one with coins in as I was always scared of choking.

The afternoon was spent with Dad playing Santa with the presents underneath the tree. We also passed round cards together while Mum brought us out drinks of cups of tea. Mum disappeared to tidy up the kitchen while the grandparents turned up and then they gave their presents out. Mum forever the hostess offered them a proper drink or a cup of tea.

Matt turned up about three o'clock to stay for the night and into the evening we split into two groups either watching the telly or playing party games in the kitchen with cards, Pictionary or Yahtzee, then Trivial Pursuit well into the evening.

At ten o'clock Granddad decided to drive back to Wells with Nan Sheila. At the same time nan Burr got up and wanted to be walked back home so Dad went with her down the road and back from Barrington Place. Matt and I yawned and went upstairs to bed.

In the morning we woke up late to my parents of whom were already up. Mum offered us a cooked breakfast and Dad asked if we wanted to watch football that afternoon over the road. Matt and I loved the idea so walked across that afternoon in the winter sun with the air cool and crisp. With our warm coats on we stood up with Dad watching Shepton play in black and white football kits.

Shepton were scoring against Wells and winning through the first half leading into half time at 2-1. The second forty five minutes nobody scored but it was a tense game that had us on the edge of our seats. We all clapped when the home team went on and won.

The week went by in a lovely lazy way with walks all together taken either across to Chew Valley Lake way and through Priddy up over the Mendips and one day out to Maesbury Ring to see where the old King Arthur's castle once stood.

For New Year's Eve the family went out to Shepton's football club for a dance for the evening. All dressed up it wasn't far for Fee and Steve to walk, with Eve, I and Mum and Dad to walk for a drink and a lovely dance. Halfway through the night the music stopped and the lights were turned on for us to see the buffet for us to stuff ourselves before the lights turned off again for us to dance all the night till the morning light.

Two days later there was an AGM with Phantoms Carnival Club the usual crowd were there and because of my snotty nose Chris called me Rudolph. I inwardly laughed as I used my handkerchief and felt accepted into the carnival club Matt had told me he'd been in for a couple of years.

Stars were in my eyes as I went into college one day really believing I could be famous one day.

Jeremiah 9: 23-24
The wise should not boast of their wisdom.

In film studies that morning there was a film by Stanley Cubrik that wasn't as shocking for the second time of watching. I'd originally watched A Clockwork Orange at thirteen and was disturbed by the violent sex scene and the attempted suicide scene. How the deranged idiot survived after the classical music drove him to jump out the window after cracking his neck I don't know. The whole idea of medically trying to stop deranged bastards ended up working for one of them who turned out to be a copper made it a satirist's disaster. As I sat there Dan and I didn't really want to watch this film and he said that he liked my knee high boots while I'd sat on the table and he also said that my boobs could do with being bigger. It made me feel like my boobs should be bigger and I wanted to be taller and told Matt that evening. In bed we made sweet, sweet loving and he jokingly said, "I'll massage them bigger," We laughed ourselves asleep, fully satiated.

In the morning college started and that day I handed in my legal assignment to be marked at the end of class. The next lesson was about turning the knobs on a radio machine to create a segment for the radio. It was hard to figure out and there was a microphone attached to speak into and you had to watch the two white disks turning on the turntable taping the show. I then had to work out how to translate it to the computer on the adobe sound fold to put with visuals later. I did this well into the lunch hour to get it right. I had only one morning assigned to me for usage on the machine I made the most of it.

In the afternoon I had to go to another building upstairs. I remember staring out the window and randomly bullet pointing everything on the white board that was written to suit what I wanted to write for our next assignment. It seemed so easy but I needed the new big words they were using to describe things properly on the new equipment we were going to have to use.

My mind was a bit vacant that day.

> *Job 20:8*
> *Like a vision at night.*

I found myself in a mock interview later and I sound to myself that I was being understood perfectly.

At the end of the day Matt picked me up and took me up his Mum's for tea before going out that evening.

Down at the Unity Club we met up with Dave, mark, Julian, Adrian and Justin and two ladies from the Golden House Chinese take away just down the road. They were beautiful and in expensive looking clothes you could tell they ran a wealthy business. We were playing killer pool of where you had to put the triangle in the middle of the table, take one turn each and had to pot one ball each time or you lost a life. you had three lives and the last one left in took all the pound coins we pooled together in the beginning to play.

> *Judges 14:12*
> *I'll bet each one of you a piece of fine linen*
> *And a change of fine clothes.*

While we'd been playing I got told of the time Matt and his friends had eaten at The Golden House restaurant and Dave had pulled Matt's boxers down. He'd flung them on the roof outside. Knowing the Chinese lady owners had been there at the time seeing his bits I got jealous and was convinced that the nicest one was only nice to Matt because she fancied him.

We played the game twice and some of the men got too competitive so I didn't mind losing to them as I'd preferred them winding each other up instead of trying to get one over on me. The drinks flowed all evening and I had been on Malibu and lemonades. Feeling all heady afterwards Matt, myself, Julian, Mark and Justin started walking home saying goodnight at each other's houses on the way until Matt and I got back up to Middlebrooks to his parents' house. I sneaked into his bed again that night. I couldn't stand the pokey camp bed and needed warm cuddles all night.

The next morning at first light I put on my nightdress that Sue had bought me for Christmas and went downstairs for a pee. I could hear moving around in the kitchen and Sue came through the hallway door and nearly collided with me coming out of the toilet. She gave that girly giggle I liked and said, "Morning Karen. Now do you want some toast?"

I said, "Yes please," and inwardly blushed. I ran upstairs cold and quickly dressed. Matt was rousing and I asked him if he wanted breakfast.

He'd said, "I'll ask Mother for something when I get down."

Then I heard her yelling up the stairs, "Get your orders in. What do you want for breakfast Matt? I'm doing toast."

"I'll have it with Marmite Mum."

She looked at me and with that look said, "Don't do it Karen. I'll do it," so I backed off from wanting to help. I loved being mothered up at Matt's anyway.

The day was cold but my body felt warm inside so I left out putting a coat on. Matt's Mum asked me did I want a coat, before Matt and I went out and I got a puzzled look in retort when I said, "No thank you."

It was a Sunday and I asked if we were going to church and Sue said, "Not today," and inwardly guffawed at Bob and Sue's idea of rebelling to me, as they'd always been good people, when they said "We'd rather have crust less toast," while they shared a secret laugh together.

That afternoon I was getting bored in my in-law's to be company while I kept watching the clock as Bob was in the garden, and Sue was reading. It seemed they had no real desire to ask me anything about myself to want to get to know me.

Psalms 142:4
No one cares for me.

At last Matt said we've got to go to our carnival meeting. Then half an hour later after saying our goodbyes we headed out the door for Meare and the pub the Railway.

Pulling into the gravelled car park we walked into the bar and were the first ones there. Matt and I had a Thatcher's each then went to the fruit machine for a quick go with a couple of quid and won some money enough for a couple of more drinks. Sat down we waited on a wooden bench not far from the fireplace by the window tucked in a corner. The concrete floor felt cold. There was a piano out by the skittle alley so I went to play some simple tunes before the others started to come in, in dribs and drabs.

Luckily the meeting started on time. It had irked me when Matt talked to the bar manager and the woman earlier by announcing their names when we first ordered and I told him before we got talking in the meeting. The chairman shot me a look so I grabbed Matt's knee for a comforting squeeze.

We discussed fundraising ideas and what was actually to come like our next event. We wanted to do ferret racing at the pub and posters were discussed for the secretary to write out. We'd discussed cart building first, then there was the treasurer's report and the chairman's report before the end of the meeting.

On the Wednesday after doing my homework at the college, as it was a study day I walked over to Matt's and got talking to his Nan waiting for him to come home and I heard her stories about her house mistress days up at Millfield school when she helped Bob with his schooling by working off half his fees. Matt came in and we had lunch together. matt fell asleep for a bit on the sofa before declaring that he wanted to go to sleep. He'd also said we'd go to Bill King's farm out in the ticks to help with building on the cart.

> *Nehemiah 4*
> *The people were eager to work.*

Once there we started painting and the men hammered things together just to do a basic underlying look to set ourselves up for an idea for the cart yet to be chosen. I'd heard of how Bill King, the owner of the famer were we were, always matched the money we made fundraising throughout the year. That meant if we made two thousand pounds he'd donate that same amount to the club.

Afterwards Matt took me home to my parents' and I got ready after tea to wash and change to go to skittles with Mum and met Tricia, the tall one, an only child, Sasha, a curly haired bubbly blonde, Rachel a brunette who smoked like a trooper, Clarrie a real matriarch, Tricia's Mum, Carolle the big lady, our captain, and Nan Sheila.

Throughout a tense game that evening I heard that one of them was looking into artificial insemination in order to have children. I thought it was Rachel looking into it and enjoyed the tension in the air that wound me up into believing I could be shit hot playing and wanted spares so badly every time I stood up to play. We went on and lost the game.

Saturday morning I went shopping with Mum over at Street to look for a wedding dress. Mum and my first stop was a hotel at the bottom of town of where I saw a massive sign on the wall saying Wedding Fayre. Inside there were dresses all around and a stand for a professional photographer. Mum and I perused the dresses. I didn't take to them as there was too much material on them and the prices were hilariously too expensive. Up town we went into a charity shop with wedding dresses in the window, a St Margaret's Hospice of where there was a whole rail of brand new wedding dresses. They were from a bridal shop that had closed and the first dress I tried on I fell in love with plenty of lace down the arms and over the chest.

> *Jeremiah 2:32*
> *Does a young woman forget her jewellery, or a bride*
> *Her wedding dress?*

It was only one hundred and fifty pounds so Mum went on to get it. It had been a very productive day which was what we wanted.

On the Tuesday I'd turned up at Matt's quite early and his Mum made us a light tea. Dressed in my favourite jeans and low cut top Matt and I excitedly headed out to skittles at the Unity Club. I got on well with Matt's friends of whom we'd catch up with enroute. Justin would join us in Ash Road, then Steve would join us in Gos Drive, Mark at his Mum's and Marcus at his Dad's. We'd go passed Merriman Park all excitedly laughing and joking.

> *Proverbs 14:22*
> *You will earn the trust and respect of others.*
> *If you work for good.*

I loved being the only female.

At the Unity Club we had to press a buzzer to get in and I'd be surrounded by good looking men in their trendy shirts all with aftershave on smelling nice. At the bar I would have Malibu and lemonade and would say hello to the rest of the team. I'd then follow them to the alley to watch. On this particular occasion Matt and I were still at the stage of not being able to keep our hands off each other and we'd spend most of the night with me on his knee snogging each other senseless. Mark and Paul, the gay couple in the team grew more and more annoyed with us.

Matt and I had ordered a taxi for before eleven o'clock to avoid after eleven charges and outside Marcus tried to stick his head in between us kissing thinking I'd kiss him instead but he smoked and his looks reminded me of Martin. I wasn't interested.

In a CJW cab Matt and I made our way back to Middlebrooks for a cuddle up in bed and a goodnight kip.

That weekend Matt and I jumped on a coach to go to Shakespeare's birthplace at Stratford-upon-Avon. Pulling up right outside a little house I was unimpressed with how little and ramshackled it looked like straight out of a Dicken's novel with its quaintness and simplicity. We went upstairs and it didn't take us long to look round.

Matt and I soon got back on the coach to go to Cadbury's World factory. I was vaguely surprised it was an actual factory I'd expected something like Willy Wonka's factory.

> *I Samuel 3:11*
> *Everyone who hears about it will be stunned.*

We saw adults in white coats and a man took us round to show us every aspect of production. We'd been promised a free chocolate bar for each of us which we were given when stood outside of the main offices. It consisted mainly of corridors really as we looked through glass at the conveyor belts too. Wandering round with the group I got more engrossed with nibbling on my chocolate till we went outside. Back on the coach we got dropped at our hotel and found ti comfortable and pleasing ready for a goodnight's rest.

Chapter Seventeen

The next morning the coach was outside ready to take us to Warwickshire. It was a longish drive before we pulled up at a large majestic looking castle, called Warwick Castle. Through the main doors we wandered through endless rooms reminding me of a museum with all the furniture and ornaments down to the last detail perfectly displayed. I ran my finger over a windowsill looking outside over the large grounds as we went through a hallway lading to a grand dining room with a chandelier in the middle of the ceiling. A long table with silver service and finest bone china all was laid out perfectly ready for a feast. Around the sides on the walls were large paintings, little soft lights and dated wall paper from previous centuries ago. There was a ballroom. Then downstairs was a drawing room, library, study, and living room, etc. On the bottom floor was a souvenir shop and we had a look round for presents. We got some postcards before the guide took us down the dungeons to see where people got imprisoned.

> *1 Thessalonians 5:12*
> *Pay proper respect to those who work among you,*
> *Who guide and instruct you.*

I was glad when we got outside to walk around the huge impressive grounds. There was a lovely big lawn stretching out to what looked like miles of trees. There were lots of colourful flowers and bushes dotted around and wide empty spaces, that we spent a good hour strolling around. It was about four o'clock when we went back to the car park to pick up the coach to go all the way home. it was a long journey. Several times I dropped off to sleep on Matt's shoulder jolting awake to every shudder of the big vehicle till we got back to Street.

I said, "Goodnight," and jumped into a car with Mum who came to pick me up.

A few days later Matt came round for me to take me out and he seemed really tired so we didn't do too much. We wandered round town hand-in-hand, kissing and cuddling, talking about the future, happy. Matt and I went up to the park and we sat down on a park bench where I laid out against his side for a while, while we dreamt up our lives together. I told him about my plans of going to university one day hoping inwardly he'd support me through my dreams. Both of us sat there for a long time. Matt dozed off. Then we went back to Mum's for tea and we had lamb chops, carrots, cabbage and mash potatoes. Matt had, had enough and decided to take his leave. My bosoms heaved pressed up against him at the door. Fiona watched and understood we were meant to be together from her happy comment.

Later on that night I had a phone call from Matt and he sounded worried saying he'd see me in a few days' time as apparently he had fallen asleep at the wheel of the car going through Pilton. The story was the car had gone on the other side of the road and a lorry beeped loudly at him from going the other way. Matt had awoken and swerved at the last minute.

>Exodus 18:7
>They asked about each other's health.

And he told me that he hated driving in the dark after that experience and would not stay too late again.

The next morning I was to start a job over at Street as a cleaner so I'd got my Mum to drive me over for my six o'clock start. I met a lady called Sheila of whom was short and dumpy with dark straggly hair. She was jolly and keen to teach me how to use a mop. Firstly I had to master a big red soft brush that was built the shape of scissors that I had to push up and down each aisle at Kwiksave. Then the mopping took place. I was shown how to dry mop by rinsing the mop out as much as possible by pushing and twisting really hard into the rounded white bit of the bucket. I even got to use a buffer to shine up the floor. I had to help with the toilets then hoover the mats by the front door.

College afterwards was a real chance to use my brains and I loved the camera class and putting photos on adobe photo shop getting to stretch my imagination.

By the end of the day my mind was buzzing and I went up to see Matt at his Mum's with a storyboard and script in my hand. I asked Matt that evening while his best friend Justin visited, if they could both star in a play I'd written for college about two male friends vying for my attention. I had a camera ready for my story to be acted out and we went up the garden after Matt discussed it with Justin first. I told them the script I had in my head and I had to get them to fight over me. It was funny in my head to see them play fighting over me.

>Exodus 2:3
>I thought that this might be the best way people
>Can spend their short lives on earth.

I could see them smiling behind their eyes but the script they kept perfect and the scene they played out all over the large back garden. I said thank you after as they did as I'd asked. I played it back to them on the video camera and they laughed. It was fun and ready for college to hand in the next day.

I handed my assignment in and was pleased but by the end of the class got it handed back with just a pass written on it in red ink.

After college up at Matt's again his Mum said that I could have my own vegetable patch. Why? As I could see that she wanted me to feel at home up there completely from my own perspective so I went up the garden with a shovel I'd found and dug out a big square patch with cabbage seeds and carrots to plant. I found sticks to put the packets on afterwards at the end of the rows. I felt elated from the physical exercise.

I went home on the bus that night and the next day college flew by as there was always something new to learn and Matt picked me up to take me to Mum's for the evening for us, Mum, Dad, Fee and Uncle Cyn to do line dancing out at a place called Doulting in a school. In the school hall we stood in line together. Mum was friendly with Lindsay the teacher and she'd been a strong leader taking us through steps to dance to first bit by bit, slowly at first before she'd put the music on to get the steps right. It had been a two steps forward routine then two steps back. A hip swivel into two steps right and a kick to two steps left and a kick with our hands on our hips. Then turn and do exactly the same routine to the side wall doing a turn to the right between each simple routine till we faced her again.

Psalms 30:11
You have changed my sadness into a joyful dance.

I could her Dad having a laugh with my Uncle in the line of whose boom was infectious and made us giggle. The next routine was fast and furious with the song 1, 2, 3, 4, 5, 6, 7, 8 that we loved the routine to. It was a lot of fun that first night then Matt dropped me back at Mum's before going home.

The next day in class we were asked to create music videos and a girl named Kate, a nice seventeen year old brunette about five foot two of medium build in sensible clothes was to do a video with me. We all paired off. Kate and I chose a song by The Proclaimers about walking five hundred miles. We had to go through magazines to get pictures to match the song so I cut out different wonders of the world like the Taj Mahal, the pyramids and a car with a girl in and Kate chose different scenes from around the world that we pasted on to black card. Then we stood each picture up on a chair, videoed them, then took the tape to the editing suite when it was our turn to dub the music over the top. Kate and I thought it was brilliant.

We showed all our videos near the end of the lesson and I felt put out that Mr Selby preferred Lee's War What Is It Good For video as he explained ours took the words too literally for our pictures. Lee had nothing but the spoils of war for his video and didn't get the tutors opinion and felt hurt.

The year drifted into the Easter weeks and I did a week's work with St Ivels in Evercreech in the laboratory. It was crappy cleaning work and didn't realise I had to work the second week and ultimately fell out with Lyn the boss over the phone when she phoned me at Matt's to find out where I was.

That evening Matt and I went to skittles at the Unity Club and I felt like having a drink. The game was a bit boring and the Malibu and lemonades were going down very easily. The team had a kitty going that was full of fine and money for the sticker upper. I grabbed this cash with the intention of tripling the money on the gambler. When I lost it all I was feeling very awkward and was hated by the team so I took myself off into another room and started shouting I liked it up the ass. Looking back none of this was cool but I'd felt like I'd been cool at the time and a bit like a party animal. I was surprised afterwards that Matt didn't dump me.

The next day I went to work and stood by a cheese factory line to put on blocks and blocks of cheese. I nibbled on the crumbled bits and as I was nibbling I thought of going home to have a shower. I was getting smellier by the minute with bits of cheese getting stuck to my clothes. My head was in the clouds and I really kept myself to myself and just kept to polite niceties with everybody. It was a ten am shift to six o'clock and I soon jumped into a friend's car from work to come on home.

Now my baby sister Eve was going out with a lad called John and that evening she'd had a phone call from him. She burst into tears yet again and I hated the lad for making my sister cry.

Leviticus 19:18
Do not take revenge on anyone or continue to hate him.

It was a Friday and I hopped on the bus after a nice shower to go see Matt and he was there when I got to his house. He said that he was going out to a skittles match and his Mum spoke up and said, "Well would you like to come to a games evening at the Methodist Church?"

I Said, "Fine."

She said, "You'll need to go to Tesco's first to get some food. Everybody supplies a little bit for a nice tea party."

"I'll get some Pringles then." I then got into the car with her and Bob to go to the church. At the church I'd said, "I'll see you in a minute," as I walked round to the supermarket and got the crisps. Back inside the hall I noticed Sue's bowl of salad. All the food looked nice. The games evening passed by quickly until twelve o'clock. I met Matt outside the Unity Club. I gave him a kiss and we walked back up to his hand-in-hand. As we were walking we stopped off for kebabs I thoroughly enjoyed it, the meat, salad and pita bread tasted nice.

A week later I jumped in a cab for a tenner to see Matt again but he wasn't in and I didn't know where the rest of his family were. I think they were in bed so I sneaked upstairs without anybody knowing and crept into his bed having forgotten he'd gone to skittles and fell asleep waiting for him to come home. He got a nice surprise and in the afternoon the next day I went home and my Uncle Roy said he'd take me to motocross that weekend.

On the Sunday Uncle Roy picked me up to take me to see my cousin Darren doing his motocross on his shit hot bike. He took me to Prestleigh Hill and drove into a field where there were load of vans and people milling about. The place looked busy. Darren and his friends had to select which bike to use for their first race of the day. I say that his numbered top was ten so I knew which number to look out for on the racecourse. I stood out of the way near the van to watch the races and Darren zipped around really fast while my uncle was ready with the camera to take promotional photographs possible for magazines. Darren was going to be followed very closely by me and as the race started I played a presenters routine in my head as he over took others and took the bends cleanly. The noise was irritating.

> *Proverbs 10:26*
> *As vinegar on your teeth or smoke in your eyes.*

It was so loud that when Darren came back after winning the side of his face was bright red apparently a bee had stung his face. He needed a cooling gel on his face and he glowed triumphantly from winning. We then packed up and went home.

Now in the evening Matt and I went line dancing and we learned a routine to the song 5, 6, 7, 8.

Now by the end of the week, because college flew by, I was going to cards night with Bob and Sue, my in-laws to be and played Chinese rummy. It was a lovely night.

A few days later it was early evening, about four thirty pm, when Mum and Dad decided to drive to Weston-Super-Mare. It had been a lovely drive through Wells and Cheddar seeing a not too intense sun in the sky, Passed the strawberry fields on the way to hitting the coastline. We parked on the beach the side of Weston where the bowling is and we walked along the sea front of where the putting green was. Mum and Dad paid for a game, after having gone for chips first, and I decided to try and impress my fiancé with my left hand playing as well as my right handed swing. I didn't do so good. Mum thought I'd played badly deliberately to help Matt look good, but I didn't need to do that as far as I was concerned Matt could play as well as the rest of us. Dad's obsession with being better than everyone else annoyed me and I found myself standing up for Matt and admitting that I was trying to impress him. Hand in hand Matt and I walked behind my parents as we'd headed back along the sea front to the car.

In the evening the next day the whole family went round to Nan Sheila's for her 70th birthday. Mum had made a lovely cake with candles on shaped like the number 70. In the kitchen everyone sat around having a good old yap.

Matt and I had been sitting in the living room on their old brown sofa. We both had a drink in our hands cuddled up. The news had been on, but Mum came in asking us to turn the telly off. Then the lights went out and Mum asked us to sing happy birthday. Now as Mum came in with Uncle Cyn and the cake Nan blew out her candles as Uncle Roy took a photograph of them in the kitchen.

I had been eager to tuck into the cake a it looked yummy. We were all offered some wine as a toast but I for once couldn't drink as I'd been aware of my surroundings for once and just wasn't interested.

I got up the next day feeling happy and sure of myself.

> *Psalms 37:4*
> *Seek your happiness in the Lord,*
> *And he will give you your heart's desire.*

I jumped into the shower singing. This was to be my wedding day. Downstairs Mum cooked me and my sisters a hearty breakfast. I'd been booked into a beautician's in the middle of town for them to do my hair and make-up. I felt calm and in control and Fee said, "I can't believe how calm you are. I'd be a barrel of nerves."

It was the 20th September 1997 and I then got changed into my wedding dress and had photos with my family on the back lawn. Dad had been cleaning the car all morning then Yonner turned up to be me chauffer. My bridesmaids got to the church first. It'd been twenty minutes after they came back for Dad and I.

I glided slowly down the aisle and felt all eyes on me. At the front nerves got the better of me and I heard clapping in the heavens over me. I just about held it together for the vows. The vicar got into a pickle and married us twice and my cousins with my Uncle Cyn laughed in the middle of the service. Apart from them there wasn't a dry eye in the church as Matt and I glided out again.

The congregation followed us from the big church in Shepton to Croscombe for the reception. The best man's speech was embarrassing.

> *Psalm 39:8, 9*
> *Don't let fools laugh at me. I will keep quiet, I will not say a word.*

Dad was proud with a little joke. Everybody laughed then I had photos in the garden.

Afterwards we went to the British Legion in Street and everyone stayed right to the end and Matt and I spent the night at The Bear Hotel.

On the Sunday after our wedding night we were looking forward to opening our presents at my new in-laws house. In their garden I'd been wearing my favourite tight white top and my snug jeans. Matt was looking casual and relaxed. All the presents were tacked on the grass on a table and Matt and I got excited as we opened each parcel.

There to watch was Bob and Sue, Gwenda, Sally, Brian, Verity, Viv and Maureen, friends of Matt's family and his brother Tom. Mum and Dad were there with my nans, Granddad Ern, Uncle Cyn, Casey and both my sisters. Everyone happily chatted away with laughter in abundance. Sue had served everyone drinks. It was the first time I'd gotten excited over things like a cutlery set from Matt's friends Mark and Dawn, and an expensive looking clock set in mahogany for the mantel piece from Gwenda. We'd taken out time going through all the towel sets given us, the toaster and the microwave from Nan Burr.

All in all it turned out to be a lovely afternoon that had stretched in to the early evening with us all either sitting on garden benches or plastic chairs eventually digging into a finger food tea.

Everyone was happy and it gave us the opportunity to have a nice send off for our honeymoon on the Monday. The build up to going back to Gran Canaria was exciting.

Our hotel was up a hill overlooking the coast. While we were there Matt and I enjoyed shopping for breakfast each day consisting mainly of soft bread, butter, jam, and bucks fizz every morning after making love each morning.

On one occasion we'd been enjoying our conjugal rites when there was a knock on our door. Matt got up to answer it with his hard-on apparent while I'd cowered under the shirts completely naked. It had been a TV repair man who'd just barged on in to see to our television set and embarrassingly sauntered out again as quickly as possible. This gave us something to giggle about for the rest of the honeymoon.

In the evening we trawled the bars round Puerto Rico and one night we saw The Four Tops and I had got our photo taken with them. I'd been determined to have a moonlight stroll along the beach one evening but someone else had caught Matt's attention. There'd been a group of Spanish youngsters on the beach and I remember seeing one girl walking into the sea completely naked which ruined my romantic evening.

One afternoon a lady stopped to talk to us talking about scratch cards that he'd said were all winners. Matt asked her if they were trying to get us to buy a time share as it wasn't the first time we'd been stopped on the way to the beach. She'd said yes.

As part of the honeymoon we'd been on a jeep safari touring the island like our holiday before but this time it wasn't a fun and I didn't like the young good looking couple in our jeep and kept calling them Mr and Mrs Perfect even when we stopped off to test some alcohol, Sambuca.

We'd even been on a ship called The Timanfaya where we'd played party games and we laughed over the fact that the lady taking the games thought I knew the man I'd been paired with for a wind the baby game as we'd looked over familiar together.

All in all it was a highly memorable honeymoon.

That Friday evening I found myself going through my husband's wall hangings I'd seen before in his old bedroom at his old family home in Street. I thought of where to hand them in the flat. The pictures were mostly of chicken and various other farm birds. I wanted to decorate the walls in the hallway so put up three side by side on one wall with nails and hammering them in with the wooden handle of my screwdriver. That was easy. There was a lovely picture of a dove on a black background that I put up on the living room wall above our breakfast bar. There was a picture of a lone Kingfisher too that I put up on the wall by the living room curtains. He also had an early to rise large picture I hammered into the wall above the fireplace. I felt really proud of myself that evening and admired my work afterward that Matt admired about me.

Deuteronomy 8:13, 14
All your other possessions have increased,
Make sure that you do not become proud and forget the Lord your God.

My desire to just get on with things as he just watched the telly.

We'd only been in the flat a couple of months in Glastonbury and I asked Matt if we could have a moving in party. I had in my mind inviting all the neighbours in our building to get to know them. Old movies went through my mind of where neighbours all knew each other and looked out for one another. I wanted that for us and there were only five other flats in our building. I'd wanted to invite the family too, but Matt put up blocks to that idea each time I'd asked him that week. I should have realised that if I'd really wanted one I should have just gone on and organised it, but I felt it had to be a joint decision. It was Matt's home too.

As we moved in the furniture from Matt's old bedroom like the ornament cabinets I found myself moving it around to suit the living room. I put his two cabinets against the back wall.

Another cabinet we bought together we bought together with a small cupboard in was put on the back wall too and I placed Matt's collectable cars in two of them and put glasses, alcohol, and Matt's farmyard ornaments on the top of the wooden cabinet. Inside the cupboard I'd envisaged putting in important documents.

The sofa was in the middle of the room with a huge telly in the corner I'd had to put a ramp under to get it up on an ugly bricked up area of which I couldn't get to the sockets underneath.

That Saturday afternoon we went up to Matt's Mum's and she gave us some money to get some curtains. I thought of our main bedroom needing some and was dead keen to get them. She gave us fifty quid on the proviso we got them fully lined.

First chance I got the following weekend I took the bus to Shepton to Roseby's a place by Haskins. Without much thought I chose a rusty coloured pair of curtains with brown shapes on reminding me of the shapes of my red curtains growing up in 10 Coombe View. A part of me wanted to see the old tiger face.

The sun was shining that next morning and Michael, another college student, and I went to a commune in a big lonely house on a corner on the way to Baltonsborough.

We walked round the back of the house to the garden and noticed many people just sitting about yapping. Michael had wanted to do the interviewing so I held the camera as he integrated with everyone in the living room with them all sat around in long flowing garments. Some of them were smoking marijuana. I'd recognised the smell. Holding the camera on the tripod I'd panned around the room until we finished until going back out to the garden of where we stopped and chatted for a while in the sunshine before walking back home. At home Matt had tea on the table ready and he told me not to wash up as he wanted to enjoy the evening with me.

At college the next day I made a tape about paedophiles. It made me feel like:

Ecclesiastes 1:2
Life is useless, all useless

and totally disgusted. I went on about how comedian like Roy Chubby Brown, I'd watched on Dad's tapes, kept going on about how they got turned on about women who'd got Brazilians. I mentioned other comedians too. Somebody in the media, about famous actresses, said there'd been a trend of women who like their vaginas bald. I realised that these celebrities just fed into the idea of keeping women childlike feeding the minds of paedophiles who groom so many young children.

That evening I dreamt of having my own little media empire of where I'd had a big mansion on a hill with a helipad to the side with a helicopter on it with KMG emblazoned in gold.

> *Deuteronomy 13: 1, 2*
> *"Prophets or interpreters of dreams may promise a miracle or a wonder, in order to lead you to worship and serve gods you have not worshipped before.*

Matt and I started Christmas Day at his parents. We got there early for our presents, with Bob, Matt's Dad, playing Santa. Then we all had a lovely traditional turkey lunch. Just before sitting down for lunch we went all over Street handing out our Christmas cards.
I'd been wearing a shiny blue shirt that day with a skirt to feel Christmassy.

When we went to Shepton at about three thirty we said hello to Mum and Dad before driving across town to Uncle Roy and Aunty Suzanne's to give them their families Christmas cards and stayed for a hot drink and a bit of a chat. We then made our excuses before going back across town and down the road to Aunty Wendy's with their cards for cousin Scott, and Lyn's family.

As the evening progressed, back at Mum's, everyone fanned out with half the family in the living room just sitting around talking while the rest of us were playing games around the kitchen table. After playing Yahtzee, when I was adding up our scores Eve's fiancé wanted to check my adding up and put a different score down to mine. I had a go at him and wore convinced that he was cheating. Everyone overheard and all decided to go home. Matt and I decided to walk my cousin Katy back to Gran's.

Come Saturday I'd cleaned that morning in the supermarket before heading home desperately needing a bloody good shower and a nice rest. I turned on the radio before sorting out a week's disaster in the kitchen.

It took a long time to clean up and didn't notice anyone had come into the flat until I felt warm familiar arms around my waist. I turned round to give Matt a kiss and afterward we sat in the living room together discussing lottery tickets. I'd said that I would use part of my mother's phone number the 3, 7, 34 and 39 and my birthday. Matt said some pretty random similar numbers and I told him that I'd go to the Co-op.

When he went back to work I walked through the high street with him and stopped at the supermarket. At the till when I'd asked for the lottery I got asked for I.D., I'd been twenty two and laughed at the time flashing my engagement and wedding ring. I reminded the lady at the till that you had to be at least sixteen to be married in order to be able to acquire the tickets and I got served. I laughed at her.

At home I put my shopping away and left the tickets in my pocket. With the radio on in the background I lazed out on the sofa reading a lovely love story from my Mills and Boon books.

I'd felt really relaxed when Matt came home that afternoon and on into the evening when it started to get dark outside Matt and I heard a door smash outside our flat and a lot of arguing. Matt wanted to know what was going on, so did I, but we were too afraid to go outside.

Deuteronomy 1:17
Do not be afraid of anyone, for the decisions you make
Come from God.

Pulling the curtains back tentatively Matt looked out the window and from behind him we noticed a removal van and a man Matt said he knew fighting some hard man. He turned to me and said that's Mark who is a postman of whom was married to an ex of his called Pauline. Apparently a blonde bombshell. I didn't need to know that I thought. This nightmare of a noise was to be the new family moving in above us.

We dared ourselves to go out after the noise died down to notice our communal front door all smashed in. There was glass everywhere and Matt bless him, bent over to pick it up. I told him to wait till I got a dustpan and brush of which I went back inside to get. I was very reluctant to go near it thinking the new tenants should have done it, but the mess was outside our front door. In the end Matt got the hoover and pushed it round in the communal area for ages trying to get up tiny shards of glass left behind.

When we sat down again Matt unburdened himself and told me that Pauline, even though married at the time, used to make out with him in the back of cabs. This used to happen after carnival do's in Glastonbury town hall.

After that nightmare of a weekend I settled into my new cleaning position at Lloyds Bank in the evenings over in a village called Street. That week was a blur what with cleaning each morning, then college all day long before the bank cleaning and shelf stacking three nights on the trot that week. I loved it though knowing I was earning a lot of money, but never losing my agenda to work in the media eventually by hanging on to my college course. Matt seemed really happy too. I felt like Matt and I were powerful couple doing the things we really wanted to do and I'd taken to long showers every morning to keep me alive and alert first thing to start each day.

Saturday finally came after my first week at the bank. I still had to clean in the morning between 6am and 8am but I decided to have a relaxing day of pampering. I ran a lovely hot bath when I got home and put in load of bubble to soap myself up. I'd put on the radio in the living room so I'd had some lovely music to listen to on Orchard FM and stayed soaking for a long time. I glided my hands all over my body with soap taking my time shaving my armpits and legs in the bath after shampooing and conditioning my hair. Then just writhed around feeling blissful and content before standing up under the shower to wash all the chemicals out of my hair. It was nearly noon by the time I got out and was feeling hungry. I had lunch and was watching telly while doing the puzzles in the TV guide by the time Matt got home.

Matt and I spent the weekend going on long walks in the sunshine and visiting our parents which felt bliss.

On the Monday during my A-levels film studies lesson we were talking about ghosts. I told everyone that on my copy, that I'd taken off the telly, of Three Men and a Baby, there was a boy standing in a window of whom shouldn't have been there. The moment occurred when Ted Danson's character and his characters mum walked by this window. Apparently the editors tried to cut it out but couldn't. Mr Selby looked as though he knew that one and I felt proud of myself actually knowing something the rest of the students didn't know.

In another lesson we watched typical music videos that we discussed as exploiting women. I didn't see it that way as far as I was concerned these women knew what they were doing. Laura inwardly made me laugh after seeing a Natalie Umbruglia video of Torn of where she was in her sweats as she pointed out that men saw her as sexy. Her confusion made me realise that she was still a virgin. Laura was only about 16 – 17 years old bless her, anyway whereas I felt like a twenty-two year old wiser than her years'.

It was February 2nd and in the morning Norm, Fiona's current beau showed up happy and horny looking. He was tall, dark, handsome, and stockily built and with a big grin on his face took Fee outside. I'd been sat by the front window and noticed a little red car outside that Norm was showing her around. I got curious, why was he looking at what I though was his red car with her.

> *Ecclesiastes 7:25*
> *I was determined to find wisdom and answers to my questions.*

When they both came in they both had red fat beamers. Fiona had just been given a car for her birthday at thirty five. They'd only been together for less than a year but I thought it was a bit over the top but sweet. Fee was happy though that was the main thing.

That evening we had an early birthday party of where we all gave presents and cards before the two love birds went to go out clubbing. They seemed good together. Apparently him being a Libran was a good sign for her Aquarian attributes.

The next day Matt and I were enjoying the throes of the honeymoon faze of our marriage and we decided to have some fun in the afternoon before I went to work after he'd come home from the bakery. We had only an hour together but bloody well made the most of it.

The following afternoon Matt decided that our food and drink reserves were getting low so we decided to do our quarterly shop to Lidl's. Matt played his part in looking for freezer foods. I looked for what could be my lunch for the next three months at this stage it was Super Noodles and tuna chunks that I liked to stock up on. Matt grabbed loads of cans. It always came to between thirty and forty pounds well within our budget.

We had some money free that weekend so when Matt finished putting everything away he sat at the dinner table and counted out some money and he reckoned we had enough to go away for the weekend then put the money back in our cup in our drinks cabinet. I had flowers, chocolate and a card that night.

It was Valentines weekend and I had to pack our clothes that evening into a great big blue bag his mother had given us. I stuffed in a lovely little flirty dress intending to go nightclubbing and we stayed at the Alexander Hotel on the sea front. It was a lovely day wandering around and in the evening we went for a lovely meal at the Ship Inn overlooking the harbour then we went nightclubbing at Rendezvous of where we danced all night long.

In the morning we'd heard there'd been a stabbing that night just down the road from us which seemed surreal as you don't expect it on your doorstep do you. The day was lovely and sunny as we walked to the amusement arcade after breakfast and making phone calls to parents on the sea front. In the arcade we got two pounds worth of two pence and put them in the two penny machines. We played together with each of us making all three slots covered to make the coins drop off the moving shelves to collect bundles of ephemerally made tokens that were ten in a bundle.

We'd had enough of Weymouth by midday and stopped off at West Bay, then Lyme Regis to play golf and to wander round the harbour before going home.

In the week I had to walk into work in the morning as Matt was in the bakery and I had a flat tyre on my bike so it had to stop raining for me, but I still had to put on my yellow rainy day clothes that was fluorescent.

In work I'd been greeted by a Margaret opening the supermarket doors and she said, "Morning Karen. How's you this morning? Alright?"

"I'm fine thanks," I said then, "You alright?"

"Oh. I'm alright," then Ange piped up from nowhere,

"We got to do a lot this morning they've emptied the warehouse for us. Do your usual first Karen."

So I got the big blue floor brush to go down and up the aisles with, then got the mop out while Margaret started in the offices and Ange used another brush for the warehouse. I always finished with the buffing machine and hoovering the produce aisle mats and the front door mats.

In college afterwards for part of an into work project there had to be an assignment on interviewer and interviewee tactics and I was put with a girl that was a bit plump and with black hair called Claire. Now we had to sit in an office on our own to get the atmosphere right and the interviews were based on our dream jobs. I went first to be interrogated. Claire asked me that if I was behind with my work would I choose it over my sister's wedding day?

I said, "No. I could catch up in the morning and still make the wedding in the afternoon." Claire called me arrogant and I was just being honest.

Job 33:3
All my words are sincere, and I am speaking the truth.

It didn't endear me to her very well and I never went through with interviewing her.

Pumping up the tyres in the afternoon on my bike I got it working again. I got it ready for the next day to ride it in, in the morning. My pride had stood me in good stead that day as I'd left Claire aghast in that office after abandoning our interviews. I made up what I would have said to her and what her pretentious answers would have been. I believed while in the library I'd done a bloody good assignment.

I'd thought about this as I came inside and sat quietly eating a curry Matt had cooked before going back out for the evening at Somerfield to do some shelf stacking until midnight. Thank God it was a Wednesday my last evening working day of the week.

After a very restful night's sleep I got up noticing that the bike my mother-in-law gave me that I knew was seen pounds from a market had the chain slipping off again. In my yellow rain suit again I put the chain back on and wiped the oil down the yellow pvc clothes. As I cycled across Safeway's car park and up the hill the chain slipped off again, so I had to stand there on the pavement putting it on again, but it wouldn't stay on this time and ended up pushing it towards Street. Finally giving up with it by Pomparle Bridge I ended up throwing it in a hedge and abandoning it there just to get on in to work. I had a whirlwind of two days running around enjoying the exercise at work.

Then that Sunday Mum gave us a ring in the morning saying there was a barbecue in the evening for Eve's birthday.

I'd said, "Great. We'll look forward to it." I turned to Matt and looked out the window at a clear blue sky. He apparently had been planning a walk over to Wells and back that day. Now because of the barbecue that very evening Matt drove and parked up at Mum's in Misburg Close into Shepton intending to get back in time for Eve's birthday.

We set out in the fields behind the St Peter's hospital walking through one high grassed field by an old ram shackled old barn weather worn by year of abuse from the weather. Then into another field where cows usually were but luckily not that day. I only assumed they were in another field all together and was pleased I remembered that bulls are colour blind and always go for blue. The third field was closed off by barbed wire leaving a thin path by the hedges filled with berries that we kept picking along the way and eating. We went over a bricked stile to a field of where I'd remind Matt each time that my family had carved our initials into a tree. Then on through a field called Friar's oven, a place used for fly tipping these days, from Shepton and on the way back across the fields on the other side of the Shepton/Croscombe/Wells road we got lost coming back and ended up, in the dark, by the mast, I decided to tell Matt to ask the next person we saw for directions. At the top of the road there was a house that I had the nerve to knock on the door of and I said, "Excuse me my husband and I are lost can you tell us how to get back to Shepton?" And they said to walk down the hill to the right road. On the way down I noticed that we were in Croscombe and we knew the way home anyway and were unhappy we'd missed Eve's barbecue.

Jeremiah 25:10
I will silence their shouts of joy and gladness.

The next day as I walked into work in Street with Matt the air was so cold I came down with a bad asthma attack, wheezing really badly and seeing the frost in the air as I forced air out of my lungs. This was about 5.30am with Matthew waling with me as he'd daren't use the car that morning because of the ice on the roads. He told me how he worried about black ice getting the vehicles that were very few and far between about to skid off the roads very easily into possibly bad accidents. I was in so much pain into work. I'd felt like ice when I turned up. Margaret opened the door and said, "You look blue in the face. Karen sit down in an office for a bit and I'll make a cup of tea to make you feel perky again."

Ten minutes later I felt myself to be able to get on and work. At college later there'd been a lad on my course called Ben who'd so called was working his last day on his studies as he was leaving for a job set up by his girlfriend's dad. I judged him and thought, "Well done," eventually through my condescending way of thinking that he used common sense but wondered why he gave up the course anyway that day in particular as he was a month away from gaining a certificate. He'd obviously put all the hard work again and that why? Sprang up again in my mind causing my brow to crease.

After I got home Matt drove us to his parents' house and I went over next door to them because I preferred to talk to his Nan, Evelyn, of whom was full of stories about her glory days of working with her son who was day released at Millfield School. It was lovely sat listening to her scenarios of how she got on with everyone she worked with and made really good friends with them all. It had been a Friday and when I saw Matt he reminded me of a party we were going to the following night that I'd been looking forward to.

In the morning I got up slumbriously and yawned realising it was nearly five thirty am. I needed to be in work for six o'clock. I threw on my clothes and raced out the door with my trainers on. I walked really fast all along the main road to the roundabout by B&Q then raced down the hill into the bottom of Street. I just made it in time for work at Somerfield. I'd finished by eight o'clock and raced back home.

All morning I pampered myself by having a long bath and took all day to find out what I wanted to wear.

By the early evening I had in my mind's eye, to wear, a very shiny dark blue short flirty dress. I got out after a shave and washing my hair to a warm home to put on my dressing gown. In the living room I dried my hair and had the hallway mirror on the floor to put on make-up too. Feeling gorgeous in my outfit with my hair up I put on my pink jacket. Matt wore a smart checked black trousers and had his gorgeous black hair slicked back.

We had a taxi booked to go down Tor Rugby Club and once there we walked up the stairs to the dance floor and bar. Hit the drinks first we moved over to the tables and chairs together and talked to a gang of girls. I even sat down with them in a bid to get to know them but they didn't speak much so I danced and sat down for a bit and Matt was with a gang of men talking to them. Twirling the drink in my hand I wanted to get on the dance floor but as no-one else was up dancing I sat there waiting for my chance. A young flirty couple got up to dance for a fast song. I kept watching Matt who'd come over to me to ask if I'd wanted to have another drink. I asked did he want to dance. He said later. I knew what he felt. There were loads of people sat down and asked him which one was Jed with the card on the table. She was a big girl in a crowd beginning to fill up the dance floor so I got up and gave it to her saying, "Happy birthday." Then Matt and I danced all night.

Two days later on a Monday after college that day I walked into the Clarks office and at down with a blonde bombshell called Georgina. We got on well. I told her that I was at college studying everything to do with the media. When I mentioned my surname she asked me if I was related to a Genge she knew in Bristol. I stated that, that was only my married name and as far as I knew I could have been. Then she started bragging that her son belonged to a famous pop band called Reef and I could start straight away and was taken to the canteen to be shown my new job. They showed me where the power points were for the hoover and buffing machine and told me what the pink, yellow, and green cloths and buckets were for.

A whole week went by swimmingly well as I threw myself into my jobs and college absolutely loving being in love with life and my husband Matthew.

That weekend I came home from Kwiksave cleaning for quarter past eight and Matt was still in bed and he told me to get packing. "We're heading off to Minehead," he'd said.

In the car the fields passed us by and through a couple of towns, then by some more fields there was a sign to Bradley Green that I fixated on feeling haunted by that name. We soon got to a farm. That first time there was a scare of foot and mouth and by the gate was a tray of water filled, with what I knew, of disinfectant. I knew from the telly I had to wash my shoes in them, but my husband never bothered. There had been a 5mph sign halfway down the hill so we had to slow up going all the way to half way down the second field. At the caravan we pulled up and tried the door. Matt had trouble with the key and had to jangle the key around for half an hour before we could get in. We looked inside and noticed a nice clean caravan with two small sofas that we knew were two small beds.

Abandoning the caravan to take off somewhere we went straight into Minehead and we parked up in Tesco's car park and wandered into the supermarket for a cooked breakfast. We ordered a big version with three of everything. I'd had brown sauce that I put on all my food. It tasted delicious.

Jeremiah 44:17
Then we had plenty of food, we were prosperous,
And had no troubles.

Then we went for a walk out towards the harbour and on the pebbles I saw quite a big duck that was bright and colourful with a red beak. Matt called him a shell duck. I liked that so did Matt. We walked round the corner from the pub and realised that we couldn't get very far that way so found a path up the hill through the woods. It was lovely.

Tired and hungry when we came back down we went to the local bakery and had some nice sandwiches, cakes, a packet of crisps and a drink that we took round to Blenheim Gardens and lazed out on the grass. Then Matt fell asleep and I snuggled up and put my head on his belly to do the same. Then his snoring actually lulled me to sleep.

When we woke up I needed a pee and went to the ladies. Afterward, through the park, we walked up a lane at the top of town through a park of where we passed couples, children, people with dogs and we chatted, cuddled and kissed. Matt and I had the whole evening planned out to go for a meal at seven thirty pm at a restaurant called the Wheelhouse.

At nine o'clock we'd finished eating and I wanted to go clubbing. We found a club and Matt didn't want to go in so Matt and I went back to the caravan. We played cards for a bit mainly a game called shit head until the wee hours of the morning.

The next day we went round Dunster castle's grounds after a late breakfast and had a lovely day. We went on home after that.

After college the following week Matt and I were off nightclubbing together. I'd had my dress-up and so did Matt. Then I put on my knee high boots to head towards Abbey Barn to pick up with a coach. I had to flash my student card to get on it and Matt had to pay.

I had no idea how far Crewkerne was but we were on the coach for a long time. As soon as we got there Matt got the drinks while I hit the dance floor and he caught my attention to get me to go to him and get my drink and so I did. I wasn't really interested in the drink and just danced for most of the evening until Matt told us to go outside and wait for the coach. We stood outside with Lee just chatting nicely until we got home.

The next day we got up quite early and decided to see Matt's Mum and Dad in the Methodist Church over in Street. This was the first time I'd gone to a Methodist service. The service was very nice as a lady called Dorcas stood up and said the sermon and led the following prayers. There was a piano player, and Elisabeth the minister. She led the communion with prayers of where I learned a new version of the Lord's Prayer. I was used to saying the trespasses but they called it sin in theirs. During communion I had a laugh with Sue over the wine she'd said, "There is no wine only blackcurrant juice. I met the flute player called Julie afterwards with all of them.

On that Saturday morning I got on the bus to go over to Street, Clarks Village for my new cleaning job. I got given a cart with a bin on the side and with cleaning cloths and cleaning bottles in the tubs. I had a dust pan and brush as well as a mop and bucket I got issued at the main head office. I'd been given orders to go to the three lots of toilets on the outskirts of the shops and just wait if someone was in a cubicle. I pushed my little cart through the crowds and to the latrines. I had to do the toilets one by one in the morning then have an hour's break so I went to Burger King and ordered cheeseburger and chips. The end of the day came quite quickly at five o'clock.

At home I jumped into the shower, then settled down for the evening with a yellow jumper I'd been knitting for Matthew. It had to be big enough to go over his body as I stitched it all together. I tried it on him afterwards and he said he looked like a banana. He obviously didn't like it. I did the same the following day round the village until I went home.

On the Tuesday that week I went into Kwiksave to clean between 6-8am before going off to college that I'd been looking forward to. I loved my job that paid for our holidays as the money went into the Building Society that was to pay nothing else. Matt had convinced me to have a separate bank account. I'd never had one before.

It felt lovely though at college learning all about putting together a camera manual and recording a show for a radio station. Then I had lunch out on the grass round the front of the college which was chips and curry sauce. It was lovely lazing out and dreaming of getting my certificate. I was looking forward to getting in the media business and going to university.

After lunch I had to research my future educational establishment but got into a tizz as my tutor told me to specialise in one area but I bloody loved all of it, even the technical sides.

After college at five o'clock I'd walk to Clarks HQ to clean the offices with my head in the clouds. Then I went to Lloyds bank as part of my job with MITIE Cleaning. Afterwards I'd gone home for tea before going over to Street again to do shelf-stacking for Somerfield. I loved the physical exercising the job gave me.

Then in the morning I went to Gladys in Street she was a lovely lady and I got to hear about her baking days and the two husbands she'd survived over at West End. I loved her to bits as I happily hoovered, dusted and got told how to iron. I didn't mind that and she told me once that the sun would shine on everything I did. I knew what she meant and felt lucky.

That evening I'd been back in Street again shelf stacking with Somerfield. I'd gone up town that afternoon with the rent book and council tax book that I love to pay off with my money.

The next day was general election day and because I'd studied all about the Natural Law Party and made a promotional video, leaflets, badges and their manifesto I decided to vote for them. Afterwards I'd noticed nine people had voted for them all together. Most people took the piss out of them for encouraging levitation.

It was exciting going up to Bristol on the bus one morning to work with not only a reporter but a photographer called Toby Melville for the day.

Matthew 5:12
Be happy and glad, for a great reward.

In the offices a handsome man with black hair introduced himself as he darted out from the editor's office. Being early in the morning Toby was keen to get on with things so we jumped in his car to go to Ashton Gate. Knowing Matt would feel jealous that I was at Bristol City's grounds. I walked by the massage room behind the stands. My eyes nearly popped out of my head as I saw some extremely fit half naked men laid out on massage tables. Toby soon dragged me passed out to the bleachers. There was a player sat outside that I'd had my photo taken with as I stood behind him draping my arms round his shoulders. In my favourite green Jaeger skirt Matt had bought me and a silky red jumper I posed with a Bristol City scarf I waved above my head.

Then we met Gary Johnson the manager. Toby and I both took a photo each and he interviewed the new manager.

The next stop was to a lady's house of where we parked outside on the road. She was going through a court case so Toby took a photo of her and all the paperwork to be used to back up her case. I thought Mr Melville was one smooth talker.

Afterward we had to make one last stop at a posh house with nice grounds. Pulling up on the gravelled driveway Toby and I made our way into a grand hall to a table with a buffet laid on for the press. I tucked into the soft sandwiches. In the hall a lot of chairs were laid out for a press conference. Not having a clue what it was about I let all those around me talk as I gazed across the grounds out of the window.

Back at the press office Toby went to do our photos and I sat at a computer with a picture of the editor on that everyone was modifying so I'd made him look a little bit fatter. Toby came back saying that my photo of Gary Johnson was better than his and that the paper were going to use it.

On the Tuesday I set off with another photographer. We went to a balloon factory of where I'd been photographed standing under a huge green dog but not much else happened.

The last three days with The Observer I spent in the office laughing about headlines the reporters came up with for stories. I remember one story of how a motorcyclist got hit by a slow moving ice-cream van. The headlines they came up with were really funny. I'd been left with the task of taking the messages left by the emergency services of the stories we were legally allowed to print.

> Matthew 5:5
> Happy are those who are humble.

I loved the camaraderie of the reporters as we'd go off to the pub next door together to have a lunch and a drink. I really enjoyed myself that week.

Chapter Eighteen

I was in the toilets cleaning at work one day when one of the men, who I normally talked to, came in to the ladies to talk to me. He'd said it was his birthday and asked me if I could kiss his cheek as it was his birthday, which I did. Next thing I knew his tongue was in my mouth and he groped me. I looked up at his crinkly old neck and he reminded me of a turtle with an ugly face. I'd felt violated and was very glad when I got home that night. The first thing I did at home was to jump in the shower to wash his hands off me. I was in the shower for two hours and when I got out I didn't feel that much better. Mat saw me pushing my body into the sofa really hard to get this pressure his hands had left on me off.

After some loving from my husband when I told him what happened I finally felt so much, physically better. It felt like my husband had healing hands.

That evening at Somerfield I was putting everything out in the health and beauty aisle when I spotted idiosyncrasies with the products and realised that customers had put them in the wrong place. I soon emptied my cage and moved everything around, faced everything up and had time to help someone else so they put me in the freezer department. They needed to throw a lot of goods away and I complained to the manager about people not doing their jobs properly and wondered why I couldn't be supervisor as I would have made sure everyone was rotating the stock properly. I was told to get on with things, so I did, and it stuck in my throat that I couldn't change things.

That Saturday after work all day round the toilets in Clarks Village it was getting me down about all my cleaning. In the end I'd had enough. I'd felt thoroughly shattered having to do three lots of toilet all day long.

Job 33:19
God Corrects people by sending sickness
And filling their bodies with pain.

The people were irritating me still going in and out as I was trying to do my job three times a day. Turned out I'd had a nice evening relaxing at home in front of the telly.

The next Monday morning I went straight from my supermarket cleaning job to college to rest for a bit of fannying about on the computers completing some work before going to Clarks HQ in the afternoon. This was where I'd cleaned the canteen and the toilets then got told to go over the science room. I wondered why it was called the science room as all I saw were COSHH posters and a man testing a pair of shoes for their reliability. I put my head down and got on with mopping all the aisles between the desks. Then I cleaned the toilets waiting for the floor to dry. I mopped the toilet floors last before grabbing a buffer. I couldn't control it very well as I kept bumping into the walls worried that I was making dents. Then I looked up and saw Georgina, my boss, of whom said, "I'll show you how to do it Karen." and instead of hurting my pride I worried about my boss not having any faith in me and she looked very frazzled and pissed off. I thought that she was on the verge of a nervous breakdown. I let her finish my job and then asked her if she was ok. She said that she wasn't and I resolved to myself to work harder for her so she wouldn't break down.

After work I met a woman who was Italian but spoke nice English. She was short, thin and dark haired, and very pleasant. Her name was Pina. I met her as we were all picking up our wage slips for the week.

When I was on my own with her I told Georgina that I couldn't work on the weekends as it was getting all too much what with cleaning every day in the mornings, going to college, and in the evenings I was at the bank and also shelf stacking late at night three days a week. She said that, that was fine and that I looked very shattered. I had to go home for tea before going back out again to the bank and then Somerfield's.

The next day was the same and on Wednesday, my study day from college I found myself knitting draught excluders while in front of the telly. I got to the point where I'd started to stuff my own snakey as I'd called my draught excluders and I wondered while finishing mine for the living room what colour to use in my spare room. I thought of the bobbly wool being used for scarves that were all the rage. The wool I got that afternoon was bobbly and purple with differing shades. I spent a whole afternoon feeling very pleased with my spurt of creativity.

Then the next day Matt and I went away to Bowleaze Cove, for a week off in a caravan for our wedding anniversary that my in-laws took to Bowleaze first just for us. That first evening Matt and I dressed up. I was in one of Mum's old best dresses that I was determined to wear a lot of times on this holiday. We went to the Ship Inn for a meal upstairs I was going to go for a stroganoff and Matt took ages over choosing. A he did so I felt more and more uncomfortably out of place as I felt too posh so we walked over the bridge to a pub we had a nice meal in for our first wedding anniversary. It turned out to be a lovely romantic evening. We discussed going over to Brownsea Island one day on the coach and we discussed seeing Bobby Davro at The Pavilion on the Saturday.

The next day was a Friday and we booked up two trips with the local coaches. One to go to Brownsea Island and one to go near the Swannery for a brilliant open air dance in some fancy gardens. We then finished the day booking up for Bobby that evening. As it was only five o'clock we went back to the caravan. I tried to initiate sex but Matt didn't want it he'd said, and I quote, "You're too loud Karen," and I felt less of a woman a I couldn't seduce my own husband.

Bobby Davro was a blast as I'd deliberately had seats in the front row and low and behold they picked women from the front row to get on stage. He asked each of us where we came from and he made a joke about each place. Bobby even tried the Somerset accent at which I burst into giggles.

On the Saturday Matt and I got up early to catch the coach to Brownsea Island. I was wearing a long sleeved velvety dark blue top and red trousers. My hair was long enough to go over my bum. We found a pebbled beach on this island and paddled my feet. We then found a clearing in some wood. It was hot that day and we made passionate love in our secluded area. I took a photo of Matt looking beautiful enough to paint as he looked very happy.

The following Monday we lazed on the beach for a while and went for long walks and in the evening when we went back to the caravan we then got changed for an evening out. We jumped on the bus over to Weymouth and went to Rendezvous a night club by the harbour. We found out, Matt and I, they were doing a karaoke and I was in a dark blue velvety shirt and my red trousers and they thought that I was a talent spotter as I'd overheard a conversation between one singer about to get up and sing.

On the last day there we got up early. Had breakfast then went on the seafront so that we could phone our parents telling them when we'd be home. Matt and I then went to a French market near The Pavilion in their car park. There were cheeses to sample and different breads like baguettes and croissants to try a little bit of with soft butter to make up ourselves. We stayed there for the most of the morning. then we jumped on the bus back to Bowleaze to get our stuff and go home.

The next day I'd been cleaning all day and by the evening I was feeling a bit lonely so I gave Martin, my ex, a ring from Lloyds bank.

> *Job 30:29*
> *My voice is sad and lonely as the cries of a jackal*
> *Or an ostrich.*

My cleaning regime was very smart so I relaxed to hearing that old familiar voice. I felt all grown up talking to him asking, "Are you married now?"

"No. I haven't got any children either."

"Are you still in your band? And do you still live with your Mum?" I'd joked.

He said, "Well yes and nowadays I play the guitar and sing in America from time to time with my old band."

I'd said, "That sounds exciting. What work do you do now?"

"Well I'm a lorry driver."

"Just like my dad," I'd thought out loud. We talked some more and then I realised I hadn't done the glass in front of the bank clerks. I'd done them so brilliantly till they shined. Then Matt came to the bank to pick me up.

The next afternoon was a Saturday and Matt told me to meet him from work as we were to walk over to Tor Leisure together to see the cricket. Once at the bar I chose an orange with lemonade with ice. I just fancied it and Matt had a driver's shandy. We then took the drinks outside to sit in the glorious sunshine to watch the cricket. We didn't talk much but when we did it was either to talk about the game or Matt wanted to talk about work. We just sat there lazily to the end of a very drawn out game.

The next day, in the morning, Matt and I jumped into the car. We were excited about a holiday to Weymouth. The car pointed towards Ilchester, then Yeovil, out onto the wide A road, round the hairpin bend and down towards Weymouth. I'd bought some lovely clothes and Matt bought his fishing kit.

We got to the Alexander Hotel after wandering past a lot of no vacancy signs. Outside the Alexander two notices caught our attention. One said fifty pounds for one night and the other promised a second night at half price if you didn't stay for breakfast. We told the proprietor about our early start for the ferry next day to go to France.

Now one whole day went by really nicely. Then the next day we had to get up at five o'clock for the ship to take us abroad. The water was calm on the boat to France our passports were needed as we alighted we only had a few hours to wander around a walled town. In and out the shops and into a café for lunch, by a Bastille and then went to the nearest beach before travelling back to Weymouth.

The next day we went to Chesil Beach with Matt's fishing kit. I sat and watched him. I felt really proud of him reeling in mackerel.

1 Samuel 2:3
Stop your loud boasting; silence your proud words.

We went home later on that day. We fell out with the hotel proprietor because he made us pay out for two nights and wouldn't go with his own sign out on his wall. We resolved never to go back there.

Getting ready to go out that Friday evening I dressed in jeans and a tight shirt. Matt looked smart in jeans and a nice purple dress shirt.

In a cab we turned up at the Unity Club in Street of where Matt got out for skittles and I'd had a peck on the lips before getting Pringles and going to the Methodist church hall for a night with my in-laws to take part in a quiz.

The hall was at the back of the church with a wooden flooring that was large. Then I went towards the noise at the back of the hall in a long carpeted room. Sat down Bob held court with the quiz as the master and we all had a good giggle as some of us just blurted out silly answers that shocked us by being correct sometimes. The serious ones took too long to answer.

At about eleven o'clock we went outside and we saw clubbers queueing outside Maxine's waiting to get in and I went up to the Unity Club for last drinks before going home with Matt.

The next day I went to the supermarket as it was open again as Kwiksave for me to go to work again as a cleaner. Now as I approached the front door I could see a new whole fruit and veg section and there was a blonde haired tall lady who looked a bit dotty putting the produce out. Ange met me at the door to take me to the staff room and introduced me to Jo so I said, "hello. How are you?" and we got chatting. That day I felt like tidying up at home after my first day back at work before slumping on the sofa to sit down to some knitting. I picked up a white jumper I was creating for Matthew. I'd put it all together bit by bit carefully sewing the separate sections all up by using the knitting needle. I'd hooked up the loops through each side of the sleeves and knitted them together loop by loop creating a new loose finish before turning it in the right way again. Which I did for every seam to put it all together. I felt pleased with the overall look as it looked like a nice big cricket jumper for Matt. Then he came home lunch time and I tried it on him but it had to be squeezed over his head as the neck wasn't big enough so he whinged. I had to throw it out, but I couldn't let go of it.

That evening Matt and I were off out to a pub in Meare by the railway to attend a skittles weekend with our carnival club. When we turned up I had a pint of Thatcher cider and sat at the bar with Matthew right by the skittle alley. Mutley put our names on the blackboard for eighteen of us who'd come out for a skittles weekend to play killer. He put on the board three lines by our names to represent three lives for each player. The first one who got up had to hit the front pin to stop from losing a life and one by one we had to hit pins down to avoid life losing until there was a player left with one life still on the board and ironically it was Mutley's son who won called Paul. Now we knew they were doing this again on the Sunday evening to raise funds for the club as each player had to pay to play.

I'd picked up several Christmas cards that weekend and finished stringing them up along the back wall behind the sofa. I was proud of three strings lining that wall full of our cards that I stood there and read from friends out at Walton, Clarks HW, Kwiksave, family and Matt's workmates. There were hundreds of them and I had time free to put out the Christmas trimmings to hang in a criss-cross shape across the ceiling using blue tack. I had some lovely dangling ornate hangings that I stuck to the ceiling. Matt came home that afternoon and we went to B&Q to get an expensive spruce tree to put up in the living room of which I whinged about knowing that it would eventually make a mess. That was how I got Matt to get an expensive tree that he'd said the needles wouldn't drop so much and I trusted him completely.

By the Wednesday I was off work for a few days. Come the evening Matt and I dressed up to go to a restaurant in Coxley called The Riverside. It was Christmas Eve that evening, and just before we'd come from the church in Shepton from the service by candlelight that was lovely and romantic singing my favourite carols and having watched the Christmas story being played out. That meal had been lovely and while we'd been there we'd discussed going up to the Methodist church for midnight mass back at Street. We went back to Bob and Sue's afterwards and stayed awake with them in the living room for ages while bathed in a golden glow for most of the night but Matt's parents nearly had to go to bed early. By eleven thirty we got up and went down town to the Methodist church of where we parked by the Golden House restaurant. There was hardly anybody in there and it was a lovely bitter sweet service. We had a good nice kip that night when we got back to my in-laws.

In the morning dressed up in my flirty little boots I sat on the left hand side of the aisle and looked up at the numbers and I sang fifty three which was a marching hymn. I sang it louder than anyone else standing on my own. Over in the other aisle there was a lady I didn't even know yet but I'd overheard her bitching about Maxine's idea of leaving the church open all day. I'd thought that she was thinking somebody would be stealing. We were praying down on our knees during the Lord's Prayer. In my head I was thinking of the person next to me and offered their inner prayers up to God.

Maxine's service was all about St James section on about love. I farted intimately no-one even looked my way. Furtively my eyes darted about I wished I hadn't done it.

> *Psalms 39:2*
> *I kept quiet, not saying a word.*

In my mind's eye I was already getting up to get my coffee. Before I knew it I'd been there and talking to anyone who'd talk to me.

Next weekend driving towards Weymouth the radio was blaring and I had been singing along thinking I'd sounded fantastic. It was probably what made Matt put his foot down a bit more though. We'd reached the treacherous hairpin bend. I'd put Shania Twain's 'Come on Over' album on the stereo listening to our song, 'Thank God We Made it' and my words were dreamily sang as eyes closed lazing in the sun warming me up through the windows.

I'd opened them again as we ground to a halt at the Lodmoor car park. Matt and I held hands along the promenade opposite enjoying the warm sea air. We both needed a drink and headed for the Co-op to get a Dr Pepper each and as we were using the same numbers every week to do the lottery we'd bought a ticket on the Wednesday before and got it checked. We were surprised to be handed seventy five pound so it was decided we'd stay the weekend in a bed and breakfast. On the seafront in Bedford House we'd enjoyed a cooked breakfast the next day talking about where'd we'd explored and what Matt and I had done the day before and how I'd danced all night at Rendezvous. It was laughter about the girl who'd lain out on the bar to have a sex on the beach that stayed with us that morning. Matt had to call his Mum on the seafront and Sue told us that she'd been about to go to the car boot sale at Ilchester with Tom, Matt's brother.

Matt and I loved wandering around the town, then to the harbour to watch the fishermen, then out to Radipole nature reserve to spy the differing species of birds and ducks using the scopes in the shop.

Along through the shops afterward we stopped at the fish 'n' chip shop we'd called Mambos by the bridge. It was lovely sitting on the harbour wall in the sunshine that evening with our food. Satiated and happy we wandered on the beach towards Bowleaze and back then found the car so that Matt could still drive in the light back home.

Ever since I'd heard that I'd had a cataract I had always been paranoid that I was going to have to wait till my eye sight in my left eye was to go completely before they did anything about it, but at twenty three I wanted to get places. I had my whole life ahead of me and I wanted to be able to drive. I kept on to my optician to help me get my cataract removed so that I could go on and see again. After much pressure Mr Springett, my optician, said that he'd write a letter to my consultant Mr Luck saying that my quality of live would improve from the removal.

Matt and I would set the alarm for half past seven to be able to speed down to Weymouth at 8 o'clock by going through Street and out to Somerton and Yeovil and onto a very fast road to take us round a very sharp hairpin bend and on into Weymouth after driving by the famous Old Spa pub and Lidl's.

When we got there we'd parked up at the largest nature reserve by the houses into Bowleaze. It meant we could walk straight round the reserve to look out across the reeds and the lake looking appreciatively for wildlife.

Genesis 40:14
But please remember me when everything is going well.

I secretly said thank you to God for it all. When we'd finished looking round at the edge of the reserve there was a bush full of little golden coloured bull finches. They looked amazing and we'd almost got scared off by a swan in our path but Matt and I waited for it to move back into the water. It was awe inspiring to see how many different birds there were.

As we got back to the car we drove to the Lodmoor car park and put a ticket on for the day. It had been a lovely stroll along the promenade passed the clock and up to a little café on the seafront of where they served us a lovely cooked breakfast and a cup of tea for me and coffee for Matt. We next hit the arcades and we each had a pot of two pence and played the two-penny machines trying to win the packet of tokens or the car key rings. We'd spend at least an hour on the games not spending much before heading off round the harbour across the bridge and stopping to look out over the Quayside. I loved looking out over the boats and as we passed to the other side of the bridge it was twelve o'clock and the road started to rise into the air to let boats and yachts in and out.

Hand in hand we'd walked into Brewers Quay and had a look round the indoor shops in the precinct. It was nice not feeling any pressure to buy and just have a look. As we came back outside into the glorious sunshine Matt and I held onto each other to walk past the bottom of Nothe Fort to see the fishermen at the end of the pier. Matt would always have a chat with them to see how many fish they'd caught and we always stopped to see them reel the fish in.

Back round the other side of the harbour we walked through the shops and I'd got some Mills and Boon books from the charity shops before progressing to where the sweet old couple were selling their pasties. I'd had a lamb and mint one and Matt had a Cornish one which we carried up to the seafront with our purchased Dr Pepper bottles to have while sat down on the beach looking out to sea. Matt lazed out on the sand afterward so I cuddled into him and we had a bit of a snooze. I woke up first and walked down to the shore to have a paddle and when I looked up Matt was awake.

We never rushed anywhere in Weymouth so by the time we got off the beach it was about five o'clock so we hit the chippy by the bridge and ate our fish 'n' chips on the wall by the harbour. That side of Weymouth was packed with people sitting outside the pub with pints in their hands and there were a group of lads diving off the harbour wall into the water. Everyone idly watched and when we'd finished our tea we took a leisurely stroll back along the seafront to the car and make our way home. I put on Shania Twain's 'Come on Over' cd in the car and I sang to all the songs as we watched the sun gradually get lower in the sky back towards Glastonbury.

Next Saturday in the morning Bob and Sue drove Matt, Tom and I off to Minehead. We hit Blenheim Gardens and posed for a photograph. I was wearing jeans, t-shirt and a hat. We played golf and Tom was getting over competitive which I didn't like. Swinging my golf club I was getting frustrated with myself.

Job 6:11
What strength have I got to keep on living?

Matt, Sue and Bob just took their time and Sue gave her usual girlie laugh. I'd felt a real part of this little family as we sat having a picnic in the park afterward. It started to rain and we headed for the car to wait for the rain to stop.

We went round the town afterwards to have a drink outside a café in the midday sun where Sue told me she preferred the café's toilet for me to go to before leaving for home.

It had been a Wednesday a gloriously hot summer's day. Matt and I got up early and headed out the door waling hand in hand together peaceful at times, chatty the next towards The Rifleman's and down the little lane to the river. Cuddling at times with my eyes sparkling up at hi, the trees, the bushes had a green vibrancy of colour. Coming to a bridge on a corner we looked out across the fields deciding to push on to Barton St David and Baltonsborough by which time we were hungry. Popping into the shop buying sandwiches, crisps and a drink which we ate making our way along the road I worried about how much I'd been eating. Thinking of my weight all the way back into Glastonbury.

I used to walk into work at Kwiksave to clean in the mornings just a stone's throw away from where I lived. I loved the fact that I could just take two minutes to get into work and two minutes to get home again two hours later.

One morning as I walked to work in the pitch dark something quite big caught my eye. I had initially thought it was a cat. Next thing I knew two wild dogs ran at me and started barking really loudly. I froze terrified if I made to move their ferocious barks would get worse and that they would move closer.

Isaiah 32:11
You have been living an easy life, free from worries;
But now, tremble with fear!

I felt trapped. I couldn't move. Next thing I knew there was a man's voice shouting at them and he called them off. I felt so relieved. None of the dogs had leads.

Thank God for Lee calling them off me, he'd said to me afterwards that he thought the dogs were mine. Why would my own dogs turn on me? If they were mine I'd have known how to control them surely?

When I got home Matt and I drove off in the car towards Somerton fisheries with two fishing rods in the car with one wedged by my front seat. When we parked up in the top car park, the fishing box, my chair, the food bags and the rods had to be taken out and carried across by two ponds one being the match lake to the canal pond.

We'd set up easily putting our reels on the ends of the rods, threading the line through the eyes and then secure the bale arm for enough thread to put the floats on first then the size twelve hook and the weights on last. Two by the float and one halfway down the line. Matt had bought me a pint of maggots and they wiggled around in my hand as I put them on my line. Casting was easy and I soon relaxed and enjoyed catching the little rud and roach counting as I went along.

Ten fishes in I'd felt like I was doing well. Matt caught a large carp and we were both putting our fish into keep nets. Not worried about catching any large fish every touch I'd had I'd caught more and more fish. I had called them little minnows and after twenty five fish caught I was well away. Matt had three large carp and glanced across at me to smile, talk, and occasionally share a kiss. Twenty fish later with the sun starting to go down over the water creating silvery lines. I didn't want to stop. Matt had enjoyed catching ten large carp going back and forth to the Match Lake and in the end as it was starting to go cold I'd counted fifty six caught fish and Matt had, had enough. We tipped our fish back into the water and packed up.

I had still felt as though my future lay in Bristol but every time I thought of that place I thought of Martin. I felt like I was going crazy. I had a wonderful husband and a place I could call my own in a town where it felt like I was on holiday, but that's just it isn't it? Holidays are not meant to last.

Romans 15:32
And so I will come to you full of joy, if it is God's will,
And enjoy a refreshing visit to you.

I put a letter for Matt to read on the computer half hoping he wouldn't really see it about how I thought my life should be lived somewhere and with someone else. All I could remember was, was that Whitchurch had felt like home.

I got on the bus and ended up at Cribbs Causeway. What on earth was I giving up? A marriage that's what and every time I thought of Matt I wanted to cry feeling disbelief that someone had actually wanted to marry me. I calmed down going round the shops and brought a phone from the Orange shop.

Outside by the buses I rang home for Matt to come and get me. I was going back to Glastonbury. I mean you can feel some where's in your future but in the moment I wanted to go home. Matt actually turned up at Cribbs minus the car. We had to walk into Bristol to get the car where Matt had abandoned it with the window down. Matt was very upset, he'd seen the written note attached to the computer telling him to switch the computer on and read the note. When we got back I actually felt relieved he never read it but I did notice that the cabinet in the bathroom had been ripped of the wall and in the living room there was a massive dent in the wall behind the sofa, of where a chair had been smashed. This shook me up to see how violent Matt could be.

Deuteronomy 1:21
Do not hesitate or be afraid.

Thankfully he hadn't aimed his violent side at me.

I tried to talk to him that I loved him but wasn't in love with him. That I saw our love as a real love, rather than an 'in the stars' love. Matt never actually understood what I was on about, so I would turn to reading my Mills and Boon books more and more as an escape to remind me that I could have carved out a major career for myself and really been somebody someday but it just wasn't meant to be my reality.

One afternoon I'd been in the scientific block of Clarks HQ, there were many posters on the wall to do with COSHH of which I thought was about chemicals. The floor that I had to wash was not very wide between long benches nailed to the floor that I couldn't move. All I had to do next was buff it up and I kept hitting the wall. I could hear a man laughing. I looked up and we got talking all about shoes and how they should be bought brand new every three months as the material retracted inwards or expanded over time which ultimately turned them into the wrong size for your feet. He also knew my Uncle in law, Uncle Mike, from on my husband's side and I told him that he was in the Middle East somewhere again working as Clarks never let him retire. I wished I had a job like that.

Psalms 73:3
Because I was jealous of the proud.

That evening Matt and I got invited up to my Mum's for tea. We were told that we were having fish. I thought lovely and was told we'd have kippers and I knew they smelled very powerful, but I told my Mum that I'd never had any before. She said that was fine.

While we were there the fish came with a bit of bread and butter. Matt picked the fish up and ate his as a sandwich with the bit of bread. I went to take one mouthful and was glad I looked at it first as it was full of bones. I sat there for an hour dissecting the bones just so that I could just eat the meat. My Mum kept going in and out of the kitchen tidying up wanting my plate to wash and she'd asked, "Haven't you finished that yet?"

"But it's filled with bones Mum and I want to eat the meat."

"Everyone's laughing at you, you know that don't you?"

"Whatever Mum. This meat is nice."

"Ok," Mum said, "But make sure you put it in the dishwasher afterwards." Which I did and I smiled to myself thinking that had been nice but never again and everyone had a laugh and a joke once I jointed them in the living room.

The next day on my lunch break at home it coincided with my husband Matthew's lunch break for once. He steamed in and went straight for the kitchen chopping things up rather loudly while I was trying to listen to the news.

"What are you chopping up?" I asked.

"Bananas," he said, "to make a milkshake."

"Ooh. Have you got ice-cream with it?" I said.

He said, "No."

So I replied, "Well why bother when you can go up to the supermarket and get a nice milkshake off the shelves?"

Matt deliberately pushed the button on the loud blender instead of answering me.

"It's healthier this way," he shouted, "Would you like some banana milkshake?"

I'd said, "Hell yeah," but was not looking forward to cleaning up the blender thinking I could cut a finger on the rotor at the bottom of the large jug. I looked up at the brekkie bar in the living room and saw my Weetabix box and smiled. I wanted to cut out the tokens on the side and the order form to get my Chicken Run characters that were basically beanie stuffed dolls. I'd been collecting them for a while and knew that postage and packaging were going to have to be paid. It was to be four pound to get hold of all the main characters that I thought would make great collector's item for myself.

The next day it was a Saturday and Fee came round to take us to Bristol shopping and we got on the bus, but before we did I encountered my ex, Martin, of whom had gotten a little bit fat and said hello. I spied a yukky green coloured Skoda parked by the pavement.

I'd said, "Is that your Skoda?"

He said, "Yes. Are you just off shopping?"

I said, "Yes." then we walked on and had a good shop round the high street then went for lunch at a nearby pub that seemed kind of quaint in an ultra-modern city. We had a wonderful meal and decided to look round a few more shops as I really wanted a dress of which eventually I found. Then Fee and I went to the Park and Ride bus and while there we got talking to a dear sweet old lady who said that she wished there were two women in her family just like us. I wondered if this sweet little old lady was actually my ex, Martin's mum. The bus soon came and Fee and I soon got on our way home with several purchases that we both felt pleased with.

I enjoyed a nice evening when I got home and Matt and I discussed going to Weymouth the next day.

In the morning, nice and early, we zoomed down the road and was soon parking near Lodmoor's nature reserve. It was still early as we walked round with our binoculars but were transfixed by a cormorant that was rather a tall black, heron shaped bird, of whom had struggled with eating an eel. You could literally see the eel struggling to get out of the bird's neck and his head kept popping up outside of the cormorant's mouth. Matt and I, especially me, wished we had a video camera. I could have made a fortune selling that clip to a studio making a nature video. the struggle between eel and cormorant took for ages and I just smiled they were in the middle of a lake right in front of us, so close we didn't even need our binoculars.

That afternoon Matt and I went into a pub along the seafront. We ordered some drinks and I leaned back comfortably into Matthew to watch a game of football on the large television at the front of the pub and ended our day at Weymouth when the game was over and we were soon on the road again.

Next afternoon I came home from work and I had lunch. I'd seen the lady upstairs son, coming back from Somerfield of where he worked. The flat was nice and quiet all afternoon while I read a book before going out again to work over Clarks.

When I came back that evening I was shattered and dying to go to sleep, but in bed that night all I could hear was sixties music pounding through the ceiling.

1 Corinthians 13:5
Love is not ill-mannered or selfish or irritable.

I moaned to Matt and he didn't want to do anything about it so I shouted through the ceiling till he heard my voice and shut up.

In the morning when I went to clean I saw this lad in work who'd had his music on above us all fucking night.

It was a Saturday that day and after cleaning I'd been itching for a bath and a shave and rushed home to have one. I turned on the taps and had lots of bubbles after washing up a week's worth of crockery and hoovering. It was nice lathering myself up and shaving myself thinking ahead to a part that afternoon. Matt came home on a break, sat down, and had something to eat and asked me what I was going to wear for the barbecue that afternoon.

Come lunch time I had a bowl of chicken soup with Matthew. I'd dressed in a nice blue summer dress.

Around five o'clock I went to the far side of our court, then to the bottom of town, up Fisher's Hill, then to Bere Lane, then to my husband's boss, Andy.

We had lovely cheeseburgers on the front lawn and I felt relaxed and at ease talking to Matt's work mates and met Dave and Theresa, a nice couple Matthew worked with. They were nice to talk to and I latched on to them and they told me that there was a ghost in their house. It sent a shiver down my spine as I traipsed through the house to the toilet. It wasn't long afterward from out in the sunshine that we went on and said our goodbyes. It had been a lovely evening.

In the morning it was a Sunday and Matt and I got into the car and went to Baltonsborough. Once there we jumped out and got to a burger van set up by our current carnival club The Dolphins. We got inside it and Matt with a man called Alan set up the food. Matt got the onions going, the other man did the burgers and I took the money. All day long we were rushed off our feet at the flower show. Hundreds of people came and went all day long in the gorgeous sunshine. I had no break all day and felt euphoric at actually being busy.

At the end of the day Alan and I took out the money and we counted all together. We were amazed that roughly we took eight hundred quid.

I went to work the next day in a good mood laughing my head off hoping no-one would make me feel embarrassed and I found old style pub glasses in a box by Kwiksave. I picked them up on the way home afterwards. I then went for the bus to Mulberry. Afterwards I came straight home and went round the Redlands Estate to see my friend Margaret for a chat and I saw her dog, a red setter. It was a soppy dog and we had a cup of tea and a long chat about our families. I sat there for ages talking about her husband Mike as well.

Later on that evening I spoke to my sister Eve on the phone and she told me she saw Robbie Williams and had sat down in a VIP seat that Lulu came over and told her off for sitting down on but Eve wouldn't budge. She met Robbie afterwards and couldn't get over how short he was.

The next day at work I couldn't resist phoning the press and told them the story.

Now two days later I saw Eve at Shepton Mallet Leisure Centre and she was mortified. She told me that the paper rung her and she couldn't lie about her fracas with Lulu. I'd upset her she'd said but we got passed it.

The next day after cleaning in the Kwiksave supermarket I went for the bus to go to the Mulberry factory. Now when I walked by the monument and Heaphy's I bumped into Matt who'd finished work early. I felt like explaining to him that I had a Cinderella syndrome. I was cleaning all the time but felt like I could do so much better.

I got on the bus and started nattering to a young girl about her life and her children. I felt oddly down hearted as the bus glided to a halt by Walton church. I walked by the shop and down to the Mulberry factory. I got out the hoover first as always and talked to everyone as I hoovered around their desks in turn. I soon cheered up. I was soon at Matt's Nan's for lunch and enjoyed her company. It had been a lovely day.

In the morning I had my usual Weetabix as I was collecting tokens for Chicken Run character toys. I got my eighth token, which was enough, to get all characters and got excited by this. I then went to go cleaning at the supermarket and afterward posted my tokens by the bus stop to go to Mulberry. I got to go through the end of line box that day and found a wallet and a belt for Matt's birthday. It cost me five pounds. I was pleased with myself.

I was soon at Matt's Nan's in Street for lunch having vegetarian pie with eggs, noodles and cooked tomato. I went cleaning for MITIE at Clarks HQ afterwards and had a laugh with the office staff. One man said he had an engineering degree and had a job in Clarks just booking up hotels for sales reps, because he had a degree it put me off looking for work in the offices there. I felt like I was good enough. I went on a computer at Lloyds bank that evening and looked at some auction sites for houses and realised that even the cheapest houses would need a lot of money to do up. The evening was a blast and I got the hoover out afterwards to whack round downstairs and upstairs. I then got the duster out to wipe the desks and counters. Then the glass partitions got wiped clean. I did the toilets next and finished early. On the way out I locked up then I went to Barclay's and did the same thing. I soon got home for tea that my lovely husband Matthew cooked, it was fish, mash and peas. Then I had a cup of tea. Matt pointed out I needed to get on and finish packing for our holiday the next day.

At the Turkish airport we were supposed to have had a car to take us to the hotel but one never showed up so Matt and I had to jump in a taxi. At the hotel we found the ride had cost a lot of money so a receipt was kept to show our rep to see if the money could be refunded. It was the middle of the night when we got to the top of the hill and the wind was howling. The next day we found a mini-bar in our room and we'd made a pact not to use too much from it as it all looked expensive.

The best parts of the holiday were spent on the beach but under the trees on our loungers, there were a lot of bugs. I wasn't impressed, so an exploration of our surroundings had been on the cards.

At the harbour there'd been a camel that I sat on to pose for a picture but the man with our camera told Matt to get on too, to ride by the water. I spied a nightclub walking round afterwards and asked Matt if we could go. I wore my wine red Donna Karan looking dress that very evening and had gotten on the stage at the night club for a drinking game while looking out over the harbour as it was open aired.

The day after we'd gone to a Turkish market and a man managed to put a necklace on me trying to sell it, but Matt said we weren't interested and they took it off. I did buy a couple of black CK jeans though.

On another night at dinner we got talking to a man named Harout of whom we played cards with one evening after waiting ages for him to finish his tea. We'd first met him in one of the bars in town and he'd been impressed with my singing, 'All I Wanna Do' by Sheryl Crow. He called me cool whereas Matt got mistook for a local lad yet again.

On another evening Matt and I saw some belly dancing in an open air location we'd gotten to on a coach. The wine was free and I'd gotten thoroughly puddled and was taking money out of the dancer's garments who'd been dancing on our table. When they called for tourists to come on stage to take part I did really enjoy myself. Back at our table there was a professional photographer taking photos of us with Turkish hats on and we received the picture straight away which I hid so as not to pay for it.

The last day while Matt and I were wandering round the town I'd gotten a Turkish fuma which was a little pitta bread wrap with lamb in and bits of salad that I sprinkled chili peppers all ground up in,

I'd really thrown myself into that holiday and so had Matt, in his way, and at least we got refunded for the taxi when we got back.

This blonde lady came up to me one afternoon at home on the forecourt and started talking to me.

I said, "Hello."

She said, "Hello my name I Susie. I know you don't I? I've seen you about." We got into a lovely conversation about her life story and how she was a hairdresser once. Then she asked me for advice about what to do with her life. She tried many things even all sorts of counselling including the local Holistic Centre. I tried to explain to her several times to just choose one thing and stick with it. She ran off at the mouth and I knew her head was stuck in the brambles, so I tried again to convince to just keep trying as hairdresser as it was obvious that she loved it. Then the woman looked like a light bulb moment went off in her head and she said, "Thank you."

I think I finally got through to her as she left. I thought that it was a weird conversation to have with some random lady desperate for advice and thought maybe word had got round that I was a fixer upper.

Leviticus 19:34
Love them as you would love yourselves.

I went indoors feeling happy I'd helped someone and the next day after work I found myself round town doing a bit of shopping.

I walked into the opticians for a check-up and had a good result about my eyesight from Mr Springett. then on the way out I bumped into Sheila Gardiner outside Desmond's solicitors. We said hi and she asked me if I wanted to work with her again in the evenings cleaning at Desmond's. I said yes. Then we reminisced about how we got together over Kwiksave and we both moaned about how we were still cleaning. I found myself confessing of how I'd love to change the world and she said, "I know how you're feeling."

"I like to think I'm my own Superhero doing nice things for everyone without them knowing."

In the back of my mind I felt like Superman. I then made a date with her to start working in the solicitors and was pleased with our meeting.

"It's my 25th birthday today." I'd said and Sheila said, "Well happy birthday to you. I must get on, John, my husband will be waiting for me."

Job 16:22
My years are passing now, and I walk the road of no return.

I said, "Bye. I'll see you again," and walked on. I smiled inwardly and looked forward to going out for a meal that night. Matt said, "We'll go to Tom Moggs tonight," I liked the place and knew we were going for a carvery. My mouth salivated with the thought of it and knew that I'd have my favourite hot chocolate fudge cake with ice-cream for pudding.

Now when I got home I had a long shower and lathered myself up. In my mind I had a long velvety navy blue dress and some nice earrings. The only shoes I could think of wearing were heeled sandals that were the same colour. I knew I had some lovely make-up and I took down the hallway mirror and put it in the living room in front of the telly with the hair dryer and spent ages primping myself. My hair felt soft and fluffy. Then I carefully put the brown eye shadow on with the brush. I tried to put mascara on lightly but stung my eye. It still worked but I had to dab my eye with a tissue. I put lippy on and a bit of cheek blusher. I felt proud of my appearance.

Deuteronomy 8:14
Make sure you do not become proud.

Then I heard Matt stamp his foot and we went out for a lovely meal.

A few weeks later it was Halloween and Matt and I had been invited to a party at one of his colleagues from work, houses over in Street. We drove over at about nine o'clock and there was a Frankenstein's monster mask on the front door. I let out a nervous giggle as I entered the house and creepy decorations were everywhere. Like big spider webs dangling down with black spiders on. There was a couple of pumpkins about with crazy faces in them. I shivered and loved the ghoul costumes everyone turned up in. I felt the skeleton costumes were the creepiest as I went into the kitchen for some alcoholic punch. Matt stood around talking and I felt the only thing left to do was dance. There was no music though so I went upstairs to the toilet and jumped out of my skin a there was a scary face on the toilet door. When I went back down I felt I had to talk and talked to Andy, Matt's boss, and it was a very good evening.

The next day Matt and I found ourselves over his Mum's in the afternoon and his Dad, Bob, asked me if I wanted to do a job for him. I said, "Yes. I'd love to."

Then Sue came in with a lot of selection boxes and told me to wrap them up. She put the pile of thirty on the floor and said they were for the boys and girls at Boys and Girl's Brigade. I had the wrapping paper given to me and I had to ask for the scissors and Sellotape. I sat there on the floor and took my time diligently wrapping them up. Matt's Mum asked me if I wanted a cup of tea and a bit of cake. I said yes and got a piece of lovely coffee and walnut cake. I sipped the hot cup of tea and soon finished it between nibbling the cake. It took me most of the afternoon to finish wrapping and felt really pleased with myself when I finished and mentally gave myself a pat on the back.

That evening Matt and I got on a coach outside the Methodist church to go to see Beauty and the Beast at the Bristol Hippodrome. The costumes were amazing. The evening was wonderful and we all came home happy. I was looking forward to seeing it again the following week with my parents.

I had a good working week. The time flew by and I knew that deep down I loved my cleaning jobs. They kept me physically fit running around lifting all the heavy black bags about.

That Saturday morning the air was fresh and as I walked home from Somerfield I whistled, going home, a happy tune after talking to Margaret and saying I'd go round her house later and see her red setter and was looking forward to seeing her husband Mike. I popped home first to tidy up and whack the hoover around. I had a week's worth of washing up to do. I loved doing it as it made my hand feel lovely and soft.

I was soon round Margaret's talking about her family. We had a cup of tea and her dog looked soppy. I told her I was going to see Beauty and the Beast that evening. We laughed and I was soon on the way home from the Redlands Estate happily whistling again.

That evening Matt drove us up to Shepton to get in my parent scar to go up to Bristol. We chatted in the car nicely and Dad got lost up a side street and made a horrible noise with the gear shaft. I jokingly said, "Crank that shaft Dad." My parents were not amused.

> *Lamentations 5:12*
> *Our elders are shown no respect.*

Then Mum piped up, "You know your Dad takes his driving very seriously. He's a class A driver." I wanted to laugh again but I daren't.

The show again was still enthralling. The sets and the music were amazing and wonderful. I loved the story of a beast turning into a wonderfully handsome man with the aid of true, true love and we all went home happy.

Two days later I was soon back at Clarks HQ doing the hoovering round the offices. I loved to chat with the office workers and do the polishing at the same time. I soon whipped round the kitchen with a cloth, mop and bucket. Then the toilets, before I emptied the bins and had to start again upstairs. I dragged the little Henry up the stairs and stopped short looking at a load of dead flies in the windowsill. I felt sick and looked for the nearest socket to hoover the flies up quickly. No way on God's earth was I going to touch them with a cloth. They were soon gone but I still found myself wretching in the toilet later as I went in there to clean. I grabbed a cup from a water cooler and squashed what I felt. My tea later made me feel better at home.

The weekend soon came and I was happy coming back from Somerfield at eight o'clock. I got home all revved up to clean all over the flat and the weeks' worth of washing up. I had a light blue shift dress on a Matt came in off his lunch break and felt me up at the sink. I inwardly smiled and finished what I was doing. I turned my head to give him a kiss.

Genesis 29:11
Then he kissed her and began to cry for joy.

"We're going up your sister's," he said and I said, "Give me a mo." And he nuzzled my neck. It tickled and I felt lovely in my dress showing off my legs with my trainers on feeling like a 80s American chick.

At Fee's she bugged me and "Why don't you want a house? Your flat should have been a starter home. I'd have gotten one by now and don't you want a garden?" I wasn't bothered but I was irritated with her comment.

Proverbs 10:26
She will be as irritating as vinegar on your teeth
Or smoke in your eyes.

I enjoyed the freedom of just having my own pace in my little flat. I loved it.

Chapter Nineteen

The next day I was in Somerfield cleaning, the other staff were all standing around talking. I got irritated seeing as I always put my head down and got on with work so I put down the hoover and joined in. They looked surprised but happy because I was talking to them. Ange came out of the offices, who was my boss, and said, "Can you put the hoover away please and go home. We've finished for the day."

Later on that day I was at Clarks headquarters being introduced to our new supervisor Lesley. I felt put out, I was educated, had been to college and couldn't work out why I couldn't have been the supervisor.

Now I'd been cleaning in the offices at the time when Lesley and Bernice walked through and I heard Lesley talking about a twin sister of whom was brainier than her whilst running herself down and I thought why, yet again, she got to be supervisor. I felt jealous.

Genesis 4:7
If you had done the right thing, you would be smiling.

I had gotten talking to the office staff again.

Later on that evening I was cleaning in Lloyds bank and used the hoover all downstairs then upstairs and I got curious upstairs about a book in the window. It had been entitled Emotional Intelligence. I knew straight away that was me. My emotions had told me all my life to go with my gut and everyone knew my exterior was an intelligent one because I always went with my gut feelings. I flicked through it briefly and realised that I didn't need to read it and put it back to get on with my work. I polished afterwards, did the toilets and put the rubbish out ready for the bin man the next day.

After work I told Matt that I wondered what oysters would taste like as they are supposed to be an aphrodisiac.

Matt said, "We'll try them another day."

The next day I was working hard slogging away at cleaning, loving the exercise looking forward to the evenings carol service with the Wednesday Wives at Matt's Methodist church.

At the church we all loved to sink al the classic carols depicting the whole Christmas story and Matt's favourite song was 'Come and Join the Celebrations, it's a very special day'. We parroted the lines over and over again and Matt and I both loved it. Then the wonderful service was over but I was happy sat next to my in-laws and their friends. The church was warm with carpeted floors and traditional pews of which I loved.

Friday came and I was soon back up the bank singing a tune to myself while lugging a heavy hoover about and putting dust up my nose spraying polish everywhere. My nose was irritated and I kept sneezing like I couldn't stop. I went to the toilet to get tissue after making my head hurt before using window cleaner to clean the clerks partitions to the public. I took the trouble that afternoon to print my CV to give to the bank as I felt that I could do simple maths and had the qualifications as I'd re-sat mathematics and felt shit hot at it.

Now at the beginning of the evening my favourite female member of staff took my curriculum vitae and I felt very optimistic hoping to get out of my cleaning jobs at last.

On the weekend I'd had a lovely time having gone out with Fee shopping in Yeovil getting some things for Christmas.

Then on the Monday working in Clarks office, workers were moaning that the handles on their doors weren't being cleaned. I thought they were being sad and laughed with a journalist over the phone at work about this.

Then a week later it came out on the page of the crossword puzzle. It said that the staff at Clarks were moaning at door handles needing to be cleaned and I felt vindicated and laughed my head off at them being shamed. I got work from the head of the canteen called Sarah. A cash in hand job and was there when they had their Christmas lunch of where they were giving speeches. I stopped to listen wondering if they'd say anything about the snippet in the paper, but they never. I thought that they'd be mortified. It didn't matter and afterward I went on to clean the canteen after getting fifty quid, cash in hand, from Sarah for helping serve food and wash up.

Now back up the bank that evening I spoke to my favourite bank clerk of whom was working late again and he told me that I had a nice CV but they weren't recruiting at the moment. I blushed, and thought at least I'd tried. Wiping my snotty nose I went to clean in a different order, as she stayed, to do the toilets first so as not to be in her way.

On Christmas Eve, Matt and I stayed up Bob and Sue's to go to midnight mass at the Methodist church. It was a good service. I loved it. Afterward I had to sleep in Tom's room on a camp bed right near to the floor that looked like it had never seen a hoover with bits all over it. I'd been really worried about my allergies to house dust and house mite.

Early in the morning everyone got dressed and the family and I sat round in the living room after breakfast waiting for Bob to play Santa and hand out gifts. Matt's Mum gave me a very lovely silky pair of pyjamas that I knew I'd never wear. We stayed for lunch and I helped wash up.

On Boxing Day Matt and I jumped into the car and headed towards Wells as we said to one another we'd follow the hunt. Out on the road heading towards Priddy we soon picked up the trail of traffic we assumed was doing the same thing. It was a long queue and we looked over the hedge and saw the men and women in their jodphurs and red jackets, white shirts and black hard hats cantering on the horses across the fields. I could hear the dogs barking and for a laugh I put on a cd I'd bought Matt for Christmas called 'Who Let the Dogs Out' by the Baha-Men and we had a bloody good laugh while stuck in the traffic, all following the same thing. We followed the hunt all morning and really enjoyed ourselves with the window rolled down blaring that tune over and over again. We soon made our way back to Matt's Mum's for lunch to have some yummy salmon. Then we got from his parents something we called a Bosnia box full of groceries for our kitchen. We just laughed and ended up having a lovely week off work together before New Year's Eve.

That Saturday evening Fiona and Steve picked us up from home. I'd primped and put on a lovely red dress with knee high boots. Matt poshed up with trousers and a new shirt to be taken to Weston-Super-Mare.

At the seaside we parked up along the front and looked for a bar to have a drink first. We found that everywhere was packed so we went into a pub. Queued for ages and I had a Malibu and lemonade. The bar was loud and we soon drunk up before going to the seafront and the Winter Gardens for our dance. In there the hall was huge and I noticed that it was mostly filled with older upper middle class people who seemed aloof but capable of dancing. There was no-ne at the bar and everyone was on the dance floor and we had a bloody goodnight.

In the week Matt and I decided to go to Weymouth even though the weather was bad. We parked up early and decided to doge the rain by going into Wetherspoon's for a hot chocolate each with all the works, but they didn't have marshmallows so I was bummed.

About eleven o'clock we walked out round the shops for a while then went to the promenade. There was loads of people about on skateboards and rollerblades and bikes. I ascertained that there was some sort of protest in the pouring rain and devil may care me ran through the middle of them laughing.

At two o'clock we went to Mambos for fish 'n' chips and felt mortified when they didn't take cards. I had to sit in the restaurant for ages when Matt went down town to get the cash back from Tesco.

I don't know why but I couldn't keep still as we went home early and contorted my legs on the dashboard of the car as the music blared off the cd all the way home.

Now that day we saw a removal van outside our flat and we introduced ourselves to a young couple moving in above us. They seemed nice and then the next day when I had the washing on in the kitchen I noticed a leak through our kitchen ceiling, passed our fluorescent light. We got worried and Matt went upstairs to tell them. They said sorry and got hold of their landlord for us and he told Matt to just bill him for the repair work. We got

Uncle Cyn to come down and fix the ceiling and he billed us for more than we paid to show their landlord that he claimed on insurance for to give back to us.

In the morning I went into Somerfield to clean with Marg and Ange and I'd gotten to know a Jo who worked in the fruit and veg section. I came home and witched on the telly to watch my favourite American shows on Channel Four; 'Everybody Loves Raymond', 'Frasier', and 'Friends' before getting on the bus to the Mulberry factory. I hoovered up all the loose bits of cotton, zips and material off the floor under the sewing machines before cleaning the toilets and polishing the foreman's desk who was Jane. Paddy was her assistant who was very nice.

Then I went to Nan's for my favourite vegetarian pie and Matt picked me up after work.

Later on I got dropped at Clarks canteen to wash the floors, hoover and clean the toilets. Then I did the same in the offices, then walked over to Lloyds bank in the high street to clean.

The next day I was up at 52, Beech Avenue to see Fee for her birthday and in her back garden I started to pick up dead branches on her lawn and putting them into bags. Fee made me think when she sarcastically said, "So you are useful for something then."

No-one had mentioned to me before that I wasn't useful. That was all I'd ever wnt3ed to be someone my sisters' could look up to. I didn't realise that before that the simplest of tasks could make me feel needed.

In the morning Matt bough me in cheese on toast with hot chocolate in bed and he also gave me a card. It was Valentine's Day and our fourth anniversary of our engagement.

"Life is a bowl of cherries," I said, "Some people are sweet, some are indigestible but when put together everyone is lovely in a piece of cake." That was in the morning. I went into the living room and there was lovely carnations in the fireplace. In three vases. I gave him a card and a great big sloppy kiss and a teddy for me to wear for him to enjoy that morning.

Later on that day we had kinky sex of where I'd played the teacher and he was the naughty boy. I sent him to the corner of the room on his knees. I left him there, then writhed all over him afterwards.

> *Leviticus 18:19*
> *Do not have intercourse with a woman during her monthly period because she is ritually unclean.*

The next day we went to Weymouth in the little YAK because I called the car that over the licence plate. It took us only forty-five minutes and I flashed my breasts, played with myself and got Matthew all turned on in the car.

At Weymouth we went round the wildlife places called Lodmoor and Radipole with our binoculars and saw a lot of birds. We also went on the beach. Matt fell asleep for two hours. We went for another walk out to the end of the harbour and saw the fisherman until three o'clock. On the way back we went back up the hill towards Nothe Fort and walked over the coastal path to see the naval base till we got to the steps to lead down to toilets. We then went to Mambos as we called it to have fish 'n' chips by five o'clock on the harbour wall.

I'd thought a lot of the parishioners at St John's church and enjoyed the services. Now one morning I sat through a lovely service and near the end I prayed for Maxine the vicar who had cancer.

Afterward I had a phone call that day from Fiona, my eldest sister saying that her and Steve were taking my husband and I to a concert that following weekend and all week it was all I could think about.

Matt and I, with Fee and Steve, turned up at the gig in Newport and at the door there was a man with an entry list.

Fiona said, "We're on the list under Eve's party."

"Who's Eve?" They said.

"She's our sister of whose boyfriend Matt is very tight with a member of the band."

"So what is your names?"

"Fiona, Steve, Karen and Matt Genge."

"You're right. You're in," and we had a lovely dance all night to Toploader and we went mad over the song 'Dancing in the Moonlight'.

In the car on the way home we finished a huge box of Terry's chocolate orange segments.

That week at work I was asked to fill in for somebody on holiday of whom worked for Barclays bank back in Glastonbury. I'd done my usual hoovering right through, polishing, especially the glass partitions and then cleaning of the toilets and kitchen as well as taking out the rubbish each evening.

I got home Friday evening full of energy and had a lovely shower and put on some jeans and a floaty top. Then Matt and I went out with his men friends to The Bear and I said to Nick "What do you think of the latest female opera artist Catherine Jenkins?" and he said, "She's got a gorgeous body," and I knew that he didn't appreciate opera so didn't pursue my questions of opera music. The men laughed and I just felt mortified. I thought that I was the hottest girl in the group. I joined in all the sex jokes the men came up with and felt sexy all evening until Matt and I went home.

On the Monday I went to Clarks canteen and in the men's someone had pooed in the urinal. I did not want to touch it so I kept filling up my bucket with water pouring it over the top setting off the urinals jet stream each time. It had gotten rid of some of it but not all of it so in the end, with my gloves on, I picked it up and put it down the toilet to flush away. I had to wash the gloves and my hands several times afterward and really sprayed the wall as well as the urinals with nice smelling disinfectant. It left me feeling disgusted.

> *Ecclesiastes 1:3, 4*
> *You spend your life working, labouring, and what do*
> *You have to show for it? Generations come and generations go*
> *But the world stays just the same.*

When I got home there was a letter from the tax man for me and I opened it. I couldn't believe my eyes I had a cheque for £400 pounds and the letter explained that I had been paying too much tax.

The next day I put it into the Post Office to build up our savings and in the afternoon Matt and I cosied up on the sofa to watch Man Utd play Chelsea. Now Matt and I had noticed a trend that when Man Utd played it was boring so we ended up having sex on the sofa.

That evening I put on my knee high black boots with a short skirt on and Matt and I went out with his mates around Street. We started off at The Unity Club and I had a Malibu with lemonade. One of Matt's mates called Mark admired my boots and openly called them kinky boots. We sat at a table and chatted happily. Then Julian, another friend, decided to go on the games machine. We all stood round and watched, me, Matt, Justin, Steve and Mark trying to help out with the games questions. We got the jackpot up to a tenner and all had a laugh. I'd kept on shouting out the answers even deliberately wrong ones to make everyone laugh.

Then we went into town and got to Wetherspoon's for tea. Most of us had steak, chips and peas. We stayed there talking for ages, then went back to The Unity Club. A couple of them got really pissed including Matthew. We called a cab and went home happy and tired.

The next day it was the beginning of Lent, so I went to church with my stomach growling. I wanted to fast for forty days and forty nights. I wondered where I could get unlevened bread to nibble on for forty days. By lunch time I felt a bit faint and a little bit sick. I tried telling Matt that I was fasting but he cooked a roast dinner anyway. I felt I had to eat it. I'd had the same delusion every year that I was going to fast.

The next day in Clarks HQ I was cleaning away talking to a couple of men going on about the national census and asked if I filled in my form yet. I'd said that I would as soon as I got home. I was mopping the floor round them at the time. One man told me he had a chalet down at Lyme Regis was he really trying to impress me with a tiny little shack? I had to go on and clean the toilets, by the window I noticed the blood bank had turned up. I dropped my work and went round to ask if I could donate. They'd asked me if I'd had any operations. I'd said four on my left eye. I had glaucoma and kerracatonis. They said I couldn't donate. Then later I went through Clarks museum to dust and hoover and got talking to the security guard of whom I liked and he asked me if I believed in angels. I said that I had a guardian angel who'd been my godmother, Aunty Nola.

I was soon home that evening getting ready to go out again. Matt and I were meeting with his family, his Mum and Dad, Aunty Chris, Uncle Mike and cousins at the Piper's Inn for a meal. I was excited to be included with his family.

Now that week Pete and Karen, friends of ours, asked us to look after their cat for a week and I awoke Matt with a start one night talking about feeding the cat in my sleep. Their cat was called Sylvia and was huge and would sit in the windowsill staring at us giving me the creeps when we'd feed her.

It was soon Sunday again and Matt had a rare weekend off so we got up early to go to a car boot sale at Ilchester. We paid our pound to get in. It was so early the grass was still wet and my feet got wet in my sandals. I wore a lovely summer dress. I looked at all the books and bought ten different Mills and Boon books for a pound and tried to look for a bargain. Matt on the other hand was looking for fishing equipment. We both enjoyed the car boot sale, but I ended up sneezing with wet feet and a bit of hayfever. By the afternoon we went to my in-laws for lunch. I'd been looking forward to a nice roast dinner. I was really hungry and we all had a nice meal. I offered to wash up afterwards happy to be of help. I talked with my mum-in-law as she got me to dry up and Matt and I stayed for a few more hours and had a cup of tea later on. When we went I said thank you for lunch. It had been really nice.

Now the weekends were my washing days for clothes and it was on my mind as Matt told me on Saturday that I'd talked again in my sleep about using the washer-dryer. We just laughed.

Nehemiah 8:10
"The joy that the Lord gives you will make you strong."

Then we decided that Saturday to go to Minehead to have nice long walks, a look around and we went up North Hill. I saw a man acting suspiciously in a fluorescent orange coat and we walked faster to get back down the hill again. Matt and I stayed for tea at the Wheelhouse and I liked the peas. I hadn't eaten any for a long time and Matt found a non-alcoholic lager. It was very nice. Then we went home through Bridgewater of where I played Anastacia's 'Left Outside Alone' very loudly with the window down.

That evening I wanted sex again. We weren't doing it that much lately and Matt said, "Look. If you cleaned the kitchen more and the flat you and I would do it more," I felt hurt.

Psalms 31:10
I am weak from all my troubles, even my bones are wasting away.

I had it in mind to hit into the housework more.

That Saturday night we drove to a very rural area, in a beautiful little village hall. I had put my favourite dress on which was blue, long and clingy. I felt very posh and womanly. It was his evening do.

We'd turned up with a fruit bowl all wrapped up in 'congratulations on your wedding day' wrapping paper and a card ready for a boogie. The hall seemed large on the inside and we placed our goodies on an end table. The dancing started pretty much straight away. I loved to dance and didn't stop till the lights went on for the buffet. Typical party food you know. We got up and danced a bit more while socialising with Matt's friends and saying our goodbyes and thank you's for a wonderful evening. We wished the couple well and made our exit. It had been a lovely evening at Dave's evening do. We were told that they had a lovely wedding ceremony.

Next day turning up at the Highbridge market Matt and I wandered around a lot of stalls all selling Xmas goodies. Delving into all the possible presents we could buy, we found gifts for all the family. Going round the market we came across a meat van of where, out the side, was a man touting for business. All the meat was displayed in lots of rows and everyone bidded for the gammon, beef, turkey, chicken and ham. We bought the gammon, beef and turkey with our Christmas party in mind. Laden down with all our gifts we went back to the car then came back to the butcher to pick up our meat. Handing over fifty quid. We were pleased with our purchases. I wanted to get all the cards too before we made our way home.

In the afternoon Matt's grandparents turned up for a hour for a spot of food and a chat. They said that they liked the sofa even though I'd had to bolster the seat up for Nan with cushions to sit on as it was low down. They enjoyed being with us before going home. Nan said that our place gave her a very peaceful feeling.

In the evening Bob, Sue, Tom, both my Nans', Granddad, my parents and my sisters crammed into the living room to enjoy our company. Tucking into a lot of food Matt had cooked, Gramp's tucked into a lot of roast potatoes that he praised Matt for. As we sat around Matt's Dad, Bob, got out bits of paper for a quiz and he did a generic one covering a lot of topics. The evening flowed well into the night and everyone went home full and happy.

It was soon summer time again and one morning Matt and I were both excited we were going to the Bath and West for the Truck fest. The sun had been shining through the curtains and the birds were singing. I felt a song in my heart. 'Morning has Broken' was going through my heart. I turned to Matt in bed and gave him a cuddle before keenly crawling out from under the duvet and getting in the shower. Slipping on something feminine I felt beautiful and proud to be with my husband while walking round endless stalls. I looked at the farmers clothes and wanted it thinking I could have anything I wanted with Matthew. Turning to him I shyly smiled upwards feeling a lot of love inside. I asked him if I could get on the ride by the main arena. It was a Mexican Hat. Turning my head sideways I saw a long queue to a black lorry of where the actress Isla Fisher, from Home and Away, was signing autographs. I didn't want to know. Coming off the fairground ride, wobbling a bit, feeling happy I heard that actress doing the announcements and we settled on the grass to watch the monster trucks and the motorbikes. This day felt wonderful as we snuggled in together.

In the morning I got up and went over to Street on the bus to do my work for the day and at lunch time over at Matt's Nan's Bob, his dad, was home for lunch. We all had lunch together that day, Bob, Sue, Gran and Gramps with me and sat round the table by the window and started to reminisce.

"At Millfield while I was there I'd heard that Ian Botham had been at the school a couple of years before and I think I met him once." Said Bob.

I thought cool and when he saw the smile on my face he told me another little story.

"While I was there an Arabian prince had been a student with me."

> *1 Kings 10:5*
> *It left me breathless and amazed.*

Matt turned up after two o'clock and mentioned that our friend Marcus was meant to be on TV on Countdown for two episodes. We moaned together that we were going to miss watching him because of work commitments.

That evening we went back for tea. Afterwards we sat around in the living room having a chat. I sat cosy on an armchair and talked animatedly about Matthew. I said to Bob and Sue, "I'd like to go down to the Methodist Hall and help run the Boys Brigade with you."

Sue came over to me and put her hand on my shoulder and said, "Don't worry all I want you to do is love my son."

"That'd be easy," and I thought that's because he's an easy man to love. I only offered to help out in that way because I wanted my in-laws to see me as an adult and an equal.

On a Sunday evening I turned up at Glastonbury's town hall to join my acting group for a quick last minute rehearsal for the paly Saints' Alive. We had the whole hall to ourselves and we practiced our lines and singing the songs. I felt happy with my role. Two hours later we got in our positions behind the curtains and we all got nervous as we heard lots of people coming to watch us. The hall filled up and there was a drum roll.

When it came to my part to dance around I sang loudly and clearly sang about sacrificing earthly things to his blood. It made me very aware of my lovely Calvin Klein jeans. When it came to my line in the script, though I fluffed it and the lady speaking to me said my line for me. I felt put out that I didn't get to say it and was aware that Matt and his parents never got to see me shine. They said, "Well done," afterward though and went on home.

The next day Matt and I had work and we had a lovely week and floated through it to the Saturday. Then in the morning Matt and I got into the car to go to Baltonsborough flower show to work in a burger van. Matt and I then took it in turns to cook and take the money with a man called Alan. It got really hectic mid-afternoon when I was taking the money and kept on having to swivel my head to keep looking at the prices so that I could add it all up. The nice smells made me hungry so at four o'clock, when it was quiet, we all had cheeseburgers that we had cooked. It had been a busy evening afterward till we had to pack up. I'd loved doing that all day and drifted off to sleep that evening out of exhaustion.

The next day on the Sunday I managed to get my ass out of bed to go to church as I never set the alarm back then and afterwards Matt and I took ourselves to my in-laws for lunch. I took with me a beige bobbly at I took ages to knit to give to my father-in-law as a present. I left it in the kitchen and he didn't seem that keen to want it, let alone wear it, which hurt my feelings.

Psalm 31:7
You see my suffering, you know my trouble.

I didn't tell him that though and stayed for some lovely food of which I emulated them for. I even washed up afterwards and gladly wiped the windowsill down and the cooker.

The next day I went to the supermarket to work in the morning and had a bit of a chat with Margaret while pushing the Clarks machine round washing the floor as she pointed out that she was going to sweep through the warehouse. I happily rushed through my work till I had to go for the bus.

At Mulberry I enjoyed my conversations with everyone as I went to each sewing machine to hoover underneath. I was happy loving my job then went into the toilets to clean and talked to Paddy and Sheila my boss.

Now that evening Matt and I went out to the Lion at West Pennard for a three course meal. I had my garlic mushrooms, my usual gammon and chips with a slice of pineapple, then chocolate fudge cake with ice-cream. Matt had a lot too and was sick on the floor by the car when we went to leave.

The next day in the evening at about five o'clock Matt asked me what did I want for tea. I told him that I wanted to go out for a meal and he said, "Let's go somewhere different." I mentioned the Poacher's Pocket and he said fine.

"Don't you want to get dressed?"

I said, "What's wrong with what I've got on?"

He said, "Won't you be cold?"

I said, "No. I'm fine." But we ended up arguing. It felt like he never understood me because he said, "I don't understand you. You put next to nothing on in the cold and cover up in the summer."

I just smiled and we went to the pub at Doulting and I had game pie with rabbit in it and it tasted quite rubbery but quite nice. We shared a drink and half an hour later we finished and decided to go to Weymouth for the day, the next day.

In the morning we jumped into the car with a picnic blanket and took off for the beach. The sun was shining and I put my hot sunglasses on and I looked in the mirror and thought I looked like a sexy celebrity who'd be on the telly one day. I fantasised about being in the movies.

At the beach I shook my touche as I wandered around hanging off Matt's arm thinking we looked shit hot as I knew Matt and I radiated heat all around all the time.

We did our usual lazing out on the beach. Matt cuddled into me and said, *Proverbs 6:10*

"I'll just take a short nap," he says; "I'll fold my hands and rest a while,"

We shared a kiss and he fell asleep. Then I got out my Puzzler and nearly filled the book. I needed a pee. I wanted to show off my figure on my own but he annoyingly woke up and said "Let me come with you." I really wanted to go on my own. Then later we went for a pasty at a sweet old couple's shop and later we had a boat trip out to see the old marine area and the prison ship. Afterwards we had fish 'n' chips on the harbour wall and I sashayed back to the car to go home.

The next day was a Sunday and we went round Nanny Sheila's. In the corner of the kitchen I noticed loads of Readers Digest books stacked up and Gramps tried to push one on me that had just come through the post. We all thought that he was fucking mad as he only bought these things in the hope he'd win thousands of pounds. He never did though. I had a cup of tea while I was there and Matt had a coffee. I had to remind Nan to put in two sugars for Matt. The news was on the telly and we sat in silence sipping our drinks and I was willing Nanny to speak.

On the Monday I cleaned in Somerfield as the supermarket had changed again. All the cleaning I did that week fucked me off. Then on the following

Sunday Matt and I got up early and decided to go to a place called Ilchester for a car boot sale. We had to pay a pound to park. I felt all flirty in a bra-less dress that was blue and in the sunshine I sashayed around rolling my hips in my little sandals. Matt looked at fishing utensils and I looked at the books and found a table full of modern day Mills and Boon books. I looked through them all. They were only five pence each so I got forty with two quid feeling happy thinking I'd love a Mills and Boon relationship that was perfect between two equals. We had a bacon sarnie while we were there and I thought of the ephemera at home that I'd been sad enough to catalogue all my Mills and Boon books in. It took all day to write out my catalogue of books that I'd started that day of all three hundred Mills and Boon books were in because I counted and in the evening I washed up the day's crockery.

The next day was September the eleventh and I'd been at work all morning but in the afternoon I turned on the news on the telly and saw to my horror the attack on the Twin Towers. It felt surreal as it was like watching a real life disaster movie and I couldn't tear myself away from the TV and I cried at the people's stories of lost loved ones. I found myself going to the fridge for a tub of ice-cream for a bit of comfort eating with my lunch before going to my next job wanting to talk about the disaster with someone to share my grief in my own sweet way of when I'd always start these discussions with a why?

> *Deuteronomy 14:1*
> *"You are the people of the Lord your God. So when you mourn*
> *For the dead, don't gash yourselves or shave the front of your head,*
> *as other people do."*

Mid-week we had a sofa coming our way and Uncle Cyn brought it in a van. He pulled up outside our flat on the Wednesday with the brown pull apart sofa that we were expecting. Nan Sheila was giving it to us for free.

Uncle Cyn and Matthew grabbed the pink beat up old sofa and put it outside under the window as they brought in each part of the sofa.

Matt and I soon writhed around on it later and I fell through the crack as we never put it together properly and it was whacked so we ended up cuddling in front of a football match that was Liverpool and Man Utd. That night we had a good fuck. Then in the morning it was a Sunday and the morning air was fresh and Matt and I had woken up early. The birds were singing loudly outside. It felt wonderful. Matt and I looked at each other and said, "Do you want to go to Highbridge Christmas market again?"

"I'd love to Matt. I need some more cards and stocking fillers."

"I thought of buying some more meat as my mother asked for some the night before last."

I yawned, "What does she need?"

"One nice gammon and pork chops and I want pork chops and pork loins too."

We soon got up there and back with all our goodies and Matt had put a joint on that morning for lunch, so we were soon tucking in to a roastie.

After I washed up Matt wanted to go fishing out at the Viaduct Fisheries. We jumped in the car and Matt stopped off at his Mum's to pick up his fishing kit. He used to take ages to sort his kit out. He'd go through old maggot boxes and just turf them out and I found myself being annoyed by these really bright blue and green bottled flies and they made me feel sick. He also went through his floats and weights. He also had to choose between lines because a lot of them got into a tangle and I offered to detangle one.

Once at the fisheries we'd turned up fully loaded and ready for action. We found a spot at the Match Lake. We looked across and saw Fiona's husband Steve on the other side fishing with someone we didn't recognise. That evening, Bob the knob, Matt's boss, called round at the flat and this was the first time I'd met him. He was of stocky build and blonde with a baby face and he asked if Matt could cover his shift in the morning.

The next day Matt and I went to Street of where I'd got some beige knee high boots from a shop called Aria. It was near Christmas and that evening I was off to have a meal at The Bear Hotel and then to go on nightclubbing. I'd bought a dress that was beige previously from Matalan in Yeovil and in my knee high boots that I bought I went out happy. The Christmas meal had been lovely before we'd queued for ages to get in Maximes. It was me and the girls from Mulberry in the factory and we had a bloody good dance before I got home in a taxi.

The next day had been Christmas Eve and at half past four Matt and I went to St Pauls and St Peter's church for a carol service. We all had candles for a candle lit service and the church was packed with families from all around Shepton. The wax from the candle ruined my shoe so I had to pick at it with nails to get it off. I was nice and cosy in a long skirt, t-shirt and jumper with my knee high boots on. When we went through Coxley, on the way home, we stopped off at the Riverside restaurant for a lovely evening meal.

Matt and I turned back afterward to go to Shepton and midnight mass at St Peters and St Paul's. Once there we got into church with Mum and once there we noticed about five other people dotted about the huge church and Matt and I were surprised when the vicar started the service with the words, "Via occulta this service." I knew that the service was mainly in Latin. I was mystified and a bit bored as there were no hymns either. I didn't even recognise the prayer being said as The Lord's Prayer.

On Boxing Day Matt and I got up early at Mum's and Dad asked if we'd like to see a football match with him and Shepton was playing. Dad stood with us by the guide ropes by the side of the pitch. I noticed a lad who was called John from school and his play was brilliant and he scored the winning goal.

Now it was our annual Christmas party at the flat and Matt had been cooking all day sausage rolls, roast potatoes, pizza and a rice dish. He even made his own coleslaw and had the slow cooker on all day with a gammon joint in. I was looking forward to eating it and it wasn't long till my in-laws turned up. Then my own family. Now Bob had brought another quiz and we had a laugh about the contents of his quiz book. Everything it seemed to me to be about dates as it was history questions and one was about which battle took place in 1066 and I blurted out The Battle of Hastings.

It was soon New Year's Eve and Matt and I had arranged to go to a proper party with all of his friends at a place called Crossways not that far from home. We all took a seven seater cab. I wore Mum's old blue dress with a blue bolero over the shoulder. All night we went back and forth from the bar to the dance floor. In my sheer tights I loved showing off my legs as they were my best feature and I remember a friend of Matt's called Steve drooling all over my legs. I kept on dancing while I watched Matt and his mates having a laugh standing around the side of the dance floor and I remember thinking that Matt was the handsomest man there.

At the end of the evening we hung around for a long time till the taxi cab came back for us.

Next day Matt was in the bath while I sat on top of the toilet seat totally naked and he was laughing at me.

"Come on and get in," he said.

I said, "Yes," and just leaned over his face with my hair flopping in my eyes and was aware of my boobs pushing up against him. I gave him a massive snog and climbed in the bath on top of him. He'd felt all slippery so I had to writhe rather hard on top of him and we laughed as his hands were all over my back. Then he grabbed my ass positioning me so he could go right inside of me. We were so wet and wild it was amazing.

In the morning I'd gone up town to go shopping and to put money down on a deposit for new glasses. I'd had twenty pound in my pocket and went into a shop called Cheap Jacks at the top of town for some boxers for Matt of where Lesley, from my Clarks days, worked.

In the Eyetech shop I walked into put my down payment on my new glasses. I'd fished in my pocket for my note but it had vanished. I went back to the Cheap Jacks and I asked Lesley if she'd seen it. Now because she said, "You shouldn't have been stupid enough to lose it." I knew that she had taken it.

Exodus 32:1-
I am angry with them.

I'd been buying blue and white wool in Cheap Jacks and after tea I started knitting a Wells City mascot using blue and white wool well into the evening.

The next day I went into Wells on the bus and I got off by Keward Close and when I walked by the Priory, a mental health institution, I felt so alive and alert thinking nothing could touch me but a very small part of me was frightened that one day I'd lose my mind. In Wells I went round several shops and met up with my Mother and we had a lovely day together. I'd bought a few things and so did Mum. Now all around town we talked nicely together and shared stories of what we'd been up to lately. It wasn't long before I got back on the bus to go home.

Matt and I had gone to London for a weekend away to celebrate Valentine's Day. When we first got there a double decker red tour bus pulled up and the first thing I'd wanted to do was go on it, but Matt wanted to explore on foot and we found ourselves walking round a massive park that we saw a horse and cart cantering through. At the bottom we found a concrete arch that reminded me of the Arch De Triomphe in Paris and several other monuments I took photos of.

Over London Bridge we came across an aquarium by the London Eye and spent a couple of hours looking round before we decided to go next door for tickets on the London Eye. We'd been walking around all day and were surprised to be standing up in a big bubble overlooking the whole of London. Well that was how it seemed as the glorious sunshine started to disappear over the horizon creating a beautiful sunset.

Back at Covent Garden we had steak and chips and got stung for thirty two pounds each. In the hotel afterward we got dressed up. Matt in trousers and shirt and me, in a long flowing velvety dark blue dress and over it a shirt. In the hotel bar we had some alcohol before heading off for the local theatre to watch 'H' from Steps playing Joseph and his technicolour dream coat. I sang along, in my head, to every song.

The next day we did more exploring and jumped on the underground not really knowing where we were going and got off at Battersea Park and wound up walking round. Matt and I found ourselves jumping in the back of a London black cab and headed back into The Strand of where we jumped out with heads spinning from stories from the cab driver. It was a wet day and we were in our coats and I stunned a squirrel with the flash on my camera in St James Park after watching a carriage going out of the Palace. It had been a wonderful experience all weekend.

That nigh lying in bed, Matt and I started kissing slowly blowing heat into each other's mouth. My arms went around his neck. The heat between kisses got hotter with his hard-on pressed up against me. I writhed around as his hand grabbed me. I turned around he grabbed my vagina yet again pushing my pert ass into his dick. His hands got rougher, and the other hand pressed over my eyes so that all there was, was sweet sensation. I pushed him away and demanded he got on top. Crouched over me I arched my back as far as it could and wrapped my legs around his waist pushing into his manhood. Driving me wild he'd caressed me all over but I didn't want it. I wanted sweet release so my legs moved up his body and wrapped my thighs round his neck bringing his head down to kiss me. Feeling frustrated I begged him to go flat on his back for me to get on top and grabbed his hands forcing him into the bed. Rubbing myself over his penis he naturally slipped inside me and there was an explosion deep inside. There was a stickiness all over the bed and I wanted to bathe myself in it. Matt got out of bed for the toilet and arched his back proudly putting his arms round the back of his head looking like a proud stag.

Matt and I arrived at a hotel on the seafront at Cyprus two days later. The hotel was situated by a barren area of land with a digger on. We soon got to our room and I jumped on the bed to test it out. I wanted to put my clothes in the wardrobe but Matt wanted to go out.

The beach was easy enough to find and there were signs for water sports we passed a young couple. The man was fat like Matt and the lady was thin she was walking far in front making the man feel small. This made me want to hold on to Matt's hand. he went on and massaged my nipple as we walked.

Next day we laid out on the beach after being in and out the sea all day. We were sound asleep on the loungers until seven thirty pm feeling fully rested and peaceful before making our way back to the hotel to get ready for tea.

The hotel was beautiful with a balcony running around the inside that I looked down over every day to see the fountain downstairs and the doors to the outside restaurant by the pool where we went to each evening. It was beautiful with the lights round the pool and with Matt and I dressing up.

One evening I'd put on my skin tight blue posh looking dress and Matt was in posh attire as we made our way to a grand hotel with a huge marquee in the grounds for a murder mystery evening. We sat on tables of six and the story was read and acted out and the tables had to work out who the murderer was. I knew the correct answer straight away but couldn't convince anyone as they came up with wilder answers. I got frustrated.

Ecclesiastes 4:6
It was like trying to catch the wind.

I was miffed afterward as another table won the champagne as my answer matched theirs and was not impressed with my team.

Later on that night I convinced Matt to go to McDonald's for a milkshake and chips but it gave my husband toothache all night. The nearest pharmacy was miles away from Limassol at Aya Napa. We went clubbing at The Castle there one evening.

One day blisteringly hot and we couldn't go outside so we had some adult fun in our room.

Fee gave birth to Liam while we were away and we saw him when we got back.

The next day I'd finished the box of the pill thinking that it was high time Matt and I started to think about having a baby. We weren't rich but were earning enough between us to be able to look after a child. Now that night I tried to initiate sex but Matt was too tired and he said to me, "Let's not do it this way. I want it all to come naturally," but deep down I wanted sex every chance we could get and I wanted ovulating sticks to plan our love life. Matt didn't want to know and I started getting frustrated with him that evening.

It was a dream one evening of where I was floating above my body in a small squared room looking at myself through a camera lense in the top left hand corner of the room. Behind the camera a two way mirror ran along the top end of the wall through which I ended up looking down at myself with my left eye where as my right eye was trained on the black and white camera version from above.

Well I know that I can look inwardly at myself from three different angles but according to Christ the Healer by F F Bosworth I should only be looking at the world through one perspective, mine.

In the comprehensive passage, God tells us exactly how to 'attend' to the words. He says, "Let them not depart from thine eyes, keep them in the midst of thine heart." Instead of having your eyes on your symptoms and being occupied with them, let not God's words, "Depart from thine eyes," that is, look at them continually and, like Abraham was strong in faith by looking at the promises of God and at nothing else. As the only way seed can do its work is by being kept in the ground, so the only way that God's 'imperishable seed' can 'effectively work in us' is by it's being kept 'in the midst of our hearts'. This does not mean occasionally, but continuously. The reason why many have failed is because they have not done this.

In 2003 we went back to Majorca and stayed in a little town near Magaluf. Matt and I had to laugh the first evening there as Matt had bumped into someone we knew. This had been going to be a nice relaxing beach holiday and we found ourselves booking up several trips with the rep the next day. There was a boat trip, a trip to the Marineland and to a casino that I'd managed to talk Matt into booking up.

The first day was lovely on the beach I'd bought my Harry Potter book to read while going in and out the sea but the water seemed a bit rough so Matt and I decided to explore.

At the other end of the island we found some trees with parrots in flying over our heads. It started to rain but I was desperate to swim so I jumped in the sea making Matt laugh.

The day after was our first island tour round the inclusive beaches set aside just for tours.

A couple of days later was the Marineland trip and I remember feeling as though Martin was there. I'd scanned the crowd watching the marine life and even thought I saw him for a briefest of moments. Matt held my hand as we watched dolphins do their tricks.

That evening we saw a lightning display all along the seafront from Magaluf from where we'd had a brilliant evening in an Irish bar.

1 Kings 10:5
It left me breathless and amazed.

The next day I'd not been in the sea five minutes before something stung me. It had been a jelly fish so we looked for a pharmacy and got some cream. That evening we had a cab to take us to the casino but we weren't allowed to take photos. I wore my sky blue callots and matching top. We played on the slots and with twenty pesos we had one game on the tables before the hordes turned up and thousands of pounds were exchanging hands. Matt and I were enthralled before we had to leave.

We went round a little market the next day when we were about to leave home.

It was a Sunday and in a boring meeting, after dancing, we were looking forward to the first carnival at Bridgewater. Our costumes hung by the side of our chairs ready to take home, but we'd needed a dress rehearsal which was why everything was rushed.

Our wigs and scary clothes on we'd worked up a sweat and Matt was told he'd go on the back of the cart high up.

At the first carnival though he freaked out over the height of his position and Elaine, Ryan's mother, went on instead so Matt got pissed all carnival.

That night after Petherton Matt got into a drinking competition with someone matching them pint for pint up at the bar. I'd watched them out of the corner of my eye while chatting with the rest of the club sitting around a large table. They then moved to the table and as Matt went to sit down he missed the chair. He'd bought a flubber a real mixture of alcoholic drinks that looked green. Determined to not let him get alcohol poisoning I swiped the drink off the table which went all over Christian. I followed Matt outside and I could hear laughter from those thinking we were up to no good. On some leaves he slipped over real hard and I felt powerless to be able to pick him up.

2 Chronicles 20:12
"We do not know what to do."

The rest of the club came out and we soon got home on the bus. Back at the flat while Matt laid down on the bed I noticed the bone on his shoulder blade sticking out. I'd told him that I'd call an ambulance. He didn't want to know but I called them anyway. Within twenty minutes they were at the door soon taking him away over their shoulders down to Yeovil hospital. The sirens blared and they went a strange route relying only on their sat nav.

Finally there Matt sat on the bed not entirely with it, with a glazed look on his face and the nurse said that he was the best well behaved drunk they'd ever had. At 05:30 Matt's Mum turned up to take us home looking worried to death. They'd showed her the protruding bone saying they weren't even going to push it in.

We still did the rest of the carnivals. Matt was ground crew and into Wells we all actually got make-up and costumes on real early and got to the cart in time for a photo with local photographer Jason Bryant. We all posed trying to look scary for our Halloween cart. The route was a success but as we got back to the party afterwards we were all a bit deflated knowing there was only two carnivals left to go. It all flew by too quick.

December soon came and Matt and I were invited round to our friends' Mark and Dawn's house. They were holding a party for New Year's Eve. I turned up in a black and white dress and knee high black boots expecting to get pissed and have a dance but it turned out to be not that kind of party and I ended up feeling awkward and out of place in my party clothes.

Ecclesiastes 9:18
Wisdom does more good than weapons.

I wished that I'd had the wisdom of knowing what to expect and stayed in cosy clothes. Don't get me wrong it was nice to hang out with these people and play Who Wants to be a Millionaire on the telly and I also met Matt's best friend's new girlfriend called Rose who seemed really quiet. There'd been on the table, in the kitchen, a few drinks and Julian and Steve was there too. I wished that I'd tried to have a conversation with Rose and Dawn as I saw, at the time, just how close those two would become, but I was just the party girl in my knee high boots.

Chapter Twenty

One day as soon as we'd finished work we bundled our belongings in the car and headed towards Street with the radio blaring. I sang along while Matt pointed the car towards Bridgewater and over the bridge towards the Cross Rifles to turn right. As we followed the winding roads we passed a sign saying Bradley Green. I could never get away from that man's name and imagined he had been born into peerage that owned a lot of land. What had I missed out on?

Matt seemed very intent on his driving. I'd been left to sing to the radio and focus on the countryside blurring past us as we drew near to Blue Anchor where the caravan was parked at Warren Farm at the top of the hill.

After dumping our things at the caravan, because it was early, Matt and I decided to go into Minehead where we parked at our usual spot in Tesco's car park. As we jumped out of the car we headed for town and heard a lot of shouting and cheering coming from the train station. We headed towards the noise and spotted a great big crowd of people watching a grown man in what I could best describe as an adult-sized baby walker pulling one of the trains. As we stayed and watched I caught the eye of a cameraman so I turned round and asked the next person to me what was going on. Everyone was watching the World's Strongest Men compete. I watched one of the strong men slip over while straining all his muscles moving a carriage along. Matt and I ended up clapping with the rest of them as the English contestant got through to the next round. The excitement dimmed as camera crew dismantled everything to move on to the next round. Matt and I headed for the town. We popped into the supermarket for drink ambling along admiring the lovely flowers and doing a spot of window shopping. We took our time and went through Blenheim Gardens stopping to play golf. It had been nice to have a laugh at our haphazard attempts at holes in one. As we headed back into town we overheard a loud compere's voice in the direction of which we headed.

By the Wetherspoon's at the centre of town the world's strongest men contestants were carrying barrels back and forth as quick as they could. Matt and I stopped to watch. There was about five contestants that we saw before we wandered off. It was such a sunny day as Matt and I made our way to a lovely café where we sat outside with cream teas watching the world go by.

The harbour was our next destination to watch the boats go in and out and to go to the Royal National Lifeboat Institutions boat house. The boat at the time was out on a rescue. As we made our way along the beach clapping was overheard coming from the Butlin's end of the beach. I walked faster towards where I knew cameras would be. Maybe we'd be filmed this time. There was an arena of where the strong men were competing over some sort of sumo wrestling, pushing each other over marked circles. This seemed more exciting with them pitting their strengths against each other and I got carried away with the cheering hoping I'd get in camera shot.

> *Genesis 6:4*
> *In those days, and even later, there were giants on the earth*
> *Who were descendants of human women and the heavenly*
> *Beings. they were the great heroes and famous men long ago.*

The whole day turned out to be highly memorable.

The next day setting the alarm for 04:00 I awoke to a dark bedroom. Springing out of bed I'd hit the shower to feel a bit more alert and fresh and clean. I grabbed my blue shirt for work and ironed it to put it on with my black trousers. Looking smart I'd thrown on my jacket and headed out the door. Walking through the back of our court, under the archway to the alley, heading towards the by-pass. I came across a drunk Tina, Geoff the scrap man's wife, coming back from somewhere along the road with some strange drunken man. They were laughing together and I just ignored them.

I was soon at the petrol station by six o'clock. The papers were stacked outside the front door and I'd dragged them in the shop to sort them out and put in the paper stand. After this a trip to the stockroom got me taking out the cigarette boxes to put behind the till. By this time the pumps were turned on, the forecourt lights were on and I was ready for business.

A car crawled into the forecourt with no lights on and a police car was behind it and the man in the first vehicle came in and asked if we sold any head lamps saying the police had told him off for not having any.

Next thing I knew the place was filled with lorries and I was still counting out the cigarettes. The men were moaning that morning that the fuel prices had gone up again but I could glaze over anything.

The day was busy with a lot of tourists and an American came in asking where Stonehenge was in Glastonbury. I'd smiled and said it was in Wiltshire about an hour's drive away. I really enjoyed working at the petrol station and was soon walking home.

In my dreams that evening I was flying high above green fields when I came across a disused railway that was poking out from the side of a green hill and by the side of the line was a beautiful little old church. There were loads of stacked books you could see through the windows. You could tell they were covered in dust.

I flew over more green fields to the side of a cliff where there was a large dead tree looking as though it would drop into the sea if it drooped over any further. Any way as I was flying over, this tree sprang to life as a giant brilliant gold skeleton of a dragon which stomped off and flapped its wings but did not fly. I promptly woke up.

Two days later I was recounting this dream to a customer and he told me that this was to do with the devil. A couple of days after this the same customer came in with passages from the King James Bible. I never read it but I politely folded it over and took it home.

That day I had read a book about an orphan who turned out to be a self-made millionaire in a M&B book. He'd grafted real hard during his whole life earning his way round the world for a bank. There'd been a beautiful woman in her own right very wealthy who met with him in America. They fell in love and he traced his family tree to a very wealthy lineage in Arabia. They did not accept him but he was glad he'd found his family tree.

I decided to write a letter to the author explaining that the ending could have been happier because he could have been accepted into his family line and changed his name again to love and be loved by his family.

In the morning that Sunday we got up early, Matt and I with his Mum, Sue, to go with her and my husband's Dad to Cheddar market. I'd felt like I'd latched on to my in-laws too hard to get them to be better friends with my parents. Round the stalls I'd picked up more Mills and Boon books and when I got home within two hours I'd read another book. That morning I'd told my mother-in-law that I'd booked Tor Leisure for a surprise part for Matt's thirtieth birthday that next Saturday evening.

On the morning of the next day Matt and I drove our car over to Street to our friend Leanne's to pick up the books she'd said were for me to be able to read. They were all Mills and Boon books.

I heard that Katy, Keith and Sue had come down from Cumbria so I gave them a ring to see if they could go out for a meal with Nan, Mum, Fee, Dad, Matt and I. We went out for the meal and then to the beach of where Katy and I rode on donkeys on Burnham beach.

Next day I leapt out of bed and jumped into the shower. It was five o'clock and I had to open the garage for six. It was an enjoyable shower and hair wash and it left me feeling refreshed and wide awake. I'd neatly pressed my uniform the night before so dressing quickly and throwing on my coat I'd headed out the door. The wind was giving me the creeps while walking in to work and the first thing I picked up as I got to the door were all the newspapers outside. When they were spread out all over the floor the light from the office seemed to be on. Richie had gotten there before me. I left him to be on the till as I put the papers out while reading all the headlines at the same time. It got really busy on the forecourt and for a while Richie seemed to be in control of the till but then he disappeared into the office as all the Ropers lorries dispersed. I went to the till and noticed there'd been a drive-off of around ninety-nine pounds. I'd called Richie but he never heard me so I felt I had to take charge. Deducing the payment had to come from a

Roper lorry I charged the amount to one of their lorry's receipts with their card details on. The rest of the day went without a hitch and Richie never came back out of the office till he left about 11:00am leaving me on my own till the next person turned up for the two o'clock shift.

Walking home afterwards I'd noticed the wind had dropped and the sun was out but there was debris that had blown all over the pavements.

At home I put on my Maroon's Five album while waiting for Matt to come home. When he did we'd wound up in the bedroom and afterward Matt started tea. He was off to skittles that night so I looked forward to an evening by myself and watching the soaps on telly.

The next day after a lovely lazy morning at home, starting with watching Channel Four in bed and then moving to the living room to watch This Morning. I'd had super noodles with tuna for lunch before tidying up and walking into work.

I'd had a spring in my step and was looking forward to working with Martin and Maria as they were genuinely nice people who loved to chat and I'd really liked Martin's stories of when he'd worked with celebrities in London. Ian popped in that day to make plans with Martin to go to his house. I was jealous of their friendship.

Psalms 73:21
When my thoughts were bitter and my feelings were hurt.

I asked them if they'd known each other before. They'd said no. Martin and Maria were finished by five o'clock leaving me on my own at the garage but at least I'd been left with the evening traffic of everyone going home from work.

Around seven o'clock I bought my usual Ginsters peppered steak pastry with crisps and a chocolate bar and an Oasis drink I'd gotten a taste for. Ivor came into the garage and we'd had a bit of a chat and I found out about his son Matt who was having his own karaoke.

I was soon all alone again when Mum came in and said hello and I'd asked how everyone was. Mum had been worried about me working on my own at night but I said that I loved my job and wasn't worried.

At the end of the night the cigarettes had to be counted and put back into boxes to take down to the store room. I'd been seven pence over on my shift closure. I'd had a good day.

I had to walk into work the next day in the dark with the wind whistling and blowing rubbish and leaves about giving me the creeps as I couldn't hear the feet of anyone walking closely behind. As I entered the petrol station the advertising signs outside had blown over so I had to pick them up. I found the papers in bundles right outside the front door, as I soon opened up. I brought them inside. It had been a typical day, asking people if they had points cards, replenishing stock and keeping the place tidy.

Martin and Maria came in and went straight into the office. Next thing I noticed was a chart taped on the office door depicting the percentage of where we'd passed on the mystery shopper. It was 98% out of a hundred. Now I knew our last two results were in the eight to ninety percent range and I deduced I could be on for a hefty bonus according to the wall chart. Today was pay day and as soon as I got home I quickly opened my payslip. I gasped. I had a tax free bonus of seven hundred pounds. My head spun. Matt and I were going to get decent presents for ourselves this year.

That day it had been the first time I'd put on Christian radio on the telly, and I had been listening to a discussion on what Christians thought of paedophiles and how they thought these criminals should be dealt with.

1 Kings 16:2
Their sins have aroused my anger.

I used the number on the screen to try and join the debate. As I had dialled the number I thought carefully about what I was going to say and when talking to the researchers I'd been thinking about the passage in the Bible about God just turning his back on certain people and told them that. When on air though I got angry and ranted that paedophiles deserved to be beaten up and killed while in prison. The radio station soon cut me off and I'd had to wait a while until I'd calmed down. It was quite a frightening but exhilarating moment for me and wondered if anything I'd said had actually been aired.

On the TV at the time there had been a series called Bad Girls I'd been following of where paedophiles were called nonces in prison and that evening the series had gotten weird portraying a ghost in the cells. I was glad the series was over after that.

One evening after being in the garage with Ian he got down pornography. The tension had been palpable, the heat was rising. men were coming into the garage to get served and one actually asked, "What's going on between you two?"

I answered as the older woman. "Nothing. I'm teaching him new things as an older sister." It had been in the back of my mind that older women, in the Bible, are supposed to see younger men as their brother.

When I got home that evening Matt and I both went to bed. I'd kissed him very slowly at first with us blowing hot air into each other's mouths with me desperately wanting to nibble his bottom lip but I refrained letting the heat of his kiss warm my belly then my loins with the warmth seeping out all over my limbs. Feeling all hot and horny I decided to trail a hot tongue down his chest encircling his navel then down to the jungle that was bathed in a gorgeous sweat. My face could have stayed there r as I'd writhed around with him flat on his back just enjoying it. Getting my tits out my bra as I'd just pushed it up I grabbed them and rubbed each one against his penis. I was so goddam hot I could have teased him forever. He pushed hard into me so I encircled him with my mouth pushing so God damned hard to get to bath my face in his hairy sweat. He tasted all man. Desperate for him to hold it I began another tit wank and slowly rubbed my nipples all up his body wanting an amazing fucking horny kiss. I straddled him while putting my hands down on him to guide him slowly enjoying the sensations of my clitoris being rubbed delicately at first while moaning and wanting to arch my back to point my tits in his face. But then sitting perfectly erect as he couldn't refrain from entering me any longer. I played with my titties encircling them with my fingers which drove Matt wild to want to push his mouth on my nipples. My body convulsed harder and harder and I grabbed his hands and pushed them back on the pillow as I gave in completely to wild abandonment coming over and over again. His pupils were fully dilated as I drowned in them enjoying my hair wishing around my face and I'm smiling. Then we came together this time and he was elevated to the point of where my face looked straight into his and I said, "I love you," really sweetly with a yellow ethereal glow about my head. Then we fell asleep together with our bodies entwined for the rest of the night.

One afternoon after work feeling the need to be loved up I threw on my cd 'Songs About Jane' album. The first song pulsated through my veins and I danced around sensually. The second song I started to feel giddy with and the pulsations through my body made me want to just lie down and writhe around to the music. Loving the sound of the singer's voice with every nuance of my body responding to the bet, the music, the words and I was singing every lyric writhing to the music. I matched the words and the sounds perfectly singing 'She Will Be Loved', loving the sound of my own voice. I'd thought of the hole Martin had left and the man on the corner was my husband Matt. Picturing him s the lover I wanted to shake off I'd felt like a real Jane.

Matt came in through the door with bags of shopping and dumped them in the kitchen. He'd seen me writhing around and put everything away.

We then went for a walk by the fire station and there was a girl who called out, "Hello Matthew," and she ignored me. I actually saw her on the way back from town and asked her why she taunted us and I sat with her getting the explanation. She'd said that her mother had known my husband at school and had always teased him about his turned out feet and his size, that was big, at school. She wanted to keep up the tradition. That was the impression I got.

1 Peter 1:6

> *Even though it may now be necessary for you to be sad for a while*
> *Because of the many trials you suffer. Their purpose is to prove your*
> *faith is genuine.*

At home we talked about going down the coast towards Minehead and on towards Cornwall. The next day we went through the long coastal road glimpsing the sea through the trees and we parked by the cliff face. Then we walked over to the river at Lynton and Lidmouth and made our way up by the water exhalting in the beauty of our surroundings. We saw the fish dart through the water. At the top both of us sat down on an outside table for a drink and two birds sat by us on a post close enough to touch. They were so tame a little blue tit and robin. That was implicit enough to round off the day before heading home.

In work the next day Martin asked me why a lady might sway from side-to-side while talking to her and I said that I'd thought perhaps she'd lost a child and was thinking of them in her arms.

The date of Tom and Lis's wedding was looming and I remember walking around my mum-in-law's garden and Lis was leading the discussion. Pointing her arms out to where she'd like garden lights through the large lawn to lead up to where they'd like the huge tent to go for the reception. We also walked around with her picturing where flowers would go too. I'd hated her commanding everyone to her attention.

The next day we'd been stewarding for carnival in the most boring spot ever along the main road to Pylle. It was a fast road. This was for the up and coming Glastonbury Festival. We were marshalling at the end of a side road that was a dead end and it seemed like we were in the middle of nowhere. The only highlight had been when a car went into the back of another. I didn't actually watch, but I'd heard the bang and saw the aftermath. The lady from the car in front got details of the driver behind and then came over to John Cullen, Matt and I. John told us not to say we'd seen anything, so the lady got back into her car, as only her bumper had been knocked, and drove away.

We had to do 24 hrs stewarding consisting of two twelve hour shifts to get a ticket for the pop festival.

When we got to the Saturday, God was smiling on us with the weather. Jessie was stewarding at John Ganes farm just opposite us. He'd made a comment about how nice my legs were as I'd climbed the gate to get in. I'd been wearing a wraparound skirt that exposed my legs when I moved. Mum and Dad had bought it as a gift from their holiday in Canada. I also heard Stuart make a comment trying to tell me that he knew I'd contacted ITN recently via email from an old computer shop that was at the bottom of town. The comment was that he knew the IRA and Loyalists were unilaterally unopposed to one another which was what I'd typed saying that ne group wanted their land back and the Loyalists just wanted our governments protection. I also added that if they went independent they could achieve both through a peace treaty with our country. I squinted at him thinking what? I was surprised he knew just before successfully negotiating the gate and heading off through the field to the main entrance for Matt and I to present our tickets. There had been several lines of queues going in and we had to show our tickets twice. Once in we spied the toilets and we were desperate to go in. They were already smelling bad and I flushed several times that blue wash to get rid of my deposit.

Once out we made our way passed the dance tent and as this tent faded into the distance as we walked across the fields I remember hearing the strains of 'Everybody move your feet and feel united' and I wished that we'd stayed at the dance tent.

We passed a huge field of tents before finding The Other Stage of where Alison Moyet was about to start singing. For an hour while standing on yellowing dried out grass in the heat we listened to her greatest hits. Then on came Joss Stone. Now Matt really liked her and her songs so we stayed and listened in a large crowd to 'You had me, You lost me'. Joss's biggest hit in the charts at the time. She looked amazing in jazzy leggings and baggy top with her lovely long flowing blonde hair. Every song had lovely words and a great beat that Matt and I found ourselves swaying to. Her set went on and on as the sweat was pouring from her face as every emotion had been on display. There was a lot of passion in her songs.

> *Genesis 40:14*
> *Please remember me when everything is going well for you.*

Afterwards there'd been a mediocre band and the crowd dispersed leaving us with a handful of others not sure where to go to next. The next band finished when we decided to go exploring and found ourselves in the children's field. We came across a story teller's tent and became enthralled with a man weaving a tale of a man made out of grass. Totally captivating it was another hour before we came out and the orange sun was going down over the horizon.

Wandering aimlessly around numerous stalls I saw a girl dressed only in a bikini standing with a man who looked like Martin and realised that had I still been with him he'd have encouraged me to dress like her too as he used to tell me I'd look good in a mini-skirt and that he'd like to spank my bottom. I'd been glad at that point that I was no-ones play thing.

It had been starting to get dark as we approached the pyramid stage from behind on the right hand side and there'd been a huge cinema screen with Boyz in the Hood just starting. I stood and watched for a while not sure of whom was about to start playing on the main stage when mat decided he'd had enough and started leading us out of the pop festival. Not liking the darkness that had descended.

We had to get cross the road to find the field with our car in that was behind John Ganes home at the back of his lorry yard. We'd stopped and chatted to those stewarding at the entrance before finding our car and making our way back out of Pilton towards Glastonbury.

On the Monday at work, from the moment I opened up, the seemingly endless queues started. Craig came in at eight and the sandwich man had completely filled up the fridges. We were swamped. All day the queues stretched across the forecourt. All sense of time felt suspended as I made my way through sale after sale. Craig could barely keep up with the food and drink flying off the shelves with putting endless supplies of stock out. I went for the toilet on the till all day. That endless queue was still there as the fridge got completely emptied. Then Steve, the sandwich man, came in with that days load and completely filled the fridge up yet again. Still all the pasties, sandwiches, chocolates, crisps, drinks were quickly diminishing yet again. It was like Craig was working on speed putting lots of water out this time as I picked my way through customer after customer tirelessly just taking my time making sure every driver got charged the correct fuel. Time hung in the air, I just wasn't interested as the sun stayed out all day giving me a God's eye view of how to handle it all.

Craig was still with me as darkness started to descend but he'd had enough and praised me for my calmness I'd showed all day. We tilled up together completely amazed at our takings and even more amazed we hadn't had a single drive off all day. The petrol station looked completely emptied of stock before we both headed off. Craig on his scooter and me in the car with Matt.

It was raining when we set off for a mini holiday for Minehead and intermittent rain giving us glimpses now and then of the sun. Bradley Green caught my eye again as I thought of him, Martin, but I didn't care I'd been with Matt for a while now and it was nice to be with someone I could have some warmth of friendship and loving with.

At the caravan park we took in our sleeping bags, duvet covers and pillows then headed into Minehead passed Dunster Castle. We sat in a large restaurant on the seafront and had a cooked breakfast and while we were there I'd had to go downstairs to the toilet.

At least the sun was out now and after we'd eaten we took a stroll towards the town. The market was on that day in the big car park by the railway station and we took our time with Matt looking at fishing tackle and me at books. I loved looking at the children's things too looking forward to the day we'd have kids.

A good hour had been spent looking at the stalls and the books on the railway platform. Because it was nice we walked towards the beach and laid out on our coats. Matt fell asleep. I needed the toilet and went across the road to the ladies. Coming back to the beach Matt had awakened wandering where I'd got to so I told him and asked if he wanted to go in the arcades. Back across the road we used a pound each on the machines with Matt on the Simpson's arcade game and me on the noughts and crosses two pence machines' Neither of us really won anything and we walked passed the pub on the corner into the high street. Matt asked if I wanted a hot chocolate so we went to our favourite café and sat outside in the sunshine still trying to come out from between the clouds. This was how we people watched and gently chatted, not intellectually but in a way that inferred cosiness. We had an amble round to the park and I needed the loo again, so I had to pass the bushes and the flowers in Blenheim to find the ladies. Matt waited for me on a bench.

The sun was still struggling to come out as we headed to the Wheel House to have tea. Matt was good at finding non-alcoholic drinks that were normally alcoholic. We'd sat by the window looking out at clouds that were getting darker and looking more ominous. We thought we'd walk round the harbour to The Old Ship Aground before it down poured where we stayed to have a couple of drinks. The trek back to the car afterwards was a wet one.

Turning in at the farm gate at Blue Anchor and driving in a 5 miles per hour limit to the bottom of the field by the caravan park owner's house, the car turned into our caravan's field. It was all set to be a stormy evening and at the caravan Matt and I got out the cards and played shit head of where you get nine cards each and try to be the first to get all your cards out. After several games we turned in but the wind had whipped up a storm and had been rocking the caravan howling around us. Hail stones were hammering on the sky light and I didn't like it so Matt held me on my bed and erratic as the weather was we moved together and made soothing love making to calm our inner storms.

In the morning light our moods were brighter along with the weather. Jumping in the car we headed for Dunster and we walked round by the castle and down to the river using Bob and Sue's National Trust card. Walking hand in hand as always and gentle cuddling we'd felt happy and contented. Heading back down the hill to the car we got a picnic out, the food having been bought the day before at Kwiksave consisting of Doritos, tomatoes, grapes, cheese and pickle rolls and drinks.

Exodus 32:6
We sat down to a feast.

Matt wanted to go home early and pop in his Mum's first on the way. His parents always greeted us at the back door and Sue would make us a hot drink.

That night it was in a dream I had felt a tingle of trepidation as I swam in a harbour full of boats as I saw his back arch out of the water. It was in the glorious yellow sky of God's own light and the dragon was predominately red but a little bit slimy green, (probably seaweed) and a bit pink in the places closest to God's glow. I wasn't in the slightest bit frightened even though I knew it was the devil's dragon. I stood on his back. He arched the rest of his back up and I just slipped under the arch where afterwards it felt like I was still standing on something. Something else went bright pink with rage. This was it, defining the moment of what was to come.

The next day Matt and I were busy that morning packing to stay at Weston-Super-Mare. Matt and I were off to Weston Wheels a haven for boy and girl racers. The carnival club were meant to do the car parking and we knew it was to be a late night.

Before going to our posts Matt and I wandered round the stalls eyeing up the expensive burger vans feeling hungry so two cheeseburgers and drinks were in order. The place had been humming with loud music with us wandering around in the sunshine. Soon us, carnivalites had to go to the parking fields to guide in the drivers.

As the sun was setting while standing at our posts the cars looked ever so fast and had blue headlamps on some and some various lights that looked illegal underneath.

Jeremiah 5:1
Can you find one person who does what is right.

I even remember one that looked like they and the back of rockets from the backs of the cars.

Jessie told me, "Show us your tits," but I never do that if my life depended on it so I pulled my bra off through my clothes and my sleeves keeping my dignity intact while waving my favourite red lacy ones at him. Which was promptly stuffed into the pocket of my big fluorescent jacket.

Feeling bored parking cars I remember getting cold and tired finding it harder and harder to help people find their cars afterwards on their way out. Matt still had to find our car at the Weston airfield up the road before heading off towards the town for the B&B. It was very basic accommodation, but comfortable enough for our needs.

The next day we never hung around long as Matt never did go much on Weston. I liked the place though.

In the afternoon I worked with a man called Michael of whom had just started working at the petrol station. He was tall, quite old and owlish looking and self-righteous I found. I got on with him well and left him on the till while I did the heavy lifting of putting the stock out. I made us a cup of tea and the time that evening just ticked by nicely and we had a little chat. Michael was a nice man and he told me that he was part of the Catholic Church. I wanted to get on and mop but Michael didn't like the state of the mop. He wanted to write a letter to martin asking for a new one.

The next day was my day off for two whole days so Matt decided we'd go off for Minehead and I thought great. We jumped into the car and flew down there and put everything away in Bob and Sue's caravan. When it had been put away it was Matt's idea to go into Minehead to have a cooked breakfast in Tesco's. The food smelled lovely and I had one fried egg, tow hash browns, two sausages, two bits of bacon and baked beans and I picked up two sachets of brown sauce.

We had a lovely day walking around Minehead. It was a beautiful place and in the evening I remember going to the toilets to brush my teeth and have a widdle and whilst walking up and back I saw the biggest full moon I'd ever seen. It took up half the sky.

> 1 Kings 10:5
> It left me breathless and amazed.

Now the next day we went and found another beach. There was nobody there and I thought of Lis my new sister-in-law to be and I remembered having been told she used to suffer from fits and had a really bad one once and forgot how to play the piano. How as that possible? I'd wanted to ask her about it but the idea that she'd forgotten how festered in my brain. I'd thought about his in the car on the way home.

The next morning I could smell burning and so I opened a window and noticed it came from outside. I saw Matt banging on the door of the Alexanders. I shouted out the window.

"What's wrong Matt?"

"There's a fire upstairs. I can see smoke everywhere."

Next thing I knew someone came out of the house to talk to Matt and then he said, "I'm going over to the fire brigade of which was just opposite us. The next thing I knew a fire engine turned up and put the fire out while Matt went on to work.

When he came back that afternoon I asked him what went on and he said, "Calm down Karen There was a fire in their bathroom. I saw it just in time as the room was full of smoke and apparently the lady there had scented candles lit all around her bath that had caught on fire to the shower curtain."

I said, "Was anyone hurt?"

"No," he said, "It just made me late for work."

"They must be glad you noticed it," and he said "Yes."

"You were a proper hero then."

It was my imagination in over drive the next day as I remember Lis having her hair cut by my mother-in-law. She was sat in Mum two's kitchen and ran her fingers through her hair and said, "Now this one's about to be cut and this one's about to be cut." This was said in just the same way Phoebe said in a famous episode of Friends of which inferred she was taking the piss out of me as she knew I liked my Friends series. I loved Friends and knew the dialogue off by heart and knew when someone was taking the piss.

In the petrol station the next day I set up easily and it was mostly men who came in of whom would talk to me and someone asked if I was from Bristol as I sounded Bristolian.

I said, "Wow. Really?"

And he said, "Yes."

I went to Nan's that afternoon and Nan Sheila gave me a brand new black Italian leather jacket. It smelled brand new so I said "Thanks." I tried it on and it fitted. I felt really pleased.

The next day I'd been enjoying my work in the garage and again it was mostly men in and the radio was blaring out the station of Orchard FM. Now one song in particular belted out the words, 'It's getting hot in here, so take off all your clothes…' I felt mortified in front of all the male customers.

Philippians 1:20
My deep desire and hope is that I shall never fail in my duty.

I didn't' know where to look.

I went up to my mother-in-law's later on that day to stay for tea. Tom and Lis was there and we all had a nice tea together. I wanted to call it dinner of which I did but they had the attitude of whatever. It was a nice tea with gammon, cheese sauce, a pineapple ring, and big chips with peas. Afterwards Sue, Lis and I decided to go in the kitchen to wash up. Lis was on the right hand side and we both dried up together. Then she asked me, "What do you see in Matt?"

I said, "I love his waddle, meaning that he's got a strong sexy jawline." They seemed happy with my answer. Lord knows what they'd been talking about.

In the morning I walked into the petrol station keen to go to work and Ian was late turning up yet again. I got fed up. Then Brian turned up for an eight o'clock start. Now Ian and I knew how to wind him up so we sat on the top shelf in the store room and had a chat. Brian yelled down, "What are you doing down there?"

"Nothing. Just going through the crisps," of which we had looked up. Really we had been on top of everything and were looking forward to the P+H lorries turning up with loads of new goodies to put out. We just laughed as we knew Brian's imagination was in hyper-drive. We finally got our asses into gear when the lorry showed up and we soon put the stock out. It was soon home time.

The next day Matt and I had a full day off of work so Matthew drove us to Weymouth as the weather was beautiful. We had the music blaring all the way down and once there we parked over at Radipole and the industrial estate. We both needed a wee and used the public toilets. Matt and I walked round the reserve and we were happy talking to the fisherman.

Afterward Matt and I walked on into town and over the harbour bridge of where we bumped into my sister Fee and Steve with little Liam in the pram and they said they were going to Brewers Quay of where we all went together. Then on to our separate ways afterwards and we said, "Have a nice day."

The following week it had been a day with lots of lorries on the forecourt and I'd been working with Adrian. I can just picture him walking through the shop with a mop and bucket in his hands. A buxom lady came in with lovely golden curly hair. She said that her name was Vicky and announced that she o a lorry. We naturally got chatting and she told me about her boyfriend that she'd met abroad. Vicky also moaned about sexism in the lorry yard but laughed it off. I was in awe of her and as she left the garage I felt the tug of wanting to live on the open road. Adrian caught my attention to talk to me. After the lorries had gone it became a slow day.

It was a Wednesday and the carnival club had to take a marshalling course of which we did in the skittle alley at The Queens Head. We had to do this to be able to work for Michael Eavis who ran the Glastonbury Festival in order to get free tickets.

Now in the morning I was working away on the till quite diligently with Maria in the office. While working on the till Martin came in with rubber gloves on and moaned about the state of the toilets. I had a good day on the till and finished at two o'clock.

I had a lovely afternoon just vegging out on the sofa reading a book, a Mills and Boon one while Matt was doing the cooking. It smelt lovely and I got hungrier and hungrier while I'd been doing a puzzle in my magazine.

After tea I washed up and then Matt and I went for a walk down Cinnamon Lane and by the river Brue stopping every two minutes so Matt could look at the fish. It was a nice evening and we had peaceful dreams.

The next day I'd had a hard day at the petrol station but at least I'd finished at the same time Matt had at the bakery. We'd decided to go out for the afternoon across the moors with our binoculars. At Shapwick we went for our long walk taking our time to stop and use our binoculars to spy the waders, types of birds, in the mud flaps. It was a long path out over the bridge with bushes either side of us but it was worth it while we occasionally held hands or moved in for cuddles. Every time I cuddled into Matt while walking he'd said I made his head spin which always sounded like a moan.

On our jaunt we'd bumped into Fee's in-laws with our nephew Liam. We always stopped to chat to say what the weather was like and swap stories of the birds we'd seen. Liam would have been in the pram. We would always say to them to have a good day and would talk to the other couples we'd bump into and ask what birds they'd seen. The swans were about and so were a couple of buzzards flying high above the trees. The weather was warm and we saw the sun start to go down as we made our way home in the car. Matt wanted an early night after tea so we both went to bed tired but happy. In the morning, while still in bed, Matt told me of a bizarre dream he'd had that him, John Cullen, Kelvin, Ryan and Jessie had been up in The Queens Head's skittle alley. In this dream they were all encircling Jesus Christ. This dream bothered me and I thought it might have been a prediction especially when the following evening I was curious to start watching a two part drama about the second coming. Now I naively thought it was going to be about Christ coming again to judge the living and the dead. It became however a drama about a scripture I'd never come across before. Apparently Christopher Ecclestone's Christ grew up with a Christian dad after his mum drunk herself to death. Christ who'd gone off on his own a lot during his life and no-one worried about it, least of all his friend Rebecca of whom he ended up sleeping with. Then just when you thought it was a wind up this Christ turned night into day in a football stadium. He looked for a Third Testament and when he couldn't find it he got his best friend to poison him with rat poison.

> *Joel 2:6*
> *As they approach, everyone is terrified, every face turns pale.*

I felt shocked and upset and really believed I'd heard a scream, coming from beyond the grave, going through my head. I really believed that Mother Mary was with me that night watching the telly not believing her eyes.

In the morning one day I got unnerved as I knew that I'd given my mother-in-law a book called The Angel of Wessex of which I'd had signed just for me. I couldn't find it so she couldn't have given it back. Now Matt wanted to go back to the Dunster Show. We jumped into the car and headed towards there. At the show I saw the author of that book again and so bought another copy that he signed yet again for me.

At the falconry display a bird went missing making us all worry but by the end of the day the bird got found.

While we had been away a neighbour called Duncan had moved in above us. He seemed really handsome and nice.

The next morning I'd had a nice bowl of porridge and got into work quickly and we had to watch out for a mystery shopper all day. We had to ask for point cards and keep the garage spotless and the shelves full up.

Towards the end of the day my lorry driver friend, Vicky, came in and asked me if I could go to an Anne Summers party at her house. I said, "That would be brilliant. When and where?"

"Next Wednesday at mine."

"What's your address?" Then she told me and I knew it was up the road from Strode College.

I anticipated this party all week and felt elated that I'd actually been asked.

On the Wednesday I got dressed up in comfortable clothes and Matt dropped me off in the car and I went upstairs into the living room with only one other person I'd recognised from cleaning days called Bernice. Everyone else seemed nice enough and we played a little game of whom we'd like to be stranded on an island with. My mind went blank. I couldn't thing of an answer. Most of them said Brad Pitt or their husbands and I just stayed intriguingly quiet saying, "I dunno," and they gave up on me. It was a brilliant evening.

Now in work the next day I was really busy on the till and only had a breather mid-morning when a handsome man, who was stickily built, and with blonde hair came in in a van delivering computer stuff. I got talking to him and he seemed very friendly and he said, "I know you don't I?"

"I don't know. Are you married to a woman called Hinde or is it Brackett?"

He laughed at me realising I was on about a really old drag act.

He said, "Elaine and her sister are fine thanks," They were Mum's old bosses at First Steps Nursery. I laughed a little bit too and had a pleasant conversation.

Now a friend called Ivor came across me in town after work and he was a typical Somerset farmer of whom stopped and talked to me about farming. I listened and talked politely.

Now a day later I walked over to Safeway to wait for Matt to come out of work and I got scared as a great big Dane pinned me against the wall on his hind legs and his front paws either side of my head. I noticed the dog was tied to a post and I stayed there for what seemed like forever, completely terrified until the owners came out and untied him. I was so glad when Matt came out of work that I flopped into his arms to walk me home.

One day while working with Ian in the garage he had gotten a top shelf magazine down yet again to waft under my nose while he worked on the till. Why he used to do this I don't know as we were both married. Trouble was this would get me turned on. I'd been paranoid at the time that my in-laws had something to do with his behaviour as he'd told me that he'd trained as an actor at college.

A customer commented that we were together but I put him straight saying that I was just being a big sister to Ian. Trouble was I'd visualised him fucking me up against the wall down the passage way. I decided to head to the toilet on my own out of harm's way. Very turned on I stayed in there pleasuring myself while I left Ian on the till. I was so pleased afterward that nothing actually happened between us as I'd convinced myself that he wasn't really interested in me that way. I always thought we could have been friends but he did confess that he had affairs.

The next day Matt and I decided to find Emerald Falls Fisheries and we got lost and a lorry in a 30mph zone over took us. We went for miles before turning towards Highbridge. Then we found the fishing ponds and Matt said, "Let's go for a walk round the ponds. I want to see what it's like here."

"Ok," I'd said and we walked round three lakes and Matt kept stopping to speak to everybody wanting to know what they were catching. We even watched one man reel in a five pound carp. Matt and I walked back to the car and drove off home.

In the evening Matt and I met up with Tom his brother and his girlfriend Lis, of whom seemed a bit strange. We'd sat outside in the courtyard of the Street Inn. Lis started on about models posing and she demonstrated a pose of where her back went rigid and she tried to act posh and above us.

Psalms 82:2
You must stop judging unjustly.

I didn't have a clue what she was on about. We sipped our drinks in silence after that and Tom broke out in speech telling us all about his day at work for Drapers. It had been pleasant enough evening.

The next day I went into work and did my thing with the work and the toilets I had to clean until the person on the till went home. Then I was stuck on my own at five o'clock. Then I had some tea of which had been a Ginsters peppered steak slice with a packet of crisps. I helped myself to a cappuccino as I'd cleaned the machine out. It was free to workers.

"I want to go to the toilet," I'd said to myself and locked the front door and came back to a loud bleep on the forecourt. It was a man just waiting to be served.

It was September time and Matt and I were flying from Bristol airport out to Majorca and this time we were staying in Magaluf. The party capital. First day there though I was looking for an umbrella as it was tipping it down. The first whole day was better as down at breakfast you could see a bright blue sky out over the sea through the windows. There was good morning written in Spanish, German and English on little bins for our rubbish on the tables.

We wasted no time finding the night life on this holiday and one night there'd been a fight between the bars and a poor young lad selling roses had his flowers kicked everywhere. I felt sorry for him. I'd been dancing at the time and dared not to venture out. That night I went on a bucking bronco and did not last long as I fell off in fits of giggles.

On the way back along the promenade there'd been an amazing lightning storm right above us and out to sea.

The next day we dared not swim and took the pedaloes out as far as a little island you could see out of our restaurant window. I made Matt pedal hard so that we could look all around it and some people had anchored their pedaloes on the shore to have a look around. We'd been gone for over an hour. This had been on the day of our anniversary and in the evening we found a lovely restaurant with a veranda looking out to sea. I'd gotten a pair of hoop earrings that would clip on that I'd dared Matt to wear for a photo making him look like a gypsy lover. We'd had a bottle of champagne with our meal and at the end of the night we realised that we'd only been charged for a standard bottle of wine. Laughing, we headed back to our hotel.

The last day there Matt and I hung around our pool right by the sea and there was music on all day by Michael Bolton. It became annoying in the end.

Proverbs 25:17
They may get tired of you and come to hate you.

The whole holiday had been wonderful.

In the morning Matt and I went to Yeovil FC grounds to queue and get tickets for an afternoon match. We then went into town and did a bit of shopping for our birthdays coming up within the next month. Then we went back to the Glovers ground to find the right stand to go in. We had sets right near the front and I had a black handbag on me. We soon got into the game with Yeovil playing Barnsley and it was a real on the edge of your seat game as loads of possible goals kept going near the nets and we kept doing Mexican Waves to keep the ball going towards the right net all the time. We even got caught up with all the chanting. Then there was a loud roar and Matt told me of a woman stripping off her top in the crowd. I never even noticed. I looked down my nose at her in my head.

Psalms 69:11
I dress myself in clothes of mourning.

The game was soon over and we got back to the car before I noticed my handbag was missing. We asked in the souvenir shop and they told us to go in the players' lounge upstairs of where I found my handbag. I was grateful no-one had stolen it.

We went to Weymouth the next day and had a long walk around out to the end of the harbour of where I witnessed a great big pink jellyfish swimming on top of the water. I couldn't take my eyes off of it. I thought of when I'd had a jellyfish sting on my leg once. Matt and I also watched the fishermen. We had a lovely day and were soon coming home to the tunes of Shania Twain's, 'Come on Over' cd. Once at home I had a phone call from my Mum and she asked me, "Have you been buying those Mills and Boon books again?" and she didn't laugh about telling me off. I said, "Yes."

"Karen," she said, "Your head's too much in the clouds. Why don't you give them up?" I felt that I'd been told off and I had been several times over the years and I just wanted to scream at Mum that I hated her.

> *Leviticus 19:17*
> *"Do not bear a grudge against anyone, but settle your differences*
> *With him.*

I'd said, "They're books I just love to read," now it felt like Mum thought, every time she'd said this, I'd married for all the wrong reasons and I hadn't. I would never ever marry for money and wanted to tell Mum over and over again that I just loved the stories as they were easy reading. It was the same old argument as before but I felt worn down and started to box them up. Mum could bloody well have them in her attic after I'd painstakingly catalogued them all.

Now the next day Matt and I went to several garages to find a new car and eyed up quite a few of them. There was a nice light blue one I fell in love with that wasn't too pricey but Matt said, "No. I like that aquamarine one."

"What the turquoise one?"

"The aquamarine one."

I said, "Same thing." We put a deposit on it and it looked like a proper boy racer car. The licence plate said K—HYG which made me call it the Kathy Genge. A Name I would have liked a little daughter called.

The next morning I went into the garage and couldn't stop telling people that my husband Matt was management material at Morrisons and that he was a baker there. I also told others that I'd love to do loads of charity work. I'd bored people to tears and I met a new lad that day called Craig who seemed quite pleasant of whom was blonde and of average build.

Now I'd been talking to Daphne whilst on the till who told me about her B&B in Bere Lane and also how she'd been to university in the Philippines. She told me about her family too.

That day when Craig had just started I really took to him but the next day I'd been doing an early shift and wanted to be finished and going home at 2pm. When he turned up it was dead on two. He made a coffee and went outside for a ciggy. He was outside for a full twenty minutes and all I'd wanted to do was go home. This was to start a trend of events.

I was so shattered when I got home that I'd wanted to collapse into bed but instead picked up my knitting to finish a draught excluder for the bedroom that I called a snakey. I finished stuffing it and put it inside the bedroom. Now that night I told Matt to put snakey by the door and he grinned at me wickedly and shook his own snakey about making me laugh before he crawled into bed.

Chapter Twenty-One

The next morning the air was crisp and light as I'd walked into work for six o'clock and later on a nice man called Alan turned up to work with me. That day our boss, Penny, asked us if we'd work all day Christmas Day for triple of our wages.

I said, "No. I always have Christmas Day off to be with my family." I really put my foot down. "It's not fair to have to work Christmas Day," and I turned to Alan. "You don't really want to work Christmas do you?" and he said, "No. I have a wife and grandchildren of whom I want to be with."

Penny heard, "Are you sure?" she'd said, "It's triple pay," but clearly I'd given Alan a back bone and we both got out of doing it.

A day later Matt and I went to Taunton to a costume hire place for carnival and we were running out of time to get them so we chose very traditional outfits. Prince costumes for girls and loads of Widow Twankies and we had one princess costume. We looked through loads of costumes that had been used in costume dramas on the telly and for Shakespeare plays. It was exciting looking round the costumes. Rita piled them into the back of her car before we came home. She took the clothes back to hers for any special readjustments. I'd had the day off to do this.

When I went back to work the next day I learned from ear wigging what happened to Martin and Maria and why they left. Apparently those two lovely people left under a cloud because someone in the garage was stealing and the area manager couldn't find the thief through them so they had to go.

That evening I'd been in the pub with Matt and Tom and Charlene amongst other friends and Charlene told me about The Dream Boys stripes doing a show at Weston and I'd said, "Wow. Can we go and see them?"

She'd said, "Yes I'd love to."

"Can we make a date?" I'd said.

"That would be nice," and nothing more was said about it. That was a Friday evening at the King Bill at the bottom of town.

The next night I went to another Ann Summers party with my Mum and my eldest sister Fiona. We got involved with a pass the parcel and the winner which was me who won two red stockings that were full of holes. I knew I was never going to wear them. There was a stand with hangers of lingerie on. I looked through them and bought a pair of pink panties that said Eat Me. While we were there two strippers came out and both were hung like horses. They even used whipped cream as part of their act. We all gave into embarrassed giggles.

Judges 9:54

> *Then he quickly called the young man who was carrying His weapons.*

The next day I had to go to work feeling happy with a spring in my step. Mum called me after work and asked me did I want to go Christmas shopping with her and Fee up at Bath tomorrow. I said, "Yes."

Then the next day Mum came to me in the same car to pick me up and we headed towards Shepton Mallet and then onto Bath. The most romantic city in the world. We parked up in Charlotte Street car park for the rest of the day and we went to the bottom of the high street first to work our way up. I had a racing green coloured skirt catch my eye first and I was there for ages trying it on, but I didn't get it. In another shop I found a nice orange patterned jumper that I decided to buy. It looked great on. I remembered when I got back to work the next day to get carnival week off just in time.

Now Bridgewater and Petherton carnival went without a hitch and I bloody loved dancing on the cart and the parties afterwards.

Then it came to being Burnham carnival on the Monday and we changed at Durston House of where Lyn got told off for surfing on top of an ironing board while we were getting changed. We had our make-up put on and were soon on the cart. It was a brilliant night.

In the morning I was completely shattered but had to get into work and started to suffer from a carnival cold as it was all over. Wells and Shepton carnivals had been wet and I'd gotten soaked through to the skin. I was coughing and sneezing everywhere. I had a handkerchief and Olbas oil that cleared my nose temporarily. My eyes were streaming all morning so as soon as the next person came in I asked them to cover for me on the till in between sneezes. They took one look at me and obliged. I was glad when work was over. I then decided to buy some oranges on the way home from work and as I walked through St John's car park I noticed my dream car. A sky blue coloured Toyota, with wings on the back, convertible.

The next day was my day off and Fiona came and got me to go to Yeovil Christmas shopping. She made me trail in and out of every single shop and I told her that I'd needed to go into Bastins for cards. The Pound shop, for stocking fillers and a pet shop because I wanted to get Matt some fish for Christmas. By the time we got there I had to choose fast they were nearly closing and I got two little gold ones I called Bubble and Squeak. I also got the bowl, and everything to go with it, even a little bridge. When we got back we went to Mum's first and I set up the present and left it in my old room till Christmas.

That evening I went round the pubs with Matt and his mates and ended up at J D Wetherspoon's in Street. Now we all ordered our own and I was on Malibu's with lemonade and we all had a laugh as we sat round one little table. Throughout the night, as we kept getting up for drinks, we started piling the classes up into a pyramid that completely over took the little table of which by the end of the night collapsed. The drink left in them and the glass went everywhere as we all just kept laughing our heads off all night.

Two days later my head felt all right again and Fiona phoned me up on a Saturday morning wanting to know if I'd go with her, Nan Sheila, Mum and Liam, my little nephew, to a garden centre.

I said, "Yes. I'd love to," and she picked me up at ten o'clock on the dot. I was surprised she'd usually turn up an hour after organised and we drove to the garden centre called Monkton Elms. At the centre there were Christmas trimmings everywhere and a walk way lined with Christmas lights leading to Santa's grotto. Little Liam was as good as gold with Father Christmas who asked if he'd been a good boy. Fee said, "Yes."

"Would you like a present?" His little face lit up and he had a bag full of tiny toys and sweets.

It was Christmas Day morn and Matt and I got to his Mum's nice and early to see his family Bob, Sue and Tom. They were all up as we got there by nine o'clock. There were lots of presents under the Christmas tree and bob played Santa to give them all out. It took up most of the morning until lunch of where they did a wonderful turkey roast dinner and afterwards I helped wash up. We stayed until about three o'clock. Then we went up to my Mum's. Once there we all had a drink and Matt and I gave our presents out. Everyone was happy. I nipped upstairs for the last gift of which was the goldfish. Matt was surprised.

"I've called them Bubble and Squeak," I'd said. Then we settled in for tea and then games for hours afterward before all us happy people went to bed.

It was New Year's Eve and Matt and I got all dressed up. I put on a retro black and white shift dress with knee high black boots as we'd been invited to Mark and Dawn's house for a party. I really thought they meant lots of music and dancing, but when we got there everyone was lounging around in front of the telly. In my party clothes I felt out of place. I got one drink and tucked into some food half way through the night. I got introduced to Matt's best mate Justin's girlfriend called Rose and we ended up playing Who Wants to be a Millionaire? Till the wee hours of the morning. Then we walked back to Bob and Sue's to sleep.

That Sunday we had an annual general meeting with carnival and I remember voting in a new top table and a man named Christian got voted in as secretary and I felt sorry for Lyn who got voted out. I knew that Christian wouldn't last the year and told Matthew. The next day Matt and I witnessed a ceiling going up in a new house being built by my sister's fiancé and a new stairway going in.

The next evening the carnival club went for a Christmas meal at The Camelot a pub restaurant on the Wells road. I sat next to a man called Jessie, an older member of the club. I dressed in a knee high beige skirt and a turquoise jumper.

After food there was a disco and I got up to dance with Jessie. I had a nice night with Jessie. Now I'd ignored Matthew all night but he seemed to enjoy himself sat down at the other end of the table. It had been a nice turkey dinner with all the trimmings.

Later on in the year Matt and I got up early on the morning of the British Heart Foundation Cycle Ride. We were both excited to take part of a major charitable event that took place in and around the surrounding villages of Glastonbury. It was exciting to watch the cyclists.

> 1 Samuel 6:13
> *They were overjoyed by the sight.*

We'd needed high visual jackets and as it had been raining Matt checked that there'd been an umbrella in the car and all he could find was his great big green fishing umbrella.

When we pulled in at the cycle ride car park across the moors at the carnival sheds, Stuart told us where our position on the route was meant to be. Luckily the drive to Coal Harbour Bridge on the road to Meare wasn't too far away. Matt pulled the car off the road on the crossroads up on the river bank. We trudged to our sanding point on the bridge as it had been tipping down with rain. An hour later the first cyclists on the shorter route started to pass us by. As our spot had been only one mile away from the finishing line we'd been told to support the cyclists with encouraging words. Matt and I clapped them as they went passed us and shouted, "Not long to go!" or "Nearly there," after helping them turn at the junction by being able to see further up the road than them.

Around lunch time a van came round with sandwiches, bits of cake, a box drink and an apple for something to eat. It was still raining but even though there'd been Matt's umbrella to stand under perched against the railings behind us. Matt kept going across the road to look down into the stream underneath hoping to see some fish.

Also across the road Matt could get a clearer view of what was coming and he started to wave cyclists across. There'd still been over a hundred riders who'd taken part in the cycle ride that year undeterred by the weather. There were even some young children who had taken part.

The 25k cyclists were beginning to start passing us and you could tell it had been them from their puffing and panting and from their questions of asking if they were near to the end. Our answer had always been the same. "Only one mile left to go."

If it hadn't been for the cyclists to talk to, the time would have dragged by, but it was soon four pm and the stragglers at the back began to pass us.

One man told us that there were two more of his friends expected until the van to pass us by to say they'd finished.

Still pouring with rain the men in the van, at the back, helping with punctured wheels called to us to stand down and yelled a thank you too. Matt and I soon jumped back into the car and headed for home.

On the Monday morning I got into work at the petrol station very early and no-one had been there yet so I was able to quietly sort all the papers and open up. By noon time Carrie, my boss, came in for work and she asked me did I want to book any holiday off.

I'd said, "Yes please," and as it was quiet I quite boldly told her I needed from third of November till the fourteenth.

"Are you going anywhere nice?" She'd said.

"Oh, it's carnival I'm going on the cart."

"That's fine," she said and as far as I knew that was my holiday booked.

Craig came in that afternoon and took ages as per usual outside having a cigarette and coffee first when he should have been working which pissed me off. Then Carrie called me back into the office and said I couldn't have carnival free because Craig already had it. I should have said, "No. You're lying," but Craig got the time off instead of me. I felt indignant they'd both swindled me out of any carnival time I'd wanted.

I finally left for home at two thirty very upset and I told Matt why as soon as I saw him. Matt suggested a trip to the fayre before tea. I said, "Yea. That would be brilliant."

We paid a pound to go in and we looked round at the hoopla stalls and the hook-a-ducks, and the cheap jack stalls as well as an amusement arcade. It was early evening with an orange sun in the sky. I felt like a kid again and asked Matt for two pound fifty to go on the Mexican Hat ride. I jumped into the cage and went whirring round and round and made myself dizzy. As I got off I felt a bit ill. I had to have some water so Matt won a bottle on the hoopla stall. The water made me feel better.

The next day was a Sunday and I managed to get my ass out of bed for church and it turned out to be a good service and afterwards I'd stayed for coffee. I'd had a pleasant afternoon with Matthew from going up his parents and seeing Gran and Gramps too. I loved them all to bits.

Then came the carnival meeting at seven thirty pm at the Queens Head and they all seemed to know that Craig conned me and Carrie to get time off work to do all carnivals. Jessie stood up for me and harped on about we should all stick together and work as a team.

The next day Matt and I were off to Aya Napa in Cyprus the most famous nightclubbing rea on the whole of the island. I thought great we could club again at The Castle night club. We spent the first day exploring our area because the back of our room looked out to sea. There were bits of rock scattered about on what could have been a lovely beach. Out the front of the hotel was a fayre that led out onto the main high street full of clubs and pubs.

We found a pub called Senior Froggy the first night there and Matt and I had a boogie on the pubs little dance floor till two in the morning although we did make it down to brekkie. We had to go a mile up the road though to find a decent beach. I'd loved vegging out on a sun bed, going in and out the sea while having a Bella on the go. The holiday was bliss and three nights in we were still ending up at Senior Froggy after going to Fred Flintstones Rock Café and opposite was The Castle a great place for a decent night club. Matt and I had been one of the first ones in and rhythm and blues played all night, but at twelve we'd had enough. We stopped at a pub and took photos of us sipping cocktails with a parasol in it and sparklers We then moved on to Senior Froggy the seventh night in. Matt got friendly with a blonde bombshell bar staff and she had to step in to one of our photographs. I felt pushed out and my ego was hurt. It had otherwise been a lovely holiday in September.

Come that October I'd been dreading turning thirty but got surprised. By the evening we went to Mum and Dad's and everyone, when I got there, yelled out surprise.

> *1 Samuel 6:13*
> *They were overjoyed at the sight.*

The whole family had been there all sat in the kitchen just waiting for me. I felt elated until Mum said we can't stay here all night, but I'd stayed long enough to have a chat with everyone and to have some food as well as a bit of my cake. Mum had lit it pretty much when I'd first walked in and they sang to me 'Happy birthday'.

Matt had gotten me to put on my poshest frock which was navy blue silky dress and I felt beautiful. Mum soon ushered me out the door again though and I'd only just eaten. We went to watch our first farce, Matt and I with Mum and Dad, at Weston-Super-Mare. The farce was set around a hotel that apparently had a leisure complex. I let out a roar of laughter in the wrong place. The action stopped on the stage as they looked in the rafters up at me and the big guy said, "It wasn't that funny," and they carried on with the script. Matt and I had a brilliant night.

The next day we went to my in-laws to see Bob, Sue, Tom and Lis. all six of us sat in the living room having a cup of tea with lemon drizzle and Lis was telling us how her and Tom got together as they'd shared the same social circle. Lis said herself that Tom thought that she was a bit of a matriarch and didn't like her very much but they grew on each other and Lis said, and I quote, "That's how the best love affairs start." I thought that she was sharing too much and didn't trust her.

That following weekend Matt and I turned up at the Golden House Chinese restaurant. I felt all happy when I knew that the in-laws with Fee and Eve with my sisters partner Matt were going to be there too. I also saw Matt's best friend Julian of whom was there with his girlfriend Rose. I told a story of when Matt's friends stripped off his boxers there once and I was convinced one of the female staff fancied him from then onwards. It was just an ego thing to hate knowing another woman had seen his bits. I thought she'd be after him after that. I said to everyone. After a delicious meal Fee and Eve wanted to take me clubbing for my 30th birthday. I loved them even more as we all stuck together on a crowded floor to boogie away all night.

The following Sunday, not the next day, we had our last dance rehearsal for Shikra taking place up in the Queens Head Inn's skittle alley. I was waving my arms about pretending to be a bird flying with the whole club doing the same thing. Towards the end they gave out the really feathery costumes and mine needed more pinning together as Anne-Marie and Rita fussed over my costume.

Next came our first carnival night at Bridgewater. The rehearsal carnival they'd called it. I flapped about on the float warming up to the music. I'd inwardly prayed a little prayer for protection for everyone before shooting off round the course. The crowd weren't very receptive but I thoroughly enjoyed it all over carnival and was surprised by the time Wells carnival on the Friday came round. It had been raining and round the route I'd spied Eve first along Union Street. Then Nan Sheila second, near the end of the route sitting in her friend's garden. Alighting off the cart we made a beeline for some food then made our way back to The Venue. Sitting near the bar I ate my burger and had an orange and lemonade. Others were singing on the karaoke but I'd had a quiz handed me that had been bought for a pound. I looked at it, filled in a few answers, and passed it round my friends to have a look. Getting up for a boogie with Matt. Lyn and Jessie were singing Build me up Buttercup. Lyn's favourite party piece. Swaying to the music all night long and having a sing song myself made the night go fast.

We were soon on the last carnival down to Weston-Super-Mare and it rained again forcing the crowds to stay indoors. Then we all went back to Pontins.

In the morning I went to the Methodist church for nine o'clock. In the church hall there were lots of stalls. There was a book stall, a table full of clothes, a tombola, a table with teas and coffees on with slices of cake and another charity stall. I'd been there helping out on my mother-in-law's book stall. I sat there with my brother-in-law's fiancé Lis, and started to chat with her.

She said, "I had an ex once called Nick of whom I used to live with."
I thought, "Ok. I'm interested."

Then she said that she'd lived with him in Yeovil and had worked as a bar mad in a night club. I felt my nose go up in the air as I'd never do that demeaning job myself.

Ezekiel 16:56
In those days you were proud.

I knew she wanted me to share about ex's in return but I'd had so many I didn't want to go on about them in front of older friends of my mother-in-law's. It would have been embarrassing. Then I went up to Sue's house for lunch and stayed there for the afternoon.

Come the evening I got into my costume for carnival and queued to get made up. We looked like big birds of prey. I thought we looked fantastic and then we all trooped outside to go along the cart route to find our cart called Shikra. Now Mr Davis was a pain in the bum as he wouldn't turn our lights on to see to be able to get on our platforms. Then we had to stand around for what felt hours freezing our butts off because he just wanted to conserve energy. When we did get going I said a little prayer for everyone's safety. I danced around for three whole hours watching the biggest crowd in the universe watching me. It felt terrific. When we all got off at the end Matt and I rushed to the pub to get changed.

Afterward with a Phil, Marcus, Sarah, and he sister we sat in the rugby club around near to the bar chatting and singing our heads off. I remember getting up and dancing once for a dance competition. I couldn't be bothered to keep dancing as the place was too packed. Matt and I stayed till about two in the morning and decided to go home before the rush because we'd have got caught in the crush.

On the Monday work had started to be a disaster that week as no-one else cleaned the toilets but me. I learned how to see to a tanker full of oil, petrol and diesel from a theory test on the computer and did it for real that same day. I wanted the certificate but never got it. I'd been on my own in the evenings that week right up to eleven o'clock. Martin and Maria went home early and Penny told me that week an old friend of hers had died called Brian of whom I'd once worked with. He'd been a lovely man.

The highlight of my week was Matt and I going fishing together at the viaduct fisheries just down the road from us at a little place called Somerton. Matt had a gentle way with me and never got irritable when I'd talk with him while fishing. I'd soon learnt my role at fishing was to provide the food even if I just had to saunter up the path by our pond to get pasties. I'd also bought the crisps as the penny finally dropped that Matt never ate anything while fishing unless I was there with the hamper. It was always lovely talking to Matt as I never felt the need to fill in the silences. We fitted together perfectly and he also let me fish.

That evening my boss from work called Penny took us staff and our partners out for a Christmas meal which was lovely.

In the morning I found out that Lis was openly using Bob, Sue and their friends and family for her own ends, which never seemed to include me. I noticed that she made a lot of effort to get to know everyone that day instead of talking to me. I heard he offer her services to do things for other people like when Bob was on the phone to someone she suggested something they could buy. Bob put his hand over the speaker bit and said, "Yes. That's a good idea Lis," then I assumed he told Gwenda.

I went to the fridge and noticed a Tupperware box with lasagne in it. My mother-in-law said, "Don't touch that it's what Lis had made for us."

When Lis spoke to me that day with no-one else around, that she'd sat with Sue and discussed lineage in her jewellery box. I got suspicious of my new in-laws relationship with Sue. Bob and Sue even discussed in front of Matt and I going over to Tom and Lis's for tea. I started to hate Lis as they were not including me in anything least of all their discussions.

Leviticus 19:18
Do not take revenge on anyone or continue to hate him.
But love your neighbour as you love yourself.

They even talked about going on holiday together just the four of them. By then I'd had enough and went across to speak with Matt's Nan instead for an hour and told her everything about Lis and she said, "Yes. I've noticed something weird go on over there too," so I started to hide my self-righteous attitude towards them.

On New Year's Eve I'd gone shopping for a new dress over at Clarks Village and found a nice red spotted dress that I tried on ready for our New Year's Eve party. I felt fantastic in it and at home I showered and shaved my pits and my legs ready for the evening. I put the dress on and Matt was faffing with a tie. He had a handsomest way about him in black trousers and a purple shirt. In the end I had to help him with the tie, and I tried to kiss him. All embarrassed and harangued he told me to get off. We were going to The Wessex Hotel with some of our friends like Jim and Val, Justin, Mark and Steve and Julian. When we got there we first got a drink and then I used the dance floor all night long as I loved to dance.

On January fifth it was a Sunday and it was our Wick CCs annual general meeting. Jo Costanza took over as secretary as she was voted in. We'd also invited in a new chairman from John to Jessie and new other officers. The meeting seemed to go on a bit too long what with the rules to have to go through and change. The treasurer had given us all copies of our funds and that took ages to explain as I'd noticed inconsistencies in the totals. We were all sat on chairs up at the Queens Head skittle alley feeling hot and stuffy.

After any-other-business we drew to a close to that meeting to start the next. A fourteen year old girl called Kirsty, who made the rules change a little bit regarding age of performers on the cart under our insurance policy. A lady named Faye had joined too. I'd had my opinions of Craig with Ryan that he was brown nosing him confirmed by Rita at that meeting. I'd had my usual orange and lemonade under my chair as Matt and I held hands all evening.

The next day I'd been told by Fee she'd got a bird bath with us sisters money and was at her house ready to be driven over to Mum's for her birthday that day.

Now in the afternoon Matthew and I came over to Mum's to see her and gave her a birthday card. I spied out the window, as Mum said thanks for it, the mermaid bird bath table, that the table was there in the undergrowth in the top left hand corner of her back garden. I smiled and though it looked fantastic.

We stayed in the kitchen with Mum and chatted until it was time to all get in our cars and travel to the Poacher's Pocket, a pub restaurant, in a place called Doulting. When we got there Uncle Cyn had already turned up with Nan Sheila with our Casey and Charlie. We met at the bar and worked out rounds together and they said, "Don't bother." I can just hear Uncle Cyn saying, "We'll all take turns to buy your Mum a drink." I felt pleased for Matt and I as finances couldn't stretch for a whole round. Then we sat in the conservatory part of the pub restaurant where lots of tables and chairs were put together for all nineteen of us. As the food came out it looked and tasted delicious and we chatted non-stop. Then a waiter came out with a cake and we all sang happy birthday. It was a wonderful evening as I felt all aglow with happiness that the whole family had come together.

The next day Fee introduced her new partner to all of us round Mum's as they'd been invited round for tea and Matt, Fee's intended, seemed too good to be true and I felt suspicious of him as I'd been looking for a flaw in his character, but decided that my jury was out about him until I could begin to warm to him. Then Mum asked Fee's Matt, of whom had his own building business, if he could convert her garage into a school room as she was doing a course called Introduction to Childcare Practices in order to be a child minder.

"Would you like to be one?" Mum asked and I said sure. I'd wanted to leave the garage then anyway as there'd been talk it was going to open for twenty four hours and start selling booze. I told this to Mum and she gave me the ephemera with this course's details and decided there and then to book onto this course myself to be able to join Mum in her new venture. We'd sat there for ages, Matt and I, and decided to go home for tea.

A week later Valentine's weekend and Matt surprised me on the Saturday in the morning with a lovely bunch of carnations that I put in a vase that was placed in the fireplace of where there was no fire just cleverly placed bricks and a shelf. that annoyed me as in a ground floor flat it didn't look right as all I saw was the wall where the fireplace should have been.

> *Proverbs 25:24*
> *Better to live on the roof than share the house*
> *With a nagging wife.*

I'd wanted to nag Matt about getting rid of it. My flowers really filled the area. Matt told me to pack. Which I did. Then we took off in the car to Weymouth for the weekend and it was brilliant.

Now when we got back my lovely carnations were still in full bloom. It was lovely to see them. I'd looked through the paper the beginning of that week and had arranged an interview for a sous chef's job at a posh place in Shepton mallet called Bowlish House. I'd arranged the interview for that day we'd come back from Weymouth so Matt took me up to Shepton.

I went into the interview prepared to answer any questions with straight to the point answers, like: "Have you had any experience?"

I'd say, "Well yes. I've been a traditional housewife for the past ten years. Chopping things up and preparing my husband's and mine meals." Then I'd thought of the why question and thought to say, "Because I want to learn even more about cooking while getting a wage at the same time."

The whole interview went to plan, then I sauntered up to Mum's where Matt said that he'd been going.

It was a couple of weeks later that my new course in ICP was booked up for. That morning at work I'd already got to know most of the staff but management had changed a lot since being there and Penny the current manager I could see myself a lot in. She was very career driven and believe din people especially me.

In the evening Introduction to Childcare Practices started up at a school called St Dunstan's. We'd worked in one of the class rooms with a great bunch of ladies of where we all had to pair up together. We chatted about childcare in general and we received lots of agenda sheets of paper to put in folders we had to bring. Our first agenda sheet we filled in about our own profiles and how and why we came to be doing the course. I told them that I was setting up a childcare business with my Mum. I wrote down that I'd finished looking, finally, for a vocation as I believed I'd found it to look after children. I had a wonderful feeling that I'd love it as I had a lovely nephew that I helped to look after and it was nothing but joy.

Our folders were full of paperwork to look at each week of the course and our profiles were supposed to be put in the front of the books.

For the rest of the week I got on well with the manager Penny as she gave me lots of space to get on with things and even promoted me to being supervisor. I felt great and on top of the world. I should have asked for a pay rise, but didn't think of it but loved handling all the cash and working with the safe.

The following week on the Tuesday it was my second session at St Dunstan's school. We made brain wave pictures of what children might need in a child care setting, like safety procedures, proper utensils in cupboards and drawers they couldn't get to and trap their little fingers in. I said that I wouldn't let them get their own scissors for safety reasons. We also came up with needing an insurance policy and needing paediatric first aid certificates. When we filled it in there was another hand-out to look at in our folders of a nursery setting and we had to ring the hazards. I spotted the sockets and ringed them as they needed special covers on them if they weren't being used as little ones could turn them on and put their little fingers in them. I found five more hazards through talking with my partner. One more was that leads were on the floor and too long as little fingers could either pull hot things on to them or little feet might have tripped over them. It was a good session.

I had a phone call from Mum that evening and she told me that Charlotte, my cousin, had gone to Rio with her sister Casey and came across an orphanage. To try and stop it closing down they pledged to send them some money to keep them going. When they got back they did a fundraising pig roast and dance. Mum told me, had we known in time we'd have gone and supported them. Mum felt proud of her niece for raising five hundred quid.

One morning I'd woken up from a weird dream of where I'd had my head on a railway track in a dark tunnel and I'd heard the loud swoosh of a modern train. My head swivelled to the right and saw a wonderfully bright technicoloured landscape right in front of me. I went up Mum's that day after work and had gotten a bit of a shock.

"Now don't break down," Mum said, "But your cousin Charlotte had died. I saw it on the news that a twenty something young lady got hit by a train up in London. Your Uncle Cyn called to confirm that it was her."

I froze in shock not really believing it, but when I saw my Mum she burst into tears. I held her in my arms and we both cried together. Words soon spread to the rest of the family that day on 24th March 2006.

Now that month finished in a bit of a blur and on the sixth April it was Charlotte's funeral. She had a cremation and I heard a beautiful singing voice that was her that everyone cried to. There were about a hundred people there to mourn her. My family were pleasantly surprised that she'd had a lot of friends. I spoke to all of them as they passed by close family when coming out of the room.

Afterward we went to the Boathouse in Bath for the wake. It was by the park and ride near a river. It had been a beautiful place. All the friends that had turned up to the funeral came to the wake and we all signed two memory books. I put down that I wished I had known her better and that she had been a very beautiful person inside and out. I'd felt full of regret about now knowing her so well and should of.

> *Ecclesiastes 1:17*
> *I found out that I might as well be chasing the wind.*

That moment will always be frozen in time to me and a few days later I'd been at home just lying about on the sofa after work listening to Maroon 5's 'Songs about Jane' album and I inwardly prayed for a lobotomy as I'd pushed a lot of regret to one side in my mind too many times in my life time. I regretted not pursuing Martin at 16 years old, beating Eve up, and the most recently scenarios and I'd never released those trapped feeling before. That evening Matt and I went to Bob and Sue's for tea and would have loved to know why my upsetting cries for Charlie were being ignored by my in-laws, especially Lis chatting away inanely. So I got up into the kitchen following my parents-in-law and just slumped into Sue's arms for a hug and the tears just poured out and I told them about poor Charlie. Lis and Tom never noticed anything was wrong all evening and didn't even care enough to ask me if I was all right when I came back into the living room to have a drink with everyone else.

The next day I found myself reaching for a packet of Lambert and Butlers to smoke and I hadn't had a cigarette since I was twenty one at work.

After work I'd been smoking on the way home. It had been raining all day and had filled the landscape drainage park down the road from work. I'd walked behind the hedge by the road and looked out over the lake by all the industrial estate buildings. I'd seen C J Whites, and looked out over the builders yards by the traffic lights while puffing on my cigarette that just felt like another extension of me. I'd felt relaxed ready to face the afternoon at home with Matt.

Now on the 29th April all the family and a couple of Casey's friends got together for her thirtieth birthday at The Thatch, a lovely restaurant at the top of Shepton. We got to meet a lovely woman called Ruth who said that she had been friends with Casey and Charlie in London. She seemed really nice, warm and friendly, a bit of a laugh like she was one of the family. We all enjoyed ourselves even with a tinge of despair in the air.

The next day was a Sunday and Matt had gone to work while I went to St John's church. It had been a lovely sunny weather day and that afternoon Matt and I went up his mother's for lunch. It was a nice Sunday roast chicken. We had a bit of chocolate torte each the chocolate hadn't been the best I'd ever ate but ate it anyway.

I soon got up declaring that I'd wanted to wash up and headed for the sink. I sorted out the mountain of washing up by the side of the sink and then Sue took over throwing food out as I washed up. Lis, my sister-in-law was on the other side drying. I distinctly remember Lis telling Sue that, "Didn't Fanny Craddock tell us once what order to wash up in?"

I thought, "Yeah, but it's common sense to me to wash the glasses in clean water first," and told them so as they'd been talking over my head about this clearly trying to look down their nose at me.

The next day at work Carrie, my supervisor and Daphne were talking about arranging to meet up nightclubbing. I got a little bit jealous and dreamt of going round town and clubbing with them. Daphne took one look at me and pointed out that my feet were smelly. It was the only fault she could find. I was almost smart in my blue Texaco shirt and black trousers unlike her who had to be immaculately dressed with all her war paint on. She told me later on that say about her family back in the Philippines and thought that we'd been getting on really well together.

A few days later Penny, the new manager, promoted me to be a supervisor officially. I didn't think to ask for a pay rise like I should have done. I was just pleased to have more control of everything 'cause I felt that it was my time to be better than I could be. That day after Penny had gone home I'd been left to deal with the money in the office and instead of giving Daphne change for notes, I sat there on the floor counting the money over and over again from the safe. There was a lot of customers in the petrol station and I'd felt under pressure to count it. In the end I thought fuck it I should have gone home half an hour ago. I put it all back and left.

On the till one day Ian was skulking behind me putting out the fags and he told me he'd get down a Maxim. My eye was instantly drawn to a black cross, whips and chains round a girl's body and I went cold. I'd finally seen sense about that boy and he stopped right by me realising that he'd pushed my buttons far too far. Feeling an icy presence about me I'd stopped working. Someone came in and shook me out of my reverie and I returned to my tasks on the till.

During work on an ordinary day in the week I remember having been offered three cups of tea from Daphne. I'd thought that I'd overheard someone talking under their breath from the other side of a shelf as no-one answered them. I wandered round the weird shops of where books on myths, magic, witches and rare stones were sold. I'd never been in these shops before and I could whiff something dodgy in the air. I went home and felt fine but in the evening I'd found myself spiritually volunteering for something. I remember jumping on the bed and touching the light bulbs saying I'd seen the light and knew all about the three-in-one, Christ, God and the Holy Spirit. A man turned up in the living room of where I'd been touching the hot lights again saying that Mum, Nan and I were the three-in-one and that anyone could understand it. Next thing I knew I'd blanked out seeing Mum and my sisters running into the flat while hearing what I thought was a helicopter whirring ready to whisk me away on holiday somewhere with my family. In reality though, it had been an ambulance. The next day as I came round there were lots of lights exploding around me and a picture of a frog in an animated light all just floating around my head in the darkness interspersed with vague orange lights.

As I came too properly Matt was with me in a room I didn't recognise and I was told that I'd been tested for all sorts of drugs and had come back clean. I'd been pumped with fifty six pills in order to bring me down. It was so nice to see Matt and I remember wandering around a carpeted corridor getting a de-ja-vu that I'd been here before. The other residents were wandering round like zombies. I'd talked to one brunette and she told me that she'd come from abroad somewhere to live in England.

That same day a car had been arranged, with a nurse to come with me, to take me to a place in Wells called Phoenix House.

I'd had quite a lot of visits from my family and Matt was there every day. They were all keen for me to come home but while I was there, during one lunch time, I bumped into my old friend, from school, Kim's mum. I asked her how Kim and Paula were doing and she glowingly told me that Kim trained to be a doctor. While we were talking over lunch a man felt inclined to talk about my gold watch, on my wrist, and how nice it was. Now I didn't know what this man was in hospital for and it occurred to me he might have been diagnosed with kleptomania, a tendency to steal. This made me look forward to going home all the more.

Matt had told me we'd go away on a holiday when I came out and thankfully I came home after a week.

It was that time of year when it was light early in the morning and when I woke up one morning the birds were singing and I looked out the window. The sky was blue but it was only five o'clock. Determined to go out I roused Matt from his sleep and told him that I wanted to go for a walk out across the moors. We jumped into the car and stopped by the Railway Inn out at Meare. Matt and I got out for a walk. The sky was clear and it felt fresh. We cuddled as we ambled along quite nicely out passed the bridge. We got home at about eight am.

Around one o'clock in the afternoon Matt and I heard that my brother-in-law had had his first child with his wife Lis. They were at Yeovil Hospital. I'd had on a short brown dress that had buttons down the front and Matt wore his shirt and trousers down to the maternity ward. Once there my eyes lit up. It was a girl who looked so tiny and vulnerable. I really wanted to cuddle her so I asked if I could hold her. Lis said yes and positioned her in my arms over a pillow for support. Matt took a lovely photo and I didn't realise till afterwards I'd left my sunglasses on. I felt so in awe of this little baby my heart went out to her.

1 Kings 10:5

It left me breathless and amazed.

They said her name was Emily. We gave Tom and Lis an anniversary card and a well done you've got a baby girl card to them too. Both parents were glowing and my little hold of her was for a long time, I was in love.

Later on that evening I'd sat at my old computer and found my creative writing side again and composed lyrics about bonking bunnies. They bonked in the morning, and bonked in the afternoon and bonked in the evening. I had a good laugh with myself while I was writing it sat in the spare room. This I did while Matt was sorting out a holiday for us over the phone. I could hear him book a hotel called The Alexander down at Weymouth and he secured a room overlooking the sea. I turned the computer off and decided to pack some things like a nice dress to go out in the evenings wearing along with sorts and a long skirt. I had my blue mottled coloured t-shirt that was skin tight and a floaty shirt amongst basic underwear plus toiletries which I did till the end of the day.

Next day Matt drove quite fast down the road to get to Weymouth and I blasted our ears with loud music on the radio and had a good sing song. Luckily the hotel had a parking space just for us round the back of The Alexander. It was a poky place and Matt's manoeuvring about was terrible. It took us ages to park.

Now we spent our days on the beach and one day when it was hot I felt the heat too much and started to burn real easily and we ascertained that my pills were aggravating a problem with the sun on my sensitive skin.

Each morning after breakfast we phoned our mothers who told us the weather was crap back home so we rubbed it in about the sun being out. Now during one phone call we were told that my sister Eve had, had a mini stroke which upset us. Thankfully it had been near the end of the holiday before we had to go back for my appointment with Dr Van Driel at Phoenix House. I told him about my sensitive skin reacting to the pills and so he changed the prescription.

On that day we went to see Tom and Lis, my brother-in-law and his wife to see how mum and child were doing.

At the house Emily was on a banana shaped pillow round her mummy's waist. They let me hold her the same way. I was in the same brown dress as before in my sunglasses for another photo. I couldn't get over how petite she was and held her for a long, long time.

A few days later Tom and Lis came round my flat on their own and they sat in one of the armchairs and Tom sat on the arm. Now I remember Lis giving me a toy dog but why? She was a grown woman giving another woman a present to try and cheer her up.

Isaiah 19:15

No one in Egypt, rich or poor, important or unknown, can offer help.

I thought that she was taking the piss. The toy didn't even look like a dog it looked like a pitiful rat. Her and Tom sat there only for about an hour before they made their excuses and left.

After a few days I was ready to face the world again and went back to work. That first day back Daphne was getting on my nerves and she made me sing. I knew why instantly what she was getting at me about making me sing an old little song that went,

"Eenie, meanie, minee, mo, catach a knicker (by that I meant thief)" I'd said to her then went on, "By its toe. If it squeals let it go."

I knew darn well it could have been misconstrued, that word knicker as nigger if not sang properly. I questioned that in my head at just the right time.

With that little song in my heart I started to think of lyrics to write about the garage and making money so that when I got home I actually printed those two songs going through my head to keep in an orange folder. I looked for the bonking bunnies to print out but I couldn't find it and really loved those lyrics.

On the first of July my eldest sister Fiona gave birth to a wonderful girl they called Lauren Charlotte, and Matt and I soon got a few necessities together as a present before we shot off to the hospital to see my new little niece. Lauren was a healthy weight that everyone called a bonnie baby as Mum and Dad were there as we got there. She had lovely chubby cheeks and was adorable. Matt and I took it in turns to hold her and we took photos. It was a momentous occasion.

The next day I woke up and it was Liam's, my little nephew's birthday. Now I'd collected stickers for a long time while working at the petrol station. I had gone about it in not the totally honest way, because the World Cup was in full swing and there were loads of tokens at the garage the people just did not want. I just wanted the right tokens for Liam so undid a lot each day, and nobody noticed, to get the right ones for him.

Now his party that day was at Wells football ground and we sat in the dance hall together putting his tokens into the book I gave him. It was a good laugh. I'd been there for his birthday.

The next day I woke early and was ready to start working with my Mum and I came across the road cleaner called Steve. We started talking about our computers and games we'd played on them and I told him about the song lyrics that I was writing. I had a good whinge about how slow my computer was working.

"Steve. Do you know of any computer games I could buy off you?"

He said, "No. I'm not in for doing it for money."

"You're not a capitalist then?"

He said, "Whoa. I know the big word, but I am not one. I'll download some one day on a disk for free."

Then he mentioned about defragmenting a self-cleaning button on my computer of which I intended to use.

I got on the next bus and went up to my Mum's and they were still decorating and putting things up in what used to be the garage to be a child minding room. I'd been pleased with the results and started to look forward to working with Mum one day. I'd spent a good day with my Mum and at the end of the day Matthew came and got me.

Now the next morning I arose to go to work in the petrol station. While walking to work through a very harsh wind god spoke softly to me and asked, "Did I want to control the weather?"

Now I'd been getting the creeps from the bad weather anyway and I said, "No," to controlling the weather because I knew it would creep me out even more if I could just click my fingers and the weather would automatically change.

By ten o'clock I was getting pissed off with people treating the place like a garage constantly asking for advice with their vehicles.

Proverbs 25:17
They may get tired of you and come to hate you.

I kept saying, "I am not a mechanic. This is a petrol station, not a garage."

At home after work I started writing song lyrics about Christ being crowned King and another one about there being a purple sky of where the whole world was turned upside down and there were triangles everywhere like the Bermuda one.

Next day when I was in the petrol station I knew Penny, my boss, was keeping an eye on me making sure I'd been alright. She was constantly putting out stock letting me stay on the till so that I hadn't felt like I'd had to do too much. She kept looking over to me and could see my face glowing as I enjoyed that aspect of my job anyway and she needed something to do.

In the evening I had to go to St Dunstan's school to do my fourth session for my ICP certificate. This session was all about diapers and how to dispose of them. I blurted out the first thing that came to mind that they should be incinerated in the back garden and everyone gave me a strange look to one another so I soon shut up.

We had two more ICP sessions after that and then the last one was about putting our folders together and writing out a contents list and numbering each page to coincide with it. I'd felt really pleased with myself and carried it all home after being told that I was ready to be a child minder and that I'd get the certificate in a month's time.

In the morning I got on the bus and went to Mum's to start child minding. There were no children there and Mum and I got to talking.

"How would you like to go about this child minding job with me?"

"What do you mean Mum?"

"Well I can't pay you. You'll have to find a little part-time job."

"Well like a job share of where receptionists do that?"

"Let me finish. I need a job share don't I or a couple of days a week in a little café?" Which was what Mum and I agreed before I'd started.

My first day at Mum's she asked me if I'd work upstairs in the bay room We'd had two children in, a little boy called Henry and an older little girl called Billie. Her mother was called Kelly of whom I'd recognised from school days. I remember looking at he and thinking she hadn't changed at all with her long blonde hair in a ponytail and her nice tom boyish shape.

Leaving her child behind after staying for a cup of tea and a chat telling us about her farm where she worked. Kelly said, "Have a nice time," to her daughter.

Billie followed Mum around all day so I had a one year old Henry to look after. He was adorable. I read him stories, changed his nappies, fed him, sang to him, and played this little piggy with his toes. He had a gorgeous smile on his little face all day until he went home with his mother. Kelly came earlier for Billie.

Chapter Twenty-Two

The next day Henry turned up smiling with his Mum and we went upstairs. Mum had got out toys for him and he was learning to put different shapes into a ball with a star, a triangle, a square and an oblong shape. We had a lovely time laughing and giggling together. He was such a sweet little boy and I read him a lovely little child's version of 'A Midsomer Night's Dream' that was about a complicated love affair.

After the day was over I went home.

The third day into child minding with Mum I came to work very keen to look after the children. Mum had Billie downstairs and I took a little baby upstairs to the little nursery and I gave him a cuddle. He was a little cuddly baby and I sat on the floor reading to him while I lovingly looked at him on the little sofa during which time he stood up. It was amazing seeing a little baby standing up for the first time and he fell of and bumped his little bottom. I freaked out and cried while cuddling him in my arms and took him downstairs to Mum who soothed him with a cold wet flannel on his forehead. He looked pink like he'd had a heat rash so Mum suggested I work with him for the rest of the day downstairs.

Mum said, "I can keep a better eye on you Karen with Henry," and he stayed happy and fun to look after for the rest of the day. Then I had to put the incident in an accident book. I soon got home and found my ICP certificate had come through the post so I put it in my folder.

It soon became Sunday and up at my mother-in-law's we did lunch Matt and I with them and it was lovely. Tom and Lis and baby Emily were there. It had been a lovely afternoon.

We had our first dance rehearsal for Genghis Khan that evening. A choreographer who'd worked the fayres with her fairground ride was teaching us the routine up in the Queens Head skittle alley. Her name was Zoe.

The next day Mum let me go up to town to look for work but I got side tracked thinking that I could still be famous one day and stopped off at the Amulet in town that was run by a theatrical group. I'd wanted to find some acting classes but couldn't find any and I soon went back to Mum's not having looked for any jobs. I told Mum that I'd looked in shop windows for someone advertising for a job.

I then went upstairs and there was a ball pit there. That day I'd had great fun with Henry laughing at throwing the balls around. Later Mum said she'd heard our laughter and was reminded about the joys of looking after children.

The next day when I went into work I was full of the joys of summer with the sun out and I had gotten into the habit of wearing sweat pants and a t-shirt with a fancy girlie colour on it. I was happy and looking forward to looking after Henry again. He was a very cute adorable little boy with chubby cheeks. In the living room I'd seen the ball pool out and Mum asked me did I want a cup of tea. I said yes and got down on the floor to witness little Henry in there and I had good fun.

I talked to Mum and told her my fears about getting another job because I believed that they could access my mental health records and would turn me down because of them. My Mum sympathised over a piece of cake with our coffees later on. We had a lazyish day and it went by nicely. I settled into the job more with Mum that seemed lovely and Mum said, "I need you to grow up and put on less tatty clothes," but I thought that bet clothes in this type of job would get ruined and told her so. She pointed out that there were black pinafores under the changing mat to put on.

Several weeks passed by and I tried getting Henry to crawl by getting down on all fours right in front of him and doing little push ups of which he'd watch and sweetly try to copy.

Towards the end of the fourth week up at Mum's Henry started to crawl backwards and I had to move some things out of the way in the baby room. I secretly smiled when I'd seen him do it and thought that I helped this little boy to crawl. I kept trying to get him to move forward by showing him again how to do it. I had a lot of fun with that agenda. We still enjoyed the ball pool while Mum had a lovely little girl to look after called Billie.

It was a Saturday and I watched the cricket with Matthew and we lazily sat around watching in the sunshine. It was nice and relaxing. While Marcus's Sarah was pregnant I bumped into her outside the Queens Head and she told me that she was being good by not giving into her cravings. In return though I told her that perhaps her craving was telling her there was a certain vitamin deficiency in the child. Sarah told me that she'd never thought of it like that.

I woke up in time for a church service the next day. It was a nice service.

One day in work with now quite a few children to look after. I remember sitting on the floor with the children at a loss as to what I should be doing so I picked up two plastic colourful balls and started juggling with them and I managed to catch the children's attention. When we'd have fruit mid-morning with the children Mum and I started having milky coffees and cake. When the children came in that morning I'd said, "Good morning cherubs," and from there on in I always called the children that.

I called mother the next day to tell her that Bob and Sue had, had a break-in at their house after Sue had taken £800 from her account for a new sofa. That morning it disappeared we all thought that she'd been watched and followed from the Post Office. I felt drawn to Lis afterwards thinking that she was the brainy one what were her views and as I'd imagined she'd have a lot to say for herself as she usually did and I had a funny feeling that she had something to do with it. This was paranoia. I slept very well that night and in the morning went up the Tor while waiting for Matt to come home. I then went with him to Tor Leisure a cricket club and we lazed out on the grass. Matt fell asleep so I got out a crafty fag. Next thing I knew a fit looking blonde was running right at us and she jumped on Matt waking him up saying, "You shouldn't sleep at a Frisbee tournament," and I got caught out with a cigarette in my hand and we continued to watch all the Frisbees being thrown about for three games being played out in front of us with lots of people running around. It was complete madness but it was wonderful with the amount of life around us. Matt had irritated me by falling asleep.

Proverbs 19:13
A nagging wife is like water going drip-drip-drip.

I wanted to nag him as he wasn't that much company.

The next day going up to Mum's on the bus I'd found myself having to stand up, as my new pills were making my knees twinge. This happened when the bus stopped just before Tin Bridge and I jolted forward. Clearly my medication wasn't right and I'd got scared every time I'd stood up especially when the bus jolted.

Psalms 6:2
O Lord; have pity on me!

I could have gone through the window or fallen over and hurt myself.

At Mum's I was feeling at a loss as to what to do with the children again so I picked up a Mickey Mouse mask. I put it on my face and started shaking each child's hand saying, "Hi, I'm Mickey Mouse. What's your name?" In an American accent just like I did when I used to read to my sister Eve in the bathroom when we were small. Each child was either laughing at me as they took my hand for a shake. The others looked at me as if I'd gone mad but I loved seeing and hearing their reactions. I had such a lovely day trying to get the children's attention.

In the morning I had an appointment to see my specialist doctor who worked at Phoenix House called Dr Van Driel of whom was Dutch. He was a handsome man and I managed to convince him that my dosage of pills were not right and I explained to him the incident on the bus so they cut me down by 0.5mg of pills. I was really pleased and got back on the bus to go to Mum's for the rest of the working day.

While walking up Bowlish Hill after getting off the bus for work I noticed the colour orange everywhere, on the bus, in the autumn leaves, the back on some trees, and in bricks. They were to remind me that I am basically a good person which is what I learned to think after being in Phoenix House. I'd gotten to Mum just in time for lunch and had a nice afternoon.

The next day was a Saturday and forensics turned up at my mother-in-law's house to take some prints. Lis was asking her a lot of questions and apparently there'd been a smell of smoke in the room after the break in and Gran's dog had barked up the garden that day. Conner with his barking never stopped them. As we realised there was no chance these people would ever be found Matt and I decided to jump in the car and go for a ride somewhere.

Now the next day it was the start of our holiday. We were going to Crete and when we got there, there were very limited amenities in our room and it was buzzing with mosquitos.

While we were out one day we went to a supermarket and found a plug-in mosquito catcher. It soon cleared the air in our very basic room. On the plus side though, we were right on the beach. There was a little café there for the residents that only served croissants and bread for toast of which we didn't have to pay for. In the afternoon we'd gotten peckish on the beach but we had to pay for lunch and I'd asked for a mocha latte of which was really nice.

One day I rode a horse along the sea front. I'd brought cigarettes from the local supermarket and when I smoked I craved chocolate and so had a magnum most days. It was nice walking to the next town on the beach that had massive swing seats and I would lie on them with a fag in my hand. Then Matt and I watched a foam party once. We stood dancing to the side of them so as not to get covered in front of the foam.

One day we got n a coach for a trip in the pouring rain because of this we just stayed in a large café all day and couldn't do what we paid for to do. We were upset.

Peter 1:6
It may now be necessary for you to be sad for a while.

I'd broken my glasses on this holiday and spent the majority of the time in my sunglasses but at night everything was blurred and had to rely on Matt a lot for my eyes.

Come our wedding anniversary for our celebrations we had a lovely meal out. I had spaghetti bolognaise and a lot of wine that made me ill.

It wasn't long after that we came home on the plane. When we got back I had to go straight to the opticians to order a new pair of glasses.

I went into the pound shop one day, back at home, with twenty pound in my pocket to put towards my expensive glasses. At the opticians I realised that the money had gone missing so I had to retrace my steps and I asked Lindsay in the shop, "Have you seen a twenty pound note? I've lost it."

She said, "You shouldn't have been that silly to lose it," and I knew instantly that she had it for herself. I felt dejected and went home unhappy how could I have gotten my money back off her.

It was the next month and on this Sunday we had dance rehearsals for carnival in the evening and the music gave me the creeps as it was about the Genghis Khan army and there was a section in the song about letting the devil take our souls. Every time they sang that it sent a cold chill up my spine.

On the Monday Matt and I got back to work and I found it hard to get out of bed and get ready for the seven thirty bus up to Shepton Mallet.

Now at Mum's little Rowan, Henry, Jasper, Adel, Billie and Lauren were there and little Adele was the eldest. They had a lovely time in the back garden playing in the sun all day. I really enjoyed myself. By the end of the day I trudged home on the bus tired but happy.

John 5:17
I too must work.

Upon looking at my tired face Matt decided to take us out for a meal. He'd suggested Wetherspoon's in Street. Once there we asked for a medium cooked steak. I didn't like it tough, chewy or pink, but I never ate it anyway as it all came out cold. I complained and got it reheated.

After a hard day's work the next day I looked forward to playing skittles with Mum's team the Rascals at tramways. Relaxing in good company with a couple of pints of fizzy orange. There was a lady called Tricia of whom I said hello to, she said, through conversation, that she lived on her own. Then there was Mandy, a friend of Mum and Dad's, of whom had been married to a Graham. I said hello to a Gill of whom was rather a large lady and he sister Christine. They lived in Shepton and Wells respectively they told me. Then there was Jan who worked as a nurse with Carolle and Julie, all of them were work colleagues who had worked at Phoenix House. Then there was Margaret who'd worked in an opticians of where she said, "I know your sister Eve I work with her."

I said hello to Cath next of whom was married to Uncle Graham. I'd asked if he was all right. Then Mum and Nan. We went on and won that skittles match.

That weekend Matt and I were in Shepton visiting Mum and we had heard on the radio that Jim Davidson was doing a live show at the Amulet in town so we had bought tickets for that evening. We'd stayed at Mum's for tea and then went across town.

There wasn't a queue when we'd gotten there and we went straight in. the soft seats let down from the ceiling were there for us to sit on and we had a warm up guy first who was a bit funny but with few people in the auditorium the claps and the laughter was not overly apparent. When Jim Davidson came out he took one look at the few people come to watch him and tried really hard to get a laugh from us. No-one felt sorry for him when he'd asked us to give him a standing ovation as he'd get extra money to help his child through school.

I'd been pleased to see him after years of watching him on TV especially as Jim had done a snooker quiz with John Virgo once that I used to like to watch. I laughed really hard completely enthralled by him and he was handsome.

The next Monday hopping on the bus I'd had fun after talking to a man on and on about his work in Shepton and he kept talking all the way up to the bottom of Mum's hill.

At the top after going round the houses doing the children's school route in reverse. I knocked on the door then Mum came downstairs in her dressing gown surprised that I was so early. It was quarter to eight early enough to be able to help Mum for once to set the house up with toys. I felt really happy and alive doing something extra useful for work as I'd been feeling not so useful for the past few days.

Mum decided to tell me that we'd have a dressing up day so got down the hat box to put on the floor in the living room. Mrs Pembro showed up with her two young boys Harry and James. Then the lawyer turned up with Katy.

"That's all of them," Mum said to me as she shut the door on another parent which I felt was rude as I'm sure Rowan's mum Stacey heard.

We took the children into the living room to show them a box covered in beige material with different clothes and hats stitched into the cover that nan Sheila had put together. We had the large hallway mirror in the living room propped up by the sofa so that each child tried on a hat mainly looking like pearly kings and queens hats. I smiled a lot at them particularly when Katy found a beret and stood in front of the mirror for ages.

It was a Saturday and I'd woken up early keen to get on with the day. Through opening the curtains I noticed that the weather was dry and the air was crisp. Putting on my jeans, a t-shirt and my favourite, cosy, navy blue cable knitted polo necked jumper. I never bothered with a coat and feeling warm headed down town for the bus.

Not having to wait too long I was soon on the Wells bus and playing back gammon on my phone. At the Wells Bus station I waited for the Weston-Super-Mare bus. Looking at my watch it was 8.30am. It was my favourite gold watch given to me years ago by Matt on our first wedding anniversary. Jumping on the 126 the bus headed out of town towards the cemetery of where I was to alight and walk down the hill to the St John's ambulance headquarters. I'd been early and met with the man there to take the paediatric course I'd turned up for. We'd had a chat about the training and Christian said that he knew my husband.

The others gradually turned up and we'd all sat in a line in front of a large window with the sun streaming through. One lady chose to be with me to practice CPR on the dummies. I warmed to her straight away as she treated me with respect.

At lunch time I'd sat in the test room on my own with my sandwiches while the others had gone next door to the café at Wells Leisure Centre.

Afterward we finished the day with a cross word we were all given first aid books to take home.

One day in work Mum got me to put this poem into little books for the children and I absolutely loved it. It was by an author called Patience Strong about 'Little Ears'. When I put this in it was near the front of what I'd been putting together a photo album and Mum also got me to photocopy a simple tick list for every folder too to show how competent the children were. There was a picture of a pencil indicating were they capable of using one. A picture of ears signifying could they take instructions, and there was another with a baby bottle, a beaker and a glass on, of which we ticked every time they achieved being able to do. I spent most of the day doing paper work that I fitted in perfectly with enjoying the children.

The next day Mum and I sorted out the medals in the morning to hang around the children's necks later. I put out the Big Toddler poster on the gate outside in the glaring sunshine happy it was a nice day.

In my red top and jeans I said good morning or tried to, to the adults as they turned up with their children. Mum got annoyed with me in the hallway with her and Carolle, a lady working with us, and told me to keep all the children out the way as more turned up. This got me irritable as the children were running everywhere. Some were practicing for later that I'd justified to myself as I couldn't control them.

Mum received the last of the collections except one from Charlotte, Grace-Anne and Oliver's mother. I watched her. We'd been raising funds for Barnardo's.

Then an hour later after organising hem we all met up with Fiona over at the cricket pitch with Liam and Lauren. We took some nice photos of us standing around together with the poster I'd made.

Then the children got led by Mum and I to run around the cricket field. It was to be three times. Little Henry and the other little ones I walked round with for one circuit. Liam and Rowan pushed themselves to do the three circuits and I ran round with them lagging behind with Rowan. When we got back to the others they all had box drinks and their medals for taking part.

It was soon holiday time and we were heading for Bulgaria. The plane landed in poor weather and Matt and I got on the coach to go to the hotel. It was night time and I'd usually pack our clothes away as soon as we got there, but was too tired upon arrival and Matt and I went straight to bed. I had to lay on the crack between the twin beds we always had to push together.

We had to put on water-proofs the next day as Matt and I headed to the beach. Matt laid out on a sunbed and while asleep I jumped on a horse and galloped along the beach next to fierce waves in the windy weather. I smiled when Matt woke as he had to pay for my ride.

In the evenings we'd go round the pubs and clubs all competing with loud music. I'd been dancing around one night, minding my own business, when a girl deliberately bumped into Matt chatting him up. Matt knocked her hands away from his pockets knowing what she was up to.

We had one day of sunshine and we'd walked the farthest along the beach that day and Matt had spotted a nude man. I laughed and felt so hot I'd stripped to my undies and jumped in the sea.

This holiday we always remembered at the wet and windy one as we made our way home.

On the Friday I'd gone into work as usual but Mum had been told about the times for the bus leaving the carnivals headquarters in Glastonbury. I'd felt tired that morning so that the children were a bit annoying, jumping on the sofa, wanting seemingly endless Bob the Builder videos, that they couldn't sit still for and one of them seemed to annoy me by throwing the toys around. One toy actually managed to hit the TV off which I couldn't have drawn attention to as Mum would've gone made.

When Matt came for me at two thirty I had a bit of a headache and was anxious to get away. Mum wished us good luck for the evening and said she hoped it wouldn't rain and gave me a hug before clambering into the car to go home.

Back at the flat I threw on my Jesters hoodie and we sauntered up to the pub early to have an alcoholic drink which helped alleviate some of the tensions in my head. Clambering on to the bus, when it turned up with Kelvin driving. Matt and I said hello loudly so that everyone on the bus could hear us. Lyn got on with us a bit worse for wear as she'd hit into her favourite doubles.

At Wells we climbed up the stairs in The Venue to go get changed into our costumes and upstairs I'd bumped into an old acquaintance from school called Emma. She'd dyed her hair blonde but I still recognised her and we got to talking about how long we'd both been in carnival and how we were both married. I'd even bumped into Marcus brown from school and said hello.

Getting into my costume I'd been getting nervous and seemed to need several trips to the toilet while having my second alcoholic drink to calm my nerves. I'd heard that it was spitting outside and next thing we all knew Kelvin was rounding us all up, after carefully put on make-up from Lyn, to walk up the Wells by-pass to get on the cart. Thankfully the cart was near the front of the line-up and because we were there early, Jason Bryant, the gazettes photographer, took a photo of us all before we boarded.

I got a real buzz dancing on the cart and would practice the routine before the start line while praying for everyone's safety that night.

> 1 Chronicles 12:40
> All this was an expression of the joy that was felt throughout
> The whole country.

I loved the music we were dancing to which was a song by Gloria Estefan that had been really upbeat. What with the rain and the heat from the bulbs around me my nose was running and my glasses were covered in rain drops and I couldn't see as I kept dancing to the crowds trying to draw them in. It didn't help that I couldn't hear much clapping but as we turned into the top of Wells high street I looked up into a flat's window above the shops and saw a familiar face. It was my sister Eve who'd created a flash in front of my eyes so I knew that she had taken a photo. This perked me up as I'd waved back at her and put even more effort into my dancing throwing my arms and legs around.

Near the end of the route I spied another familiar face and gave a wave to my Nanny Sheila never missing a beat with my routine. I knew my make-up had run from the rain and my back felt like it was burning up. I was sneezing come the end when we all went to get off right back to where we'd started but on the other side of the roundabout.

The whole carnival club were glad to get out of the rain back at The Venue and were incensed we'd had to pay a pound each to get back in but another club had put on the karaoke for the evening and a quiz. Never one to pass up the opportunity I had a good old sing song on the karaoke once I'd got changed enjoying my own voice.

The camaraderie of the carnival clubs were apparent and Lyn and Jessie got up to sing their usual 'Build Me Up Buttercup', and 'Sweet Caroline'.

On the way home on the bus we were all still singing while some of us fell asleep. A good night had been had all round and as Matt and I got dropped Matt decided to moon everyone on the bus before I got up and followed him down the alley back to our little flat.

It had been snowing for a few days and everywhere was white. Matt had taken a couple of pictures of the scene just outside our flat, our car dusted with snow, the white on the grass and the ice on the courtyard. Matt had done a lot of work getting in all the prizes from the shops, restaurants, hairdressers and pubs around town. I'd spent hours writing out posters and letters to theme parks, zoos and local attractions. I had gotten a lot of vouchers from.

The day came for our carnival Christmas bingo and John turned up at home with his van and a couple of helpers Rita and Keith to fill it with our spare room's collection of goodies. Keith tried to wind em up by telling me they'd take my piano away as a prize, but I just laughed it off.

At the Town Hall where we'd all met up with the rest of our club the prizes were all laid out strategically on the stage and around the table where the bingo caller Jessie was going to sit. Tables had been laid out in front of the stage for raffle prizes to be placed on.

There was a great big chocolate cake as one of the main prizes on the end table. The door opened at six thirty to let in what we hoped would be our regular large crowd but due to the snow only a handful of our regulars showed up. It was a quiet night but Jessie's banter seemed to keep everyone amused as he called out the numbers.

Halfway through we had a break to pass around free wine and mince pies that we'd stored in the back room from where we normally run our bars. Afterwards the club regrouped to sit together taking part in the bingo ourselves to raise extra funds. We always had a laugh sitting together. This was when we'd sold the last of our raffle tickets and so a couple of us had to tear up the stubs, fold them, and put them in the wooden tombola. For the second half of the bingo we changed callers to Eddie. He would try to crack jokes too but they were more near the knuckle. The evening had been a success.

I read in the journal about a drama group called Theatresaurus and there was a phone number to ring to talk to someone called Ros. I gave them a call and found out they met every Wednesday at a place called Seagar Hall in Wells. I was told that I was welcome to come for eight pound a session. I had always wanted to act and Ros said she was a professional drama teacher at Millfield. I thought that this was my chance as personal coaching was offered to get through possible auditions.

> *Psalms 31:24*
> *Be strong, be courageous, all that you hope in the Lord.*

When I attended the first session everyone seemed to know one another and were really nice. There was a game we played where we all stood around in a circle and had to copy a single movement from someone who was looking at you. The first movement was a twitch but as we copied each other each time the movements got more exaggerated.

We were also given a part of a script from a book called the Caucasian Circle, and the group was assigned particular characters each to do a read through with. The ended happily and I felt I'd learned a brand new story and learnt brilliant acting techniques to find out how to pick up on cues as to when to speak or act.

On the day of Rheann's wedding I'd turned up at the bottom of Mum's hill and walked up towards Rheann's mother's house to ask where the wedding was actually going to be. Her mother told me it was to be held at Shepton's registry office. I had dressed smartly that morning with my nicest black jacket on over a khaki coloured blouse and with black trousers. Walking all across town I'd gotten there just as the bride arrived and I went over and said hi. Rheann then asked me if I could stay and go to Bowlish House with them afterwards as a guest had pulled out. Very happy I said yes.

The ceremony was lovely from sitting at the back and they'd taken their vows in a little hall decorated with flowers. Rheann was in white and looking wonderful next to her gloriously Mediterranean skin. They'd signed the register looking blissfully happy before gliding back down the aisle. Rheann had said I'd made her day by showing up and everyone hung around outside afterward for photos. I wasn't in any until we went over to Bowlish House and out into the garden. The usual family shots were taken until it was my turn with a handful of Rheann's other friends and I was happy to be a part of this wonderful day.

> *Deuteronomy 27:7*
> *And be grateful in the presence of the Lord your God.*

We sat down to eat afterward and luckily the food that had been ordered for the no-show guest was just what I liked to eat. I started giggling with Glyn, Rheann's brother, that I'd successfully gate crashed a wedding and all the toasts were made before we all went back to Rheann's Mum's house afterward. Once there I was finally introduced to Meesha and Moneesha her cousins, the one who I though Rheann had made up all those years ago.

I was finally happy that Rheann had found someone who made her happy and it was ironic that her husband was called Matt too.

That Wednesday morning I got into work nice and early to help Mum set up the toys. Now Carolle suggested I wrote out alphabet books that day for the children. Mum had an alphabet book with black letters in order from A to z of which I felt the need to photocopy to make the books quicker for our six children. Photocopying each page took up a lot of ink so I found myself reaching for a black marker to write out every letter one by one. This task took me most of the day in between looking after two girls called Khya and

Ivy who'd started with Mum and I that week and we were looking after my niece Nancy.

Ivy was a lovely red haired girl with a thick Irish accent. Khya was of slight build and had long blonde hair, and seemed very intelligent. She always reminded me of someone who'd go on and work for spooks, a spy team on the telly. That first day with them I'd learned all about their soft temperaments and how to get round them. I was looking forward to seeing them the next day.

In the morning I bounded up the hill eager to start work and was greeted by a warm hug from Mum and a "Good morning. Lovely to see you. Come on in." This lifted my spirits even further and when I got into the school room I put out all the ephemera for the children to draw on. Ivy came in first with her mum, Nicky, who was lovely in her navy blue top and black trousers uniform for her job that day. When Khya turned up with her mother and Nancy I took them all into the school room. Then pulled out a handful of pens. One of each colour. We sat round a little round blue table from Ikea as I handed out each colour because I'd asked which pen they wanted.

Khya said, "That one, please," and pointed to one.

I'd said, "This is pink," I looked her in the eyes and she repeated the word pink back at me to learn the colour. I turned to Ivey, "Which one?" I'd asked and she pointed to one, "This blue one?" I asked and she just said, "Yes," cheekily. I expected her to repeat the word blue so I kept on until she said it and smiled back at her. We were there for a long time before going and finishing off the end of the day in glorious sunshine.

On the Friday it peed down with rain and we stayed indoors playing ball games throwing the coloured plastic balls into the coloured plastic bowls to sort the reds from the blues and the purple and the orange ones to teach them their colours.

The Saturday was amazing thinking of children. I got on the bus and chatted to a nice lady called Julie about her life as a nun and she told how she loves Jesus passionately and in her heart the woman knew she'd be his wife one day free from poverty and enslaved by sins of the flesh. Fun times were ahead she told me. "I could feel it in my heart and soul. I've been chaste for too long. I felt I was dying," then she confessed she had cancer.

"What type of cancer?" I tentatively said back and Julie replied, "Terminal," I then bit back tears and offered a silent prayer up to God for her and thought about that wonderful woman who'd given up her whole life up to God all day. My shopping was stinted that day as I thought about how selfish I was being so I just concentrated on getting nice gifts for everyone for Christmas. In my heart I knew that woman on the bus was going to her true love soon.

Sunday evening came far too fast and in the evening myself and my husband went to the carnival shed down on the wild moors stretching as far as the eyes could see meeting the moon and stars that evening. The big barn doors opened and we stopped in to view a large carnival float decked in Victorian street scenes with big candle lit street lamps down the side. Round the inside of the building were planks of wood attached to metal poles as scaffolding. Now there were stairs to get to stand on it and the choreographers got on there. I walked upstairs to the top of the scaffolding and got slight vertigo so I went back down stairs. Now Jenny the secretary helped with the choreographers and we all stood in the only area that was clear of wood chippings and tools and desks. We all looked up to them. I got a crook in my neck looking up at them and enjoyed dancing for the next hour. Then there was a meeting afterward of where I'd zone out and just chip in when I wanted to. They looked at me as though I was thick sometimes. I didn't care, then I'd make them feel small with a poisoned dart coming straight from the heart as they'd tried to make me confused. That man Stuart was an intellectual who would waffle. I always knew basically what he was on about so that was my dart I'd slap him down to make him look confused.

In the morning in work I sat down with the ephemera again and dished out the pens again giving two choices like the pink or the brown and they'd have to point to the right colour they asked for.

That afternoon on New Year's Eve I got ready for a party in a red dress and red lucky thongs with a matching bra. Matt and I were off to our local the Queens Head for a karaoke and a dance. Lots of locals and our carnival club were there having loads of booze and a laugh, a brilliant sing song and a dance. I got in the middle of a group of dancers and flashed my thong. I exclaimed out loud that I got lucky in those every time. I even followed Matt to the toilet and when we both came back we said we did it in the men's. At midnight I phoned everyone on my mobile wishing them a happy New Year, even my doctor and then I grabbed Charlene's big boobs while dancing. It was a brilliant night.

On the third of January Fee had taken a lovely photo of the children sat in front of their Christmas tree at home. On the back was a thank you note for all their presents. I put it all in Liam's photo album.

I had woken up one Sunday at eight am realising I'd enough time to wash my hair. I jumped into the shower that woke me up. Dressing carefully for church in a purple skirt and shirt I made my way across St John's car park.

Inside the church I'd made my way to the front so that the picture of Christ in the stain glass window was in full view. We heard the notices for the week from the vicar David and then the organist struck up the tune for the first hymn and stood up to sing as the choir wafted incense up the aisle and up my nose.

Proverbs 10:26

He will be as irritating as smoke in your eyes.

I'd knelt for the prayer of preparation and meant that my heart and mind be totally open to God for forgiveness.

As the service wore on two gospel readings were read out before another hymn. Then there was the sermon and Rev'd David Macgeoch drew on his family life to paint a lovely picture of how a Christian should be. I just stared at the depiction of Christ the Teacher willing him to send me a message just for me through the reverends words.

Before I knew it we were standing again for a hymn I'd actually sung before. Belting out the words this was my favourite part of the service, very few were in the congregation so much so they actually matched the amount of people in the choir. I stood still for the peace and let others come to me to shake my hand. I'd felt embarrassed slightly doing this as I'd just blown my nose with a bit of tissue. Embarrassment over I let the lady at the end of the pew beckon me up to the front for communion. Back at my seat I remember praying for the next person's prayers sat next to me as I could not think of a single prayer for myself and finished by saying the Lord's Prayer under my breath.

I was happy when the wafting incense made its way back into the vestry and confident enough to get a coffee at the back of the church. Someone came up to me through judging my size and asked me if I was pregnant. I didn't know where to look as I'd been going through the early menopause and had been turned twice for adoption. I'd plainly said, "No." to the woman, promptly finished my coffee and headed for home to cook lunch.

After tea that evening and washing up I felt as horny as hell and climbed on Matthew on the sofa. We were both full of heat coursing through us. I had to undo his zipper very quickly so fast I just writhed around on his dick that came hard so fucking quickly. His hands went up my top and my breasts softened as my nipples went hard. In fact my whole body softened and quivered so fucking much my head felt fuzzy and my eyes blurred over. Afterwards I felt thoroughly shagged. Matt looked like he wasn't with it and he had to go out the door to skittles.

When he came back later he told me that Glyn, the barman up at Queens, told him that he looked thoroughly shagged.

The next day began in a daze as I walked up through Mum's estate to her house while I cleverly started recognising the same names I'd made for the usual licence plates like; Fuck the Fox for the F66TFX and nice saxophone for N36 SXP on the vehicles I passed.

It was a nice day. It went swimmingly with Mum and I being outside all day with the back lawn cluttered with toys for the children. There were bikes, a trampoline, a Wendy house in the trees, and loads of retainers casually haphazardly strewn about everywhere. The children would dart about from toy to toy which made the atmosphere electric as I'd stop and play games with them in between like running around the lawn with them all and dancing round the washing pole.

Mum and I talked together on and off that day and she'd been telling me how Dad had started taking canoeing lessons at the local swimming pool once a week in preparation for one of their up and coming holidays.

The next morning the phone rang early and got me out of bed. It was a Saturday for Christ's sake. I'd wanted a lie in. Fee had been on the other end of the line asking if I could go out with them that day and where would I like to go for a walk. I suggested out Meare then she decided to take us out for a meal somewhere. I said that would be fine and I'd asked when she replied, "I'll be there about ten thirty. Please wait in. I'm coming with the girls they'll bring their scooters."

I said, "See you later. Bye," and hung up. I sat and watched Friends all morning waiting for her to turn up. My eyes kept turning to the window while I was twitching every five minutes for Fiona to turn up in her silver car.

At eleven there was a banging on the door. Fiona barged in needing the toilet. "The girls," she said, "Are waiting in the car." I waited for her while picking up my handbag and putting a coat on. "Let's get going," she said while primping herself in front of the mirror. I followed her out and in the car I'd noticed the girls, Lauren and Nancy not in their seat belts as per usual, so I told them to put their belts on. I even reached over the mess in the car to help Lauren click her belt in. Frightened they'd get hurt if they'd had an accident.

Flying down the road, as Fiona was a fast driver, we were soon at Ham Wall. The girls got out their scooters within five minutes of Nancy being on hers I ended up having to carry it along. The path was gravelly, there were buses and lots of trees wither side all shade of luscious green. I took a photo of beautiful Lauren in her pink leggings and stripy jumper posing on her scooter.

Fee and I talked about the children and where to go for lunch. We stopped at an information point and sat down for a rest and read all about the birds that could be spotted. Nancy started to get bored and along came Matthew. He'd finished work early, found my note and came to be with us. It was a lovely day weather wise and Matt suggested a pub lunch at a place called The Rose and Portcullis for a carvery. Matt and I got in our own car afterwards and led the way.

At the pub we went inside to sit down at a great big pine table near the hearth that was lovely and warm. We had a laugh then queued up for our lunch out in the restaurant that was nice and spacious with big windows all around that you could spy the garden through it. Matt and I eyed up the delicious food and had a slice of each meat. A bit of turkey, gammon and beef. The girls spied the little play park outside and afterwards we all went to watch them play on the swings and the climbing frames. I got a few nice pictures of them.

Fiona bundled her little family into their car afterward and said goodbye to take them all back home. Matt wanted to drive over his mother's. We went over there and had a cosy little chat while with the children and Tom and Lis. We soon rushed on for a carnival meeting up at Queens that had been boring.

It had been May Bank holiday the following day and Matt and I decided to go to a fete over at Brookside School. It was a modern looking building and we parked behind the wire fence where normally the teachers put their cars. It was a brisk morning and inside the hall there were lots of people milling about looking at lots of stalls. A pinball machine caught my eye with a five pound sticker on it. I immediately though of Liam of whom was approaching six years old. I went on and bought it. Matt wasn't bet pleased as it was a proper arcade sized game, but we managed to take the legs off and put it into the back of the car. I'd been really pleased about my purchase and Matt had gotten other little things.

By the Monday morning after a crammed packed weekend I felt tired on the bus up to Mum's. Too many children seemed to be turning up that morning and my head began to swim so I said a little prayer for the day to go well without any accidents. Jasper and Adele, a fellow child minders brother and sister were with us as well as our own which amounted to fifteen children. I took charge of the nappies for the day and started off with one pooey nappy first thing that morning.

The children got split into three groups. I had five of them in the living room with lots of toys and Cbeebies on in the background. Carolle had five in the school room doing some work and Mum was supervising five at a time in the garden.

We ushered them all outside to sit on the grass for fruit and drink. Carolle and I sat with all of them while Mum finished by making our hot drinks and bringing out cakes for us adults.

Job 5:5
Hungry people will eat the fool's crops.

The whole day went on and passed without any incidents. By the time I'd got home I was exhausted and picked up my knitting in front of the news. I'd been creating a nice stripy pink, brown, yellow and beige cardigan for Lauren and was pleased with how it was coming along while Matt made tea. The aromas smelt delicious coming from the kitchen and I looked forward to the rest of the working week.

By Saturday I'd really enjoyed myself and Matt and I took ourselves to my in-laws to see little Emily for her second birthday. The whole garden was alive with children playing all around it. There was a gazebo up. Jono, a relative of Lis, had a guitar he'd been strumming on. In the middle of the lawn there were bedclothes strewn about for the babies to crawl on and a big table by a small copse of plum trees with lots of parcels on so I placed our present and card on. Up the garden I did a cartwheel to impress the children but no-one was looking but I felt happy at still being able to do one as I'd separated from the party for a bit.

There were two pass the parcel games that were fairly ran so that all the children got presents. The adults just sat around chatting and stuffing their faces. I tried to mingle and talk to everyone. The day went by really quickly.

By Wednesday that week Mum had talked of going to New Wine, a Christian Festival with Eve but I'd wanted to go there with her, but Mum said that Eve asked to go with her that evening so I took myself home on the bus that afternoon a little bit jealous.

> *Job 5:2*
> *To worry yourself to death with resentment could*
> *Be a foolish, senseless thing to do.*

The next day Eve popped by in Mum's before work to say thank you for the night before. I'd heard how they'd both hit the wine at the Bath and West and how they'd joined in the Christian worship singing for most of the evening. Eve told me how she felt spiritually lifted from the experience and of how Matti, her ex, was starting to become a distant memory. She'd felt a certain release from having felt angry about splitting from her fiancé Matti. We were talking over coffee and the day went by slowly. We only had in two children who were happy enough playing with each other running around together with their baby dolls. They liked to dress them and put them in buggies while wearing the little green and pink princess shoes each. Both the girls were really sweet.

Then in the evening Matt and I prepared dinner together and had vegetables with pork chops and a bit of gravy. It tasted delicious.

The next day was a Saturday and I hopped on the bus to go to Wells that morning. I'd had nothing better to do so I went in to Fat Face and found some lovely red leggings that were expensive. I tried them on and they looked sexy emphasising my best features, my legs.

In another shop I looked at lacy underwear thinking that I'd like complete sets, matching panties with bras, but it was all too expensive. I went round a charity shop called St Margaret's Hospice and loved looking at the books and a blue top caught my eye that was all soft and flirty. I had a lovely shopping day before going home. The whole afternoon we spent up Mum-in-law's.

In the morning I went to church and sat in my usual seat on the left hand side of the aisle behind the numbers. The service started and I looked up and saw a stranger asleep at the bottom of the aisle. I'd overheard someone saying, "They shouldn't be in here," and I gasped in horror thinking it was one of the best places for them to be.

Ten minutes later a policeman turned up and took him on. I felt sorry for him as clearly he was homeless and asked why t myself someone before had said, to my mind, a nasty comment.

After he got moved on we went on with the service I'd really wanted to get up and talk to him, but didn't have the guts. The service was about John the Baptist and of how he anointed Jesus with water but had to be anointed by the Holy Spirit first. I always liked that story and could picture in my mind's eye two men by the River Jordan.

I then waited for my chance to sing a really nice hymn before getting up for communion wine of where I'd felt more spiritually connected to God. The service went on and ended. Then I floated out on a fluffy white cloud back home to do lunch.

Matt came home at a quarter to three and we sat down to a nice hot roast dinner. Afterwards we decided to go up the pub early that day and ended up playing pool with Jeremy and Chris and this was the first time we'd heard that Jeremy was going out with a much younger girl called Sarah.

While playing pool several times they had on a Babe channel in the background while I tried to impress the men with playing left handed but they didn't notice.

After three or four games we played darts and I was really crap with my darts either going on the floor or on to the wooden doors at the side or rebounding off the walls. I found it funny as the men took the game far too seriously. It had been a nice afternoon and Matt and I went for kebabs afterwards for tea.

In the morning it turned out to be a nice day at work which blurred the days all week into a nice working week. Come the weekend Matt and I went to the pub called The Crown at the bottom of town. It was a lovely big pub with a karaoke machine playing with loads of people waiting to sing. Matt Morse got up to sing a really deep throated song and I remembered that he'd had a recording deal once with a label in Germany. Then asked myself why it went wrong. My other friend JP was there singing Little Bird by the Eurythmics and I grinned and bore it to sing along with him so it sounded nice to my ears then emulate him by clapping afterwards. Then I got up and sang 'Something Beautiful' by Robbie Williams. It sounded amazing to my ears as everybody clapped. Afterwards some man congratulated my singing and again I thought great I found a fan. They did a pick a key raffle but my Matt never won. So we went home.

During the next day I found myself knitting Lauren's cardi with pink and beige wool without a pattern but I had actually measure her the day before for it to fit.

That day an invitation to Lucas's christening came through the door for in a couple of moths' time and Matt and I were both asked to be his godparents. Matt and I were really pleased and flattered to be asked.

We started to pack our suitcases for our next holiday to Rhodes.

The weather was balmy as we stepped off the plane in the early afternoon and the journey on the coach wasn't that long as I sang along to All Saints 'Never Ever' on the radio. Rhodes seemed peaceful and idyllic with beautiful flowers and bushes dotted about in amongst long stretches of hotels and greenery.

We turned up a hill towards our hotel and promptly got off with another oldish couple. I'd have loved to be able to put all our clothes away and tried out the bed but Matt wanted to explore. We walked down our hill passed by a few bars, cafes and restaurants to a big hotel on the sea front of where we wandered through the grounds wondering where the beach was.

A couple of days later we had the bus route sussed for the beach in the next town. A route we were to take every day. One evening Matt and I stayed in that town to do the karaoke and I'd gotten the chance to hog the microphone all night. A couple of lads came in to the bar making too much noise and were told not to be so rude as I was singing. Outside we heard a band marching through playing loudly and we followed behind to the bus stop.

At the hotel one evening Matt and I decided not to go out and I did karaoke at the hotel. I sang Bonnie Tyler's 'I need a Here' and got talking to a lady afterwards who was a bit shy but wanted to sing a song with me I'd never heard of before so I talked her into singing a bit of Abba. We sounded really good together. I'd been on the Blue Lagoons all night. Towards the end of the holiday I finished The Order of the Phoenix while I laid out on the sunbed and on the bus Matt and I pressed the bell far too early and annoyed the bus driver when we said that he was dropping us at the wrong place. We walked through the back of an empty hotel not finished being built about a mile away from our town. It had been a bit creepy walking by lots of trees surrounding the place and were completely exhausted by the time we got back. In our bar we'd gotten chatting to two other couples and had their photo taken with us.

We had been to the next town to us again of where the harbour was. The shops were hidden behind what looked like castle walls and again there were endless flowers and beautifully coloured bushes dotted about. We toyed with the idea of going out on a boat but couldn't book anything up within our remaining time frame. I'd had a paddle on a small stretch of beach and took a photo of a statue of two dolphins. It was such a lovely laid back sort of holiday we both said we'd come again.

Looking at the photos when we'd got home I'd forgotten that there'd been a lovely large house for sale near our hotel and I'd taken a photo of the 'for sale' sign with the number to ring on it. Well, maybe one day, I'd thought.

Back on home soil relaxing on the sofa I fancied knitting the rest of Lauren's cardigan but couldn't find it. I looked everywhere and started annoying Matt to try and find it for me. It should have been for Lauren's birthday. With nothing else to do I decided to go shopping up town and I stopped off several times in different shops looking either t the books in charity shops and the clothes. I walked round for ages until I found the Woolworth's shop and once in there I noticed the sop was closing down. There were lots of cards so I bought family ones for the future and notice that the full set of Cold Feet was there. An old brilliant English series following three couples lives. It was all knocked down to six quid so I got it and with the cards I spent a tenner. I was elated I'd gotten so much with such little money.

Chapter Twenty-Three

That afternoon Matt and I went over to Street to be with his friends at a bar called the Unity Club to sit down with them and watch an England world cup match against Portugal. The only thing that made the football bearable was the electric atmosphere of men shouting out at the telly and sank back into Matt's comforting arms while watching it. While both of us made two drinks last throughout the whole of the game. The score became two to one against Portugal.

We stayed for a while afterward with his friends before heading off home in the car. The next day I got up to jam and toast in the morning. Then while waiting for the seven thirty bus that Friday morning I got talking to Steve, the street cleaner, of whom was moaning yet again about the mess he had to clean up in the high street. He told me of how a badger had been seen that morning outside the Somerset Kebab House as takeaways had been strewn over the floor as the bin had spilled out over.

"I'd been amazed," I said, "If I'd seen a badger." Steve explained that how vicious they are and how he'd seen one up at the park that morning. I'd held on and couldn't talk any longer in that conversation as the queue for the bus was going down and I needed to leave so I said, "I gotta leave."

Trying to keep a clear head up at Mum's when I'd got there after dozing on the bus twice I found that only two children were in that day called Callie and Rowan. They were in the back garden of where they had a toy car each. Callie was really sweet as she sang a Lily Allen song, "It's not OK and I think it's really mean…," It was a number one at the time and hearing a two year old girl singing this very clearly made me want to wind her up to get her singing all of it as the song was about sex and I knew she didn't know that. This made me inwardly smile and kept me singing the chorus of that song all day. At one point though Callie had had enough while Rowan was desperate to win at hide 'n' seek. There were several places in the garden to hide; in the Wendy house, behind three trees, behind the bushes, under the patio chair and tables, and beside the garden shed. I deliberately peeked out trying to find him counting down from ten each time. I always knew where he was but liked to go round the houses to find him making Rowan believe that he was good at hiding. The neighbour Wendy looked over the fence and said, "Hello Karen. How are you today?"

I'd said, "Fine thank you. How's Matthew and Mel?"

Wendy pointed out that Mel was having the day off as she ran her child minding business with her son and daughter.

After having had lunch outside a band started playing next door. I knew that it was Matthew and his friends rehearsing for something called Battle of the Bands. They were so loud and the singing sounded brilliant. The beat was pulsating though my veins and I found myself singing along out loud. It stopped me from talking with the children of whom were happy doing their own things. Rowan was playing in the sand and Callie was using a watering can to water the flowers. I smiled inwardly enjoying the sounds of the next door neighbour's band and Mum came out and said, "I wrote some lyrics for them once and gave it to them hoping they'd write some music to go with it."

I'd written some song lyrics myself after coming out of hospital and told Mum. She was interested in reading them so I said I'd bring them in. This had been near the end of the day. Callie had to go home at five but was still there at quarter past and I had to run for the bus.

Down the bottom of the hill I rang Nan Burr and she answered. We had a good chat and I invited her to go to Weymouth with Matt and I that weekend. She mentioned that the weather was meant to be good on the weekend. I was still talking to her after getting on the bus but lost the signal as we drove through Croscombe.

At home I started routing out my song lyrics to have a look through them but didn't get round to taking them up Mum's till the Friday.

Mum looked through the lyrics in the orange folder that Friday afternoon and with Eve there they both looked at it. The both liked the Teddy Bear War years but believed the lyrics ran more like a poem but I explained to them that Julian Lennon's 'We Are A Rock Revolving Around A Golden Sun's' tune had been going round inside my head when I wrote it.

The next morning Matt and I looked forward to a day at Weymouth beach getting excitedly into the car with Nan who'd come across to Glastonbury on the bus. Heading down the road we all talked pleasantly together. When we reached the beach we parked up by the arcades and walked to get on the sand together. I'd led the way into the sea for us all to have a paddle as Nan had asked for one with us. Pulling her skirts up, she went in up to just below her knees. I had to roll up my trousers to above my knees and Matt stood and watched us at the edge of the water. I'd never seen Nan look so happy. Her twinkling blue eyes amongst her long heavily crinkly face with permed grey hair smiled at me as she told me about her Dougie and his daughter who had a boat in Weymouth. We'd told her to book with our favourite hotel for the night called The Alexandra on the seafront of which we left her there for the evening.

Just before we went home Matt and I got a take away at the chip shop we always called Mambos by the bridge and sat by the harbour with haddock and chips. We watched a golden glow move from the east to west slide down in an arc over the sky slowly huddling together happy knowing Gran was left in a nice hotel having tea.

Thessalonians 5:13
Be at peace among yourselves.

On the way back I'd had on one of my favourite cd's blaring loudly and sang to Shania Twain's 'Looks Like We Made It', really sweetly meaning every single word that resonated through my heart. When I got home there was the phone ringing and I picked it up jubilant someone's actually called me. My little heart beat fast hearing my own little sister Eve's voice and she had a bloody good chat about clothes and her up and coming hen weekend. Then she asked me if I wanted to go shopping with her as Eve said, "I need a new bra every time I go away. Can we go round Clarks Village tomorrow?"

I said, "Yes," and my little face lit up. "What time?" I'd said.

"Ten o'clock."

"That's fine." I put the phone down and went to bed happy that night.

In the morning I woke up extra early jubilant that my sister was coming to take me shopping. She turned up early and honked the horn to get me running outside slinging my handbag over my shoulder feeling like a little school girl. Jumping in the car we were soon parked up and got out. Eve talked me into buying a lovely white top with a black frill around the neck in Monsoons. It was a bit see-through so I was prompted to buy a brand new white bra from Marks and Spencer's. Eve then took me into New Look on the high street to get a black summer jacket. I'd ended up with new black shoes too. Eve wanted lunch with me but I said that I had to go home but as I walked back I regretted my decision as I'd seen her slumped shoulders from behind walking off.

Proverbs 5:12
Why would I never learn?

That evening I saw an advertisement for acting classes for the next day. I turned up in the early evening and one other woman turned up with lovely auburn curly hair of whom was voluptuous. The lady running the course asked us why we were taking acting classes.

I simply said, "I'd like to train to be the best at what I do," the other lady said she was doing it to gain personal confidence. We started off doing arching movements down on our hands and knees learning self-control skills. We then had to take an emotion each and act it out. I decided to play the victim afterward the other woman said she really believed I was upset and nearly found herself comforting me over it. The tutor then asked us to fight. I knew that the teacher wanted a real bitch fight to get off on so I thought of Bridget Jones and Darcy and Dick faces fight and went for a playful kick. The other lady kicked back and ended scene. The fight was rubbish.

That same day I walked up Glastonbury high street and spotted a multi-coloured dress on the dummy in the cancer research shop window and I just had to try it on. I deduced it would go well with black leggings for when I'd go out on the tiles up in London. I did try it on and it was a size eighteen but it suited my shape straight off. I'd love the look of it and felt happy.

The whole week at work went by slowly as I willed the weekend on to go on Eve's hen do.

That Saturday morning along the bottom of the high street I popped in the pasty shop as it advertised bacon butties. I ordered one with a cup of tea and sat outside waiting for the bus at a table. Nibbling away it felt like a grand start for the whole weekend.

Soon on the bus I played on my mobile phone going through Facebook. I got off at Fee's and posed for someone to take a photograph outside her house with my suitcase while dressed in my new white top and jean shorts.

At London we looked for our Travel Lodge and I found myself staying in a room with a large girl named Marie. That night we went to a restaurant with a tally dummy in a tuxedo outside of it. Inside I had mussels for the first time then we all stayed for a disco and danced all night.

In the morning Marie moaned about me snoring all night and then we all met downstairs for a cooked breakfast.

The day passed with us going round London on the underground which scared Fiona. We ended up at the Strand for cakes and tea before running for the Victoria Line to go on home.

That next day I'd arranged for Jim to come round from work to play on the piano. He was tall, albino looking, very fit. Everyone had warned me about him but I put on sexy shorts and a tight top thinking I could handle him. Now he was from the carnival club and had kept on he wanted to learn guitar and needed to learn the notes on the piano first. It started ok at first but then we came into the living room when he wanted a drink. He asked me if I wanted a massage. I wanted to say no but we sat down on the sofa and he pushed me on my front and massaged me anyway. I eventually found the strength to say no and sat at the table instead. he got out a twenty pound note and told me to get my tits out. I found the strength to say no even louder then and wondered what sort of relationship he'd had with my Nan in carnival before which was why I'd trusted him. Then he went home.

The next day I'd had a lovely lie in then a nice long soak in the bath washing my hair and shaving my under arms and legs. I stood up under the shower while the bath water drained away to wash out the two in one shampoo and conditioner. It was a warmish sort of day as I slipped on my jeans with a summery top and sandals. Turning on the taps in the kitchen I'd run a bowl of hot soapy water to wash up the crockery and cutlery from the day before. Doing this always dried my hair out so I gave it a nice long comb afterward to clear the last of the knots.

Lazing out on the sofa I looked through my What's On TV magazine and did the puzzles while catching up on Emmerdale omnibus.

Having had an early lunch I went round town afterwards and bumped into Ivor, Matt Morse's dad and had a chat about his farming and when we'd go up the pub next for Matt's karaoking. There was a karaoke that night. I told him we were going up my in-law's that afternoon and while I was there Emily and I played a killing bears game around the garden Lis, Emily's mum, became concerned over our shouting, pretending to be scared and puta stop to our game that we'd been happy playing. Matt and I stayed for tea but said we couldn't stay too long as we were going out.

That evening I'd been on the wine and got up and sang three times, my usual Valerie by Amy Whitehouse, Mercy by Duffy, and Empire State of Mine. It had been a good night.

The afternoon came the next day and Matt and I went round my Mum-in-law's and Lis and Tom were there. We'd been invited to lunch and afterwards when Sue washed up Lis and I decided to help out by drying up. Lis offered a nice dress and white shoes to wear on Eve's wedding day. She went upstairs to get them after being in the kitchen. They looked lovely and I said thanks.

The wedding came that weekend and Mum, Fee, Eve and I went to a beauticians/ hairdressers. I got make-up done and I felt pampered before going home to dress up. Matt and I soon met everyone at St Thomas in Wells church. It was a lovely sunny day and we went on to have photos afterwards in the grounds. Then Eve and Jeremy started the route to Wells Cathedral School for the reception and evening do. I enjoyed the food and later on the dancing. Matt did nothing but knock back wine all afternoon.

At the night time Matt took me up to the Queens Head in Glastonbury and he'd drunk so much he nearly cracked his head when falling off the bar stool. He'd been a disaster.

Ezekiel 16:58
You must suffer for the obscene,
disgusting things you have done.

In the morning my head was banging with a hangover as I'd been drinking the night before. I checked my purse for some money and had a flash back to losing money on the gambler the night before. I checked my purse for some money and had a flash back to losing money on the gambler the night before. I was running late for the bus that morning and dressed without showering. The whole day looked as though it was going to be a disaster as I had a snotty nose all the way up Mum's. At her house at number ten there was a chance to play all day up at the park because the early weather had been nice, but by the time all the children turned up the clouds had come over and the whole sky went black. All day we had fun playing games. I stayed that night for skittles with Mum and Nan's team, The Rascals, and we played at Wells Rugby Club of where I'd gotten a ten spare and I declared to myself that, that was my favourite alley.

All night I had a really nice sleep but the door down stairs woke me up in the morning with the door flap going with mail being pushed through. I ran downstairs for the toilet and had a look at the paperwork. One piece of mail was a large brown envelope. It said on the top St John's Ambulance and it had my name on so curiouser than the curious I ripped it open and found a three page certificate that was my paediatric first aid document. Mum told me to take a frame and put it in there, then hang it on the wall of which I did.

The day ended up going swimmingly as I'd floated around on hot air.

Down town in the morning I stood by the bus stop and a big ten foot tall black man came my way and he told me that he was a Rastafarian by looking directly at me and he told that I'd been lied to. I scrunched my eyes up and thought so what, everybody lies and I didn't have a clue what he was on about so I never even asked.

I was keen to get into work and my eyes lit up at little Rowan in that day and outside I took some lovely pictures of the children playing. Rowan loved trying to climb the tree but didn't quite get it and I talked to Nany, my youngest niece, that day about who she liked and she said Rowan.

It started snowing the next day and it settled everywhere nice and deep. I couldn't go to work so I stayed at home and with Matt later on we went up his mother's. A lovely scene greeted me in the garden as Sue was there with Emily posing by a massive snowman with a woolly hat on, scarf, buttons and a carrot for a nose. Tom was there, my brother-in-law, and they'd spent most of the afternoon putting it together in the back garden.

They went indoors. Took their shoes off and coats and Sue suggested to have some hot chocolate. We said yes and had lots of cream and sprinkles on top.

Starting the next day, all fired up to teach the alphabet books and wanting to do work with the children all day. I got there at Mum's door and tapped on the glass as I'd forgot my key. I was extra early as it was only a quarter to eight. Mum came rushing downstairs in a towel wrapped around her and with a turban on her head she'd said, "I've just got out the shower. You're nice and early," and she gave me a hug. Then ushered me into the kitchen. "Would you like a cup of tea?"

"Yes please," and Mum said, "Whack the kettle on then I'll make it in a minute."

Moving into the school room I got down my evidence folder and found I'd only got a handful of pictures. It was nearly a year later since I'd started it for most weeks there was only one picture of things we'd made and tried to use it for new ideas for things to do with the children. I'd gotten to the letter O in the alphabet with cute pictures coloured in with the letter beside it that they'd stuck on coloured paper. Some of them were still on the wall waiting to be taken home. The other corkboard had my June in Bloom poster on it with loads of flowers on it and the English and Latin names underneath.

Maisie and Tom came in with their mother. Then William came in and his mum Emily showed off the new little baby who was a few days old of whom they called Poppy. I thought it was sweet and my little face lit up.

Sat round the table later with Haydn as well I'd drawn out some pigs and cut them out. they were all very studios concentrating with their pink pens. Rachel, one of our quiet ones looked up at me and said Mum. I told her to say that to her Mum as she picked her up today. It was hard work getting Haydn to colour in but he knuckled down eventually. I got talking to him about Star Wars and Peter Pan and other films. He said he wanted to be Darth Vader. It was a bit weird at first so I said, "Don't you want to be the good guy like Luke Skywalker?"

Jeremiah 5:1
Can you find one person who does what is right?

Haydn didn't know who that was. He soon got up from the table and then William and they had a light saber so I gave William a toy screwdriver from the tool box for them to have a weapon to run around with. Maisie stayed at the table while the boys enjoyed themselves. She wanted to colour in a gorgeous little picture of a princess with Rachel. While they drew I cut out the letter P's they coloured in and stuck them and the pigs to coloured paper and underneath I wrote the name pig in bold letters. The names and dates went on them. Then I pinned them to the wall to take a photo for my evidence folder to show Ofsted.

By the afternoon we'd all had lunch and was tidy again ready for action and adventure. Mum wanted their food to go down so they sat on the bottom of the stairs to play the wheels on the bus for over an hour. They bloody loved it.

Then parents started turning up one by one and Mum went outside to their car to look at little Poppy and cooed over her for ages. Mum said to me, "Do you want a lift home with them?"

I'd said, "Yes," then they took me to Wells where I took the bus.

I went to Street the next day in the afternoon on the bus from Shepton to the dentist by Vine Surgery round the back of Green Bank swimming pool. I was going to register as a patient because my previous one was German of whom had been too far out at Somerton and was expensive. Walking into the reception area I asked for a registration form. I sat down, filled it in there and then. It was a bloody long form I had to tick about family medical histories as well as my own.

I felt happy that I'd done this then I took the bus on home. When I'd gotten home Matt was there putting the tea on. It smelt really delicious and I told him I needed another driving instructor so Matt gave me a calling card he'd gotten from a driving instructor when he came into Morrisons that day. So I gave him a ring and booked up an appointment for two days' time. I sat down for tea and it was delicious.

Two days later I was getting excited about my up and coming first driving lesson with Guy.

1 Samuel 6:13
They were overjoyed at the sight.

When I first met him he was tall and lean with a good sense of humour. During the lesson of where I'd got used to the new stick shift and the gadgets in the car. I joked with him that it was like a James Bond car full of brand new gadgets. He'd had a little mini that was electric blue with a silver stripe down the side.

Driving round town there was a dog that went to run out into the road. I had to swerve and nearly hit a parked car on the other side of the road. Thankfully I never while down the bottom of Northload Street. Guy liked to tell me stories of the days he spent taking my brother-in-law, Tom, out driving. He was a bloody good laugh.

In the week Matt and I went up Queens for a drink and met with other men on Matt's skittle night. Charlene was there with Kate getting louder and louder on lots of booze. We were having a laugh about sex scenarios. Charlene was always full of it and I shocked her when I'd get blunt and honest about the subject as she kept on about giving black eyes and I said, "Well Matt and I have actually said bite me to each other during sex before and nearly done it on my boobs.

When Michaela, the landlady, got a word in edge ways she told us about having a vicars and tarts evening that's because I'd just shut everybody up. She was planning it for two weeks' time. Matt had a mad look in his eyes and we discussed getting a skirt from his Mum and a nice blouse. Michaela said she had some wigs but I had in the back of my mind a blonde curly wig I used in dress-up scenarios with the kids at work.

Two weeks later in the early evening Matt had bought some balloons and I blew them up as he got changed into his outfit. The balloons I blew up were huge and he stuffed them into his blouse. He'd even bough some kitten heeled shoes from a charity shop. He looked fucking hilarious. Then he asked me if he could use my lipstick. I wondered if Matt was going to have a shave. He said, "No." and asked again for my lipstick. I'd only had

Lancôme Paris make-up and I kept on trying to stall him wanting it as it's fucking expensive. In the end I caved expecting him to just whip it over his lips really quickly but he pressed real hard and ruined it. I was livid. We went on out anyway. At the bar the other men were all in tarts outfits, mainly long skirts, blouses and wigs. Someone kept mistaking Glyn for me, Karen, because of his hair which I felt was insulting.

Genesis 19:5
"Where are the men who came to stay with you tonight?"

Michaela picked up several air ambulance, and BIBIC collection pots for the men to wonder from pub to pub getting pissed. I stayed drinking at the pub all night with the girls getting reports of what the men were up to going round to The Becketts first, then The George and Pilgrim, and The Crown and The Backpackers. Not many people were about that night but when they eventually got back two collection pots were completely filled.

The following Saturday Matt and I met Fee and the girls Lauren and Nancy when queuing to get into Tor Leisure's Medieval Fayre. We paid for my nieces to get in and started looking into some of the tents with them saying we'd give them a pound to get what they wanted. Lauren actually chose to pay to see the Jester of whom I though wasn't that good with his cheesy jokes and age old tricks.

Afterwards all five of us decided to walk further round the grounds. I'd spied a burger stall and Matt and I decided to queue for the pig roast. We lost Fee and came across some belly dancers. I'd tried to do their dance moves as we watched them gyrate to the music in their jangly long flowing garments. Straight afterward was the battle re-enactment followed by the falconry display.

We caught up with Fee and the girls again while watching the jousting. There were four knights competing for a goblet by firstly knocking a sign around, then riding by objects to hook up off the floor followed by trying to knock each other off their horses. The costumes were of medieval design with dragons and vivid colours. One was predominantly in black, the typical evil knight to boo at.

Afterward, round the stalls, Lauren and Nancy spotted face painting and got butterflies on their faces. Fee said that they had, had a lovely afternoon before we hugged and kissed saying our goodbyes.

Starting the next day I had a phone call at seven thirty and got me out of bed. I looked at the clock quickly and though, "Shit." I had ten minutes to run for the twenty to eight bus. I grabbed the phone angrily it was Mum and I stood there in a stunned silence as she spoke. Then told me there were no children in that day and even though Matt was at work I had to find something to do. My first thought was great, I can go back to bed and have a longer sleep, so I crawled back under the duvet and slept soundly dreaming of the children at work doing cute little things like playing their pirate games.

Waking up I found some knickers on the floor and put them in the wash basket. There was change everywhere all over the floor and over the chest of drawers and Matt and mine's bedside cabinets. I'd had enough as I'd walked into the living room there was change on the breakfast bar. I decided to get some change pots and went through the coins in my head, the two pound coins, the pound coins, fifty pence pieces, the twenties, tens, fives, twos and pennies and ascertained that I need four pots to put the coins in. I wrote on the tops when I got them, two coinage numbers on each one and started to full them up with all the change I found. I tidied the whole flat until Matt came home and we went to Mother-in-law's for tea and cake.

On the phone on the way back I phoned the local radio station for a song by George Michael and Mary J Blige called 'As' but couldn't remember the title correctly and they made me feel silly when they said that they couldn't find the song.

> *2 Samuel 24:10*
> *"I have acted foolishly."*

We went home and Matt reminded me he had to do his fertility tests so got out a test tube for his samples. I had to have him a long wank and he came, filled the tube completely and made a mess all over the bed but we put the cap on afterwards.

Then two weeks later the results of the test came back through the post and the letter stated a lot of medical jargon that basically said he was infertile. We were mortified.

> *Peter 1:6*
> *Be glad about this, even though it may now be necessary*
> *For you to be sad for a while because of the many kinds*
> *Of trials you suffer.*

I knew I had a low egg count that four in every five cycles I'd actually produced eggs so we decided to go for IVF treatment. We got the ball rolling with making another doctor's appointment and they told me I had to go for three blood tests which were made for two weeks' time. I never believed I could get pregnant naturally after that.

Matt and I were talking to Zip on the way back after I told him I had a low egg count and I refused to tell that Matt couldn't reproduce. We went home and held hands on the top of the bed and said a little prayer together. Afterwards, both depressed, we fell deeply into a long sleep. Then the next day, very early, I got up, showered, dressed and breakfasted, then remembered the block of cheese in the fridge Matt told me to take to my sisters for my brother-in-law's party that very evening.

I stopped off at Tesco and bought a card and a present. Then at the bottom of the hill I got off the bus and walked to Beach Avenue where my sister lived. Round at her house the family was in the main bedroom upstairs giving cards so I gave Matt mine and he said thanks and smiled when I said the cheese was downstairs.

Later on that night there was a great spread and a brilliant dance. Eve's friend Kelly B was there with her fiancé and I talked to her for a while and had a bloody good dance with her thinking we were friends.

A few days later it was a Friday at Mum's and I'd brought my little suitcase up trailing it loudly through town and up the hill to Mum's as I was staying the night to go the skittles award night.

At work Mum confessed she couldn't get out that night with me. Though she arranged my lift for the evening with my Uncle Graham of which I accepted. I'd bought a black low cut top and black trousers and heels with a bit of make-up on. The day panned out nicely with the children as they played really well together running around for most of the day with plastic swards playing at being pirates. They were really adorable.

After lunch they calmed down a bit and watched Pirates Ahoy! With Scooby Doo, all afternoon. I kept looking at the kids and talking to them. I could tell Keeley was a bit scared so took her to the school room to do some work.

That evening I had a lovely shower, put on my sexy outfit, put on the slap and was ready for the evening. Uncle Graham was on time and as he pulled out I said goodbye to Mother who told me to go have fun and have a nice evening. All the way there I had a heart-to-heart with my Uncle and we felt close for a while till we got out at Wooliton and the pub/restaurant/hotel, Crossways. As we pulled up Mandy and Graham got out their car and so did Jan and Margaret with Carolle. We all said hello and walked into the bar together. I said goodbye to Uncle Graham and said, "See you later."

In the bar area we posed for photos after the award ceremony with a massive cup. I took my photos on my phone with us all looking jubilant. We just talked and talked all night sat around on the nice comfy sofas until it was time to go home.

The next day I was shopping over Street for a present for Matt and came across an advertisement in a travel shop window. It was for tickets to go to see Kylie Minogue at the 02 in London. I looked at the price and thought that Matt was worth it. I'd paid there and then.

There'd been a week at work that was wearing me down as Mum had been moaning about the state of Fee's home.

Psalms 69:20
Insults have broken my heart, and I am in despair.

How she always wanted household chores done when Mum visited. Mum had also moaned about Carolle using all her paper for blotting and all I'd really wanted to do was stop her bitching really looking forward to the weekend's concert.

Matt and I turned up at The Angel Place in Bridgewater for the coach to take us to London that weekend. There'd been a queue, obviously it had been a popular trip. The coach turned up by an Express Tesco's to let us all off and we headed for the Dome after getting drinks at the supermarket.

We were in awe of the large auditorium and showed our tickets. I began to get vertigo and began to wheeze the higher we climbed to get to the back row practically in the rafters. Looking down to the stage Kylie was barely a dot belting out all our favourite tunes and had dancers flying out over the stage. I'd had to watch the performance mainly through the zoom on my camera while taking pictures. Thoroughly enjoying 'Especially for you' at the end and we soon found ourselves making our way back.

Come the next Saturday I was all excited getting dressed up in white leggings and a nice flirty top that was purple. Then Michaela turned up in her car to take me to Paignton. In the car there was Julie, Becky and Sarah, Julies twin sister, they were all black haired, short and friendly. In the car on the way down they put on Dream Coats and Petticoats cd that we all sang to and chatted round. Becky kept waving to the other cars and pissing them off.

At the B&B Julie and I shared a room. Becky and Sarah were next door and Michaela was downstairs. We went for drinks at Henry's bar the first night and met with a couple called Jer and another Sarah of whom bough a round of blue shots all night and I got puddled. We went for a take away afterward and met Steve the seagull and we laughed as Becky went skinny dipping.

That night Julie and I chatted for ages and I told her the story of when my family had Mist Blue the budgie.

The next day we went round the shops and then in the afternoon we cruised the coastline on the way home. I had to get dropped off at skittles with carnival at Westonzoyland of where they'd started when we got there. The game got thrown away by Ryan and Chelsie.

It was on a Friday morning up at Mum's when I felt so happy I could have died as I'd had one child to look after by myself called William. I read to him in the morning then he kept looking for his favourite toy in the basket at the bottom of the shelves. I knew which one so I took everything out and helped him find a charaterly dressed little monkey. I turned the white little handle then stood the money up on his feet led down on the floor with

William to watch the response and it flipped over backwards. William loved it.

At break time Mum told me how Eve and Nan Burr went to the Bath Spa the day before and had a swim in the pool and to have a bit of pampering. I felt jealous as I'd loved someone inviting me to swim with them at Bath. I looked at Mum with squinty eyes and returned to looking after William for the rest of the day.

The weather was warm so I slung my jumper and coat in a bag and went home.

Next January getting all glammed up for the evening ahead on my own with Matt at football with Dad and Jeremy in Yeovil I started to feel tired. Then rested on the sofa as I waited for my lift from Kelvin. I'd woken with a start when the phone rang. It was Matt ringing from Westlands he said that he was on Stuart's phone and where was I? Apparently Kelvin had called them wandering where I was apparently he'd been knocking on the door for ages while I'd been asleep. Matt told me to call his brother for a lift of which he did and took me there just in time for the meal. It had been a brilliant Gangs carnival club evening.

The next day Matt and I ventured out into slightly bad weather having spent most of the morning indoors just to do something and ad gone over to Tor Rugby Club in Glastonbury to their fete.

Shrouded in mist we wandered round about five stalls when bumping into Nick, a tall classically handsome friend of Matt's with his wife, Gemma, who was a brunette of average size, and their children.

Matt saw a CAB counsellor that afternoon and he told me someone would be calling round the flat sometime to assess us.

Eve popped by the flat to see me quickly, and pointed out to me the state of the cooker that was covered in bread crumbs, and then promptly left and hurt my feelings. I'd just stayed up Mum's for the night and was angry. Matt hadn't kept the flat clean. I wished Eve had stayed for my company.

Exodus 32:9
I know how stubborn these people are.

Over at Sue's that evening one of their female friends popped by and I blurted out, "Hello Gwenda." The lady turned to me and looked sharply my eyes had blurred over but they began to clear and I realised that the woman wasn't who I thought it was and recognised her as Janice from next door. I felt awful, but at least she left me alone with my thoughts to feel normal again without her publicly showing me up as being wrong. I stayed for another hour with Matt just talking to Bob and Sue.

In the morning Matt and I threw a suitcase in the back of the car and headed off fo Weymouth for a holiday. It was a beautiful day and longing for excitement a frisson went through my head as the car sped down the road. The radio was blaring and my favourite Maroon 5 song came on. 'Moves Like Jagger' that I sang really loudly and tried to sound like Christina Aguilera dancing around in my seat. Then I put on Justin Timberlake. The sound of it was hot and horny. I could see Matt tensing up at the wheel as I placed my hand on the top of his leg. Driving down the road Lidl's was there and we decided to pop into the supermarket for a cheap drink. We got out the car and looked around the store and I chose a strawberry milkshake and Matt had a banana one.

Back at the car I kicked back and sipped while Matt drove off. He had swigged his back in two minutes and I enjoyed every bit of the delicious coolness of mine.

The sky was azure blue and the road came alongside the beach. Avoiding the side lane for the buses we got stuck in traffic and people were honking horns to try and pass one another. One car actually went into the bus lane and sped off towards the other end of the promenade.

We eventually parked up by the Pavilion. Matt had to pay twelve pounds for all day. Getting out of the car I slung on the grey coat Eve had given me once for my birthday. Matt put on his fleece so as to brace ourselves from the windy weather.

Along the seafront we stopped in a newsagents and I got a Bella magazine and a pen for later on the beach. Matt got a Lucozade that we both had to carry round together. I rolled my magazine up to put in my pink handbag. We wandered around for a bit over by the harbour down over to Radipoles nature reserve. We talked about what to do that day and Matt wanted to go over Nothe Forte side to see the fishermen on the pier.

Our whole day was taken up with walking around laughing and joking, cuddling and kissing. We went to a restaurant in the evening and walked to a bar for the rest of the night and saw a band on the seafront.

For the rest of the week it had been lovely and sunny. One day was a whole day on the beach and Matt stretched out and went to sleep for most of it. I read about real life sad stories, some were bloody humbling and scary and I loved doing the puzzles one by one. I needed a drink and to go to the toilet. When I came back with a beverage for Matthew too he was talking in his sleep so I pushed up my trouser legs to have a paddle in the sea. I walked for a long way along the sea edge and then turned round, walked out further to wade back to where I thought we were. Matt came out to greet me. That had been a lovely day.

During the week we'd seen an old fashioned horse and carriage with two brown stallions at the front making me think of Cinderella. It was outside the court house as we walked towards the Co-op and I saw a beautiful woman in it in a traditional lily white bridal gown with a long train down the back and lots of ruffles of whom alighted with whom I assumed was her father. I turned to Matt to remind him that we always see a wedding on our holidays. By the end of the week we'd had enough and were ready to go home. Sinking into Matt's arms we walked back to the car on the last day and headed back.

In the New Year it was a Tuesday after work and I walked round Fiona's down the bottom of the hill. At hers there were the children Lauren, Liam and Nancy. They were playing with their Christmas toys with a mess everywhere. Fee offered me a hot drink and I had a cup of tea. The children, I'd had to hear Fee tell them, to thank me for their Christmas presents. I didn't like that I'd have rather I had the 'thank you's' without the prompting. Fee, before I went home on the bus, gave me a picture postcard of the kids with a thank you for our Christmas presents on.

At home I got ready for skittles in my hit 'n' hope top that was blue wiggling into tight jeans then putting on flatter shoes ready for the evening. Cars had been arranged and Matt and drove to the Royal British Legion over in Street. We sat down in the balcony area on some chairs round a table. Matt ordered the drinks and I had a pint of orange and lemonade and a bag of salt 'n' vinegar crisps with a pickled egg. Munching away it tasted delicious while waiting for my turn to throw the balls down the alley. I got up and visualised someone's face of whom I hated. It was Lis and I smashed the ball down and got a nine. My score had been really good that night at thirty five. I was pleased with that.

We all sat round chatting having bread, cheese and onions until we all dispersed and went home.

Jumping out of bed at seven o'clock the next day I'd felt surprisingly alert. Pulling on my jeans and my warm carnival hoodie I'd headed out the door towards the corner shop for Emma to pick me up in her car. We had to be at Pilton Park as early as possible but when we got there we'd ended up waiting in the car for ages until the green Living Homes van turned up at which point Emma and I got out of the car. We'd chatted happily all the way there but had to focus on clearing out the garage of a lady called Jenny further into the village. While piling the van high with masses of bric-a-brac Jenny offered a cup of tea for when we finished clearing everything out for her. She was a nice lady and loved to chat telling us which stalls she'd wanted everything to go on back at the park. Saying thank you for our teas we'd made our way back to where the fete was going to be.

By the time the van was emptied the morning was nearly over and the wooden sides of the stalls had to be put up. Jessie had been driving the van and through him and a couple of local men all five us managed to put all six stalls together and the skittle alley. I'd been my usual macho self and had lifted some concrete blocks to secure the metal barriers up with. By one o'clock all the bric-a-brac we'd collected was set out on the selected stalls and we started to relax.

Matt turned up straight after work and we'd walked round the stalls together and bumped into Mum, Dad, Fee and the kids. I had a go on the tombola, bought a few bits and pieces and Matt and I, plus Mum and Dad took turns on the skittle alley not doing very well.

After a catch up and in the drinks tent big Oliver, from work, came in with his Mum, Tracy and they said hello. It was nice to see them. My family told me they'd had enough and were heading home but Matt and I had to stay to clear up all the rubbish and put down the white tables, that had been out for the bar. On collapsing the chairs put in heaps by the inside of the tent I caught up with Emma again to lay out the long tables ready for a meal in the evening. Matt had gone outside with the rest of the men to take down the stalls and put them in the back of the green van. They disappeared after that to take the stalls back to where they came from and by the time they'd got back we were all ready for the evening crew to come down and take over for the dinner and dance. Our day's work was finally over and I jumped into our car leaving Emma to drive home by herself.

That Friday morning, a week later, I woke up at Mum's house ready to go on an intensive driving course for the weekend.

Dad said, "Wait downstairs in the hallway," after I'd got ready to go. Patiently standing there Sally's driving school turned up. Next thing I knew there was a beep from outside and I ran out the door to get inside the car. Strapping up, my foot hit the pedal to the metal and the driving instructor told me which way to go to Barnstaple. It was a nice flat area in which to drive in round the town I just hated when we had to go over a long sleeping policeman to park up by the test centre. I'd done well that first day and the instructor was pleased.

Second day into the course we drove further afield round some estates trying to anticipate where the test routes would go.

Job 38:3
Now stand up straight and answer the questions I ask you.

Now I'd used some natural remedy Fee told me to use on my tongue to relax me. That turned out to be a mistake as I'd been too relaxed and fucked up reversing out of the parking bay. I did keep going and everything was so laid back I ended up making several mistakes. It was obvious I'd failed my test.

That evening when I got back from driving I noticed Matt had found a channel called Pick TV with reality shows on and I noticed Angela Griffin, from Coronation Street, in the back of an ambulance going from one incident to another. I liked her style of presenting. It was a programme I actually found myself getting in to.

In the week I phoned up my previous driving instructor Guy and booked up an appointment for Friday. The lesson itself seemed easy and Guy couldn't work out why, again, I couldn't pass myself so I had to tell him about my mistakes. The mistakes being bumping into things.

I woke early the next morning to toast and jam. Then I made a cup of tea for Geoff, the scrap man, and he quipped that people would talk as we sipped our teas together outside. Afterwards I'd done a good day's work with Mum at our nursery.

In the evening Mat had cooked a heavy meal so we walked up town, passed Silver Street by the bottom of the Tor and down Bere Lane and back into the bottom of the high street to walk off our tea while walking hand in hand and cuddling from time to time.

The next day was a Saturday and the phone rang of which got me out of bed. Fiona was on the end of the line asking if I'd come out with her for the day round Cheddar reservoir. Fee was to bring her girls Lauren and Nancy. She'd said Nancy would be in her pram. I'd said yes and Fee said that they'd turn up after ten o'clock.

Still waiting at eleven twenty while watching the television I kept looking out the window for the familiar sight of my sister's silver car. At eleven thirty I breathed a sigh of relief not realising till then I'd been holding my breath for ages when the Where Nobody car turned up I'd made the name up out of the licence plate letters.

Pulling up under a myriad colour of leaves on the trees we all got out of the car. I got the pram out for Nancy and Fee pushed her around the mile circumference of the reservoir. I walked with my goddaughter Lauren stopping every now and again to stare out across the water to recognise each winged creature trying to tell Lauren the different names for each one. At one stop, with my goddaughter looking very beautiful in her yellow dress and her wind swept hair billowing out behind her I stopped and took a photo with the wall and the water in the background. It was a lovely photo. Trekking on further to do the whole circumference we looked all around across the lush green fields with the arboretum of hedges and trees framing at the front and the back creating a wonderful picture.

Fee asked did I want to come back for lunch at hers that afternoon. Nancy was beginning to get cold in her thin denim jacket over her dress and began shivering. Luckily we were all nearing the car park. I'd helped with putting the buggy back into the automobile and helped strap the girls in. Through the long drive way back onto the road Fee just flew home to where she made us all sandwiches while I flicked on the kettle for us girls to have a cup of tea while Nancy insisted on having blackcurrant juice. This I made and gave out as my sister served up the food and about an hour later Matt came to pick me up to take us round my Mother's house. I'd recognised the big blue car outside Mum's as we pulled in as Eve's car. We walked straight into the house and heard a lot of childish talk. Pippa, my new born niece, was being held in her mother's arms in the kitchen. I got to hold the lovely bundle too.

I remembered feeling happy for my little sister and proud of her for finally achieving everything she'd ever wanted.

> *Deuteronomy 27:7*
> *Be grateful in the presence of the Lord your God.*

I vaguely recollect it was that day when Mum suggested that Eve, Fee, I and her spend some alone time together to perhaps all go to the cinema once a month together at Wells Regal Cinema.

That Wednesday we did exactly that and met up in the bus stations car park to go watch a film called Bridesmaids together. It was, what I thought, about a woman having a bit of a break down. My Mum and my sisters had the same opinion afterward that we shared walking back to the car to go home.

That Thursday Mum sent me home from work early after I'd told her I had a driving lesson with Guy of whom took me round Weston to drive. He just wanted me to get used to the roads there.

Back at Mum's later we all had tea before I jumped into the shower for a hair wash before skittles that evening and the Britannia in Wells. We played against Aunty Wendy's team and lost. It was still nice to see her. Her team was called The Castaways. It had been a good evening.

Two days later, on the Saturday, I decided to take the bus over to Wells and went towards Lidl's to visit my sister Eve's house in St Andrew's Walk. She wasn't in as Nan answered the door saying that my little sister had gone out. Nan Sheila then said that Eve had given her a copy of her front door key for when Nan would go shopping over Lidl's and had to wait for Uncle Cyn to pick her up. We both stayed as long as we could till Eve came home and made us cold drinks and showed off her new magnets on the fridge with her and a bunch of friends on, and a picture of sweet, innocent Pippa on. It wasn't long before I made my excuses. Jumped on the bus and then went home.

One evening Matt and I went up town to the Queens Head for a drink with our friends and I bumped into Valerie.

I said, "Hello. How are you?" And she talked to me and said, "Hello. Would you like to come down to The Mitre with me?"

I said, "Yes," and followed her down to the pub The Mitre. She offered to buy me a drink. She looked gorgeous with her red hair and nice figure. I accepted the drink and we went over to the fruit machine together. Valerie put in some coins and we took it in turns to push the buttons. We got onto the winner board and I pushed her to go higher and I pushed the button to go up the board more when she was distracted and we won seventy five pound. I was pleased that I helped her and she offered to buy me another drink. Feeling contrary I didn't want another drink from her even though she'd won the money. I wanted her to keep her winnings so I dipped into my own purse. I then got talking to Shane Avery and started having a go at him about something feeling a bit drunk. Next thing I knew Matt came in the bar looking for me and he'd said Maxine came looking for him. He'd been worried about me he'd said and I told him that I was a big girl. I could take care of myself. We then walked home together.

The next day at work few children were in and Mum and I found ourselves talking a lot.

Mum said, "I'm thinking of having a girls night on Fridays of where we teach each other about our hobbies and how to make things."

I'd said, "That's a good idea Mum."

"I've asked my friend Lizzie to come on over with her crepe paper to show us how to make flowers."

I'd said, "I'll look forward to it."

Mum got worried about a friend and told me about her situation with her husband who was possessive and never let her out. I then tried telling Mum about my friend Elisabeth of whom I'd met at Theatresaurus who'd taken the bar and perhaps she could help Mum's friend out. I'd been thinking of the legalities of her situation and tried to explain that to Mum. She wasn't listening but Mum poo-pooed my idea and I left the conversation alone thinking I hadn't explained myself properly.

> *Jeremiah 15:5*
> *Who will stop long enough to ask how you are?*

I felt confused then we went back to looking after the children for the rest of the day.

That evening I went on the internet at home and I found Bristol City football club tickets for Matthew's birthday. I clicked on a picture of the sets for a decent view point and then went on the Badgerline website to research bus time tables to be able to get to Ashton Gate and back. I felt pleased with myself and anticipated the tickets to come through the post in a couple of days.

Two days later Matt and I went for a walk down a footpath of a place called Godney. The car was parked on a gravelly spot with a handful of vehicles parked by. Walking cuddling together we came across a couple called Pam and Albert of whom were my nephew Liam's Gran and Gramps of whom was with them. We got chatting to them about the birds and wildlife we'd seen and then walked on after they'd said, "We'll see you again," and Matt said, "See you again. Bye."

Then we went a lot further down the path looking across ponds and fields topping every now and again for a cuddle and a chat. We stayed until the sun started to go down to watch the starlings. There was a flurry of birds overhead so we stood rooted to the spot with a few others watching clouds of birds in the air blocking out the last of the sun. There were thousands of them and they danced in the air as a collective over the wetlands creating one big black cloud before settling in the reeds. It was amazing.

We had a lovely roast dinner when we got home to warm ourselves up and settled down for the evening.

Chapter Twenty-Four

Three days later my driving instructor Guy turned up in the morning. He'd said to take me round the test route in Weston-Super-Mare. Out of the centre we went over a bridge and on a roundabout and then we found the coastal road. I loved ring and did everything I was told. The whole experience felt nice and leisurely until we went on a housing estate of where we attempted parallel parking of which I got first time. The weather had been lovely and I drove home happy with the test coming up in a few days' time.

The next day was my 36th birthday and I went into work up my Mum's happy. Poppy, Rachel and Jacob were in and we had our usual fruit and drinks mid-morning when Fiona, Eve and Nans' turned up for coffee to see me. They gave me presents. Eve's was a gorgeous green scarf to go with my camel coloured coat. Fee and Mum gave me nice presents too so did the nans'. Then Mum came in, turned off the lights and everyone sang happy birthday. It was a nice sponge cake with plenty of icing on and several candles of which I blew out while wishing I had children of my own. The cake was delicious and I wanted more. We all had a glass of wine each and said cheers. The children had their juice with us.

It was a lovely morning with the children going on and playing happily. Then lunch time came and I sorted out the children's food by opening up tin foil, putting Poppy's hot food in the microwave. While I was doing this I kept eyeing up my cake and nabbed a slice again for myself. The working day had been easy and I soon got home.

Matt had a surprise for me when I got back that evening and he told me to dress up. We were going out for the evening and jumped into the car and headed for Coxley. We stopped off at the Indian restaurant and my parents were there with huge grins on their faces.

Dad said, "Happy birthday Karen," with a wink and a cuddle. Then Mum gave me a cuddle and said, "Happy birthday," and we sat down in the lounge with aperitifs and we clinked them together and said cheers. We were all happy then the waiter came over to take us to our table. They gave us a menu and we laughed and joked. I chose a lamb korma, a very hot one, and everyone else had a hot 'n' spicy dish too. We had a toast and clinked our wine glasses together and said, "Cheers. Let's eat up."

The wine flowed, and the conversation was happy all fucking night. The meal was delicious, the waiters were efficient and polite and kept their distance properly. Then the bought out a cake and everyone sang happy birthday. I was ecstatic and had a wonderful night.

Two days later my driving test was down Weston-Super-Mare and for once I drove in my own car with Matthew but we went round and round in fucking circles. I couldn't find the test centre and it fucking rained. It was a disaster, so two hours later we gave up the ghost and went home.

Job 15: 12, 13
But you are excited and glare at us in anger.

That evening I dressed up in a low cut blacktop and red trousers and heeled boots to go to an Ann Summers party up at the Queens Head at the top of town.

When I got there I waited in the front bar with a Southern Comfort and lemonade in my hand. Charlene was there waiting for Annabel to turn up as it was her party. When everyone got there we went into the back bar in the semi dark with soft disco lights on with music in the background from the juke box. Annabel dished out the Ann Summers catalogues for us to peruse as we sat there and chatted about Fifty Shades of Grey and talked about our sex secrets. I wouldn't give the game up though and kept them guessing about mine and Matt's smut raising my fucking eyebrows in the right places. I went on and ordered a gorgeous black lace teddy, as I was thinking about a present for Matt's birthday. We then played a card game that asked each in turn about sex secrets. In turn five scenarios were given us and we had to choose from several answers as to which was most relevant to us. My scene was above five different sex scenes of where I had to choose two answers that would have proved if I was a prude or a liberal. I answered prudishly but had a very liberal real answer in my head and I smiled secretively. It was a brilliant night and a couple of days later my present for Matt turned up just before his birthday.

I'd phoned Guy my driving instructor that day to cancel any more lessons as I'd taken my test nine times and didn't want to do it anymore.

The next day from throwing some food together, a blanket and some drinks Mum and I headed down the road holding Maisie, Tom and William's hands. We walked past Mum's neighbours, Wendy, then the ones who shared their vegetables with Mum and Dad, then Aunty Wendy's with the caravan outside. We soon came to the pathway behind the community hospital that led to the fields.

Mum and I brought bags to collect blackberries, conkers and acorns in. the first bushes we came across were ripe with berries and the children soon started copying us and eating them. The little scamps, we were trying to collect them so that the children could have their own bags full to take home.

Out across the fields the three of them kept up quite well and Mum pointed out the tress where the acorns could be found and where the Horse Chestnut trees were. I just happily kept going asking Mum where to put the picnic blanket next to a hedge. Mum wanted to go on and show them the owl house. They seemed happy enough to want to sit down as Mum told me to go on and put the blanket down. Mum took out the crisps for the children and I waited patiently with the boys and Maisie for drinks and my chocolate bar.

The morning went by quite quickly out in the sun as the box of children's fruit came out then some of their sandwiches as they were hungry. Then we sang some nursery rhymes that the children were good at singing. Mum looked at her mobile for the time and it was passed noon, time to go to the owl house at the top of the first field. by the time we got back there was two hours left before William, the first one who was due to leave, went home.

As per usual the twin's mother turned up late as she'd been a teacher at Wells Cathedral School. She'd told us that her children's parents either turned up late or wanted to stay for a chat.

In the morning I went to Mum's happy and little Rachel was there the sister to a girl named Katy. She was ever so quiet but I loved her to bits and she made friends with the other children by giving them the toys she picked up. I used to try and get her to talk with me. She was two years old and she said to me that morning, "Mum." I was happy to hear her speak and so I said say that to your mummy when she picks you up that afternoon. She nodded ascent and I couldn't wait for her mummy to turn up to see if she'd say it to her.

It was nearly lunch time so I gathered the children together in the school room for a bit of a sing song as Mother put together their lunches. I could tell Rachel wanted to join in and I got a few 'La's' from her. She was really sweet.

At half past two the parents started to show up and I kept the other children out of the way in the living room. Rachel had been in the school room. Her mother just walked in through the front door without knocking. I saw Rachel walk towards her and I heard her as clear as day saying, "Mum," to her mother. I felt the tears of joy spring from her mother's lips.

Not long afterwards her mum, Sue, decided to be a stay at home mum.

I was staying up Mum's for the night for skittles and I'd brought my noisy little suitcase that I dragged along on wheels up on the bus. It had been an early start getting on the six thirty bus from Glastonbury and then the seven o'clock bus from Wells and it had been cold too.

The day went slowly and we managed to pack in doing a lot with the children, like reading to them, sitting with them while they coloured in their alphabet pictures, etc. It had been quite a productive day.

In the evening I helped Mum with tea and while Dad sat in the living room with his, while watching the news, Mum and I would sit up to the dining room table. We talked about our day and what we did with the children. It was pleasant before I got up and washed up while Mum had gone upstairs to get changed for skittles. I'd changed after finishing in the kitchen into my blue and white shirt that was the Rascals uniform. Mum and I had grabbed our coats and handbags and jumped into the car heading for the sleepy little village of Croscombe passing the quaint little pubs and the village shop. Just on the outskirts we had to do an emergency stop as a large stag ran out into the road. It stopped and stared at us through the bright glare of the headlights.

> *1 Kings 10:5*
> *It left us breathless and amazed.*

We had to wait an age for it to move and it made Mum drive a bit slower into Wells and out towards the Britannia Inn on the Bath Road.

We were the last ones to turn up at skittles so Mum went out to the alley to say we were there as I'd get in the drinks. We'd both had a pint of orange juice and lemonade and I'd always had ice in mine. Strictly Come Dancing was on the telly at the time so we'd discussed this, holidays, the music that was playing and we'd learned about the cat that turned up at Tricia's. The evening had flowed lovely and we'd actually won the game. I'd had a score up in the thirties and Mum had hit in the forties so we were happy with the outcome and at the end of the evening I got some of the lasagne put out for us for Nan Sheila. I'd got some for myself with a little bit of salad. Mum wouldn't eat and we had to wait for Tricia to eat a bowl too before taking her and Nan home with us.

At about eleven o'clock we were finally back and we found Dad still up watching telly so we told him about the stag we'd seen. Exhausted after my long day I used the bathroom first and went on to bed.

We set the alarm the next day to wake up early at about eight am to chuck on our carnival tops and jeans. We brushed our hair and ran out the door ready for a good piss up. We were missing Liam's scout march into Wells for Remembrance Sunday. At the town hall we jumped on the bus and shouted Wick Army one by one to those going. The bus Kelvin was driving sped up the Street by-pass to pick up the next lot of us ready on the grass. All chattering away happily Kelvin parked near the high street and we all jumped out heading for the Carnival Inn Wetherspoons for a hearty breakfast. Lyn Caddey had started the trend of Wick Army.

Then we went across o to the New Market Inn to have a bit of a dance and to meet up with other clubs. I started on the Cinzano and lemonades which was going down really nicely. A couple of pubs down the road we were at the Cross Rifles by the roundabout. More and more carnival clubs were gathering together then we took off to the right of the pub and up the road Damon jumped on a cone in the middle of the roundabout make a good picture. We'd all had nicknames put on t-shirts for this. I had sexpot because I thought I looked sexy and Matt was called Marmite because of his love for it.

We made it on to the River Parrott having had some in fighting in the pub on the way around the pool table. By the river as per usual someone had been threatening to throw Lee, this time, in the river. I worried every year that one day someone would really be thrown in and drowned. Ryan jumped in the pub through the window.

Along route we'd played Postman's knock on some terraced houses doors and Paisley, an ex-girlfriend of Lees, joined in. Matt had picked up a TV in someones front garden and dropped it a few houses down the road.

We came out The Parrot and across the bridge into town and we kicked the footballs about outside the sports shop. It was a bottle that was kicked that went into the spokes of somebodies bike and sent them flying. We were laughing about how Charlene had gone into the children's play area at The Bunch of Grapes going on their trampoline and getting stuck in the Wendy house.

> *1 Samuel 3:11*
> *Everyone who hears about it will be stunned.*

We moved around from pub to pub near St Mary's church and in the Golden Ball I noticed a fireman's pole. Our club were the first ones in there but the place soon filled up. After a bit of a dance we moved onto KFC of where I'd had a spicy chicken wrap and laughed at Reg losing his baked beans all over the floor. The others were laughing at how Ryan and Lee had gone into the video shop to ask for gay porn and how they'd knocked a video stand flying.

We went to another pub that had music and a bit of a dance floor but everyone was so well gone that Sophie had been saying, "I'm sorry, so sorry," all the time she was drunk and outside this pub she'd slumped onto the floor. Reg tried to revive her with a glass of water and was, inappropriately, I'd thought, straddling her on the floor trying to get her to drink.

Eventually we all found ourselves hanging around on the pavement waiting for our driver Kelvin to say we could go home. Ryan passed out on the pavement hitting his head as he fell.

Then we all ambled back to the bus to let Kelvin drive us home. I'd felt oddly detached from it all that day and had enjoyed the mayhem.

For Mum's sixtieth birthday, Fee and Eve were asked to invite all Mum's friends and our family. They were having trouble tracking everyone down so Mum ended up helping them out with friends' phone numbers. We started the day for Mum with a poster put up outside on the front gate with yellow 60th balloons. As soon as mum saw it I was there with the camera. Mum came outside with her knee high boots, checked shirt and pink jumper on all happy and full of hope.

In the early evening the whole family greeted the birthday girl in the lounge of the restaurant of Bowlish House. I was wearing my wine red shiny dress and matching bolero with make-up on. I'd sat with my Nan Burr and a handful of Mum's friends chatting idly waiting to be called into dinner. The room was decked out lovely with helium balloons, decadent name cards and beautifully arranged napkins. Mum looked beautiful with a natural radiance making everyone feel happy just to be there to share her big day. We all talked as the conversations flowed then we burst into song as the tasty looking cake came out while Mum made a wish and blew her candles out. Then she made a speech thanking everyone for coming. It was a wonderful evening.

That weekend I went to Abbey Hill in Yeovil to a steam fayre, with lots of vehicular mechanisms with a carnival club called Keykids. Amy, Ryan, Charlene and Tom were there. A lovely little family unit.

Matt and I helped to spread out the bouncy castle on the grass and Tom began pumping the large buoyant castle up bit by bit. Matt, Charlene, and I were still unfolding parts of the huge slide encouraging the air to come through the fabric. It was such a lovely day but we'd been placed quite a way from all the mains stalls, but at least the pitch had been gained through a large discount. We stood with the bouncy castle for most of the day either taking money or moving a flap of material across the slide constantly to keep it smooth.

Amy, Charlene's daughter, was getting bored so I offered to walk with her around the stalls and we got chatting. I learned that Amy liked animals so we went into a farm animal's tent to look at various chickens, and guinea pigs, etc., on display. In another tent I asked her if she'd like cakes as I got us some little fairy ones each. She was telling me about her lack of a boyfriend but wasn't really that bothered and I'd said, "Good for you, they're too much bother anyway and at thirteen you've still got time." We also talked about school and then got onto the topic of likes and dislikes, then we found a haberdashery tent of where Amy soon started looking at the beads and the strings, or the elastic to go with them. I'd been distracted by the jewellery and found myself buying a matching earring and necklace set that was predominantly silver with purple stones in. The earrings were dangly and I put them straight on and the necklace to match my purple flowered summer top and light purple cut off trousers. I'd felt real lady like and summery with my heeled sandals on too. Gravitating back to where I'd left Amy she was struggling to find the money for all the bits and bobs she'd wanted so I gave her a pound towards it. I also gently stated that, that was the last I was going to spend on her. She seemed happy with that.

Half an hour later of wandering round the tractors and hay bale machinery we found ourselves back at the bouncy castle. Matt was dishing out doughnuts from work and we were all laughing at the mess they made down Pat's top. Matt had hinted he'd put extra jam, as he was a baker, just for us and laughed his head off. It was all in good fun then he went off with Ryan, Amy's brother, to let him have a ride on his tractor being displayed in the main arena. By the time he got back Charlene wanted to walk with me round the stalls and we had a bit of a chin wag. She ended up buying a new little generator to help either put on their caravan that was stationed on site as they were staying a couple of days or to help pump up their bouncy slide.

Matt and I stayed till the end of the day to help deflate the massive slide and stayed round yapping for a bit before taking off to find our car again in the top field. Tired but happy the roads were clear on the way back.

Next day at work I'd asked Mum what she wanted in her sandwich, as I'd have made her whatever she'd have asked for, but seeing as she wanted to just take over I was put off offering to make sandwiches again.

On the Saturday that week was Henry's, Tom and Lis's little man's, christening and I dressed up and Matt put on a suit. At the Methodist all the first person I'd noticed was little Henry in a grey suit and shirt running around on a toy red and yellow car. His friends were playing on the other toys.

The christening had been sedate with Lis's family being godparents. Sue, her mum. Helen, and his Uncle Rob. I remember taking lots of photos and back in the hall Henry, with his friends, started to play the piano on a long yellow bench. With their backs to me I took a cute photo.

On the other side of the hall was the cake and Tom, Lis, Henry and Emily all posed to cut it for photos. I took a much better photo of the family later on all sat on the floor. It had been such a lovely day.

A week later Matt and I went to watch a local derby football match at Yeovil. Sat on the side by the car park we watched a real grudge match with the score 1-1 at the end and there was a pitch invasion. Fists started flying and I got a bit worried standing next to it and tried to urge Matt out of the stadium. Matt had wanted to watch but was scare that we'd get dragged into it all and end up hurt. I never did like fighting. As soon as we got into the car I was shaking on the way home glad to have gotten away.

Matt and I were off to Butlin's on a slightly chilly but sunny morning. We had the window slightly down and the radio playing. Heart FM were running their usual Who's On Heart? Competition where three celebrities said Who's On and Heart and you had to guess their names. I'd tried phoning through about a hundred times by this point and had achieved talking to Toby Anstis, the presenter, by the time we reached Tesco's car park. This was where Matt got out to get us drinks while I'd been talking about our holiday to Toby and he asked me if I'd seen the Butlin's robot. I didn't know what he was on about as we hadn't arrived at our holiday destination by then.

In our chalet we'd turned on the telly most mornings and got into a programme called heir hunters making us wonder if anyone would ever want to track us down.

Ecclesiastes 7:25
I was determined to find wisdom and the answers to my questions.

In the evenings we'd watch tribute acts like a Stereophonics act and a Tina Turner act that were both fantastic. I was having omelettes with a full cooked breakfast in the mornings and pancakes afterwards.

One morning we saw a rabbit on the grass outside of where we were staying. It didn't rain once on holiday and one day along Minehead's promenade thee was a pirate posing for photographs so Matt and I had our photos taken with him with his real parrot as a memento. It was a lovely holiday but not quite warm enough to get into the sea but the Butlin's site had proved enough entertainment.

One morning my mind was made up and I started worrying about my husband's faith and I had to deliver some words to him from God. I'd thought that he was spiritually blind so I started to share everything I could remember from Bible passages about Jesus ministry. I told him about the sower and explained it to him, then the Baptism and temptation of Jesus. he was baptised by John and got taken to the desert to be tempted to won the world. I had a lot of other passages in my head and we ended up missing out on going to a carnival social down at Yeovil of where we had several awards to pick up. Three whole days were taken up talking about them. In the end I'd felt that I'd passed a message onto him from God. I needed confirmation that he'd received the message that I'd had to pass on.

That Sunday evening Matt and I went to a carnival meeting up at the Queens head and it went slowly as I took it all in.

In the morning I got up and went to work up at my mother's. Rowan, Katy, Callie and little Oliver were there. I took them in the school room for a reading and Katy wanted Postman Pat she really liked him. Then we had fruit, juice, and milky coffees for Mum and I with a slice of cake.

Now we did lots of work that day and Jessie picked me up from mothers in the evening and he let me drive for miles to Burnham out across the moors and we had a laugh. This was my first lesson with Jessie then we turned round and went home again.

Matt and I struggled with getting the doctors attention to get IVF and I had to get my blood type. This was our third try and I went there convinced they'd tell me what blood type I was but they never said anything.

The next day I went round Fee's after work. It had been snowing heavily and our children ran around in the snow throwing snowballs, but they did make a large snowman together. Mum put on a blue scarf, black buttons, a carrot and little stones as the mouth. We had a lot of fun and I took photos for their little progress books. They looked really sweet.

It was Valentine's week that week and Jessie came round to take me driving. He'd offered advice the last time I'd seen him to get a basque and stockings and suspenders for a present for Matt. Now I went on and got it all that week. It was a resort for sex as it was waning. Matt never used to look at my presents. Jessie kept on for me to wear it so he could take a photograph. I hated it and told him to take it off his phone of which he did. Matt went on and didn't appreciate my gift on Valentine's Day.

I'd gone to work the next morning and in the afternoon Mum and I settled down from all the mornings activities to watch a film called Peter Pan with the children who had Quavers to munch. They were good as gold while Mum and I had a cup of tea. I told my Mum that I was going to have a driving lesson that evening with Jessie of whom was going to pick me up from Mum's. He had a bit of a chat with Mum about carnival days before we took off in the car. I drove in the dark and nearly hit a parked car by the pavement in Street. I'd had enough this was to be my last lesson before I gave up.

On the Tuesday I went to work with nothing else on my mind but playing with the children. Nancy, my niece, was in today and I knew we'd have fun at some point with tickle monster. The day soon flew by and then in the evening I went up town to do some kick boxing. I'd felt a bit intimidated by the other women and men there though and worried about my glasses being broken.

> Matthew 6:27
> *Can any of you live a bit longer by worrying about it?*

I tried very hard to orchestrate punches and kicks in a safe way without hurting anyone but failed in feeling anger like the others felt.

I'd been into Hades, the land of the dead, a few times in my dreams. It can seem like you're in a black tunnel and any lights you do see, I believe, are God's own lights shining through the people there. Some have a real yellowy golden glow about them, but most have a white light about them that can be tinted slightly with a bit of blue. If I did see places other than faces alive with colour then a soul was about to leave Hades to go into heaven.

I'll share one dream in particular I experienced in Hades of where I'd initially flew in through the pitch dark countryside into a building where there was a teacher. The teacher had several souls standing to attention each with their own individual lights about them. I heard a pupil say, "Oh my god," in a way which inferred a major personal epiphany had just occurred. I remember the reply of the teacher, "You can only say that once!" that was said very sharply. A powerful force pushed me very had quickly out of the building. Then it felt like I was creeping through a hedge backwards on my hands and knees through the pitch dark of the surroundings just to get out of there. I promptly woke up. Thankfully it had all been a dream.

That Saturday I turned up at the Bishop's Palace with Matt saying we were with Wick Carnival Club. Spying the marquee and the swans through the archways I'd guessed where to go and led Matt to the back end of the large white tent. The hook-a-duck was already set up and so were the face paints. Intent on getting practice in, in painting a child's face after a couple of hours I got my chance. A child had asked for a tiger face. Noticing my hesitancy the Mum hinted at me to get on with it. With a bit of orange make-up all over the face and lines and dots in black I'd thought that I'd done a good job, but Emily and Georgia thought otherwise. Feeling scorned I got up with my camera and proceeded to find the decorative swans I'd missed round town. The witch looked fantastic and so did the others I missed. Snapping happily in and around the grounds I soon found my way back to the little plastic ducks of which I had more fun with anyway while having a laugh with Sue and Keith.

The paddling pool was soon tipped up on the grass with the yellow ducks packed away. At least I cheered up by then when Matt was pulling me away to leave. We said our goodbyes and see you at the next meeting.

On the Thursday I got up to Skyfall by Adele and in the dark it gave me the creeps. I'd been getting up very early for work, and laid in to hear the song getting a chill up my spine. I turned my radio alarm clock off after to get straight in the shower.

In work later I'd had a good day and looked forward to going to one of my children, I'd childminded birthdays. When we'd finished for the day big Oliver's mum said she'd give us a lift to her house for the party. I went through her house and in the kitchen I got offered a drink to take outside in the sunshine. I stood around and chatted with the other mums while watching a party of children either running around or on the trampoline. Matt came over to pick me up.

Back at home I decided to walk up town to the Whiteheads newsagents and spoke with Tubsy the owner and talked about carnival and I asked if Wendy with the children were all right while buying a Wispa.

That Saturday I hopped on the bus and went over to Street at the Methodist hall for one of their coffee mornings. My Mum-in-law and Lis, my sister-in-law were already there. Lis was selling expensive looking artefacts from where Tom, her husband, worked at Cheddar in a warehouse. They were collecting money for Fibromyalgia researchers as Lis suffered with that condition. My Mum-in-law Sue was selling her books and bric-a-brac while I played with my niece and nephew, Emily and Henry. I also helped out with cooking tea cakes. Helen was there, Lis's half-sister, and she gave me her number to go horse riding with her.

Next day feeling half asleep I dragged myself out of bed intending to go to church. Not bothering to look at the time I'd slung on my jeans, warm clothes and my bright fluorescent jacket to face the cold air.

In church I placed my coat by the side of me and I'd fumbled in my purse for all of my small change to put in an orange packet at the end of the pew. My order of service fell to the floor and I'd had to bend over to pick it up while everyone else started singing. They were two verses in before I'd found the hymn in my book and didn't really feel with it that morning.

Completely zoning out to Robin's sermon I'd stared at the picture of Christ in the window working out what he needed me to hear. Robin sticking steadfastly to a doctrine service actually helped me to clear my mind and my spirit started to feel uplifted. Sniffing the air I reached into my pocket for a tissue and the next hymns cheered me up as I'd sang along. I'd been sitting on the right hand side of the church that morning with a whole pew to myself and shred the peace with those immediately around. I was beginning to recognise some faces in church but was rubbish at memorising names.

The communal wine and bread gave me a feeling of inclusion while knelt down with the others either side of me as I'd said my 'amen's' and felt cheered walking back to my seat. I still had to reach for my coat as I'd felt cold seeing that the clouds were forming outside.

As I started to walk towards the back of the church for coffee a lady called Caroline, of whom you couldn't mistake for anyone else in her lovely attire, came up to me and commented on my choice of coat that was my fluorescent carnival coat. Embarrassed, I'd left not having any coffee thinking that perhaps I needed a new coat.

I went to the library one morning and I'd ordered a book about a reporter called Kate Adie, 'The Kindness of Strangers'. The book they'd said on the computer was in Wells and would take a couple of days to get to me. As I'd sat there ordering it myself without any help I came across a man I'd known from my Theatresaurus days and he said that he was writing his life story as he'd grown up on the streets.

The next morning I showered and changed ready to go to work. Then I walked down to the bus stop and saw a young lad waiting for the bus. He had been in a school uniform.

"What school are you off to?"

"Wells Blue," he said.

"Do you know of a redheaded lad called Liam Smith?"

"I don't know I'm twelve."

"Oh, my nephew's ten."

"I don't know him," but we soon got on the bus together.

In work that day up at Mom's we'd spent most of the day out in the garden. The children got on and occupied themselves really well. I'd tried to get them to play football and noticed that there were eight footballs of varying size and colours. I ended up kicking them all around the garden make round shapes with them. This got me absentminded about there being eight earths or eight solar systems. I did wonder if God's first works were The Big Bang Theory that he'd whispered into the sun and when the first planet appeared within the fourth ring around the sun it became the first earth. But then there'd been three other planets behind it and when the first earth moved to the fifth ring round the earth the planet behind it became the second earth, so that every time a planet passed through the fourth ring it became another earth.

It was lunch time by the time I stopped wondering about the universe, but I remembered what I'd been thinking as I'd passed round the food to the children.

I'd had far too much time to think that morning so put more effort into playing with the children that afternoon.

Next day I went to see my consultant Dr Van Driel with my husband Matt and I got more curious than ever to know what exactly I had wrong with me.

Ecclesiastes 7:25
I was determined to find wisdom and the answers to my questions.

I needed to know. It had been seven years since my first diagnosis of me just having been on a natural high. I actually asked the man outright. He'd said that it was a chemical in-balance on the brain. My brain went into over drive had I had too much acid or something in my diet messing my mind up. I'd given up Coca-Cola years ago because of phosphoric acid a poisonous substance. At this time I was still drinking Dr Pepper with kebabs and I read phosphoric acid on the side of the can. I decided to give the drink up.

My next door neighbour Penny asked me if I'd like to go to an Aster Communities meeting. She'd asked me if there was something I'd like to change in the area where we lived and I said that there could be something like a concrete plant pot on the pavement outside our front window. I'd said that because cars were constantly parking right under our front window. Penny told me that she'd asked to get the street lamp removed from right outside her bedroom window, and she'd been on about getting posts in the ground alongside our flat to stop people from parking on the grass. I was convinced as we'd had a long discussion.

In the morning on the bus into Wells I realised that I had to get a present and a card for Valentine's Day so I walked into Tesco's and found a heart shaped pillow, a bottle of wine, a card, and a box of chocolates just for Matt.

It was a Wednesday and only three children were in. I spent most of the morning keeping Keeley occupied and away from the other children as she seemed tired and inclined to be more likely to bite. I liked Keeley anyway and sat with her in the school room for most of the morning as she did a lot of drawing and other work like her alphabet book. I felt pleased with her progress. Nancy came round in her cute little pink ballet outfit and I decided to take a photograph before she went to lessons for the first time.

That evening, after work, I was pleased to be greeted at home with a lovely anniversary of our engagement card and a big bunch of flowers in the fireplace. Matt said that he'd decided to cook salmon as a romantic dinner. I decided to dress up in a black low cut top and black trousers, Matt dress in shirt and trousers and we enjoyed our wine.

The next day I'd gotten a letter in the post from a woman called Katherine explaining that there was to be a reunion for the class of '92'. I deduced that her maiden name must have been James as she was the girl I'd pulled the hair out of in a French lesson once. There was a number on the letter to ring to say if I could attend and if there were others she could contact through me. I thought of Rheann but didn't have any address or phone number for her. I wondered if they'd been in touch with Becky too as it would have been nice to see her again. I also thought of Damion, my old school crush, and hoped he'd be there.

At Charlton House, in Shepton, where the reunion had been taken place I'd first got talking to Saffron who'd said she'd always felt sorry for me at school. I didn't want to know why and left her aghast as I'd told her I hadn't even recognised her.

In my black low cut top, black trousers and with plenty of make-up I'd felt better looking than most of the other women. Nicky Bennett said hello at the bar and we got to talking just like old friends. The most popular boy in school once could still make me blush before making my excuses at seeing Becky, one of my old school friends turn up. As Becky and I got talking I'd noticed Emma Baber, Sarah, who would have been once Dyer, and Dawn Muscroft at our table. Emma had brought an old photo album along and I'd been the only one who bought her husband along. I turned to Matt engrossed in conversation with Trevor Edwards who looked like he hadn't aged a day since school. He'd been asking Matt about joining our carnival club.

I turned back to Dawn going on about how we'd been related through marriage once when my cousin Scott had married her sister Karen and they'd had a couple of boys together.

I was happiest reminiscing with Becky though and were both a bit sad that Rheann hadn't made it, but with three children and no means of transport, we'd understood why.

At the end of the evening I said thank you to Catherine for a lovely get to together and she told me to thank a Liz, who'd come from Australia, who'd helped organise it all, which I did.

Emma asked me if I'd remembered Liz and I simply said that she seemed a nice lady. Emma took that as a no. I said goodbye to those I'd talked to and Matt and I went on home.

I'd wanted a second confirmation to be able to say to everyone of how I'd grown through faith. Mum had wanted Eve and Fee to get confirmed for years and we finally got to the day when all four of us were to be confirmed. The whole family turned up to the church excited. I'd fantasised that a reporter would be there to talk to our family that was getting confirmed together. Yet again there had been no Lord's Prayer said reminding me of my first confirmation.

We'd been introduced to the others getting confirmed and the church had been packed for fourteen adults and children to make their vows with God.

I'll always remember talking to one old lady who'd lived in Africa for years called Diana.

Deuteronomy 4:9
Be on your guard! Make certain that you do not forget,
As long as you live, what you have seen with your own eyes.

I'd been surprised that such an aged lady would come to faith so late in life and Toby, seeing us talking, told me to look out for her.

As Fee, Eve, Mum and I stood up in front of the congregation we realised Diana was a bit deaf as she asked the vicar Toby to repeat himself. Fee, Eve and I just secretly smiled as our promises were made to God to uphold the Christian faith.

We'd lined up at the back of the church near the font ready to be flicked water at which was a bit of a shock, but apparently I couldn't have the sign of the cross on my forehead at my second confirmation.

Dressed in my favourite suede skirt, and matching in colour jumper with a white shirt I felt happy to be with my sisters finally devoting themselves to the Christian faith.

At the end of the service Mum, Fee, Eve and I were given thick dark blue new edition Bibles and I asked Toby why the Lord's Prayer had never been said. He told me it shortened the serve not being used.

I draped my arms round Matt on the way out and Mum thought she'd been recognised by the Bishop present as he'd officiated at her first confirmation. It had been such a lovely evening as we all made our way home.

On the Monday while clearing up the toys after work Mum had asked me to box everything up and put it back into the shed. I'd brought down the hoover to get up the bits on the living room carpet and in the hallway. Trudging back upstairs with the hoover afterwards I then had to pick up the gloriously thick white rug to put under the fireplace that was up on the wall. The cushions had to be brought back down for the two sofas Mum had.

I'd put the TV on afterwards and watched Pointless knowing Dad would want to watch when he came home. By six thirty we'd eaten a lovely cooked meal and Dad and I watched the news before Mum came in having washed up.

I'd gone upstairs then to find Mum's laptop to play The Cradle of Rome game linking all the different pictures together. I'd been getting towards the final level under Aunty Nolas name. Realising the time I changed quickly into my jeans and My Rascals top to play skittles. We had to win tonight to stay near to the top of the table.

Jumping in the car with my handbag and my coat on Mum drove us through Croscombe out to ten bath Road side to Wells and the Britannia Inn.

I'd gotten the drinks first while Mum went through to the alley with our raffle prizes to put on the table behind us. Making my way through the doors with two pints of orange juice and lemonade in my hands wasn't easy so the lady at the bar held the door open for me. Mum was already on the alley playing, so I said hello to everyone and reached into my purse for my three pound to play and chose my raffle tickets. I'd had the numbers eleven to fifteen and felt lucky as I'd eyed up the prizes. I was to play after Tricia who'd gotten eight pins down, Mum and Mandy had gotten the same so the pressure was on to do well. My first ball went down the side but I'd been determined to do well with the two remaining balls. My second throw hit down six pins with three remaining at the back of the diamond. I caught one made the others wobble but ended up with a score of seven.

Sitting back down with the team next to Tricia and Mum we watched the rest of the players do well and we ended up with an accumulative score of fifty six. The team started off well.

While sipping my orange drink I discussed the programme I was watching called Marchlands with Tricia who'd been watching it too saying how creepy it was as the story was about a ghost and had been set in the eighties. I asked Mandy how her husband Graham was and apparently he had Man Utd football team playing on the telly at home. I knew Mandy would ask me about Matt and I'd said that he was fine and playing his own skittles match back at the King William back home in Glastonbury.

Three rounds in Mum got up to get the next drinks and I chatted with Nan Sheila for a bit hearing of how Fee had turned up with the kids at her house that day. Then of how Nancy made Nan laugh trying to get some biscuits from Nan's musical biscuit tin blaring out A Little Less Conversation by Elvis Presley. I'd turned round and high fived Margaret for getting a nine. Carolle, our captain, was telling everyone how her daughter Melonie was pregnant with her first grandchild.

The rest of the evening flowed and at the end we were all happy that the game was won by us.

The next day Matt and I decided to walk across town to Tor Leisure that had a massive bar area with a skittle alley. On the walls were up and coming events such as the R I T S day, their Karaoke nights, and up and coming bands to be played there. It had been about three o'clock in the afternoon when we got there and the television in the corner of the bar was silently showing a football match. We'd noticed barely anyone there and decided to shoot some pool on one of the two tables. At least by the door some sun was shining through and I'd decided to start playing my game left handed. Matt potted first and started hitting down the red balls. It had been awkward to try the shots I'd had available right handed anyway. I'd soon won the first game.

Racking the balls up in the triangle as Matt didn't know how it was my turn to play first. For each of my turns I'd been alternating between right handed and left handed play. I lost the second game. We went to a third game and ended up with the score 2-1 to me. We soon took our drinks outside on the benches to look out over the huge grounds belonging to the Leisure Centre and watched the sun go down behind the trees before deciding to head home.

In church, on the Sunday, I'd sat where the sun was streaming through the windows glad that I was making the most of the morning. The dulcet tones of Larry's sermon were pleasing to the ear while wondering what god's message had been for me that morning. It put me in a thoughtful mood. Going through my stressed, suicidal, and depressed site on Face book, after church, a girl had said she'd had no friends at school so I advised he to join a church youth group.

Mum told me the previous week to write to the head teacher of a school called St Aldhelms. It sounded like a lovely village C of E Primary and as Mrs Thomas worked there. She was someone we both knew from having child minded her daughter Iris, I decided to compose a letter. Apparently Hannah had been impressed in my ability to look after her daughter and had already requested that I help her in her class room anyway. A letter was to be a mere formality.

Outlining my love of working with children, the qualifications I'd taken and the basic roles I'd undertaken as a child minder, the third attempt at this letter was my final one. Quite pleased with what I'd written the following morning the letter was popped into the post.

On the bus into work I noticed James, from my summer skittles team, get on by the cemetery and we exchanged pleasantries. I soon noticed that a head set was on his ears. So clearly he'd been listening to music while making his way to the back of the bus making a conversation impossible. I daydreamed looking out the window at the sun coming up.

At work there'd been Tom, Maisie and a little boy named Liam of whom was usually very quiet. We all played lovely that day and while in the school rom trying again to gently coax a conversation from Liam. I asked him what his favourite programme was very quietly, almost under his breath, I quite distinctly heard the words Bob the Builder which bought happy tears to my eyes. It was lovely to finally hear this little two year old speak and I told his Mum later on that day when his mum came to pick him up.

The following week we had the pirates' film on the telly called Ships Ahoy! And I encouraged Keeley to go in the living room with the boys. By the time the film had finished Mum had cut up the fruit and told the children to go out to the kitchen. My usual milky coffee was on the table with a bit of my favourite farmhouse cake. Mum had the same.

After snack time the morning passed by quite quickly with the three of them, Keeley, Evie and William playing nicely until Jacob showed up dead on lunch. It was tough keeping them occupied until they went home.

After tidying up the living room I sat down and watched Pointless waiting for Dad to come home so that we could all have tea then Mum and I would get ready for our evening skittles match. It was going to be the knock out final.

All night long it was a tensely close game right up until the sixth hand of where we drew and had to play a seventh hand. We started and got thirty three pins with twenty four balls! Our worst hand all night. The other team got up and hit down forty seven pins and won. We, as a laugh, blamed it on a dolly they had that looked like one of those voodoo dollies, but the game ended on good terms as we had won second prize.

That night a prophesy of the future came to me in a dream about the Holy City, but because I was looking down on a road I only saw plenty of feet running around. I'd been particularly fascinated with something else I'd seen which was a chriogenetically engineered fragmented head bobbing up and down on the road. Like the head of a hologram but the head of a real person talking to me. I recognised the face from somewhere. They'd looked like an older version of a child I'd looked after called Keeley.

I'd been reading the Bible after work the next day, the bit about one side of your brain hearing your mother's voice, and the other side your father's voice. I could ascertain from my own mind that Gran's voice could sometimes be heard through the top of my mind. Logically the Devil's desire had to be heard in the mind too of which the access, that I put down on a brain map, came through behind the left ear. God's voice of sanity had to hold all your thoughts together and I placed his voice somewhere in the back of my mind, which made a very clear looking biblical brain map. I felt quite pleased at my take on the biblical passages I'd been reading in bed.

The next year Mum and I went to the football club into Wells to meet with the Rascals to play the final in our knock out cup.

> *Proverbs 16:7*
> *When you please the Lord, you can make your enemies into friends.*

The tables had been pushed together for us to sit round and Carolle had already put the names on the board. I was a bit put out that I wasn't in the team and had to watch. I'd aimed my moaning at our captain Carolle for most of the evening.

Half way through the evening and saying we could be winning by now if I was playing I stood up by the table to watch the bottom of the alley to see the pins go down. The captain played anchor woman and before she sat down I got talking to her about the patients that had been at The Priory and she told me something very interesting. As we were talking Carolle made a point of standing behind my left ear orating a lot of obscenities after which I got told that some patients actually hear those sort of words externally.

As I sat down a bit dazed I'd realised that my biblical brain map I had come up with was right. There was no moaning from me after that as I got back into following the game. On the fifth hand we'd clawed a lot of pins back with a sixty-four hand. It felt like we were out to win at last and by the time the last player of the second team got up to play she needed a spare to bet us. We all waited with baited breath as she hit seven pins with her first ball. The next ball hit the remaining two down. A spare became imminent but the last ball went right through the middle. Carolle congratulated the whole team.

I had awoken very early one morning unable to sleep. Something had been drawing me to the computer like a moth to a flame to begin typing. Feeling like my brain was awash with the Holy Spirit my fingers seemed to have a life of their own as they began to transcribe a conversation I'd been having with God in my head.

GOD: "In the Bible there was a get-out clause for those who would become lazy and apathetic."

KAREN: "IT'S THE WRONG WORD!" (I'd been thinking of the word complacent but God took over my typing).

GOD: "It was about the meek inheriting the earth which is why the vast majority of people turned their backs on their faith, because they thought that because they were basically good people they didn't have to be Christians."

KAREN: "ORIGINAL SUBLIMINAL MESSAGE GOING ON HERE!" (I'd been thinking about God's original message to us through the natural colour of orange).

GOD: "The next get out clause Karen, provided, is that there had to be worldwide peace before the next 500 years start." (meaning worldwide peace started several hundred years ago in the heavens of where the original twelve disciples, as spirits appeared on no-man's land at the beginning of world war one, the land of Armageddon) Now as Christians we want worldwide peace right? So this is the final test."

KAREN: "The judgement days have been happening already haven't they through us and the way we judge ourselves? Thank you God. I know now there will only be a handful of people only judged by yours truly. At least this way friends of Christians that they have been praying for can be dealt with by them around them only. It's been going through my head a lot recently that carol about where the meek souls shall receive him still then the dear Christ enters in…

GOD: "I'm starting to think that certain other things should have been left out of the original Bible because we should have had forever to figure everything out. Karen's made me believe in the power of protection through words hell was the wrong word because when you preach fear you're pushing others away and I didn't want that. I should have just encouraged those who believe that when you're dead you're dead there's just no more second chance for some people. Karen knew the last word God is going to say at the end of it all. Sorry. The only thing I did wrong in creating us was to teach people how to judge one another in the wrong way."

At which point I got up from my computer and went back to bed. I slept soundly all morning and was roused from sleep by the sound of people outside. It had nearly been midday. Getting out of bed I yawned, stretched, and just chucked on my clothes which was shorts and a black and white flowery top. Having lunch I had the radio on and started dancing and singing to 'Moves like Jagger' my favourite song at the time. Deciding to go up town to get some washing powder to do our weekend wash.

By the time Matt got home the flat was hoovered through with the jocks and socks wash going round in the washer-dryer. Matt asked if I was ready. I said yes but I soon got told to put jeans on for stewarding into the night up at Pilton with Battle of the Bands. A competition organised by Michael Eavis for bands to be able to win a place on a stage at Glastonbury Festival.

Once there Matt and I grabbed our fluorescent jackets and put them on. Matt had bought crisps, doughnuts, and a drink for later. It was going to be a long afternoon. Locals kept turning up in their cars taking up spaces for the bands and roadies so that they could get their free tickets for the local festival. I didn't get irate for once. Matt dealt with most people turning up in their vehicles while I'd had the list of bands in my hand to mark off as they came in. It was soon all over.

Chapter Twenty-Five

After the hellish year I'd had of where the IVF treatments hadn't worked I'd been feeling particularly distraught one evening while Matt was at skittles. There was an anger that had built up inside of me and I knew that if I went looking for trouble that evening I'd have let someone beat me to death. Feeling trapped by my own desires my fingers found themselves dialling 118500 for The Samaritans. I had to let this build-up of emotions have some sort of release. A lady introduced herself as Jane and in a calm controlled manner she'd kept me talking and I let out all my inner frustrations as I didn't want to trouble my family with any of this. I'd explained that my sister Eve was finally happy with a family of her own to deal with. Fiona had her own problems with her children and I just believed that my sisters, my Mum and even my Mum-in-law who'd all had their children just wouldn't understand my emotional pain. I'd been convinced that my IVF treatments hadn't worked because I'd believed they never had enough oxygen. I'd kept Jane talking for over an hour feeling more and more calmer as I talked. I thanked Jane for the phone call afterwards and felt emotionally spent as I took myself off to bed.

The next day I'd told my Mum that I'd phoned The Samaritans. She looked upset so I explained that I hadn't wanted to do anything stupid. I'd just needed someone to talk to. Mum made me realise that you only call the Samaritans when you feel suicidal and again I reassured her that I would never do anything like that. Mum let the matter drop and I wished I'd never said anything although a part of me had wanted Mum to be aware I'd been feeling upset.

> *1 Peter 1:7*
> *So your faith, which is more precious than gold, must also be tested,*
> *So that it may endure.*

Mum did say one more thing though, that I could call her or my sisters anytime. I said that I knew.

A couple of days later a phone bill came through the post and Matt and I balked at the amount as it had been over a hundred and ninety pounds. Apparently that Samaritan phone call had cost over a hundred pounds just because I'd let 118 500 put me through to them. My resolve was to never call them again.

I'd stewarded on the Saturday from one pm onwards. The sun slowly fell out of the sky showing a clear night full of stars and Stuart turned up on shift. He started stewarding with me and while looking at the sky Stuart started pointing out the constellations to me.

It was Sunday the following day and miraculously got up in time for church. The service had been about the ministry of John the Baptist and remember hearing the vicar quote the passage about how the next Messiah coming after him will anoint with the Holy Spirit.

After church I bought some roast potatoes, some veg and meat for a roast dinner for when Matt got home.

The next day I went into work and the boys were in who were William, Finley, Haydn and Jacob. We made some leaf rubbings before elevenses and afterwards I had to rush to the toilet upstairs as we were going to go out for the rest of the day. As I came downstairs William was standing outside the toilet and he said that it looked orange. I froze to the spot wondering what he was on about. He'd been looking at a white door. He also said that he saw the sign of the fish.

1 Kings 10:5
It left her breathless and amazed.

I said to William, "Look again and take a step back. What colour is the door now?"

He'd said "White."

"And can you see the symbol of a fish?"

He'd said, "No Karen. It's gone."

It wasn't long until we were all out the door going to the fields. Jacob was on a go slow with me so I had to hold back with him and he got distracted by something in the hedge at the bottom of the field. He pointed at it and said the word fish. I mentally dismissed this and urged Jacob to keep up with the rest. I thought at the time that he was one of the Kings line as in the Bible.

Afterwards I pulled my hair together behind my head and we only got as far as the second field of where there were hay bales the children wanted to jump on. Haydn picked up loads of hay in his hands and posed as a scarecrow. I took a photo for his book. We decided not to go any further after this and went back to the first field for our picnic.

It wasn't long before all of us made our way back to Mum's over the crumbling wall, by the bottom of the hospital and up passed the houses on the estate to Misburg Close. The children soon all went home.

While we were tidying up the toys strewn around the living room Mum began to flick through the channels on the TV for a film to watch but soon gave up. Mum and I soon sat down thoroughly exhausted and then out of nowhere Mum started to tell me about a film based on a true story. It was about the Ming Dynasties and how the beautiful Geisha girls in the harem were waited upon hand and foot. One lady had escaped this world by having a baby by the royal type of king in order to have private quarters. There had been another lady though who'd had her legs chopped off and had been placed in a vase for the rest of her life. That haunted me and made me feel blessed.

Reading about the Holy City that night I thought of how the world was two thousand years ago and how oppressive society had been and thought of the depression that must have been about the poor and needy. John must have been depressed and so this vision encapsulated the deep needs of a man desperate to bring heaven to a very real hell on earth. It had to be a real vision though because as far as I knew there were only ten months to the year back ten as October was originally the eighth month, but they foresaw twelve months in a year to come through the blossoming on the tree of life.

At home that next day, in the evening, Matt and I sat on the sofa. I climbed on top of his lap writhing around till I found his arousal under me. I'd arched my back and took my top and my bra off. Matt looked at me with his pupils dilating, smoke got in his eyes. I'd felt slumberous and heat coursing through my veins. I arched my back again as he stroked the sides of my back, slowly encircling the indent at the bottom of my spine driving me wild. I ran my fingers through my hair as we felt each other. He made to pull me forward to suckle my nipples gently nicking them to get hard. The heat was so powerful I'd had convulsions desperate for another release. I'd fumbled with his zip urgently brushing my hands down his boxers. Matt held me still while with the other hand removed to free his penis after his jeans and his underwear fell to the floor round his ankles.

After our lovemaking we went to the pub for our carnival meeting and as soon as we walked through the door Glyn, the manager, looked at us both looking dishevelled and said to Matthew, "You look thoroughly shagged."

The next morning Mum told me, with a glint in her eyes, that England was playing football that night in an international game. We got out four, A4 bits of paper and small bits of card. Mum held one bit of card over one side of the paper. I did the same on the other side and we left a horizontal gap of which the children painted red. The paint was quick drying and we did the same again vertically to make it look like an England flag. Afterwards we rolled the side of the flags around straws and 'voila' I'd said after putting names and dates on them.

The next day was a Friday and I was up at St Aldhelms with a Mrs Reed first telling me to cut up circles and then cut them into three segments. I'd got into a muddle tough as I started putting several circles together to cut up in one go. When I got to put twenty triangles into each cup for thirty children I ended up needing help. Mrs Reed, Sarah, a trustee, and I had to sort them out properly before the lesson started. Mrs Reed called me Mrs Muddle like in the test we were setting. By the end of the day I was really tired before I had to run for the bus.

That evening my first Neighbourhood Panel Zone 20 meeting took place just down the road from where we lived in a small hall I never knew existed. Sat round tables all pushed together we all introduced ourselves. I said that my name was Karen and I'm an Aster Communities tenant in Glastonbury. Representing Aster was someone called Steve. Elaine was the chairwoman, vice chairwoman was Gill. Penny, my neighbour, introduced herself, there was a blind woman called Lisa of whom was the secretary, and a coloured man named Amos. There were a couple of other housing association tenants too. This had been their AGM and I got voted in as a panel member with full voting rights. Penny did recommend me as a treasurer but I wouldn't do it knowing full well I couldn't be responsible for all the money.

When we were all elected a handful of people came to for handouts as we had thousands of pounds to give to community projects. We decided to vote on four key areas of how to help in the community. The first area was tackling worklessness, improve social environment, partnership work and prevent anti-social behaviour and fear of crime.

The people who'd applied had asked us for a tea project set up for locals to drop into a place for tea parties and an application was made by a couple using a local church to run activities, we also had someone from Wookey Hole who wanted to run Christmas outings. We funded all three and I felt pleased to be a part of such a generous group.

The end of the meeting descended into chaos though as Penny started to have a go at Lisa with her saying, "It's a scary place to be if I'm actually in control of your emotions." Penny turned herself into somebody who was not very well liked as the meeting was wrapped up and I was just desperate to walk home. Hating confrontations I did just that.

In the evening I got picked up by my best friend Julie to go to our friend Michaela's house. When we got there we got out the car and went to our friends little flat.

When we got in we were offered a drink and Julie and I had lemonade. Then we all sat down in front of the television and we shared our gossip. I talked of my family and gossiped about a woman called Charlene, of whom was my main piece of gossip. Michaela would make me laugh when she'd go on about her family, especially her grandchildren and she'd show us some pictures. Michaela and Julie liked to talk about their work too as carers. I really enjoyed their company and we'd have a meal together while all the time we'd have channel ten on in the background on the telly. We loved to watch Doc Martin. This would be a lovely few hours and that night Julie and I finally got home around midnight.

A few days later Matt and I were on a plane to Cuba for our holiday. The Blau Costa Verde was massive and had its very own part of the beach. On the first day there we booked up our trips. Strolling round the grounds that second night a lot of the hotel was still being built and we couldn't get over the size of the place. We had two decent sized pools too.

On the beach all the activities were free so we went on the catamaran three times which was fun. During that first week Matt was determined to banish my fears of swimming with the fishes so that I could go on and swim with the dolphins. Each morning at breakfast we'd take some bread rolls to go to the beach with to feed the fish. We hired snorkels and it was amazing as blue long nosed fish came up around us, little yellow fish, dark brown flat fish, some tiny pink fish would follow us around for our bread and I really enjoyed myself.

The hotel offered entertainment every evening and we got to know a young Canadian couple named Mike and Louise. Mike was a live wire and encouraged us to play water sports in the pool. We really came alive that holiday and played games on the beach too like boules, water balloon games, and darts.

We were soon on our trip to see the dolphins. Matt and I got surprised when part of the trip was to go on speed boats and were left to drive them ourselves. I soon took the steering wheel and gave Matt a white knuckle ride round the estuary.

Later on we had to clamber on a passenger boat of where I'd lost the camera in the sea. The skipper bless him retrieved it for us though and told us to put it in a bag of rice when we got back to the hotel. This boat took us to a semi-captive area for the dolphins. Luckily there was a shop where I'd bought a fun camera.

> Isaiah 32:11
> You have been living an easy life, free from worries;
> but now, tremble in fear.

Wetting myself in the water with the dolphins when one brushed against my leg they felt solid and hard but as everyone else was rubbing their tummies. I found the strength to do it too. We'd had to pay an extra twenty for tricks and I grabbed their fins to be pulled around in the water. Matt paid to be flipped into the air by them. Terrified as I had been I was still glad that I'd swam with them and we came away with a professional photo of us with them.

One day on a coach there was a guide telling us about the poor locals of whom were paid four pounds a month in our money and how they were desperate to leave the island. Some locals had sold everything they had even their homes to be able to leave. We went by a bus in a field of where he'd said a family went to live after a bad storm blew down their home. These people lived on tips from working in the hotels and asked for what we wouldn't want any more at the end of our holidays. We were being taken to a market and we saw an old mustang, Corvette, and Cadillac that I took photographs of. At the market we bought our gifts to take back home.

On the last night there, a security guard made a beautiful rose out of grass of which prompted me to go back to our room for some money to give him.

Before going to the plane the next day Matt had taken a bag full of toiletries and clothes we didn't want to a security guard down by the beach of whom had asked him for these things in the week. Despite the locals being very poor they were lovely people always willing to share their stories.

There'd only been one storm all holiday of where we'd been stranded at the hotel bar when the chairs and tables blew around the pool and things got smashed. We heard it. The rain even put us knee deep in water around the bar.

Mike had given us his Facebook name to get in contact with him afterward.

On the way home the nine hour flight took far too long. The telly's weren't working. The lights were dimmed so much I couldn't see to do my puzzles or read my books. I had to keep annoying Matt to stop him sleeping just for some company, and even from London it took us so long to get back it was lovely to finally be in our little flat. At home I put my rose in a little vase in the kitchen window.

Mum had organised, with other child minders in our area, to go over her neighbour Wendy's house for the day with Katie, Freya, Maisie, Tom, William and Evie. I'd sat with them to start off with and watched them play on the fort, or on trikes, around the garden. Then I'd sat by the table with my crowns on for them to sticker and draw on. I'd spent most of the morning cutting them out. It was a lovely hot day. this day was to signify Kate and Prince William's nuptials.

We had our own area on the grass to sit on and have lunch together with lots of other children. I took photos of our children for their books. They played some more before we were one of the groups who were the last ones to leave as some of them had been due to go home.

It had been a lovely start to the day as Mum and I went round Fee's after work to go to her Kate and Will's party in a tent in the garden. Rachel and Anne, my sister-in-law's were there and Rachel had gone blonde. I thought it suited her.

Fee had decorated the tent with pictures of Kate and Wills on the tent walls. We all sat around talking together and tucking into some lovely food. By then my Matt had turned up and I got chatting to Anne, Fee's eldest sister-in-law. I then proceeded to talk to Rachel about her work over at Clarks warehouse. I asked her if she know my Matt's best friend Justin, she said yes. I had always liked these sisters, but then turned to talk to Nan Sheila sat with Nan Burr. It was a pleasant evening and I helped Fee wash up in the kitchen afterward and stacked the dishwasher.

I used to have the children lovely playing wheels-on-the-bus on the bottom three steps of the stairs. I would tell them to put their seat belts on and we'd sing the wheels-on-the-bus song until I'd announce where we were going. Then the children would tell me about the chickens, and stray animals in the road, so we'd all honk on our horns to get them out of the way. I would always aske before we'd start the game where they would like to go on the bus. Their favourite places were the park and the beach. I'd pretend to give them beach bags with swimming costumes, towels, buckets and spades, sun hats and sun lotion. I'd always pretend to give them money for ice-creams, and they'd go off and pretend to go swimming, and building sandcastles, etc. This was always a favourite game. Sometimes I'd suggest we went to farms and I gave them all carrots for the donkeys, or apples for the horses and the children would have great fun pretending to feed the animals. We'd soon gave up for mid-morning fruit.

That weekend I'd been invited to go to St John's AGM up at The Abbey house at the top of town. I was pleased and excited at being able to go.

> Matthew 5:3
> *Happy are those who know they are spiritually poor.*

I'd showered and hair washed. I'd put on my favourite suede skirt with a white blouse and a sleeveless beige jumper that had a pretty white pattern on. Pulling on my knee high suede boots I walked up town. We'd been asked if we'd wanted a roast dinner afterwards but Matt didn't want to go and he'd said that he'd rather cook.

At the meeting the room was crammed pack with people all waiting to either be re-elected into their positions in the church or for the meal afterwards. I'd found a seat not far from the front of the room and as the Reverend David Macgeoch went on about the church finances I put my hand up to speak. I'd asked if the church raised funds through the local carnival. The meeting soon wrapped up and I'd been pleased to have been a part of it.

Matt did a lovely roast dinner at home and that evening we had a carnival meeting down at The Mitre. Struggling yet again to see the other people's faces through the poor lighting of the room and with my ailing eyesight the meeting droned on mainly about our up and coming fundraising events like the extravaganza and how much building still needed to be done. The meeting, surprisingly, closed early and Matt and I went for kebabs before going home.

I went up the Tor the next morning and met with a man so vulnerable he looked close to tears. I asked him how he was doing. He said that it was the anniversary of his wife's death fifteen years prior. We got chatting and he told me that he kept going for his family while all the while a white pink ethereal glow was around him and I saw an arm. He told me that sometimes he still actually felt her warm embrace. The moment looked priceless so I tactfully made my excuses and went down the Tor.

That evening I took a meeting with the carnival club down the shed where the cart was built and it was really low key. I stayed on after the meeting when a lady called June asked those, who hadn't got their costumes yet, to stay behind. I'd expected that Sunday to pick up my finished costume but she said that she had to make alterations. June panicked me as the first carnival was in five days' time.

By the Thursday I was down at the cart again and started panicking I wouldn't get my costume in time. Come Bridgewater I'd had no collar on my costume. I had to complain about frayed edges, and June put on wide shoulder pads to cover up her mistake.

As part of a dream, that next morning, I saw the great Holy City from a distance. It's been built in this dream but was under cover set back from some dark green shrubbery hovering in the heavens somewhere over Texas.

That was a vision of the Holy City, God told me, and that day I had a meeting with my favourite vicar David at St John's church. I came to him with visions and dreams and the Bible passage Peter 1:20 and he looked at me to say, "You could make it as a prophetic minister like Iain is."

I felt elated that he had such confidence in me. Then I went away and thought about what he'd said. It really made my day.

The next day the carnival club had all met up at Charlton Inn in Shepton. I'd gone home to Glastonbury after work as Matt had wanted me with him on the bus back to Shepton Mallet. Out in the skittle alley I'd been getting nervous but stayed off the drink so that I wouldn't have to pee the moment I got on the float. I'd felt awash with something bigger than me as we all clambered on the Showtime cart. my costume reminded me of Mo-Mo from on Cbeebies even though I was meant to be a character from Starlight Express with my shiny blue and silver costume.

While I was dancing on the cart practicing, before getting to the start line, I felt that I'd been awash with the Holy Spirit and as we passed the fields I was convinced that I could just walk off the moving cart right across the fields and that night would turn into day.

While passing the place en-route, where my family usually stood, opposite the petrol station, I couldn't see them and was convinced that I'd been anointing the crowd with the Holy Spirit as I danced to the music. I kept looking for Mum, Dad, Uncle Cyn, Fee, Matt, and the girls and Liam, but I never saw them.

In work the next day I'd asked Mum what she had thought of the cart and told her our ranking in getting any trophies. I'd asked her where they'd been standing, Mum told me at the usual spot and apparently Nancy had followed the cart for a bit to catch my attention, but I explained my misgivings and Mum replied that Nancy had been hurt because I never waved back.

The Bath and West, after carnival, the night before was filled with carnivalites dancing and drinking the night away and I'd bumped into Damon. He told me that he was doing well in Masqueraders and I told him that I'd been appointed Vice Chairman in his place. He'd wished me good luck.

Work was quiet at Mum's on the Friday and I was keen to be picked up by Matt to get to Wells carnival. At the start of the procession, whilst we were beginning to walk up the by-pass, I saw a beam of light in the sky. Matt and I wondered if it was a laser beam coming from a nightclub. Anyway I had a bizarre thought that someone would pretend to blow up the moon, and then a laser would pretend to project a new moon in the sky and with the original moon still there it would look like two moons came to replace the first one. I mean, let's face it, without the moon there would be no day or night and therefore no seasons to be able to create anything to grow. It had been a Bible passage I'd based these ideas on.

A couple of days later I remembered of having dreamt of being on a golden beach with red Amethyst stones washed up on the shore and there was a helicopter hovering overhead. God spoke to me saying, "It is said that when we all touch a bright red Amethyst, for a moment, we all stop spreading the seed of life."

This had been before I'd had a very strong vision of me standing in a red bricked room of where my book had lain open upon the page of living in the moment. Two girls passed through, looked at it briefly, and went to walk off, but one hung around in the distance. Then two boys came into the room and opened the book on the pages of The Seeds of Trust, one dissipated but the other one got more and more enthralled with another book with lots of Biblical references down the bottom and only his form, like an apparition, hung around with his nose just lightly touching the book. I then looked up and saw Jesus straining against what looked like veins running through the earth trying to create a new tree of life.

The red bricked walls changed slightly to look like the inside of a cave made out of clay and I stomped my foot and said, "Jesus why don't you just come down from there and walk out," but he wouldn't answer. This vision hung around in my mind for over three weeks and during these weeks I saw another cave like room with somebody in a coma with a nurse sitting vigilantly. This would be the basis on which I agreed with God there should be a holistic place called The Amethyst Room inside of the Holy City.

After this vision I sat on the floor and prayed to find out if God actually wanted me to work with children. I needed to find out if He actually trusted me. I needed to know what my calling was. I prayed for fucking ages until baby chicks started to appear in front of my eyes until I made up a list of how to get God to trust me.

In the morning, the next day, I spent my time cleaning the flat when I had a phone call it was from my sister Fiona and she asked me what was going on in Glastonbury. I'd said the Frost Fayre all down the high street. She said, "I'll see you after lunch. Don't go out will you?"

"No. I'll be in. What time?"

"About three o'clock," she'd said.

When she got to me we went straight up town and I paid for Lauren, Liam and Nancy on a swing ride. We bumped into Liam's dad with his half-brother Daniel. It turned out to be a very nice evening before we started to walk back to mine.

"Karen. There's Santa in Wells next weekend. Meet you there?"

"I'd love to."

In the week I went to my fifth Aster Communities meeting and we gave two thousand pound to three deserving causes in the community. I really enjoyed giving my point of view and helping to build up the amounts for the causes I thought could really make a difference. I was really happy doing this and the week flew by. Before I knew it, it was the weekend again and I waited in for Fee to go to Wells. I saw Santa with reindeer with the girls and took a photo of them on a waltzer. We had a wonderful time as Santa on his sleigh with the reindeer went through town.

At four thirty, the next day, it was a Sunday and my in-laws and I, with Matt, were at the Methodist church to take part in a Christingle service, We all had the oranges with the red ribbon round and cocktail sticks with raisins on and a candle in the top.

The congregation sang beautifully to all the Christmas carols and we heard the nativity story of the three wise men, the kings and shepherds who came to worship the young baby Jesus. I loved the atmosphere when all the lights went out and all you could see was the candles and the story played out in front of you. There was no communion but they had the Lord's Prayer which made us feel united.

Joshua 24:22
"You are your own witnesses to the fact that you
Have chosen to serve the Lord."

After tea, that day, Matt and I went into Wells to look at the Christmas decorated houses and we saw a brilliant one just off the Bath road on an estate. Once there we met up with Fee, Mum, Lauren and Nancy. I took a photo of my nieces in front of the bright lights. The well that was lit up, reindeer, Santa sleigh, icicles and a massive seven pointed star over the garage. It was beautiful.

A week later Julie, Michaela, and her sister Sonia, and I met up one evening at Brent House for a carvery. Julie and I wore Text Santa hats and we lined up together to get our food. As we sat down we asked each other what we had been up to. I asked Michaela about her girls and son. We had a brilliant conversation all night. Julie, Sonia, and I looked at bags placed by our plates. Michaels said, "Open them. They're my little treats for you." I opened mine and there were a handful of little chocolates. I couldn't help but eat the lot. Then we sat around for a while with heavy tummies before saying our good nights.

The next day I went on the internet and scrolled down through the international news feed and came across comments on a biblical website. The name Scott came up and he was advertising himself as a born again Christian of whom was looking for a friend. I talked on this site with him and he seemed genuine enough to befriend. I thought that I really loved Christian Americans because they are always talking about their faiths and don't get easily embarrassed.

On Christmas Eve the whole family went to the carol service at St Thomas into Wells. I would have loved to sit in the middle near to the front row but everyone wanted the seats to the left-hand side of the church. It was a lovely service. They had the usual little actors and actresses playing the parts of the animals, my sister Eve and her husband playing Mary and Joseph with my nice Pippa playing the role of Jesus. My other nephew Liam, and nieces, Nancy and Lauren, played a shepherd and angels. They were all very good and we had a very peaceful service.

We had some nice presents on Christmas Day round my in-laws and up my parents. My favourite was a voucher to go for a spa day at Charlton House in Shepton. I was very pleased and gave my Mum a warm hug.

Afterwards Christmas week was quiet and for New Year's Eve, Fiona wanted us all around hers, so Matt and I took a cooked gammon joint and some bread with a few drinks. We played on the Wii all evening having a dancing game. The children and I did very well to an Abba song to keep a dance routine going. Later on we saw the New Year in with Gary Barlow.

I began the New Year of 2014 doing a Somerset Total Communications course at the Shepton Mallet leisure centre. Mum was rehearsing, at the time, just down the road with Liam, my eldest nephew, for a late Christmas pantomime called Aladdin. Mum and I had agreed that I was to walk to St Pauls School after my course to get a lift home.

At the course I got to know other child minders and some teachers. They gave us agenda sheets and asked us to do homework. We had to choose a child we were working with to do a character assignment to learn about the child.

The next day at work I began to study Noah and his expressions of whom was the newest child in my sister Eve's family. Over the week I noticed I could write a lot about his expressions and learn the hand signs he made when he wanted things and would make his whole little body tense up.

At the next meeting the tutor was impressed by my observations. I stayed the night at Mum's and in the morning, when I got back from Shepton, there was a man who seemed to be living in the garage opposite our flat. I went to talk to him and his name was Steve. He spoke to me about playing his guitar, but he didn't have it on him. He also told me there was a friend of his called Mike of whom he didn't trust. Matt came by then and confirmed this opinion. I'd had it in my mind to invite Steve in to stay in our spare bedroom, but wanted to ask Matt later on to agree to that first.

When we had tea though, Matt cooked too much and put it on a spare plate for Steve. He told me that he'd need to trust Steve before letting him in the flat.

The next day I went to Charlton House with Mum to have a pamper day. It was a Xmas present. We had massages, a swim in the pool, a lunch, and cream teas mid-morning. We even brought a book each to sit around with mid-treatments. My book was 'Getting Over Mr Right'. I even used the gym for twenty minutes. The next day in the morning I'd seen Steve again and he was drinking alcohol outside of Hawthorns. I took it as normal for him as I'd often seen him with a bottle of wine in his hand. I tried to get him to reminisce about good times in his past. He said that he'd been happy in Wales where he used to live, walking across the vast countryside. God had asked me to get him to go back there. Reminiscing I'd thought was a good way to go.

That same day I'd scrolled through Newsfeed on my phone and noticed a comment from a friend called Callum with a hot 'n' steamy picture about hot kisses. I put down that I'd had the hottest and the coolest thinking about Matt and Martin respectively.

I'd been worried that day about whether God trusted me. My calling was never clear but I really thought I'd had it with children even though I'd felt something bigger than me was always looming. I had to have a leap of faith into some great unknown.

Now in the morning I prayed really hard for my calling and to know god trusted me. I went to Tesco's with the children and Mum found an old fiver in her purse. She was going to go to the bank to change it. I said to go to customer services and make a fuss. Mum kept saying she'd got it from the cash machine. I pointed out that cash machines don't give out fivers. Mum thought about this and reasoned she must have got it when she saw the Cantibles Ladies Choir in St Thomas church on the weekend as she'd handed over a twenty and got two fivers back.

We stopped at Costa Coffee for a latte and a cappuccino, because the drinks were balancing in the pram we didn't go down the old railway track hill we normally run down in park because of a potential spillage.

At the duck pond we took out miniature doughnuts for the children. Haydn didn't like his but had his crisps instead. With the let over doughnut in our hands we noticed a mummy duck coming towards us with her ducklings so we decided to break up the remaining doughnut for the duct to feed her babies. My aim at targeting the ducklings was very good as I threw my remains to the ducks and the children did the same. The seagulls kept trying to get the little family's food but another family had come across us and started throwing bread specifically to the seagulls and the other ducks, so that we could continue to feed the little ducklings.

On the way through the park before we'd gotten to the pond Fin spotted a black little Scottie dog barking up a tree and he was worried that the dog was going to climb the tree and catch the squirrel. I explained that dogs don't climb trees to reassure him. We all stopped to watch the spectacle.

After feeding the ducks the boys wanted to play pirates and became Peter Pan and Captain Hook, making the bandstand their ship and the shrubbery around it Neverland. They found sticks for swords and loved chasing me around their ship. A lot of fun was had, but just as we were about to leave the park Fin fell over. We put them straight into their prams and left the park. Through distracting Fin we helped with is crying by talking about other things. We calmed him down and walked back through the Ridgeway estate. We talked about the cars we passed, the chickens, and a motorbike we passed and made it back for lunch.

The following week I was soon up at St Aldhelms school. I'd worked hard all morning putting homework into children's bags and running around looking for children's computers to do the children's spelling lessons with them.

In the afternoon a new teacher showed up called Elisabeth. I met her on the lunch break and shook her hand as we introduced ourselves. Hannah looked pleased with me. Now during registration I looked at Elisabeth and thought I could have some fun with her. Instead I felt torn in all directions all lesson as the children approached me for everything. There was one little girl who drew her family to show where her home is. I knew the teacher wanted a picture of a house, and even though she heard me I said to the girl, "That's acceptable," as I thought her family were her home no matter where she lived. The day was soon over.

The next day Matthew and I went fishing. We were at the Emerald Falls fisheries at Highbridge. Matt fished at the Ruby pond first and had many large fish. I'd betted with him that he'd wind up saying he'd caught a tonne by the end of the day. It had been such a lovely sunny morning.

We'd taken a picnic with four of Matt's Morrisons rolls that he bakes so well, crisps, scotch eggs, and the red Oasis drinks, Summer fruits.

I had taken a 'Take a Break' to read as I could never find Tattlers, the National Enquirers. At least there were many a good puzzle in the real people's magazines that I used to love, to relax and enjoy. Matt's favourite publications were fishing magazines, the local Gazette, and The sun newspaper. I used to love reading the Dear Deidre column and having a bit of a laugh.

Anyway, Matt decided he'd had enough of catching the carp that afternoon so we'd moved around to the Sapphire pond. We were eating apples for lunch when I suddenly got the idea to break the last bit of it to feed the fish with. They looked interested at first and began to suck on the bits. Matt even got a bite on his line with a bit of his apple, but the fish seemed to want to just spit it out. It was a bit of a giggle and helped spread the day out a bit.

The next day it had been pouring down with rain and it was on a day when I'd been going round to different schools with my CV to ask for voluntary work when I passed a hedgehog on the pavement just at St Dunstan's school gate. I thought nothing of it as I went into the academy to hand over my envelope, but as I came out of the building a man called Veejay Sharmar came towards me. He asked me if I could stay with the hedgehog as the poor things face was covered with blood and because a cat was wandering nearby we'd thought that the two animals had clashed. Mr Sharmar asked in the school for the NSPCA number or the Secret Worlds phone number. They had told him to pick the animal up, put them in a box and wait for someone to come from Secret World to pick the poor animal up. As I had been waiting for him a lady asked me if I needed to borrow her umbrella. I said yes as we stood near the trees. The lady told me that she used to work for Secret World. Veejay went to a friend's house for a box and a blanket and let his friend pick the hedgehog up. I was told someone could come for him in less than two hours' time.

Exodus 23:4-5
"If his donkey has fallen under its load, help him get the Donkey to its feet again; don't just walk off."

I had been at my Mum's working and afterward Matt picked me up and we went round Fee's to see her with the children. We told her about a homeless man we'd befriended called Steve. He'd been sleeping rough in a garage opposite us and we'd taken him out food and a cup of tea once in a while. We'd exchanged mobile phone numbers. He was a pleasant man.

Now Fee had told me about someone who'd collapsed outside her house and of how she had called an ambulance that soon came and helped him. We stayed there for a little while and I helped Nancy with her reading. Then we went home.

A few days later it was Fiona's 40th birthday and they'd arranged a birthday meal at Crossways. Right the whole family went there for a really nice meal. Then the cake came out that we all sang to Fee happy birthday with.

At St Aldhem's school the next day I had a birthday card to give to my old friend from school days Becky who lived nearby. I didn't see her until after school and then I gave it to her. We had a chat about her children and her husband Richard.

At half past four I got into Wells and signed on with the job centre and they gave me an evidence book to fill in to say that I was actually looking for work.

The next day I went with Mum, Lauren and Nancy up to Ridgeway Park and the girls climbed up the climbing ropes to the top. I took a lovely photo of them the next day.

That evening I went to King Bill and spoke with my friends Michaela and Julie. Apparently Michaela's Kate was expecting her second child. I felt a bit jealous.

That Sunday it was Valentine's Day and Matt and I went to Weymouth. It was romantic and I left some clothes behind. It bothered me.

Now on my phone I had Facebook and my friend Casey put on there that he'd been spending Valentine's alone. I put on there, in response, that had I been twenty years younger and single I'd volunteer to keep him company that evening. I laughed.

In the morning I woke up and heard God say to me to apologise to Eve for the hurt I put her through at fifteen. I cried over this and up at Mum's that day, after work, Eve offered to take me home. I thought that apologising would be uninterrupted in the car. I wanted her to say it was all right. She did but I scared her until I got her to pull over near to home and I walked the rest of the way home. I really wished I'd never brought up the subject.

On the bus next day I flew up to St Aldhem's and when there on a lunch break I helped out a girl named Demi and her friend. They'd had an accident of where the friend had hurt her knee and they asked me for an ice pack. I'd told them it was in the staff room. I sent them there as I was working. They came back disgruntled so I told Demi to knock on the door again. When they came back they had the ice pack and they shared it and both gave me a hug in turn and my boss Hannah saw it. It felt implicit.

Now that weekend on the Sunday I wore my fluorescent jacket into church. There was a lady there called Caroline and she picked on my coat. I suddenly realised I'd have to get a new one of which I did in the week.

One afternoon I was on Facebook and I remember sending a message to my friend Scott from Florida telling him about a dream I'd had of where I was in a supermarket with a massive TV, somewhere in Japan, showing a channel called God cam showing people's good deeds. He liked that idea.

On the next Sunday in Church we all stood round in the apse, at St Thomas's, saying our vows to God. I looked at Jo, one of Eve's friends, who wasn't particularly a church going person, and felt a stab of jealousy as I hadn't been chosen to be godparent as she had.

After the service while taking photos of Noah I'd asked Jeremy to hold Noah over the holy water while I snapped away. We went to the hall next door for food and I itched to play the piano. Feeling like a trust up turkey in my turtle neck white top, with my aquamarine dress and matching jacket I made my way to that piano and began playing. The children gravitated towards it and I left them to it with one child making a racket on the keys for over an hour. He was told off several times and my nerves were grating.

> *Judges 2:2*
> *But you have not done what I told you.*
> *You have done just the opposite!*

Matt and I made our excuses after handing over our christening present to Eve's little boy Noah and left.

It was Palm Sunday when I got into Wells on the bus a week later. It was a sunny day and I caught up with everyone converging on a piece of grass by Budgeons to be with my family. It was a church service and we had two real donkeys. They told us the story of a donkey waiting to be chosen by a master. They were chosen by Jesus along with his baby colt. I talked to Nanny Sheila and hung back from the group that Mum, Fee and the children were in. It turned out to be a lovely service.

That evening I'd been reading through Revelations until I came to the Holy City. I presumed that it had been John the Baptists vision but no matter how many times I read it there wasn't any mention of children and became baffled. This city was meant to be completely filled with jewels too which seemed a totally impractical place to live and decided that I wouldn't want to live there.

Another thing that confused me was that it seemed to be a hiding place from all those who desperately needed the guidance of faith. So what if the tradesmen that came to the gates swore. I'd thought that all adults said the occasional swear word of which would leave very few, the so-called privileged, the chance to live there. I then went to bed thinking about what to wear the next day.

On the bus in the morning I'd heard a siren. Not knowing the difference between an ambulance, cop car, or fire engine siren I silently said a prayer for all those involved, in Jesus name, to be safe and well. Sirens always worried me.

As soon as I'd gotten up Bowlish Hill to Mum's she'd already had a plan in place for us all to go across the fields that day. Waiting for all the children to come in Mum flitted between the hallway and the kitchen packing a blanket, crisps, and drinks.

The walk itself lasted quite a while as Jacob had been walking slowly. He'd been really sweet. It had been a lovely day.

The next Sunday I had awakened at just the right time to go to church. It was a lovely service and right near the end, even though the church was completely packed, there was enough chrysanths given out to all the women there. It was Mothering Sunday. I choked back a tear as the vicar had said that the flowers were for all the Mums and Aunties. I thought of all my nephews and nieces. It reminded me of a little note I'd pushed through my vicar's door previously of a concern I'd had with an unknown, personally, family to me in the parish. I walked home in the glorious sunshine with my little flower pushed in my buttonhole on my coat. I didn't want to get in the long queue for the hot drinks that morning.

I'd had a light lunch later on and waited for Matt to finish work. He came home happy so we fooled around on the bed. As we'd been fooling around I'd seen Jesus's face as clear as day! He was right there in between our heads as we were kissing. I turned my head from side to side to shake off the vision. I couldn't. In the end someone's name popped into my head and I managed to block this vision out, so that we could keep kissing. Jesus's eyes had been shining out to me a light blue colour, but then he'd turned his head slightly so that his hair partially blocked his face and then I saw what looked like a very large pear drop in his eyes as he winked at me. Matt and I finished kissing. I gave my Mum a ring to see what she was doing. Mum said that she was taking the Nans to Cheddar's garden centre to drop them off to look around and let them idle the time away with a tea and a slice of cake while she and my sister's family were to walk round the reservoir. I kept my flower in my coat as Matt and I headed out, in the car, to meet up with my family there.

At the reservoir we'd parked up on the far side under the trees and we met up with my family part way round getting out of their cars by the skate park. It was a lovely walk looking out over the fields and the water lapping up by the wall. The children were good on their bikes as we walked the circumference of the reservoir. Nancy saw, what Dad called raisins, on the floor and we told her that rabbits must have been about. We'd noticed the sheep grazing in nearby fields and their new born lambs. It was such a lovely warm afternoon. We didn't notice the time till we'd got back to Mum and Dad's car. We all said our goodbyes as my parents looked at their watches and were amazed to see that it was five o'clock. They said they'd better get back to the Grans at the garden centre and Fee piped up and said, "Doesn't the centre close at four on a Sunday?"

Mum looked aghast as this news sank realising the Grans wouldn't be very pleased at having to have hung around there waiting for an hour and they shot off in their car to pick them up. The rest of us just stood around laughing as we gave each other a hug before Fee got in her car with her little family and left.

Matt and I held hands again to walk round by the yachting club house to our car secretly laughing to ourselves that Nan Burr would have a lot to say to Mum when she'd get to them.

It had been such a lovely day that when we got back in the evening I placed my lovely flower in a little vase in the kitchen windowsill with my flower from Cuba and I took a picture on my phone to remind me of some very special people.

It was two days after Easter Sunday and I had just started a new job in a nursery in the baby room. It was on the understanding it was only casual work in case anything more permanent came up. I didn't mind as I needed the money and there was also the hope I could go on and further my training with them for a CACHE Level Three diploma. Anyway, I'd been there that day on the understanding that they had needed me to work all day. At two o'clock they were letting me go and that I could work that Thursday and Friday. I was thrilled. It was a start.

> *Nehemiah 8:17*
> *And everybody was excited and happy.*

I came out of Kickers and Dribblers to phone my husband to see where he was to pick me up and I caught him at the fishing ponds in Somerton. He'd said that he was packing up between four to five o'clock. I walked over to his Mother's house and knocked twice but she wasn't in. I'd tried my husband's keys in the lock but they didn't work as keys were in the lock on the other side of the door. Just across the road the Yeovil bus pulled up of which I knew went through Somerton where my husband was fishing. I got on. The six pounds and forty pence was nothing to get to see my husband who went to the car to get me my fishing rod. I was a bit worried about getting a bit smelly before I'd been due to go out with my friends, Julie and Michaela, that evening and wasn't too keen after using Matt's rod in his swim first. I'd then been reminded of the parable in St John's parable about having fishing on one side of the boat, so I'd switched my hands when Matt had come back to use my own rod in my own swim.

Then I had said, "I'll actually eat my shoe if I caught a fish," and lo and behold though after just ten minutes of fishing I'd had a bite. The rod started to bend nearly in half. Time and time again I had to reel the fish in then let the line out. Each time my shoulder was beginning to hurt. My husband eventually came to me with the landing net and another ten minutes later he actually scooped this beautiful eight pound fish out the water. I couldn't believe it. To me it was huge and the largest fish I'd ever caught!

> *1 Samuel 6:13*
> *They were overjoyed at the sight.*

I had Matt take a photo of me with it to go in our wildlife photo album.

That evening I'd first met a Dalibor Moyse on Facebook on Explore God website. There was a question about if there'd ever be a cure for cancer. Dalibor, being a bio-chemist from Florida had four cases of cancer sufferers being cured by asparagus therapy. This was back when I was on Facebook a lot and still collecting friends and Dalibor sounded like a cool person to be friends with. He had a lot of paranoid ideas about what governments hide that I saw on his home page. One article on his home page was a quote from Pablo Picasso saying that the meaning of life was to give away your gift. I tried to talk with Dalibor on chat that as a Christian you should never give away your god given gifts. I got the impression that Dalibor believes in God, but not so much in people, but I believed that God works through and in and with everybody whether they believe in Him or not.

Carnival was providing not a lot to do at this time except our meetings once a fortnight and because of a job one of our members I wondered if Dalibor worked for the MOD. One thing he had asked for was for cancer sufferers to try the asparagus therapy and provide him with more successful case studies. Well, I'd thought at the time that glaucoma was a cancer of the eyes and so perhaps I should trial this asparagus therapy myself. I went to the supermarket and found Kingfisher canned asparagus. I picked up three cans, bought them and took them home. I tried to tell my husband, Matt, about asparagus therapy but as his Dad and Gran died of cancer of the stomach during those last five years he didn't want to know I tried it anyway and would separate the juice in the can from the asparagus and make a meal, like soup, out of the asparagus and I would put the juice in a flask in the fridge as a drink to heat up later. It was quite nice.

I went to see a really nice lady doctor about headaches I'd been having and she explained to me about the medication very clearly. I told her of the asparagus therapy as a cure for cancer. She said thank you. I'd asked her if I could find out if I had stomach cancer as my tummy played me up. The doctor gave me a number to ring.

At home on the phone a lady said that they didn't do cancer tests for those over sixty and she wound me up.

I told her, "I'll tell that to the next child who's dying of cancer shall I?" and slammed te phone down. "What a job's worth." I'd said to myself.

Exodus 32:10
I am angry with them.

I had only been concerned about my stomach.

Chapter Twenty-Six

In a dream I had of the future once there were two great big Sherman Tanks looking like warships, because they were on the water, firing their last weapons.

Which led to another dream of the future when the last bomb will be dropped on a government building in the middle of some beautiful green fields with a narrow, perfectly flat lane leading to it. As the building went up in smoke, the smoke and everything formed into the shape of a massive mushroom.

The next day I was talking to Steve, the street cleaner, on the way to the bus that morning. Because of the new hat I'd been wearing, it was a straw hat with a dark brown band around it he'd said it looked like I should have a gun. He'd been telling me that teenagers had been going round town shooting pellet guns at signs and shooting these guns up at the park. Steve told me that he'd found a dead squirrel shot in the head with a pellet. He told me that he had called the police and the council and that they didn't want to know. He had kept a photo of the poor creature. I told him he should have called the RSPCA or any other animal charity.

When I'd got to Mum's, Keeley, Fin and Haydn were already there causing mayhem. The boys had pretend guns and were running around pretending to shoot the bad guys. It was a game. Fin's mum didn't like it but Mum and I saw no harm in their innocent playing. I took my suitcase upstairs in my room as I was going to stay the night for skittles. Keeley got some paper to do a lot of drawing on and asked to do her alphabet book. At least she needed me to do this s I'd told her to stay in the lines and I dotted the lower case letters out for her to draw round.

I heard through the wall that Scooby-Doo was on again. The day went swimmingly.

In the morning I was in a buoyant mood. The sun was shining and Mum told me to look for the sun tan lotion in the school room cupboard and to find some hats. Finding out the stripy hats with sunglasses on attached to the front for the children. I went in search of straw hats for Mum and I.

The children turned up one by one and the buggies were pulled through the kitchen out the front door by me and put them up outside the living room window. I'd had my usual one in the front double buggy and Mum had the side by side one.

The usual two girls were split up and the boys got split up to. I asked the eldest girl to be my eyes as we crossed the roads and she enjoyed being put in charge. Haydn and I talked about the different flowers we passed and counted the snails he could see. The children always had better eyesight than me.

Mum never told me till the last minute that she wanted an awful lot of photos from Boots and so Evie still had to be on alert. Keeley made to grab for a jar with a Walt Disney princess on the bottom shelf and was horrified that it was a bottle of vitamin pills.

The day at the park was wonderful chasing the children down the old railway, stomping around in the bandstand and stopping briefly at the swings and the slides before we headed towards Ridgeway Park. The girls loved the little train while the boys competed for attention on the swings. Mum and I then sat to drink out of our flask while all the children had gotten on the train at that point.

Back in their buggies going by Nan's house from under the bridge, the four children munched happily on their Quavers. Waiting for a break in the traffic I ran across the road and up to the doctors to wait for Mum. Feeling the strain of pushing the older children up the incline passed the Old Noah Fry building they talked of getting out at the next park but Mum wanted us to get back.

The kids jumped out of their buggies in front of the house while I collapsed them and pulled them back through the kitchen up to the garden shed.

That evening Pointless was on as I sat with Dad while Mum cooked the tea. I had been looking forward to skittles and we won that evening. I had a brilliant night.

Now the next day was a Friday and I had a good day at work. That evening my mum-in-law invited us round for tea. It was nice food and we soon withdrew to the living room. My Mother-in-law had to go out and the phone rang leaving Matt and I, and Tom and Lis in the living room. We soon went home.

It was Easter time and we made baby chicks. We cut out two bits of a broken egg and put a pin in the corner. We drew the baby chicks for them to colour in on the end of a thin bit of paper to move about up and down inside the egg.

By the end of the day they went home with Easter cards, Easter biscuits and painted crosses.

Now after work Matt took me to a new place to fish called Windmill Ponds. I tried to talk with Matt saying I needed to have a confrontation with Lis so I could be polite, but tell her what I thought of her. It turned into an argument because Matt got scared at the thought of a confrontation. I ended up screaming at him, "But I hate her and just wanted her to understand me."

What I wanted to say was, "Look I know you use people for what you want. use me. you can make a friend out of me if you want a baby sitter," that was all I'd ever wanted to say to her.

I got on the bus one morning and headed out to Doulting on the 161 to the school St Aldhem's. I had a lovely morning sorting the children out with their problems and setting homework.

Now during the lunch break a little boy called Rio was being disruptive and went under a table pulling all the chairs over to him as a barricade. I whipped under the table and sweet talked him about his favourite biology book and I sat with him going through it afterward. The teachers said thanks to me.

Now in the evening it was our first game of summer skittles at the King Bill in Glastonbury and started a tradition of calling out seven just like Len off Strictly Come Dancing. We laughed all night and won our game.

The next day after child minding with Mum, I missed the quarter to four bus and started to walk home. By Dinder the bus went passed me and so I continued to walk to Dulcote and I saw my sister Eve's car pull into her driveway, so I walked up to her house. She went into the garden.

"Where's Pippa?" I asked.

"Oh. In the car she's fast asleep. I leave her in there. What gave you got on? Trousers would look better." I was in my sweat pants and felt insulted and pushed on to the back foot and replied, "It's dangerous to leave her in the car anyone on Google Earth can see your habits with Pippa and could time it right to kidnap her." I'd felt a genuine concern but she said, "I don't want to hear it."

"Well I don't want to be attacked about my dress sense. It's not important." I walked off then but Eve said she'd take me into town for the bus and I went on home.

That afternoon I went up to my Mother-in-law's house and Lis paraded around a handbag. She said that she got it off her mother-in-law's friend. I got angry, was she ever going to treat me like a human being. I knew I had to be wealthy to get her attention and she knew what I was thinking and said accusingly, "Well how do you get what you want?" I wanted to scream at her "Through a lot of bloody hard work."

That evening I went to skittles and an all ladies team were practicing and they came out moaning that cat poo was down the shoot as it was coming out on the balls. We had to wait while they cleaned it. We went on and claimed the game as they wouldn't play.

The next day there was a play being performed in the Abbey grounds depicting the life story of Jesus Christ. I had to be a steward with a man named Daz of whom I laughed and flirted with. I called him Mr Willis. He called me Mrs Genge as we patrolled around the grounds. It was a gorgeous sunny day at Glastonbury Abbey and on the Monday when I went into work I took Haydn to Barrington Place Park while Mum stayed at home with Keeley. I'd really hit it off with three year old Haydn and we could talk about anything as his brain seemed as colourful as mine. On the Saturday in the morning I got up to the alarm clock and I ended up going to church to help with a Kermis which was basically a fete. While I was there they put me on children's books. I stood there and spread them out so that everyone could see what books there were. I'd had a Horrible Histories book I'd told James, of whom was the vicar's son, that the book would be a laugh to teach him about history. His dad interrupted and said, "I don't believe in that."

Then I came across my old drama teacher from school called Mr Casey and we had a chat.

Then the lady next to me said "Would you like to look around. I'll look after your stall."

I went up to the tower to face a fear of vertigo.

Isaiah 32:11
But now tremble with fear.

It was terrifying but I made it to the top and was really scared.

Later on that day I was up my in-laws but most of them had gone out and Lis my sister in law was there having an intense conversation with a lady called Gwenda and I felt left out. Why couldn't she talk like that with me? I'd have loved a decent conversation with her.

One afternoon I was sitting on the sofa with my husband and the windows were open. A cat was walking on the window ledge that looked black and it came in and sat on my lap. I looked at it again and it was ginger. Now I had to see Dr Van Driel and I told him about the cat and visions I'd had. I told him that possibly they were hallucinations, manifestations of me taking my pills and was angry yet again at having to take them.

The next day Matt and I took a card and present to our best man's, Justin's house for their little girls birthday. Turned out her birthday was a month later. Back at home Matt knew something was afoot with my pills.

"I've got to get off them." I'd said and we had an argument. Next morning I started writing a plan to get off my pills by whittling them down to every two days then three days and four days until I got off them. Then I put on my Goodnight Sweetheart series and for the umpteenth time I had the voices of St Peter and St Paul in my head getting me to speak as Gary and Phoebe in an awful cockney accent. I went up town and found Bach White Chestnut. It was supposed to be for loud noises in your head. I went home and tried it in water and my head fizzed and the voices left. I felt euphoric.

Then the next morning the sun was out at five and I washed and dressed and put tree radio stations on. Two on Heart FM and another on Premier Christian Radio thinking I could mess other people's noises in their heads. No neighbour complained.

That weekend Dad phoned me up with some bad news as he said they'd found Nan slumped in her kitchen obviously as she'd washed up looking at her beautiful garden and the birds outside. Dad said her heart must have given out and I cried on the phone.

On that morning afterwards I came across GenG Kad Et Po Lis^-^SMK pLM ^-^ on Lis's Facebook page. I noticed lots of Middle Eastern women speaking in a foreign language and I couldn't work out what the web page was all about. Had I rumbled Lis doing something she shouldn't have? I never did trust my sister-in-law and this had been confirming suspicions of something wrong going on.

That afternoon I went up my mother-in-law's for lunch and I looked at Lis wondering whether or not to ask her about her Facebook page.

Then the next day Pippa, my little niece, came into school with Mum early and was ready to dominate. She was a lovely, adorable child, cute like a button, but didn't know how to shut up. She wanted to do everything for everyone especially at fruit time and she wouldn't sit down or kept still. Pippa brought in the plates. I brought in the fruit to stop it falling everywhere and when it was biscuit time she was the first one to get up and pass the biscuit tine bus around. I found it irritating but by the time her mother Eve came to get her I told my sister that Pippa was a very gracious little girl in her nanny's home and Eve was pleased with that.

That afternoon was the funeral of Nan Burr, but I had to go to see Dr Van Driel, my consultant, at The Bridge. I'd been dressed in a dark navy blue velvety dress. Matt had been in shirt and suit. I had a bit of paper that had all the times I'd hurt my head on. He said thanks and photocopied it and gave it back.

At the funeral afterwards Fee stood up to give an eulogy just for nan that sounded like it came from the heart. Then Eve stood up and gave her eulogy too and she made me cry. It was a lovely service.

We all went on to the Con Club for the wake and a lot of people were there. I made a point of talking to everyone and afterwards Mum told us she was proud of us girls.

A few days later the family convened at Nan's house to choose what to do with her chattels. I chose several things and had to comfort Eve.

I'd started that weekend getting ready for Nan's two piece suite, cabinet, pouffe and table to be delivered. The old green suite had to be moved out first. I'd gotten talking to my neighbour Jason and I'd managed to talk him into helping me manoeuvre the old sofa and chair out of the flat. I was amazed that we ended up getting it out really quickly through careful negotiations.

2 Chronicles 25:8
It is god who has the power to give victory or defeat.

We sat on the sofa outside together talking to one of his friends and I made them a hot drink mainly to say thanks.

Afterwards I started clearing out our oversized cabinet and tried to sort out the glasses, the ones to keep, and the others to throw away, on the living room carpet.

Matt came home and I tried to tell him my system with the glasses as I boxed a lot of stuff in a plastic box to take to the Cancer Research shop. Matt was a bit miffed as I hadn't made proper arrangements to bring down the new furniture and was moaning about where we were going to sit, but we had two chairs.

Matt and I went for a walk later on up the road to the Chalice Well and came back over Windmill Hill. As we were strolling along I remember two oriental looking tourists behind us taking photos of us two famous people. When we got back it was quite late and Matt was telling me to take my pills yet again and again I told him that I was an adult and that I didn't have to take them if I didn't want to. This lead to an almighty argument. Sick of fighting over this issue I decided to go for a walk to get some space. I had to really put my foot down to not get Matt to follow me. Thinking about it this walk I went on was in the middle of the night. I know I had some pretty random thoughts going through my head, probably the words from our argument going round and round. I came across four large visions of Jesus in black and white. He was in white robes and so were a bunch of children around him. I had felt so mad I'd flung my engagement ring in a bush. At the top of Bere Lane I tried to coax a foreign looking lady across the road as she looked lost. I thought she was the original Sarai. I remember feeling the need to pray to Mecca to get her to understand me. I can recall being picked up by an ambulance after that. I kept calling it a rickety old bus and asking them, because they had a mobile, if I could call my husband to tell him I was on my way to Musgrove hospital. They had said that I couldn't call anyone till I got to the hospital. After this my memory became blank as the next thing I knew I was waking up in a place called Rydon. I didn't think anyone knew where I was so I was glad I had my mobile on me. I'd acknowledged to myself that this was a strange place to be in. I spent my days feeling a bit lost and disorientated trying to work out the way the land lied.

The first day there of being at Rydon Ward Two, I had overheard a woman calling me posh. I was curious about her. Next thing I knew she appeared at my door with a beautiful red rose. Everyone up to this point was struggling to understand me as I had come to the hospital spouting Latin, Arabic, or something. My nephew thought I sounded Italian over the phone. It was alien sounding to my own ears. I'd seen my friends, Julie and Michaela, in Rydon, my sister Fiona, and her husband brought flowers when they came, my mother-in-law would bring my husband regularly. My Mum showed up once. Nan Sheila had called in the evenings and she basically told me to tow the line and I would come home. Eve called some evenings too.

I was taken aback and was pleased that another patient would do something so nice like give me that rose. During my first meal, in the hospital, I got talking to a patient called Dominic to whom I asked, "Voulez-vous couche avec moi se soir?" he laughed saying he knew that one. He had told me he'd been waiting for five years in hospital for his girlfriend to come and visit him. I didn't have the heart to tell him what I'd thought that really she probably just didn't want to know him anymore. Dom told me that he had brothers and sisters who lived all over the world who wouldn't come and visit him as well. I was getting phone calls from friends and family all the time I was there wanting me to stop sounding foreign and to come home.

I knew that I was speaking in tongues really the minute a cleaner looked up and told me she could speak in tongues too. I kept looking out for her afterwards, but I never came across her again after that.

I did shout at the nurses a couple of times thinking they were incredibly naïve about some things and I don't know what I was shouting about one day when five of them jumped on me in a room I hadn't been in before. This frightened me so I felt that I had to shout back to defend myself in a blind rage as they pushed me further onto the floor. At which point I told a man, twice my size to stop hurting my arm.

In the end I asked the two remaining restrainers that if I pretended to be asleep would they please leave me alone. I apologised afterward to the girl I'd spat in the face of and explained that they'd terrified me as I had never experienced being retrained before. Feeling calmer I had the chance to have the chaplain pray for me when I went downstairs once to what if thought would be a church service. Another patient had been learning tunes on the hospital's keyboard for us to sing contemporary music to.

I'd been allowed knitting needles and made a line of triangles with a nurse and two other patients.

My phone went missing while I was at Wellsprings hospital, amongst other things, and just before I left I confronted Robyn over my phone snarling at her saying that I was only there because I was afraid of my own temper. On my way out she came to me with a bag of cherries that I thought that would be nice for my husband, so I said thanks to her and to the nursing staff, giving them my flowers, for putting up with me.

I moved onto St Andrews in Wells to be closer to my husband and family. Here was far more relaxed and I actually got to go outside for walks. I had told Caroline, a nurse, one I could finally connect with, all about myself as she shared parts of her life with me. I'd learned to nibble my food here to help fill in time and Mum had given me some paper to make posters with for her retirement part and for what I thought was going to be my home coming party too. By now the funny accent and different languages I'd been speaking had disappeared. It had been so nice to have visitors and my husband Matt came more often here to see me.

I had to have an assessment with the consultant before I went home and they'd asked me if I'd heard voices. I said no. But I had heard voices and something in my mind was telling me to say that St Peter and St Paul were talking to me.

I soon went home first to Mum for the weekend which was lovely as I'd felt like I didn't want to be anywhere else the next day. Then I went back to Glastonbury to the marital home of where my husband was now my carer.

I soon heard all about how the new furniture was moved in as soon as I got home from hospital, especially Nan's big sofa and chair. It had been a nightmare, apparently, to get in as three doors had to be taken off their hinges and were actually removed. I had miscalculated the actual size of it but at least they'd all had a big laugh, and said it was never to be removed.

I was so pleased to be home and had some new ideas for things to do with my lie, like one day if I had enough money I could train to be a paediatric nurse, though my first thought was to change my wardrobe. A lot of my dresses were to go to be replaced with leggings and to be more girlie with pink knickers.

Not long after I'd come out of St Andrew's Mum told me that she wanted to spend some more time with me. There was talk of her coming to my flat regularly to help me organise my home. By this time I was calling my home a bit of a black hole as things kept going missing. I desperately needed a place for everything so that I could put my hands on things as and when I needed them. My memory felt like it was going.

One day we arranged to go off somewhere together and Mum chose Cheddar. Together we decided to go round the town as we had never explored the high street shops before. Like my life had gaps in it and I'd finally accepted my brain needed fixing. I'd finally conceded I needed my pills and had started taking them regularly again. A lot of the shops were closing as it was getting into early evening but we found ourselves in clothes shops. God was telling me to get some leggings to prepare myself for being a yummy mummy.

I surveyed the jewellery and told my Mum, yet again, that I needed a dressing table at home in my bedroom. Mum said I could have an earring stand of hers. She'd offered her idea of help.

I found some nice quarter-length brown leggings. I was looking for red socks and pink knickers but instead I came across some knitting patterns in a charity shop. I looked through them for sock patterns. Mum told me that it was tricky knitting socks as you needed either four needles or rounded needles. The book I picked up looked like it was written in the eighties. The woman on the front had big curly hair and a huge pair of pink socks that looked more like leggings. I also bought some wool. I had started knitting a pair of red socks at home and had lost the pattern. I figured that all sock patterns were the same. I had nicked a book from Mum's full of patterns. In the end I had acquired three sock patterns. Mum and I was going to go up the Gorge for tea and cake but decided to go back to Shepton for a hot drink. My red socks were going to be hard work to knit, kinda like how hard my life had always been, but no matter what I had always persevered.

That evening Matt and I played our last summer skittles match at the King Bill at the bottom of town. I liked that alley and played really well on it as well as the rest of the team. We'd had a good run that season and come out of it on a high.

Right. Three days later I went to church and heard a heart rendering sermon by Diana about how a murderer got forgiven by his victims Mum. I cried. It really moved me to tears as the mother knew how not to hold onto a lot of anger that she could have held onto for the rest of her life. It was the best service I'd ever been to.

Matt took my eldest nephew Liam fishing two days later and Liam fell into the river from off the banks as the grass hadn't really been cut back. Matt was incensed and decided, when he got home, to get hold of a reporter. He got hold of Jason Bryant, a local photographer, of whom was prepared to do a segment on him.

A few days later Matt took him to where he'd fished for a photo shoot and Jason wrote about the lack of keeping the sides of the river banks safe for fishermen.

That evening I'd had a dream that was bathed in a yellow glow, to stop this dream from feeling scary I suppose, as it was about Armageddon raging all around me and my sisters while we were huddling together under my king-size wooden bed, crouching on my yellow carpeted floor.

I took this to mean that if everyone took to the trees or churches with wooden doors or benches in well then they could feel safe during said time. I need to remind everyone that Armageddon is actually a place where the kings will gather. Here is my list of kings I invited back in. Number one was St Peter, number two St Paul, three St John, four St Matthew, five St Mark, six St Luke, seven St Andrew, eight St Bartholomew, nine St Leviticus, Ten St Philip, eleven St Thomas and twelve St Saviour. I wanted them to come back in glory to judge the living and the dead. I'd done this through simple prayers to try and bring on the thousand years peace as predicted.

The next day after I'd written this down I went to see my little niece Nancy at Croscombe School of where she was taking her Rainbow pledge. Fee, Eve and Mum were there beaming with pride and taking photos. Nancy was in her element. This was a nice Friday evening.

It was a Saturday morning and Matt and I went across the moors by the Railway Inn at Meare and parked up opposite. Then we walked along the path towards the bridge. Matt and I were arguing about fighting on the news that I didn't agree with. I said perhaps they were all spiritually blind and I kept quoting the passage from the Bible of Amos 8: 10, 11, 12. We were arguing the entire walk and I wanted to get back for a charity football match in the afternoon.

Proverbs 15:1
A gentle answer quietens anger, but a harsh one stirs it up.

That had been me. Now I'd talked to a child sat on the wall next to my friend Charlene and enjoyed watching Bristol Rovers and Glastonbury FC.

Now two days later it was Baltonsborough Flower Show and Matt and I met up with Sue, Tom, Lis, Emily and Henry. We went round loads of stalls and had a burger. We paid for Emily and Henry to go on a merry-go-round then they had a ride on the donkeys. It had been a lovely day and on the Thursday winter skittles season had started again and our first game was at the Britannia in Wells. Tricia pointed out that the fish in the aquarium were in the dark. I said perhaps they had to turn off the hot light occasionally so they could freely swim without having to avoid the heat underneath or by brushing the sea weed as it needs cool water.

We kept losing each hand and I had to keep wetting my fingers to moisten the board for the chalk to work. I got a score of thirty five, at least I was pleased with that.

Four our seventeenth wedding anniversary Matt and I couldn't make our minds up whether to go to Minehead or Weymouth for the weekend. We reasoned that there would be more to do at Weymouth. We knew the best restaurants were at Weymouth for our anniversary meal. There was trouble looking for a bed and breakfast for the night as nearly every place to stay along the seafront had their no vacancy signs in the window. After about the twentieth B&B that did have the vacancy sign up we finally found a double bedroom that was on the seafront, trouble was the place had no car parking. We asked the proprietress anyway if there was anywhere we could park for free, she said that there was free parking by the church and down behind hers near to The Park pub on the road side. Matt and I drove round for ages in this part of town before settling for a space passed the Wetherbury Inn. This was a new area of Weymouth we'd never explored.

We went for a walk along the seafront and talked about what to do for lunch. I always liked having a pasty from the pasty shop but when we got into town, and walking passed the shops, I noticed the M&S shop and suggested going in there for sandwiches. They were very nice. I had still been nibbling my sandwich as we walked past the moored boats by Nothe Fort. This was where we heard a child's voice on a microphone saying what a great day she'd been having so we followed the noise to the top of Nothe fort. There was a marque with a band playing inside, they sang 'Valerie'.

There was free tea and coffee, and lots of families with children playing with lots of different activity sets. The band played three more songs as we sipped our free hot drinks. The organiser came on stage to announce the Weymouth Baptist church was holding a service next morning. Matt and I decided that we would go. As we came out of the tent we made our way to Brewers Quay and went for a walk back to the bed and breakfast to get ready to go out for dinner. Everywhere was packed and we finally found a small table for two at the Old Rooms Inn by the harbour.

It had been a lovely meal and the atmosphere had been noisy, but there were lit candles and dimmed lighting for a romantic effect. We strolled around town afterward to find a band playing in a not too full pub, which was scarce, and as we got tired Matt and I thought about turning in.

Up with the dawn we went downstairs for a nine o'clock cooked breakfast then made our way to the church service. The songs were happy and they showed a short film of the day before activities. Usual prayers for the world were said and as per usual I kept repeating the Lord's Prayer under my breath to help me concentrate. We made to leave and got talking to a couple of nice people keen to introduce themselves which rounded off this very pleasant morning. We watched the squirrels remembering when Matt got attacked by a couple one and made our way back over the bridge towards the town.

We went into the shops for a bit and I bought some pink knickers before we walked over to Weymouth Tower to be able to look out right over the bay. It was the last thing we did before making our way home.

THE END

THE EPILOGUE

The only time we had a budgie it lived in its cage in the dining room. We used to occasionally let him fly around the house. It flew away when someone left the window open. When my husband was six years old he told me that a blue budgie was found in a hedge in his family's front garden. He vividly remembers the bird sitting on his finger. I'll always wonder if it was Misty Blue finding my mate.

OTHER BOOKS IN THE SWING SET SERIES

Utopia; Shropshire
Come join James and Karen dragging the Saints and Jesus into the 22nd century through love affairs and friendships.

Utopia; Ethiopia
Come join Karen in her quest of utopia through trials and tribulations in her ultimate goal of having a wonderful marriage to Jesus. Then see how the dynasty of Karen and Jesus survive.

Utopia; Arabia
Come join the adventures of Sherie Marie, a lovely Muslim girl, in her quest for her ultimate goal of marrying Jesus.

Lightning Source UK Ltd.
Milton Keynes UK
UKHW01f1058280818
327916UK00001B/203/P